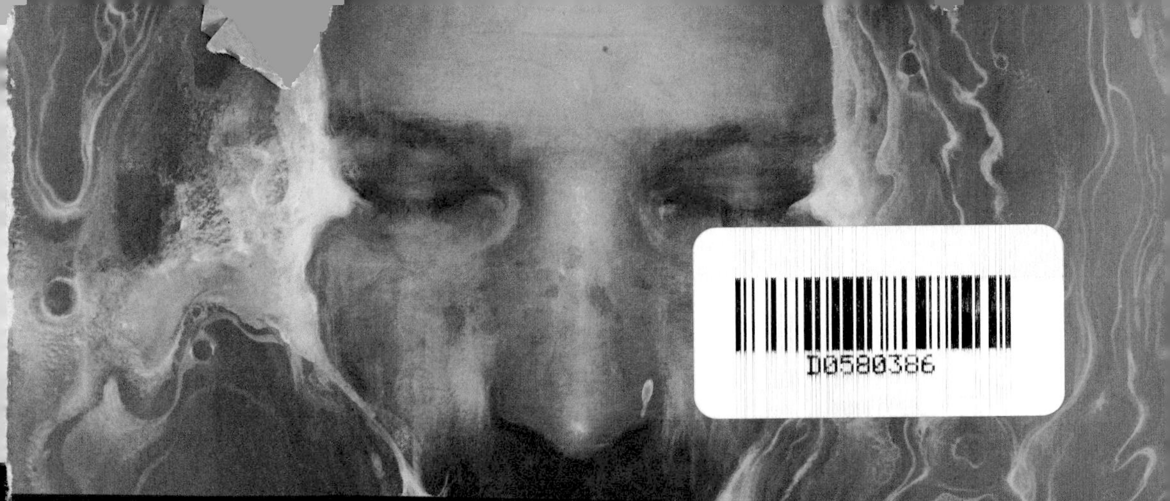

FABLES: THE GOOD PRINCE

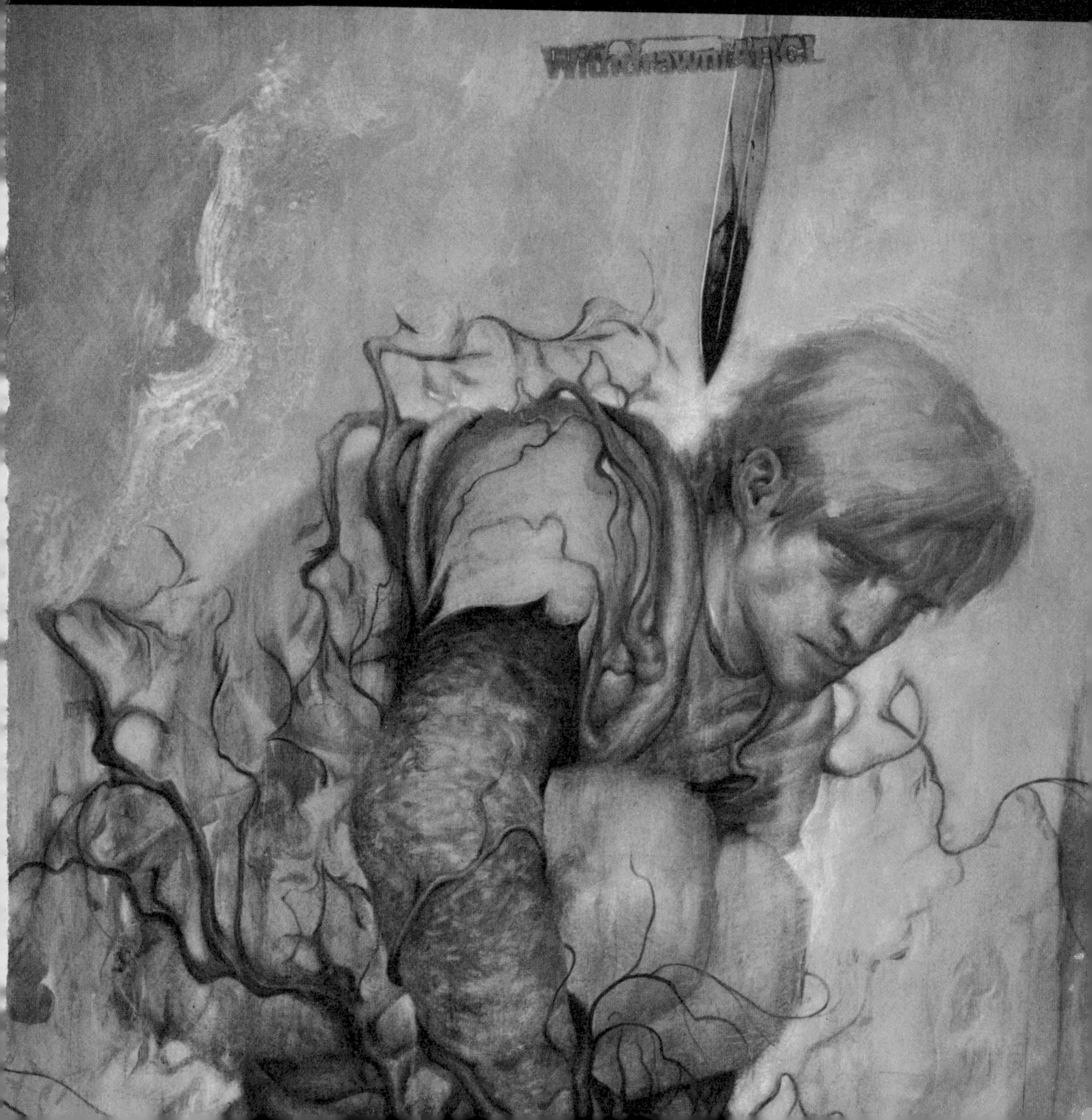

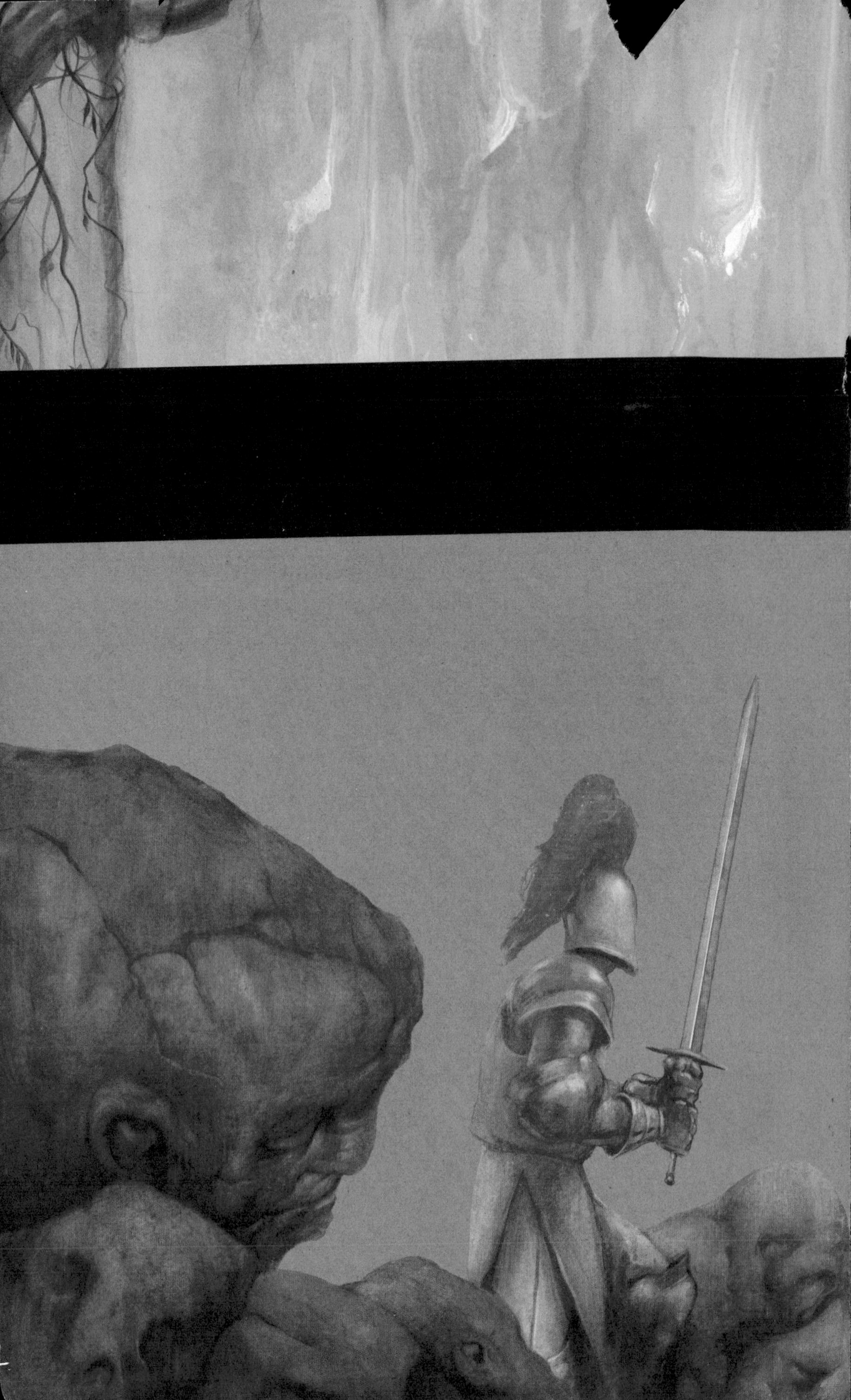

Table of Contents

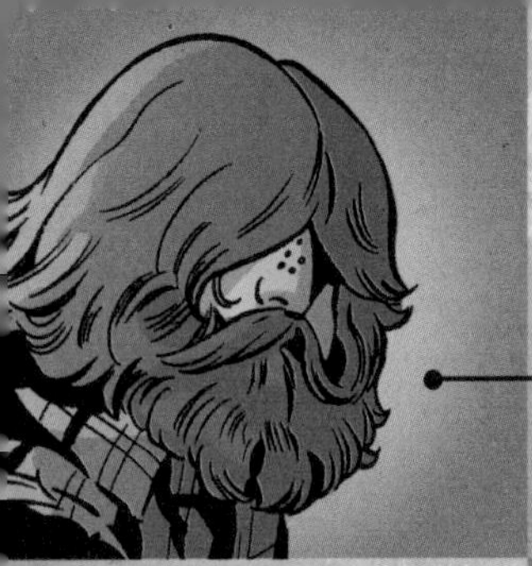

WHO'S WHO IN FABLETOWN

FLYCATCHER

He was the Frog Prince before becoming the Woodland Building's lowly janitor.

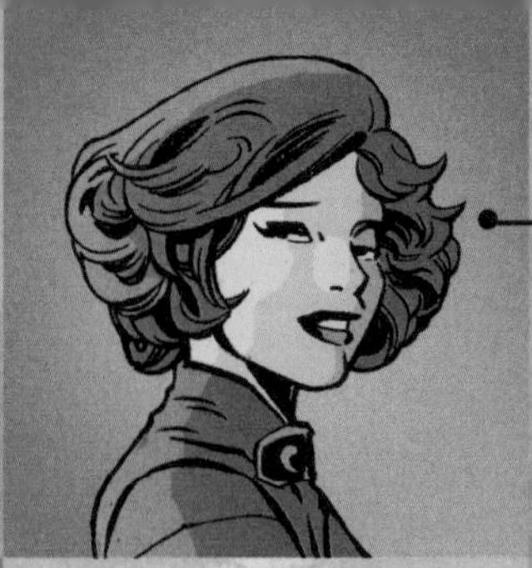

RED RIDING HOOD

It's pretty clear she has thing for Flycatcher, but she prefers that you use his real name, Ambrose.

FRAU TOTENKINDER

She's the witch with a thing for gingerbread houses, but now she serves Fabletown — doesn't she?

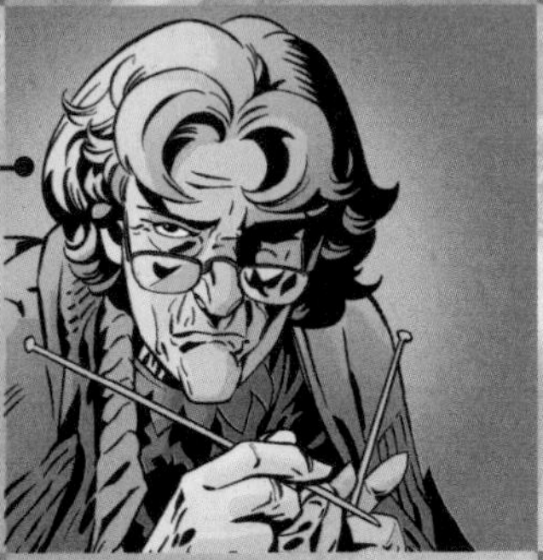

BIGBY

He's the big bad wolf, and now a husband and father.

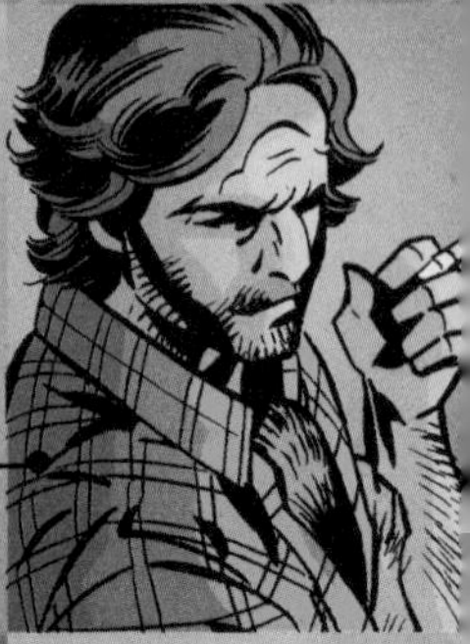

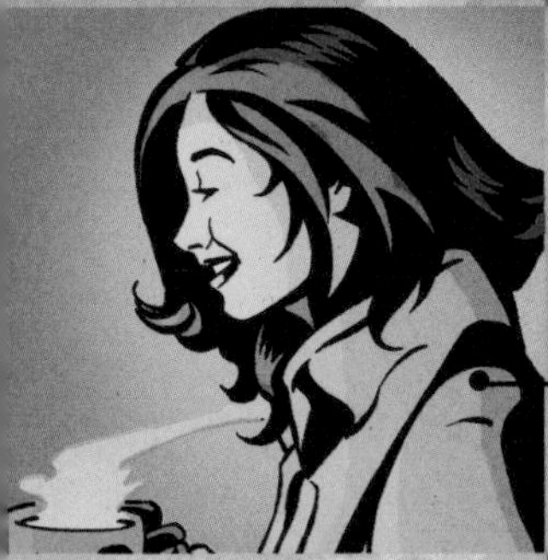

THE CUBS

There are seven of them, but only six that most know about.

SNOW WHITE

She's married to Bigby and is the mother of seven unruly kids.

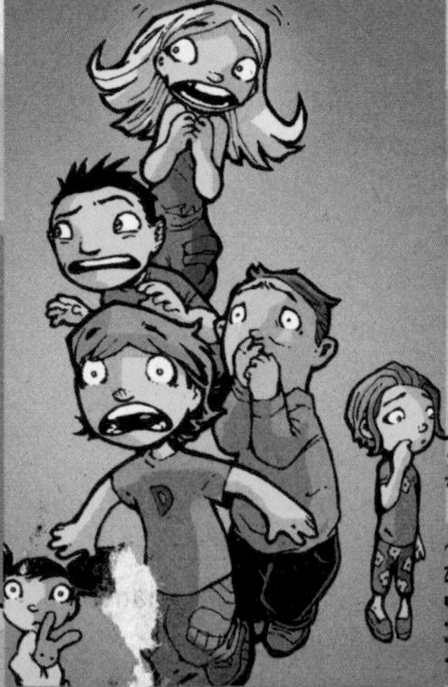

SHERE KHAN

A terrible tiger from *Jung* *Book* fame, killed by Sn White up at the Farm.

PRINCE CHARMING

A womanizer of note, he's also the duly elected mayor of Fabletown.

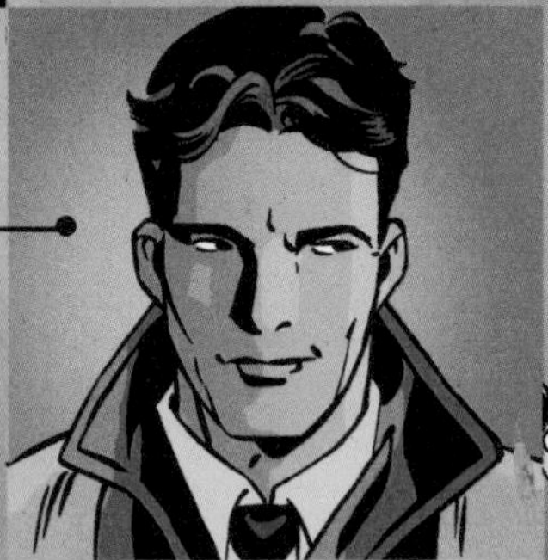

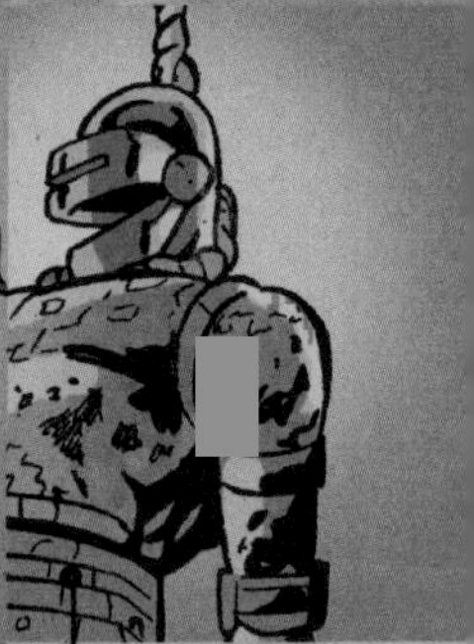

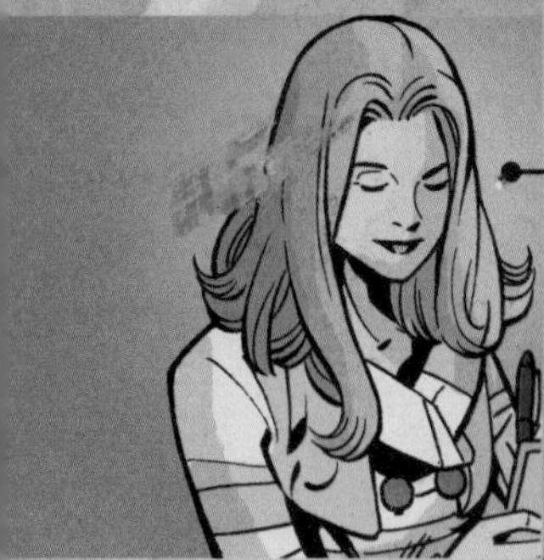

BEAUTY AND THE BEAST

She's the deputy mayor. He's the town sheriff. What a lovely couple.

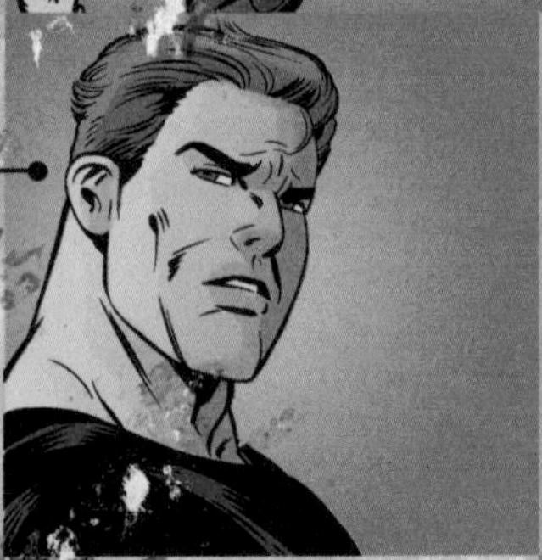

THE FOR… KN…

His pa… he's be… in the Wo… office fo…

BUFKIN

A monkey of the flying variety. He works in the business office.

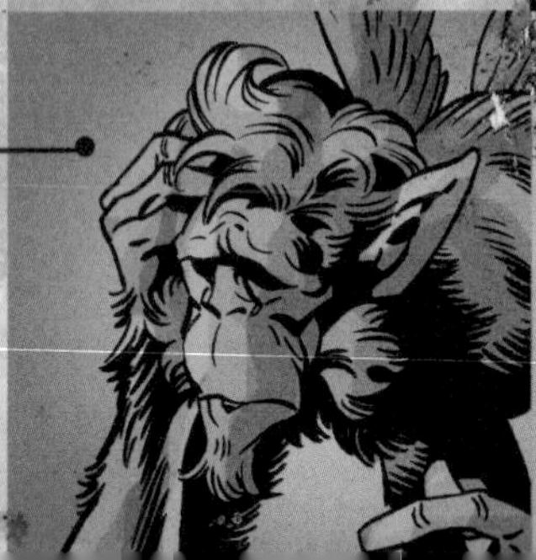

KAY

He can see all the evil anyone has ever done just by looking at them — at least when he hasn't gouged out his own eyes.

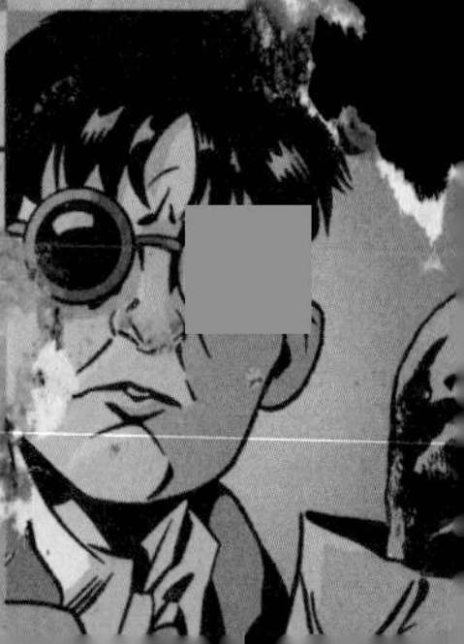

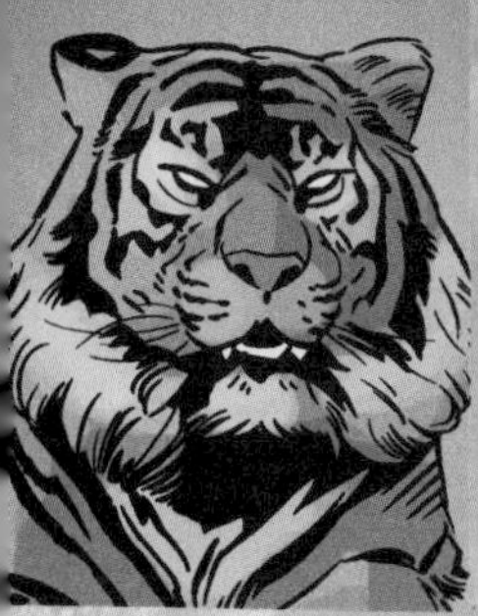

TRUSTY JOHN

A trusted member of Fabletown until it was discovered he was a spy for the Adversary. He was forced to jump alive into the Witching Well.

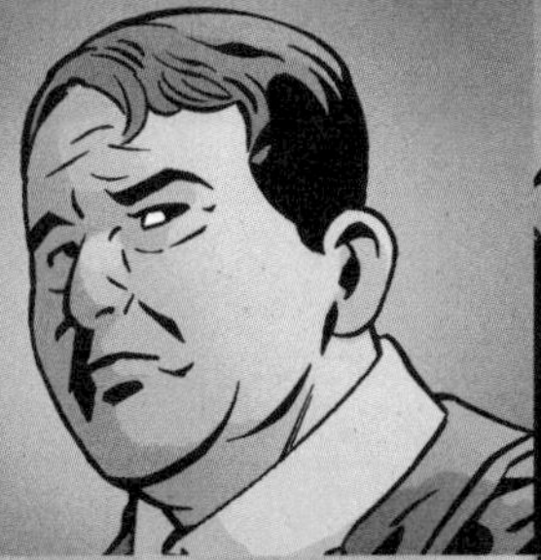

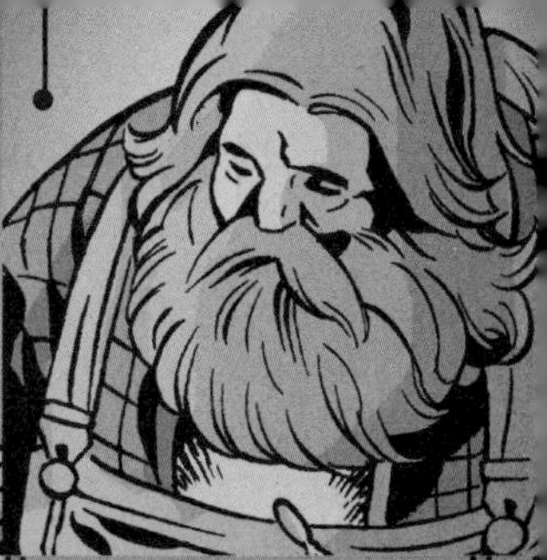

WHO'S WHO IN THE HOMELANDS

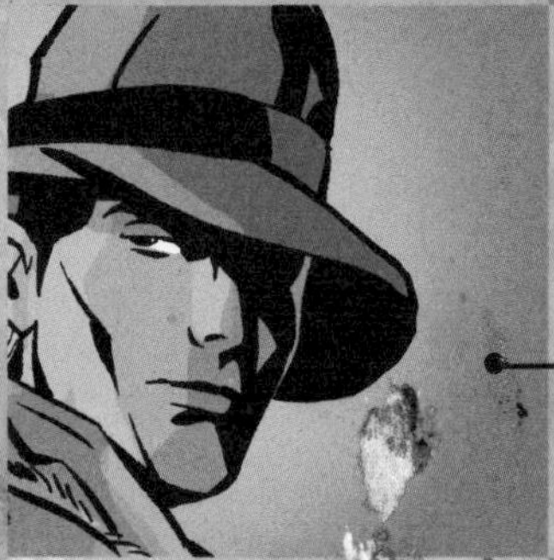

THE EMPEROR

He's a puppet, but a mighty one — the figurehead for an empire that spans over a hundred worlds.

HANSEL

The Empire's dreaded Witchfinder General, he's now their ambassador to Fabletown.

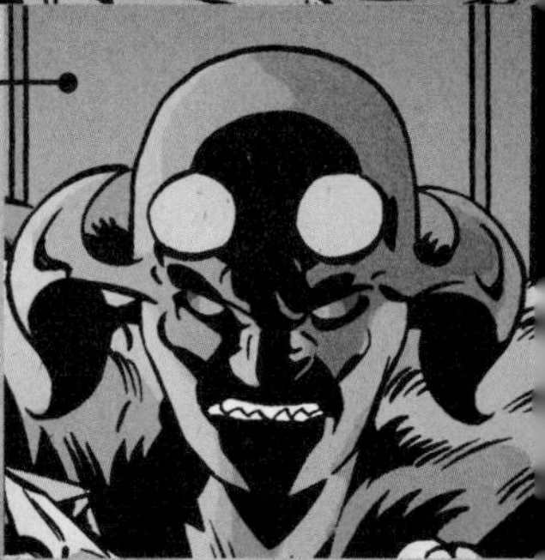

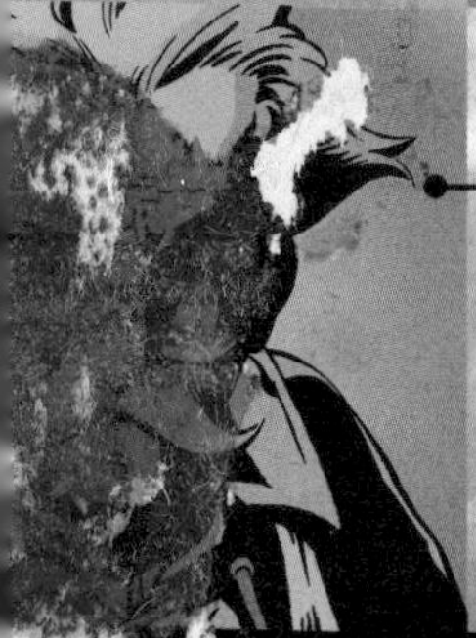

GEPPETTO

He seems just a lowly woodcarver, but he's the legendary Adversary and the true power behind the imperial throne.

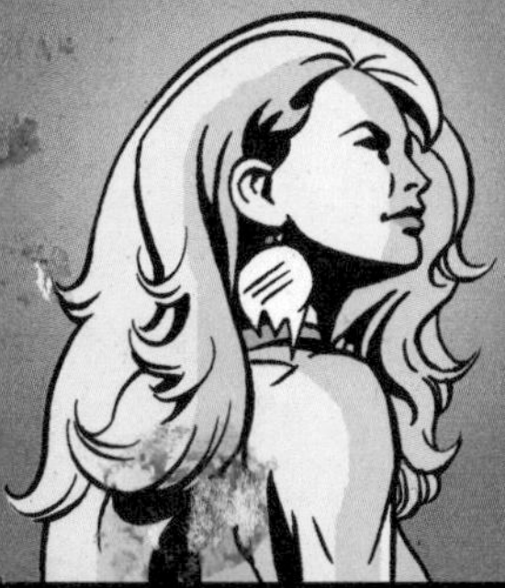

THE SNOW QUEEN

One of Geppetto's most trusted advisors, her powers are vast and her heart is wicked through and through.

THE STORY SO FAR

For centuries Fabletown and the Empire have gotten along in a state of mutual distrust, keeping a wary eye on each other. But recently the winds of war have begun to blow. The Adversary wants the exiles in Fabletown either brought back into the fold or slaughtered if they continue to hold out. Invasion plans are being drawn up while Fabletown seems none the wiser. In the meantime, Flycatcher, Fabletown's most lowly and humble citizen, has recently recovered lost memories of how his wife and family were brutally slaughtered during the Adversary's initial conquests of the Fable Homeworlds so many long ages ago...

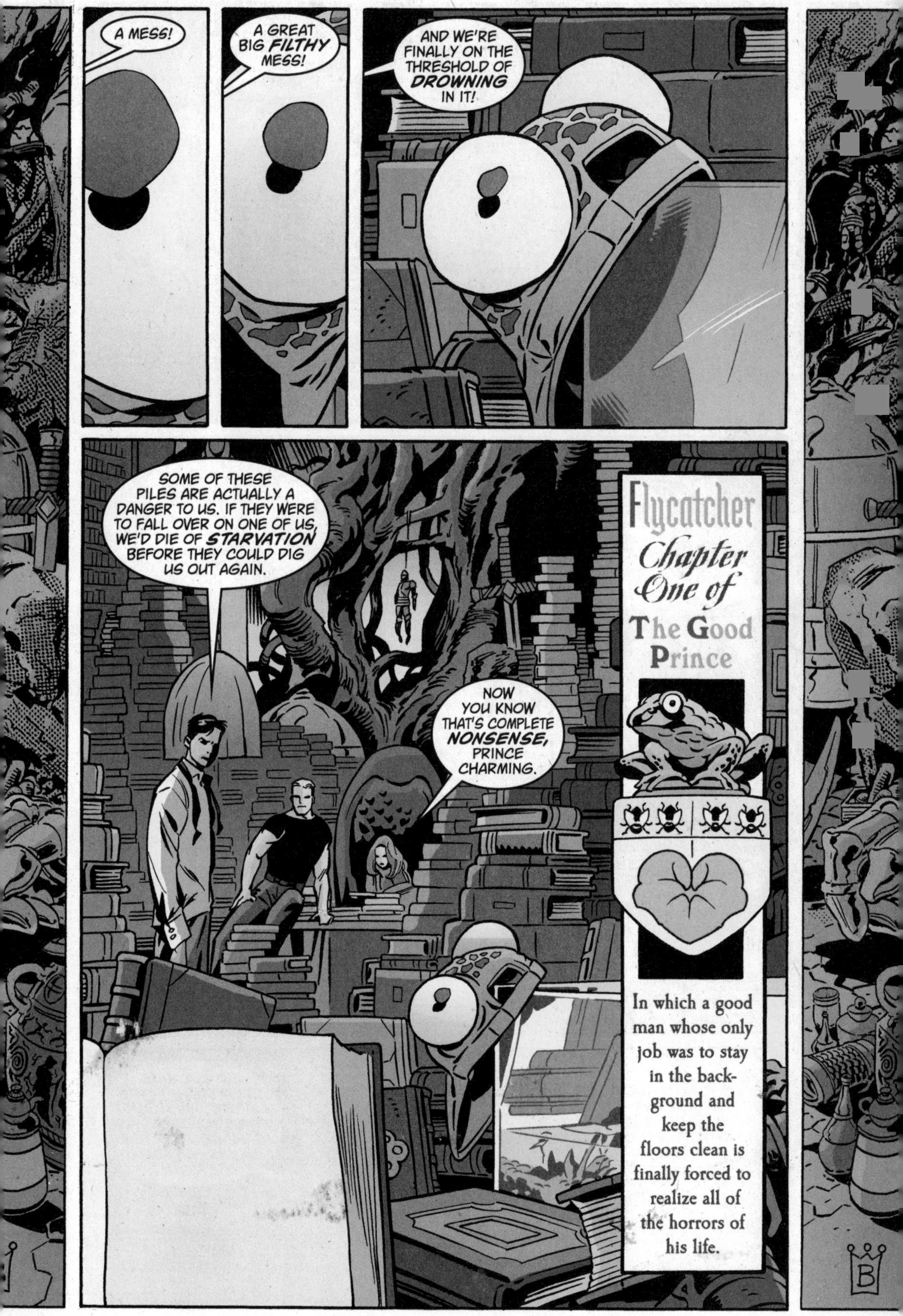
A MESS!
A GREAT BIG FILTHY MESS!
AND WE'RE FINALLY ON THE THRESHOLD OF DROWNING IN IT!
SOME OF THESE PILES ARE ACTUALLY A DANGER TO US. IF THEY WERE TO FALL OVER ON ONE OF US, WE'D DIE OF STARVATION BEFORE THEY COULD DIG US OUT AGAIN.
NOW YOU KNOW THAT'S COMPLETE NONSENSE, PRINCE CHARMING.
Flycatcher
Chapter One of
The Good Prince
In which a good man whose only job was to stay in the back-ground and keep the floors clean is finally forced to realize all of the horrors of his life.

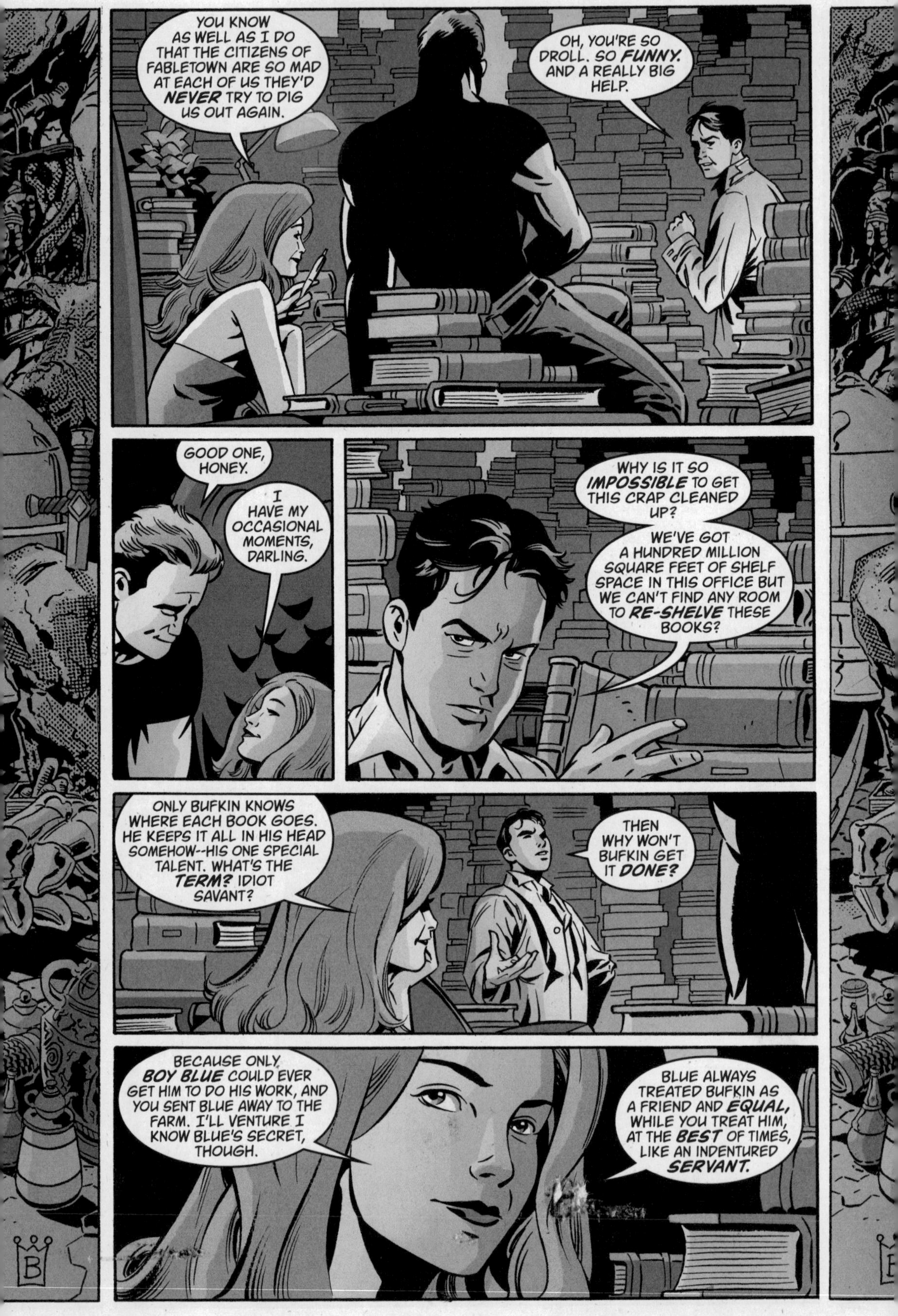
YOU KNOW AS WELL AS I DO THAT THE CITIZENS OF FABLETOWN ARE SO MAD AT EACH OF US THEY'D NEVER TRY TO DIG US OUT AGAIN.
OH, YOU'RE SO DROLL. SO FUNNY. AND A REALLY BIG HELP.
GOOD ONE, HONEY.
I HAVE MY OCCASIONAL MOMENTS, DARLING.
WHY IS IT SO IMPOSSIBLE TO GET THIS CRAP CLEANED UP?
WE'VE GOT A HUNDRED MILLION SQUARE FEET OF SHELF SPACE IN THIS OFFICE BUT WE CAN'T FIND ANY ROOM TO RE-SHELVE THESE BOOKS?
ONLY BUFKIN KNOWS WHERE EACH BOOK GOES. HE KEEPS IT ALL IN HIS HEAD SOMEHOW--HIS ONE SPECIAL TALENT. WHAT'S THE TERM? IDIOT SAVANT?
THEN WHY WON'T BUFKIN GET IT DONE?
BECAUSE ONLY BOY BLUE COULD EVER GET HIM TO DO HIS WORK, AND YOU SENT BLUE AWAY TO THE FARM. I'LL VENTURE I KNOW BLUE'S SECRET, THOUGH.
BLUE ALWAYS TREATED BUFKIN AS A FRIEND AND EQUAL, WHILE YOU TREAT HIM, AT THE BEST OF TIMES, LIKE AN INDENTURED SERVANT.

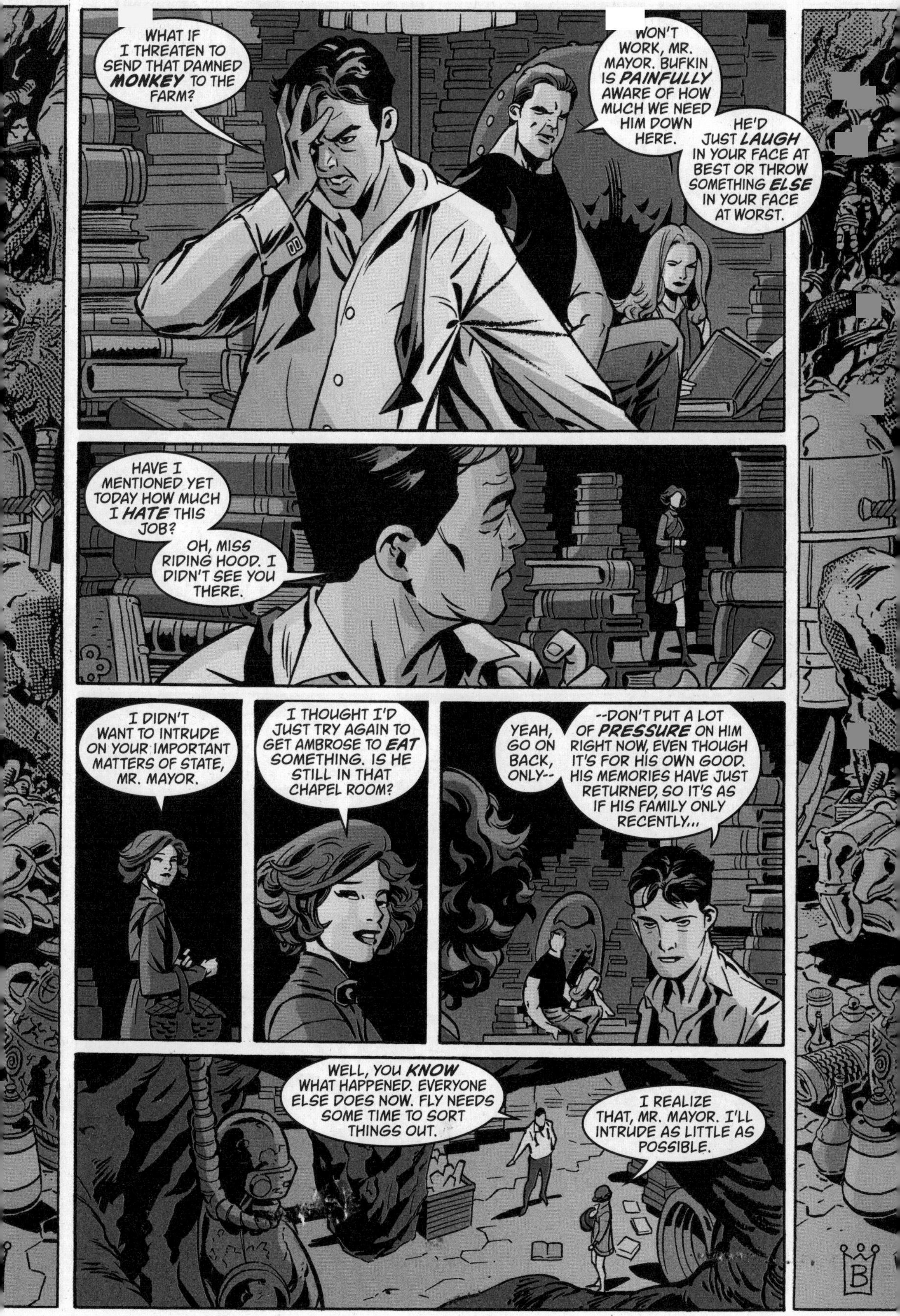
WHAT IF I THREATEN TO SEND THAT DAMNED MONKEY TO THE FARM?
WON'T WORK, MR. MAYOR. BUFKIN IS PAINFULLY AWARE OF HOW MUCH WE NEED HIM DOWN HERE.
HE'D JUST LAUGH IN YOUR FACE AT BEST OR THROW SOMETHING ELSE IN YOUR FACE AT WORST.
HAVE I MENTIONED YET TODAY HOW MUCH I HATE THIS JOB?
OH, MISS RIDING HOOD. I DIDN'T SEE YOU THERE.
I DIDN'T WANT TO INTRUDE ON YOUR IMPORTANT MATTERS OF STATE, MR. MAYOR.
I THOUGHT I'D JUST TRY AGAIN TO GET AMBROSE TO EAT SOMETHING. IS HE STILL IN THAT CHAPEL ROOM?
YEAH, GO ON BACK, ONLY--
--DON'T PUT A LOT OF PRESSURE ON HIM RIGHT NOW, EVEN THOUGH IT'S FOR HIS OWN GOOD. HIS MEMORIES HAVE JUST RETURNED, SO IT'S AS IF HIS FAMILY ONLY RECENTLY...
WELL, YOU KNOW WHAT HAPPENED. EVERYONE ELSE DOES NOW. FLY NEEDS SOME TIME TO SORT THINGS OUT.
I REALIZE THAT, MR. MAYOR. I'LL INTRUDE AS LITTLE AS POSSIBLE.

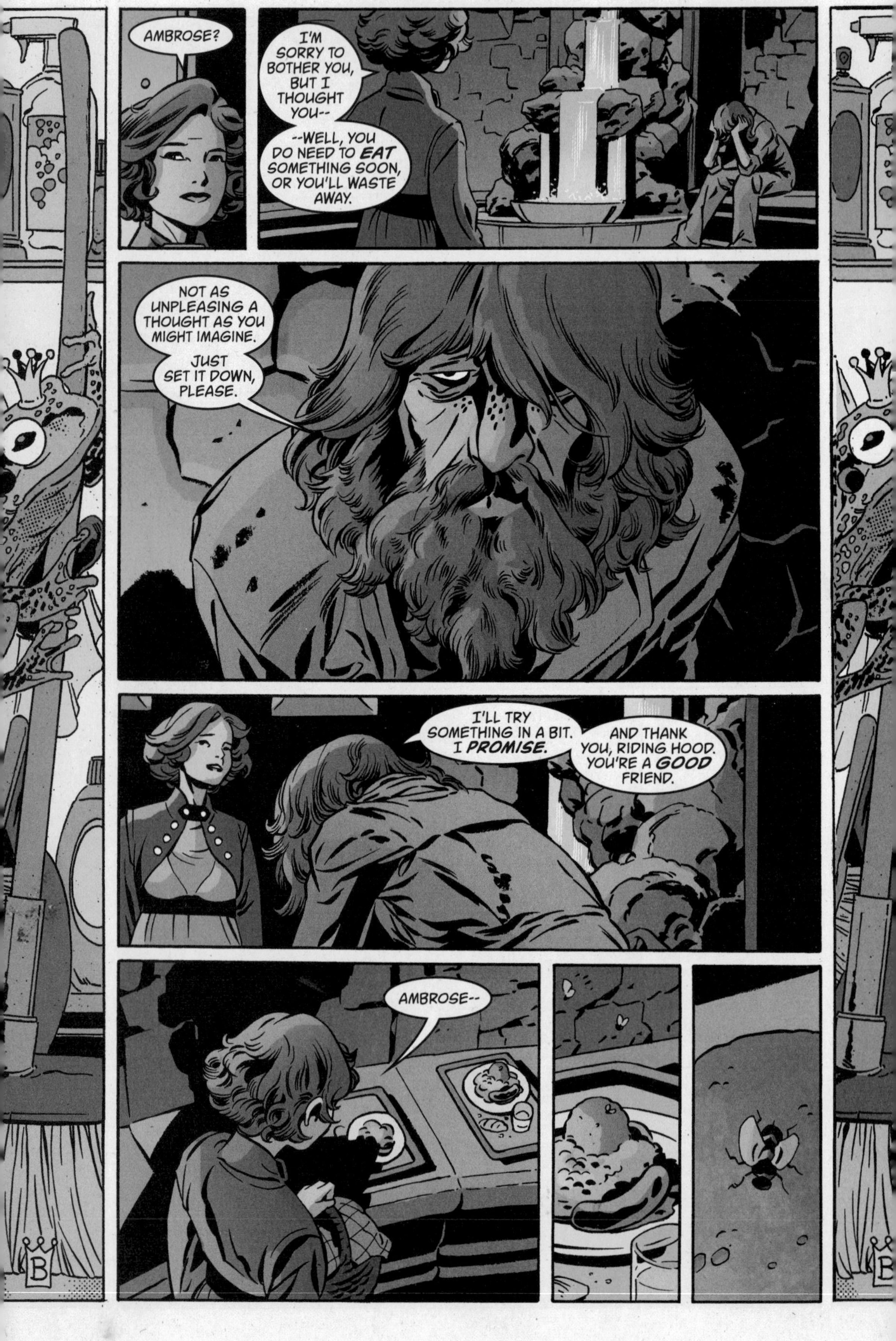
AMBROSE?
I'M SORRY TO BOTHER YOU, BUT I THOUGHT YOU--
--WELL, YOU DO NEED TO EAT SOMETHING SOON, OR YOU'LL WASTE AWAY.
NOT AS UNPLEASING A THOUGHT AS YOU MIGHT IMAGINE.
JUST SET IT DOWN, PLEASE.
I'LL TRY SOMETHING IN A BIT. I PROMISE.
AND THANK YOU, RIDING HOOD. YOU'RE A GOOD FRIEND.
AMBROSE--

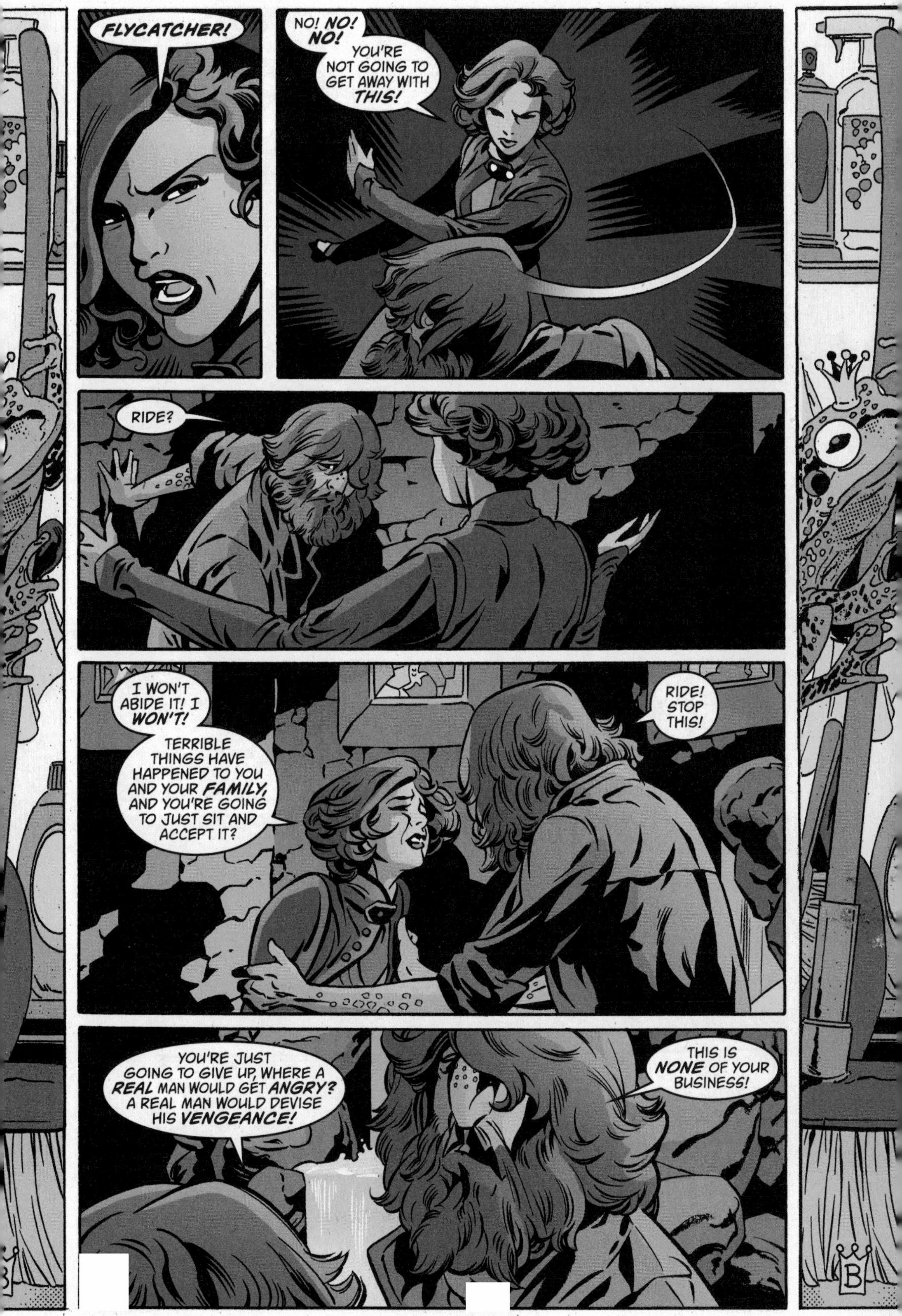
FLYCATCHER!
NO! NO! NO!
YOU'RE NOT GOING TO GET AWAY WITH THIS!
RIDE?
I WON'T ABIDE IT! I WON'T!
TERRIBLE THINGS HAVE HAPPENED TO YOU AND YOUR FAMILY, AND YOU'RE GOING TO JUST SIT AND ACCEPT IT?
RIDE! STOP THIS!
YOU'RE JUST GOING TO GIVE UP, WHERE A REAL MAN WOULD GET ANGRY? A REAL MAN WOULD DEVISE HIS VENGEANCE!
THIS IS NONE OF YOUR BUSINESS!

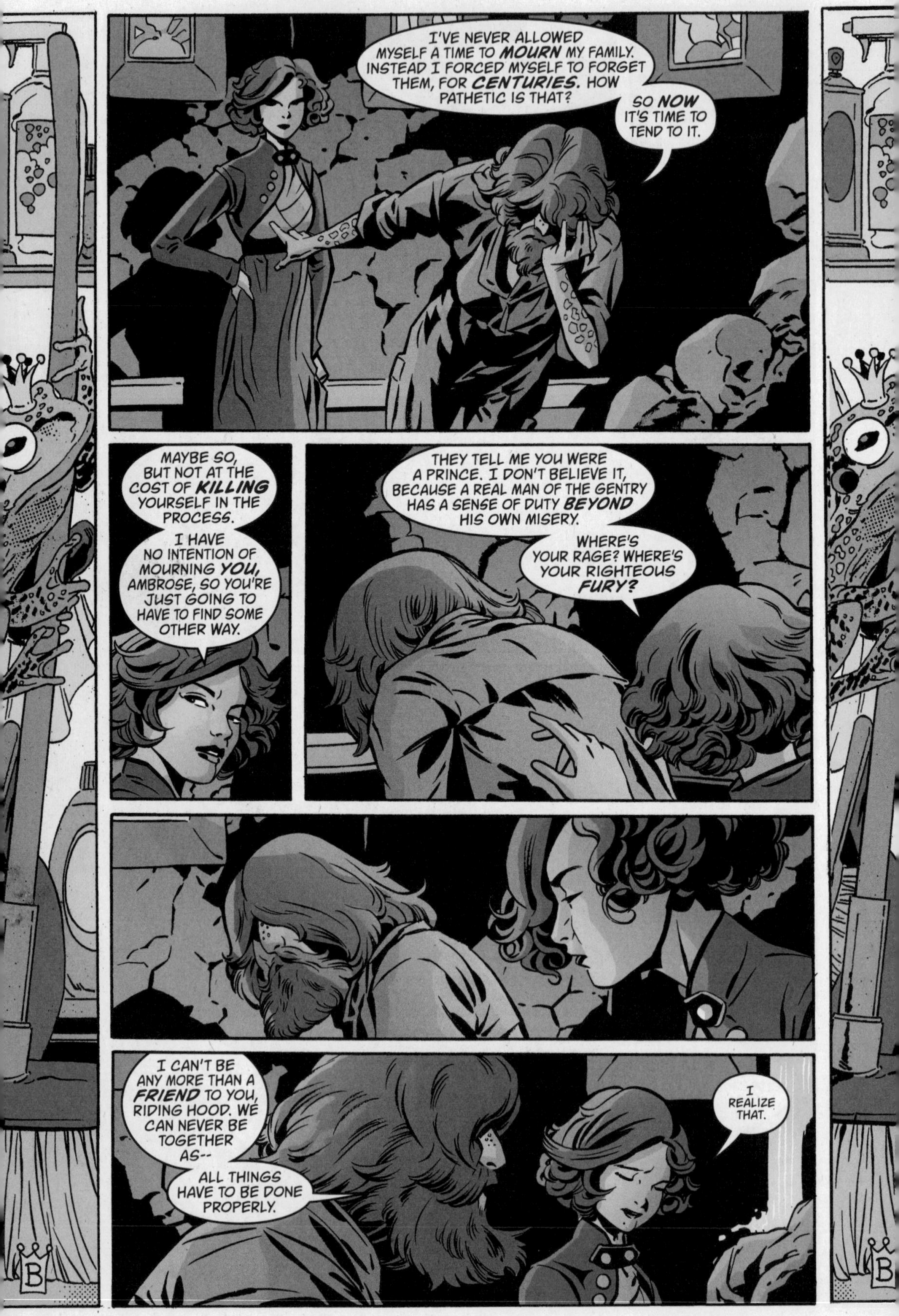
I'VE NEVER ALLOWED MYSELF A TIME TO MOURN MY FAMILY. INSTEAD I FORCED MYSELF TO FORGET THEM, FOR CENTURIES. HOW PATHETIC IS THAT?
SO NOW IT'S TIME TO TEND TO IT.
MAYBE SO, BUT NOT AT THE COST OF KILLING YOURSELF IN THE PROCESS.
I HAVE NO INTENTION OF MOURNING YOU, AMBROSE, SO YOU'RE JUST GOING TO HAVE TO FIND SOME OTHER WAY.
THEY TELL ME YOU WERE A PRINCE. I DON'T BELIEVE IT, BECAUSE A REAL MAN OF THE GENTRY HAS A SENSE OF DUTY BEYOND HIS OWN MISERY.
WHERE'S YOUR RAGE? WHERE'S YOUR RIGHTEOUS FURY?
I CAN'T BE ANY MORE THAN A FRIEND TO YOU, RIDING HOOD. WE CAN NEVER BE TOGETHER AS--
ALL THINGS HAVE TO BE DONE PROPERLY.
I REALIZE THAT.

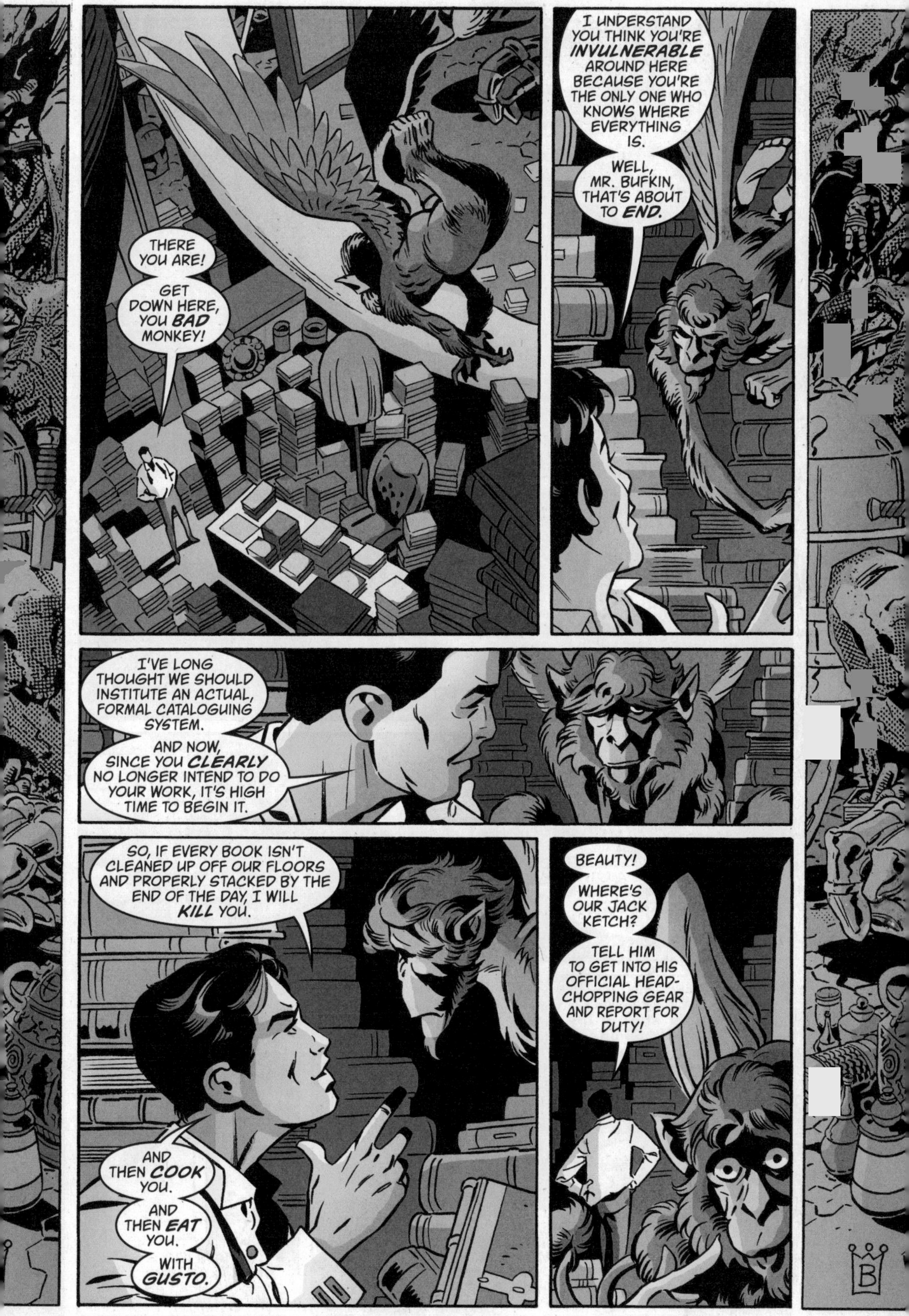

THERE YOU ARE!
GET DOWN HERE, YOU BAD MONKEY!
I UNDERSTAND YOU THINK YOU'RE INVULNERABLE AROUND HERE BECAUSE YOU'RE THE ONLY ONE WHO KNOWS WHERE EVERYTHING IS.
WELL, MR. BUFKIN, THAT'S ABOUT TO END.
I'VE LONG THOUGHT WE SHOULD INSTITUTE AN ACTUAL, FORMAL CATALOGUING SYSTEM.
AND NOW, SINCE YOU CLEARLY NO LONGER INTEND TO DO YOUR WORK, IT'S HIGH TIME TO BEGIN IT.
SO, IF EVERY BOOK ISN'T CLEANED UP OFF OUR FLOORS AND PROPERLY STACKED BY THE END OF THE DAY, I WILL KILL YOU.
AND THEN COOK YOU.
AND THEN EAT YOU.
WITH GUSTO.
BEAUTY!
WHERE'S OUR JACK KETCH?
TELL HIM TO GET INTO HIS OFFICIAL HEAD-CHOPPING GEAR AND REPORT FOR DUTY!

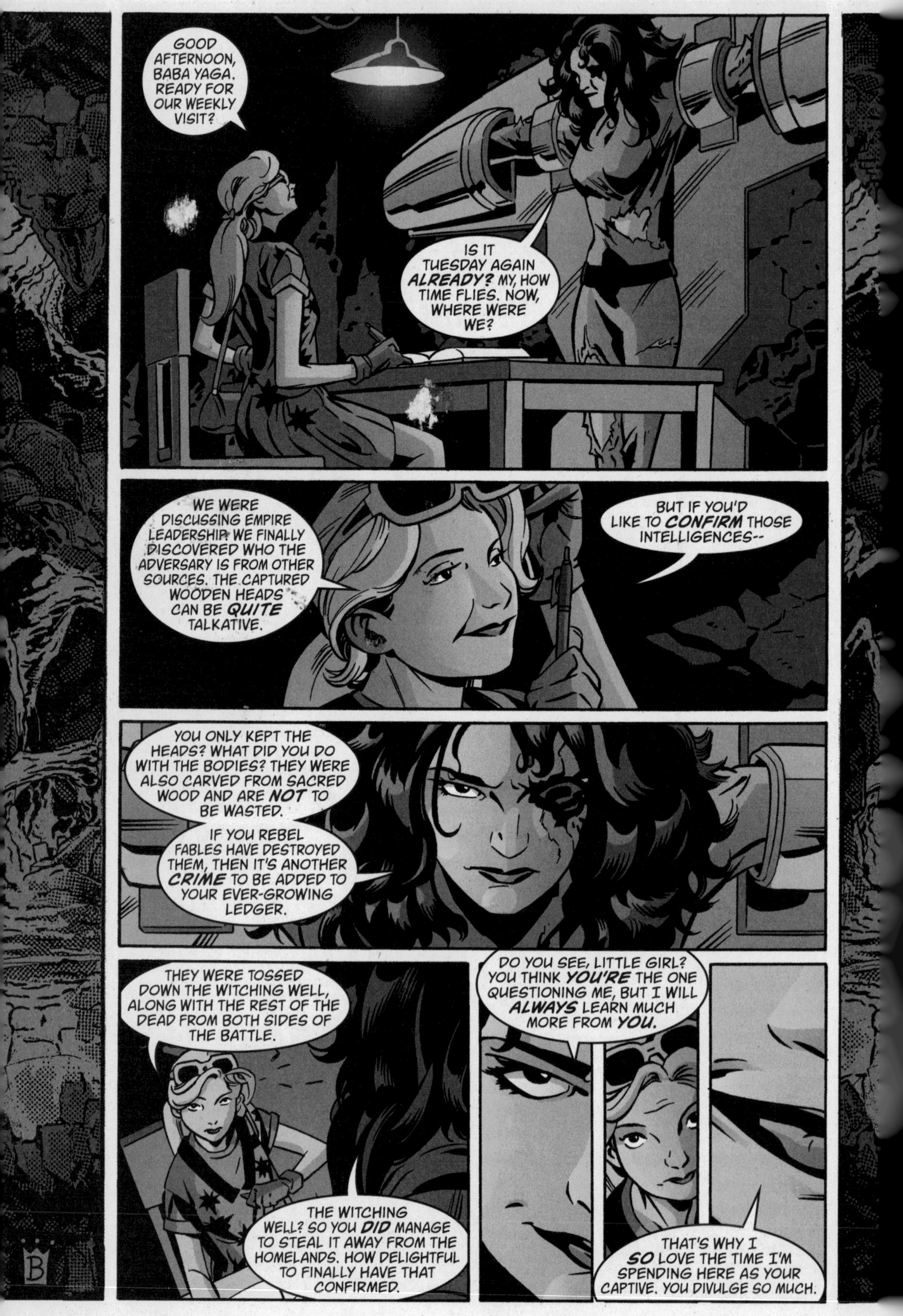
GOOD AFTERNOON, BABA YAGA. READY FOR OUR WEEKLY VISIT?
IS IT TUESDAY AGAIN ALREADY? MY, HOW TIME FLIES. NOW, WHERE WERE WE?
WE WERE DISCUSSING EMPIRE LEADERSHIP. WE FINALLY DISCOVERED WHO THE ADVERSARY IS FROM OTHER SOURCES. THE CAPTURED WOODEN HEADS CAN BE QUITE TALKATIVE.
BUT IF YOU'D LIKE TO CONFIRM THOSE INTELLIGENCES--
YOU ONLY KEPT THE HEADS? WHAT DID YOU DO WITH THE BODIES? THEY WERE ALSO CARVED FROM SACRED WOOD AND ARE NOT TO BE WASTED.
IF YOU REBEL FABLES HAVE DESTROYED THEM, THEN IT'S ANOTHER CRIME TO BE ADDED TO YOUR EVER-GROWING LEDGER.
THEY WERE TOSSED DOWN THE WITCHING WELL, ALONG WITH THE REST OF THE DEAD FROM BOTH SIDES OF THE BATTLE.
THE WITCHING WELL? SO YOU DID MANAGE TO STEAL IT AWAY FROM THE HOMELANDS. HOW DELIGHTFUL TO FINALLY HAVE THAT CONFIRMED.
DO YOU SEE, LITTLE GIRL? YOU THINK YOU'RE THE ONE QUESTIONING ME, BUT I WILL ALWAYS LEARN MUCH MORE FROM YOU.
THAT'S WHY I SO LOVE THE TIME I'M SPENDING HERE AS YOUR CAPTIVE. YOU DIVULGE SO MUCH.

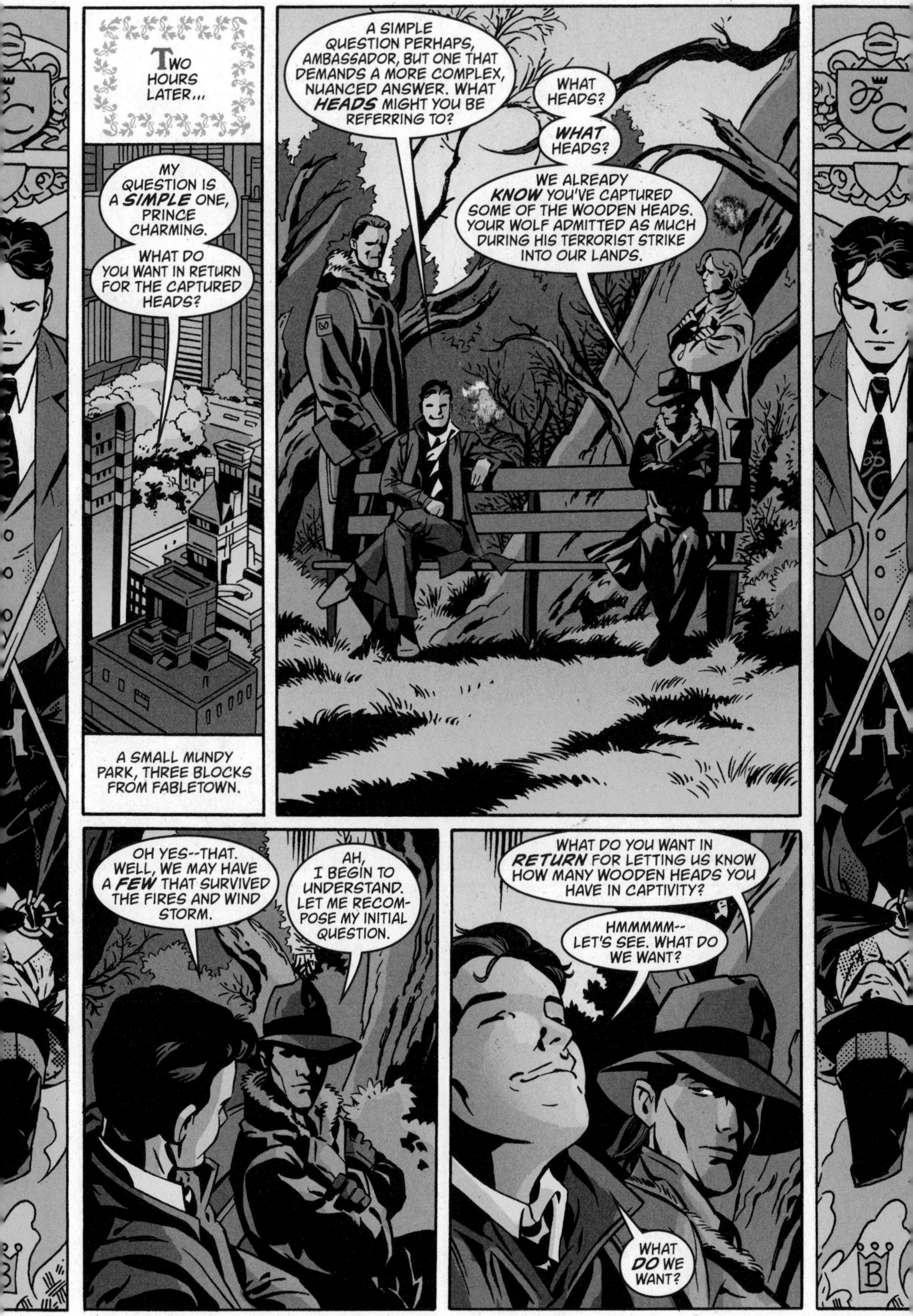
TWO HOURS LATER...
MY QUESTION IS A SIMPLE ONE, PRINCE CHARMING.
WHAT DO YOU WANT IN RETURN FOR THE CAPTURED HEADS?
A SMALL MUNDY PARK, THREE BLOCKS FROM FABLETOWN.
A SIMPLE QUESTION PERHAPS, AMBASSADOR, BUT ONE THAT DEMANDS A MORE COMPLEX, NUANCED ANSWER. WHAT HEADS MIGHT YOU BE REFERRING TO?
WHAT HEADS?
WHAT HEADS?
WE ALREADY KNOW YOU'VE CAPTURED SOME OF THE WOODEN HEADS. YOUR WOLF ADMITTED AS MUCH DURING HIS TERRORIST STRIKE INTO OUR LANDS.
OH YES--THAT. WELL, WE MAY HAVE A FEW THAT SURVIVED THE FIRES AND WIND STORM.
AH, I BEGIN TO UNDERSTAND. LET ME RECOMPOSE MY INITIAL QUESTION.
WHAT DO YOU WANT IN RETURN FOR LETTING US KNOW HOW MANY WOODEN HEADS YOU HAVE IN CAPTIVITY?
HMMMMM-- LET'S SEE. WHAT DO WE WANT?
WHAT DO WE WANT?

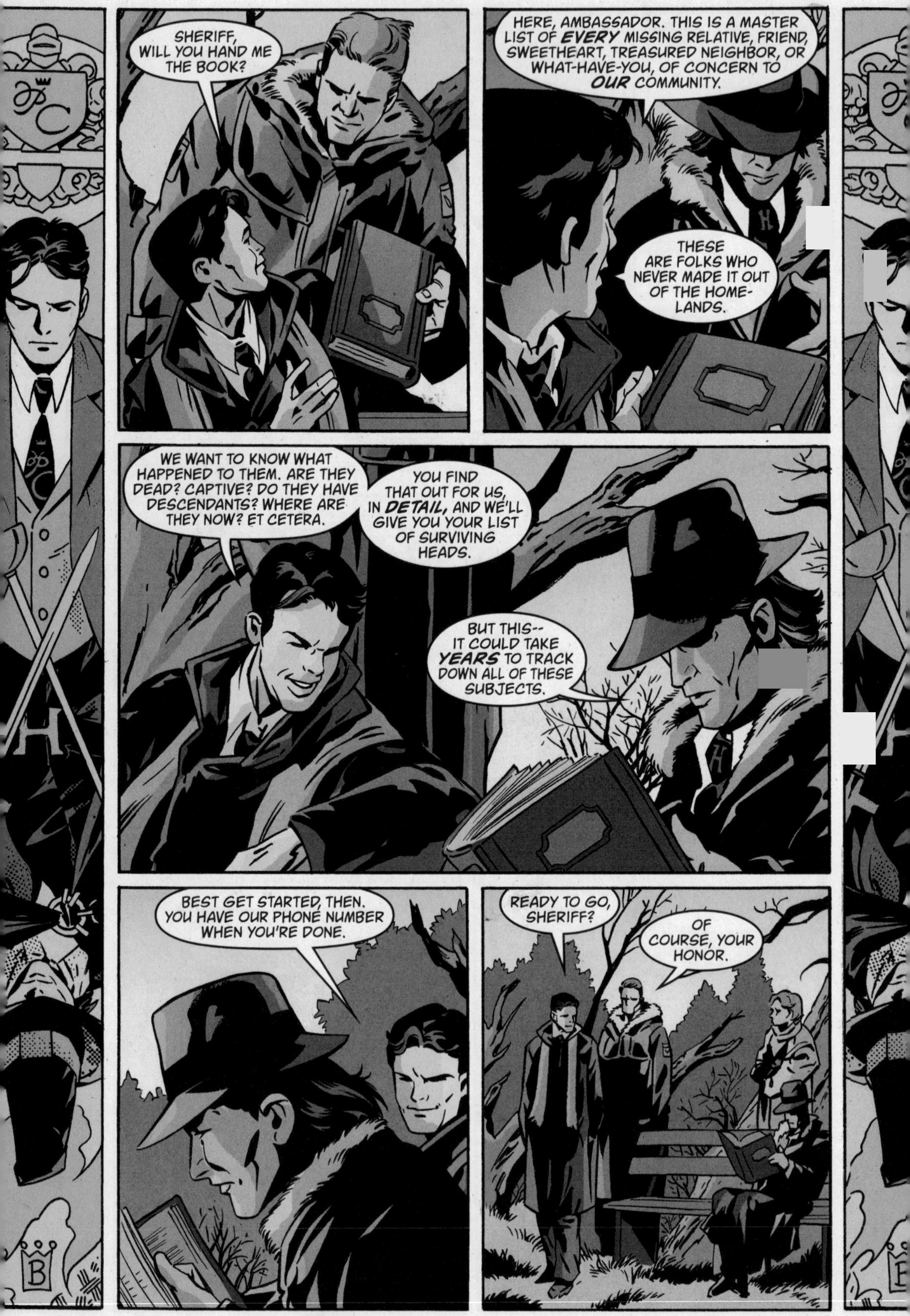
SHERIFF, WILL YOU HAND ME THE BOOK?
HERE, AMBASSADOR. THIS IS A MASTER LIST OF EVERY MISSING RELATIVE, FRIEND, SWEETHEART, TREASURED NEIGHBOR, OR WHAT-HAVE-YOU, OF CONCERN TO OUR COMMUNITY.
THESE ARE FOLKS WHO NEVER MADE IT OUT OF THE HOME-LANDS.
WE WANT TO KNOW WHAT HAPPENED TO THEM. ARE THEY DEAD? CAPTIVE? DO THEY HAVE DESCENDANTS? WHERE ARE THEY NOW? ET CETERA.
YOU FIND THAT OUT FOR US, IN DETAIL, AND WE'LL GIVE YOU YOUR LIST OF SURVIVING HEADS.
BUT THIS-- IT COULD TAKE YEARS TO TRACK DOWN ALL OF THESE SUBJECTS.
BEST GET STARTED, THEN. YOU HAVE OUR PHONE NUMBER WHEN YOU'RE DONE.
READY TO GO, SHERIFF?
OF COURSE, YOUR HONOR.

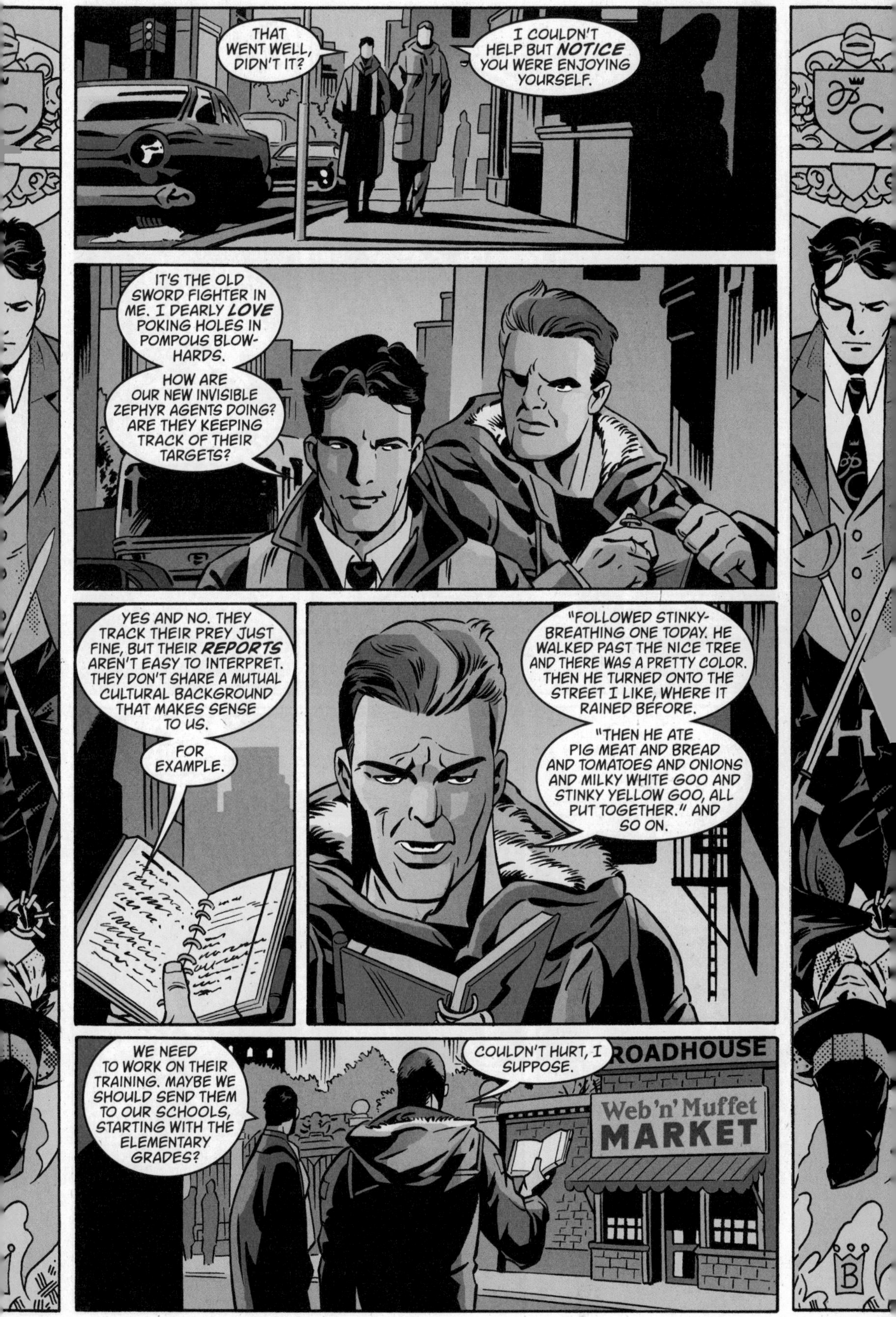
THAT WENT WELL, DIDN'T IT?
I COULDN'T HELP BUT NOTICE YOU WERE ENJOYING YOURSELF.
IT'S THE OLD SWORD FIGHTER IN ME. I DEARLY LOVE POKING HOLES IN POMPOUS BLOW-HARDS.
HOW ARE OUR NEW INVISIBLE ZEPHYR AGENTS DOING? ARE THEY KEEPING TRACK OF THEIR TARGETS?
YES AND NO. THEY TRACK THEIR PREY JUST FINE, BUT THEIR REPORTS AREN'T EASY TO INTERPRET. THEY DON'T SHARE A MUTUAL CULTURAL BACKGROUND THAT MAKES SENSE TO US.
FOR EXAMPLE.
"FOLLOWED STINKY-BREATHING ONE TODAY. HE WALKED PAST THE NICE TREE AND THERE WAS A PRETTY COLOR. THEN HE TURNED ONTO THE STREET I LIKE, WHERE IT RAINED BEFORE.
"THEN HE ATE PIG MEAT AND BREAD AND TOMATOES AND ONIONS AND MILKY WHITE GOO AND STINKY YELLOW GOO, ALL PUT TOGETHER." AND SO ON.
WE NEED TO WORK ON THEIR TRAINING. MAYBE WE SHOULD SEND THEM TO OUR SCHOOLS, STARTING WITH THE ELEMENTARY GRADES?
COULDN'T HURT, I SUPPOSE.
ROADHOUSE
Web'n'Muffet MARKET

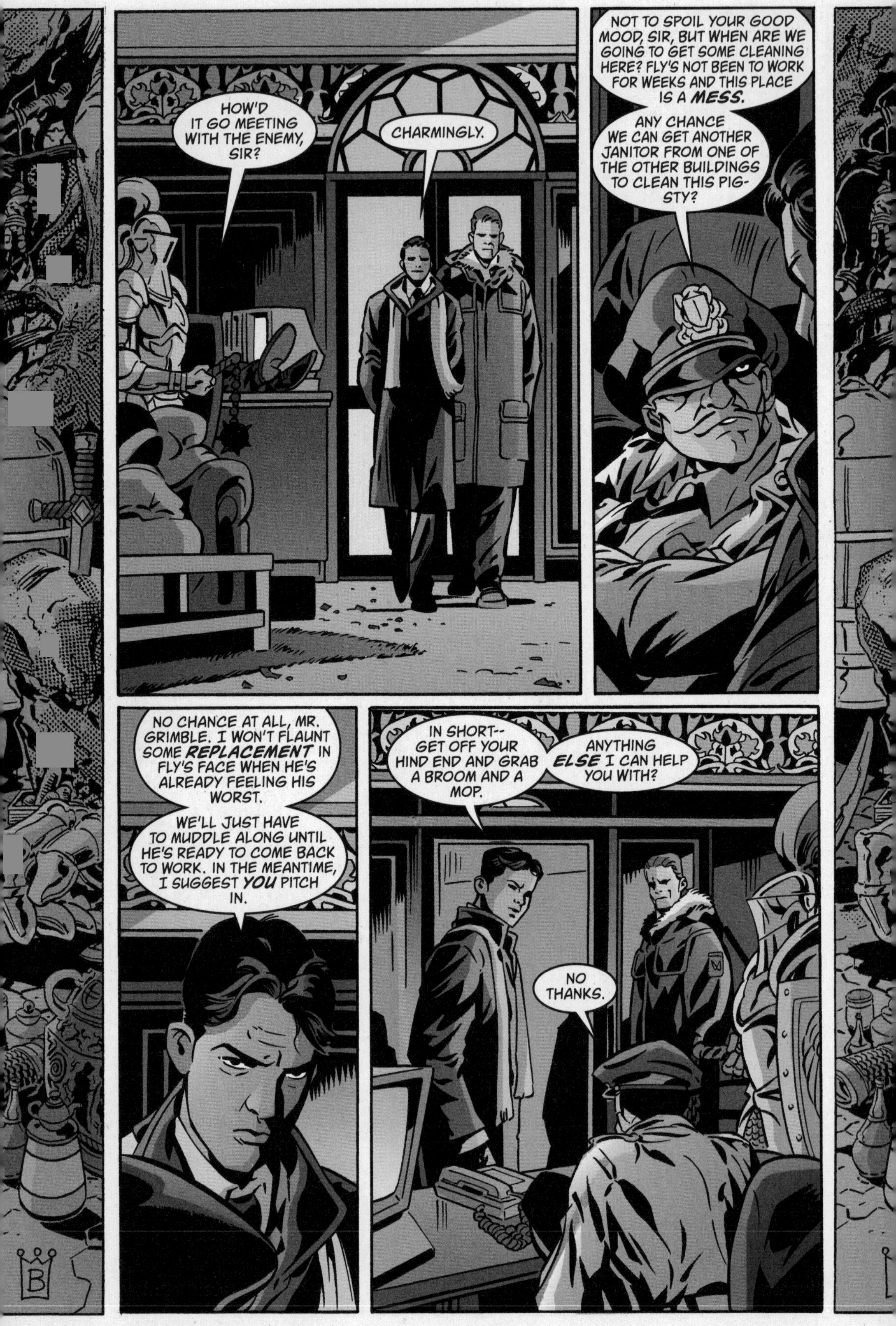
HOW'D IT GO MEETING WITH THE ENEMY, SIR?
CHARMINGLY.
NOT TO SPOIL YOUR GOOD MOOD, SIR, BUT WHEN ARE WE GOING TO GET SOME CLEANING HERE? FLY'S NOT BEEN TO WORK FOR WEEKS AND THIS PLACE IS A *MESS.*
ANY CHANCE WE CAN GET ANOTHER JANITOR FROM ONE OF THE OTHER BUILDINGS TO CLEAN THIS PIG-STY?
NO CHANCE AT ALL, MR. GRIMBLE. I WON'T FLAUNT SOME *REPLACEMENT* IN FLY'S FACE WHEN HE'S ALREADY FEELING HIS WORST.
WE'LL JUST HAVE TO MUDDLE ALONG UNTIL HE'S READY TO COME BACK TO WORK. IN THE MEANTIME, I SUGGEST *YOU* PITCH IN.
IN SHORT-- GET OFF YOUR HIND END AND GRAB A BROOM AND A MOP.
ANYTHING *ELSE* I CAN HELP YOU WITH?
NO THANKS.

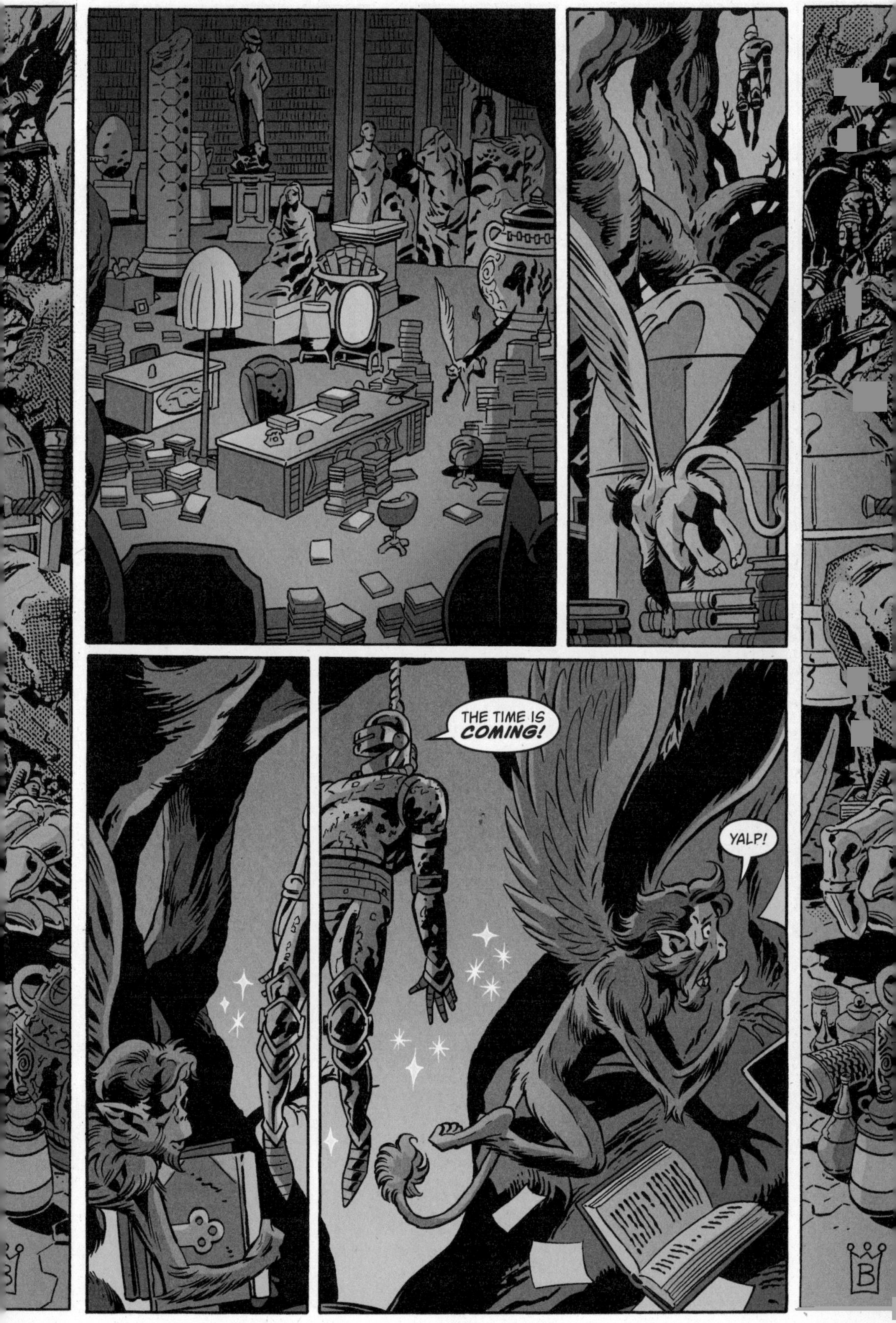
THE TIME IS COMING!
YALP!

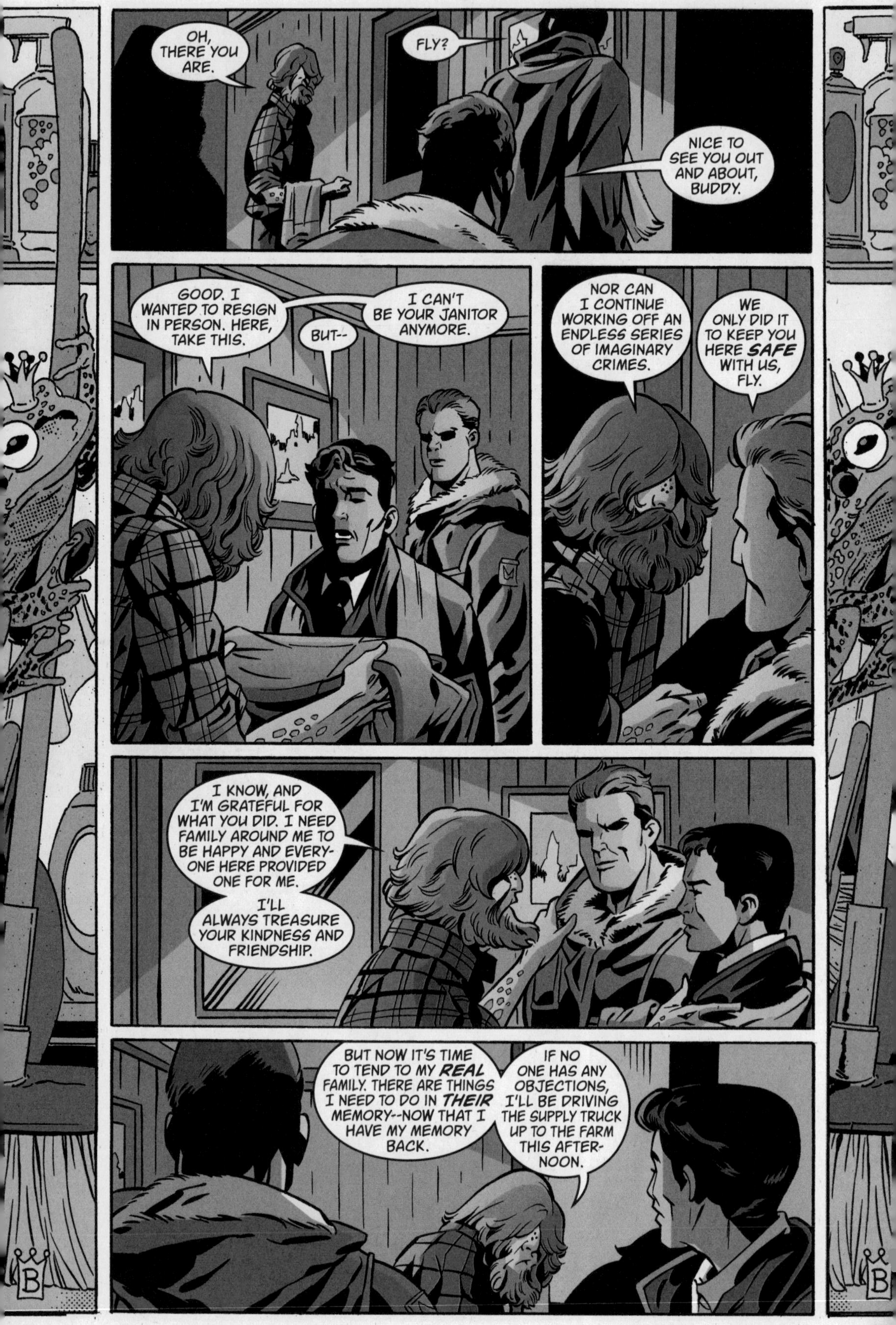

OH, THERE YOU ARE.
FLY?
NICE TO SEE YOU OUT AND ABOUT, BUDDY.
GOOD. I WANTED TO RESIGN IN PERSON. HERE, TAKE THIS.
BUT--
I CAN'T BE YOUR JANITOR ANYMORE.
NOR CAN I CONTINUE WORKING OFF AN ENDLESS SERIES OF IMAGINARY CRIMES.
WE ONLY DID IT TO KEEP YOU HERE SAFE WITH US, FLY.
I KNOW, AND I'M GRATEFUL FOR WHAT YOU DID. I NEED FAMILY AROUND ME TO BE HAPPY AND EVERY-ONE HERE PROVIDED ONE FOR ME.
I'LL ALWAYS TREASURE YOUR KINDNESS AND FRIENDSHIP.
BUT NOW IT'S TIME TO TEND TO MY REAL FAMILY. THERE ARE THINGS I NEED TO DO IN THEIR MEMORY--NOW THAT I HAVE MY MEMORY BACK.
IF NO ONE HAS ANY OBJECTIONS, I'LL BE DRIVING THE SUPPLY TRUCK UP TO THE FARM THIS AFTER-NOON.

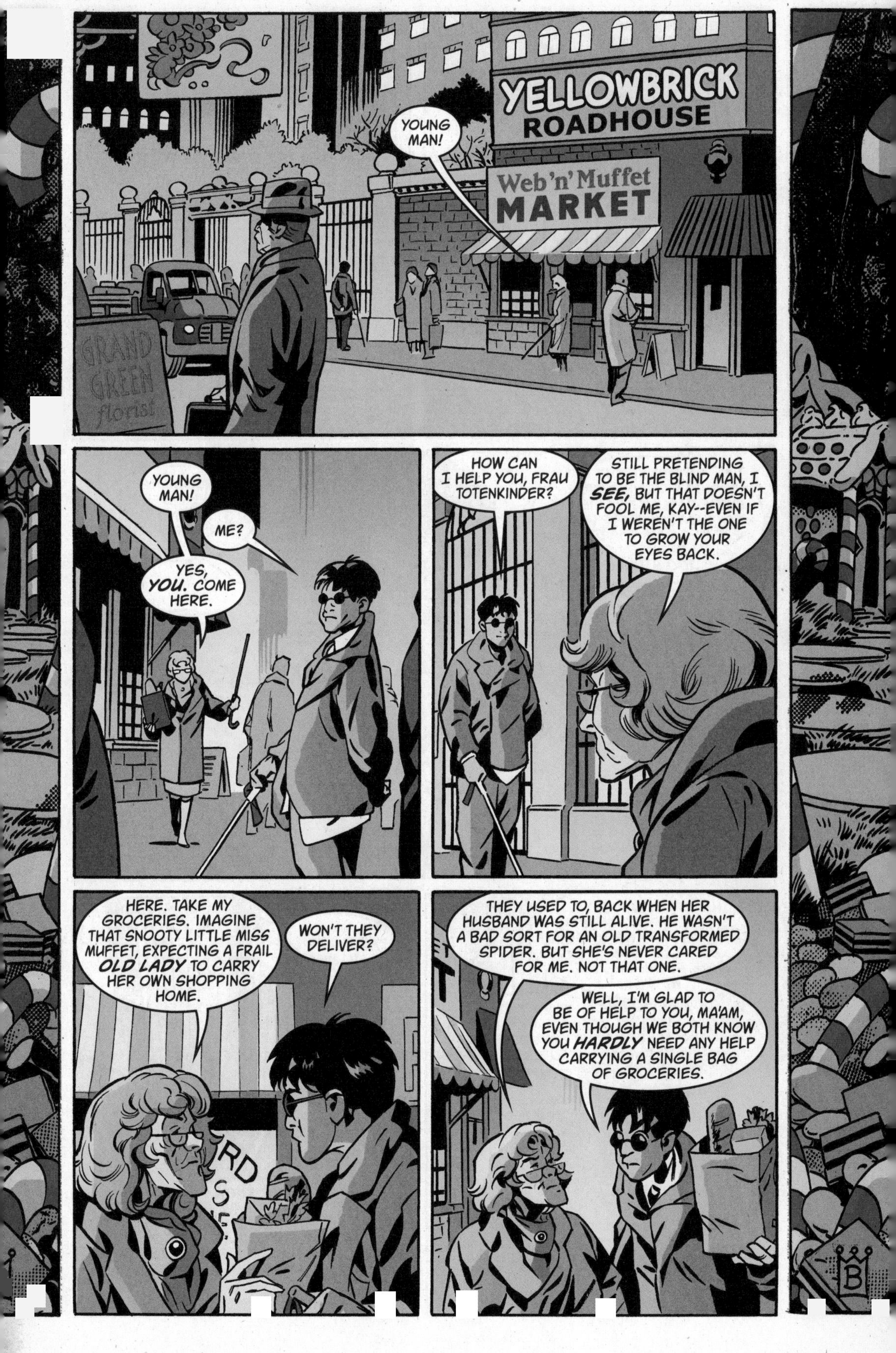

YELLOWBRICK ROADHOUSE
Web 'n' Muffet MARKET
GRAND GREEN florist
YOUNG MAN!
YOUNG MAN!
ME?
YES, YOU. COME HERE.
HOW CAN I HELP YOU, FRAU TOTENKINDER?
STILL PRETENDING TO BE THE BLIND MAN, I SEE, BUT THAT DOESN'T FOOL ME, KAY--EVEN IF I WEREN'T THE ONE TO GROW YOUR EYES BACK.
HERE. TAKE MY GROCERIES. IMAGINE THAT SNOOTY LITTLE MISS MUFFET, EXPECTING A FRAIL OLD LADY TO CARRY HER OWN SHOPPING HOME.
WON'T THEY DELIVER?
THEY USED TO, BACK WHEN HER HUSBAND WAS STILL ALIVE. HE WASN'T A BAD SORT FOR AN OLD TRANSFORMED SPIDER. BUT SHE'S NEVER CARED FOR ME. NOT THAT ONE.
WELL, I'M GLAD TO BE OF HELP TO YOU, MA'AM, EVEN THOUGH WE BOTH KNOW YOU HARDLY NEED ANY HELP CARRYING A SINGLE BAG OF GROCERIES.

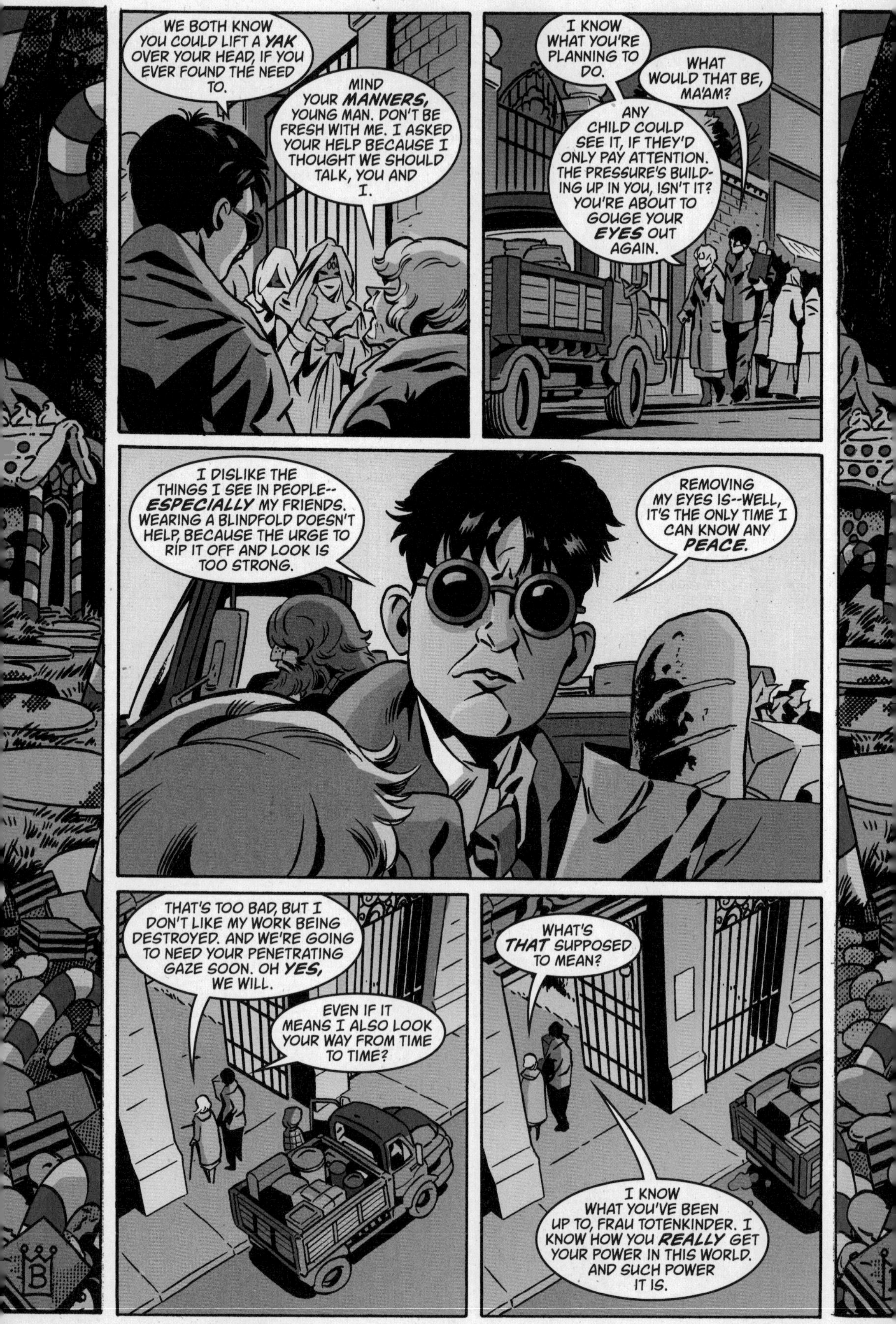
WE BOTH KNOW YOU COULD LIFT A YAK OVER YOUR HEAD, IF YOU EVER FOUND THE NEED TO.
MIND YOUR MANNERS, YOUNG MAN. DON'T BE FRESH WITH ME. I ASKED YOUR HELP BECAUSE I THOUGHT WE SHOULD TALK, YOU AND I.
I KNOW WHAT YOU'RE PLANNING TO DO.
WHAT WOULD THAT BE, MA'AM?
ANY CHILD COULD SEE IT, IF THEY'D ONLY PAY ATTENTION. THE PRESSURE'S BUILD-ING UP IN YOU, ISN'T IT? YOU'RE ABOUT TO GOUGE YOUR EYES OUT AGAIN.
I DISLIKE THE THINGS I SEE IN PEOPLE-- ESPECIALLY MY FRIENDS. WEARING A BLINDFOLD DOESN'T HELP, BECAUSE THE URGE TO RIP IT OFF AND LOOK IS TOO STRONG.
REMOVING MY EYES IS--WELL, IT'S THE ONLY TIME I CAN KNOW ANY PEACE.
THAT'S TOO BAD, BUT I DON'T LIKE MY WORK BEING DESTROYED. AND WE'RE GOING TO NEED YOUR PENETRATING GAZE SOON. OH YES, WE WILL.
EVEN IF IT MEANS I ALSO LOOK YOUR WAY FROM TIME TO TIME?
WHAT'S THAT SUPPOSED TO MEAN?
I KNOW WHAT YOU'VE BEEN UP TO, FRAU TOTENKINDER. I KNOW HOW YOU REALLY GET YOUR POWER IN THIS WORLD. AND SUCH POWER IT IS.

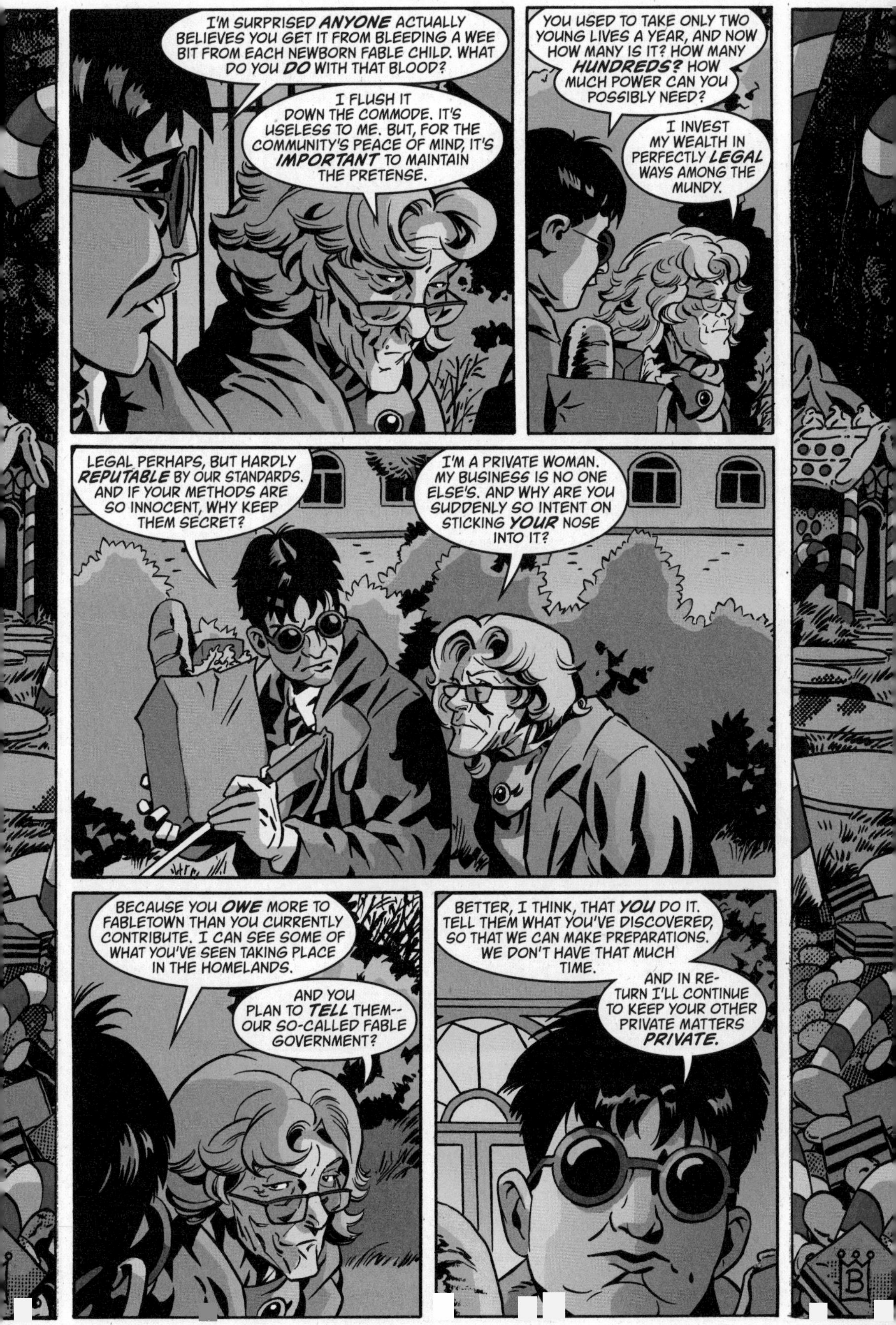

I'M SURPRISED ANYONE ACTUALLY BELIEVES YOU GET IT FROM BLEEDING A WEE BIT FROM EACH NEWBORN FABLE CHILD. WHAT DO YOU DO WITH THAT BLOOD?
I FLUSH IT DOWN THE COMMODE. IT'S USELESS TO ME. BUT, FOR THE COMMUNITY'S PEACE OF MIND, IT'S IMPORTANT TO MAINTAIN THE PRETENSE.
YOU USED TO TAKE ONLY TWO YOUNG LIVES A YEAR, AND NOW HOW MANY IS IT? HOW MANY HUNDREDS? HOW MUCH POWER CAN YOU POSSIBLY NEED?
I INVEST MY WEALTH IN PERFECTLY LEGAL WAYS AMONG THE MUNDY.
LEGAL PERHAPS, BUT HARDLY REPUTABLE BY OUR STANDARDS. AND IF YOUR METHODS ARE SO INNOCENT, WHY KEEP THEM SECRET?
I'M A PRIVATE WOMAN. MY BUSINESS IS NO ONE ELSE'S. AND WHY ARE YOU SUDDENLY SO INTENT ON STICKING YOUR NOSE INTO IT?
BECAUSE YOU OWE MORE TO FABLETOWN THAN YOU CURRENTLY CONTRIBUTE. I CAN SEE SOME OF WHAT YOU'VE SEEN TAKING PLACE IN THE HOMELANDS.
AND YOU PLAN TO TELL THEM--OUR SO-CALLED FABLE GOVERNMENT?
BETTER, I THINK, THAT YOU DO IT. TELL THEM WHAT YOU'VE DISCOVERED, SO THAT WE CAN MAKE PREPARATIONS. WE DON'T HAVE THAT MUCH TIME.
AND IN RETURN I'LL CONTINUE TO KEEP YOUR OTHER PRIVATE MATTERS PRIVATE.

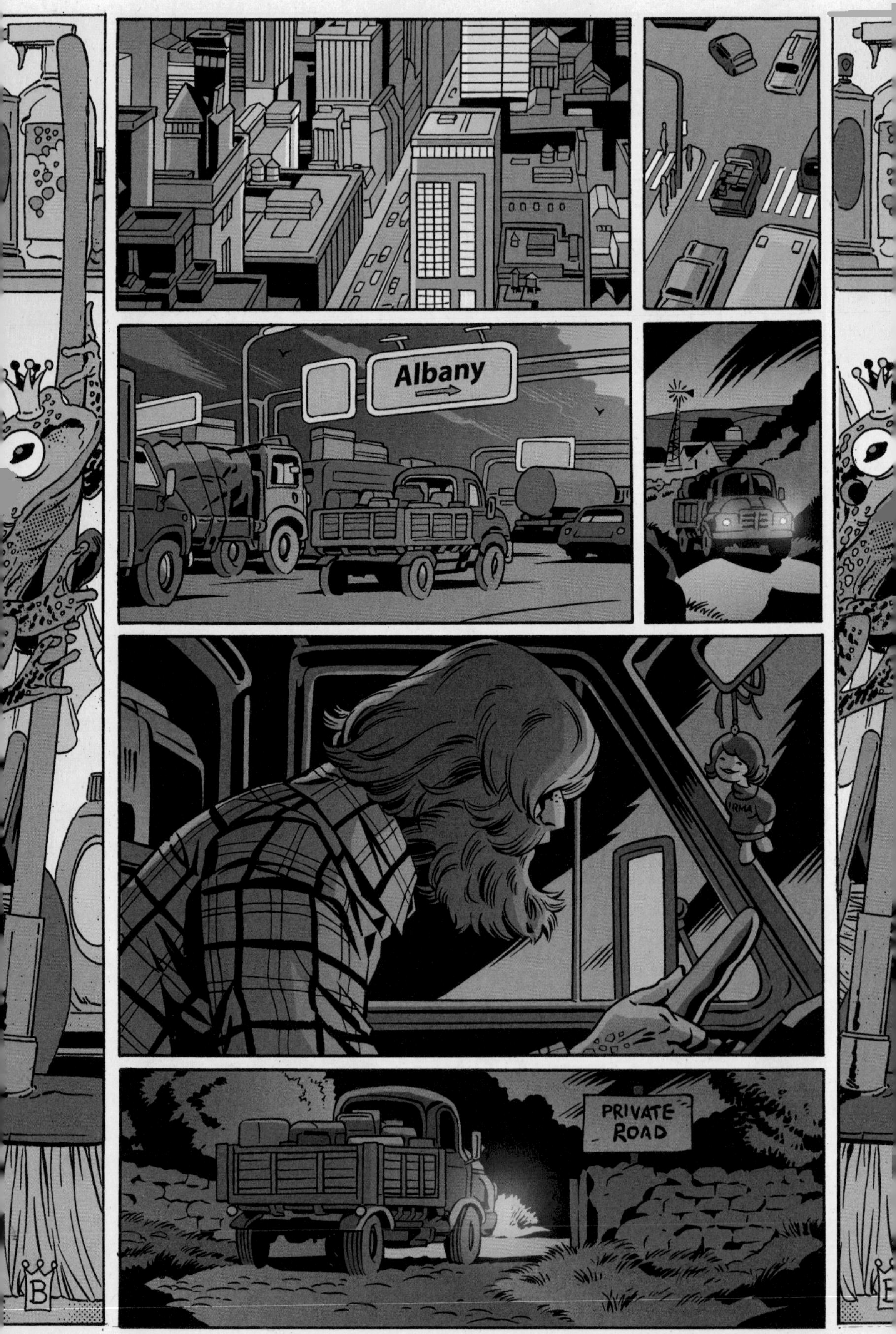
Albany
PRIVATE ROAD

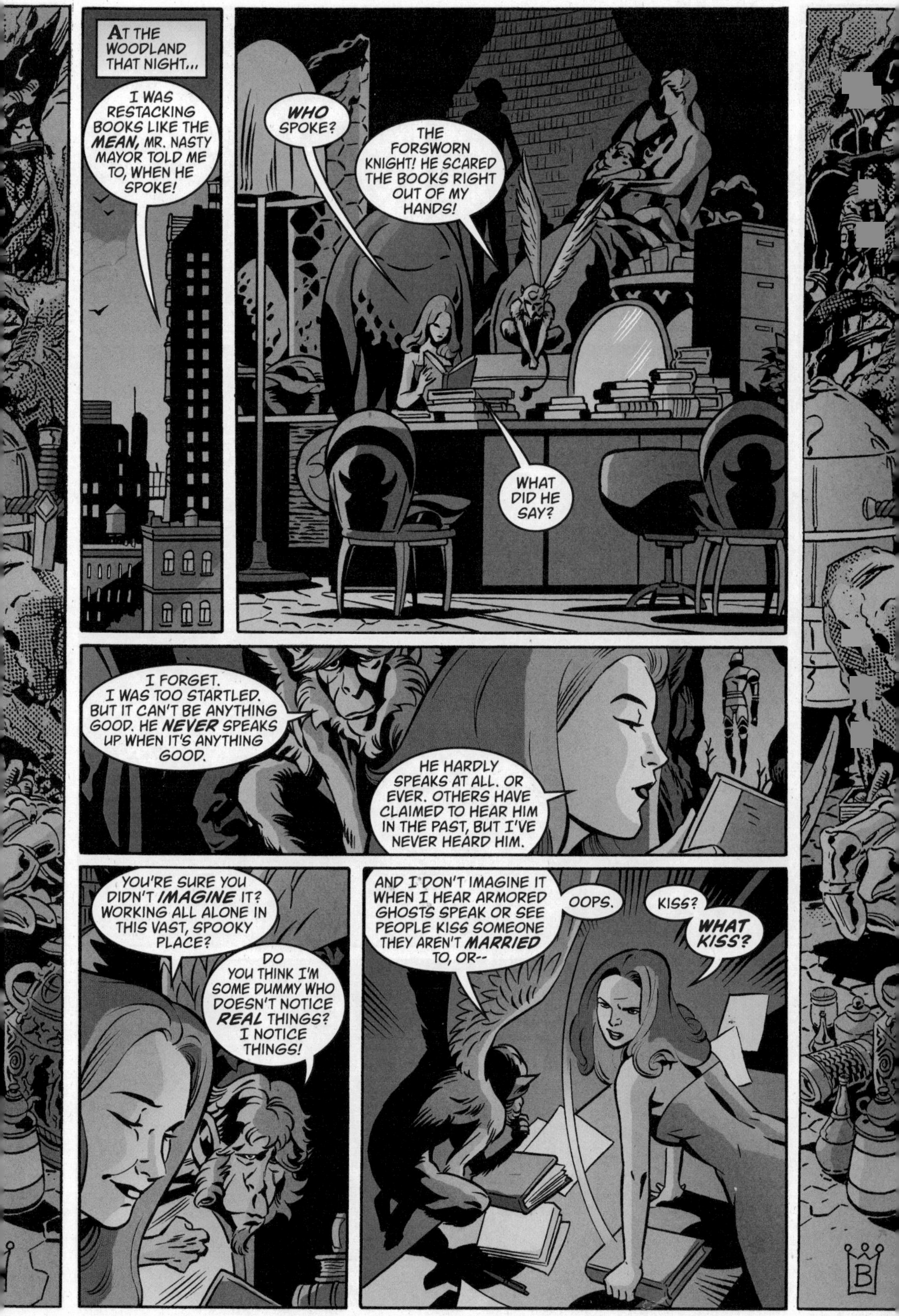
AT THE WOODLAND THAT NIGHT...
I WAS RESTACKING BOOKS LIKE THE MEAN, MR. NASTY MAYOR TOLD ME TO, WHEN HE SPOKE!
WHO SPOKE?
THE FORSWORN KNIGHT! HE SCARED THE BOOKS RIGHT OUT OF MY HANDS!
WHAT DID HE SAY?
I FORGET. I WAS TOO STARTLED. BUT IT CAN'T BE ANYTHING GOOD. HE NEVER SPEAKS UP WHEN IT'S ANYTHING GOOD.
HE HARDLY SPEAKS AT ALL. OR EVER. OTHERS HAVE CLAIMED TO HEAR HIM IN THE PAST, BUT I'VE NEVER HEARD HIM.
YOU'RE SURE YOU DIDN'T IMAGINE IT? WORKING ALL ALONE IN THIS VAST, SPOOKY PLACE?
DO YOU THINK I'M SOME DUMMY WHO DOESN'T NOTICE REAL THINGS? I NOTICE THINGS!
AND I DON'T IMAGINE IT WHEN I HEAR ARMORED GHOSTS SPEAK OR SEE PEOPLE KISS SOMEONE THEY AREN'T MARRIED TO, OR--
OOPS.
KISS? WHAT KISS?

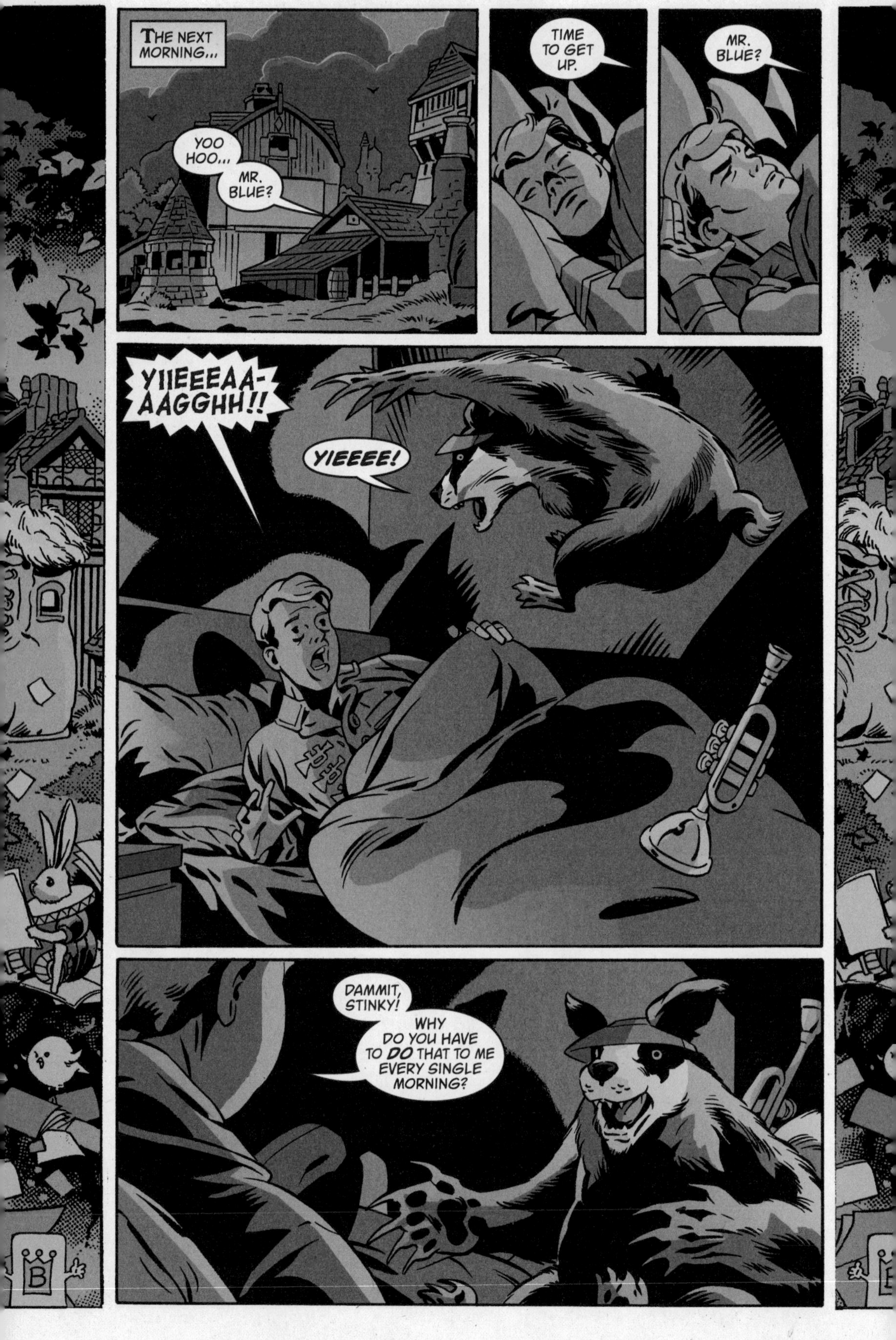

THE NEXT MORNING...
YOO HOO...
MR. BLUE?
TIME TO GET UP.
MR. BLUE?
YIIEEEAA-AAGGHH!!
YIEEEE!
DAMMIT, STINKY!
WHY DO YOU HAVE TO DO THAT TO ME EVERY SINGLE MORNING?

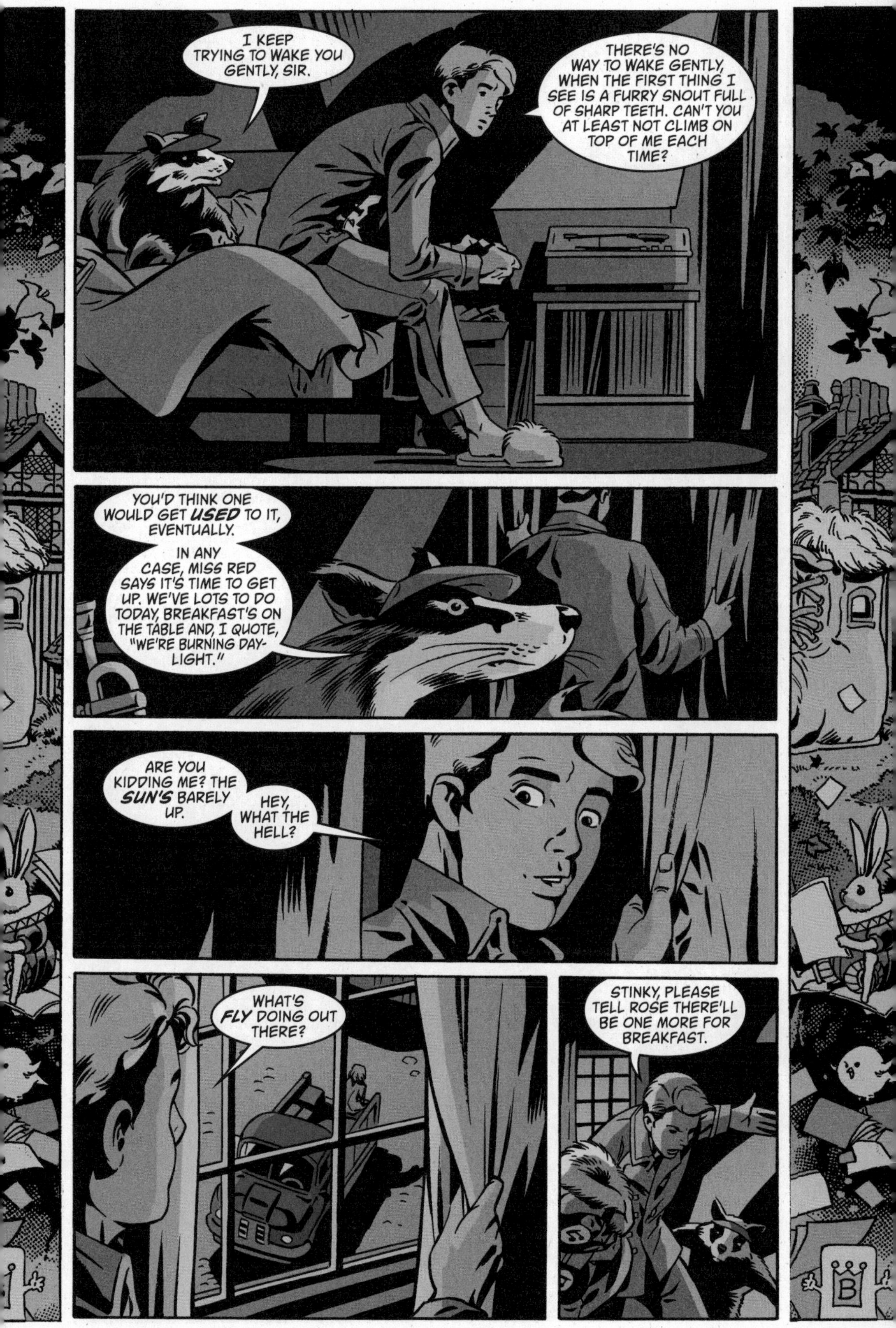
I KEEP TRYING TO WAKE YOU GENTLY, SIR.
THERE'S NO WAY TO WAKE GENTLY, WHEN THE FIRST THING I SEE IS A FURRY SNOUT FULL OF SHARP TEETH. CAN'T YOU AT LEAST NOT CLIMB ON TOP OF ME EACH TIME?
YOU'D THINK ONE WOULD GET USED TO IT, EVENTUALLY.
IN ANY CASE, MISS RED SAYS IT'S TIME TO GET UP. WE'VE LOTS TO DO TODAY, BREAKFAST'S ON THE TABLE AND, I QUOTE, "WE'RE BURNING DAY-LIGHT."
ARE YOU KIDDING ME? THE SUN'S BARELY UP.
HEY, WHAT THE HELL?
WHAT'S FLY DOING OUT THERE?
STINKY, PLEASE TELL ROSE THERE'LL BE ONE MORE FOR BREAKFAST.

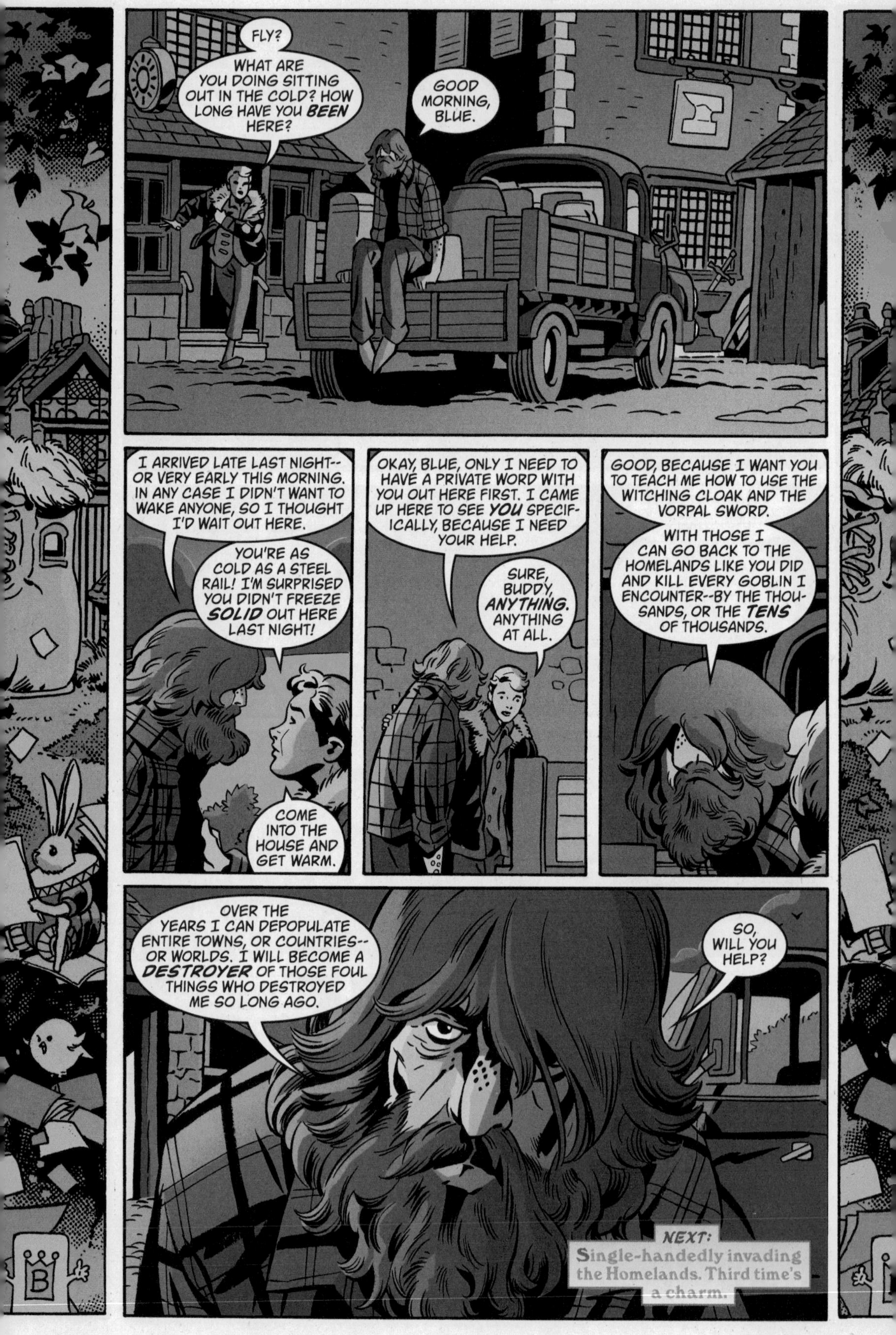
FLY?
WHAT ARE YOU DOING SITTING OUT IN THE COLD? HOW LONG HAVE YOU BEEN HERE?
GOOD MORNING, BLUE.
I ARRIVED LATE LAST NIGHT--OR VERY EARLY THIS MORNING. IN ANY CASE I DIDN'T WANT TO WAKE ANYONE, SO I THOUGHT I'D WAIT OUT HERE.
YOU'RE AS COLD AS A STEEL RAIL! I'M SURPRISED YOU DIDN'T FREEZE SOLID OUT HERE LAST NIGHT!
COME INTO THE HOUSE AND GET WARM.
OKAY, BLUE, ONLY I NEED TO HAVE A PRIVATE WORD WITH YOU OUT HERE FIRST. I CAME UP HERE TO SEE YOU SPECIFICALLY, BECAUSE I NEED YOUR HELP.
SURE, BUDDY, ANYTHING. ANYTHING AT ALL.
GOOD, BECAUSE I WANT YOU TO TEACH ME HOW TO USE THE WITCHING CLOAK AND THE VORPAL SWORD.
WITH THOSE I CAN GO BACK TO THE HOMELANDS LIKE YOU DID AND KILL EVERY GOBLIN I ENCOUNTER--BY THE THOUSANDS, OR THE TENS OF THOUSANDS.
OVER THE YEARS I CAN DEPOPULATE ENTIRE TOWNS, OR COUNTRIES--OR WORLDS. I WILL BECOME A DESTROYER OF THOSE FOUL THINGS WHO DESTROYED ME SO LONG AGO.
SO, WILL YOU HELP?
NEXT:
Single-handedly invading the Homelands. Third time's a charm.

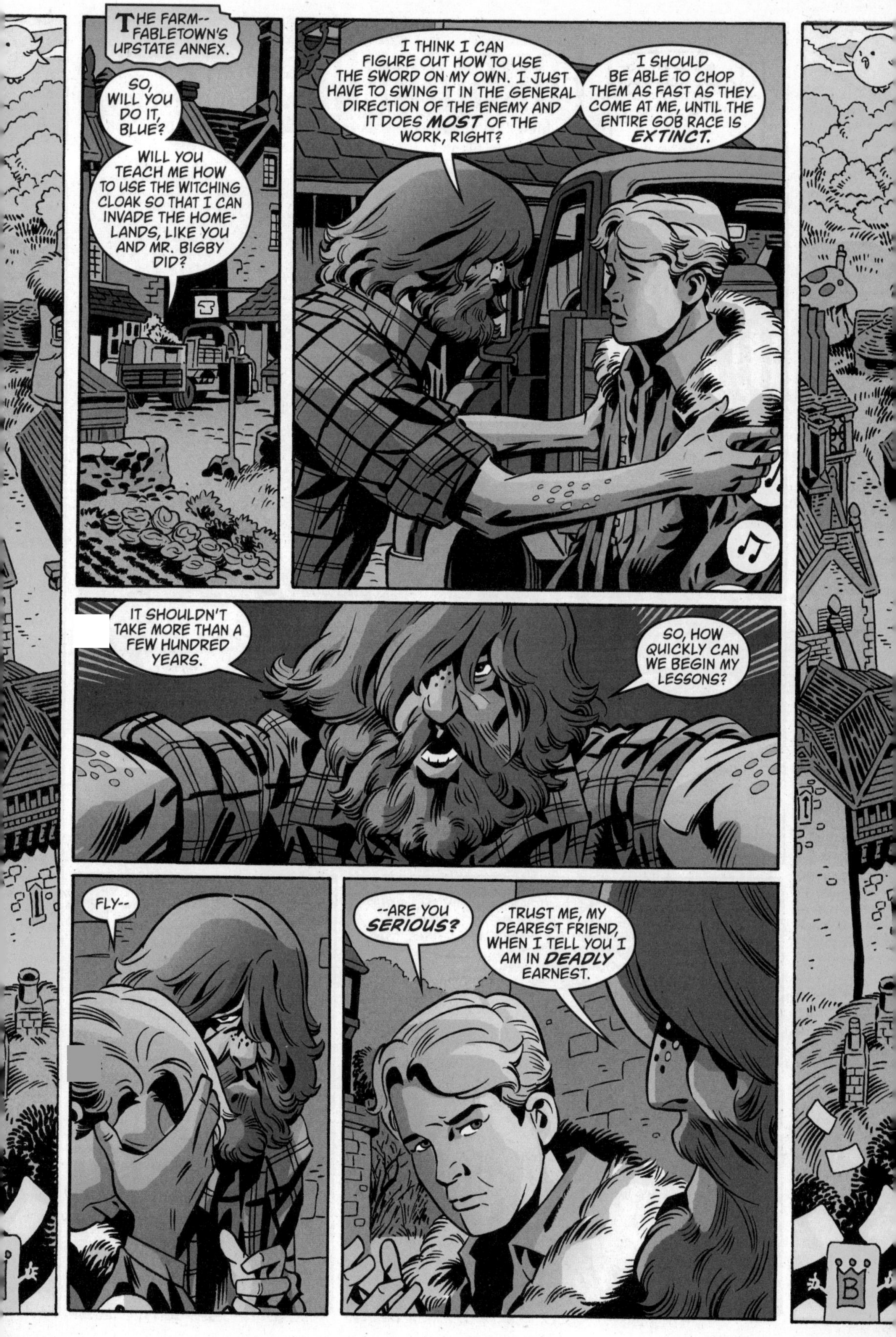
THE FARM--FABLETOWN'S UPSTATE ANNEX.
SO, WILL YOU DO IT, BLUE?
WILL YOU TEACH ME HOW TO USE THE WITCHING CLOAK SO THAT I CAN INVADE THE HOMELANDS, LIKE YOU AND MR. BIGBY DID?
I THINK I CAN FIGURE OUT HOW TO USE THE SWORD ON MY OWN. I JUST HAVE TO SWING IT IN THE GENERAL DIRECTION OF THE ENEMY AND IT DOES MOST OF THE WORK, RIGHT?
I SHOULD BE ABLE TO CHOP THEM AS FAST AS THEY COME AT ME, UNTIL THE ENTIRE GOB RACE IS EXTINCT.
IT SHOULDN'T TAKE MORE THAN A FEW HUNDRED YEARS.
SO, HOW QUICKLY CAN WE BEGIN MY LESSONS?
FLY--
--ARE YOU SERIOUS?
TRUST ME, MY DEAREST FRIEND, WHEN I TELL YOU I AM IN DEADLY EARNEST.

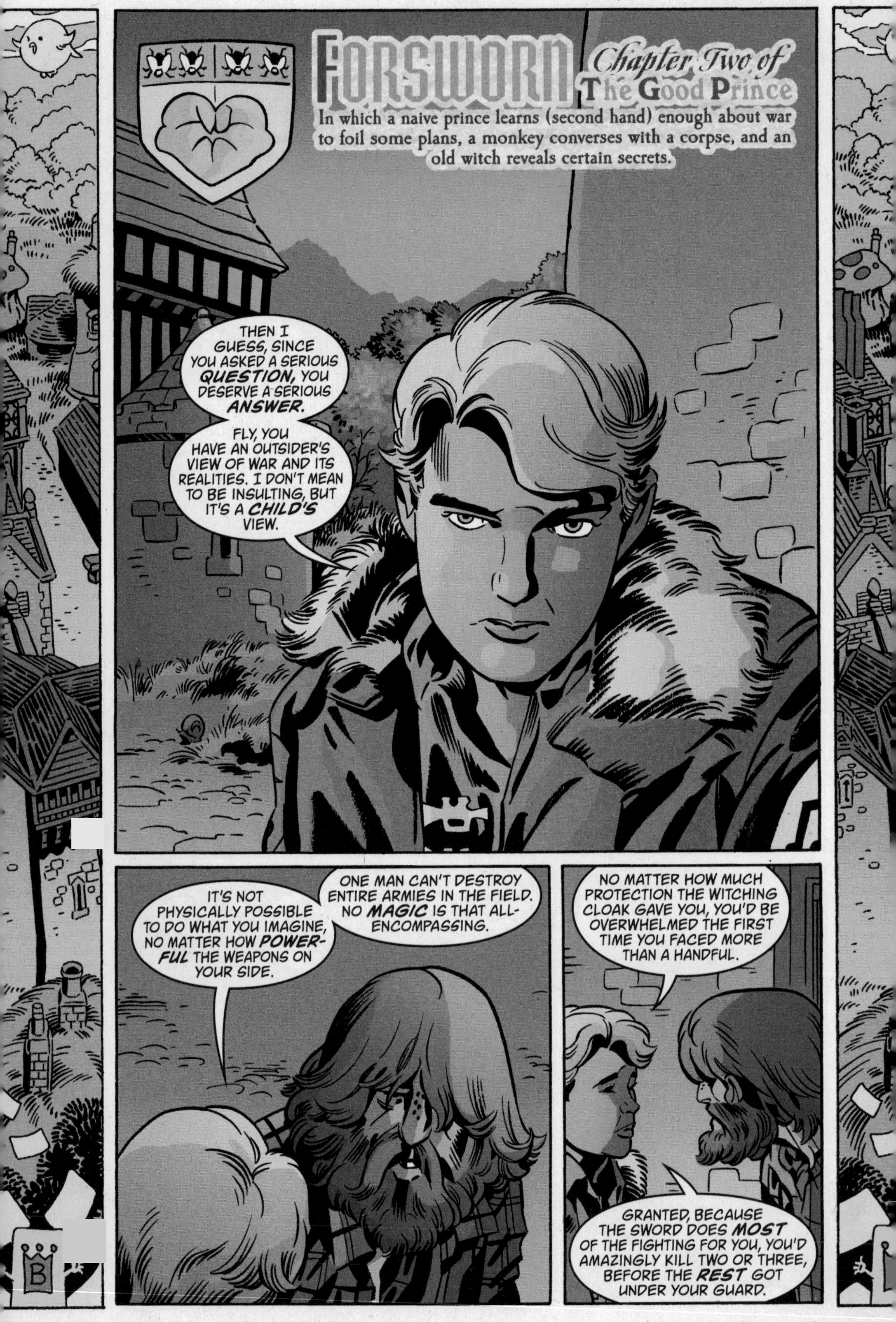
FORSWORN Chapter Two of The Good Prince
In which a naive prince learns (second hand) enough about war to foil some plans, a monkey converses with a corpse, and an old witch reveals certain secrets.
THEN I GUESS, SINCE YOU ASKED A SERIOUS QUESTION, YOU DESERVE A SERIOUS ANSWER.
FLY, YOU HAVE AN OUTSIDER'S VIEW OF WAR AND ITS REALITIES. I DON'T MEAN TO BE INSULTING, BUT IT'S A CHILD'S VIEW.
IT'S NOT PHYSICALLY POSSIBLE TO DO WHAT YOU IMAGINE, NO MATTER HOW POWER-FUL THE WEAPONS ON YOUR SIDE.
ONE MAN CAN'T DESTROY ENTIRE ARMIES IN THE FIELD. NO MAGIC IS THAT ALL-ENCOMPASSING.
NO MATTER HOW MUCH PROTECTION THE WITCHING CLOAK GAVE YOU, YOU'D BE OVERWHELMED THE FIRST TIME YOU FACED MORE THAN A HANDFUL.
GRANTED, BECAUSE THE SWORD DOES MOST OF THE FIGHTING FOR YOU, YOU'D AMAZINGLY KILL TWO OR THREE, BEFORE THE REST GOT UNDER YOUR GUARD.

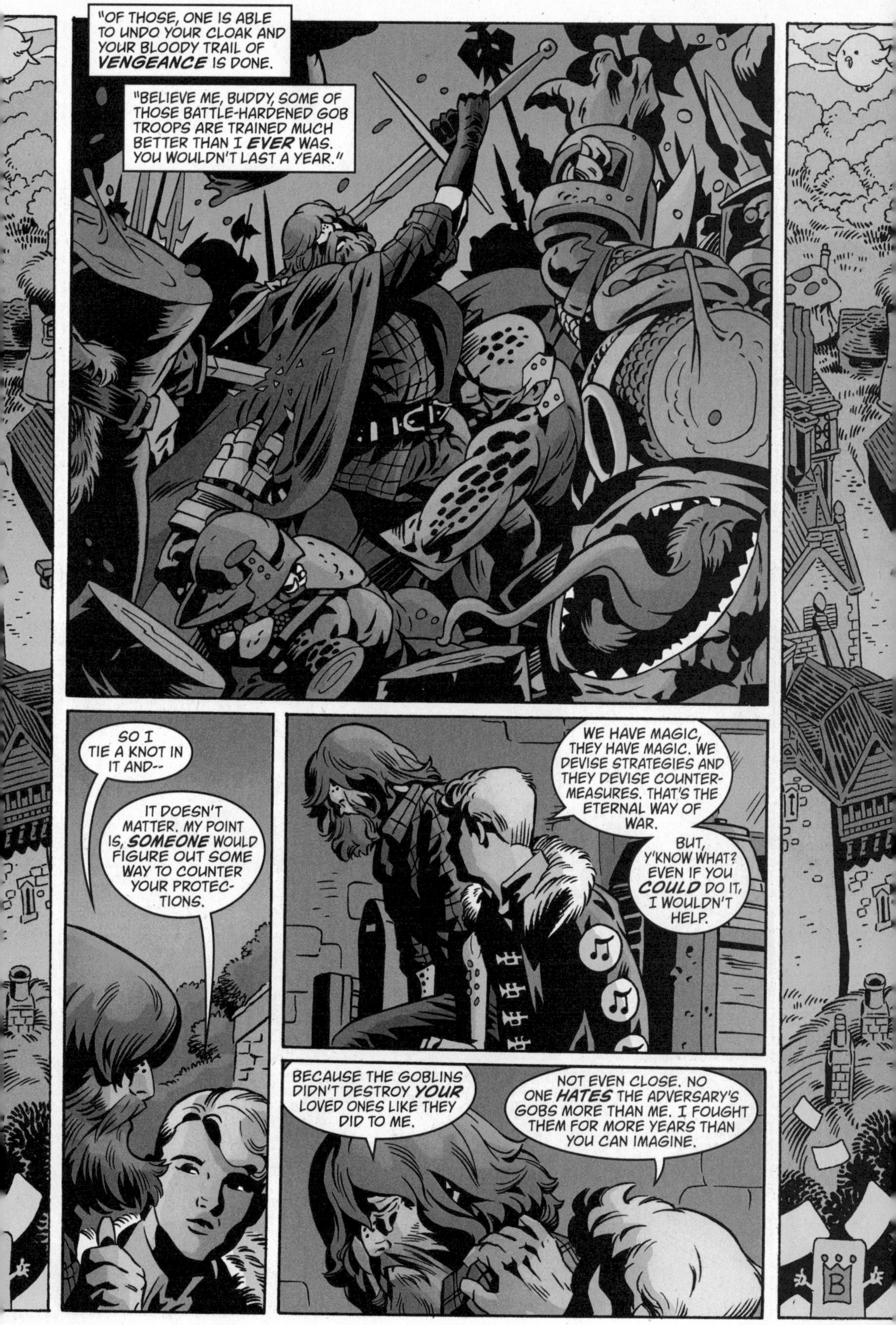
"OF THOSE, ONE IS ABLE TO UNDO YOUR CLOAK AND YOUR BLOODY TRAIL OF VENGEANCE IS DONE.
"BELIEVE ME, BUDDY, SOME OF THOSE BATTLE-HARDENED GOB TROOPS ARE TRAINED MUCH BETTER THAN I EVER WAS. YOU WOULDN'T LAST A YEAR."
SO I TIE A KNOT IN IT AND--
IT DOESN'T MATTER. MY POINT IS, SOMEONE WOULD FIGURE OUT SOME WAY TO COUNTER YOUR PROTECTIONS.
WE HAVE MAGIC, THEY HAVE MAGIC. WE DEVISE STRATEGIES AND THEY DEVISE COUNTER-MEASURES. THAT'S THE ETERNAL WAY OF WAR.
BUT, Y'KNOW WHAT? EVEN IF YOU COULD DO IT, I WOULDN'T HELP.
BECAUSE THE GOBLINS DIDN'T DESTROY YOUR LOVED ONES LIKE THEY DID TO ME.
NOT EVEN CLOSE. NO ONE HATES THE ADVERSARY'S GOBS MORE THAN ME. I FOUGHT THEM FOR MORE YEARS THAN YOU CAN IMAGINE.

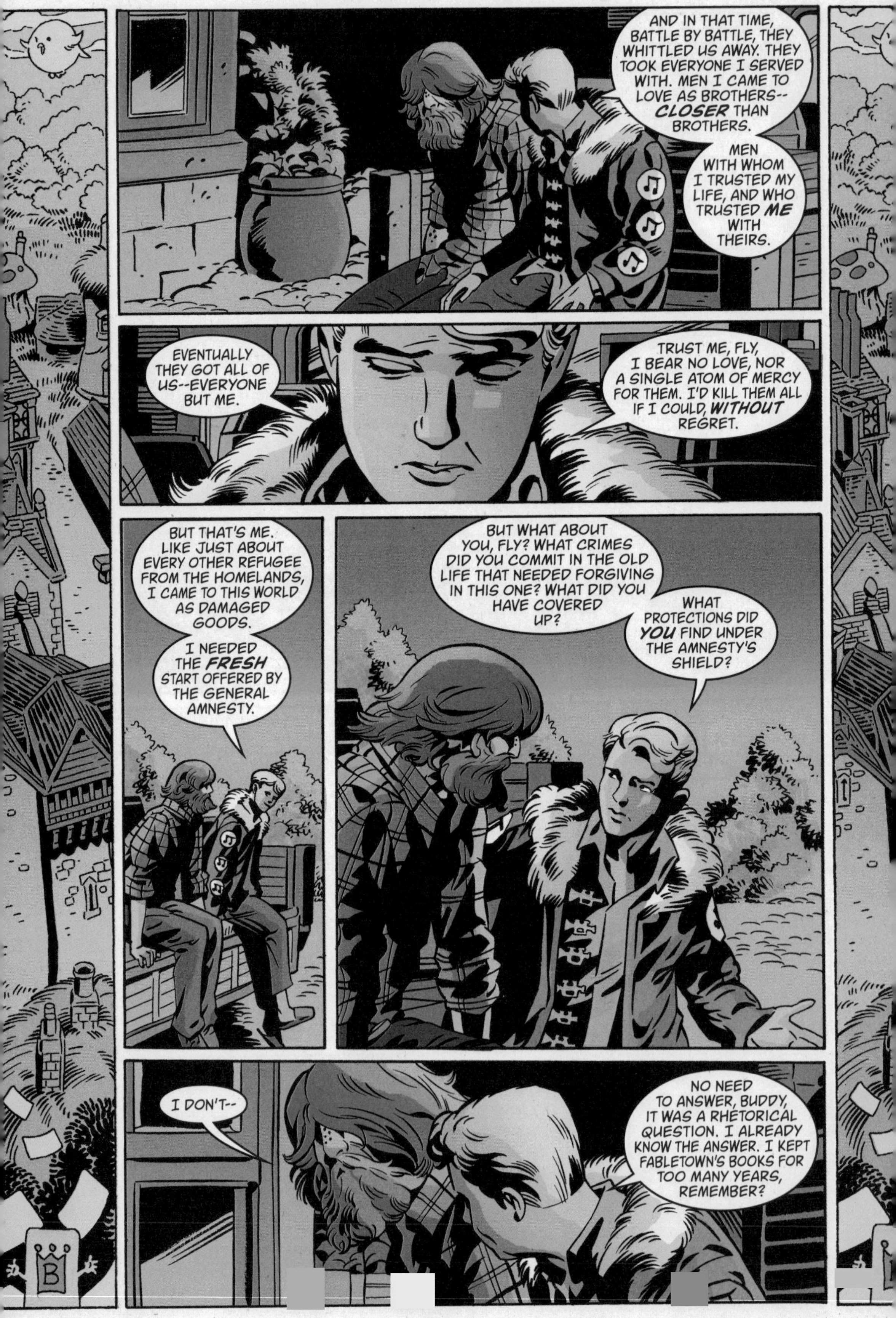
AND IN THAT TIME, BATTLE BY BATTLE, THEY WHITTLED US AWAY. THEY TOOK EVERYONE I SERVED WITH. MEN I CAME TO LOVE AS BROTHERS-- CLOSER THAN BROTHERS.
MEN WITH WHOM I TRUSTED MY LIFE, AND WHO TRUSTED ME WITH THEIRS.
EVENTUALLY THEY GOT ALL OF US--EVERYONE BUT ME.
TRUST ME, FLY, I BEAR NO LOVE, NOR A SINGLE ATOM OF MERCY FOR THEM. I'D KILL THEM ALL IF I COULD, WITHOUT REGRET.
BUT THAT'S ME. LIKE JUST ABOUT EVERY OTHER REFUGEE FROM THE HOMELANDS, I CAME TO THIS WORLD AS DAMAGED GOODS.
I NEEDED THE FRESH START OFFERED BY THE GENERAL AMNESTY.
BUT WHAT ABOUT YOU, FLY? WHAT CRIMES DID YOU COMMIT IN THE OLD LIFE THAT NEEDED FORGIVING IN THIS ONE? WHAT DID YOU HAVE COVERED UP?
WHAT PROTECTIONS DID YOU FIND UNDER THE AMNESTY'S SHIELD?
I DON'T--
NO NEED TO ANSWER, BUDDY, IT WAS A RHETORICAL QUESTION. I ALREADY KNOW THE ANSWER. I KEPT FABLETOWN'S BOOKS FOR TOO MANY YEARS, REMEMBER?

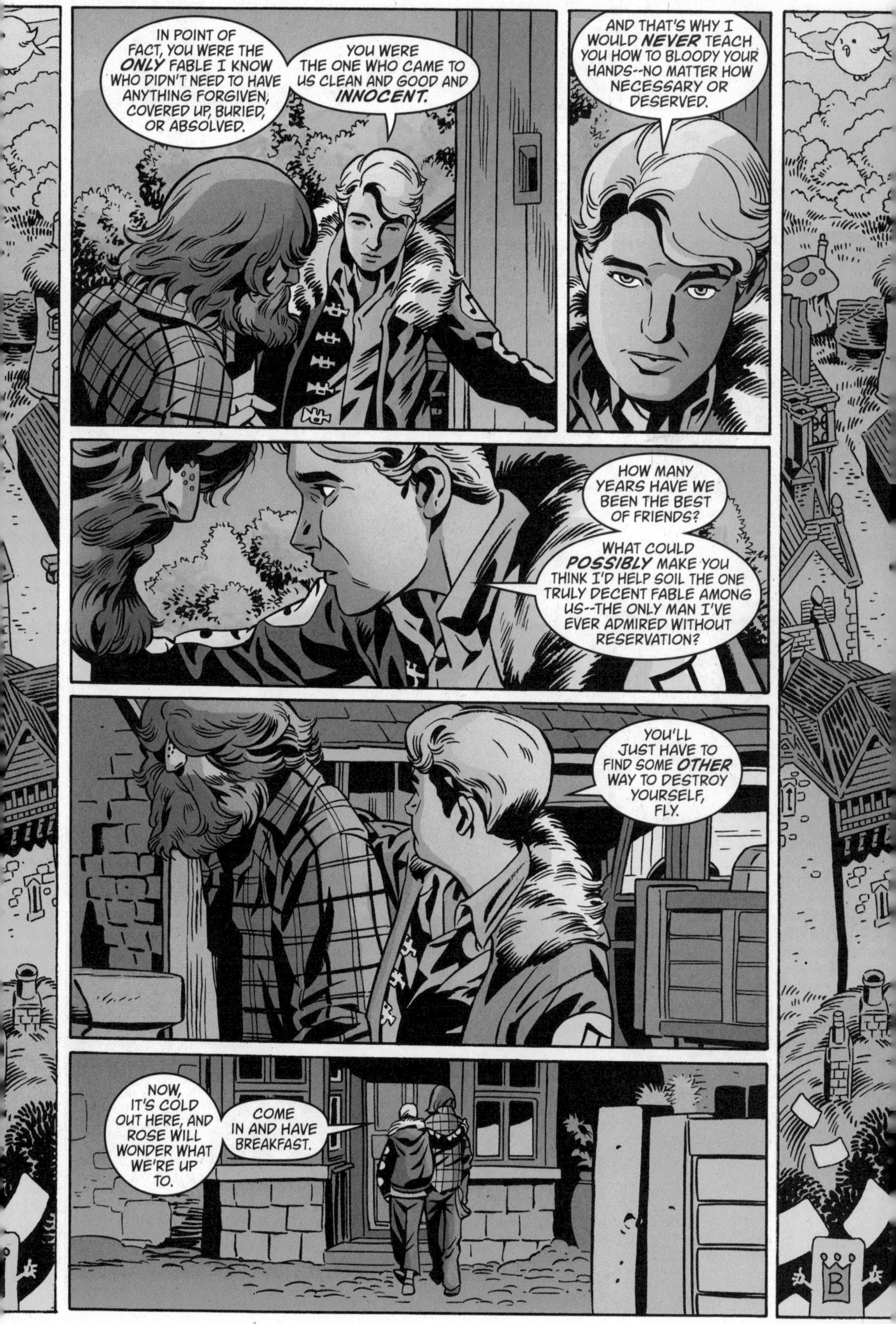
IN POINT OF FACT, YOU WERE THE ONLY FABLE I KNOW WHO DIDN'T NEED TO HAVE ANYTHING FORGIVEN, COVERED UP, BURIED, OR ABSOLVED.
YOU WERE THE ONE WHO CAME TO US CLEAN AND GOOD AND INNOCENT.
AND THAT'S WHY I WOULD NEVER TEACH YOU HOW TO BLOODY YOUR HANDS--NO MATTER HOW NECESSARY OR DESERVED.
HOW MANY YEARS HAVE WE BEEN THE BEST OF FRIENDS?
WHAT COULD POSSIBLY MAKE YOU THINK I'D HELP SOIL THE ONE TRULY DECENT FABLE AMONG US--THE ONLY MAN I'VE EVER ADMIRED WITHOUT RESERVATION?
YOU'LL JUST HAVE TO FIND SOME OTHER WAY TO DESTROY YOURSELF, FLY.
NOW, IT'S COLD OUT HERE, AND ROSE WILL WONDER WHAT WE'RE UP TO.
COME IN AND HAVE BREAKFAST.

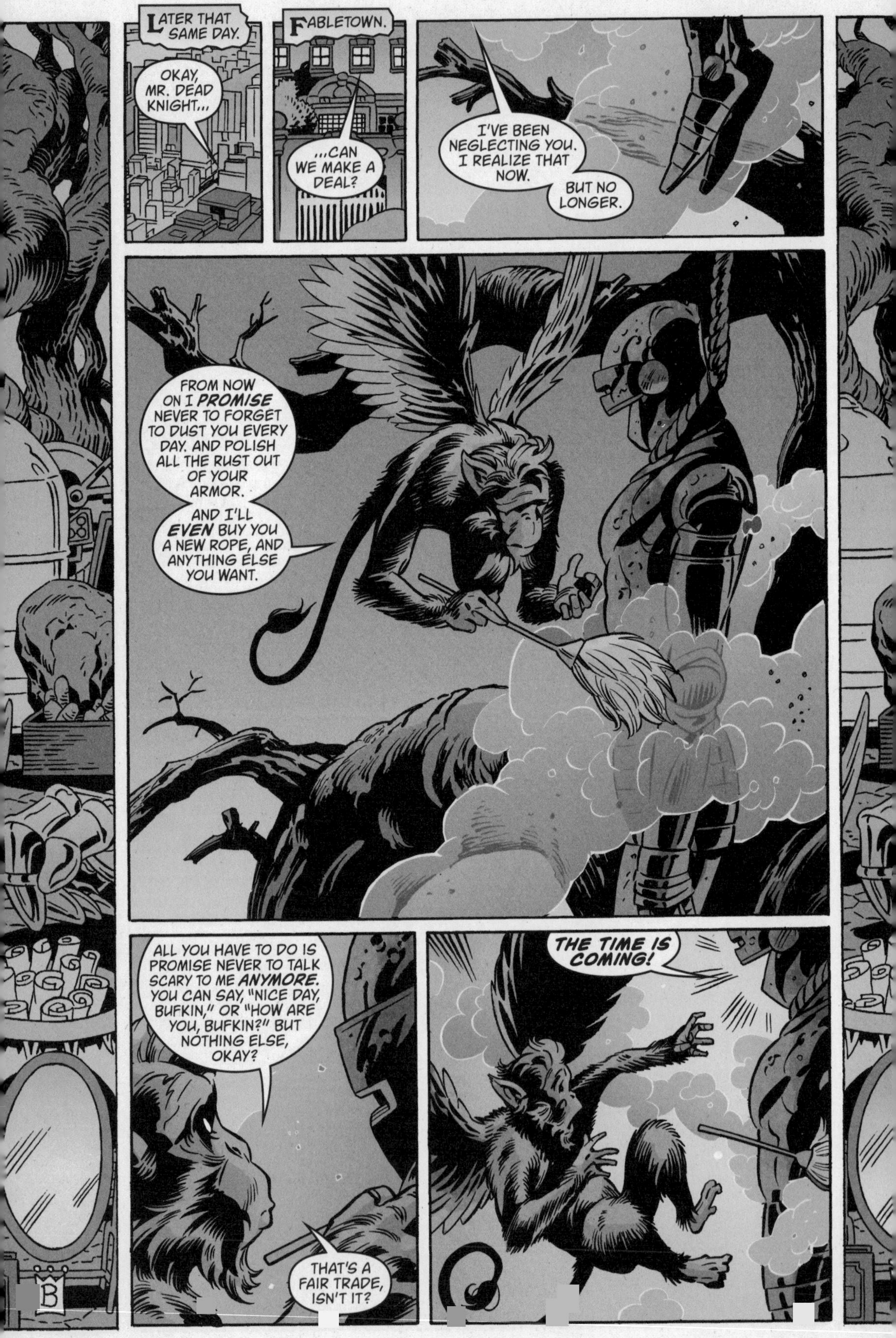

LATER THAT SAME DAY.
OKAY, MR. DEAD KNIGHT...
FABLETOWN.
...CAN WE MAKE A DEAL?
I'VE BEEN NEGLECTING YOU. I REALIZE THAT NOW.
BUT NO LONGER.
FROM NOW ON I PROMISE NEVER TO FORGET TO DUST YOU EVERY DAY. AND POLISH ALL THE RUST OUT OF YOUR ARMOR.
AND I'LL EVEN BUY YOU A NEW ROPE, AND ANYTHING ELSE YOU WANT.
ALL YOU HAVE TO DO IS PROMISE NEVER TO TALK SCARY TO ME ANYMORE. YOU CAN SAY, "NICE DAY, BUFKIN," OR "HOW ARE YOU, BUFKIN?" BUT NOTHING ELSE, OKAY?
THAT'S A FAIR TRADE, ISN'T IT?
THE TIME IS COMING!

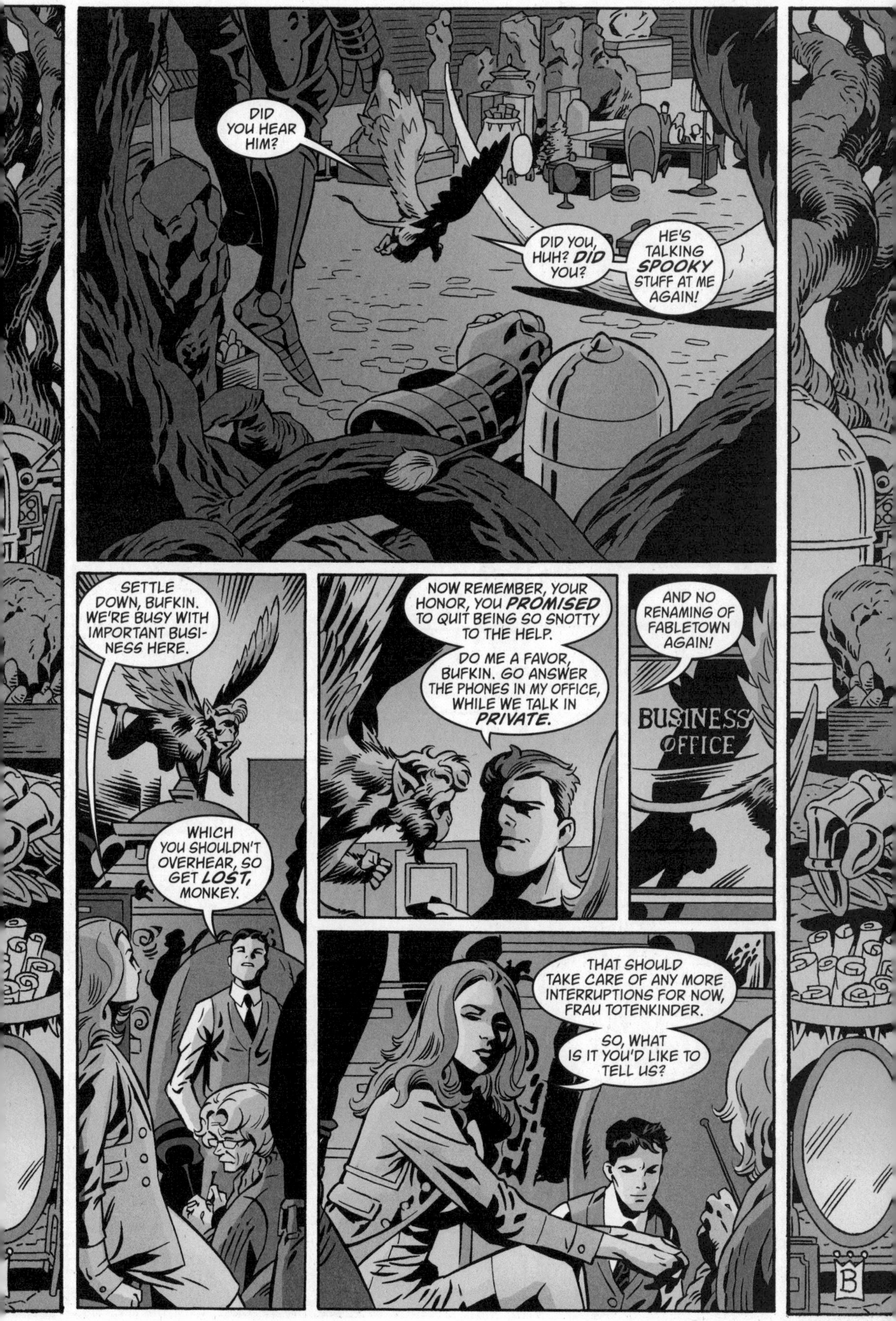
DID YOU HEAR HIM?
DID YOU, HUH? DID YOU?
HE'S TALKING SPOOKY STUFF AT ME AGAIN!
SETTLE DOWN, BUFKIN. WE'RE BUSY WITH IMPORTANT BUSINESS HERE.
WHICH YOU SHOULDN'T OVERHEAR, SO GET LOST, MONKEY.
NOW REMEMBER, YOUR HONOR, YOU PROMISED TO QUIT BEING SO SNOTTY TO THE HELP.
DO ME A FAVOR, BUFKIN. GO ANSWER THE PHONES IN MY OFFICE, WHILE WE TALK IN PRIVATE.
AND NO RENAMING OF FABLETOWN AGAIN!
BUSINESS OFFICE
THAT SHOULD TAKE CARE OF ANY MORE INTERRUPTIONS FOR NOW, FRAU TOTENKINDER.
SO, WHAT IS IT YOU'D LIKE TO TELL US?

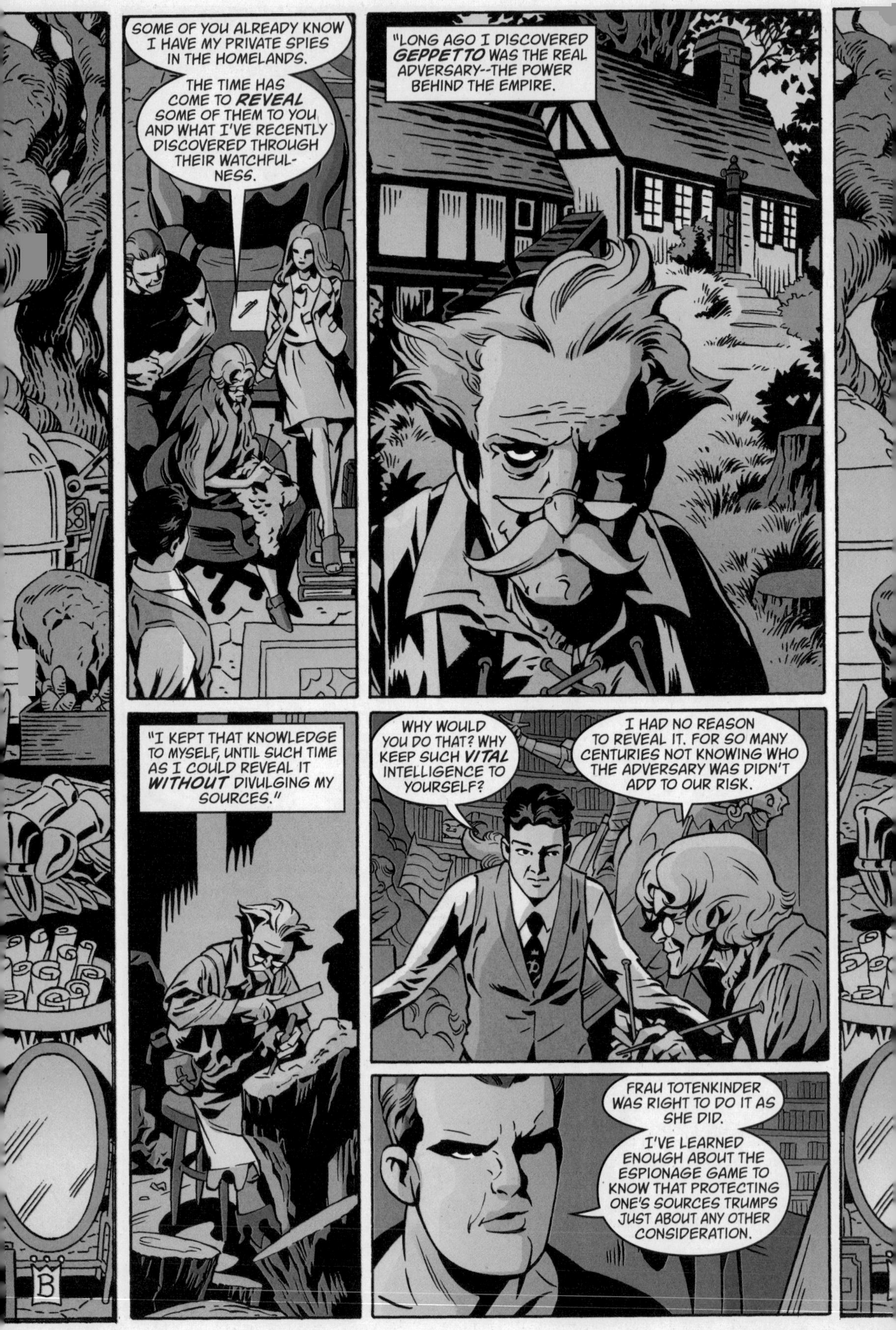
SOME OF YOU ALREADY KNOW I HAVE MY PRIVATE SPIES IN THE HOMELANDS.
THE TIME HAS COME TO REVEAL SOME OF THEM TO YOU AND WHAT I'VE RECENTLY DISCOVERED THROUGH THEIR WATCHFUL-NESS.
"LONG AGO I DISCOVERED GEPPETTO WAS THE REAL ADVERSARY--THE POWER BEHIND THE EMPIRE.
"I KEPT THAT KNOWLEDGE TO MYSELF, UNTIL SUCH TIME AS I COULD REVEAL IT WITHOUT DIVULGING MY SOURCES."
WHY WOULD YOU DO THAT? WHY KEEP SUCH VITAL INTELLIGENCE TO YOURSELF?
I HAD NO REASON TO REVEAL IT. FOR SO MANY CENTURIES NOT KNOWING WHO THE ADVERSARY WAS DIDN'T ADD TO OUR RISK.
FRAU TOTENKINDER WAS RIGHT TO DO IT AS SHE DID.
I'VE LEARNED ENOUGH ABOUT THE ESPIONAGE GAME TO KNOW THAT PROTECTING ONE'S SOURCES TRUMPS JUST ABOUT ANY OTHER CONSIDERATION.

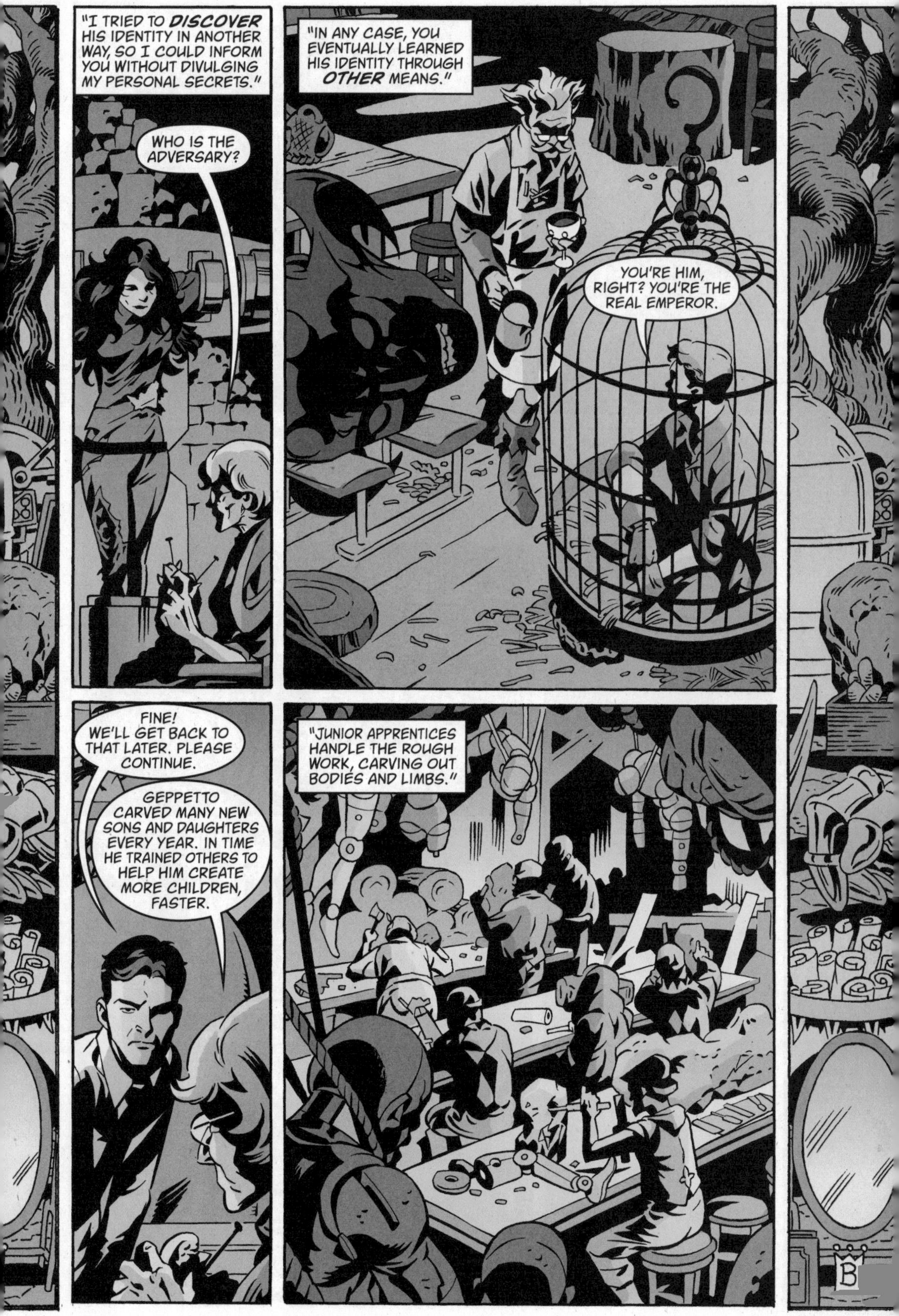
"I TRIED TO DISCOVER HIS IDENTITY IN ANOTHER WAY, SO I COULD INFORM YOU WITHOUT DIVULGING MY PERSONAL SECRETS."
WHO IS THE ADVERSARY?
"IN ANY CASE, YOU EVENTUALLY LEARNED HIS IDENTITY THROUGH OTHER MEANS."
YOU'RE HIM, RIGHT? YOU'RE THE REAL EMPEROR.
FINE! WE'LL GET BACK TO THAT LATER. PLEASE CONTINUE.
GEPPETTO CARVED MANY NEW SONS AND DAUGHTERS EVERY YEAR. IN TIME HE TRAINED OTHERS TO HELP HIM CREATE MORE CHILDREN, FASTER.
"JUNIOR APPRENTICES HANDLE THE ROUGH WORK, CARVING OUT BODIES AND LIMBS."

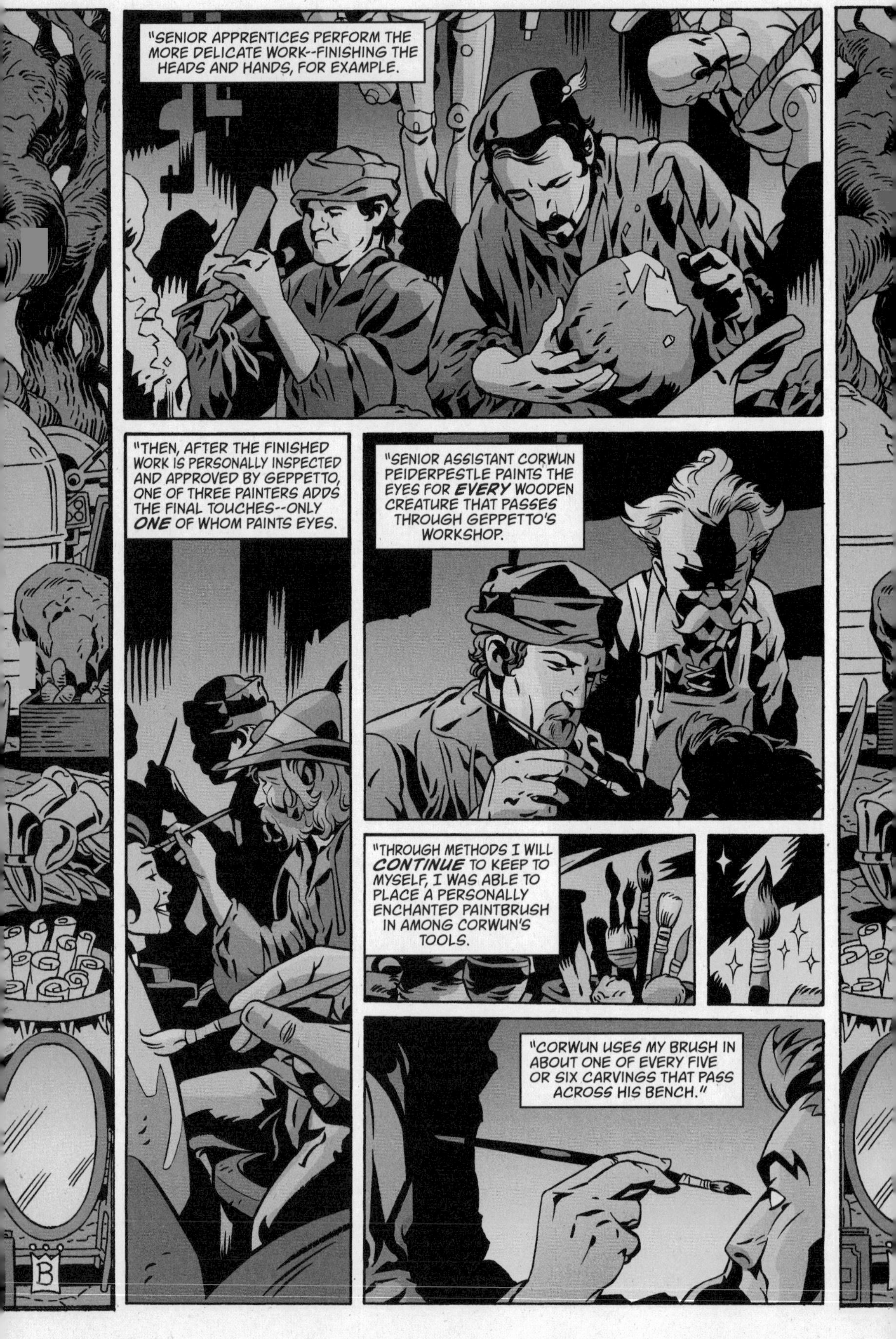
"SENIOR APPRENTICES PERFORM THE MORE DELICATE WORK--FINISHING THE HEADS AND HANDS, FOR EXAMPLE.
"THEN, AFTER THE FINISHED WORK IS PERSONALLY INSPECTED AND APPROVED BY GEPPETTO, ONE OF THREE PAINTERS ADDS THE FINAL TOUCHES--ONLY ONE OF WHOM PAINTS EYES.
"SENIOR ASSISTANT CORWUN PEIDERPESTLE PAINTS THE EYES FOR EVERY WOODEN CREATURE THAT PASSES THROUGH GEPPETTO'S WORKSHOP.
"THROUGH METHODS I WILL CONTINUE TO KEEP TO MYSELF, I WAS ABLE TO PLACE A PERSONALLY ENCHANTED PAINTBRUSH IN AMONG CORWUN'S TOOLS.
"CORWUN USES MY BRUSH IN ABOUT ONE OF EVERY FIVE OR SIX CARVINGS THAT PASS ACROSS HIS BENCH."

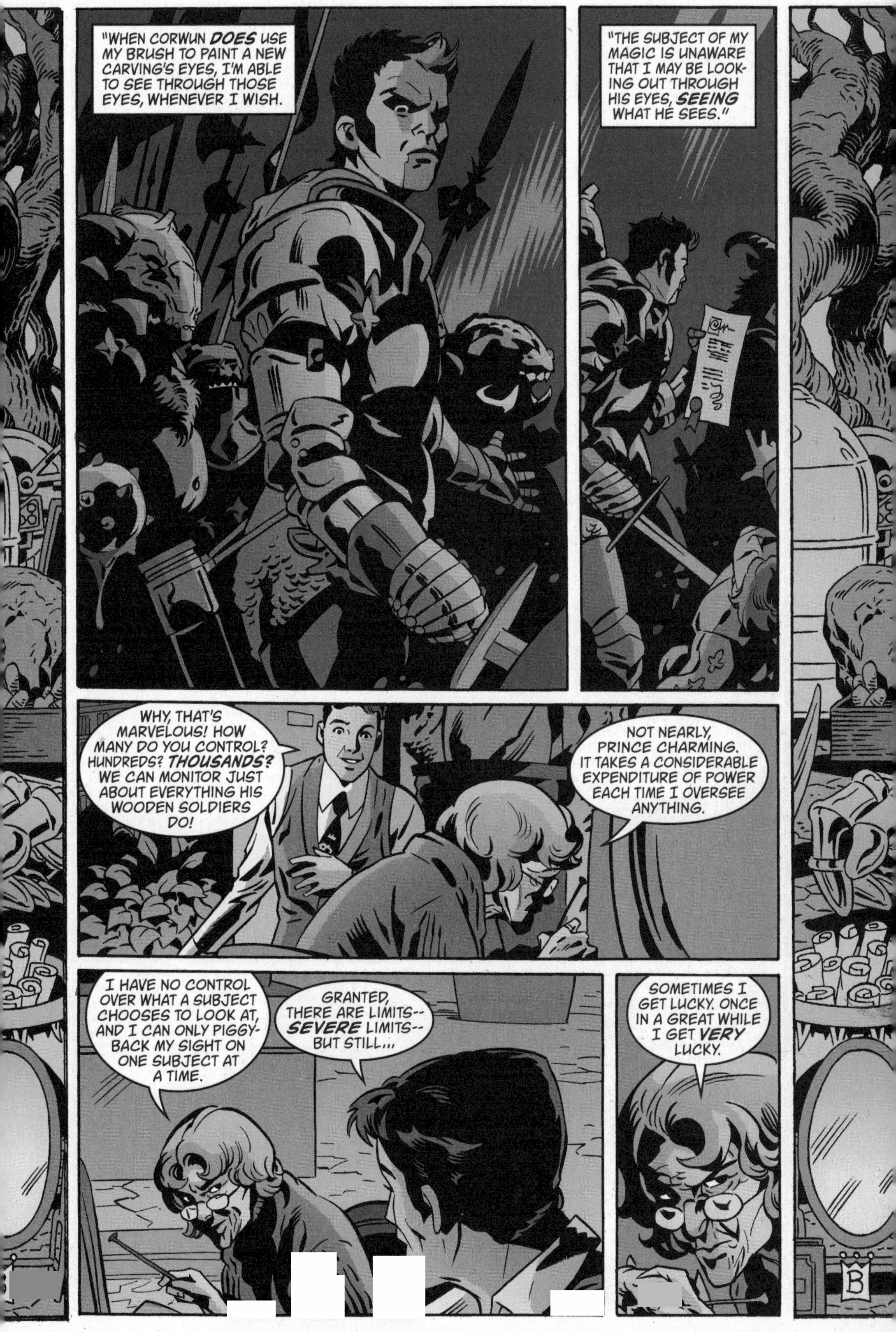
"WHEN CORWUN DOES USE MY BRUSH TO PAINT A NEW CARVING'S EYES, I'M ABLE TO SEE THROUGH THOSE EYES, WHENEVER I WISH.
"THE SUBJECT OF MY MAGIC IS UNAWARE THAT I MAY BE LOOKING OUT THROUGH HIS EYES, SEEING WHAT HE SEES."
WHY, THAT'S MARVELOUS! HOW MANY DO YOU CONTROL? HUNDREDS? THOUSANDS? WE CAN MONITOR JUST ABOUT EVERYTHING HIS WOODEN SOLDIERS DO!
NOT NEARLY, PRINCE CHARMING. IT TAKES A CONSIDERABLE EXPENDITURE OF POWER EACH TIME I OVERSEE ANYTHING.
I HAVE NO CONTROL OVER WHAT A SUBJECT CHOOSES TO LOOK AT, AND I CAN ONLY PIGGYBACK MY SIGHT ON ONE SUBJECT AT A TIME.
GRANTED, THERE ARE LIMITS-- SEVERE LIMITS-- BUT STILL...
SOMETIMES I GET LUCKY. ONCE IN A GREAT WHILE I GET VERY LUCKY.

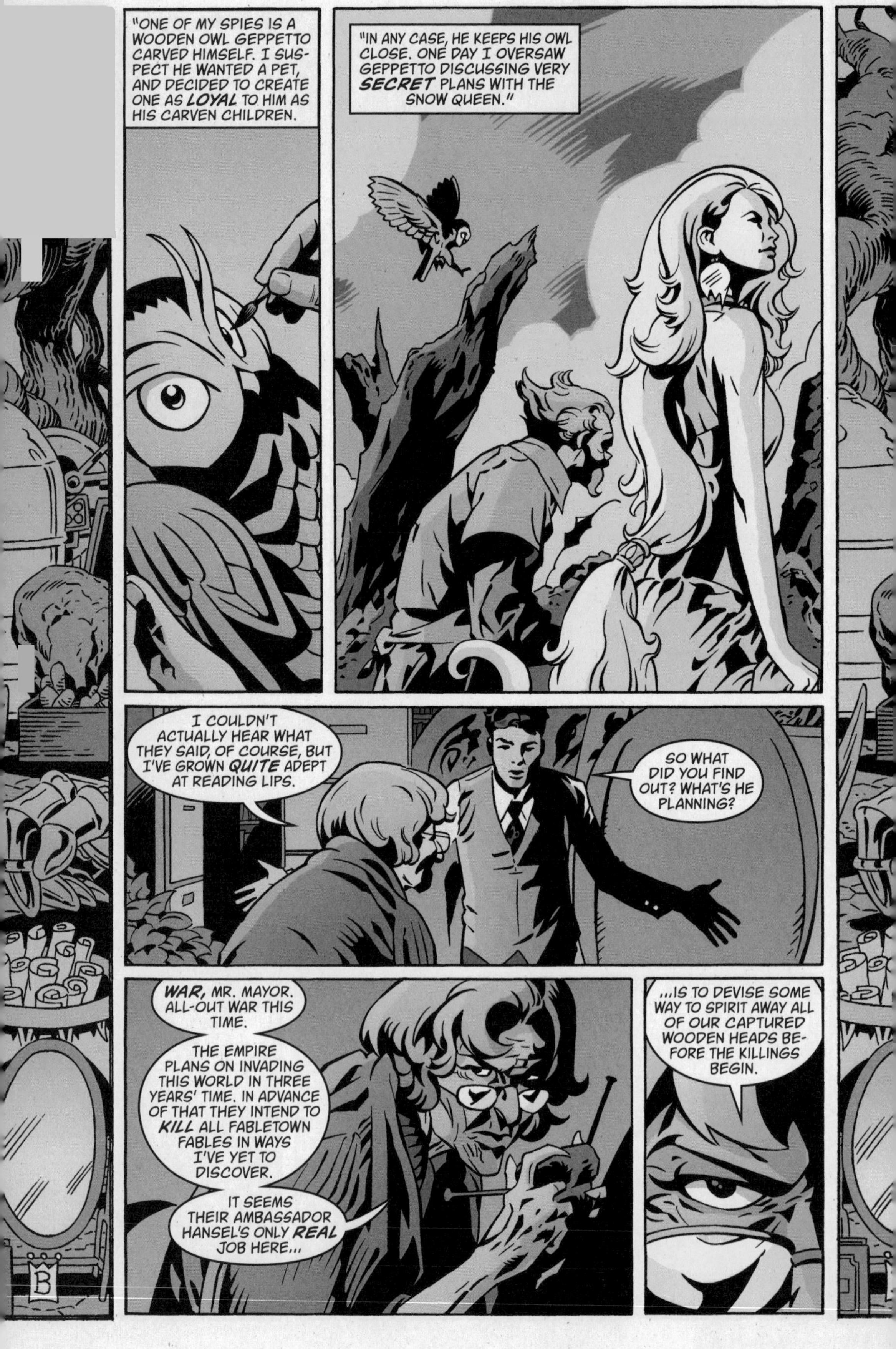
"ONE OF MY SPIES IS A WOODEN OWL GEPPETTO CARVED HIMSELF. I SUSPECT HE WANTED A PET, AND DECIDED TO CREATE ONE AS LOYAL TO HIM AS HIS CARVEN CHILDREN.
"IN ANY CASE, HE KEEPS HIS OWL CLOSE. ONE DAY I OVERSAW GEPPETTO DISCUSSING VERY SECRET PLANS WITH THE SNOW QUEEN."
I COULDN'T ACTUALLY HEAR WHAT THEY SAID, OF COURSE, BUT I'VE GROWN QUITE ADEPT AT READING LIPS.
SO WHAT DID YOU FIND OUT? WHAT'S HE PLANNING?
WAR, MR. MAYOR. ALL-OUT WAR THIS TIME.
THE EMPIRE PLANS ON INVADING THIS WORLD IN THREE YEARS' TIME. IN ADVANCE OF THAT THEY INTEND TO KILL ALL FABLETOWN FABLES IN WAYS I'VE YET TO DISCOVER.
IT SEEMS THEIR AMBASSADOR HANSEL'S ONLY REAL JOB HERE...
...IS TO DEVISE SOME WAY TO SPIRIT AWAY ALL OF OUR CAPTURED WOODEN HEADS BEFORE THE KILLINGS BEGIN.
B

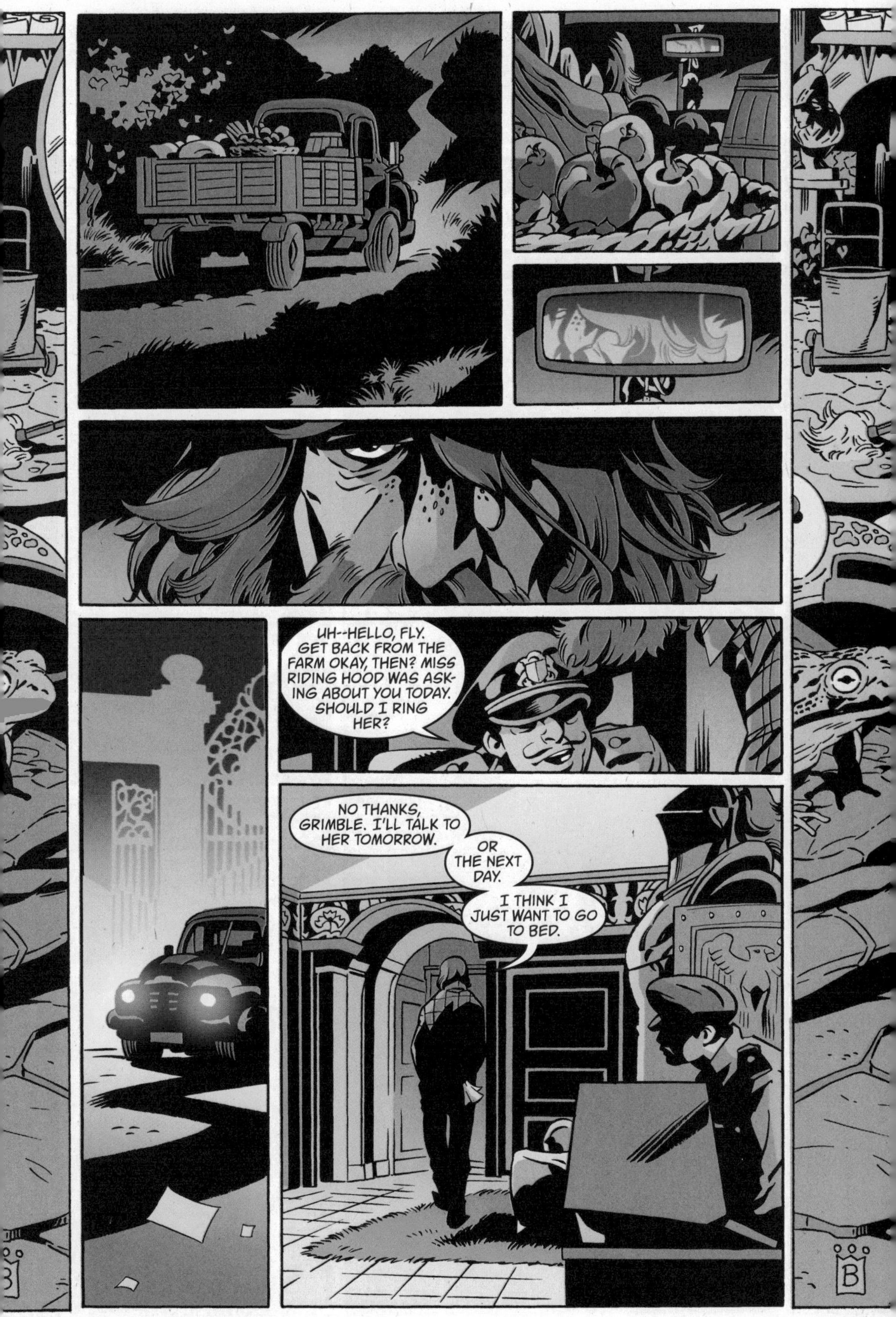
UH--HELLO, FLY. GET BACK FROM THE FARM OKAY, THEN? MISS RIDING HOOD WAS ASKING ABOUT YOU TODAY. SHOULD I RING HER?
NO THANKS, GRIMBLE. I'LL TALK TO HER TOMORROW.
OR THE NEXT DAY.
I THINK I JUST WANT TO GO TO BED.

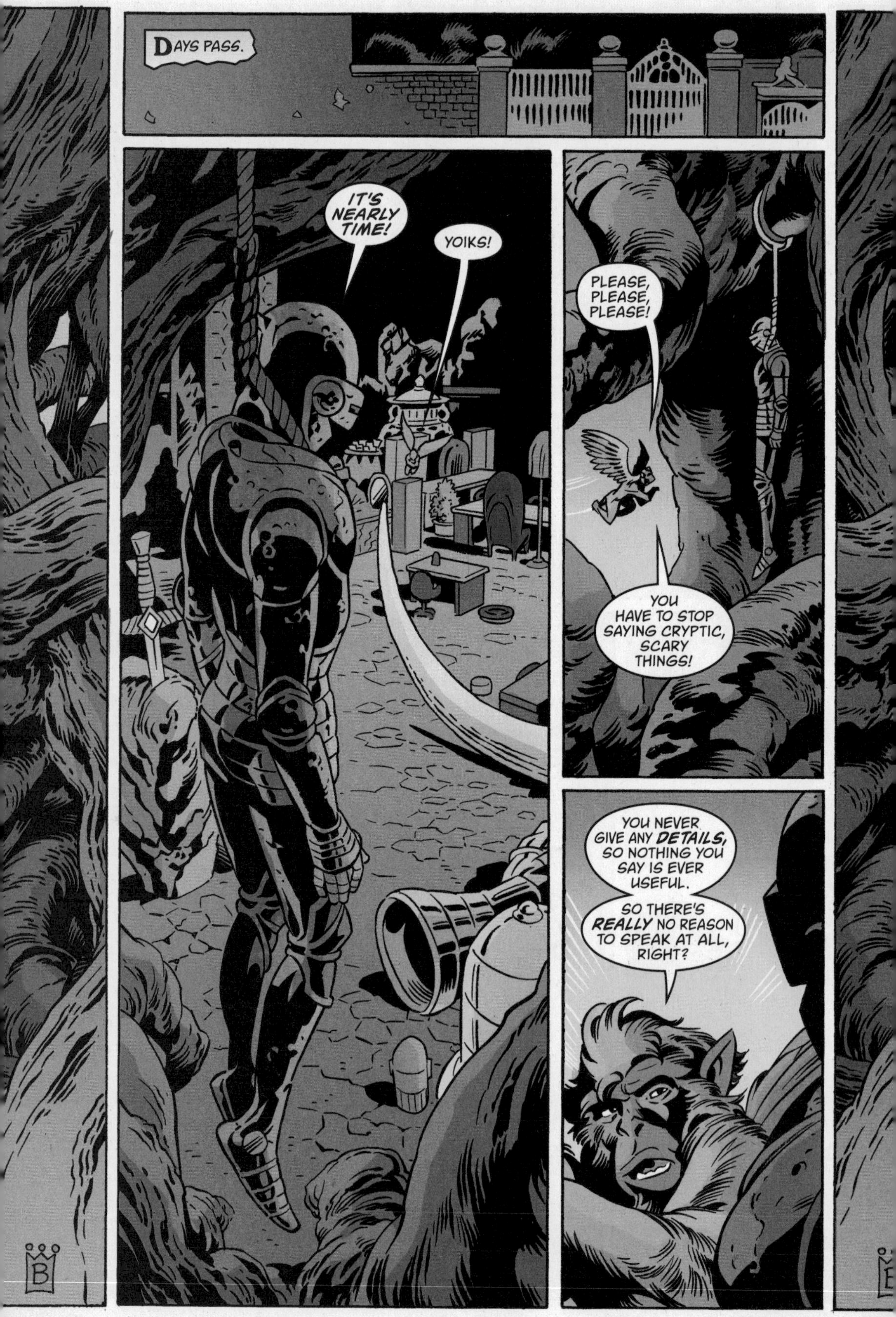
DAYS PASS.
IT'S NEARLY TIME!
YOIKS!
PLEASE, PLEASE, PLEASE!
YOU HAVE TO STOP SAYING CRYPTIC, SCARY THINGS!
YOU NEVER GIVE ANY DETAILS, SO NOTHING YOU SAY IS EVER USEFUL.
SO THERE'S REALLY NO REASON TO SPEAK AT ALL, RIGHT?

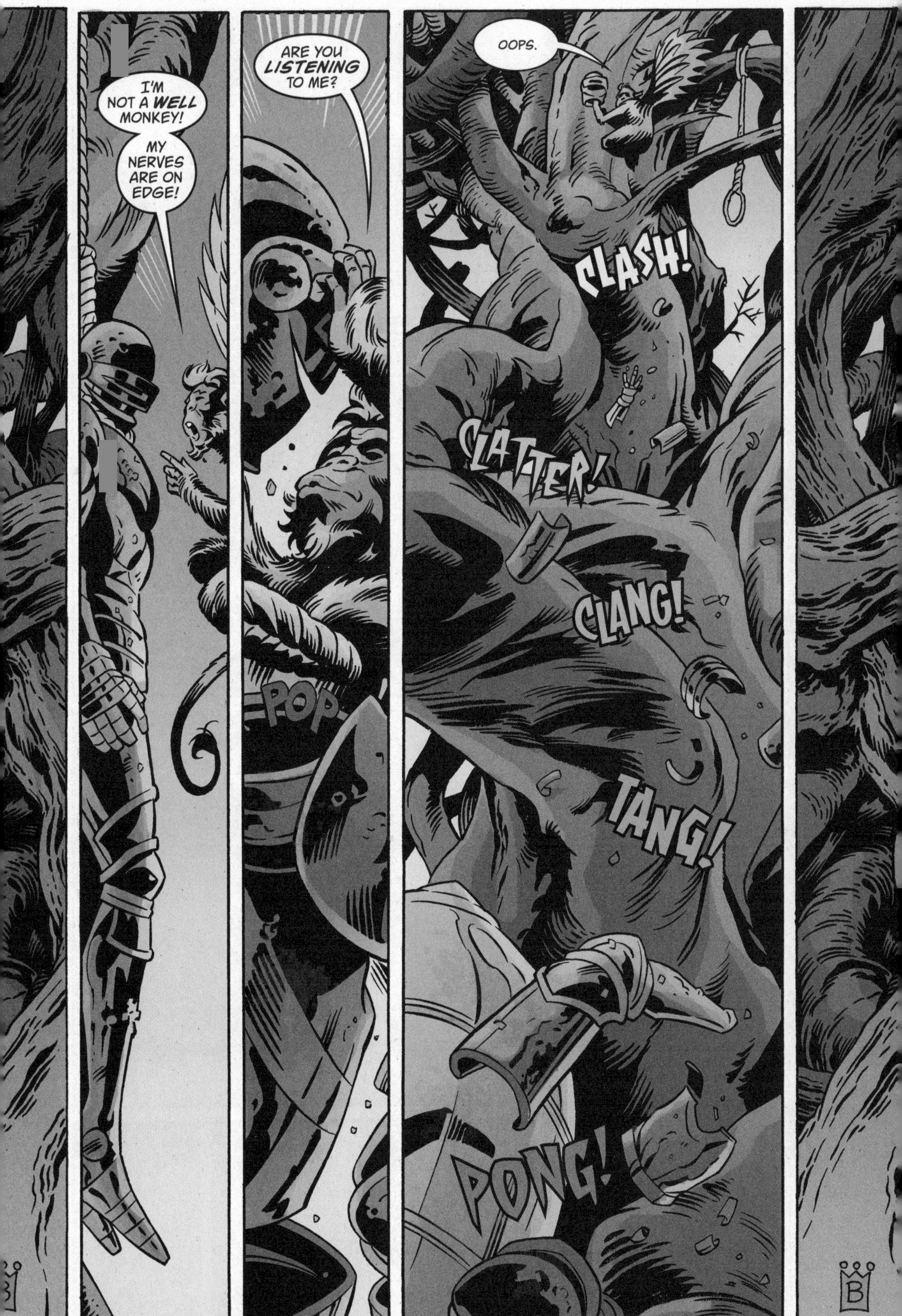

I'M NOT A WELL MONKEY!
MY NERVES ARE ON EDGE!
ARE YOU LISTENING TO ME?
POP
OOPS.
CLASH!
CLATTER!
CLANG!
TANG!
PONG!

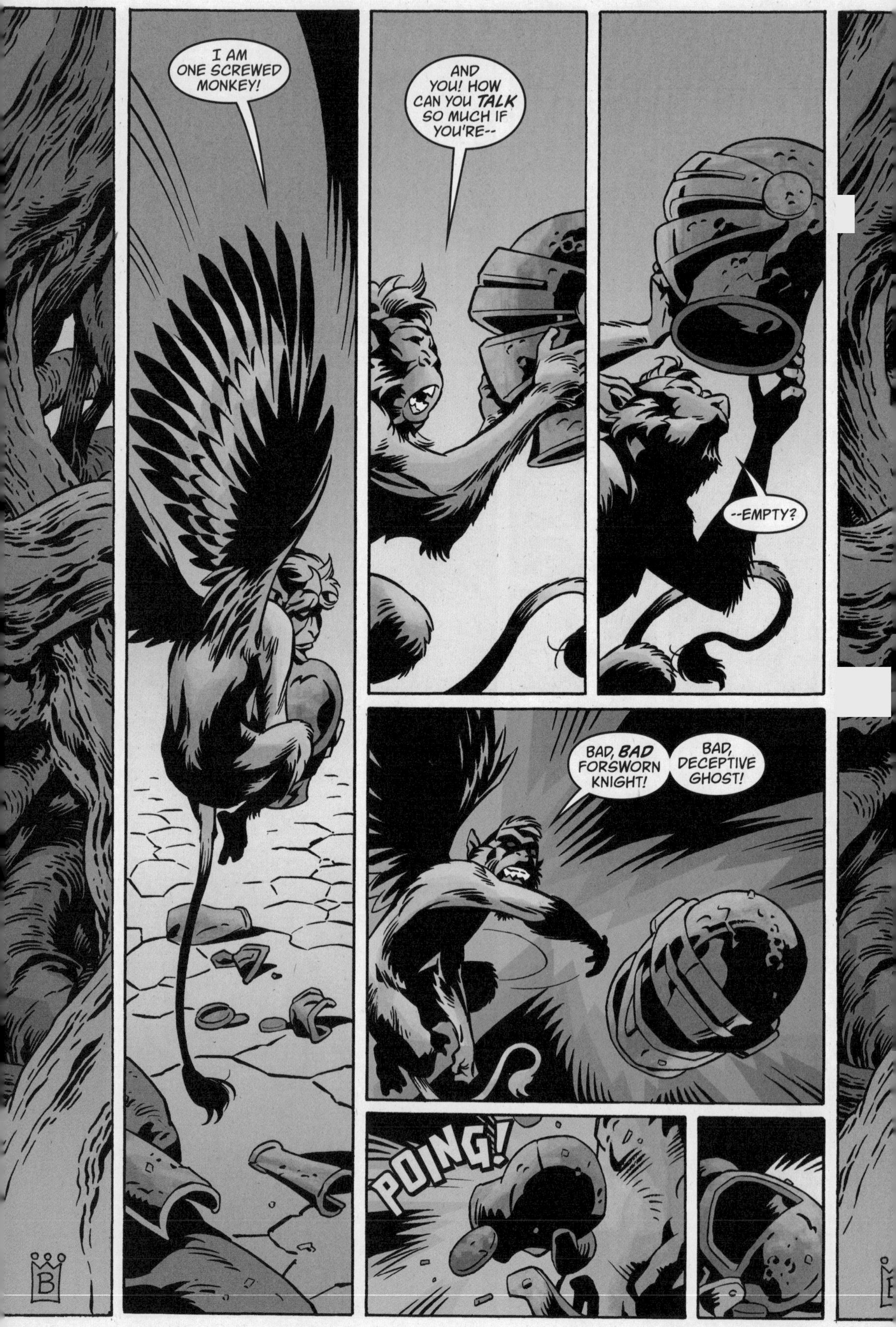
I AM ONE SCREWED MONKEY!
AND YOU! HOW CAN YOU TALK SO MUCH IF YOU'RE--
--EMPTY?
BAD, BAD FORSWORN KNIGHT!
BAD, DECEPTIVE GHOST!
POING!

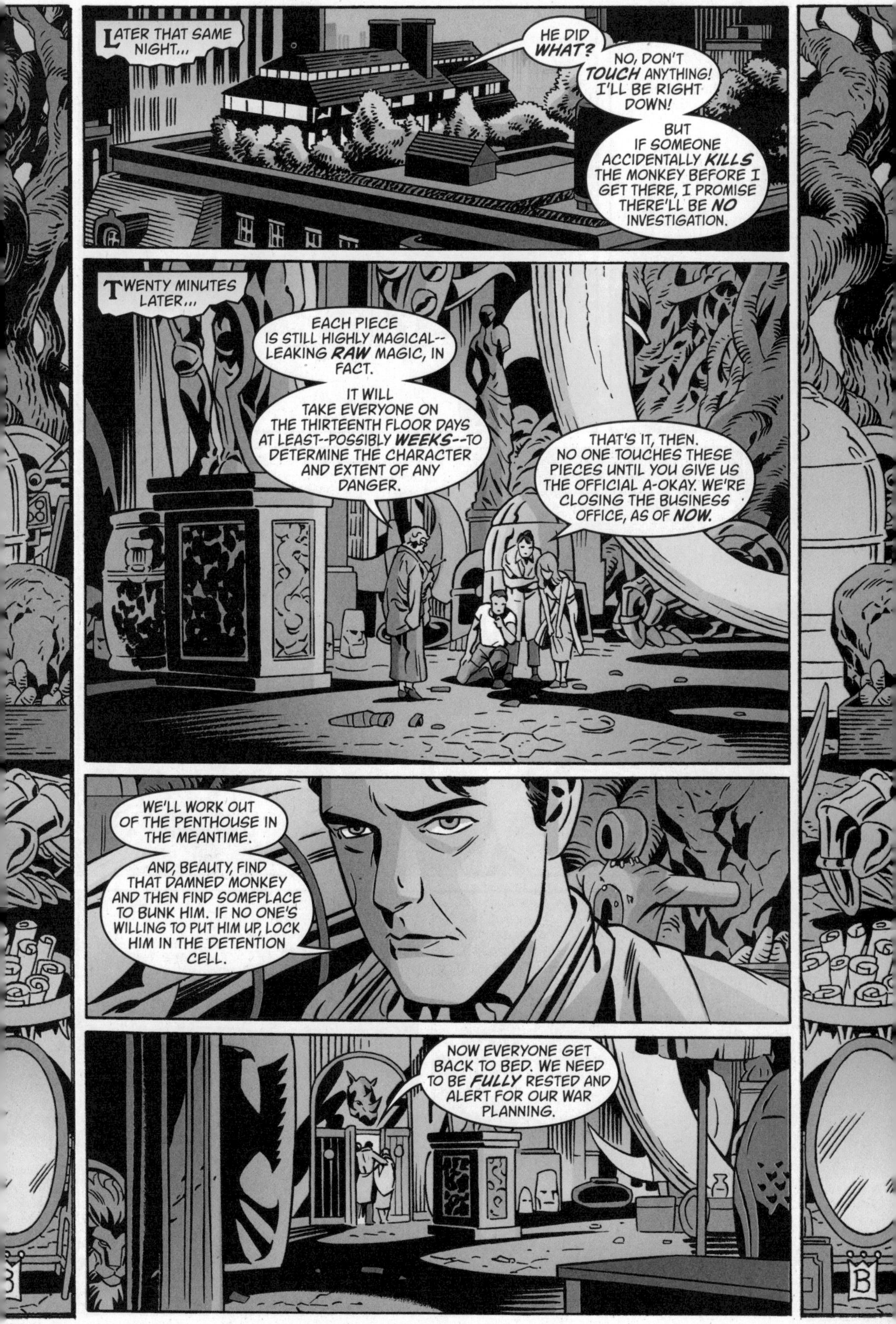
LATER THAT SAME NIGHT...
HE DID WHAT?
NO, DON'T TOUCH ANYTHING! I'LL BE RIGHT DOWN!
BUT IF SOMEONE ACCIDENTALLY KILLS THE MONKEY BEFORE I GET THERE, I PROMISE THERE'LL BE NO INVESTIGATION.
TWENTY MINUTES LATER...
EACH PIECE IS STILL HIGHLY MAGICAL--LEAKING RAW MAGIC, IN FACT.
IT WILL TAKE EVERYONE ON THE THIRTEENTH FLOOR DAYS AT LEAST--POSSIBLY WEEKS--TO DETERMINE THE CHARACTER AND EXTENT OF ANY DANGER.
THAT'S IT, THEN. NO ONE TOUCHES THESE PIECES UNTIL YOU GIVE US THE OFFICIAL A-OKAY. WE'RE CLOSING THE BUSINESS OFFICE, AS OF NOW.
WE'LL WORK OUT OF THE PENTHOUSE IN THE MEANTIME.
AND, BEAUTY, FIND THAT DAMNED MONKEY AND THEN FIND SOMEPLACE TO BUNK HIM. IF NO ONE'S WILLING TO PUT HIM UP, LOCK HIM IN THE DETENTION CELL.
NOW EVERYONE GET BACK TO BED. WE NEED TO BE FULLY RESTED AND ALERT FOR OUR WAR PLANNING.

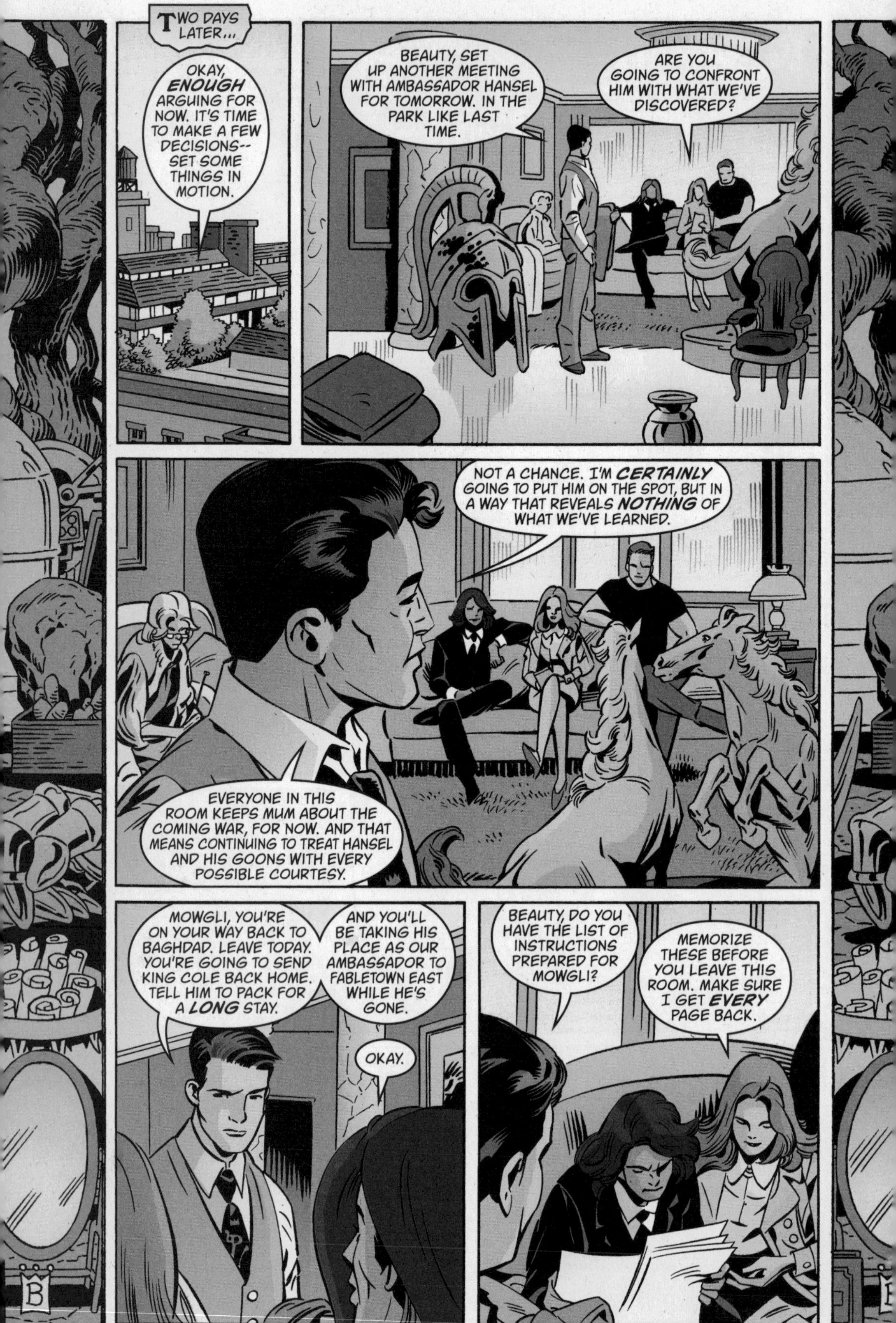
TWO DAYS LATER...
OKAY, ENOUGH ARGUING FOR NOW. IT'S TIME TO MAKE A FEW DECISIONS-- SET SOME THINGS IN MOTION.
BEAUTY, SET UP ANOTHER MEETING WITH AMBASSADOR HANSEL FOR TOMORROW. IN THE PARK LIKE LAST TIME.
ARE YOU GOING TO CONFRONT HIM WITH WHAT WE'VE DISCOVERED?
NOT A CHANCE. I'M CERTAINLY GOING TO PUT HIM ON THE SPOT, BUT IN A WAY THAT REVEALS NOTHING OF WHAT WE'VE LEARNED.
EVERYONE IN THIS ROOM KEEPS MUM ABOUT THE COMING WAR, FOR NOW. AND THAT MEANS CONTINUING TO TREAT HANSEL AND HIS GOONS WITH EVERY POSSIBLE COURTESY.
MOWGLI, YOU'RE ON YOUR WAY BACK TO BAGHDAD. LEAVE TODAY. YOU'RE GOING TO SEND KING COLE BACK HOME. TELL HIM TO PACK FOR A LONG STAY.
AND YOU'LL BE TAKING HIS PLACE AS OUR AMBASSADOR TO FABLETOWN EAST WHILE HE'S GONE.
OKAY.
BEAUTY, DO YOU HAVE THE LIST OF INSTRUCTIONS PREPARED FOR MOWGLI?
MEMORIZE THESE BEFORE YOU LEAVE THIS ROOM. MAKE SURE I GET EVERY PAGE BACK.

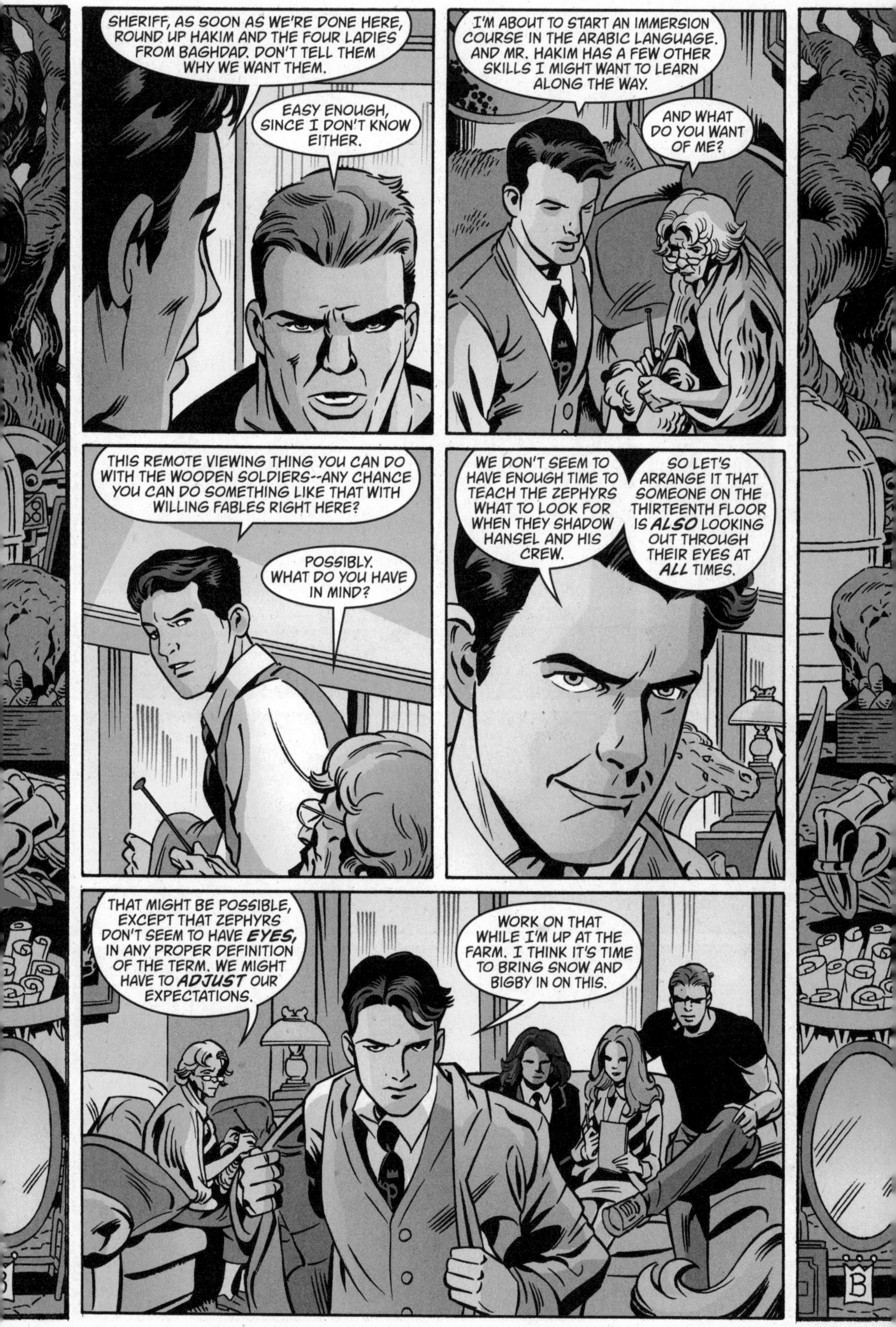
SHERIFF, AS SOON AS WE'RE DONE HERE, ROUND UP HAKIM AND THE FOUR LADIES FROM BAGHDAD. DON'T TELL THEM WHY WE WANT THEM.
EASY ENOUGH, SINCE I DON'T KNOW EITHER.
I'M ABOUT TO START AN IMMERSION COURSE IN THE ARABIC LANGUAGE. AND MR. HAKIM HAS A FEW OTHER SKILLS I MIGHT WANT TO LEARN ALONG THE WAY.
AND WHAT DO YOU WANT OF ME?
THIS REMOTE VIEWING THING YOU CAN DO WITH THE WOODEN SOLDIERS--ANY CHANCE YOU CAN DO SOMETHING LIKE THAT WITH WILLING FABLES RIGHT HERE?
POSSIBLY. WHAT DO YOU HAVE IN MIND?
WE DON'T SEEM TO HAVE ENOUGH TIME TO TEACH THE ZEPHYRS WHAT TO LOOK FOR WHEN THEY SHADOW HANSEL AND HIS CREW.
SO LET'S ARRANGE IT THAT SOMEONE ON THE THIRTEENTH FLOOR IS ALSO LOOKING OUT THROUGH THEIR EYES AT ALL TIMES.
THAT MIGHT BE POSSIBLE, EXCEPT THAT ZEPHYRS DON'T SEEM TO HAVE EYES, IN ANY PROPER DEFINITION OF THE TERM. WE MIGHT HAVE TO ADJUST OUR EXPECTATIONS.
WORK ON THAT WHILE I'M UP AT THE FARM. I THINK IT'S TIME TO BRING SNOW AND BIGBY IN ON THIS.

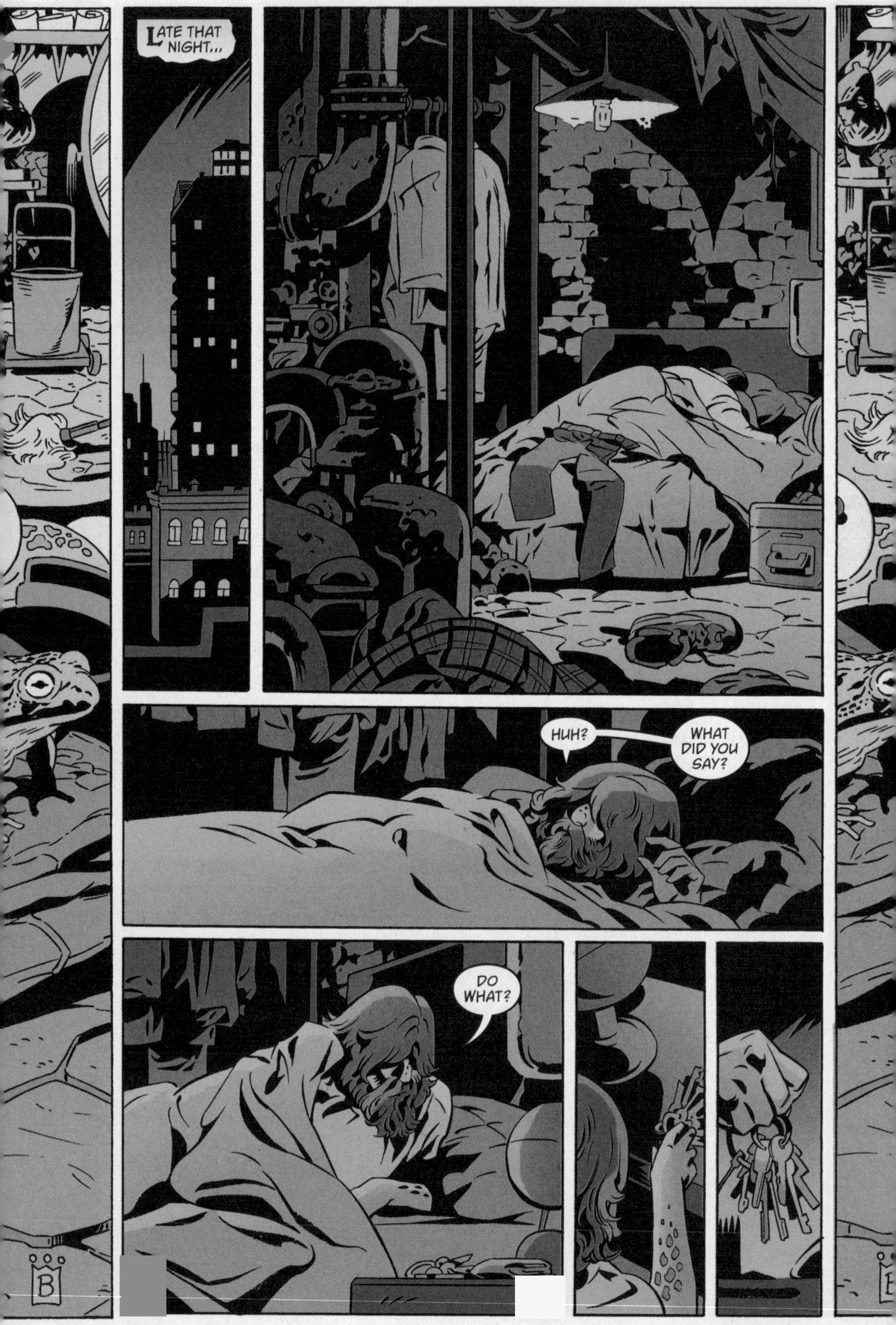

LATE THAT NIGHT...
HUH?
WHAT DID YOU SAY?
DO WHAT?

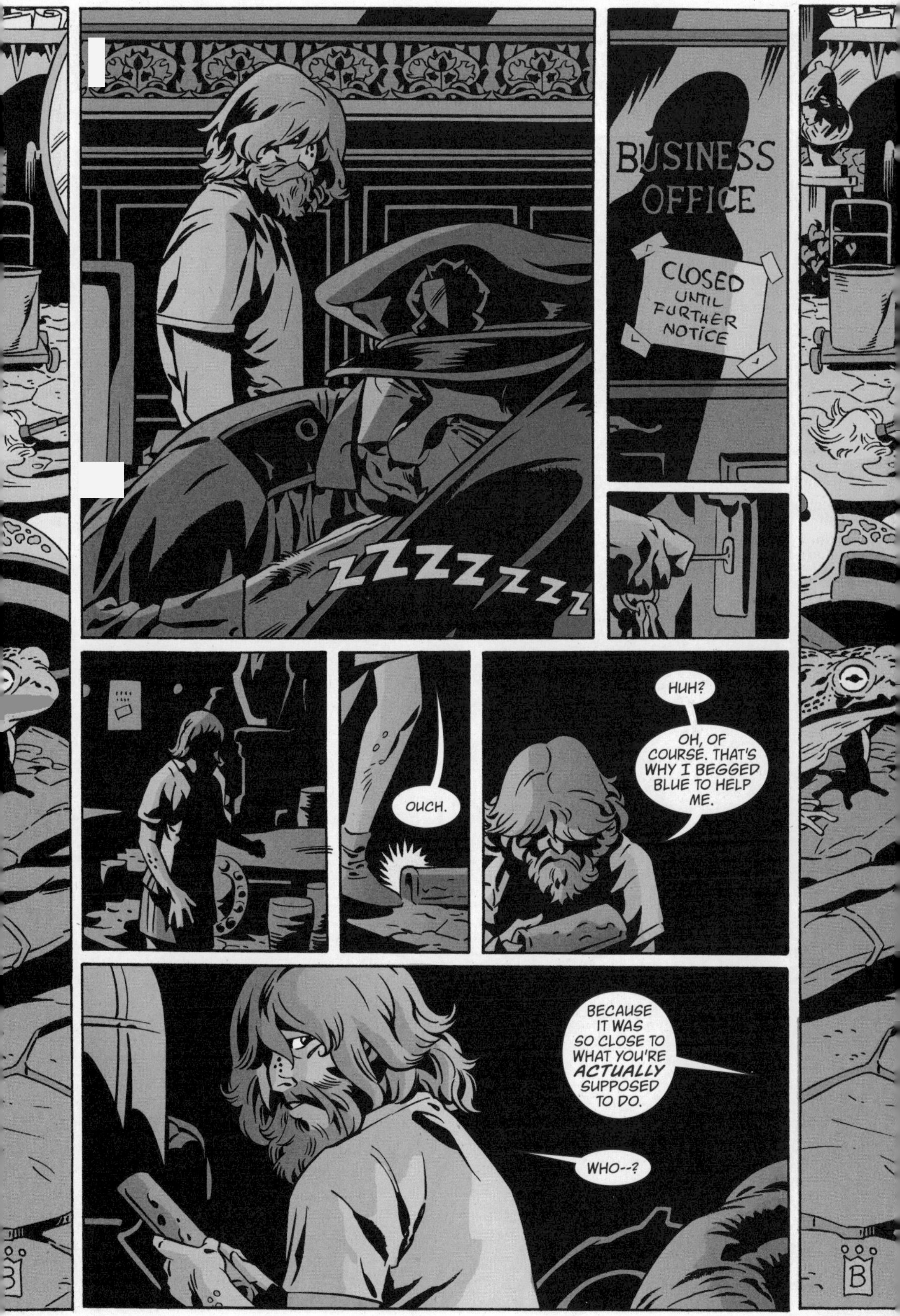
BUSINESS OFFICE
CLOSED UNTIL FURTHER NOTICE
ZZZZZZZZ
OUCH.
HUH?
OH, OF COURSE. THAT'S WHY I BEGGED BLUE TO HELP ME.
BECAUSE IT WAS SO CLOSE TO WHAT YOU'RE *ACTUALLY* SUPPOSED TO DO.
WHO--?

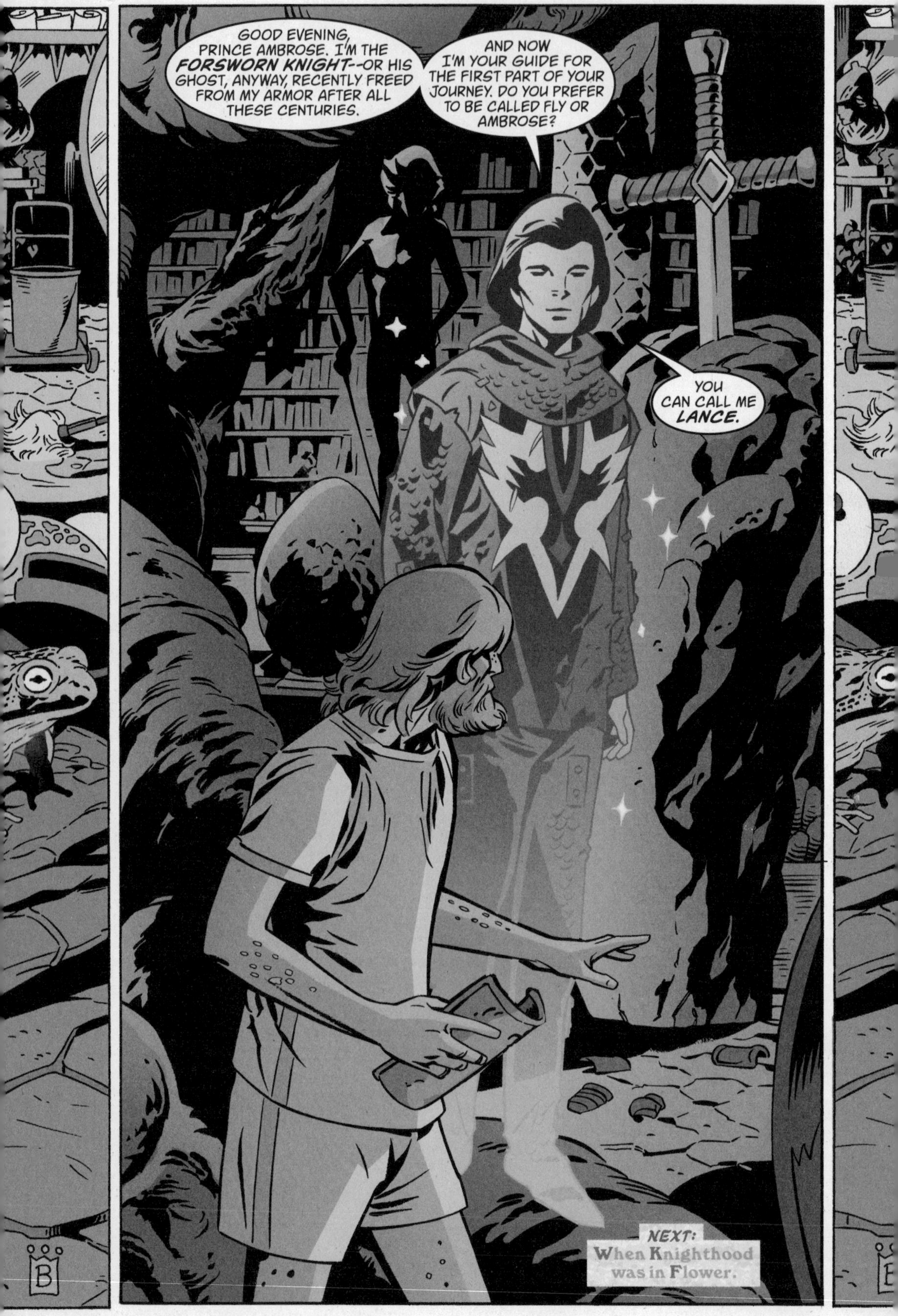
GOOD EVENING, PRINCE AMBROSE. I'M THE FORSWORN KNIGHT--OR HIS GHOST, ANYWAY, RECENTLY FREED FROM MY ARMOR AFTER ALL THESE CENTURIES.
AND NOW I'M YOUR GUIDE FOR THE FIRST PART OF YOUR JOURNEY. DO YOU PREFER TO BE CALLED FLY OR AMBROSE?
YOU CAN CALL ME LANCE.
NEXT: When Knighthood was in Flower.

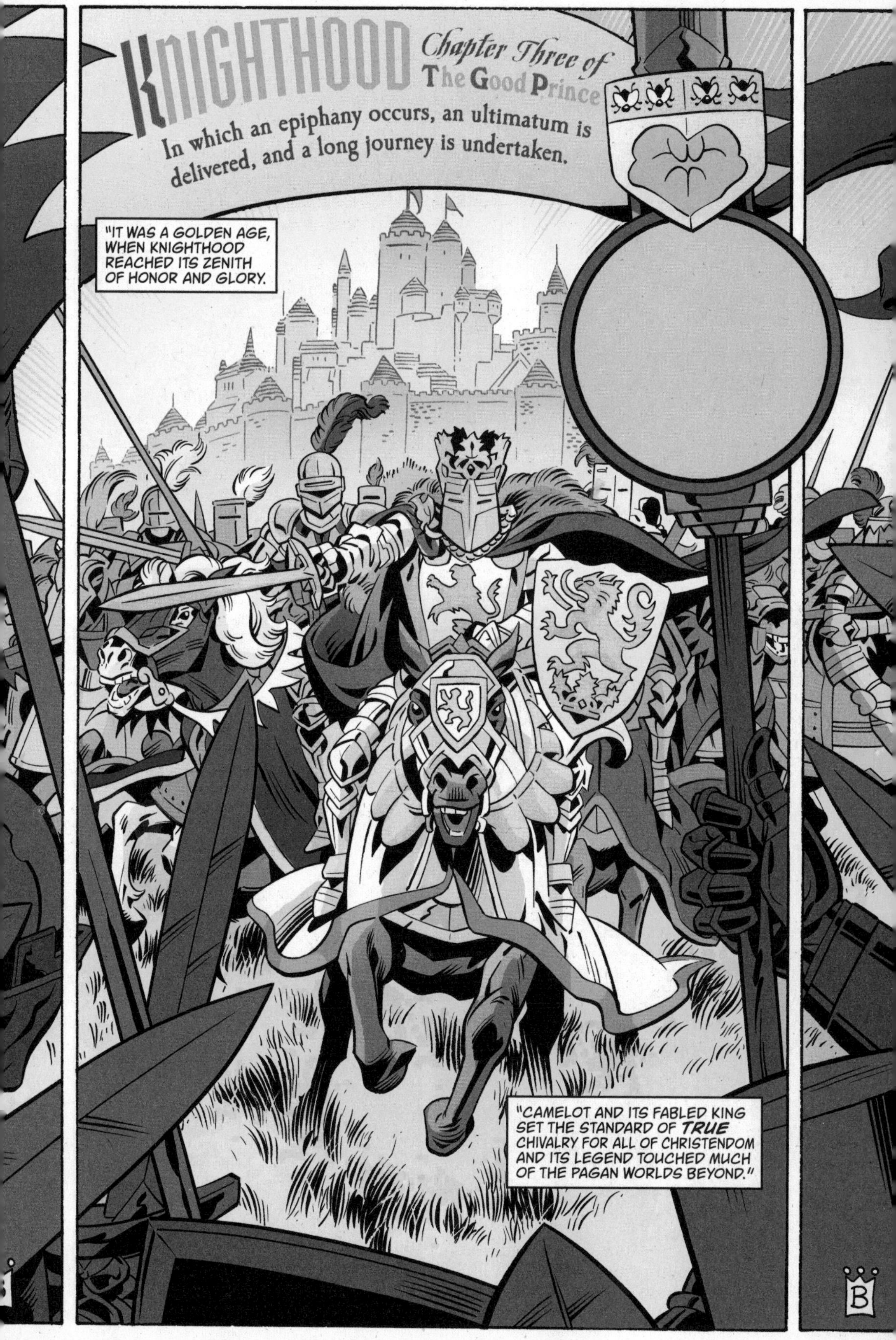
KNIGHTHOOD
Chapter Three of The Good Prince
In which an epiphany occurs, an ultimatum is delivered, and a long journey is undertaken.
"IT WAS A GOLDEN AGE, WHEN KNIGHTHOOD REACHED ITS ZENITH OF HONOR AND GLORY.
"CAMELOT AND ITS FABLED KING SET THE STANDARD OF TRUE CHIVALRY FOR ALL OF CHRISTENDOM AND ITS LEGEND TOUCHED MUCH OF THE PAGAN WORLDS BEYOND."
B

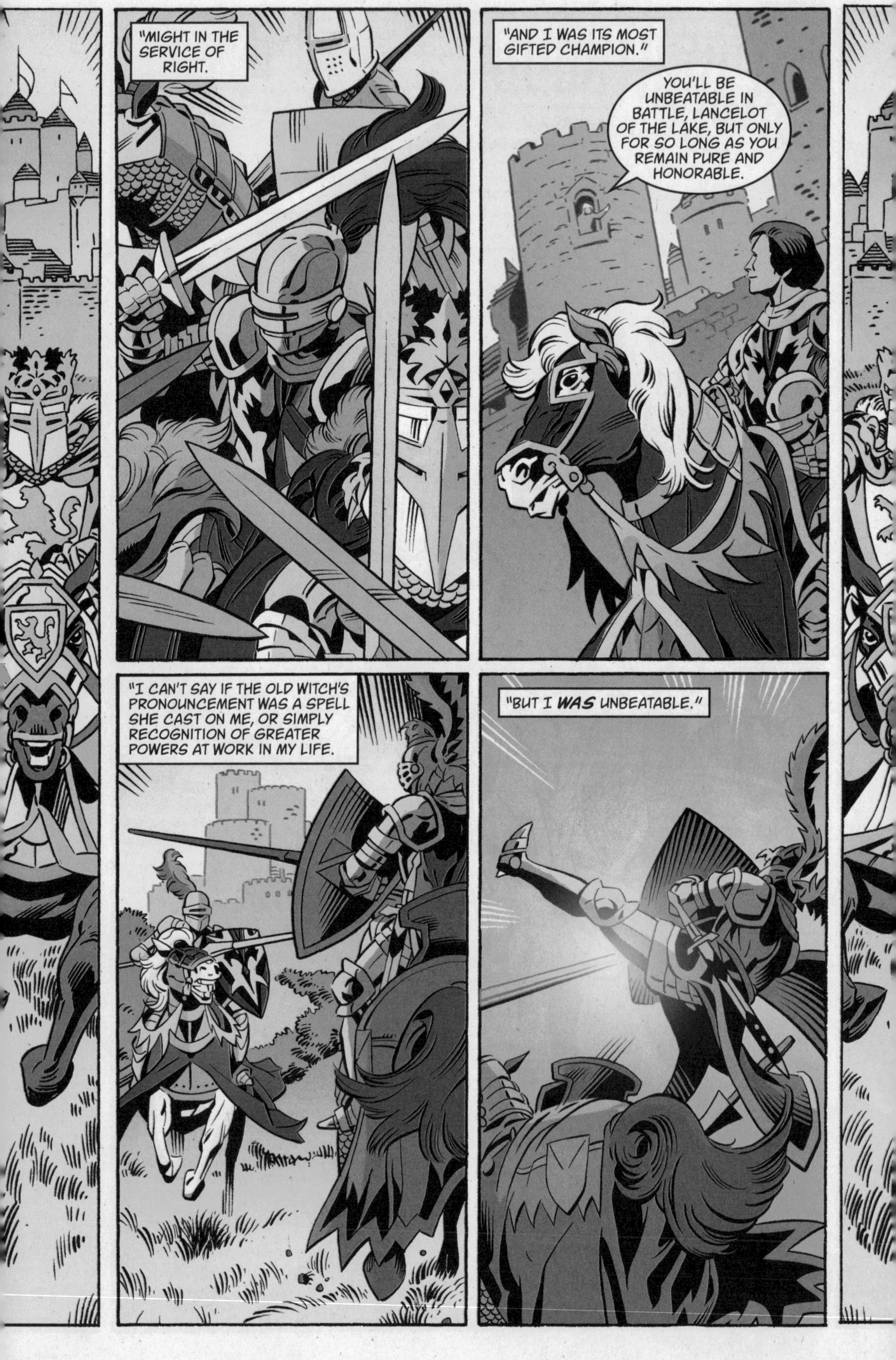
"MIGHT IN THE SERVICE OF RIGHT.
"AND I WAS ITS MOST GIFTED CHAMPION."
YOU'LL BE UNBEATABLE IN BATTLE, LANCELOT OF THE LAKE, BUT ONLY FOR SO LONG AS YOU REMAIN PURE AND HONORABLE.
"I CAN'T SAY IF THE OLD WITCH'S PRONOUNCEMENT WAS A SPELL SHE CAST ON ME, OR SIMPLY RECOGNITION OF GREATER POWERS AT WORK IN MY LIFE.
"BUT I **WAS** UNBEATABLE."

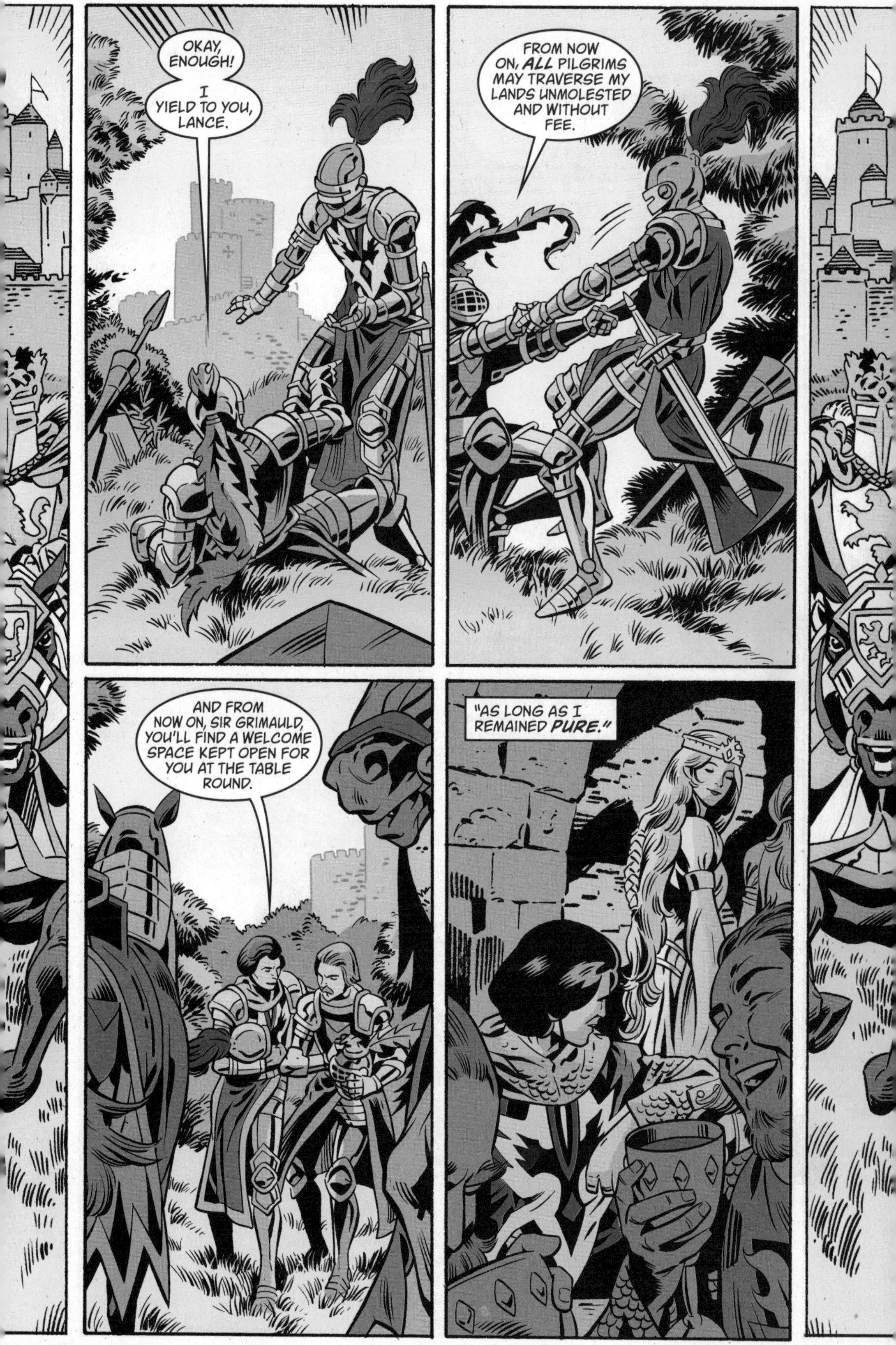
OKAY, ENOUGH!
I YIELD TO YOU, LANCE.
FROM NOW ON, ALL PILGRIMS MAY TRAVERSE MY LANDS UNMOLESTED AND WITHOUT FEE.
AND FROM NOW ON, SIR GRIMAULD, YOU'LL FIND A WELCOME SPACE KEPT OPEN FOR YOU AT THE TABLE ROUND.
"AS LONG AS I REMAINED PURE."

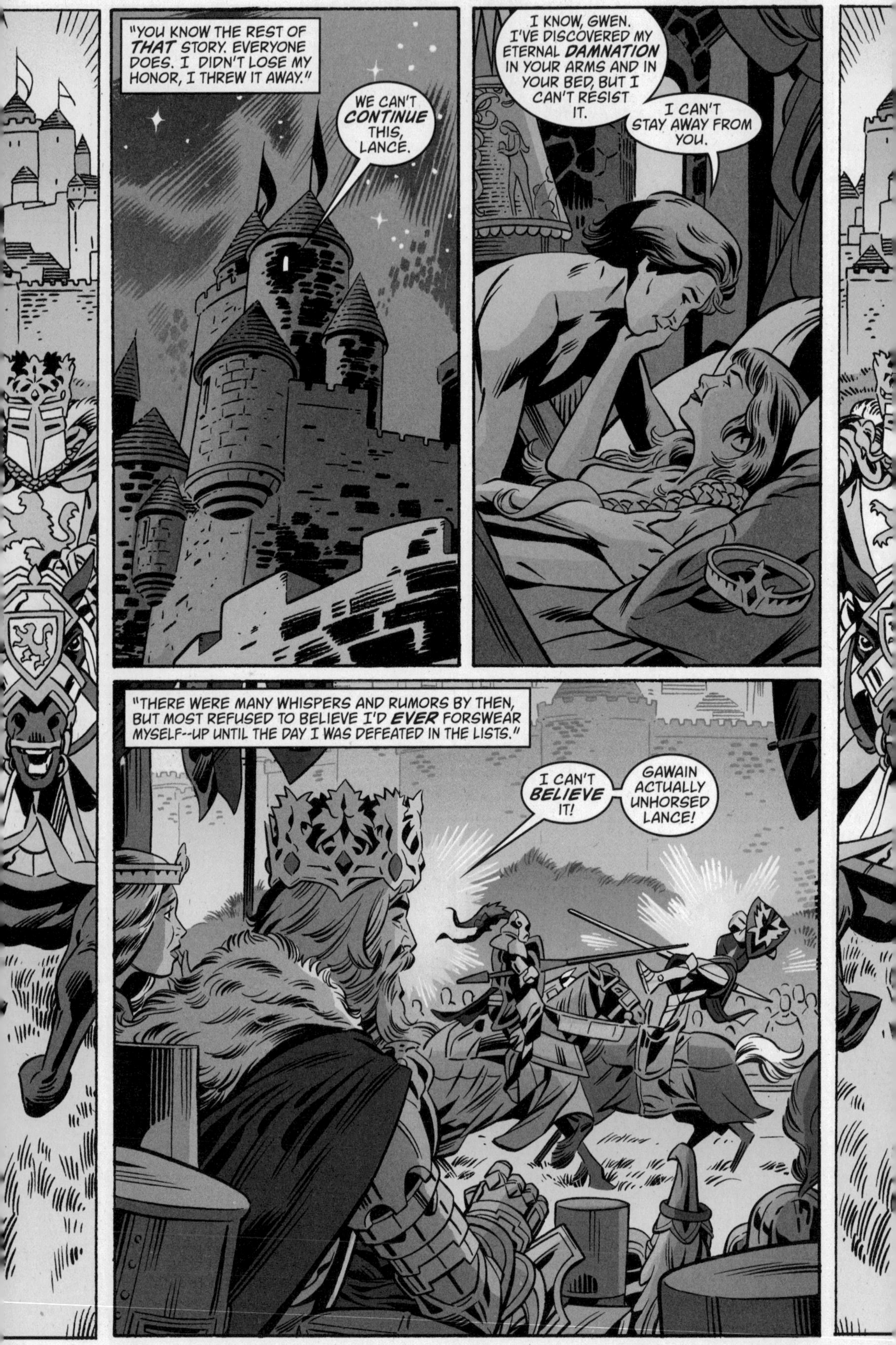
"YOU KNOW THE REST OF THAT STORY. EVERYONE DOES. I DIDN'T LOSE MY HONOR, I THREW IT AWAY."
WE CAN'T CONTINUE THIS, LANCE.
I KNOW, GWEN. I'VE DISCOVERED MY ETERNAL DAMNATION IN YOUR ARMS AND IN YOUR BED, BUT I CAN'T RESIST IT.
I CAN'T STAY AWAY FROM YOU.
"THERE WERE MANY WHISPERS AND RUMORS BY THEN, BUT MOST REFUSED TO BELIEVE I'D EVER FORSWEAR MYSELF--UP UNTIL THE DAY I WAS DEFEATED IN THE LISTS."
I CAN'T BELIEVE IT!
GAWAIN ACTUALLY UNHORSED LANCE!

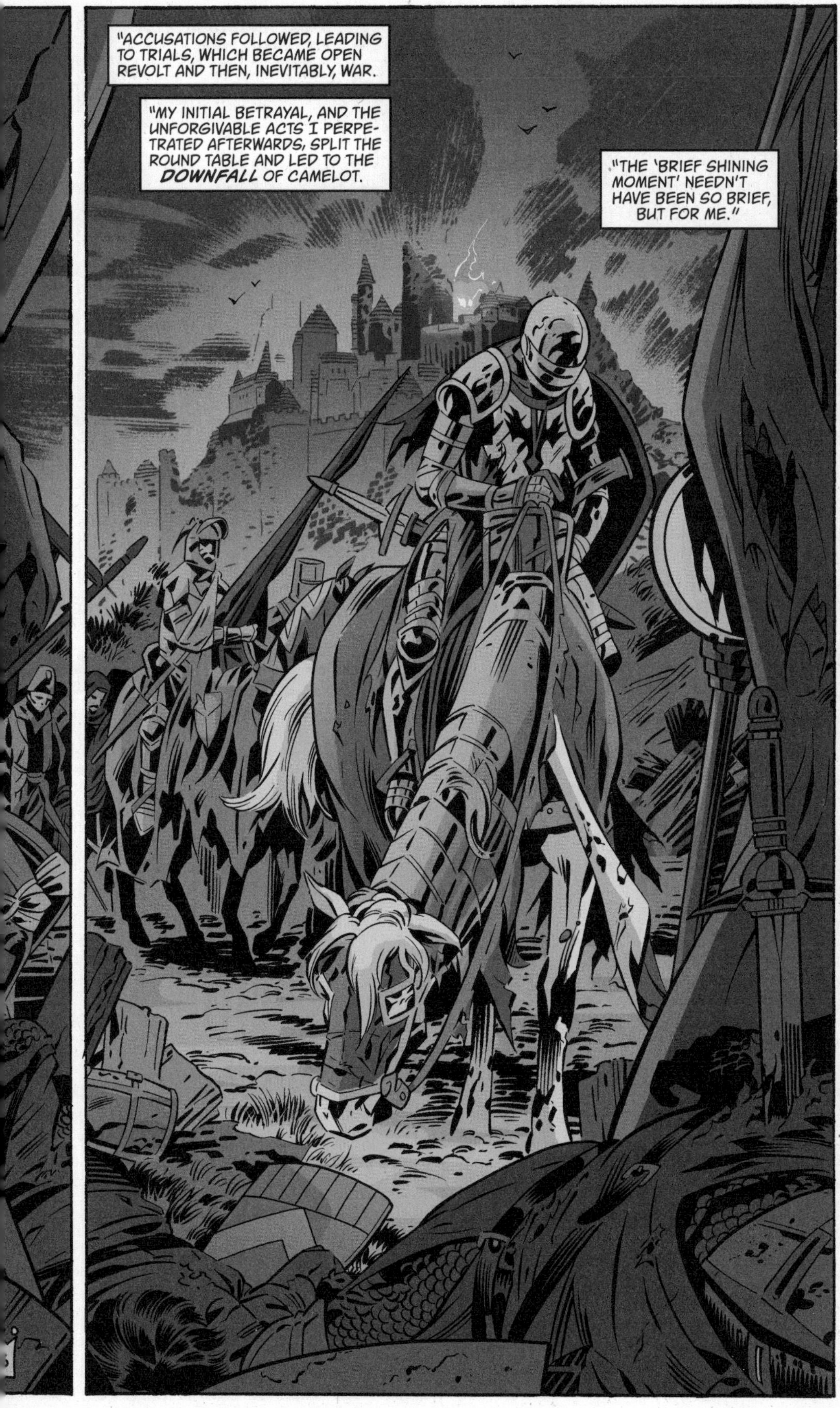
"ACCUSATIONS FOLLOWED, LEADING TO TRIALS, WHICH BECAME OPEN REVOLT AND THEN, INEVITABLY, WAR.
"MY INITIAL BETRAYAL, AND THE UNFORGIVABLE ACTS I PERPETRATED AFTERWARDS, SPLIT THE ROUND TABLE AND LED TO THE DOWNFALL OF CAMELOT.
"THE 'BRIEF SHINING MOMENT' NEEDN'T HAVE BEEN SO BRIEF, BUT FOR ME."

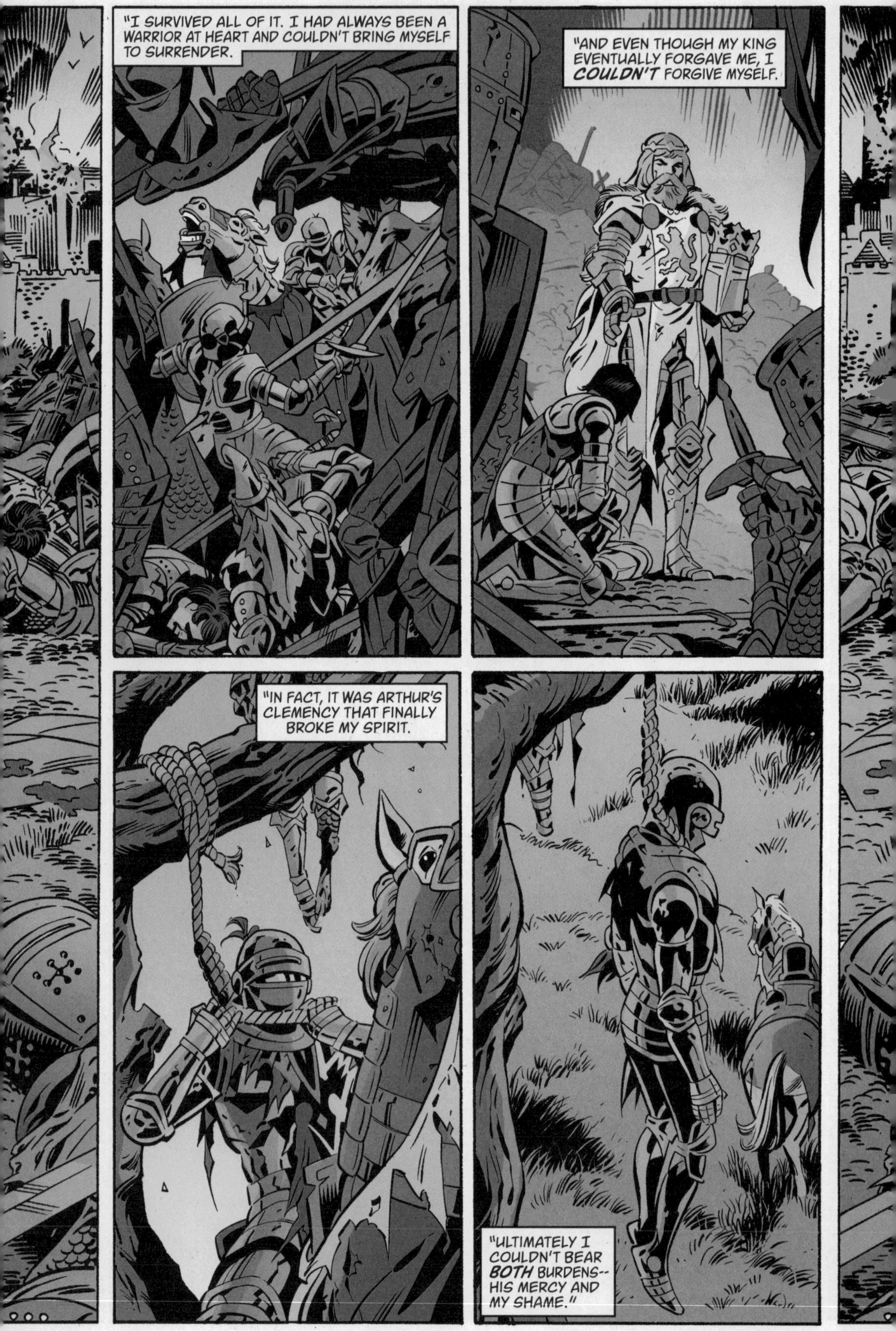
"I SURVIVED ALL OF IT. I HAD ALWAYS BEEN A WARRIOR AT HEART AND COULDN'T BRING MYSELF TO SURRENDER.
"AND EVEN THOUGH MY KING EVENTUALLY FORGAVE ME, I COULDN'T FORGIVE MYSELF.
"IN FACT, IT WAS ARTHUR'S CLEMENCY THAT FINALLY BROKE MY SPIRIT.
"ULTIMATELY I COULDN'T BEAR BOTH BURDENS-- HIS MERCY AND MY SHAME."

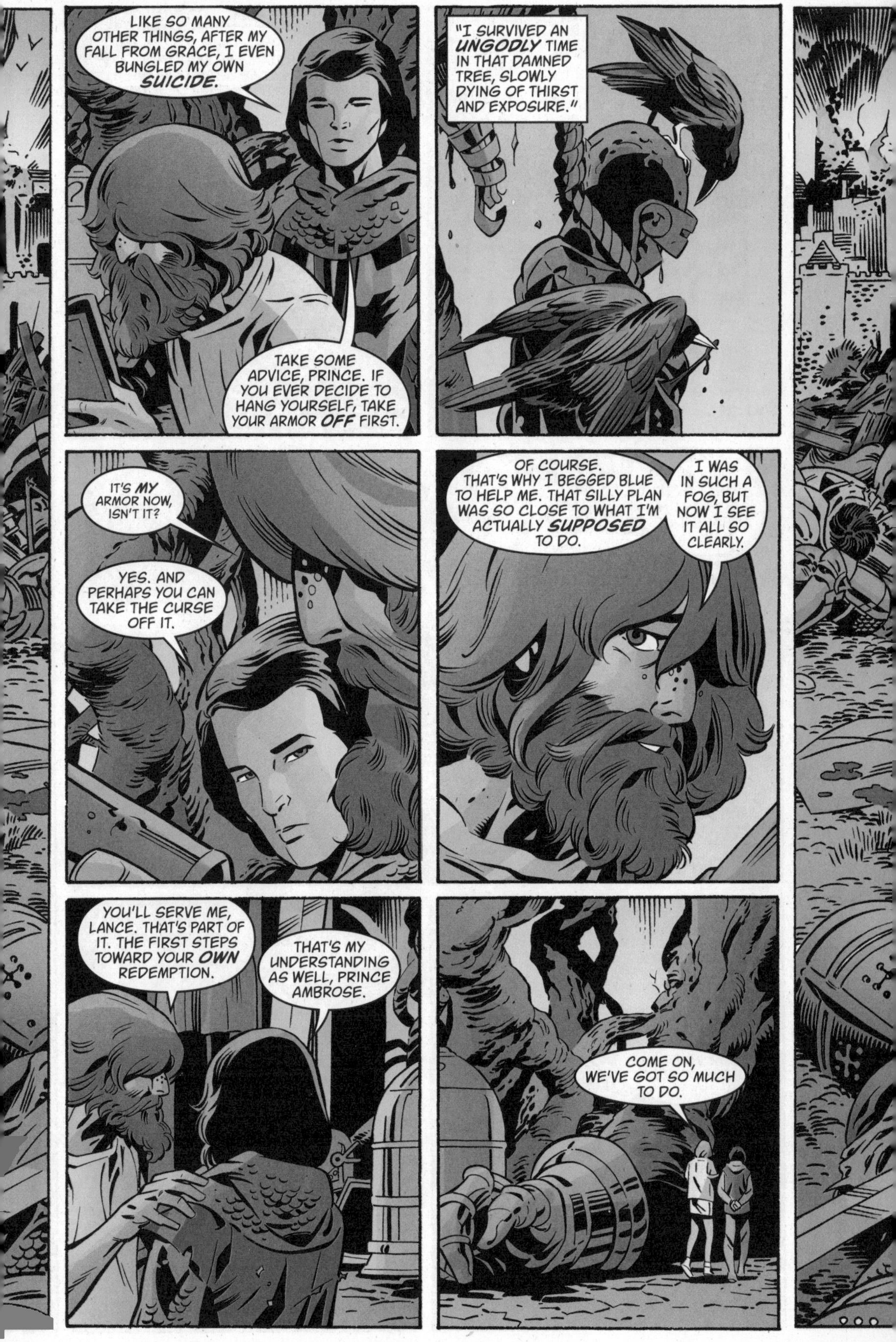

LIKE SO MANY OTHER THINGS, AFTER MY FALL FROM GRACE, I EVEN BUNGLED MY OWN SUICIDE.
TAKE SOME ADVICE, PRINCE. IF YOU EVER DECIDE TO HANG YOURSELF, TAKE YOUR ARMOR OFF FIRST.
"I SURVIVED AN UNGODLY TIME IN THAT DAMNED TREE, SLOWLY DYING OF THIRST AND EXPOSURE."
IT'S MY ARMOR NOW, ISN'T IT?
YES. AND PERHAPS YOU CAN TAKE THE CURSE OFF IT.
OF COURSE. THAT'S WHY I BEGGED BLUE TO HELP ME. THAT SILLY PLAN WAS SO CLOSE TO WHAT I'M ACTUALLY SUPPOSED TO DO.
I WAS IN SUCH A FOG, BUT NOW I SEE IT ALL SO CLEARLY.
YOU'LL SERVE ME, LANCE. THAT'S PART OF IT. THE FIRST STEPS TOWARD YOUR OWN REDEMPTION.
THAT'S MY UNDERSTANDING AS WELL, PRINCE AMBROSE.
COME ON, WE'VE GOT SO MUCH TO DO.

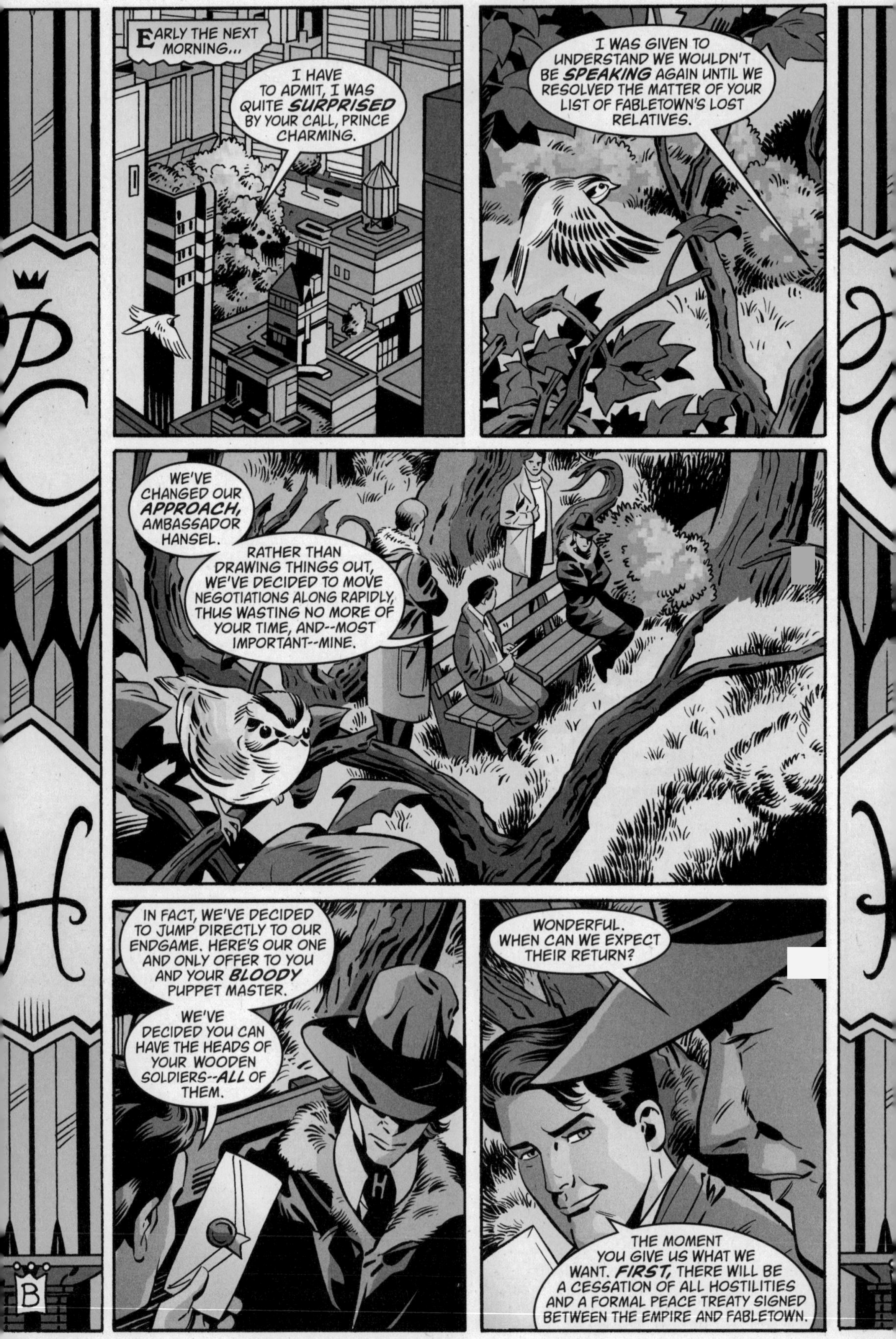
EARLY THE NEXT MORNING...
I HAVE TO ADMIT, I WAS QUITE SURPRISED BY YOUR CALL, PRINCE CHARMING.
I WAS GIVEN TO UNDERSTAND WE WOULDN'T BE SPEAKING AGAIN UNTIL WE RESOLVED THE MATTER OF YOUR LIST OF FABLETOWN'S LOST RELATIVES.
WE'VE CHANGED OUR APPROACH, AMBASSADOR HANSEL.
RATHER THAN DRAWING THINGS OUT, WE'VE DECIDED TO MOVE NEGOTIATIONS ALONG RAPIDLY, THUS WASTING NO MORE OF YOUR TIME, AND--MOST IMPORTANT--MINE.
IN FACT, WE'VE DECIDED TO JUMP DIRECTLY TO OUR ENDGAME. HERE'S OUR ONE AND ONLY OFFER TO YOU AND YOUR BLOODY PUPPET MASTER.
WE'VE DECIDED YOU CAN HAVE THE HEADS OF YOUR WOODEN SOLDIERS--ALL OF THEM.
WONDERFUL. WHEN CAN WE EXPECT THEIR RETURN?
THE MOMENT YOU GIVE US WHAT WE WANT. FIRST, THERE WILL BE A CESSATION OF ALL HOSTILITIES AND A FORMAL PEACE TREATY SIGNED BETWEEN THE EMPIRE AND FABLETOWN.

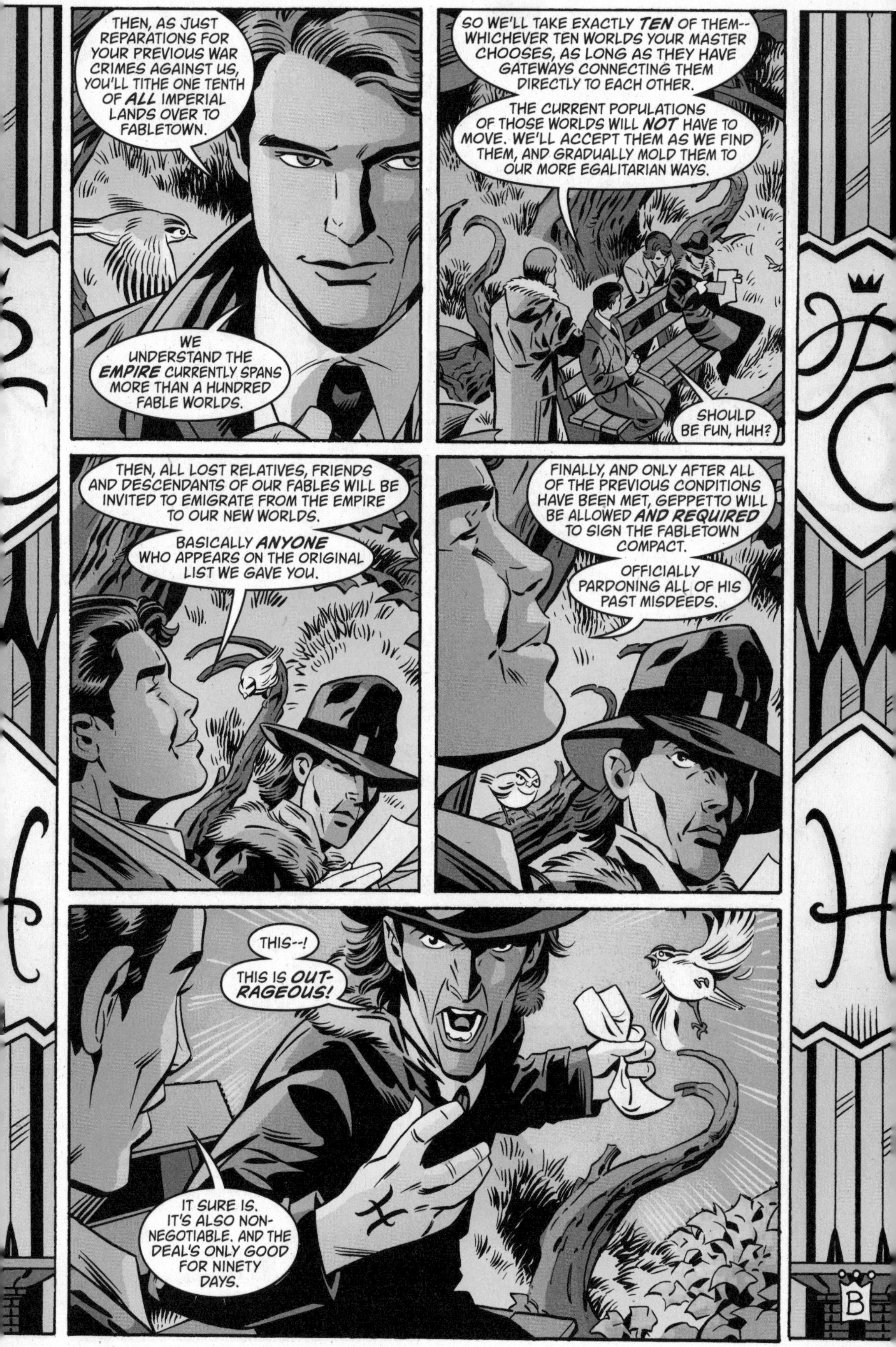
THEN, AS JUST REPARATIONS FOR YOUR PREVIOUS WAR CRIMES AGAINST US, YOU'LL TITHE ONE TENTH OF ALL IMPERIAL LANDS OVER TO FABLETOWN.
WE UNDERSTAND THE EMPIRE CURRENTLY SPANS MORE THAN A HUNDRED FABLE WORLDS.
SO WE'LL TAKE EXACTLY TEN OF THEM--WHICHEVER TEN WORLDS YOUR MASTER CHOOSES, AS LONG AS THEY HAVE GATEWAYS CONNECTING THEM DIRECTLY TO EACH OTHER.
THE CURRENT POPULATIONS OF THOSE WORLDS WILL NOT HAVE TO MOVE. WE'LL ACCEPT THEM AS WE FIND THEM, AND GRADUALLY MOLD THEM TO OUR MORE EGALITARIAN WAYS.
SHOULD BE FUN, HUH?
THEN, ALL LOST RELATIVES, FRIENDS AND DESCENDANTS OF OUR FABLES WILL BE INVITED TO EMIGRATE FROM THE EMPIRE TO OUR NEW WORLDS.
BASICALLY ANYONE WHO APPEARS ON THE ORIGINAL LIST WE GAVE YOU.
FINALLY, AND ONLY AFTER ALL OF THE PREVIOUS CONDITIONS HAVE BEEN MET, GEPPETTO WILL BE ALLOWED AND REQUIRED TO SIGN THE FABLETOWN COMPACT.
OFFICIALLY PARDONING ALL OF HIS PAST MISDEEDS.
THIS--!
THIS IS OUT-RAGEOUS!
IT SURE IS. IT'S ALSO NON-NEGOTIABLE. AND THE DEAL'S ONLY GOOD FOR NINETY DAYS.
B

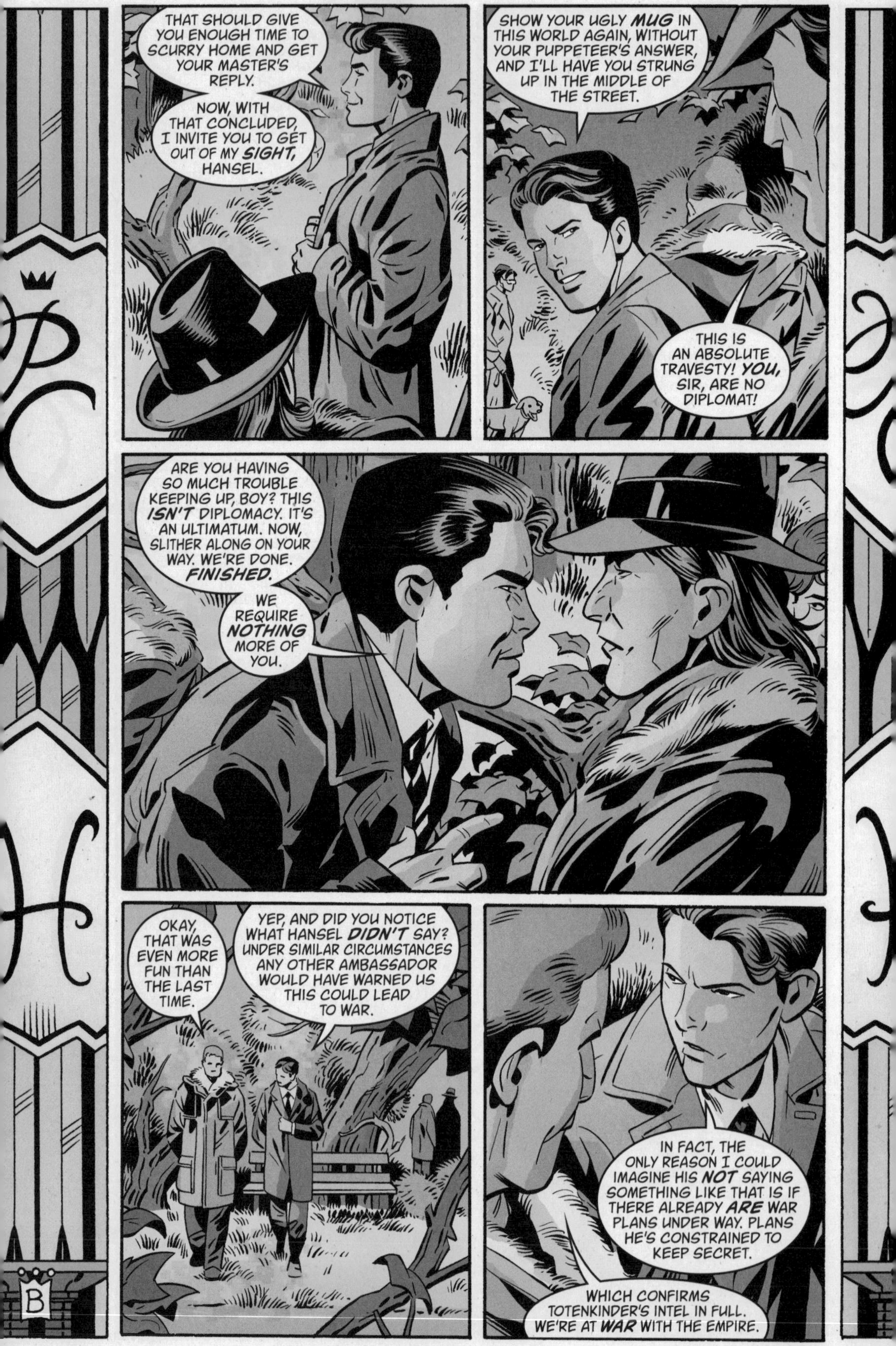
THAT SHOULD GIVE YOU ENOUGH TIME TO SCURRY HOME AND GET YOUR MASTER'S REPLY.
NOW, WITH THAT CONCLUDED, I INVITE YOU TO GET OUT OF MY SIGHT, HANSEL.
SHOW YOUR UGLY MUG IN THIS WORLD AGAIN, WITHOUT YOUR PUPPETEER'S ANSWER, AND I'LL HAVE YOU STRUNG UP IN THE MIDDLE OF THE STREET.
THIS IS AN ABSOLUTE TRAVESTY! YOU, SIR, ARE NO DIPLOMAT!
ARE YOU HAVING SO MUCH TROUBLE KEEPING UP, BOY? THIS ISN'T DIPLOMACY. IT'S AN ULTIMATUM. NOW, SLITHER ALONG ON YOUR WAY. WE'RE DONE. FINISHED.
WE REQUIRE NOTHING MORE OF YOU.
OKAY, THAT WAS EVEN MORE FUN THAN THE LAST TIME.
YEP, AND DID YOU NOTICE WHAT HANSEL DIDN'T SAY? UNDER SIMILAR CIRCUMSTANCES ANY OTHER AMBASSADOR WOULD HAVE WARNED US THIS COULD LEAD TO WAR.
IN FACT, THE ONLY REASON I COULD IMAGINE HIS NOT SAYING SOMETHING LIKE THAT IS IF THERE ALREADY ARE WAR PLANS UNDER WAY. PLANS HE'S CONSTRAINED TO KEEP SECRET.
WHICH CONFIRMS TOTENKINDER'S INTEL IN FULL. WE'RE AT WAR WITH THE EMPIRE.

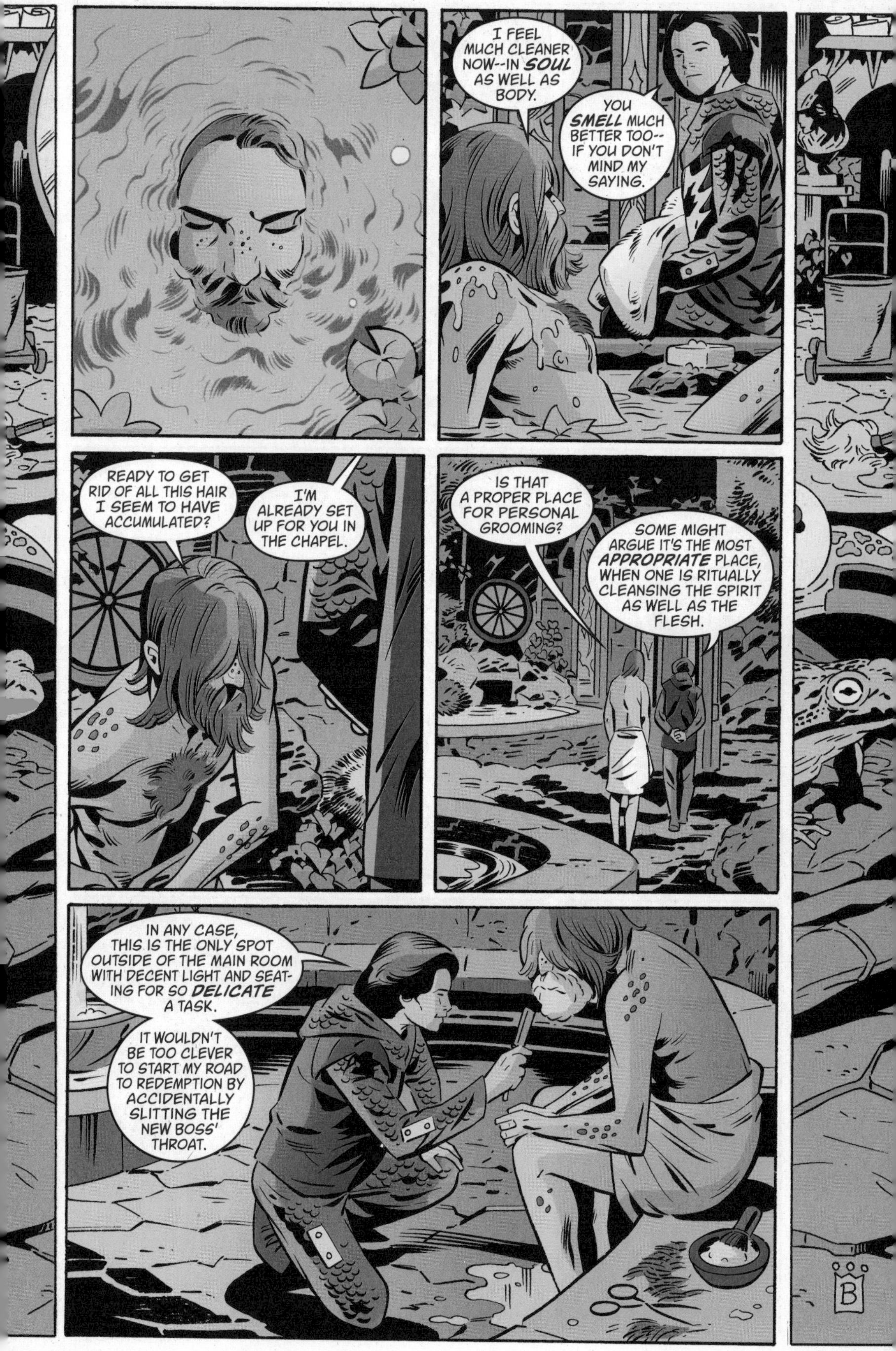

I FEEL MUCH CLEANER NOW--IN *SOUL* AS WELL AS BODY.
YOU *SMELL* MUCH BETTER TOO-- IF YOU DON'T MIND MY SAYING.
READY TO GET RID OF ALL THIS HAIR I SEEM TO HAVE ACCUMULATED?
I'M ALREADY SET UP FOR YOU IN THE CHAPEL.
IS THAT A PROPER PLACE FOR PERSONAL GROOMING?
SOME MIGHT ARGUE IT'S THE MOST *APPROPRIATE* PLACE, WHEN ONE IS RITUALLY CLEANSING THE SPIRIT AS WELL AS THE FLESH.
IN ANY CASE, THIS IS THE ONLY SPOT OUTSIDE OF THE MAIN ROOM WITH DECENT LIGHT AND SEATING FOR SO *DELICATE* A TASK.
IT WOULDN'T BE TOO CLEVER TO START MY ROAD TO REDEMPTION BY ACCIDENTALLY SLITTING THE NEW BOSS' THROAT.
B

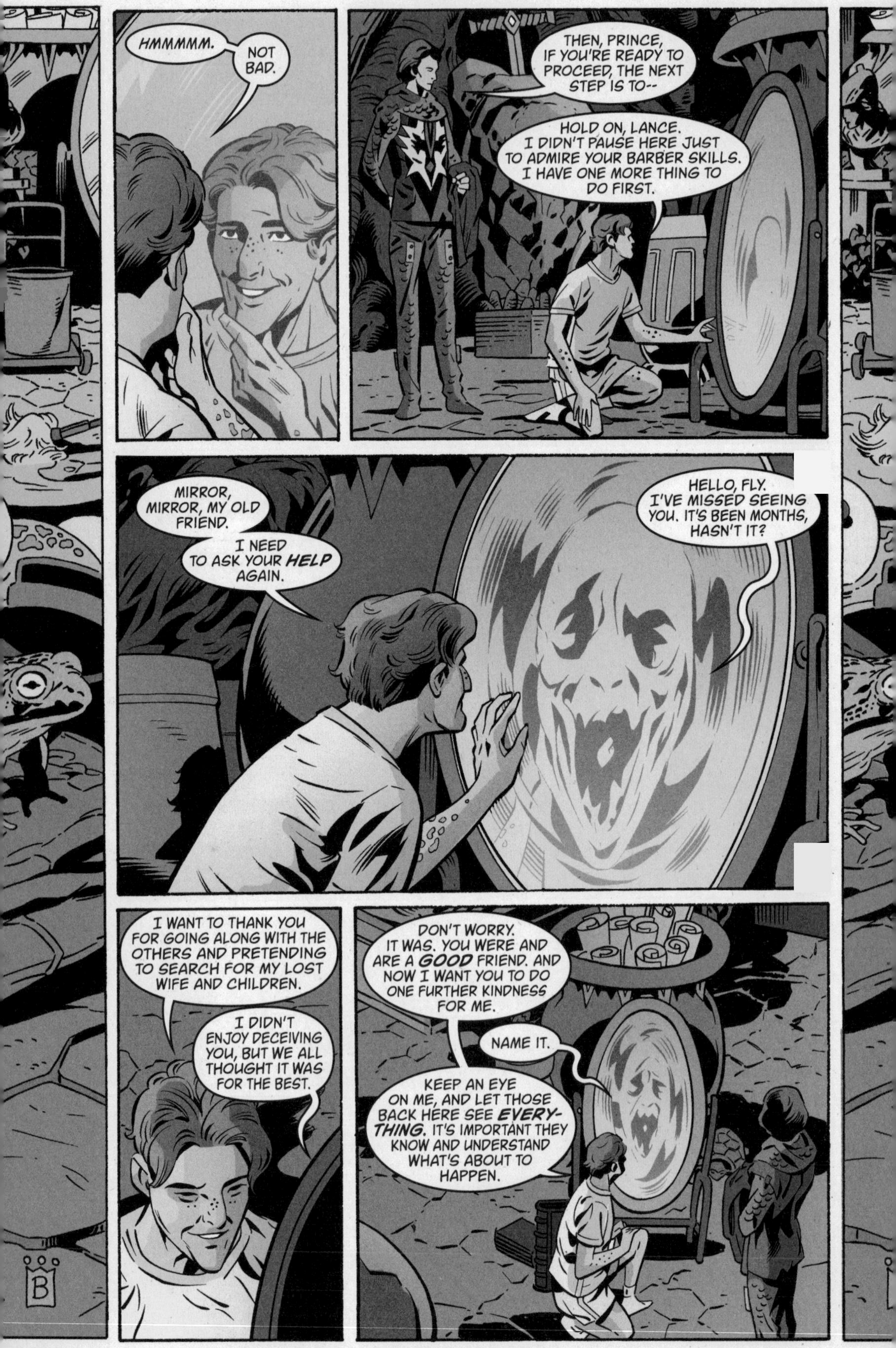
HMMMMM.
NOT BAD.
THEN, PRINCE, IF YOU'RE READY TO PROCEED, THE NEXT STEP IS TO--
HOLD ON, LANCE. I DIDN'T PAUSE HERE JUST TO ADMIRE YOUR BARBER SKILLS. I HAVE ONE MORE THING TO DO FIRST.
MIRROR, MIRROR, MY OLD FRIEND.
I NEED TO ASK YOUR HELP AGAIN.
HELLO, FLY. I'VE MISSED SEEING YOU. IT'S BEEN MONTHS, HASN'T IT?
I WANT TO THANK YOU FOR GOING ALONG WITH THE OTHERS AND PRETENDING TO SEARCH FOR MY LOST WIFE AND CHILDREN.
I DIDN'T ENJOY DECEIVING YOU, BUT WE ALL THOUGHT IT WAS FOR THE BEST.
DON'T WORRY. IT WAS. YOU WERE AND ARE A GOOD FRIEND. AND NOW I WANT YOU TO DO ONE FURTHER KINDNESS FOR ME.
NAME IT.
KEEP AN EYE ON ME, AND LET THOSE BACK HERE SEE EVERYTHING. IT'S IMPORTANT THEY KNOW AND UNDERSTAND WHAT'S ABOUT TO HAPPEN.

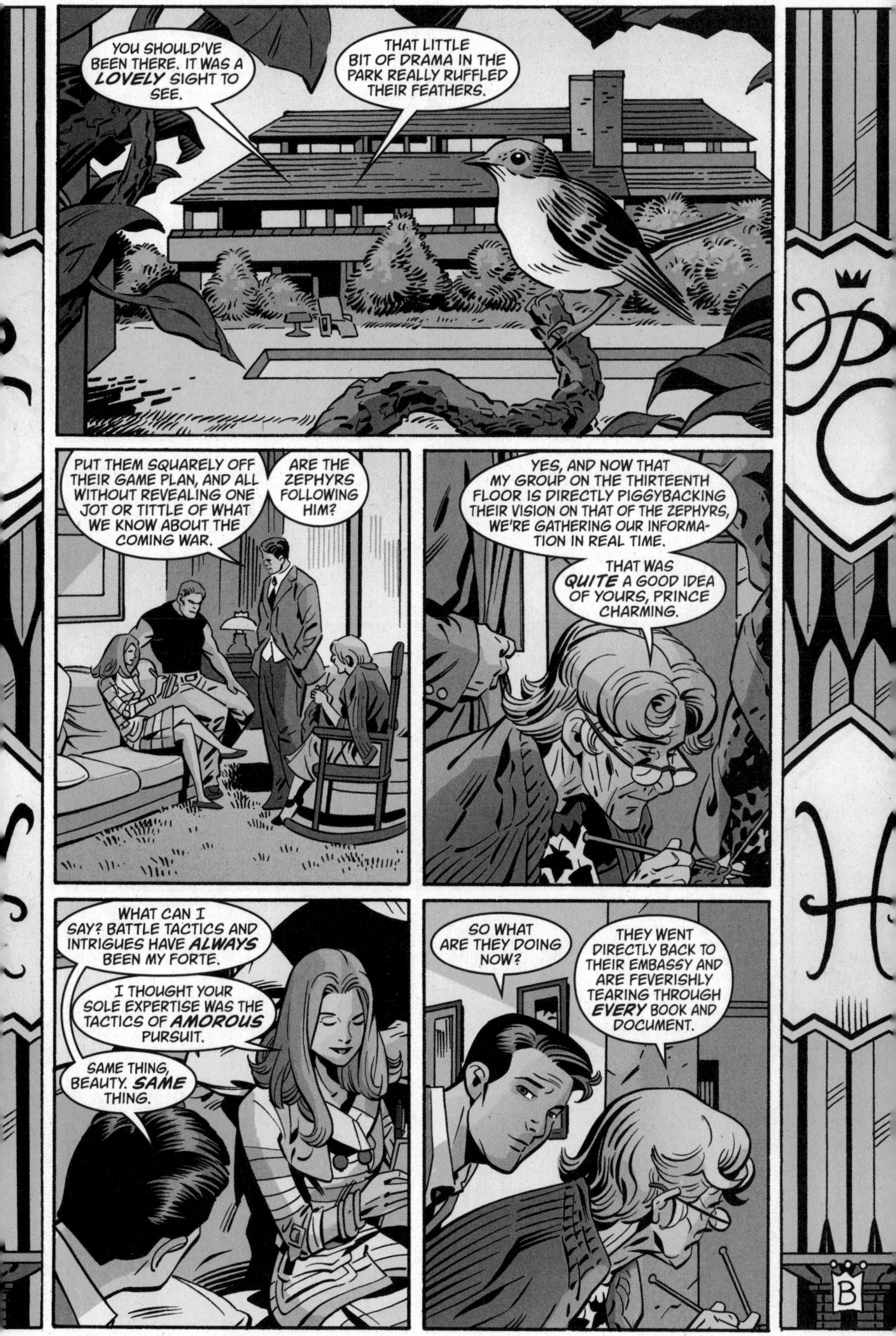
YOU SHOULD'VE BEEN THERE. IT WAS A LOVELY SIGHT TO SEE.
THAT LITTLE BIT OF DRAMA IN THE PARK REALLY RUFFLED THEIR FEATHERS.
PUT THEM SQUARELY OFF THEIR GAME PLAN, AND ALL WITHOUT REVEALING ONE JOT OR TITTLE OF WHAT WE KNOW ABOUT THE COMING WAR.
ARE THE ZEPHYRS FOLLOWING HIM?
YES, AND NOW THAT MY GROUP ON THE THIRTEENTH FLOOR IS DIRECTLY PIGGYBACKING THEIR VISION ON THAT OF THE ZEPHYRS, WE'RE GATHERING OUR INFORMATION IN REAL TIME.
THAT WAS QUITE A GOOD IDEA OF YOURS, PRINCE CHARMING.
WHAT CAN I SAY? BATTLE TACTICS AND INTRIGUES HAVE ALWAYS BEEN MY FORTE.
I THOUGHT YOUR SOLE EXPERTISE WAS THE TACTICS OF AMOROUS PURSUIT.
SAME THING, BEAUTY. SAME THING.
SO WHAT ARE THEY DOING NOW?
THEY WENT DIRECTLY BACK TO THEIR EMBASSY AND ARE FEVERISHLY TEARING THROUGH EVERY BOOK AND DOCUMENT.

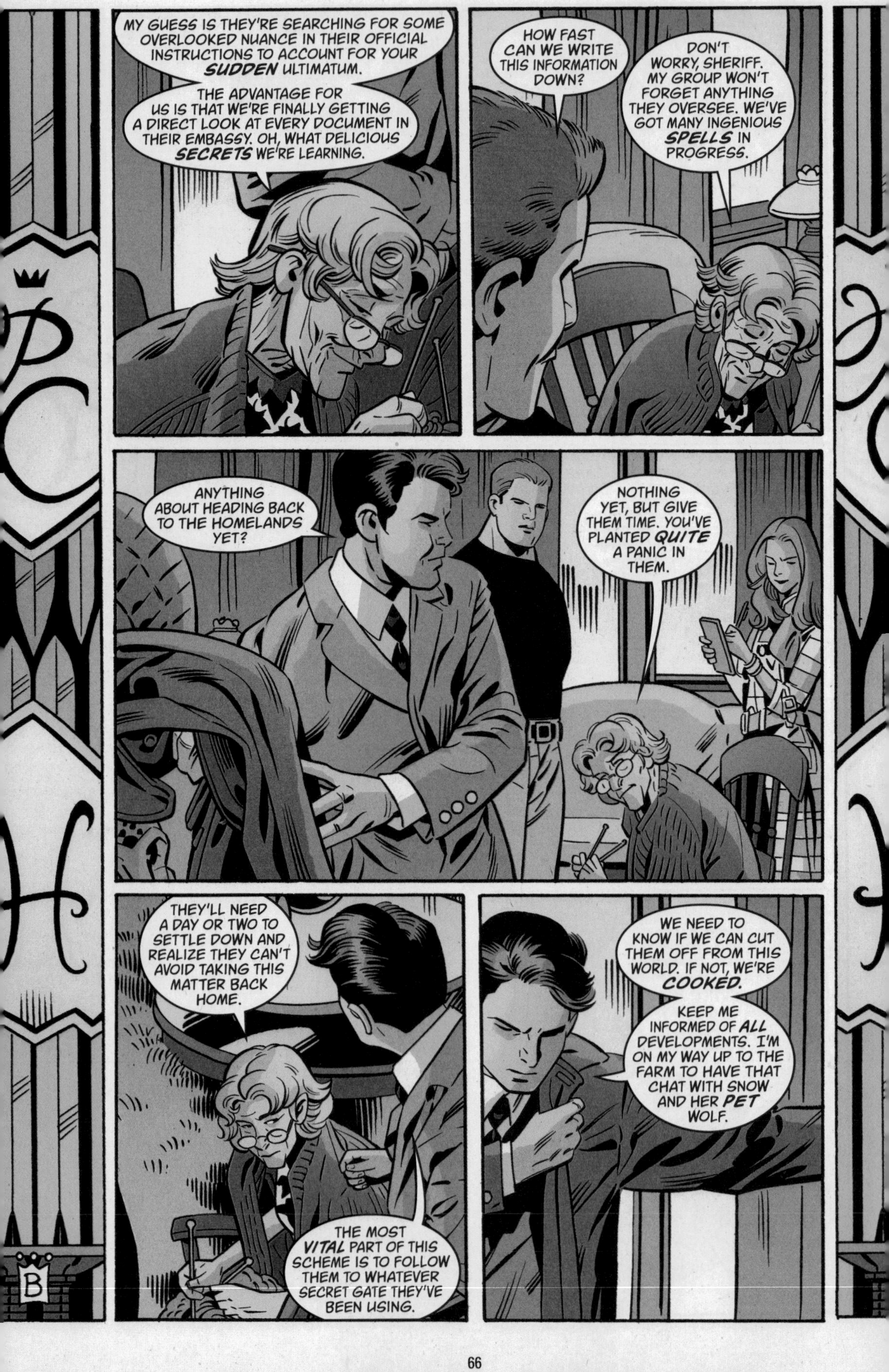
MY GUESS IS THEY'RE SEARCHING FOR SOME OVERLOOKED NUANCE IN THEIR OFFICIAL INSTRUCTIONS TO ACCOUNT FOR YOUR SUDDEN ULTIMATUM.
THE ADVANTAGE FOR US IS THAT WE'RE FINALLY GETTING A DIRECT LOOK AT EVERY DOCUMENT IN THEIR EMBASSY. OH, WHAT DELICIOUS SECRETS WE'RE LEARNING.
HOW FAST CAN WE WRITE THIS INFORMATION DOWN?
DON'T WORRY, SHERIFF. MY GROUP WON'T FORGET ANYTHING THEY OVERSEE. WE'VE GOT MANY INGENIOUS SPELLS IN PROGRESS.
ANYTHING ABOUT HEADING BACK TO THE HOMELANDS YET?
NOTHING YET, BUT GIVE THEM TIME. YOU'VE PLANTED QUITE A PANIC IN THEM.
THEY'LL NEED A DAY OR TWO TO SETTLE DOWN AND REALIZE THEY CAN'T AVOID TAKING THIS MATTER BACK HOME.
THE MOST VITAL PART OF THIS SCHEME IS TO FOLLOW THEM TO WHATEVER SECRET GATE THEY'VE BEEN USING.
WE NEED TO KNOW IF WE CAN CUT THEM OFF FROM THIS WORLD. IF NOT, WE'RE COOKED.
KEEP ME INFORMED OF ALL DEVELOPMENTS. I'M ON MY WAY UP TO THE FARM TO HAVE THAT CHAT WITH SNOW AND HER PET WOLF.

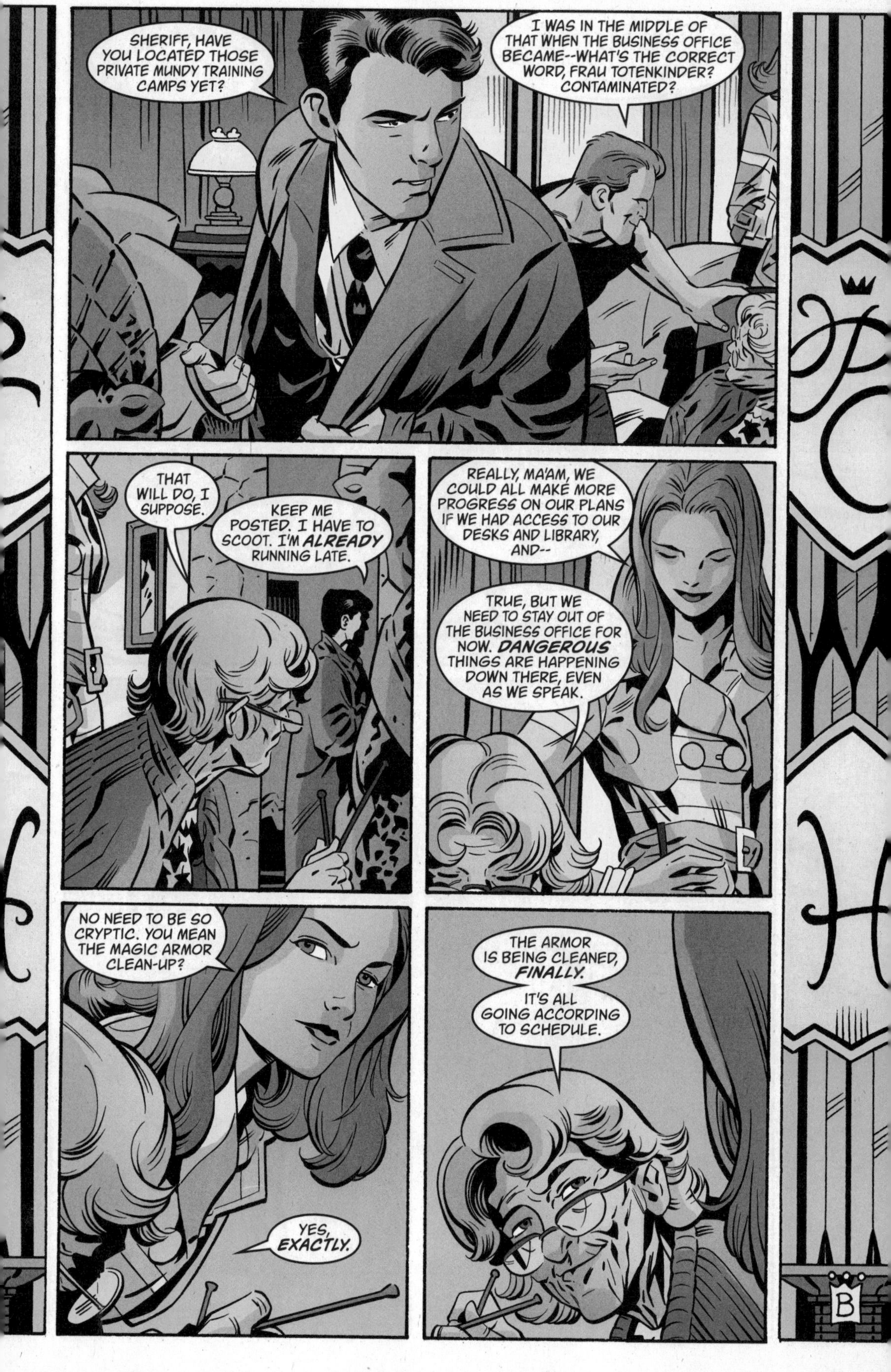

SHERIFF, HAVE YOU LOCATED THOSE PRIVATE MUNDY TRAINING CAMPS YET?
I WAS IN THE MIDDLE OF THAT WHEN THE BUSINESS OFFICE BECAME--WHAT'S THE CORRECT WORD, FRAU TOTENKINDER? CONTAMINATED?
THAT WILL DO, I SUPPOSE.
KEEP ME POSTED. I HAVE TO SCOOT. I'M *ALREADY* RUNNING LATE.
REALLY, MA'AM, WE COULD ALL MAKE MORE PROGRESS ON OUR PLANS IF WE HAD ACCESS TO OUR DESKS AND LIBRARY, AND--
TRUE, BUT WE NEED TO STAY OUT OF THE BUSINESS OFFICE FOR NOW. *DANGEROUS* THINGS ARE HAPPENING DOWN THERE, EVEN AS WE SPEAK.
NO NEED TO BE SO CRYPTIC. YOU MEAN THE MAGIC ARMOR CLEAN-UP?
YES, *EXACTLY.*
THE ARMOR IS BEING CLEANED, *FINALLY.*
IT'S ALL GOING ACCORDING TO SCHEDULE.

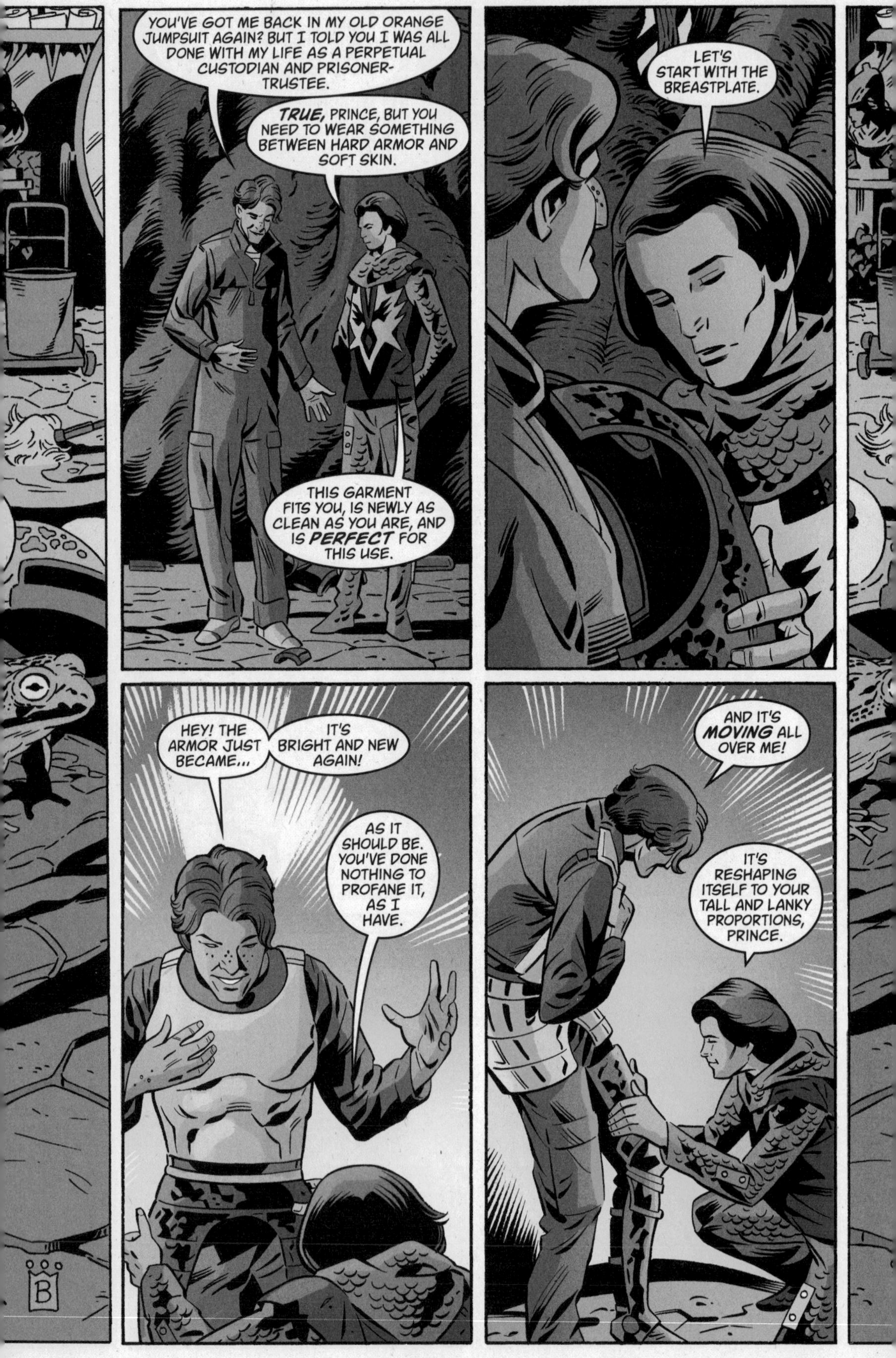
YOU'VE GOT ME BACK IN MY OLD ORANGE JUMPSUIT AGAIN? BUT I TOLD YOU I WAS ALL DONE WITH MY LIFE AS A PERPETUAL CUSTODIAN AND PRISONER-TRUSTEE.
TRUE, PRINCE, BUT YOU NEED TO WEAR SOMETHING BETWEEN HARD ARMOR AND SOFT SKIN.
THIS GARMENT FITS YOU, IS NEWLY AS CLEAN AS YOU ARE, AND IS PERFECT FOR THIS USE.
LET'S START WITH THE BREASTPLATE.
HEY! THE ARMOR JUST BECAME...
IT'S BRIGHT AND NEW AGAIN!
AS IT SHOULD BE. YOU'VE DONE NOTHING TO PROFANE IT, AS I HAVE.
AND IT'S MOVING ALL OVER ME!
IT'S RESHAPING ITSELF TO YOUR TALL AND LANKY PROPORTIONS, PRINCE.

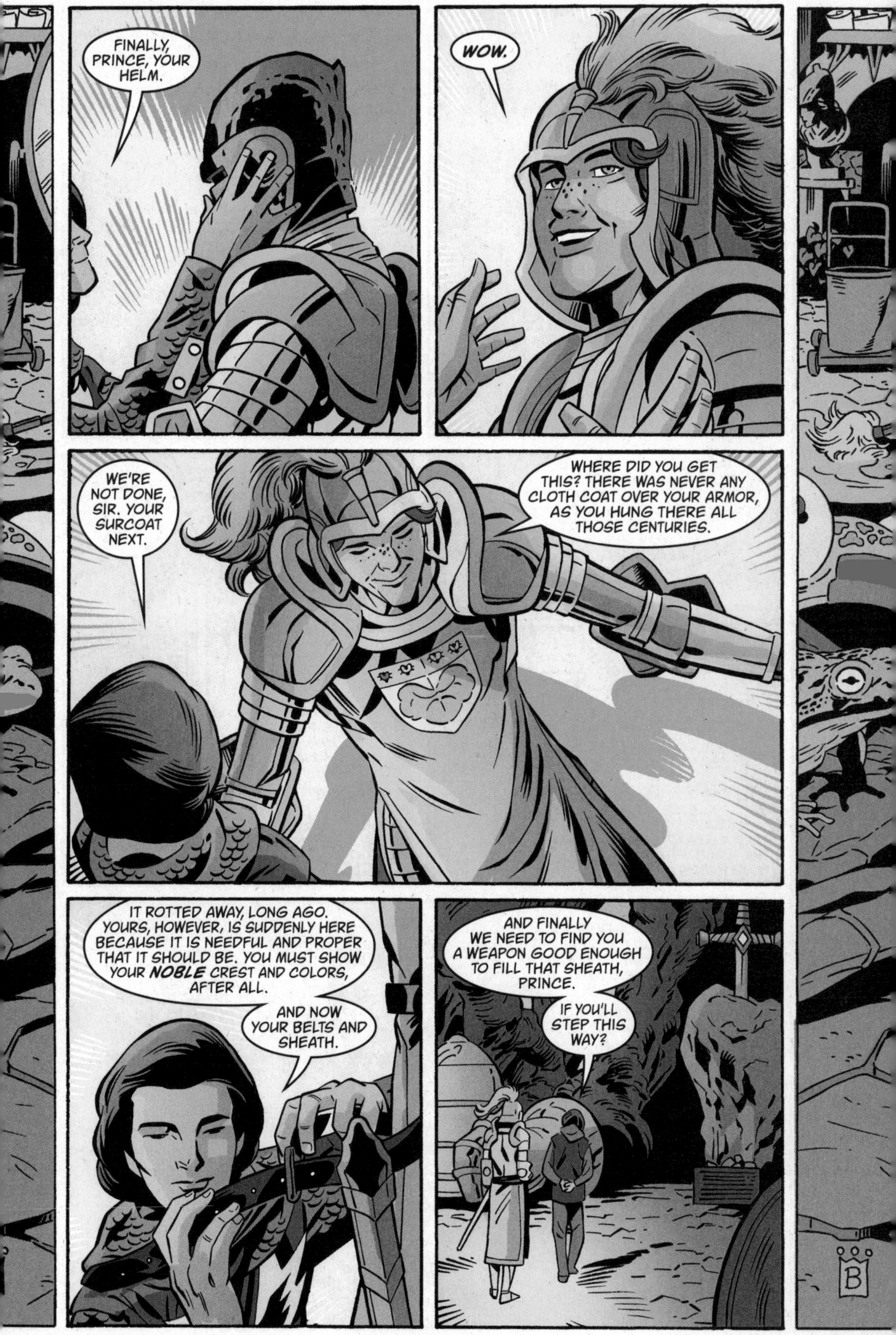
FINALLY, PRINCE, YOUR HELM.
WOW.
WE'RE NOT DONE, SIR. YOUR SURCOAT NEXT.
WHERE DID YOU GET THIS? THERE WAS NEVER ANY CLOTH COAT OVER YOUR ARMOR, AS YOU HUNG THERE ALL THOSE CENTURIES.
IT ROTTED AWAY, LONG AGO. YOURS, HOWEVER, IS SUDDENLY HERE BECAUSE IT IS NEEDFUL AND PROPER THAT IT SHOULD BE. YOU MUST SHOW YOUR NOBLE CREST AND COLORS, AFTER ALL.
AND NOW YOUR BELTS AND SHEATH.
AND FINALLY WE NEED TO FIND YOU A WEAPON GOOD ENOUGH TO FILL THAT SHEATH, PRINCE.
IF YOU'LL STEP THIS WAY?

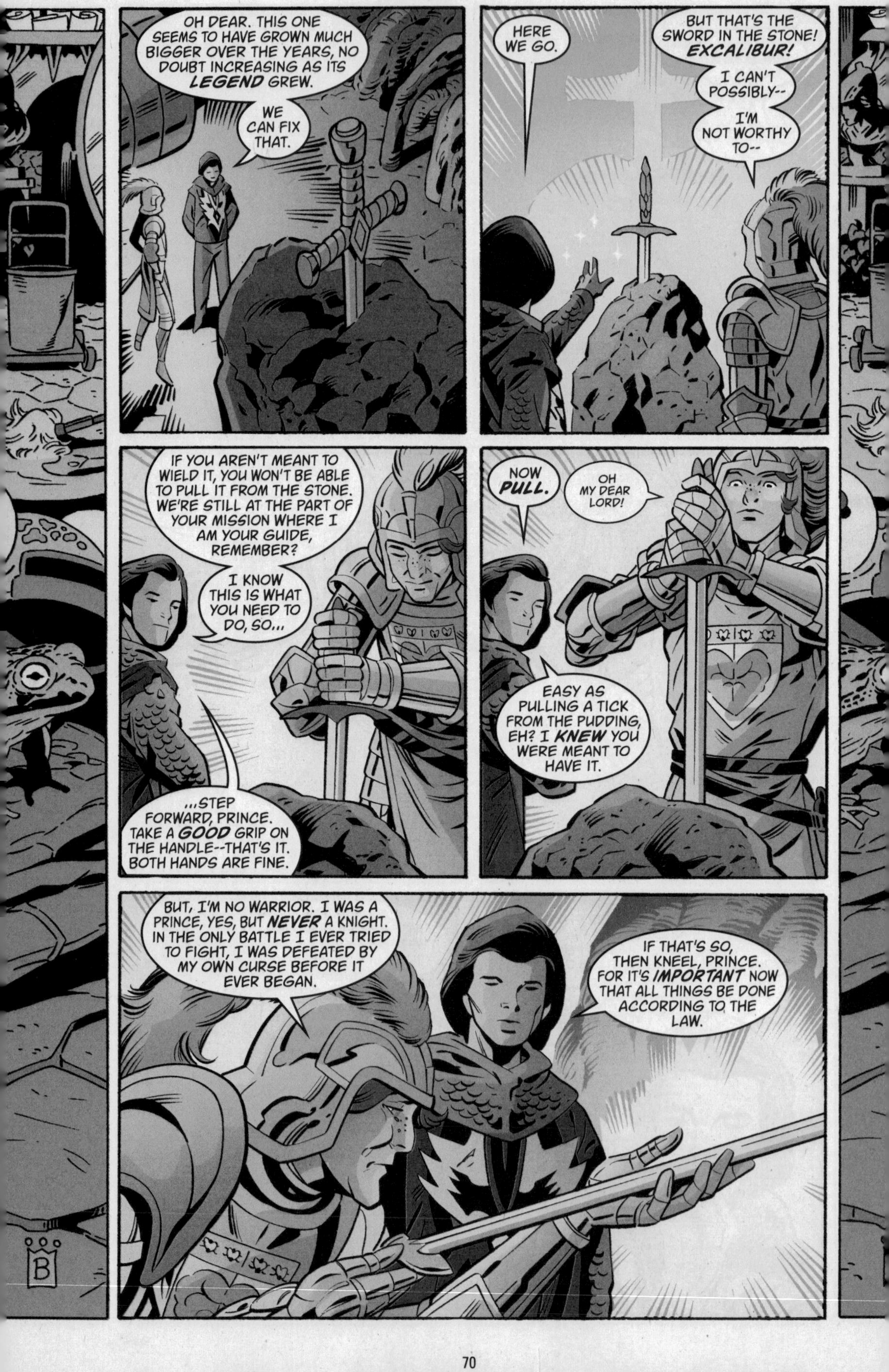
OH DEAR. THIS ONE SEEMS TO HAVE GROWN MUCH BIGGER OVER THE YEARS, NO DOUBT INCREASING AS ITS LEGEND GREW.
WE CAN FIX THAT.
HERE WE GO.
BUT THAT'S THE SWORD IN THE STONE! EXCALIBUR!
I CAN'T POSSIBLY--
I'M NOT WORTHY TO--
IF YOU AREN'T MEANT TO WIELD IT, YOU WON'T BE ABLE TO PULL IT FROM THE STONE. WE'RE STILL AT THE PART OF YOUR MISSION WHERE I AM YOUR GUIDE, REMEMBER?
I KNOW THIS IS WHAT YOU NEED TO DO, SO...
...STEP FORWARD, PRINCE. TAKE A GOOD GRIP ON THE HANDLE--THAT'S IT. BOTH HANDS ARE FINE.
NOW PULL.
OH MY DEAR LORD!
EASY AS PULLING A TICK FROM THE PUDDING, EH? I KNEW YOU WERE MEANT TO HAVE IT.
BUT, I'M NO WARRIOR. I WAS A PRINCE, YES, BUT NEVER A KNIGHT. IN THE ONLY BATTLE I EVER TRIED TO FIGHT, I WAS DEFEATED BY MY OWN CURSE BEFORE IT EVER BEGAN.
IF THAT'S SO, THEN KNEEL, PRINCE. FOR IT'S IMPORTANT NOW THAT ALL THINGS BE DONE ACCORDING TO THE LAW.

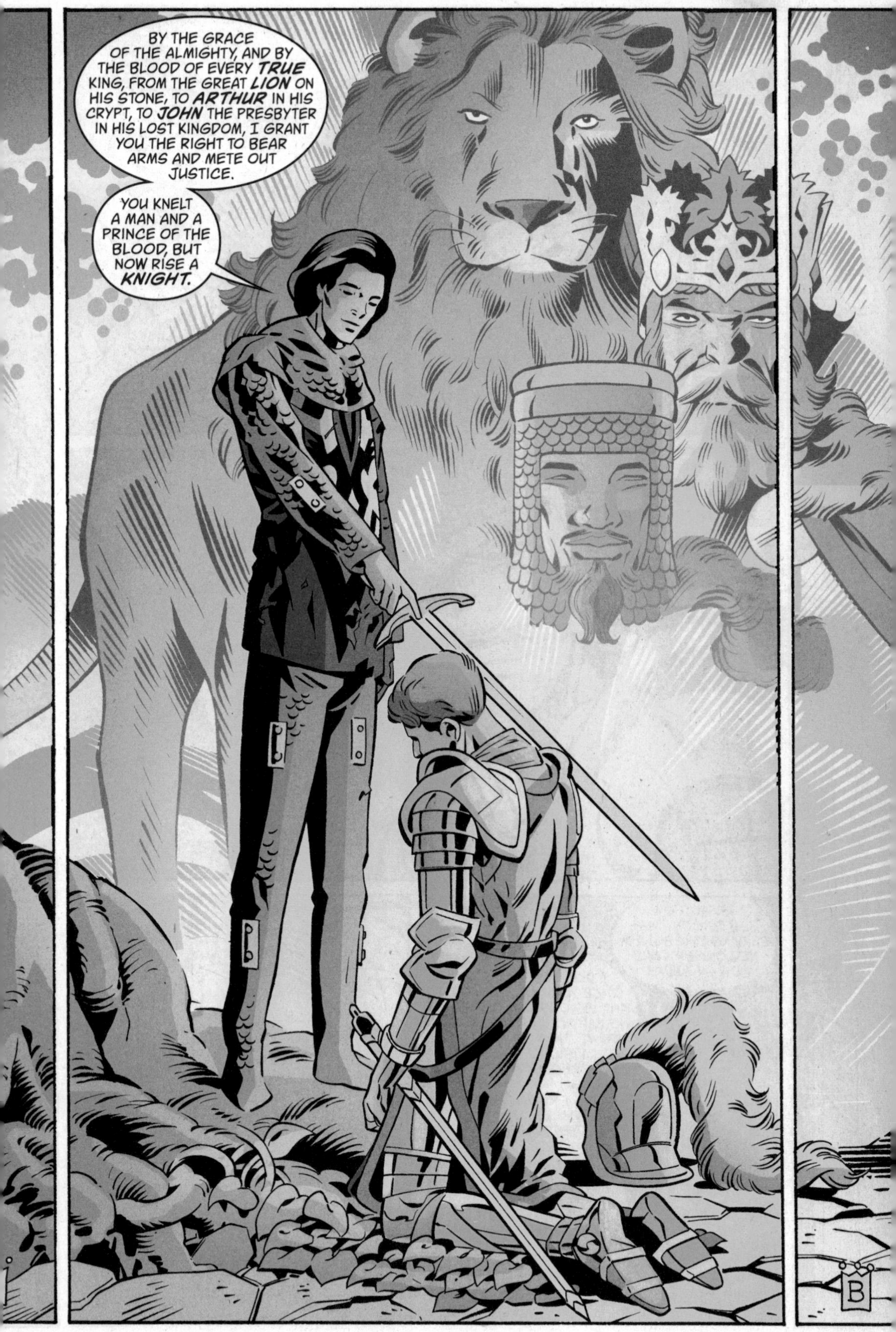
BY THE GRACE OF THE ALMIGHTY, AND BY THE BLOOD OF EVERY TRUE KING, FROM THE GREAT LION ON HIS STONE, TO ARTHUR IN HIS CRYPT, TO JOHN THE PRESBYTER IN HIS LOST KINGDOM, I GRANT YOU THE RIGHT TO BEAR ARMS AND METE OUT JUSTICE.
YOU KNELT A MAN AND A PRINCE OF THE BLOOD, BUT NOW RISE A KNIGHT.

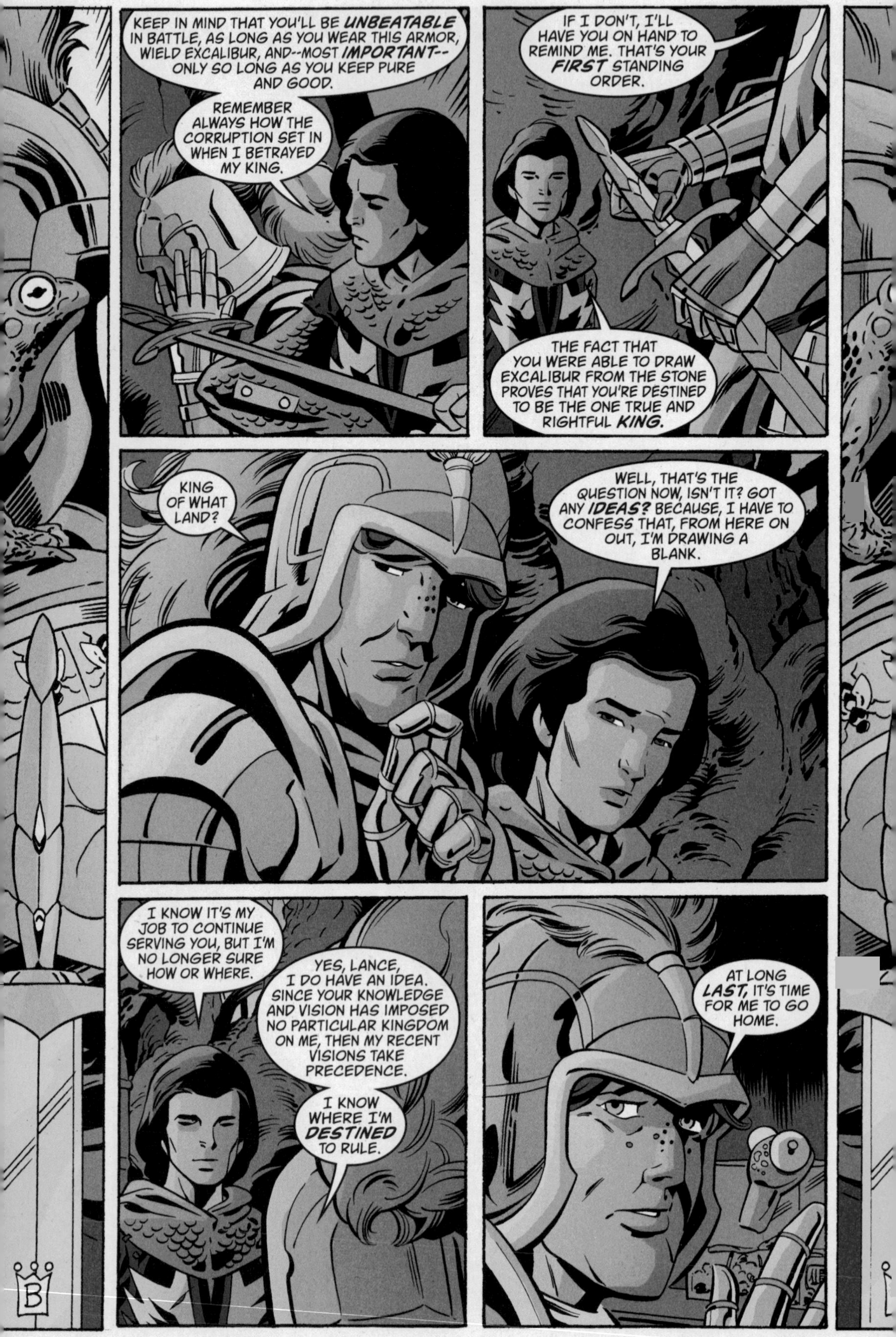
KEEP IN MIND THAT YOU'LL BE UNBEATABLE IN BATTLE, AS LONG AS YOU WEAR THIS ARMOR, WIELD EXCALIBUR, AND--MOST IMPORTANT--ONLY SO LONG AS YOU KEEP PURE AND GOOD.
REMEMBER ALWAYS HOW THE CORRUPTION SET IN WHEN I BETRAYED MY KING.
IF I DON'T, I'LL HAVE YOU ON HAND TO REMIND ME. THAT'S YOUR FIRST STANDING ORDER.
THE FACT THAT YOU WERE ABLE TO DRAW EXCALIBUR FROM THE STONE PROVES THAT YOU'RE DESTINED TO BE THE ONE TRUE AND RIGHTFUL KING.
KING OF WHAT LAND?
WELL, THAT'S THE QUESTION NOW, ISN'T IT? GOT ANY IDEAS? BECAUSE, I HAVE TO CONFESS THAT, FROM HERE ON OUT, I'M DRAWING A BLANK.
I KNOW IT'S MY JOB TO CONTINUE SERVING YOU, BUT I'M NO LONGER SURE HOW OR WHERE.
YES, LANCE, I DO HAVE AN IDEA. SINCE YOUR KNOWLEDGE AND VISION HAS IMPOSED NO PARTICULAR KINGDOM ON ME, THEN MY RECENT VISIONS TAKE PRECEDENCE.
I KNOW WHERE I'M DESTINED TO RULE.
AT LONG LAST, IT'S TIME FOR ME TO GO HOME.

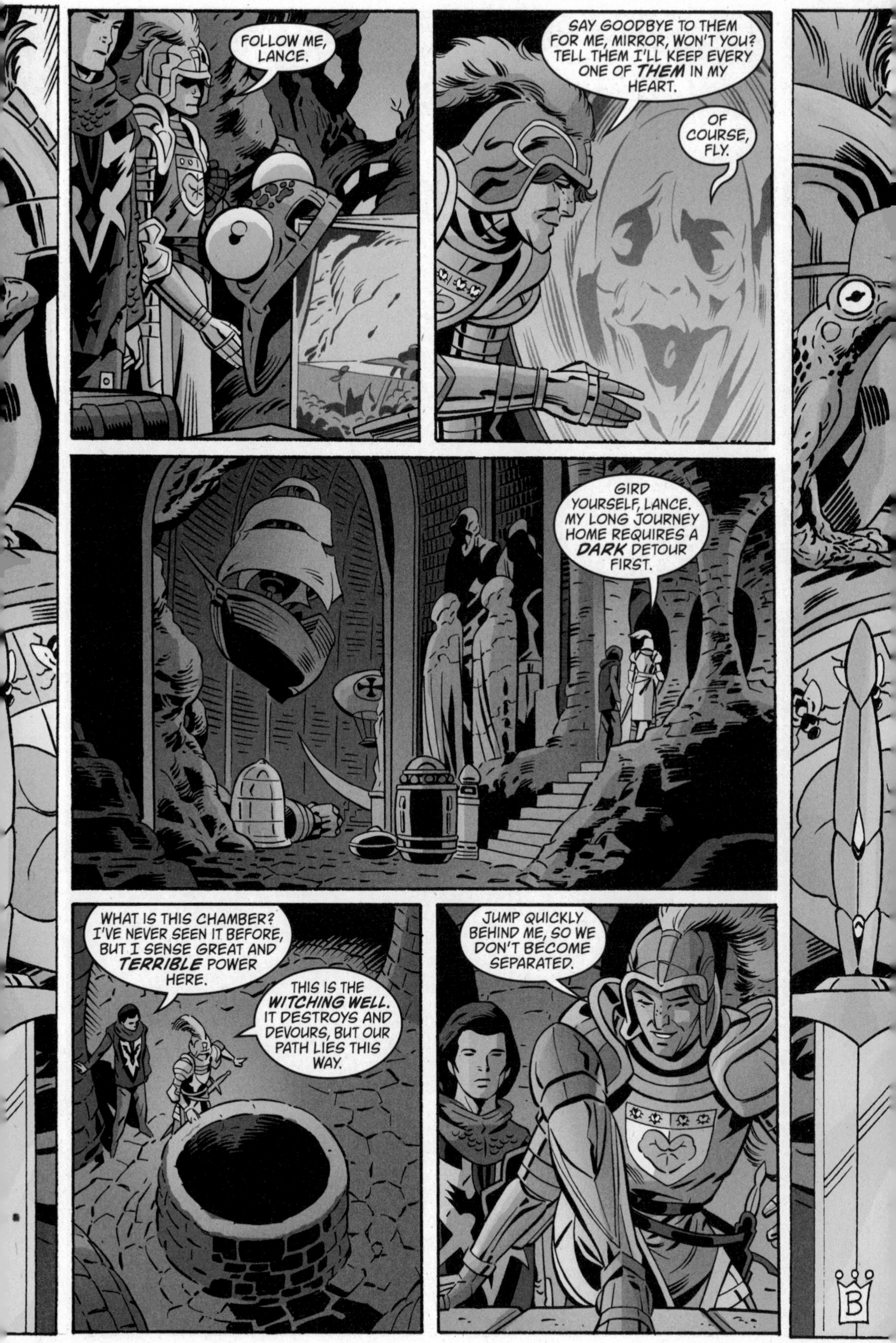
FOLLOW ME, LANCE.
SAY GOODBYE TO THEM FOR ME, MIRROR, WON'T YOU? TELL THEM I'LL KEEP EVERY ONE OF THEM IN MY HEART.
OF COURSE, FLY.
GIRD YOURSELF, LANCE. MY LONG JOURNEY HOME REQUIRES A DARK DETOUR FIRST.
WHAT IS THIS CHAMBER? I'VE NEVER SEEN IT BEFORE, BUT I SENSE GREAT AND TERRIBLE POWER HERE.
THIS IS THE WITCHING WELL. IT DESTROYS AND DEVOURS, BUT OUR PATH LIES THIS WAY.
JUMP QUICKLY BEHIND ME, SO WE DON'T BECOME SEPARATED.

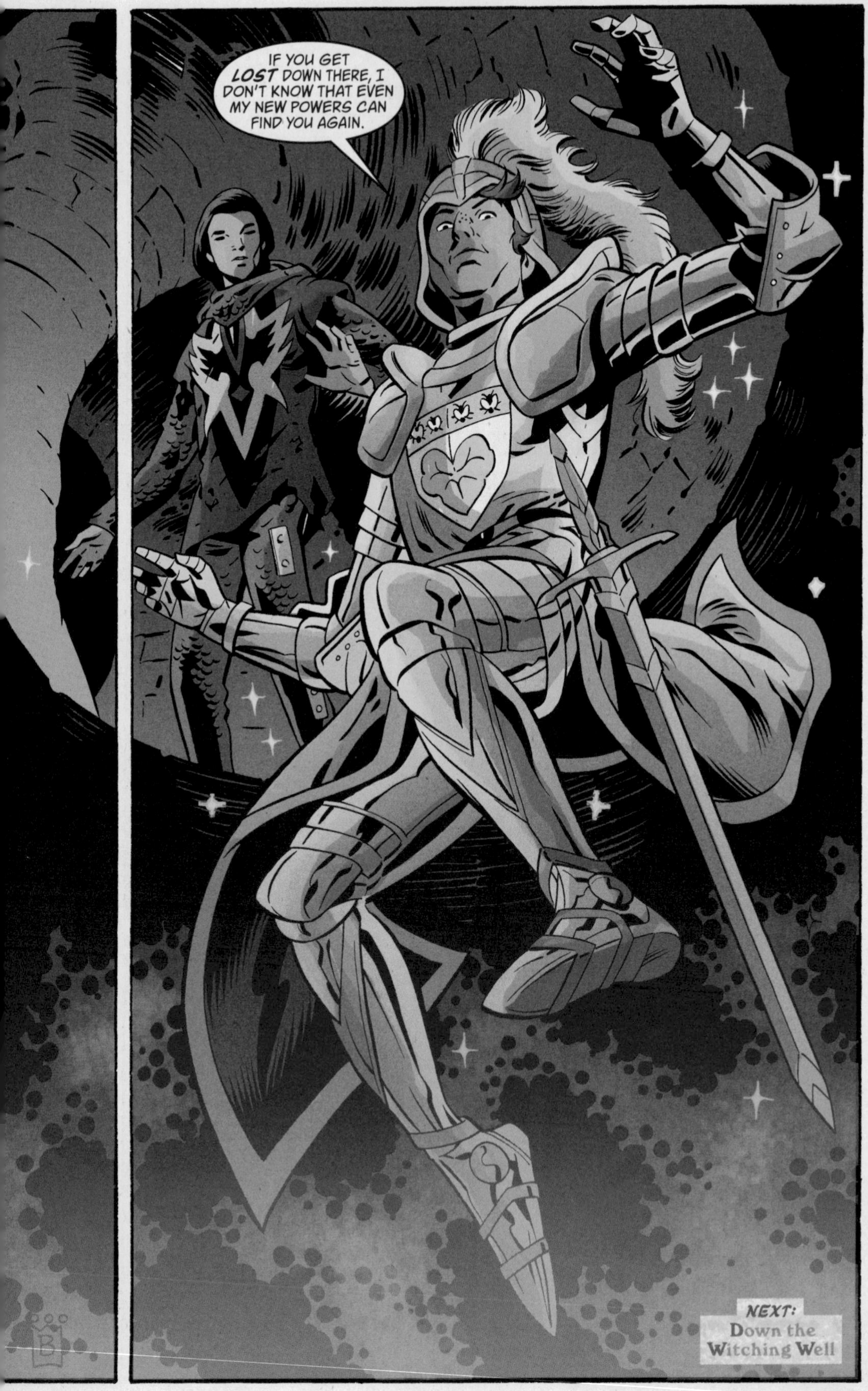
IF YOU GET LOST DOWN THERE, I DON'T KNOW THAT EVEN MY NEW POWERS CAN FIND YOU AGAIN.
NEXT:
Down the Witching Well

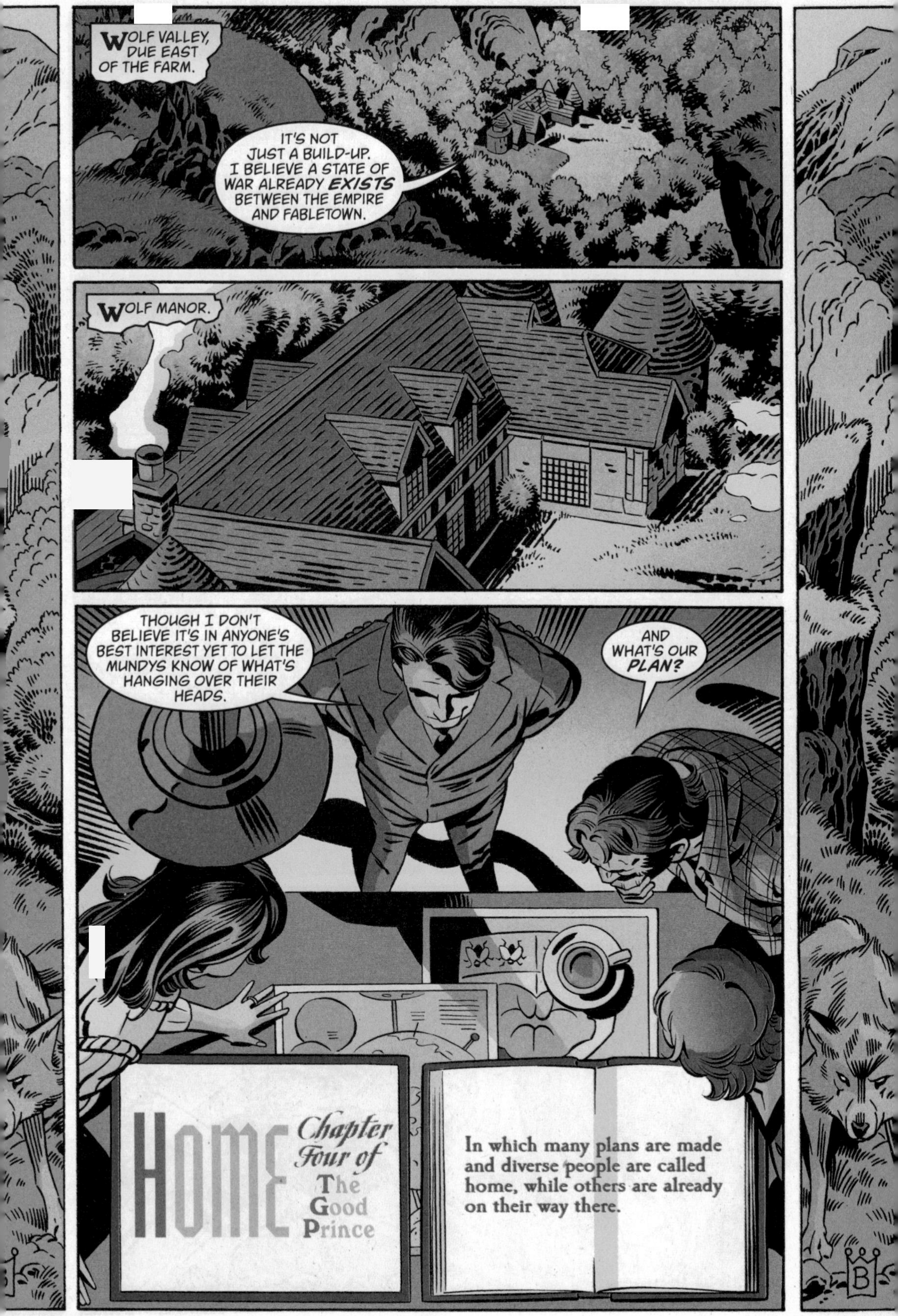
WOLF VALLEY, DUE EAST OF THE FARM.
IT'S NOT JUST A BUILD-UP. I BELIEVE A STATE OF WAR ALREADY EXISTS BETWEEN THE EMPIRE AND FABLETOWN.
WOLF MANOR.
THOUGH I DON'T BELIEVE IT'S IN ANYONE'S BEST INTEREST YET TO LET THE MUNDYS KNOW OF WHAT'S HANGING OVER THEIR HEADS.
AND WHAT'S OUR PLAN?
HOME
Chapter Four of The Good Prince
In which many plans are made and diverse people are called home, while others are already on their way there.

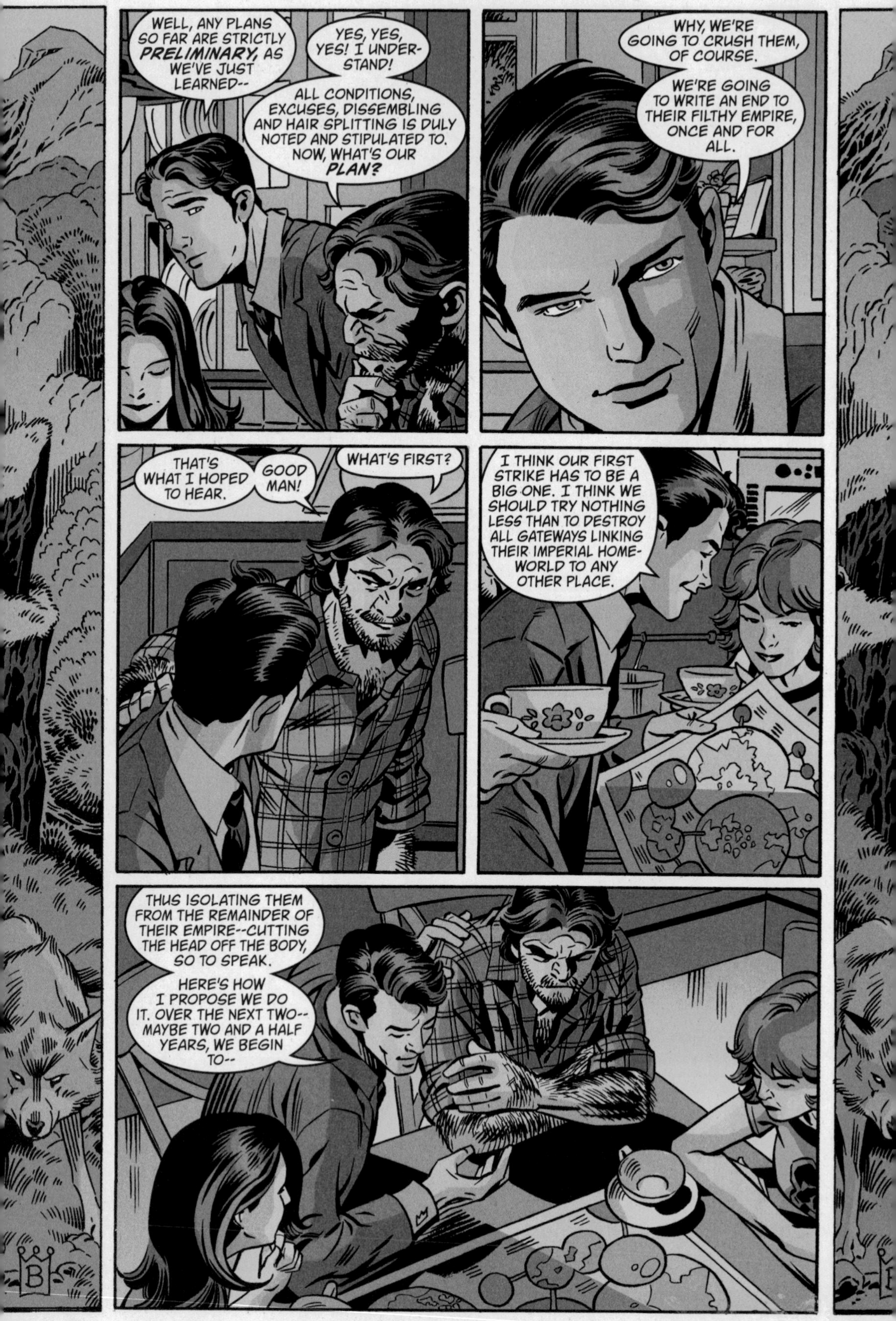
WELL, ANY PLANS SO FAR ARE STRICTLY PRELIMINARY, AS WE'VE JUST LEARNED--
YES, YES, YES! I UNDERSTAND!
ALL CONDITIONS, EXCUSES, DISSEMBLING AND HAIR SPLITTING IS DULY NOTED AND STIPULATED TO. NOW, WHAT'S OUR PLAN?
WHY, WE'RE GOING TO CRUSH THEM, OF COURSE.
WE'RE GOING TO WRITE AN END TO THEIR FILTHY EMPIRE, ONCE AND FOR ALL.
THAT'S WHAT I HOPED TO HEAR.
GOOD MAN!
WHAT'S FIRST?
I THINK OUR FIRST STRIKE HAS TO BE A BIG ONE. I THINK WE SHOULD TRY NOTHING LESS THAN TO DESTROY ALL GATEWAYS LINKING THEIR IMPERIAL HOMEWORLD TO ANY OTHER PLACE.
THUS ISOLATING THEM FROM THE REMAINDER OF THEIR EMPIRE--CUTTING THE HEAD OFF THE BODY, SO TO SPEAK.
HERE'S HOW I PROPOSE WE DO IT. OVER THE NEXT TWO--MAYBE TWO AND A HALF YEARS, WE BEGIN TO--

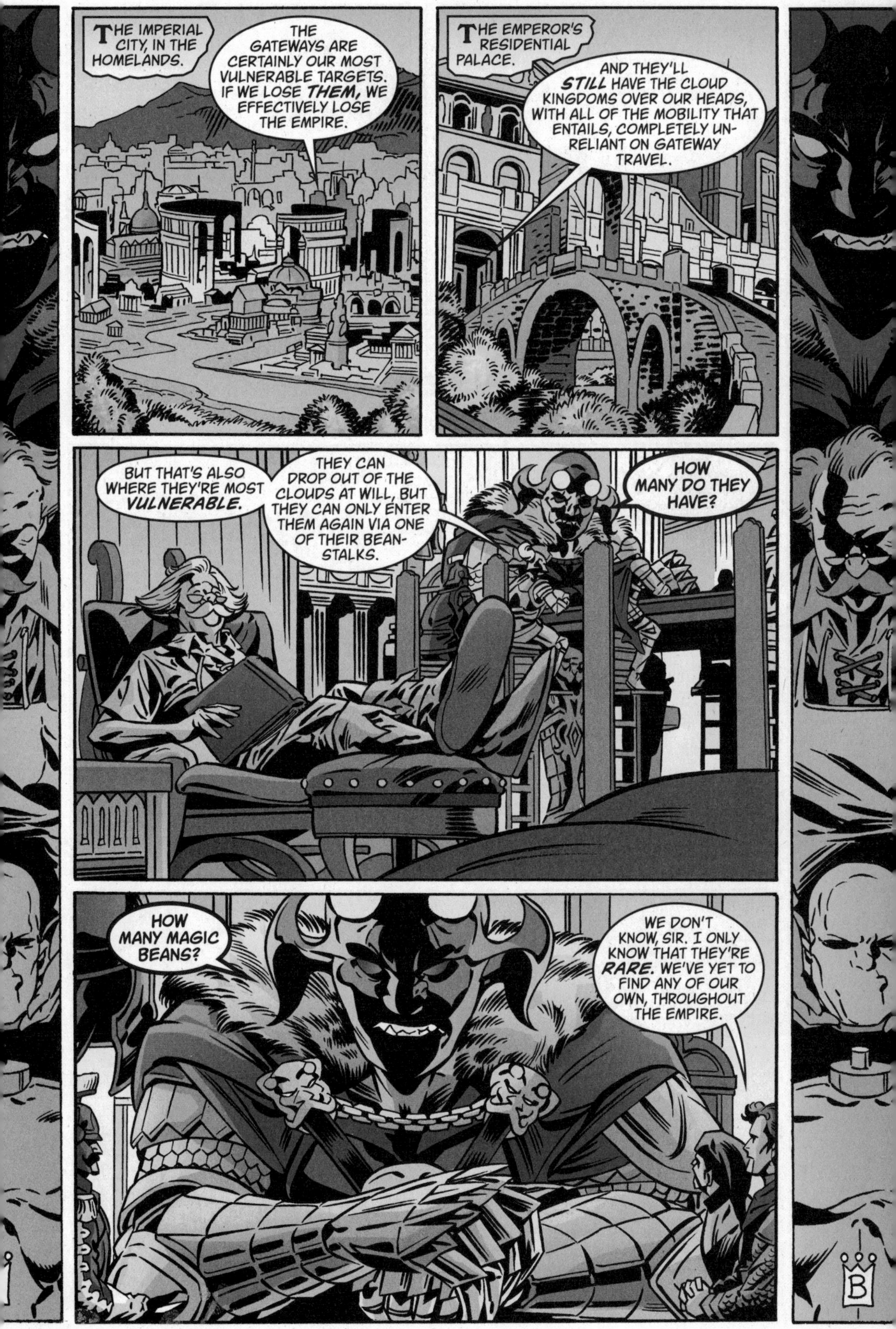
THE IMPERIAL CITY, IN THE HOMELANDS.
THE GATEWAYS ARE CERTAINLY OUR MOST VULNERABLE TARGETS. IF WE LOSE THEM, WE EFFECTIVELY LOSE THE EMPIRE.
THE EMPEROR'S RESIDENTIAL PALACE.
AND THEY'LL STILL HAVE THE CLOUD KINGDOMS OVER OUR HEADS, WITH ALL OF THE MOBILITY THAT ENTAILS, COMPLETELY UN-RELIANT ON GATEWAY TRAVEL.
BUT THAT'S ALSO WHERE THEY'RE MOST VULNERABLE.
THEY CAN DROP OUT OF THE CLOUDS AT WILL, BUT THEY CAN ONLY ENTER THEM AGAIN VIA ONE OF THEIR BEAN-STALKS.
HOW MANY DO THEY HAVE?
HOW MANY MAGIC BEANS?
WE DON'T KNOW, SIR. I ONLY KNOW THAT THEY'RE RARE. WE'VE YET TO FIND ANY OF OUR OWN, THROUGHOUT THE EMPIRE.

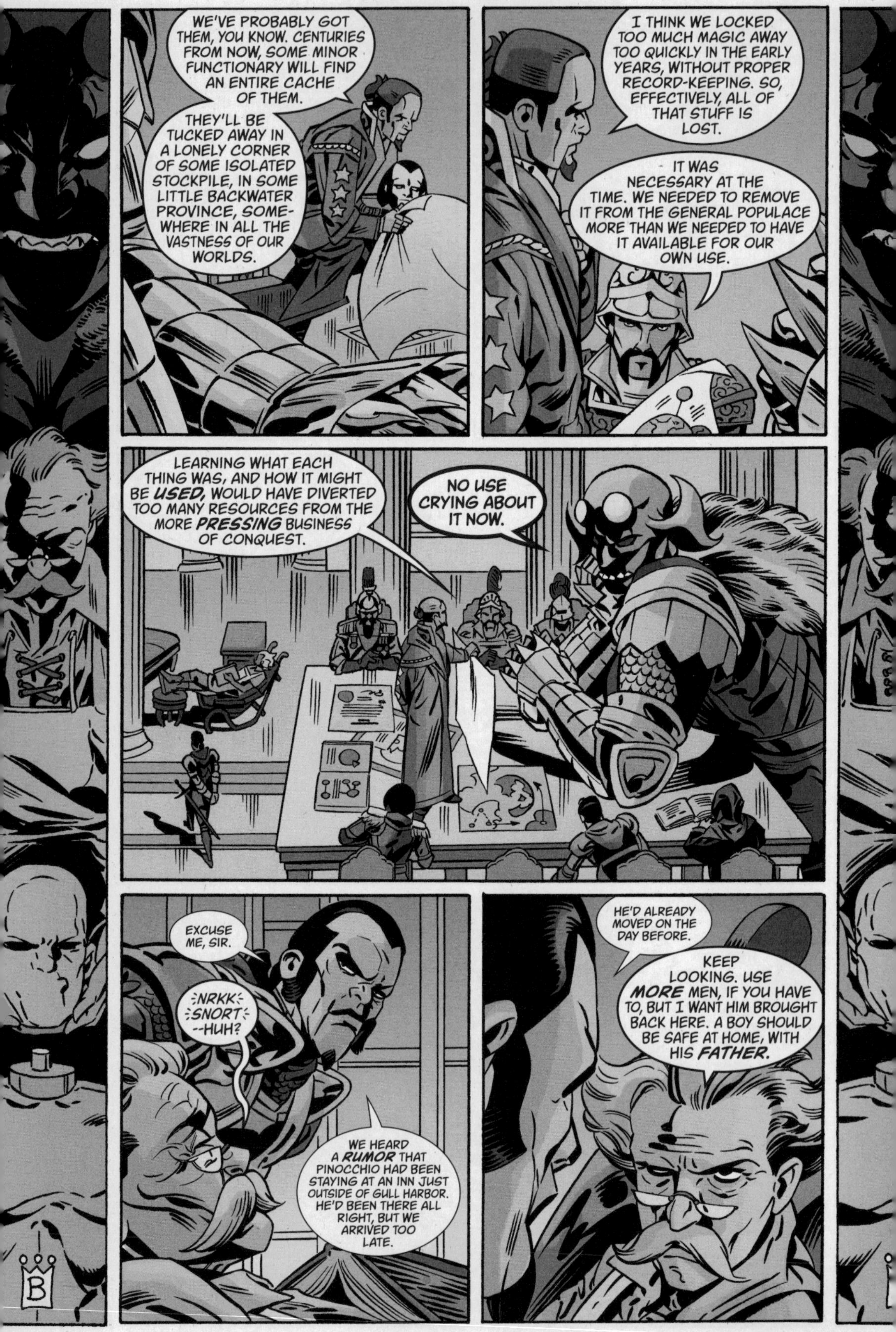
WE'VE PROBABLY GOT THEM, YOU KNOW. CENTURIES FROM NOW, SOME MINOR FUNCTIONARY WILL FIND AN ENTIRE CACHE OF THEM.
THEY'LL BE TUCKED AWAY IN A LONELY CORNER OF SOME ISOLATED STOCKPILE, IN SOME LITTLE BACKWATER PROVINCE, SOME-WHERE IN ALL THE VASTNESS OF OUR WORLDS.
I THINK WE LOCKED TOO MUCH MAGIC AWAY TOO QUICKLY IN THE EARLY YEARS, WITHOUT PROPER RECORD-KEEPING. SO, EFFECTIVELY, ALL OF THAT STUFF IS LOST.
IT WAS NECESSARY AT THE TIME. WE NEEDED TO REMOVE IT FROM THE GENERAL POPULACE MORE THAN WE NEEDED TO HAVE IT AVAILABLE FOR OUR OWN USE.
LEARNING WHAT EACH THING WAS, AND HOW IT MIGHT BE USED, WOULD HAVE DIVERTED TOO MANY RESOURCES FROM THE MORE PRESSING BUSINESS OF CONQUEST.
NO USE CRYING ABOUT IT NOW.
EXCUSE ME, SIR.
NRKK SNORT --HUH?
WE HEARD A RUMOR THAT PINOCCHIO HAD BEEN STAYING AT AN INN JUST OUTSIDE OF GULL HARBOR. HE'D BEEN THERE ALL RIGHT, BUT WE ARRIVED TOO LATE.
HE'D ALREADY MOVED ON THE DAY BEFORE.
KEEP LOOKING. USE MORE MEN, IF YOU HAVE TO, BUT I WANT HIM BROUGHT BACK HERE. A BOY SHOULD BE SAFE AT HOME, WITH HIS FATHER.

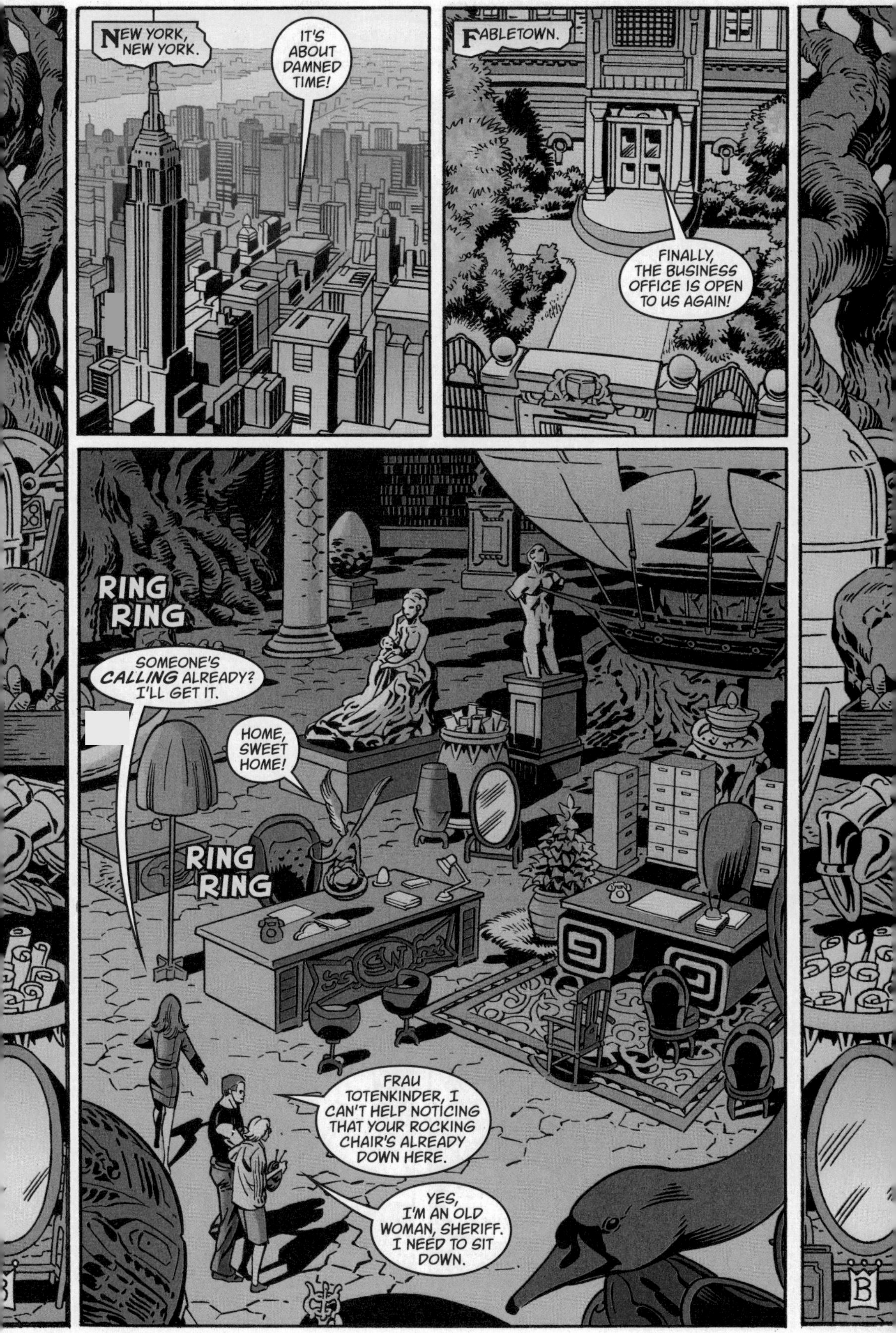
NEW YORK, NEW YORK.
IT'S ABOUT DAMNED TIME!
FABLETOWN.
FINALLY, THE BUSINESS OFFICE IS OPEN TO US AGAIN!
RING RING
SOMEONE'S CALLING ALREADY? I'LL GET IT.
HOME, SWEET HOME!
RING RING
FRAU TOTENKINDER, I CAN'T HELP NOTICING THAT YOUR ROCKING CHAIR'S ALREADY DOWN HERE.
YES, I'M AN OLD WOMAN, SHERIFF. I NEED TO SIT DOWN.

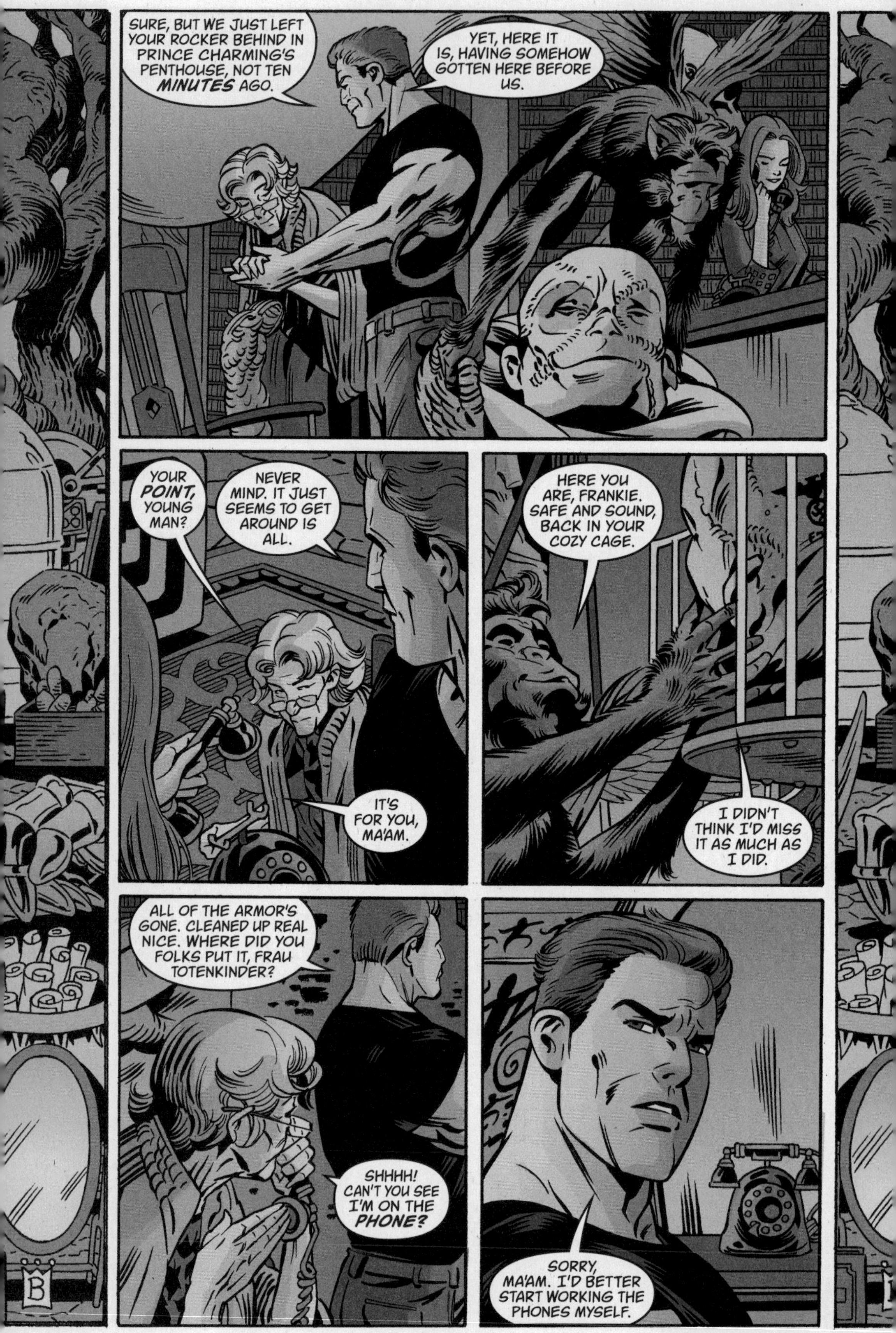
SURE, BUT WE JUST LEFT YOUR ROCKER BEHIND IN PRINCE CHARMING'S PENTHOUSE, NOT TEN MINUTES AGO.
YET, HERE IT IS, HAVING SOMEHOW GOTTEN HERE BEFORE US.
YOUR POINT, YOUNG MAN?
NEVER MIND. IT JUST SEEMS TO GET AROUND IS ALL.
IT'S FOR YOU, MA'AM.
HERE YOU ARE, FRANKIE. SAFE AND SOUND, BACK IN YOUR COZY CAGE.
I DIDN'T THINK I'D MISS IT AS MUCH AS I DID.
ALL OF THE ARMOR'S GONE. CLEANED UP REAL NICE. WHERE DID YOU FOLKS PUT IT, FRAU TOTENKINDER?
SHHHH! CAN'T YOU SEE I'M ON THE PHONE?
SORRY, MA'AM. I'D BETTER START WORKING THE PHONES MYSELF.

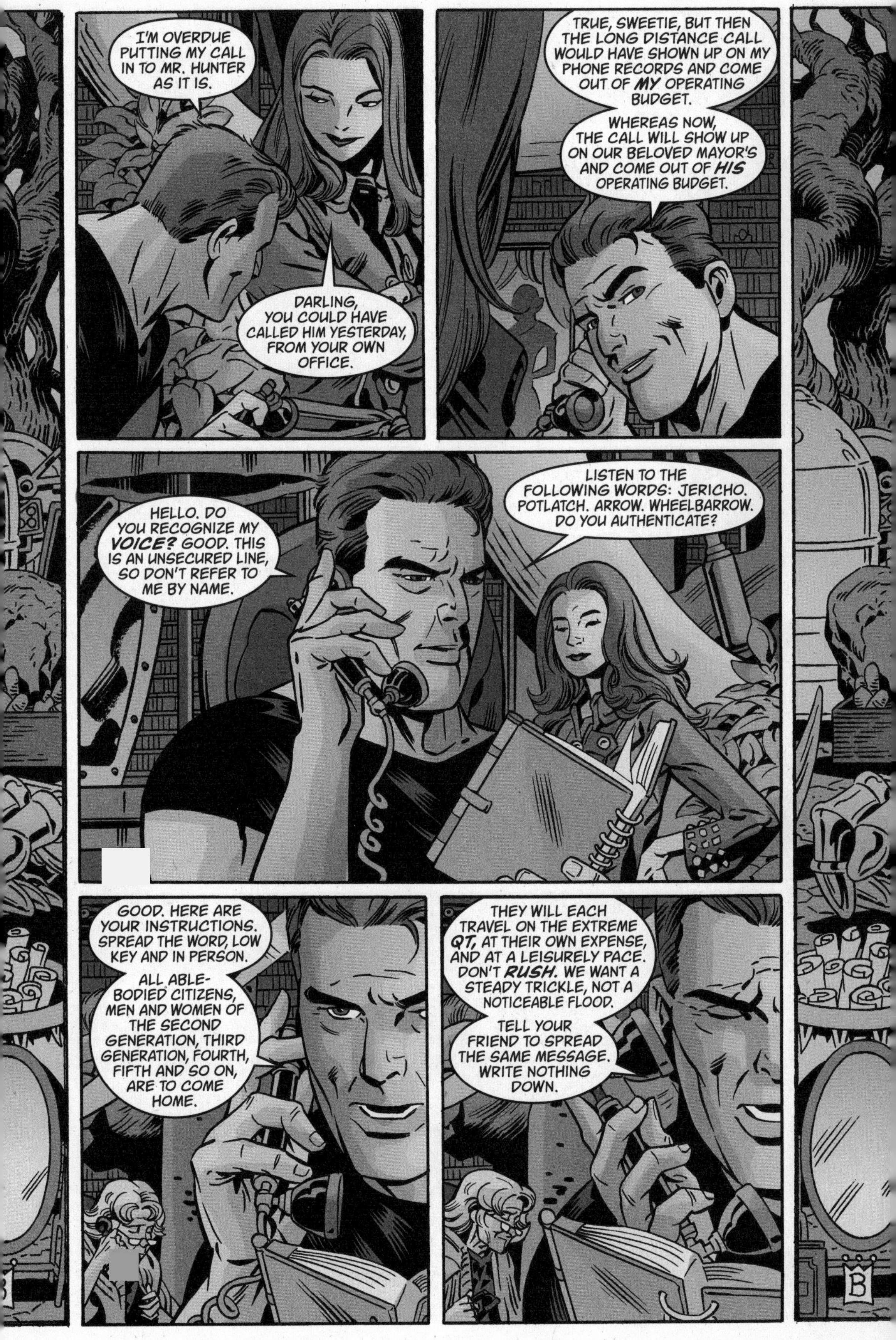
I'M OVERDUE PUTTING MY CALL IN TO MR. HUNTER AS IT IS.
DARLING, YOU COULD HAVE CALLED HIM YESTERDAY, FROM YOUR OWN OFFICE.
TRUE, SWEETIE, BUT THEN THE LONG DISTANCE CALL WOULD HAVE SHOWN UP ON MY PHONE RECORDS AND COME OUT OF MY OPERATING BUDGET.
WHEREAS NOW, THE CALL WILL SHOW UP ON OUR BELOVED MAYOR'S AND COME OUT OF HIS OPERATING BUDGET.
HELLO. DO YOU RECOGNIZE MY VOICE? GOOD. THIS IS AN UNSECURED LINE, SO DON'T REFER TO ME BY NAME.
LISTEN TO THE FOLLOWING WORDS: JERICHO. POTLATCH. ARROW. WHEELBARROW. DO YOU AUTHENTICATE?
GOOD. HERE ARE YOUR INSTRUCTIONS. SPREAD THE WORD, LOW KEY AND IN PERSON.
ALL ABLE-BODIED CITIZENS, MEN AND WOMEN OF THE SECOND GENERATION, THIRD GENERATION, FOURTH, FIFTH AND SO ON, ARE TO COME HOME.
THEY WILL EACH TRAVEL ON THE EXTREME QT, AT THEIR OWN EXPENSE, AND AT A LEISURELY PACE. DON'T RUSH. WE WANT A STEADY TRICKLE, NOT A NOTICEABLE FLOOD.
TELL YOUR FRIEND TO SPREAD THE SAME MESSAGE. WRITE NOTHING DOWN.

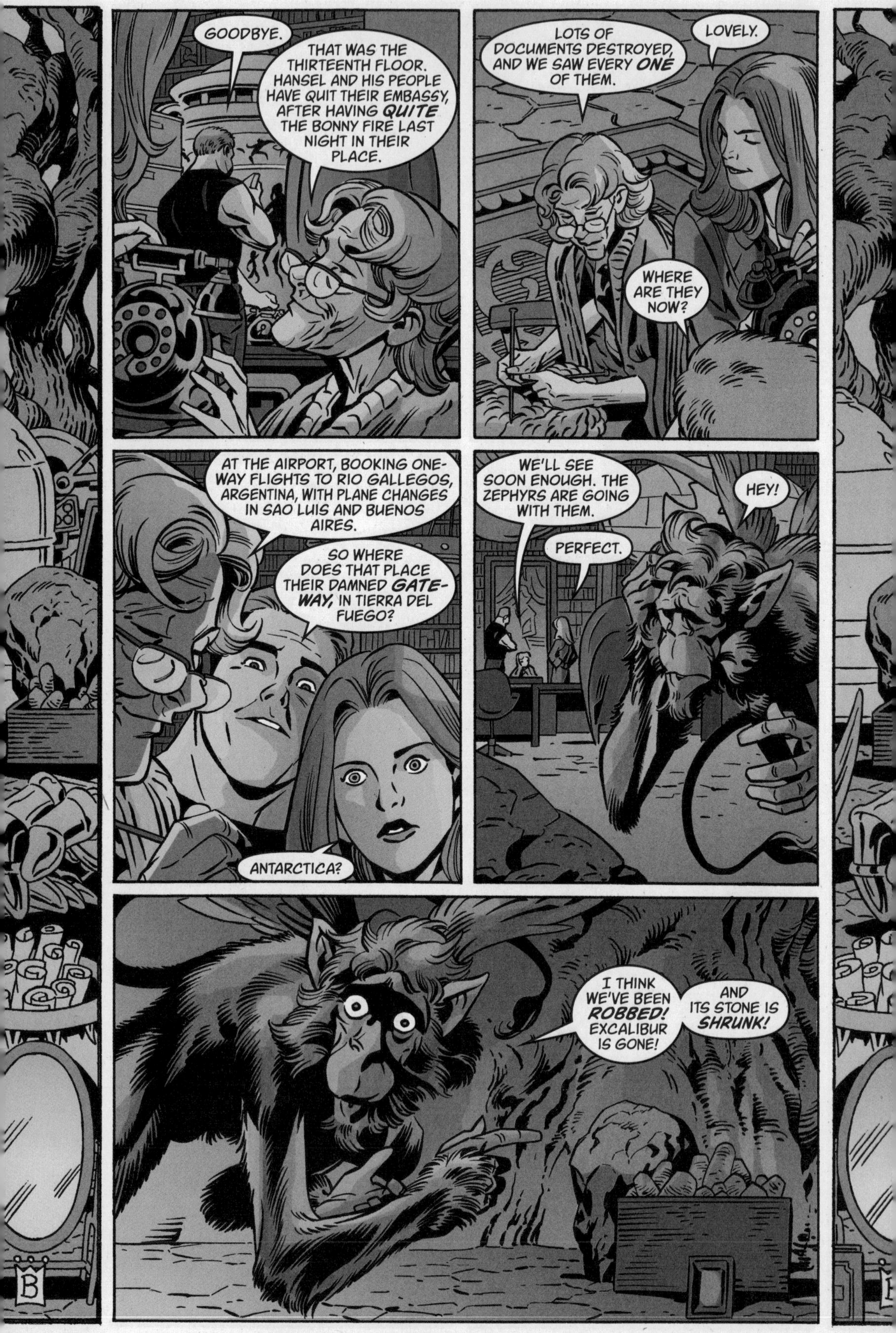
GOODBYE.
THAT WAS THE THIRTEENTH FLOOR. HANSEL AND HIS PEOPLE HAVE QUIT THEIR EMBASSY, AFTER HAVING QUITE THE BONNY FIRE LAST NIGHT IN THEIR PLACE.
LOTS OF DOCUMENTS DESTROYED, AND WE SAW EVERY ONE OF THEM.
LOVELY.
WHERE ARE THEY NOW?
AT THE AIRPORT, BOOKING ONE-WAY FLIGHTS TO RIO GALLEGOS, ARGENTINA, WITH PLANE CHANGES IN SAO LUIS AND BUENOS AIRES.
SO WHERE DOES THAT PLACE THEIR DAMNED GATEWAY, IN TIERRA DEL FUEGO?
ANTARCTICA?
WE'LL SEE SOON ENOUGH. THE ZEPHYRS ARE GOING WITH THEM.
PERFECT.
HEY!
I THINK WE'VE BEEN ROBBED! EXCALIBUR IS GONE!
AND ITS STONE IS SHRUNK!

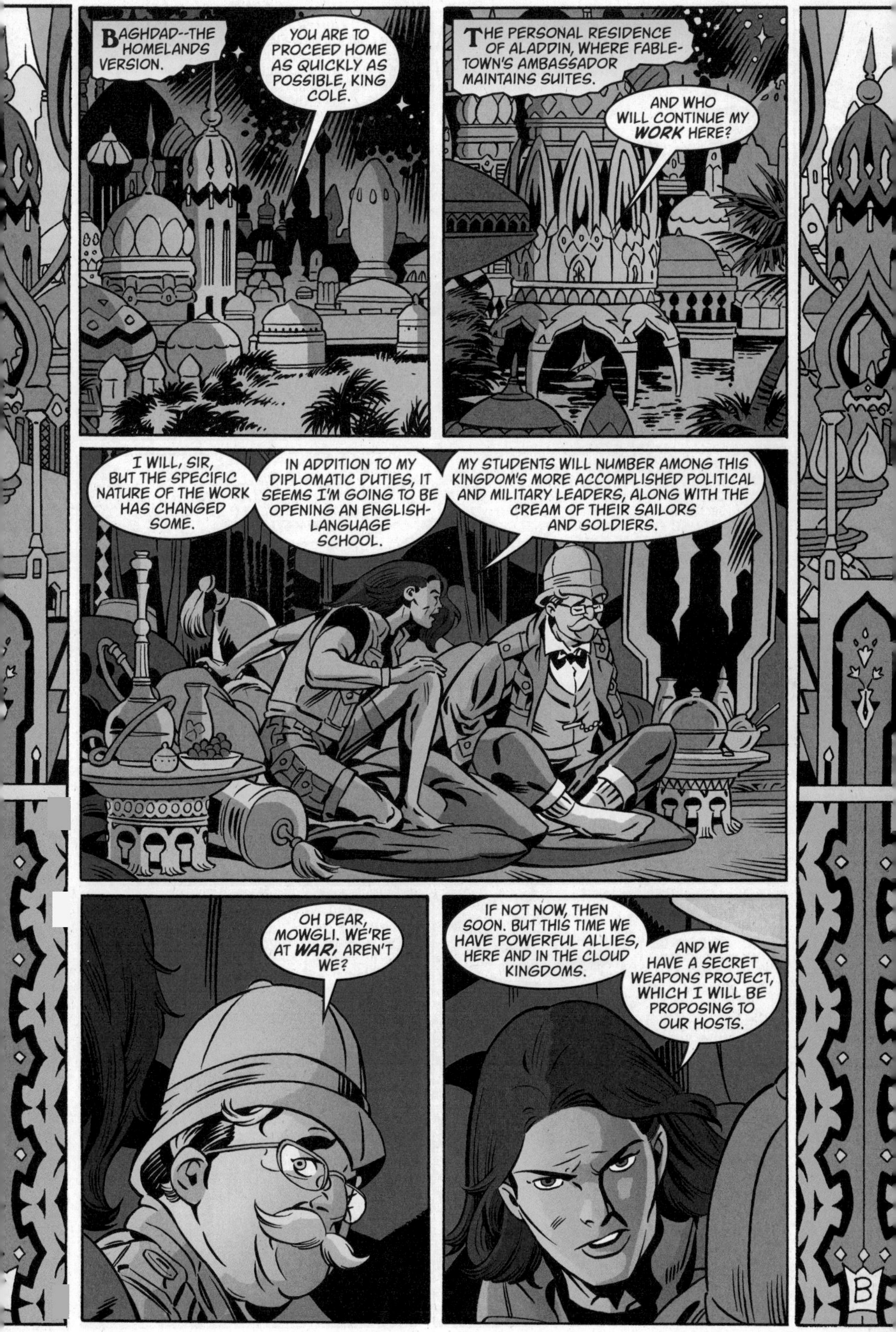
BAGHDAD--THE HOMELANDS VERSION.
YOU ARE TO PROCEED HOME AS QUICKLY AS POSSIBLE, KING COLE.
THE PERSONAL RESIDENCE OF ALADDIN, WHERE FABLE-TOWN'S AMBASSADOR MAINTAINS SUITES.
AND WHO WILL CONTINUE MY WORK HERE?
I WILL, SIR, BUT THE SPECIFIC NATURE OF THE WORK HAS CHANGED SOME.
IN ADDITION TO MY DIPLOMATIC DUTIES, IT SEEMS I'M GOING TO BE OPENING AN ENGLISH-LANGUAGE SCHOOL.
MY STUDENTS WILL NUMBER AMONG THIS KINGDOM'S MORE ACCOMPLISHED POLITICAL AND MILITARY LEADERS, ALONG WITH THE CREAM OF THEIR SAILORS AND SOLDIERS.
OH DEAR, MOWGLI. WE'RE AT WAR, AREN'T WE?
IF NOT NOW, THEN SOON. BUT THIS TIME WE HAVE POWERFUL ALLIES, HERE AND IN THE CLOUD KINGDOMS.
AND WE HAVE A SECRET WEAPONS PROJECT, WHICH I WILL BE PROPOSING TO OUR HOSTS.

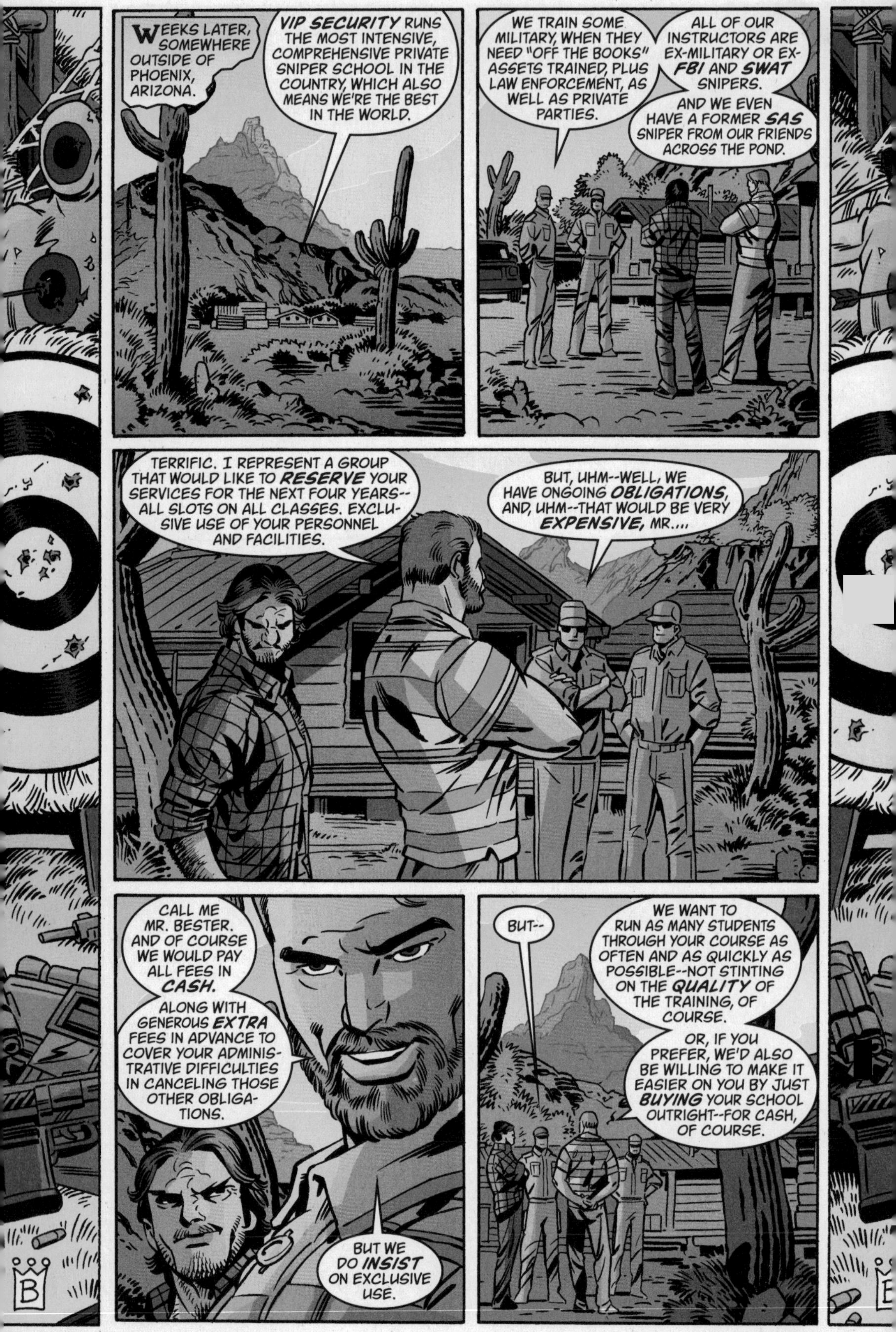
WEEKS LATER, SOMEWHERE OUTSIDE OF PHOENIX, ARIZONA.
VIP SECURITY RUNS THE MOST INTENSIVE, COMPREHENSIVE PRIVATE SNIPER SCHOOL IN THE COUNTRY, WHICH ALSO MEANS WE'RE THE BEST IN THE WORLD.
WE TRAIN SOME MILITARY, WHEN THEY NEED "OFF THE BOOKS" ASSETS TRAINED, PLUS LAW ENFORCEMENT, AS WELL AS PRIVATE PARTIES.
ALL OF OUR INSTRUCTORS ARE EX-MILITARY OR EX-FBI AND SWAT SNIPERS.
AND WE EVEN HAVE A FORMER SAS SNIPER FROM OUR FRIENDS ACROSS THE POND.
TERRIFIC. I REPRESENT A GROUP THAT WOULD LIKE TO RESERVE YOUR SERVICES FOR THE NEXT FOUR YEARS--ALL SLOTS ON ALL CLASSES. EXCLUSIVE USE OF YOUR PERSONNEL AND FACILITIES.
BUT, UHM--WELL, WE HAVE ONGOING OBLIGATIONS, AND, UHM--THAT WOULD BE VERY EXPENSIVE, MR....
CALL ME MR. BESTER. AND OF COURSE WE WOULD PAY ALL FEES IN CASH.
ALONG WITH GENEROUS EXTRA FEES IN ADVANCE TO COVER YOUR ADMINISTRATIVE DIFFICULTIES IN CANCELING THOSE OTHER OBLIGATIONS.
BUT WE DO INSIST ON EXCLUSIVE USE.
BUT--
WE WANT TO RUN AS MANY STUDENTS THROUGH YOUR COURSE AS OFTEN AND AS QUICKLY AS POSSIBLE--NOT STINTING ON THE QUALITY OF THE TRAINING, OF COURSE.
OR, IF YOU PREFER, WE'D ALSO BE WILLING TO MAKE IT EASIER ON YOU BY JUST BUYING YOUR SCHOOL OUTRIGHT--FOR CASH, OF COURSE.

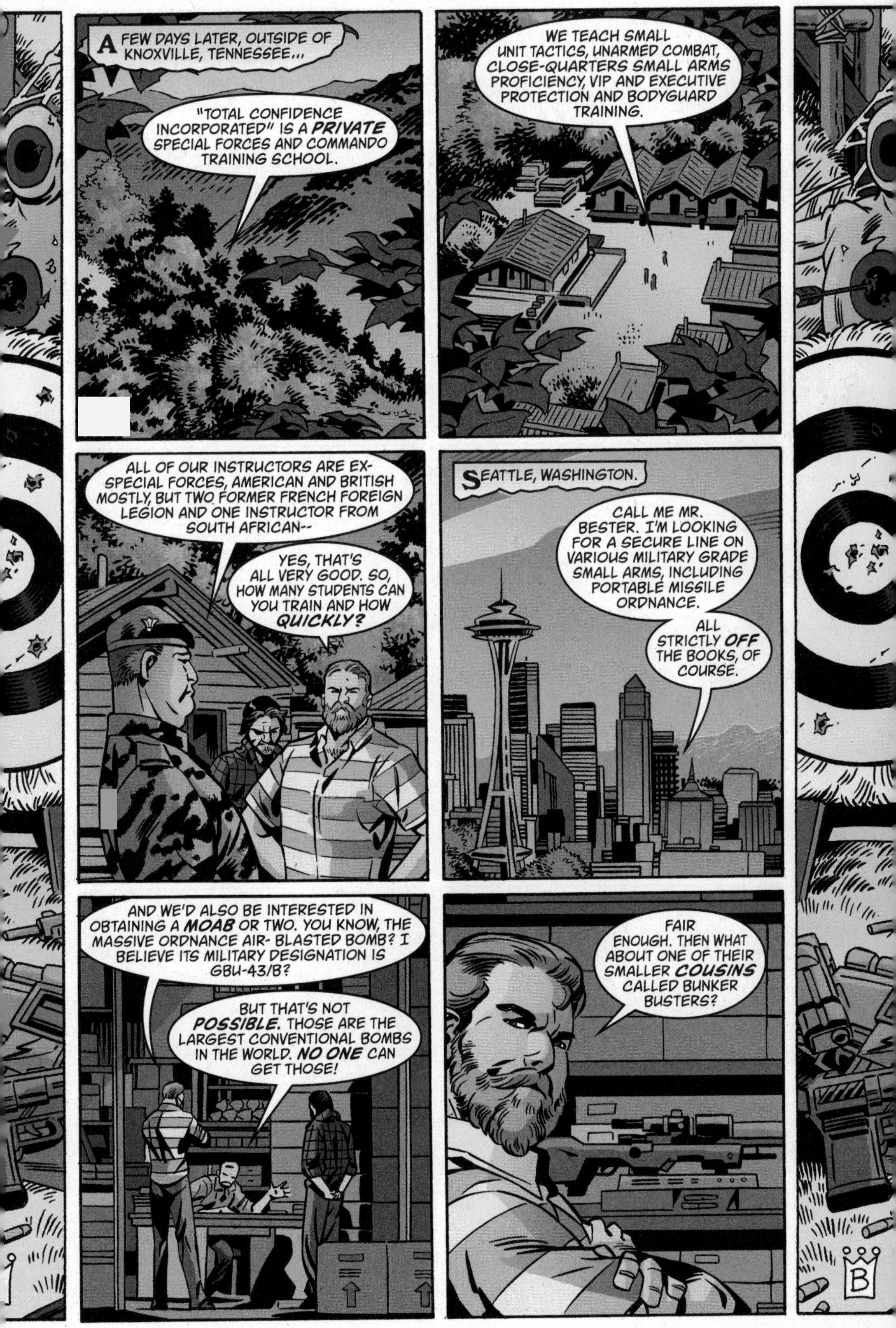
A FEW DAYS LATER, OUTSIDE OF KNOXVILLE, TENNESSEE...
"TOTAL CONFIDENCE INCORPORATED" IS A PRIVATE SPECIAL FORCES AND COMMANDO TRAINING SCHOOL.
WE TEACH SMALL UNIT TACTICS, UNARMED COMBAT, CLOSE-QUARTERS SMALL ARMS PROFICIENCY, VIP AND EXECUTIVE PROTECTION AND BODYGUARD TRAINING.
ALL OF OUR INSTRUCTORS ARE EX-SPECIAL FORCES, AMERICAN AND BRITISH MOSTLY, BUT TWO FORMER FRENCH FOREIGN LEGION AND ONE INSTRUCTOR FROM SOUTH AFRICAN--
YES, THAT'S ALL VERY GOOD. SO, HOW MANY STUDENTS CAN YOU TRAIN AND HOW QUICKLY?
SEATTLE, WASHINGTON.
CALL ME MR. BESTER. I'M LOOKING FOR A SECURE LINE ON VARIOUS MILITARY GRADE SMALL ARMS, INCLUDING PORTABLE MISSILE ORDNANCE.
ALL STRICTLY OFF THE BOOKS, OF COURSE.
AND WE'D ALSO BE INTERESTED IN OBTAINING A MOAB OR TWO. YOU KNOW, THE MASSIVE ORDNANCE AIR-BLASTED BOMB? I BELIEVE ITS MILITARY DESIGNATION IS GBU-43/B?
BUT THAT'S NOT POSSIBLE. THOSE ARE THE LARGEST CONVENTIONAL BOMBS IN THE WORLD. NO ONE CAN GET THOSE!
FAIR ENOUGH. THEN WHAT ABOUT ONE OF THEIR SMALLER COUSINS CALLED BUNKER BUSTERS?

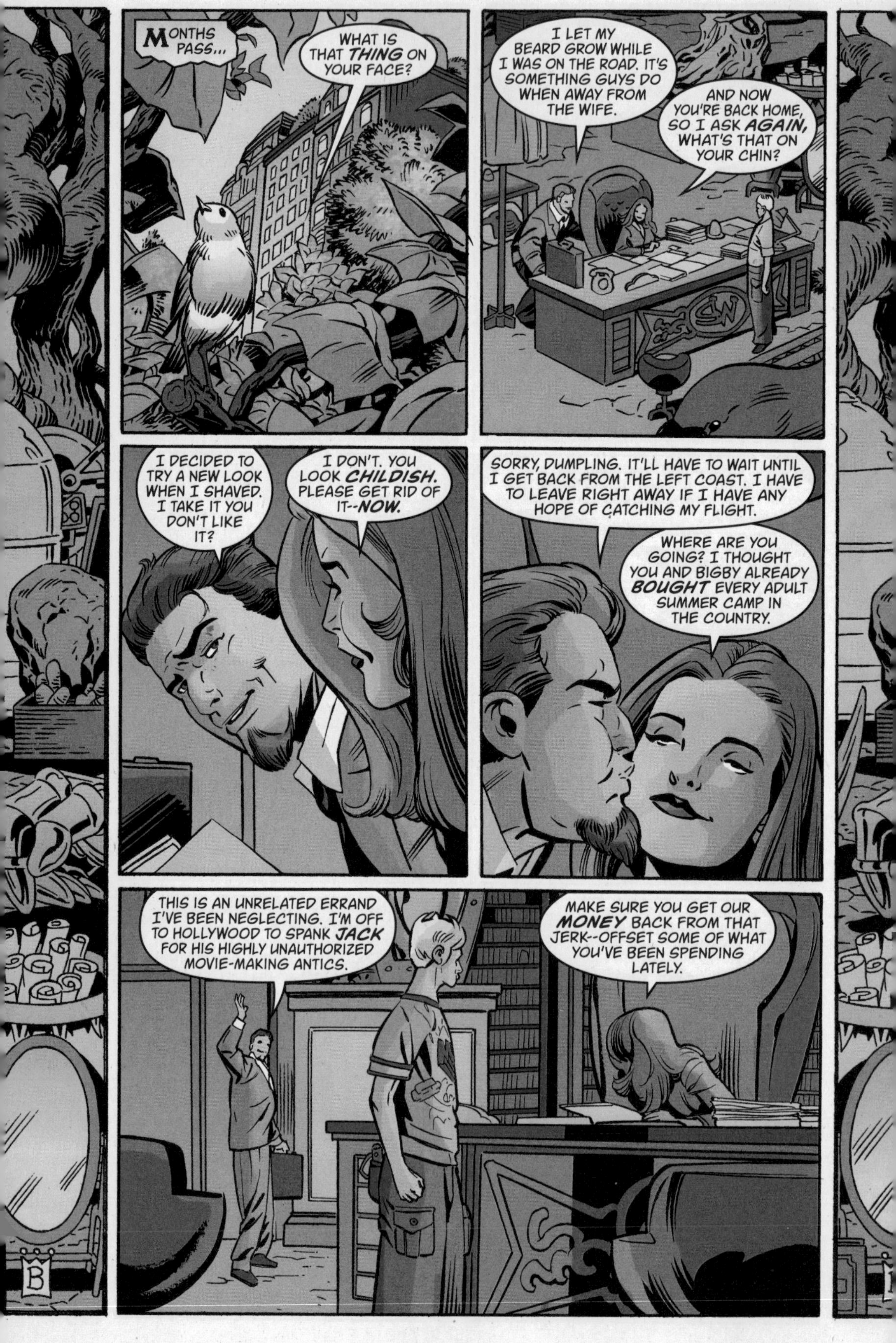
MONTHS PASS...
WHAT IS THAT THING ON YOUR FACE?
I LET MY BEARD GROW WHILE I WAS ON THE ROAD. IT'S SOMETHING GUYS DO WHEN AWAY FROM THE WIFE.
AND NOW YOU'RE BACK HOME, SO I ASK AGAIN, WHAT'S THAT ON YOUR CHIN?
I DECIDED TO TRY A NEW LOOK WHEN I SHAVED. I TAKE IT YOU DON'T LIKE IT?
I DON'T. YOU LOOK CHILDISH. PLEASE GET RID OF IT--NOW.
SORRY, DUMPLING. IT'LL HAVE TO WAIT UNTIL I GET BACK FROM THE LEFT COAST. I HAVE TO LEAVE RIGHT AWAY IF I HAVE ANY HOPE OF CATCHING MY FLIGHT.
WHERE ARE YOU GOING? I THOUGHT YOU AND BIGBY ALREADY BOUGHT EVERY ADULT SUMMER CAMP IN THE COUNTRY.
THIS IS AN UNRELATED ERRAND I'VE BEEN NEGLECTING. I'M OFF TO HOLLYWOOD TO SPANK JACK FOR HIS HIGHLY UNAUTHORIZED MOVIE-MAKING ANTICS.
MAKE SURE YOU GET OUR MONEY BACK FROM THAT JERK--OFFSET SOME OF WHAT YOU'VE BEEN SPENDING LATELY.

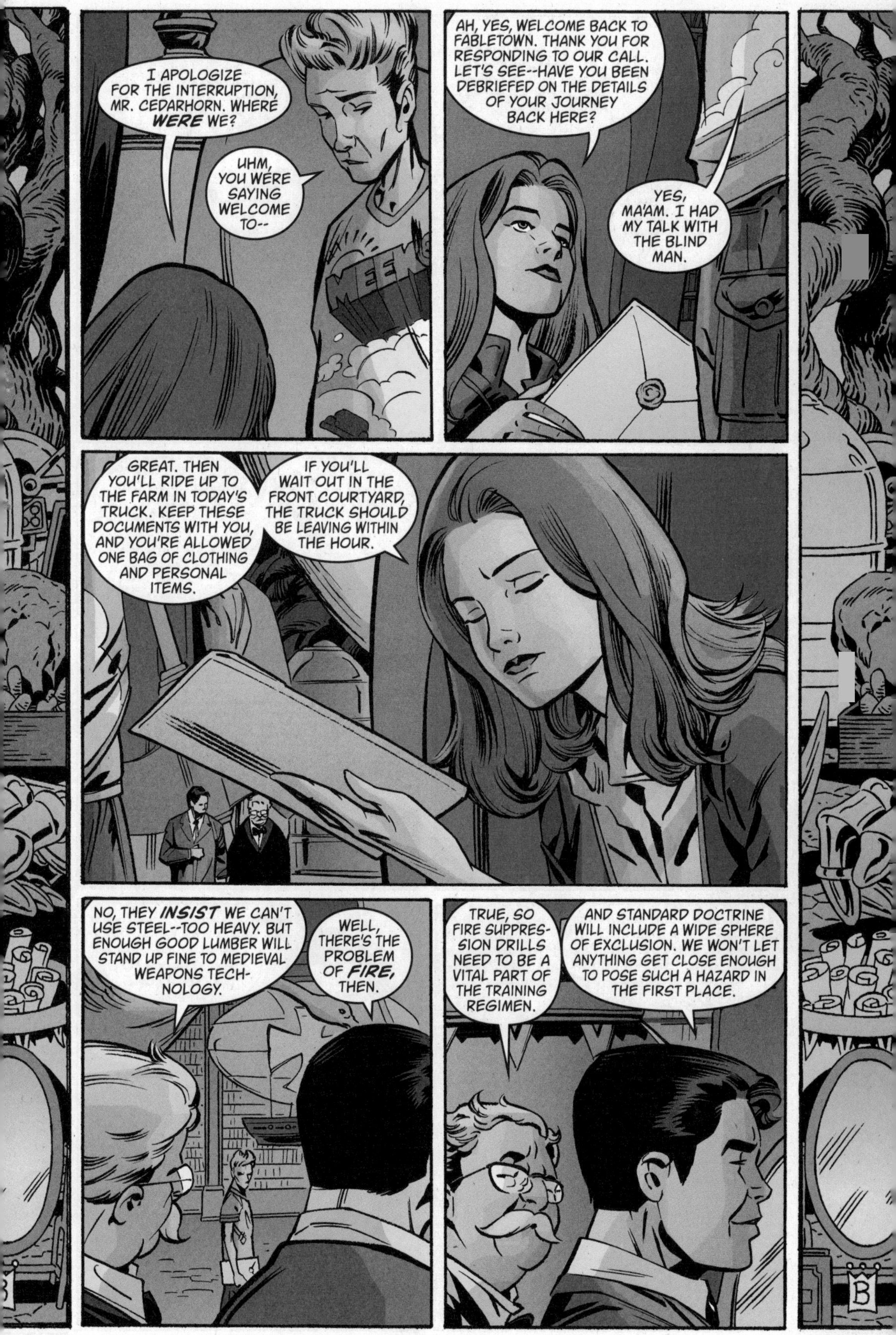

I APOLOGIZE FOR THE INTERRUPTION, MR. CEDARHORN. WHERE WERE WE?
UHM, YOU WERE SAYING WELCOME TO--
AH, YES, WELCOME BACK TO FABLETOWN. THANK YOU FOR RESPONDING TO OUR CALL. LET'S SEE--HAVE YOU BEEN DEBRIEFED ON THE DETAILS OF YOUR JOURNEY BACK HERE?
YES, MA'AM. I HAD MY TALK WITH THE BLIND MAN.
GREAT. THEN YOU'LL RIDE UP TO THE FARM IN TODAY'S TRUCK. KEEP THESE DOCUMENTS WITH YOU, AND YOU'RE ALLOWED ONE BAG OF CLOTHING AND PERSONAL ITEMS.
IF YOU'LL WAIT OUT IN THE FRONT COURTYARD, THE TRUCK SHOULD BE LEAVING WITHIN THE HOUR.
NO, THEY INSIST WE CAN'T USE STEEL--TOO HEAVY. BUT ENOUGH GOOD LUMBER WILL STAND UP FINE TO MEDIEVAL WEAPONS TECH-NOLOGY.
WELL, THERE'S THE PROBLEM OF FIRE, THEN.
TRUE, SO FIRE SUPPRES-SION DRILLS NEED TO BE A VITAL PART OF THE TRAINING REGIMEN.
AND STANDARD DOCTRINE WILL INCLUDE A WIDE SPHERE OF EXCLUSION. WE WON'T LET ANYTHING GET CLOSE ENOUGH TO POSE SUCH A HAZARD IN THE FIRST PLACE.

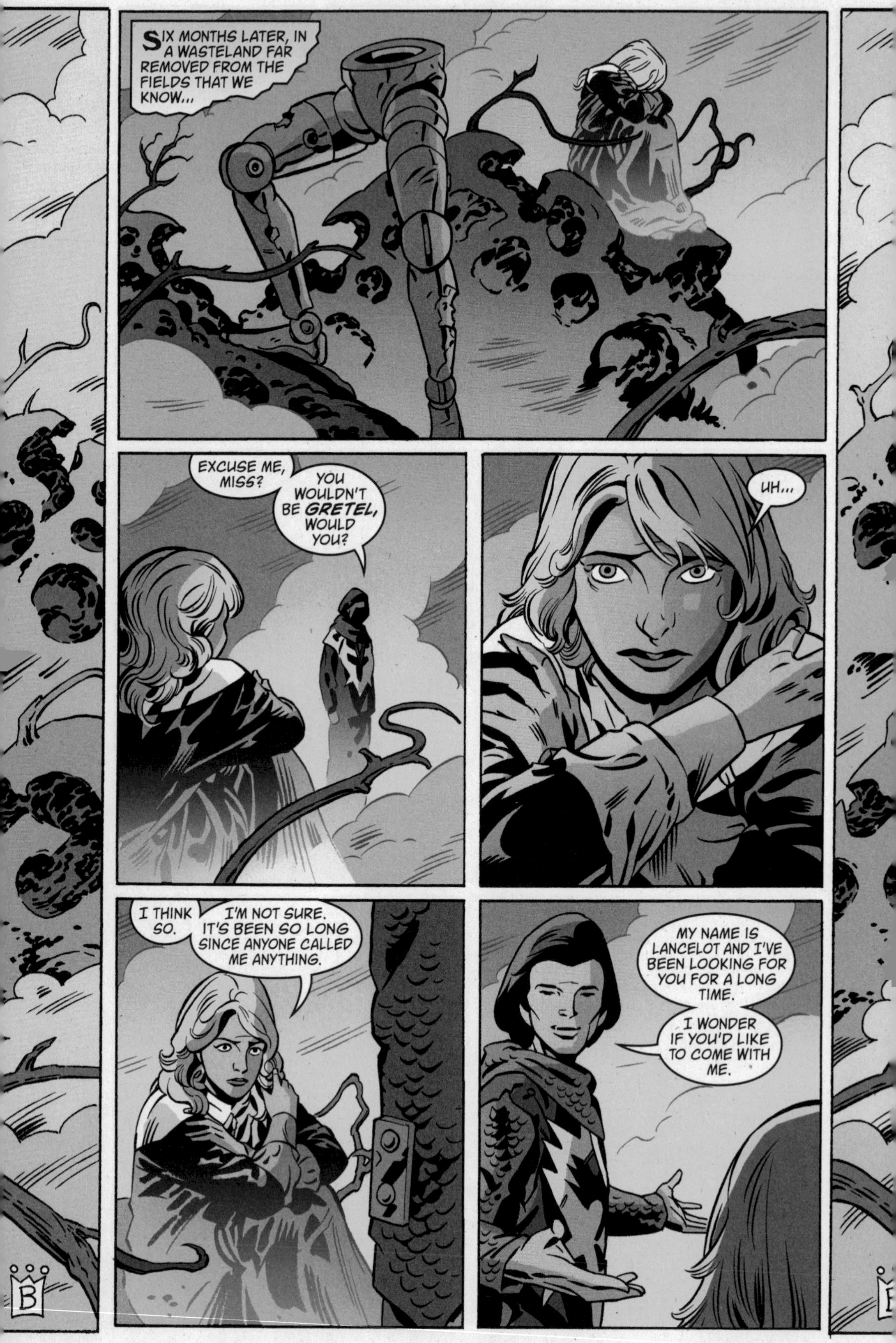

SIX MONTHS LATER, IN A WASTELAND FAR REMOVED FROM THE FIELDS THAT WE KNOW...
EXCUSE ME, MISS?
YOU WOULDN'T BE GRETEL, WOULD YOU?
UH...
I THINK SO.
I'M NOT SURE. IT'S BEEN SO LONG SINCE ANYONE CALLED ME ANYTHING.
MY NAME IS LANCELOT AND I'VE BEEN LOOKING FOR YOU FOR A LONG TIME.
I WONDER IF YOU'D LIKE TO COME WITH ME.

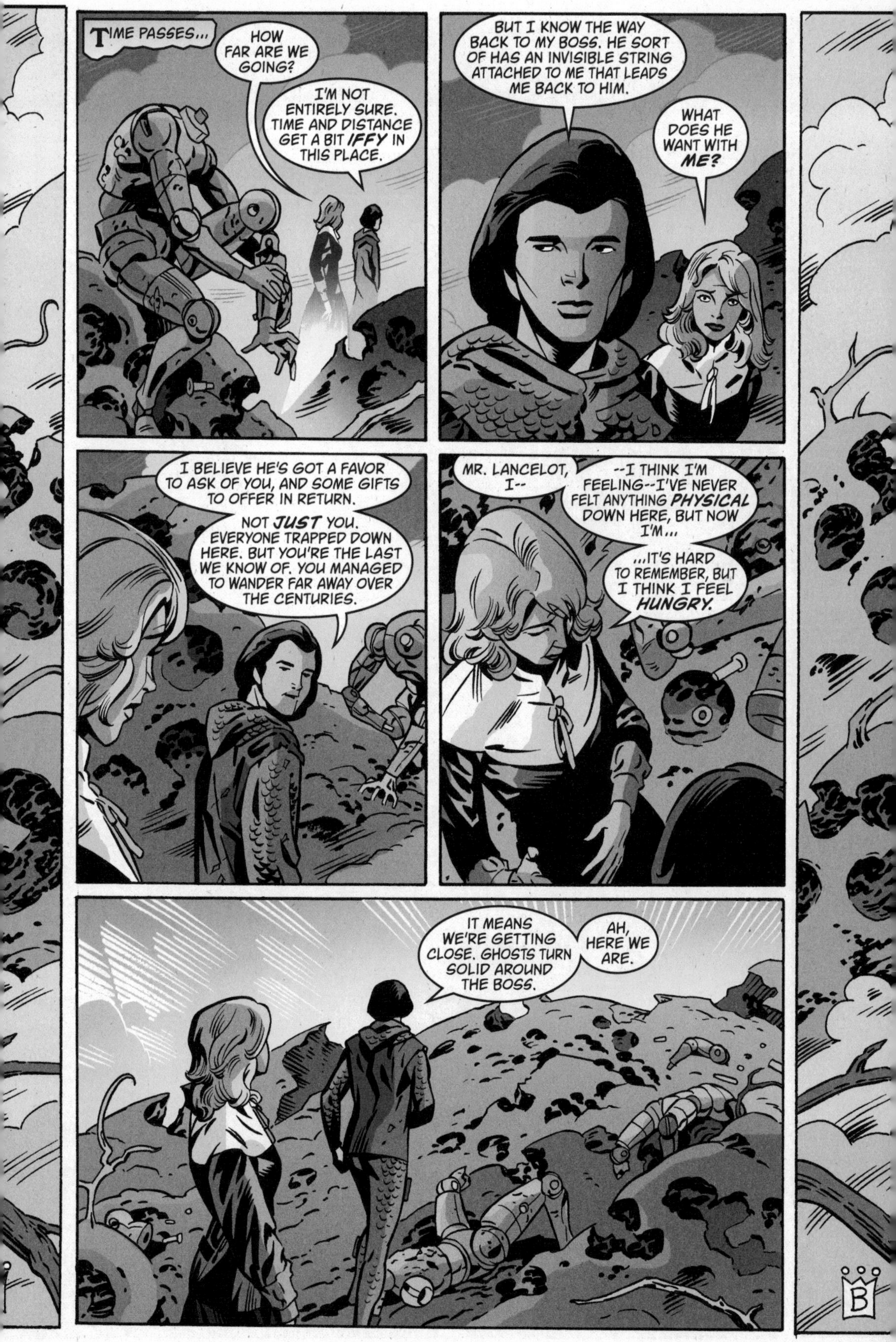
TIME PASSES...
HOW FAR ARE WE GOING?
I'M NOT ENTIRELY SURE. TIME AND DISTANCE GET A BIT IFFY IN THIS PLACE.
BUT I KNOW THE WAY BACK TO MY BOSS. HE SORT OF HAS AN INVISIBLE STRING ATTACHED TO ME THAT LEADS ME BACK TO HIM.
WHAT DOES HE WANT WITH ME?
I BELIEVE HE'S GOT A FAVOR TO ASK OF YOU, AND SOME GIFTS TO OFFER IN RETURN.
NOT JUST YOU. EVERYONE TRAPPED DOWN HERE. BUT YOU'RE THE LAST WE KNOW OF. YOU MANAGED TO WANDER FAR AWAY OVER THE CENTURIES.
MR. LANCELOT, I--
--I THINK I'M FEELING--I'VE NEVER FELT ANYTHING PHYSICAL DOWN HERE, BUT NOW I'M...
...IT'S HARD TO REMEMBER, BUT I THINK I FEEL HUNGRY.
IT MEANS WE'RE GETTING CLOSE. GHOSTS TURN SOLID AROUND THE BOSS.
AH, HERE WE ARE.

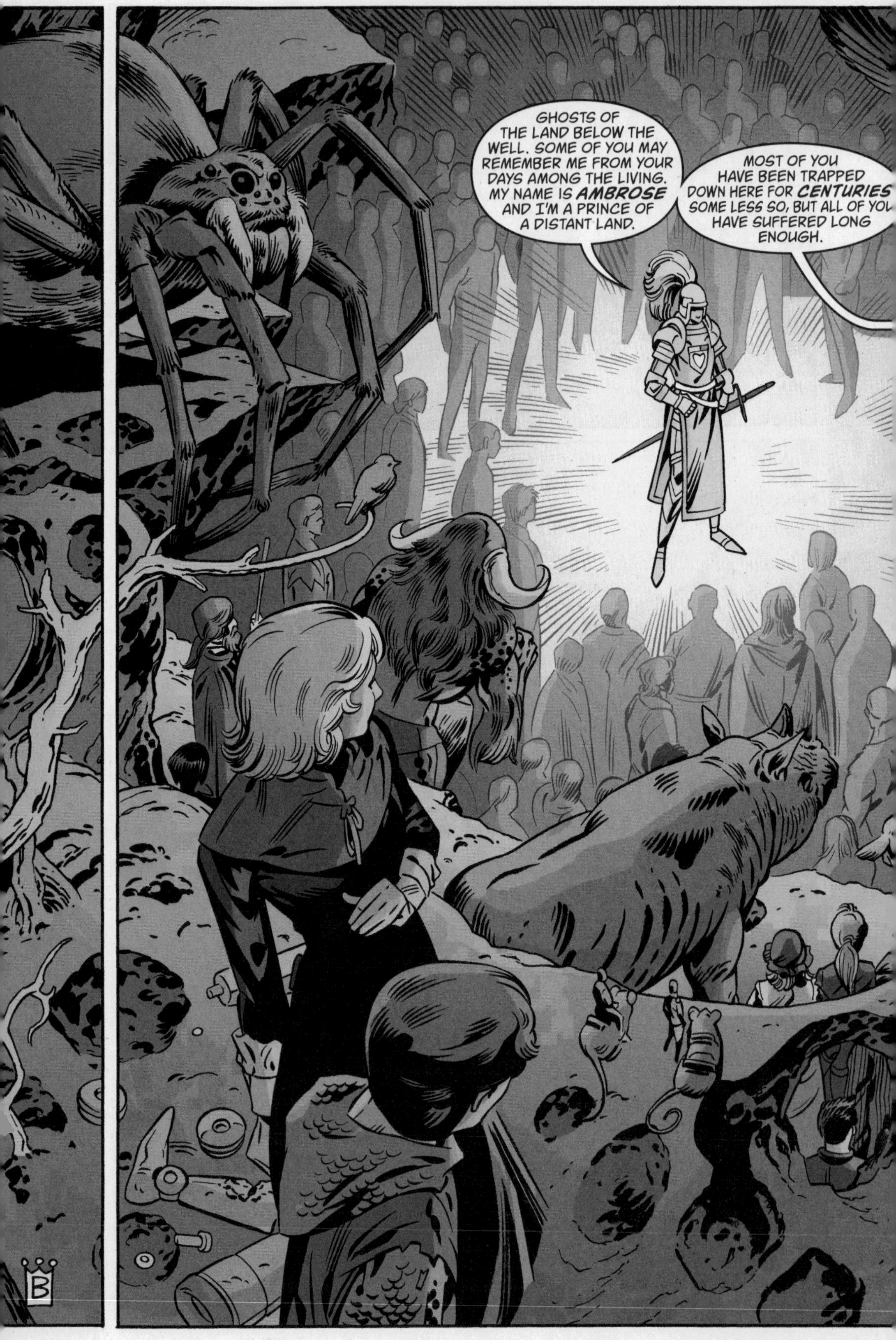
GHOSTS OF THE LAND BELOW THE WELL. SOME OF YOU MAY REMEMBER ME FROM YOUR DAYS AMONG THE LIVING. MY NAME IS AMBROSE AND I'M A PRINCE OF A DISTANT LAND.
MOST OF YOU HAVE BEEN TRAPPED DOWN HERE FOR CENTURIES SOME LESS SO, BUT ALL OF YOU HAVE SUFFERED LONG ENOUGH.

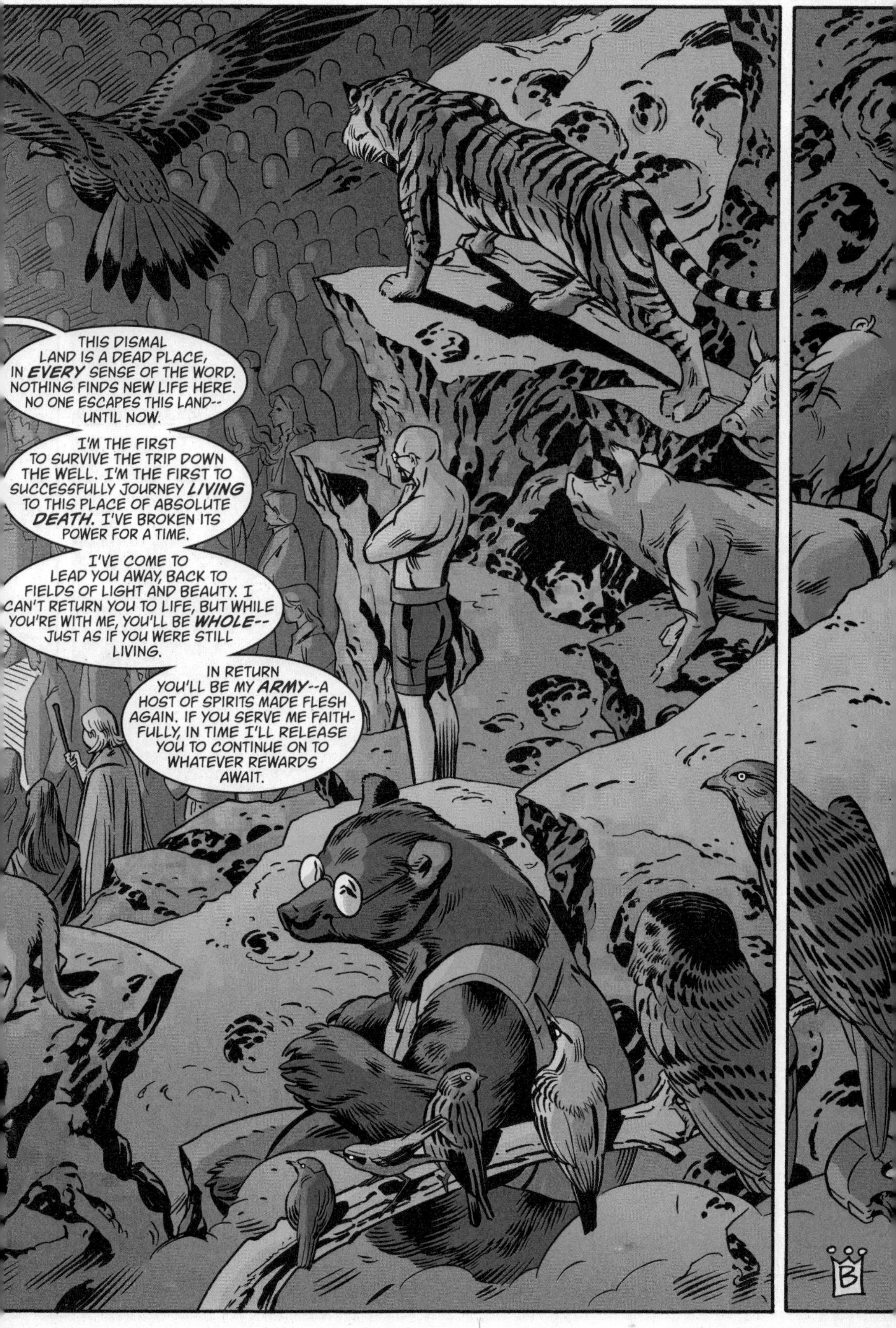
THIS DISMAL LAND IS A DEAD PLACE, IN EVERY SENSE OF THE WORD. NOTHING FINDS NEW LIFE HERE. NO ONE ESCAPES THIS LAND-- UNTIL NOW.
I'M THE FIRST TO SURVIVE THE TRIP DOWN THE WELL. I'M THE FIRST TO SUCCESSFULLY JOURNEY LIVING TO THIS PLACE OF ABSOLUTE DEATH. I'VE BROKEN ITS POWER FOR A TIME.
I'VE COME TO LEAD YOU AWAY, BACK TO FIELDS OF LIGHT AND BEAUTY. I CAN'T RETURN YOU TO LIFE, BUT WHILE YOU'RE WITH ME, YOU'LL BE WHOLE-- JUST AS IF YOU WERE STILL LIVING.
IN RETURN YOU'LL BE MY ARMY--A HOST OF SPIRITS MADE FLESH AGAIN. IF YOU SERVE ME FAITHFULLY, IN TIME I'LL RELEASE YOU TO CONTINUE ON TO WHATEVER REWARDS AWAIT.

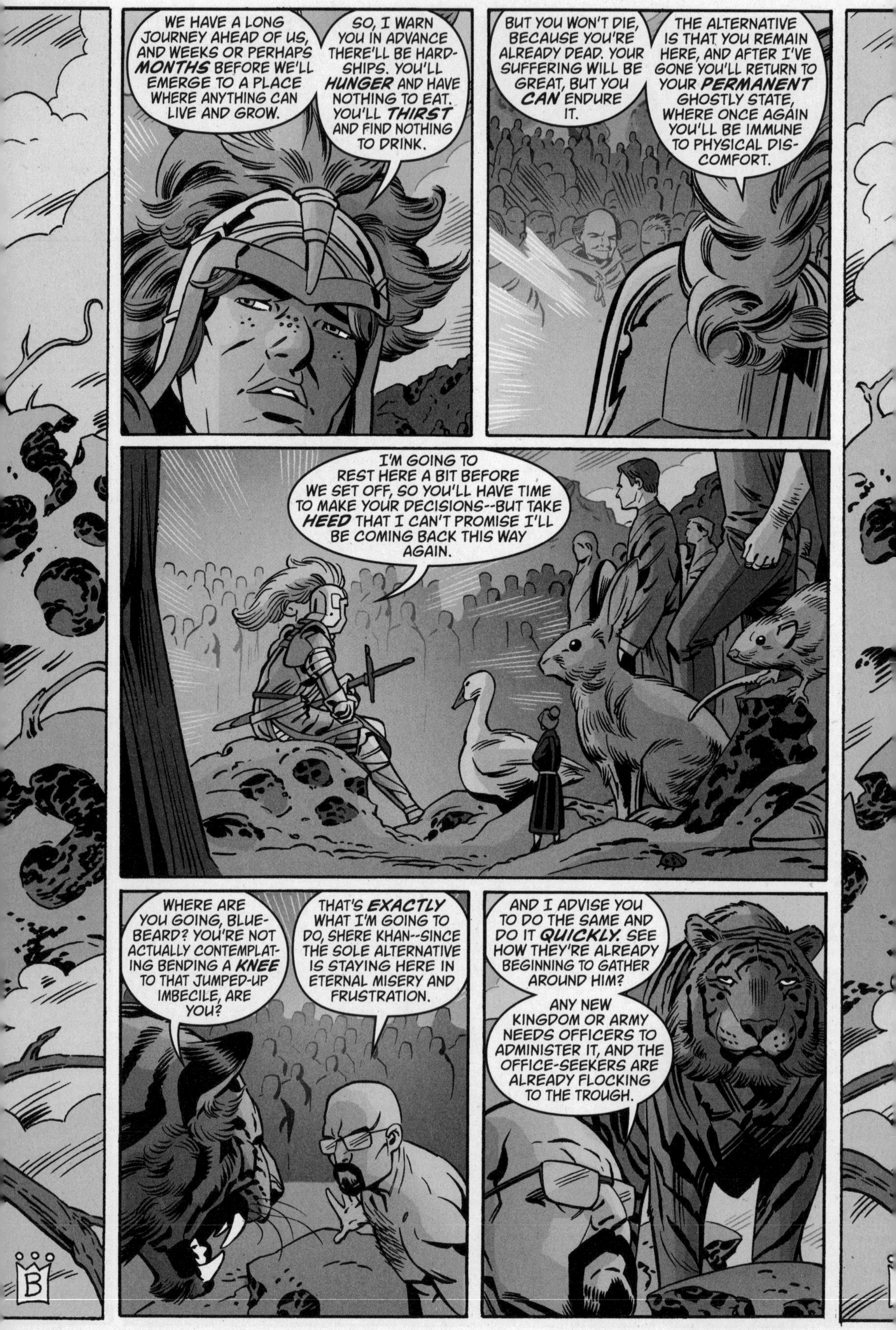
WE HAVE A LONG JOURNEY AHEAD OF US, AND WEEKS OR PERHAPS MONTHS BEFORE WE'LL EMERGE TO A PLACE WHERE ANYTHING CAN LIVE AND GROW.
SO, I WARN YOU IN ADVANCE THERE'LL BE HARD-SHIPS. YOU'LL HUNGER AND HAVE NOTHING TO EAT. YOU'LL THIRST AND FIND NOTHING TO DRINK.
BUT YOU WON'T DIE, BECAUSE YOU'RE ALREADY DEAD. YOUR SUFFERING WILL BE GREAT, BUT YOU CAN ENDURE IT.
THE ALTERNATIVE IS THAT YOU REMAIN HERE, AND AFTER I'VE GONE YOU'LL RETURN TO YOUR PERMANENT GHOSTLY STATE, WHERE ONCE AGAIN YOU'LL BE IMMUNE TO PHYSICAL DIS-COMFORT.
I'M GOING TO REST HERE A BIT BEFORE WE SET OFF, SO YOU'LL HAVE TIME TO MAKE YOUR DECISIONS--BUT TAKE HEED THAT I CAN'T PROMISE I'LL BE COMING BACK THIS WAY AGAIN.
WHERE ARE YOU GOING, BLUE-BEARD? YOU'RE NOT ACTUALLY CONTEMPLAT-ING BENDING A KNEE TO THAT JUMPED-UP IMBECILE, ARE YOU?
THAT'S EXACTLY WHAT I'M GOING TO DO, SHERE KHAN--SINCE THE SOLE ALTERNATIVE IS STAYING HERE IN ETERNAL MISERY AND FRUSTRATION.
AND I ADVISE YOU TO DO THE SAME AND DO IT QUICKLY. SEE HOW THEY'RE ALREADY BEGINNING TO GATHER AROUND HIM?
ANY NEW KINGDOM OR ARMY NEEDS OFFICERS TO ADMINISTER IT, AND THE OFFICE-SEEKERS ARE ALREADY FLOCKING TO THE TROUGH.

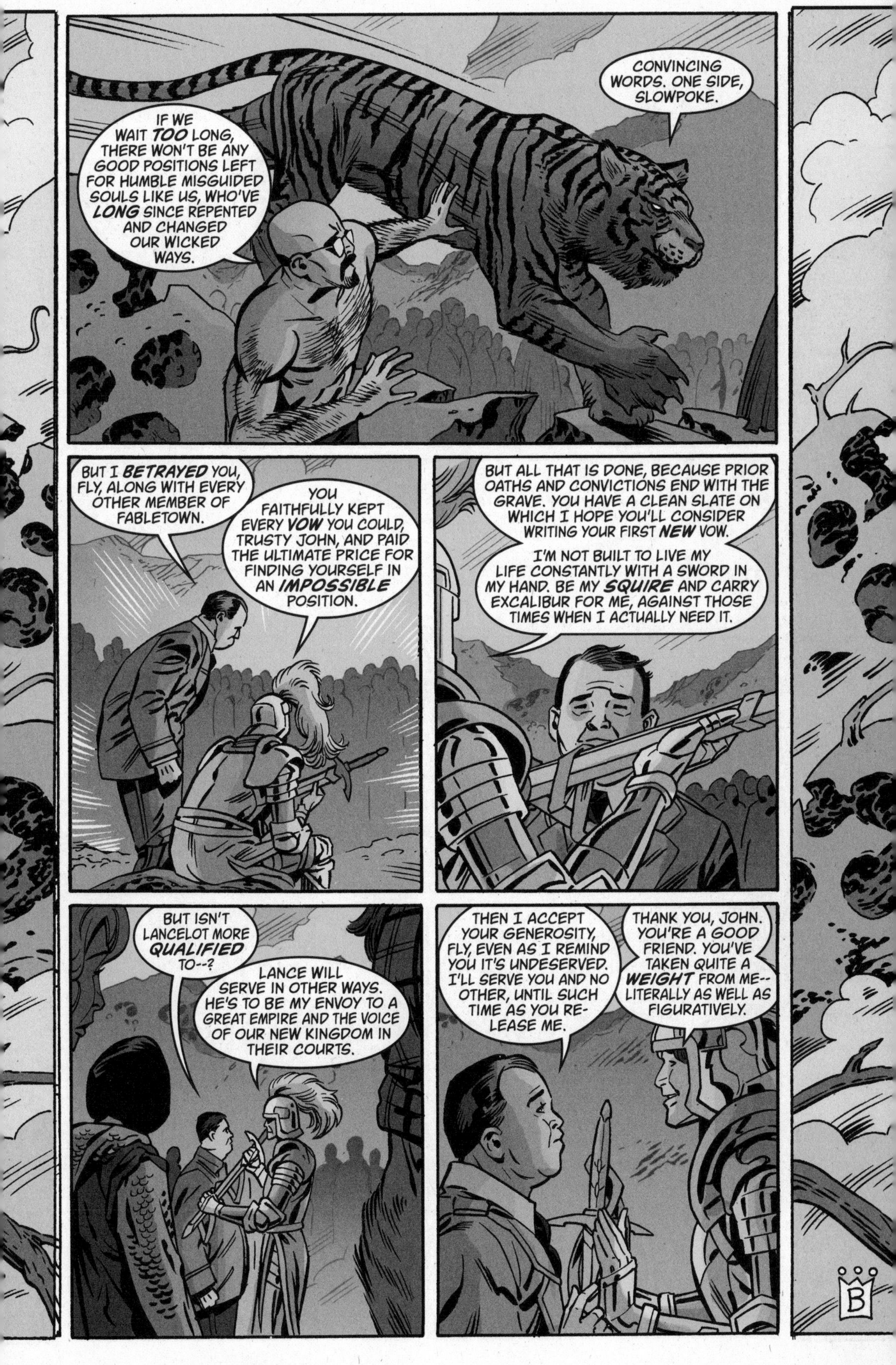
IF WE WAIT TOO LONG, THERE WON'T BE ANY GOOD POSITIONS LEFT FOR HUMBLE MISGUIDED SOULS LIKE US, WHO'VE LONG SINCE REPENTED AND CHANGED OUR WICKED WAYS.
CONVINCING WORDS. ONE SIDE, SLOWPOKE.
BUT I BETRAYED YOU, FLY, ALONG WITH EVERY OTHER MEMBER OF FABLETOWN.
YOU FAITHFULLY KEPT EVERY VOW YOU COULD, TRUSTY JOHN, AND PAID THE ULTIMATE PRICE FOR FINDING YOURSELF IN AN IMPOSSIBLE POSITION.
BUT ALL THAT IS DONE, BECAUSE PRIOR OATHS AND CONVICTIONS END WITH THE GRAVE. YOU HAVE A CLEAN SLATE ON WHICH I HOPE YOU'LL CONSIDER WRITING YOUR FIRST NEW VOW.
I'M NOT BUILT TO LIVE MY LIFE CONSTANTLY WITH A SWORD IN MY HAND. BE MY SQUIRE AND CARRY EXCALIBUR FOR ME, AGAINST THOSE TIMES WHEN I ACTUALLY NEED IT.
BUT ISN'T LANCELOT MORE QUALIFIED TO--?
LANCE WILL SERVE IN OTHER WAYS. HE'S TO BE MY ENVOY TO A GREAT EMPIRE AND THE VOICE OF OUR NEW KINGDOM IN THEIR COURTS.
THEN I ACCEPT YOUR GENEROSITY, FLY, EVEN AS I REMIND YOU IT'S UNDESERVED. I'LL SERVE YOU AND NO OTHER, UNTIL SUCH TIME AS YOU RE-LEASE ME.
THANK YOU, JOHN. YOU'RE A GOOD FRIEND. YOU'VE TAKEN QUITE A WEIGHT FROM ME--LITERALLY AS WELL AS FIGURATIVELY.

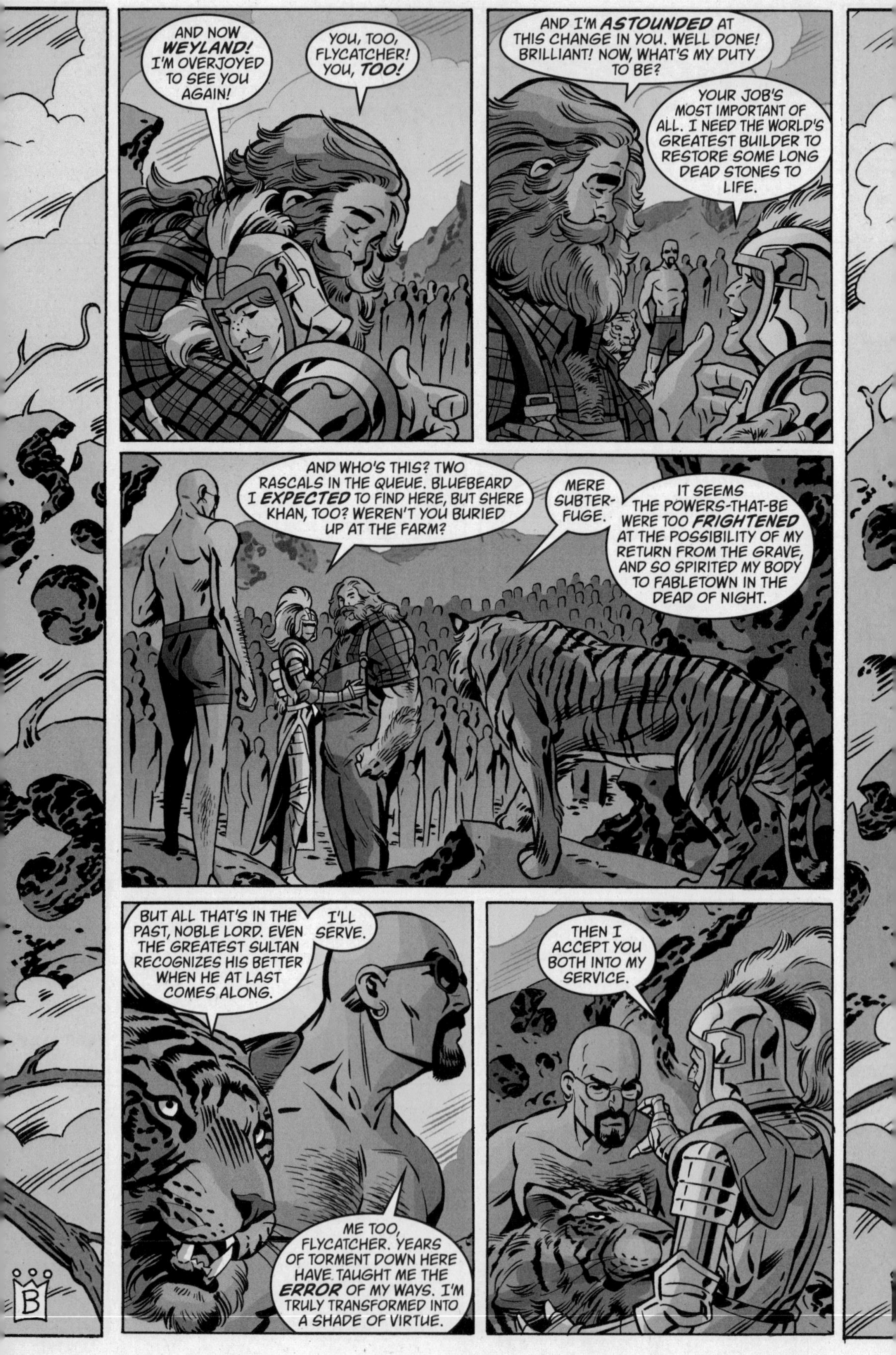
AND NOW WEYLAND! I'M OVERJOYED TO SEE YOU AGAIN!
YOU, TOO, FLYCATCHER! YOU, TOO!
AND I'M ASTOUNDED AT THIS CHANGE IN YOU. WELL DONE! BRILLIANT! NOW, WHAT'S MY DUTY TO BE?
YOUR JOB'S MOST IMPORTANT OF ALL. I NEED THE WORLD'S GREATEST BUILDER TO RESTORE SOME LONG DEAD STONES TO LIFE.
AND WHO'S THIS? TWO RASCALS IN THE QUEUE. BLUEBEARD I EXPECTED TO FIND HERE, BUT SHERE KHAN, TOO? WEREN'T YOU BURIED UP AT THE FARM?
MERE SUBTERFUGE.
IT SEEMS THE POWERS-THAT-BE WERE TOO FRIGHTENED AT THE POSSIBILITY OF MY RETURN FROM THE GRAVE, AND SO SPIRITED MY BODY TO FABLETOWN IN THE DEAD OF NIGHT.
BUT ALL THAT'S IN THE PAST, NOBLE LORD. EVEN THE GREATEST SULTAN RECOGNIZES HIS BETTER WHEN HE AT LAST COMES ALONG.
I'LL SERVE.
ME TOO, FLYCATCHER. YEARS OF TORMENT DOWN HERE HAVE TAUGHT ME THE ERROR OF MY WAYS. I'M TRULY TRANSFORMED INTO A SHADE OF VIRTUE.
THEN I ACCEPT YOU BOTH INTO MY SERVICE.
B

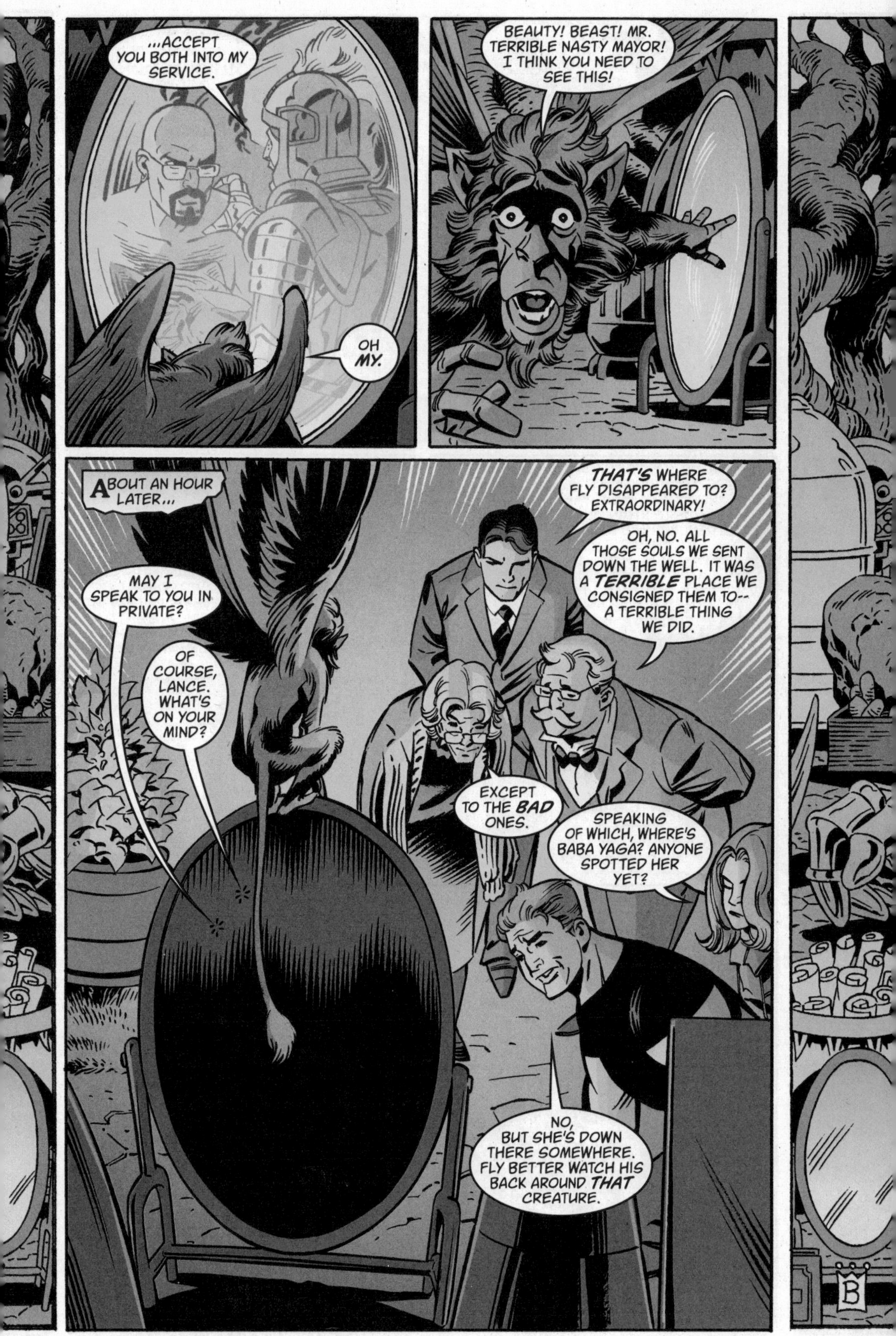
...ACCEPT YOU BOTH INTO MY SERVICE.
OH MY.
BEAUTY! BEAST! MR. TERRIBLE NASTY MAYOR! I THINK YOU NEED TO SEE THIS!
ABOUT AN HOUR LATER...
THAT'S WHERE FLY DISAPPEARED TO? EXTRAORDINARY!
OH, NO. ALL THOSE SOULS WE SENT DOWN THE WELL. IT WAS A TERRIBLE PLACE WE CONSIGNED THEM TO-- A TERRIBLE THING WE DID.
MAY I SPEAK TO YOU IN PRIVATE?
OF COURSE, LANCE. WHAT'S ON YOUR MIND?
EXCEPT TO THE BAD ONES.
SPEAKING OF WHICH, WHERE'S BABA YAGA? ANYONE SPOTTED HER YET?
NO, BUT SHE'S DOWN THERE SOMEWHERE. FLY BETTER WATCH HIS BACK AROUND THAT CREATURE.

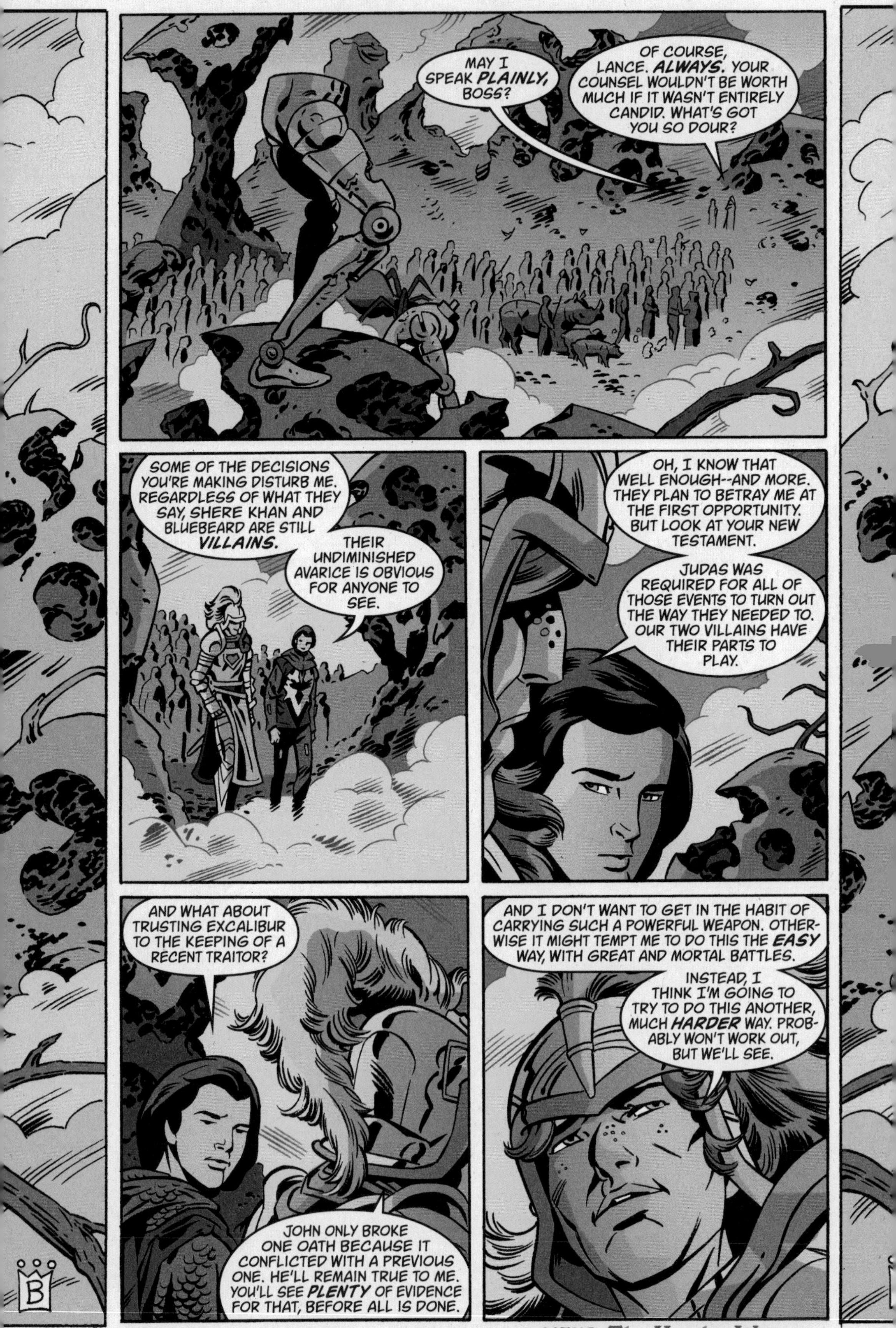
MAY I SPEAK PLAINLY, BOSS?
OF COURSE, LANCE. ALWAYS. YOUR COUNSEL WOULDN'T BE WORTH MUCH IF IT WASN'T ENTIRELY CANDID. WHAT'S GOT YOU SO DOUR?
SOME OF THE DECISIONS YOU'RE MAKING DISTURB ME. REGARDLESS OF WHAT THEY SAY, SHERE KHAN AND BLUEBEARD ARE STILL VILLAINS.
THEIR UNDIMINISHED AVARICE IS OBVIOUS FOR ANYONE TO SEE.
OH, I KNOW THAT WELL ENOUGH--AND MORE. THEY PLAN TO BETRAY ME AT THE FIRST OPPORTUNITY. BUT LOOK AT YOUR NEW TESTAMENT.
JUDAS WAS REQUIRED FOR ALL OF THOSE EVENTS TO TURN OUT THE WAY THEY NEEDED TO. OUR TWO VILLAINS HAVE THEIR PARTS TO PLAY.
AND WHAT ABOUT TRUSTING EXCALIBUR TO THE KEEPING OF A RECENT TRAITOR?
JOHN ONLY BROKE ONE OATH BECAUSE IT CONFLICTED WITH A PREVIOUS ONE. HE'LL REMAIN TRUE TO ME. YOU'LL SEE PLENTY OF EVIDENCE FOR THAT, BEFORE ALL IS DONE.
AND I DON'T WANT TO GET IN THE HABIT OF CARRYING SUCH A POWERFUL WEAPON. OTHERWISE IT MIGHT TEMPT ME TO DO THIS THE EASY WAY, WITH GREAT AND MORTAL BATTLES.
INSTEAD, I THINK I'M GOING TO TRY TO DO THIS ANOTHER, MUCH HARDER WAY. PROBABLY WON'T WORK OUT, BUT WE'LL SEE.

NEXT: **The Harder Way**

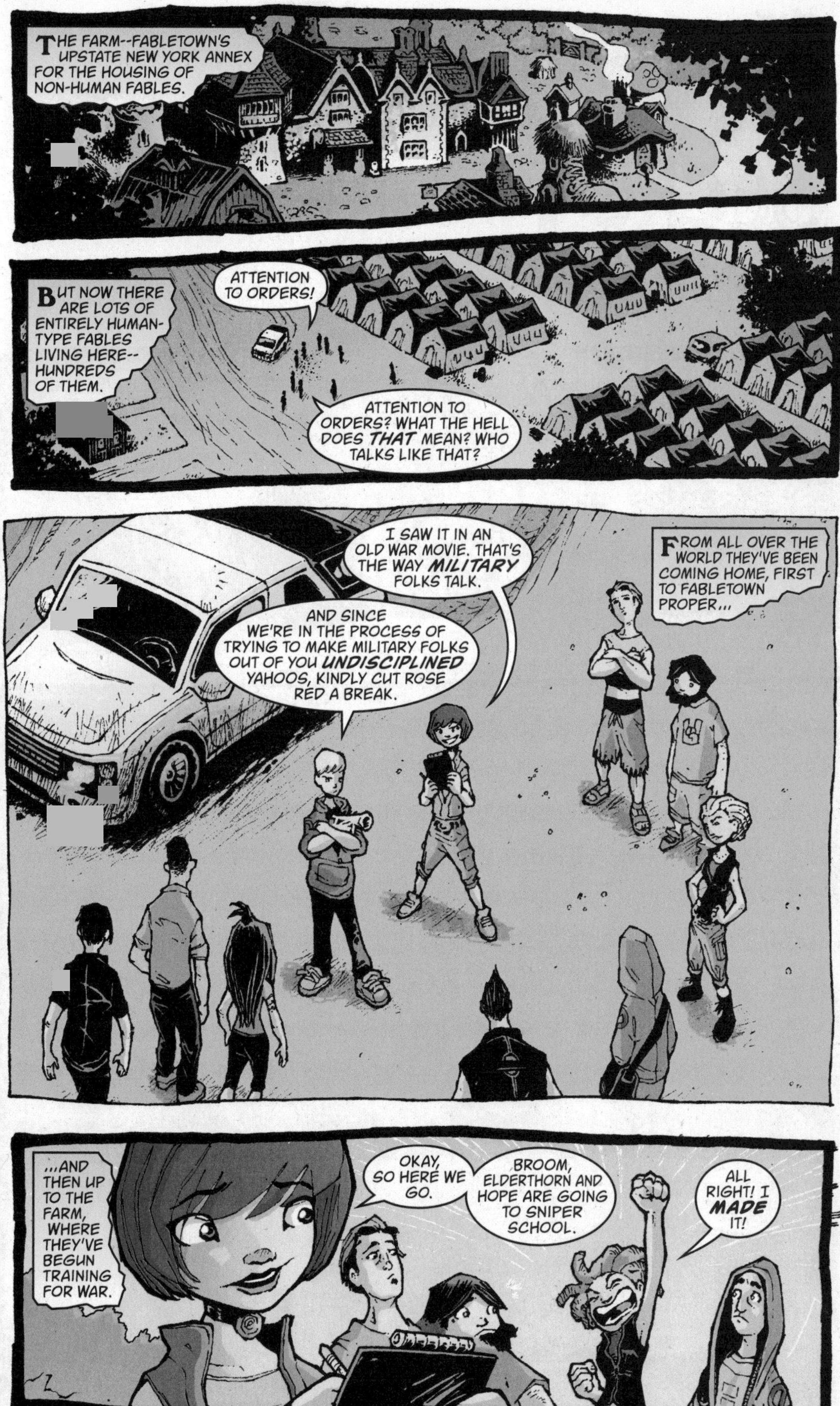
THE FARM--FABLETOWN'S UPSTATE NEW YORK ANNEX FOR THE HOUSING OF NON-HUMAN FABLES.
BUT NOW THERE ARE LOTS OF ENTIRELY HUMAN-TYPE FABLES LIVING HERE--HUNDREDS OF THEM.
ATTENTION TO ORDERS!
ATTENTION TO ORDERS? WHAT THE HELL DOES THAT MEAN? WHO TALKS LIKE THAT?
I SAW IT IN AN OLD WAR MOVIE. THAT'S THE WAY MILITARY FOLKS TALK.
AND SINCE WE'RE IN THE PROCESS OF TRYING TO MAKE MILITARY FOLKS OUT OF YOU UNDISCIPLINED YAHOOS, KINDLY CUT ROSE RED A BREAK.
FROM ALL OVER THE WORLD THEY'VE BEEN COMING HOME, FIRST TO FABLETOWN PROPER...
...AND THEN UP TO THE FARM, WHERE THEY'VE BEGUN TRAINING FOR WAR.
OKAY, SO HERE WE GO.
BROOM, ELDERTHORN AND HOPE ARE GOING TO SNIPER SCHOOL.
ALL RIGHT! I MADE IT!

"the Birthday Secret"

In which we momentarily turn away from the incredibl events taking place down the Witching Well to mark an important event in the lives of the Wolf Cubs.

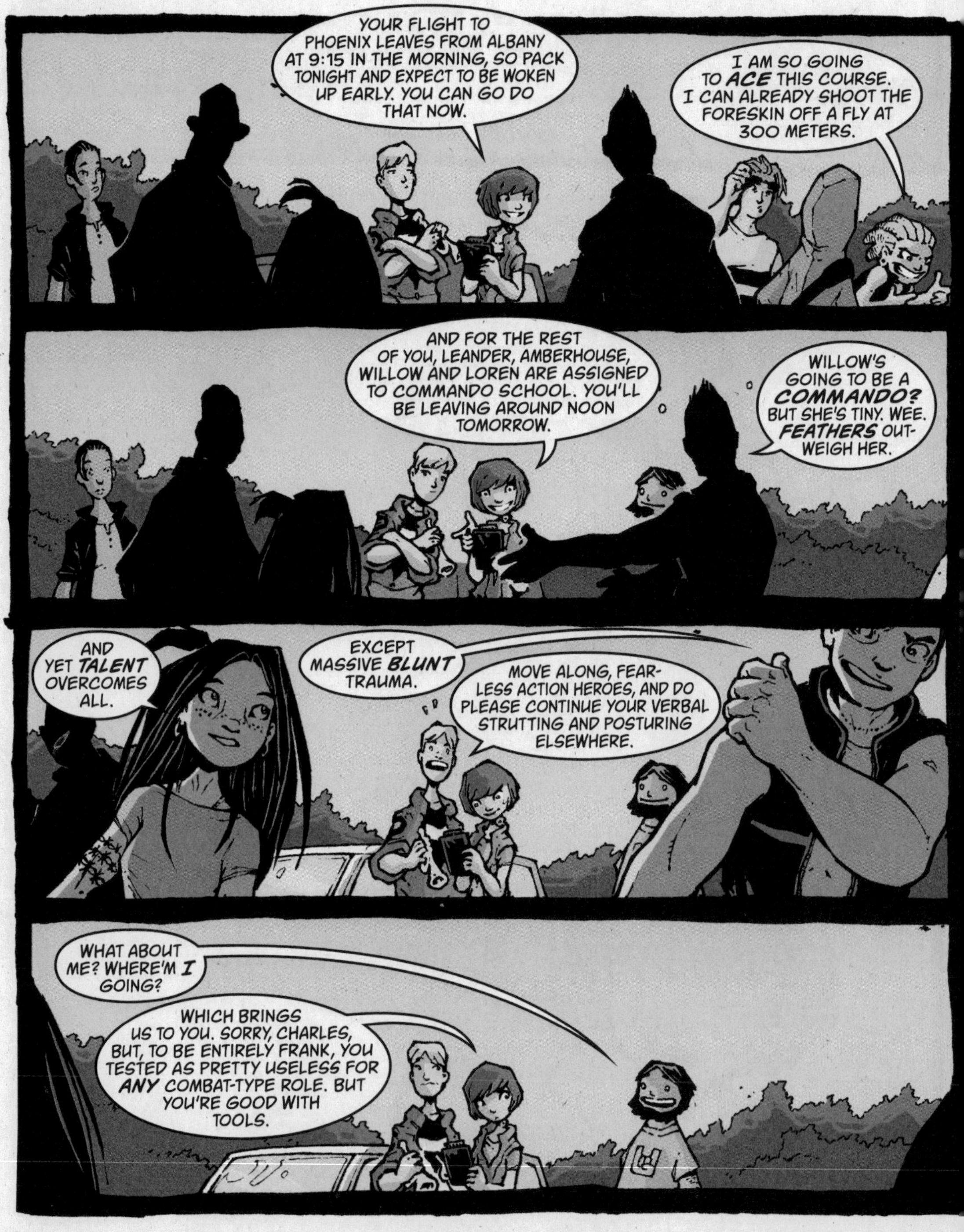
YOUR FLIGHT TO PHOENIX LEAVES FROM ALBANY AT 9:15 IN THE MORNING, SO PACK TONIGHT AND EXPECT TO BE WOKEN UP EARLY. YOU CAN GO DO THAT NOW.
I AM SO GOING TO ACE THIS COURSE. I CAN ALREADY SHOOT THE FORESKIN OFF A FLY AT 300 METERS.
AND FOR THE REST OF YOU, LEANDER, AMBERHOUSE, WILLOW AND LOREN ARE ASSIGNED TO COMMANDO SCHOOL. YOU'LL BE LEAVING AROUND NOON TOMORROW.
WILLOW'S GOING TO BE A COMMANDO? BUT SHE'S TINY. WEE. FEATHERS OUT-WEIGH HER.
AND YET TALENT OVERCOMES ALL.
EXCEPT MASSIVE BLUNT TRAUMA.
MOVE ALONG, FEAR-LESS ACTION HEROES, AND DO PLEASE CONTINUE YOUR VERBAL STRUTTING AND POSTURING ELSEWHERE.
WHAT ABOUT ME? WHERE'M I GOING?
WHICH BRINGS US TO YOU. SORRY, CHARLES, BUT, TO BE ENTIRELY FRANK, YOU TESTED AS PRETTY USELESS FOR ANY COMBAT-TYPE ROLE. BUT YOU'RE GOOD WITH TOOLS.

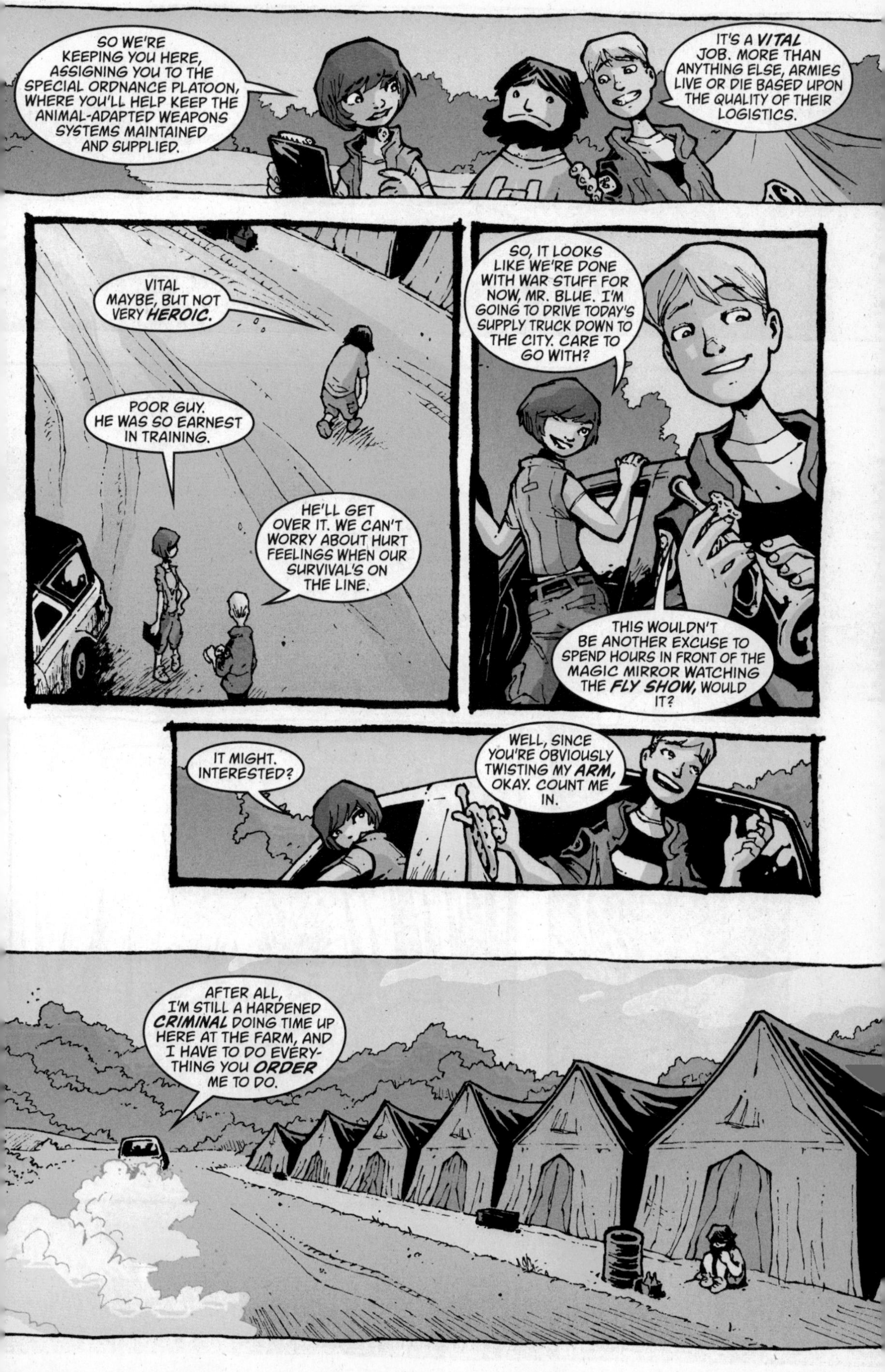
SO WE'RE KEEPING YOU HERE, ASSIGNING YOU TO THE SPECIAL ORDNANCE PLATOON, WHERE YOU'LL HELP KEEP THE ANIMAL-ADAPTED WEAPONS SYSTEMS MAINTAINED AND SUPPLIED.
IT'S A VITAL JOB. MORE THAN ANYTHING ELSE, ARMIES LIVE OR DIE BASED UPON THE QUALITY OF THEIR LOGISTICS.
VITAL MAYBE, BUT NOT VERY HEROIC.
POOR GUY. HE WAS SO EARNEST IN TRAINING.
HE'LL GET OVER IT. WE CAN'T WORRY ABOUT HURT FEELINGS WHEN OUR SURVIVAL'S ON THE LINE.
SO, IT LOOKS LIKE WE'RE DONE WITH WAR STUFF FOR NOW, MR. BLUE. I'M GOING TO DRIVE TODAY'S SUPPLY TRUCK DOWN TO THE CITY. CARE TO GO WITH?
THIS WOULDN'T BE ANOTHER EXCUSE TO SPEND HOURS IN FRONT OF THE MAGIC MIRROR WATCHING THE FLY SHOW, WOULD IT?
IT MIGHT. INTERESTED?
WELL, SINCE YOU'RE OBVIOUSLY TWISTING MY ARM, OKAY. COUNT ME IN.
AFTER ALL, I'M STILL A HARDENED CRIMINAL DOING TIME UP HERE AT THE FARM, AND I HAVE TO DO EVERYTHING YOU ORDER ME TO DO.

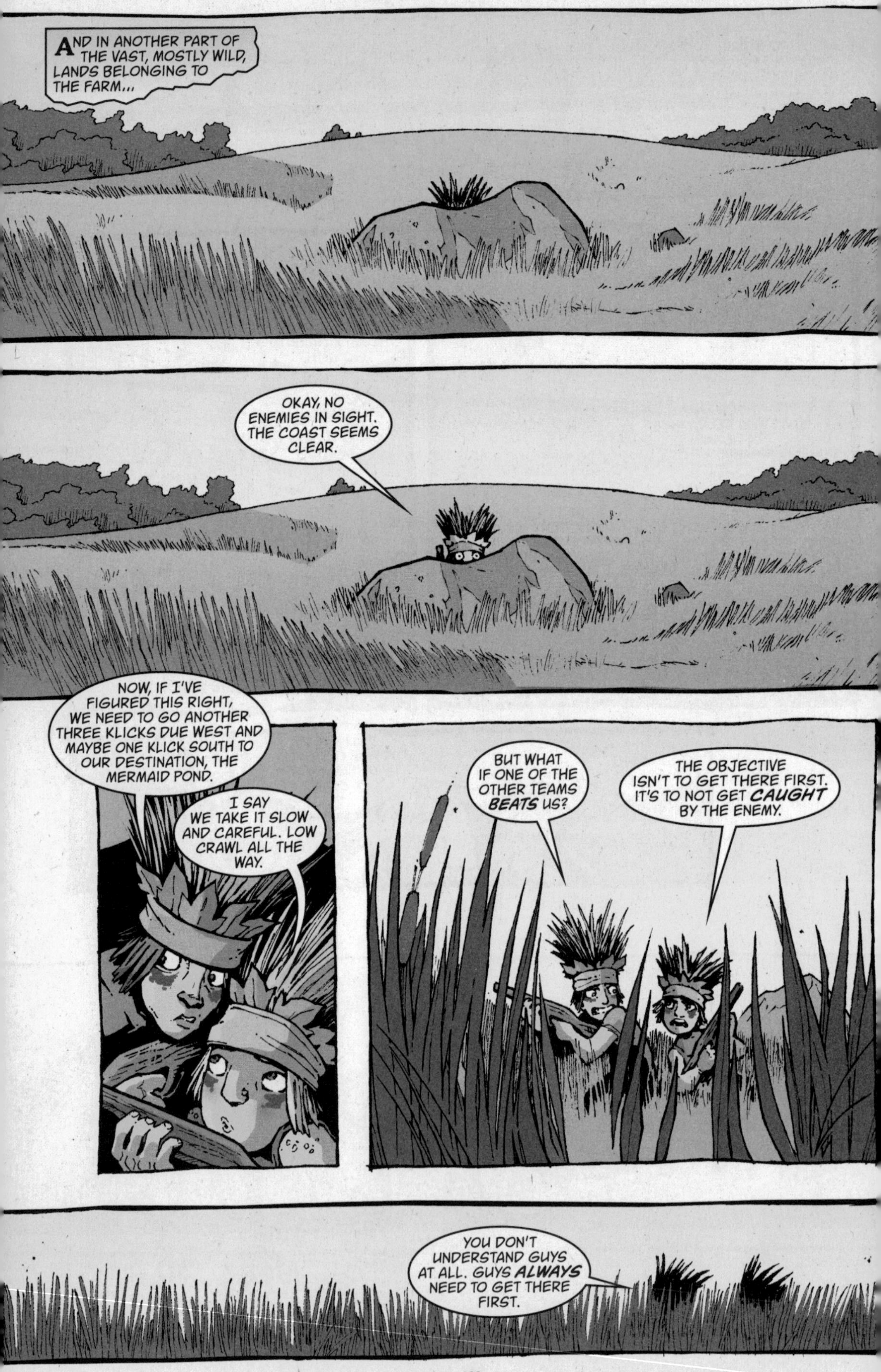
AND IN ANOTHER PART OF THE VAST, MOSTLY WILD, LANDS BELONGING TO THE FARM...
OKAY, NO ENEMIES IN SIGHT. THE COAST SEEMS CLEAR.
NOW, IF I'VE FIGURED THIS RIGHT, WE NEED TO GO ANOTHER THREE KLICKS DUE WEST AND MAYBE ONE KLICK SOUTH TO OUR DESTINATION, THE MERMAID POND.
I SAY WE TAKE IT SLOW AND CAREFUL. LOW CRAWL ALL THE WAY.
BUT WHAT IF ONE OF THE OTHER TEAMS BEATS US?
THE OBJECTIVE ISN'T TO GET THERE FIRST. IT'S TO NOT GET CAUGHT BY THE ENEMY.
YOU DON'T UNDERSTAND GUYS AT ALL. GUYS ALWAYS NEED TO GET THERE FIRST.

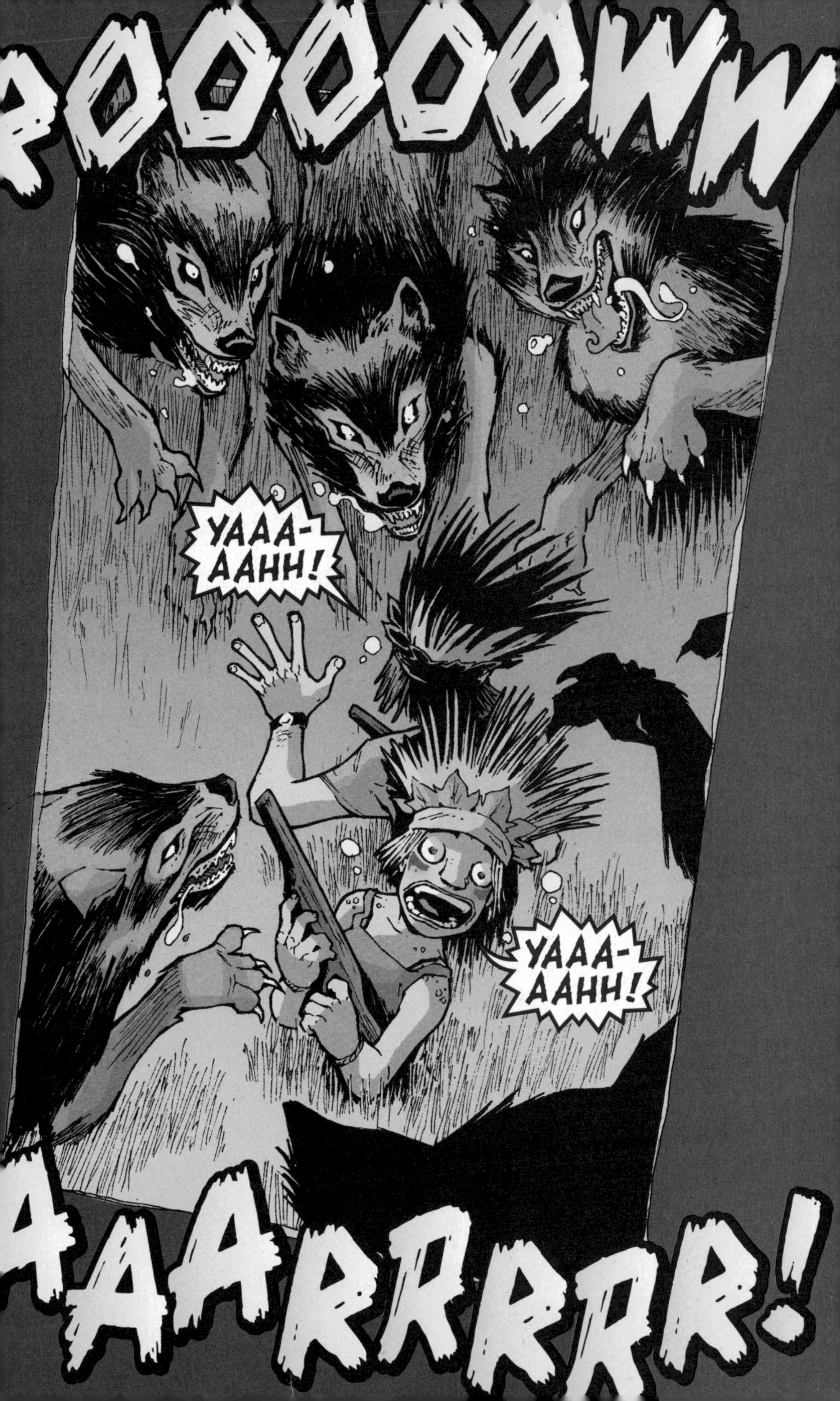
ROOOOOWN
YAAA-AAHH!
YAAA-AAHH!
AAARRRRR!

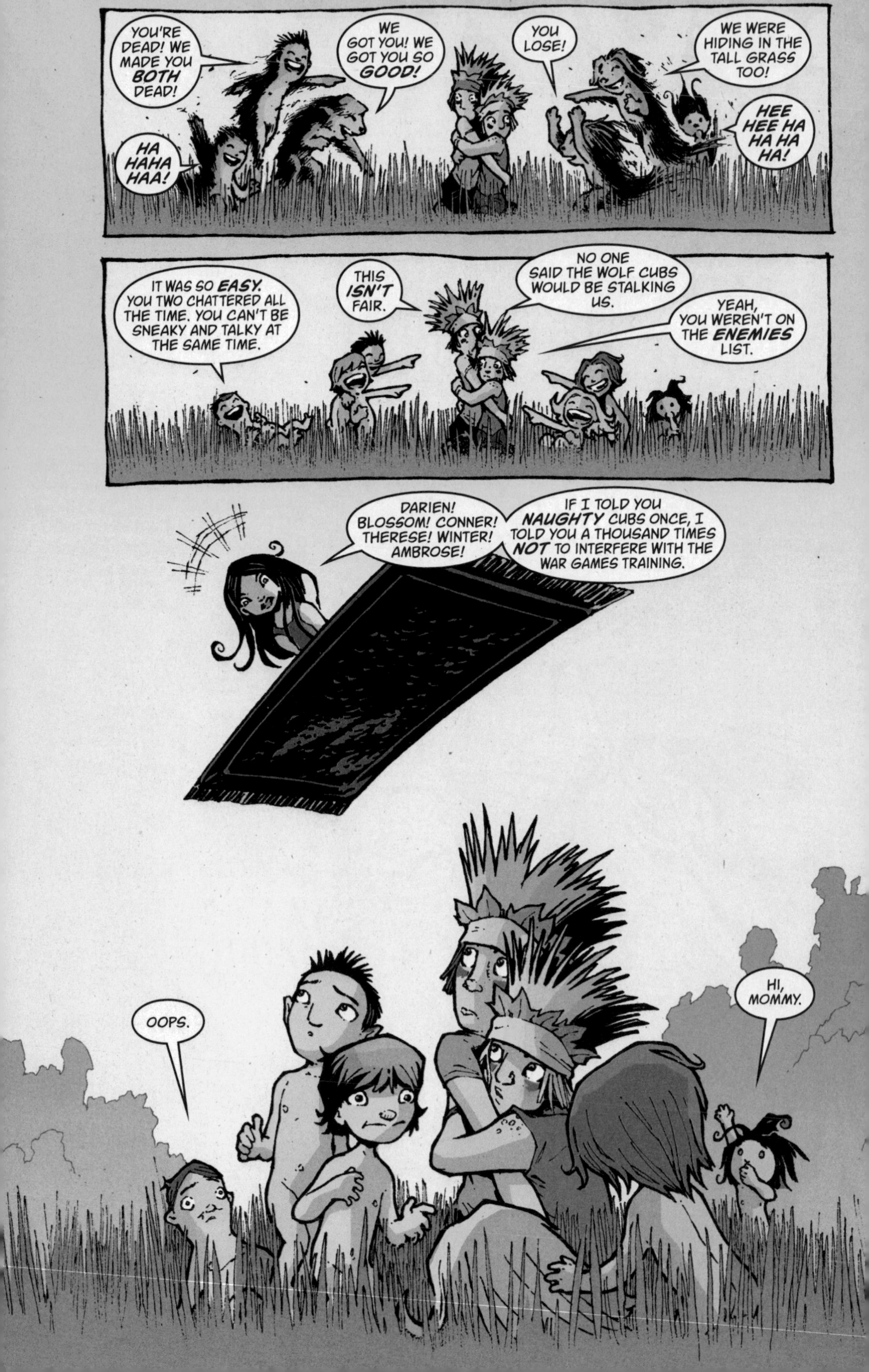

YOU'RE DEAD! WE MADE YOU BOTH DEAD!
HA HAHA HAA!
WE GOT YOU! WE GOT YOU SO GOOD!
YOU LOSE!
WE WERE HIDING IN THE TALL GRASS TOO!
HEE HEE HA HA HA HA!
IT WAS SO EASY. YOU TWO CHATTERED ALL THE TIME. YOU CAN'T BE SNEAKY AND TALKY AT THE SAME TIME.
THIS ISN'T FAIR.
NO ONE SAID THE WOLF CUBS WOULD BE STALKING US.
YEAH, YOU WEREN'T ON THE ENEMIES LIST.
DARIEN! BLOSSOM! CONNER! THERESE! WINTER! AMBROSE!
IF I TOLD YOU NAUGHTY CUBS ONCE, I TOLD YOU A THOUSAND TIMES NOT TO INTERFERE WITH THE WAR GAMES TRAINING.
OOPS.
HI, MOMMY.

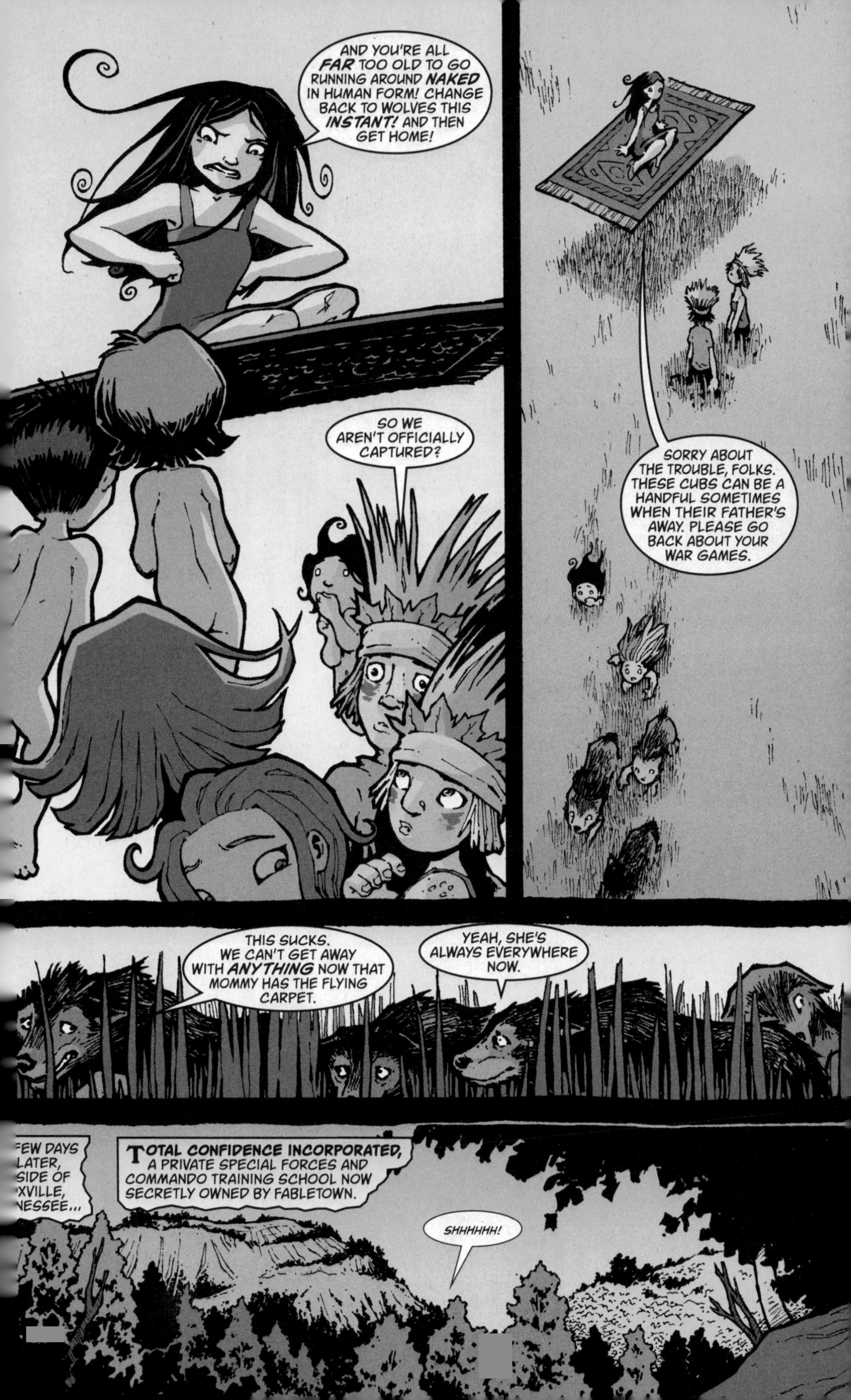
AND YOU'RE ALL FAR TOO OLD TO GO RUNNING AROUND NAKED IN HUMAN FORM! CHANGE BACK TO WOLVES THIS INSTANT! AND THEN GET HOME!
SO WE AREN'T OFFICIALLY CAPTURED?
SORRY ABOUT THE TROUBLE, FOLKS. THESE CUBS CAN BE A HANDFUL SOMETIMES WHEN THEIR FATHER'S AWAY. PLEASE GO BACK ABOUT YOUR WAR GAMES.
THIS SUCKS. WE CAN'T GET AWAY WITH ANYTHING NOW THAT MOMMY HAS THE FLYING CARPET.
YEAH, SHE'S ALWAYS EVERYWHERE NOW.
FEW DAYS LATER, SIDE OF XVILLE, NESSEE...
TOTAL CONFIDENCE INCORPORATED, A PRIVATE SPECIAL FORCES AND COMMANDO TRAINING SCHOOL NOW SECRETLY OWNED BY FABLETOWN.
SHHHHHH!

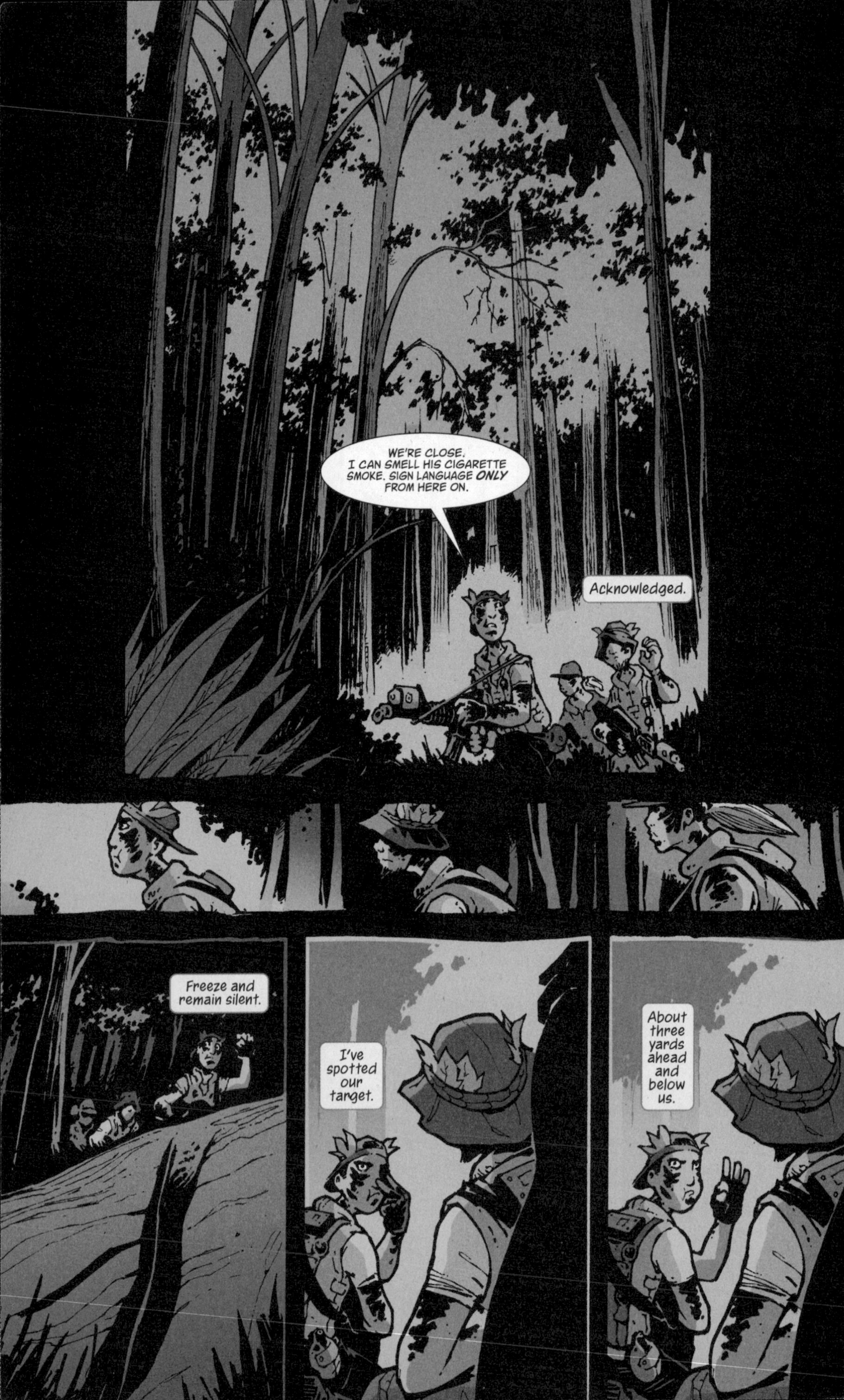
WE'RE CLOSE. I CAN SMELL HIS CIGARETTE SMOKE. SIGN LANGUAGE ONLY FROM HERE ON.
Acknowledged.
Freeze and remain silent.
I've spotted our target.
About three yards ahead and below us.

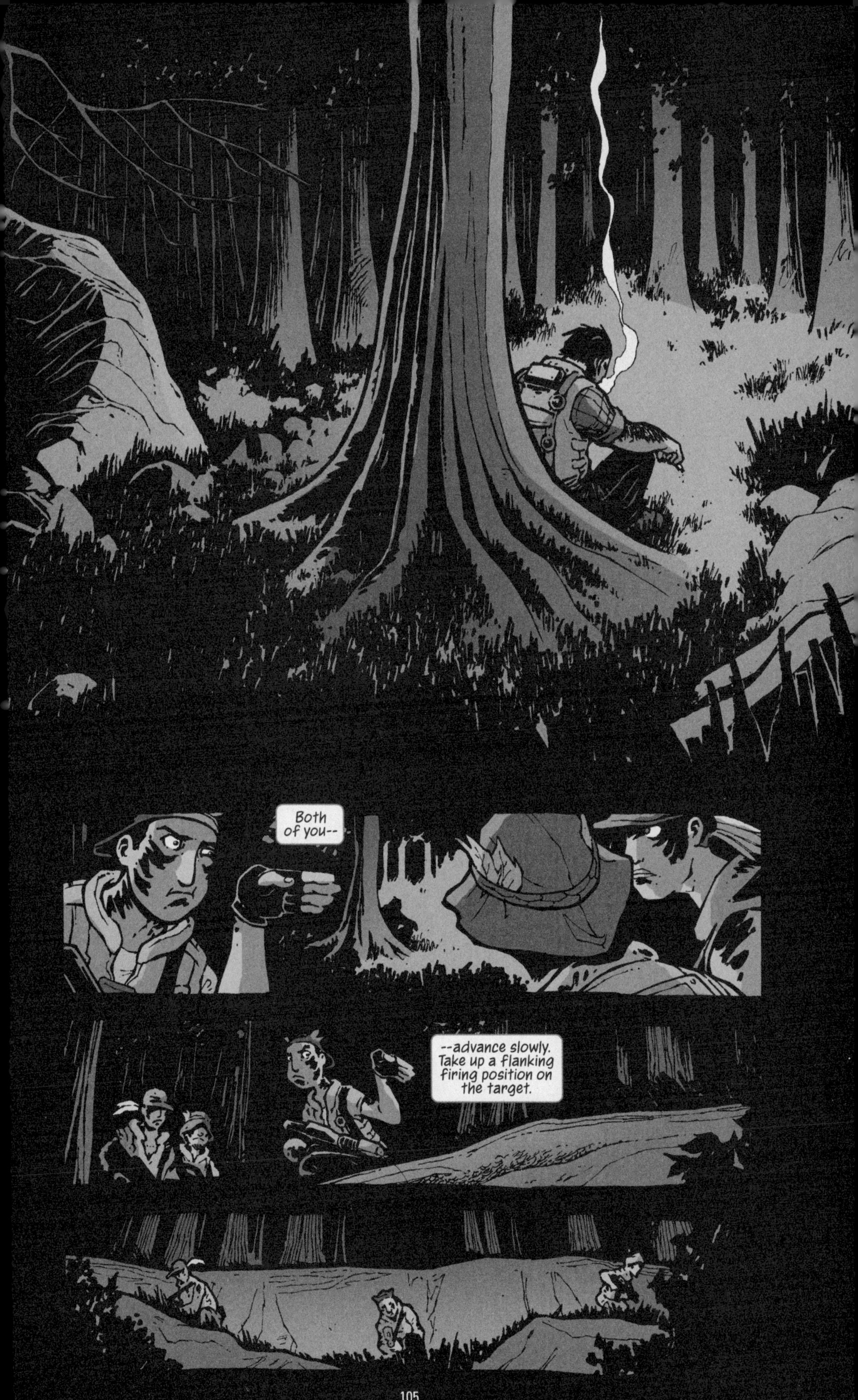
Both of you--
--advance slowly. Take up a flanking firing position on the target.

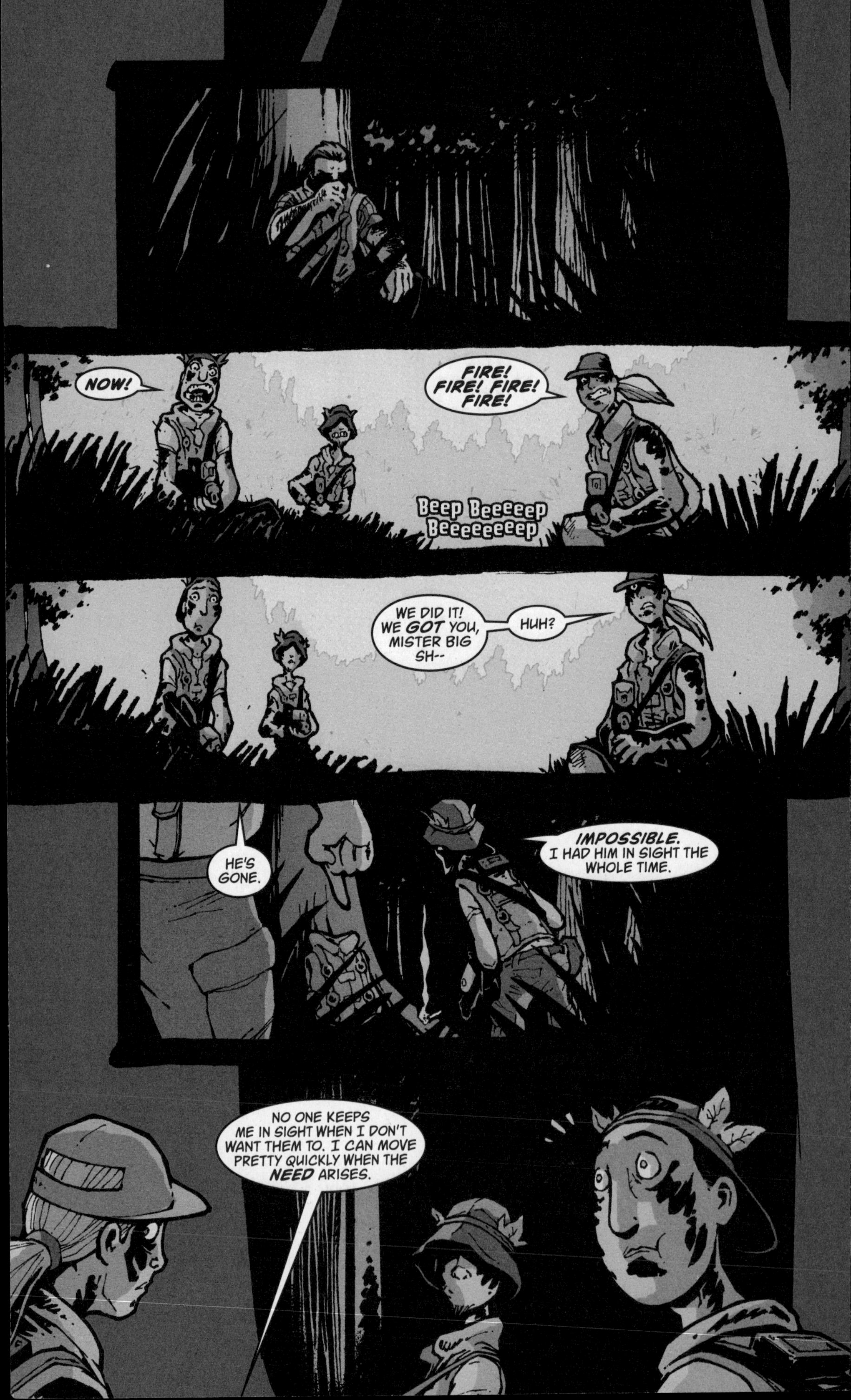
NOW!
FIRE! FIRE! FIRE! FIRE!
Beep Beeeeep Beeeeeeeep
WE DID IT! WE GOT YOU, MISTER BIG SH--
HUH?
HE'S GONE.
IMPOSSIBLE. I HAD HIM IN SIGHT THE WHOLE TIME.
NO ONE KEEPS ME IN SIGHT WHEN I DON'T WANT THEM TO. I CAN MOVE PRETTY QUICKLY WHEN THE NEED ARISES.

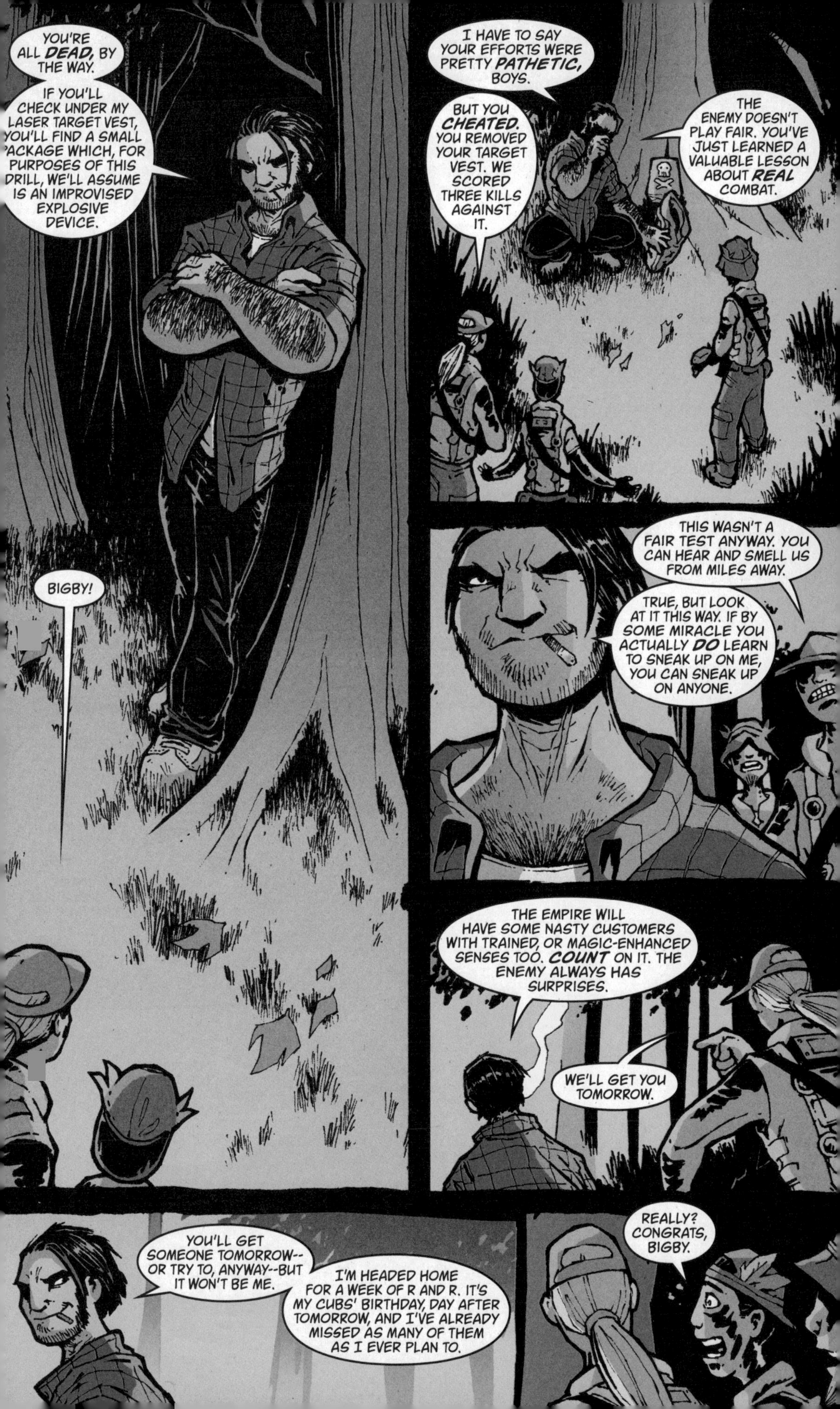
YOU'RE ALL **DEAD,** BY THE WAY.
IF YOU'LL CHECK UNDER MY LASER TARGET VEST, YOU'LL FIND A SMALL PACKAGE WHICH, FOR PURPOSES OF THIS DRILL, WE'LL ASSUME IS AN IMPROVISED EXPLOSIVE DEVICE.
BIGBY!
I HAVE TO SAY YOUR EFFORTS WERE PRETTY **PATHETIC,** BOYS.
BUT YOU **CHEATED.** YOU REMOVED YOUR TARGET VEST. WE SCORED THREE KILLS AGAINST IT.
THE ENEMY DOESN'T PLAY FAIR. YOU'VE JUST LEARNED A VALUABLE LESSON ABOUT **REAL** COMBAT.
THIS WASN'T A FAIR TEST ANYWAY. YOU CAN HEAR AND SMELL US FROM MILES AWAY.
TRUE, BUT LOOK AT IT THIS WAY. IF BY SOME MIRACLE YOU ACTUALLY **DO** LEARN TO SNEAK UP ON ME, YOU CAN SNEAK UP ON ANYONE.
THE EMPIRE WILL HAVE SOME NASTY CUSTOMERS WITH TRAINED, OR MAGIC-ENHANCED SENSES TOO. **COUNT** ON IT. THE ENEMY ALWAYS HAS SURPRISES.
WE'LL GET YOU TOMORROW.
YOU'LL GET SOMEONE TOMORROW--OR TRY TO, ANYWAY--BUT IT WON'T BE ME.
I'M HEADED HOME FOR A WEEK OF R AND R. IT'S MY CUBS' BIRTHDAY, DAY AFTER TOMORROW, AND I'VE ALREADY MISSED AS MANY OF THEM AS I EVER PLAN TO.
REALLY? CONGRATS, BIGBY.

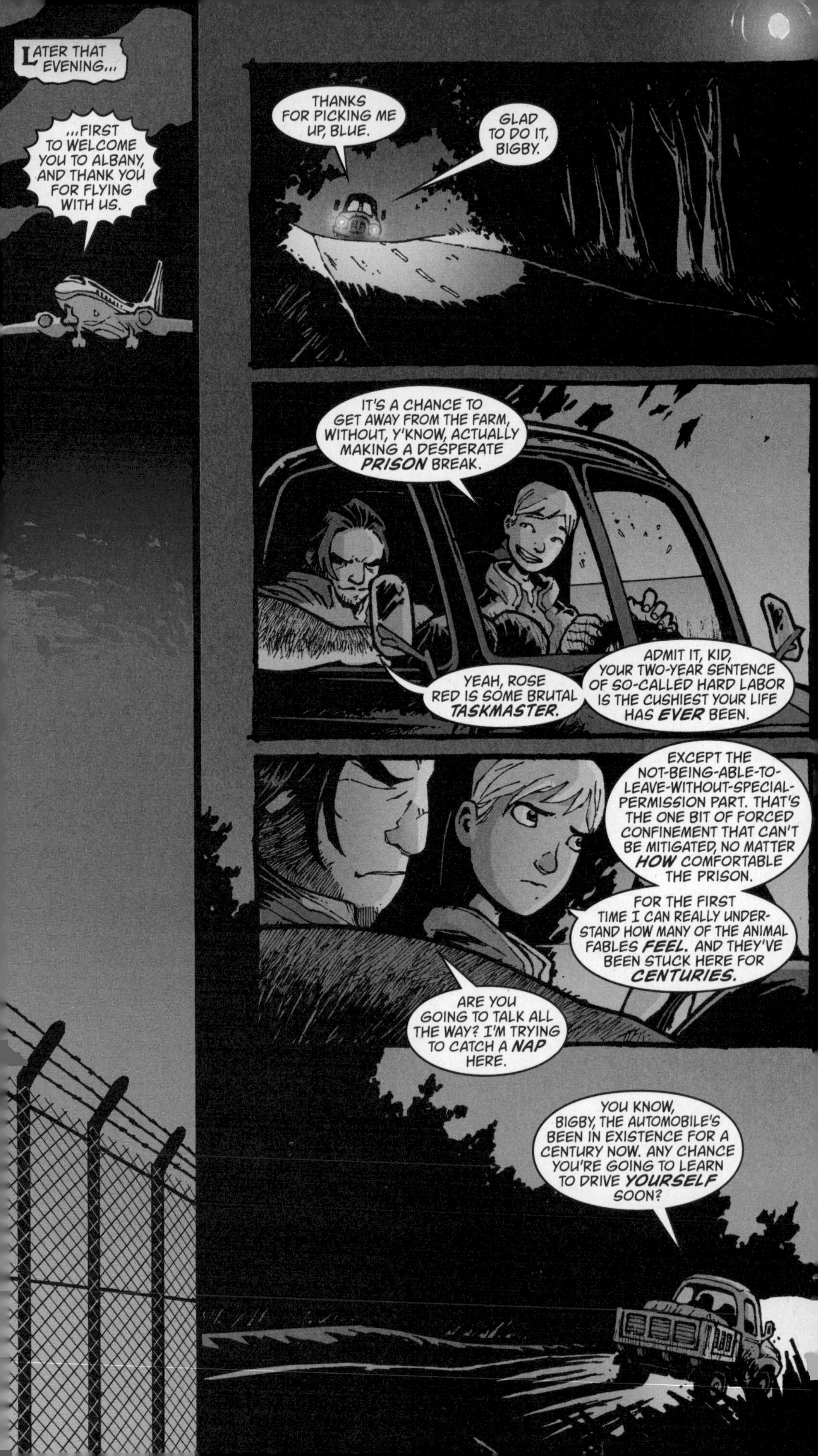
LATER THAT EVENING...
...FIRST TO WELCOME YOU TO ALBANY, AND THANK YOU FOR FLYING WITH US.
THANKS FOR PICKING ME UP, BLUE.
GLAD TO DO IT, BIGBY.
IT'S A CHANCE TO GET AWAY FROM THE FARM, WITHOUT, Y'KNOW, ACTUALLY MAKING A DESPERATE PRISON BREAK.
YEAH, ROSE RED IS SOME BRUTAL TASKMASTER.
ADMIT IT, KID, YOUR TWO-YEAR SENTENCE OF SO-CALLED HARD LABOR IS THE CUSHIEST YOUR LIFE HAS EVER BEEN.
EXCEPT THE NOT-BEING-ABLE-TO-LEAVE-WITHOUT-SPECIAL-PERMISSION PART. THAT'S THE ONE BIT OF FORCED CONFINEMENT THAT CAN'T BE MITIGATED, NO MATTER HOW COMFORTABLE THE PRISON.
FOR THE FIRST TIME I CAN REALLY UNDERSTAND HOW MANY OF THE ANIMAL FABLES FEEL. AND THEY'VE BEEN STUCK HERE FOR CENTURIES.
ARE YOU GOING TO TALK ALL THE WAY? I'M TRYING TO CATCH A NAP HERE.
YOU KNOW, BIGBY, THE AUTOMOBILE'S BEEN IN EXISTENCE FOR A CENTURY NOW. ANY CHANCE YOU'RE GOING TO LEARN TO DRIVE YOURSELF SOON?

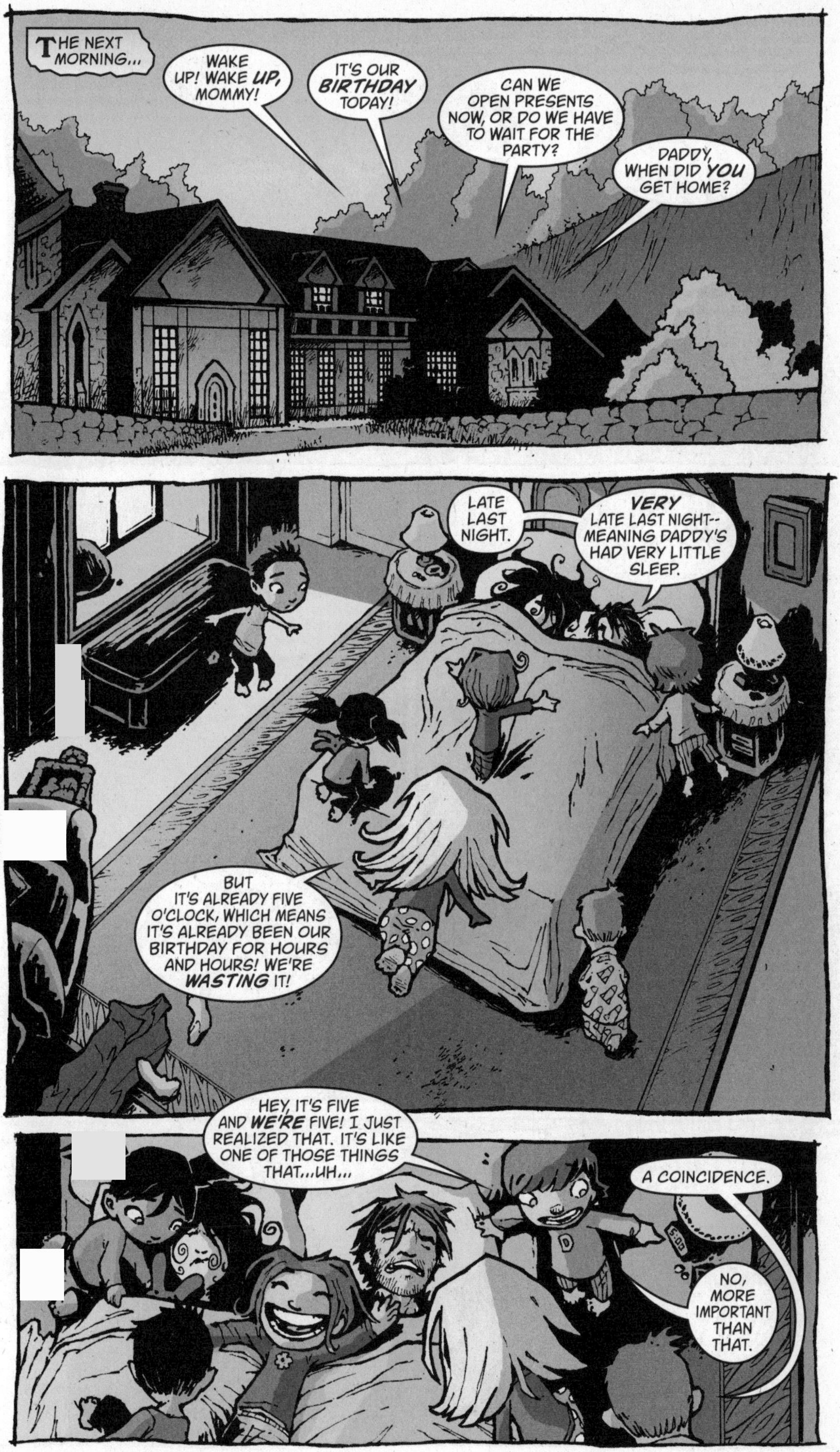
THE NEXT MORNING...
WAKE UP! WAKE UP, MOMMY!
IT'S OUR BIRTHDAY TODAY!
CAN WE OPEN PRESENTS NOW, OR DO WE HAVE TO WAIT FOR THE PARTY?
DADDY, WHEN DID YOU GET HOME?
LATE LAST NIGHT.
VERY LATE LAST NIGHT-- MEANING DADDY'S HAD VERY LITTLE SLEEP.
BUT IT'S ALREADY FIVE O'CLOCK, WHICH MEANS IT'S ALREADY BEEN OUR BIRTHDAY FOR HOURS AND HOURS! WE'RE WASTING IT!
HEY, IT'S FIVE AND WE'RE FIVE! I JUST REALIZED THAT. IT'S LIKE ONE OF THOSE THINGS THAT...UH...
A COINCIDENCE.
NO, MORE IMPORTANT THAN THAT.

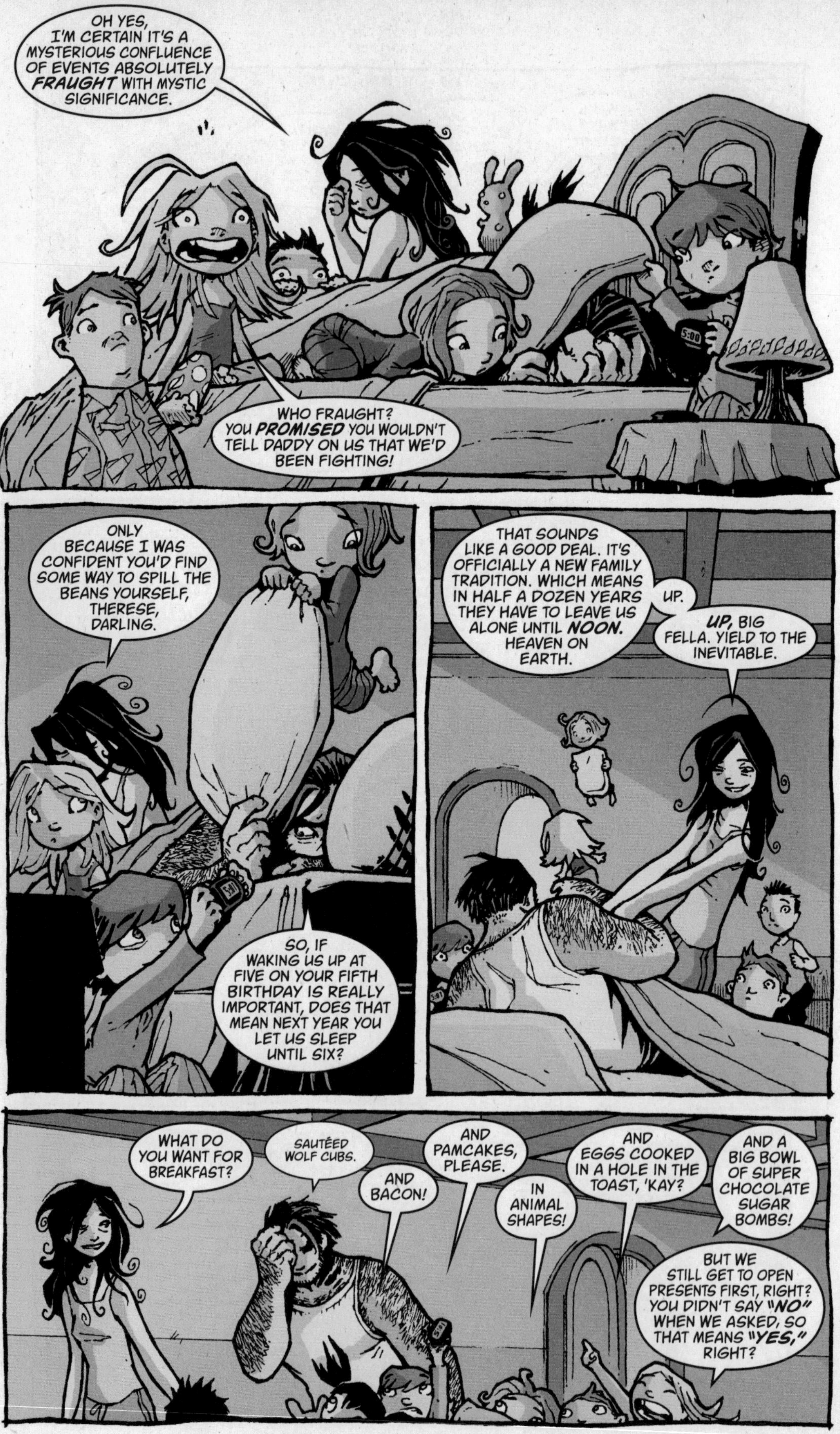
OH YES, I'M CERTAIN IT'S A MYSTERIOUS CONFLUENCE OF EVENTS ABSOLUTELY FRAUGHT WITH MYSTIC SIGNIFICANCE.
WHO FRAUGHT? YOU PROMISED YOU WOULDN'T TELL DADDY ON US THAT WE'D BEEN FIGHTING!
ONLY BECAUSE I WAS CONFIDENT YOU'D FIND SOME WAY TO SPILL THE BEANS YOURSELF, THERESE, DARLING.
SO, IF WAKING US UP AT FIVE ON YOUR FIFTH BIRTHDAY IS REALLY IMPORTANT, DOES THAT MEAN NEXT YEAR YOU LET US SLEEP UNTIL SIX?
THAT SOUNDS LIKE A GOOD DEAL. IT'S OFFICIALLY A NEW FAMILY TRADITION. WHICH MEANS IN HALF A DOZEN YEARS THEY HAVE TO LEAVE US ALONE UNTIL NOON. HEAVEN ON EARTH.
UP.
UP, BIG FELLA. YIELD TO THE INEVITABLE.
WHAT DO YOU WANT FOR BREAKFAST?
SAUTÉED WOLF CUBS.
AND BACON!
AND PAMCAKES, PLEASE.
IN ANIMAL SHAPES!
AND EGGS COOKED IN A HOLE IN THE TOAST, 'KAY?
AND A BIG BOWL OF SUPER CHOCOLATE SUGAR BOMBS!
BUT WE STILL GET TO OPEN PRESENTS FIRST, RIGHT? YOU DIDN'T SAY "NO" WHEN WE ASKED, SO THAT MEANS "YES," RIGHT?

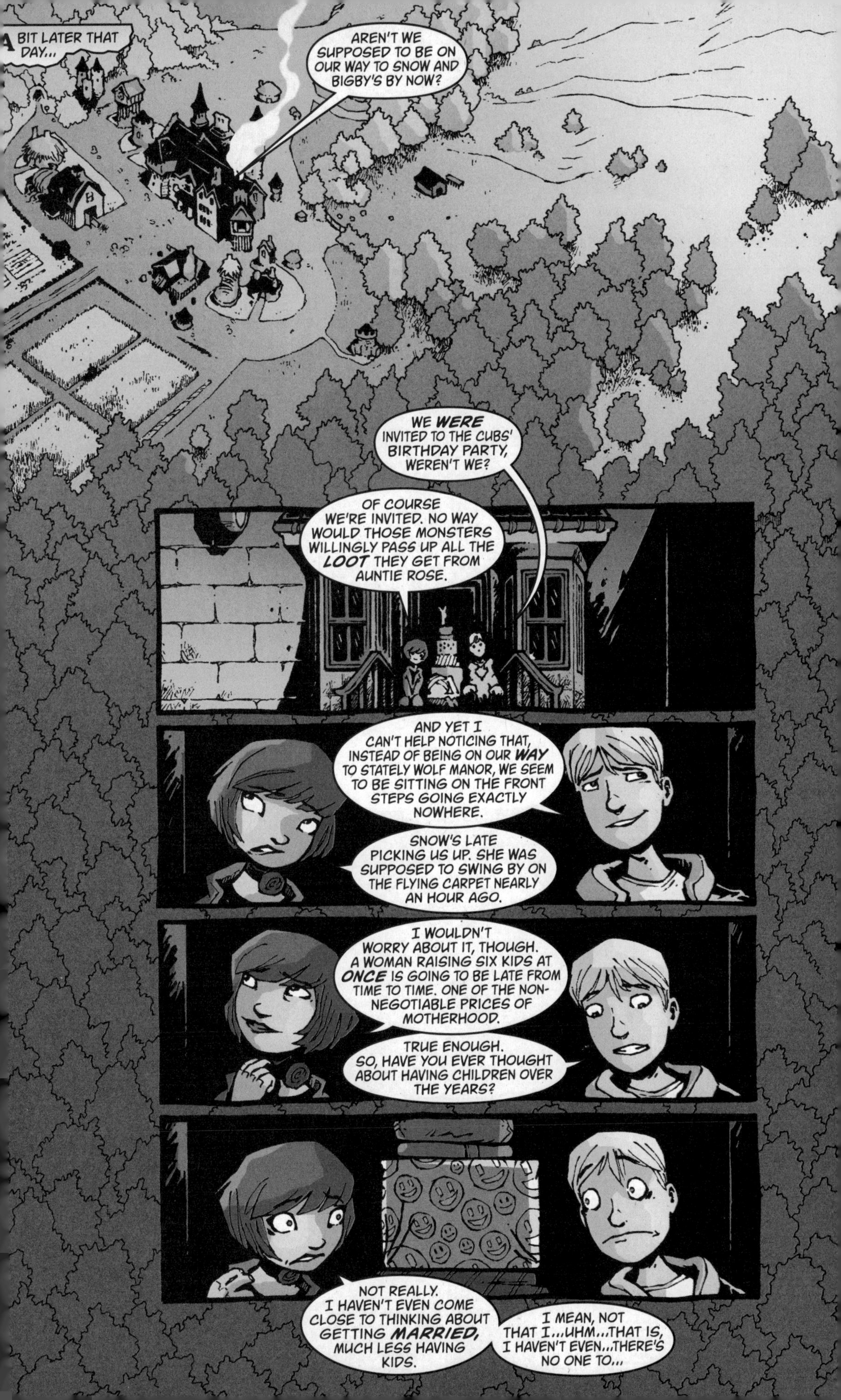
A BIT LATER THAT DAY...
AREN'T WE SUPPOSED TO BE ON OUR WAY TO SNOW AND BIGBY'S BY NOW?
WE WERE INVITED TO THE CUBS' BIRTHDAY PARTY, WEREN'T WE?
OF COURSE WE'RE INVITED. NO WAY WOULD THOSE MONSTERS WILLINGLY PASS UP ALL THE LOOT THEY GET FROM AUNTIE ROSE.
AND YET I CAN'T HELP NOTICING THAT, INSTEAD OF BEING ON OUR WAY TO STATELY WOLF MANOR, WE SEEM TO BE SITTING ON THE FRONT STEPS GOING EXACTLY NOWHERE.
SNOW'S LATE PICKING US UP. SHE WAS SUPPOSED TO SWING BY ON THE FLYING CARPET NEARLY AN HOUR AGO.
I WOULDN'T WORRY ABOUT IT, THOUGH. A WOMAN RAISING SIX KIDS AT ONCE IS GOING TO BE LATE FROM TIME TO TIME. ONE OF THE NON-NEGOTIABLE PRICES OF MOTHERHOOD.
TRUE ENOUGH. SO, HAVE YOU EVER THOUGHT ABOUT HAVING CHILDREN OVER THE YEARS?
NOT REALLY. I HAVEN'T EVEN COME CLOSE TO THINKING ABOUT GETTING MARRIED, MUCH LESS HAVING KIDS.
I MEAN, NOT THAT I...UHM...THAT IS, I HAVEN'T EVEN...THERE'S NO ONE TO...

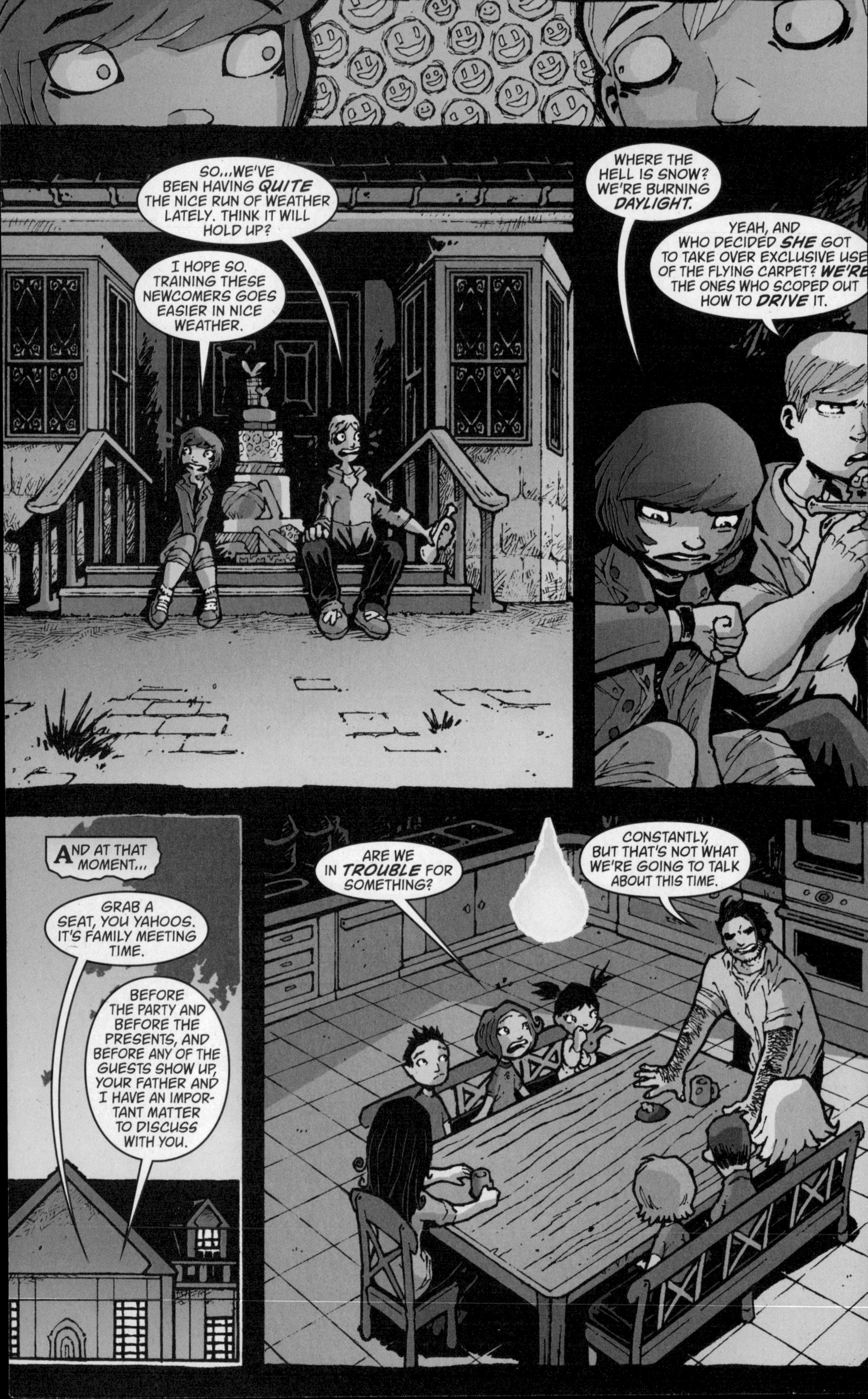
SO...WE'VE BEEN HAVING QUITE THE NICE RUN OF WEATHER LATELY. THINK IT WILL HOLD UP?
I HOPE SO. TRAINING THESE NEWCOMERS GOES EASIER IN NICE WEATHER.
WHERE THE HELL IS SNOW? WE'RE BURNING DAYLIGHT.
YEAH, AND WHO DECIDED SHE GOT TO TAKE OVER EXCLUSIVE USE OF THE FLYING CARPET? WE'RE THE ONES WHO SCOPED OUT HOW TO DRIVE IT.
AND AT THAT MOMENT...
GRAB A SEAT, YOU YAHOOS. IT'S FAMILY MEETING TIME.
BEFORE THE PARTY AND BEFORE THE PRESENTS, AND BEFORE ANY OF THE GUESTS SHOW UP, YOUR FATHER AND I HAVE AN IMPORTANT MATTER TO DISCUSS WITH YOU.
ARE WE IN TROUBLE FOR SOMETHING?
CONSTANTLY, BUT THAT'S NOT WHAT WE'RE GOING TO TALK ABOUT THIS TIME.

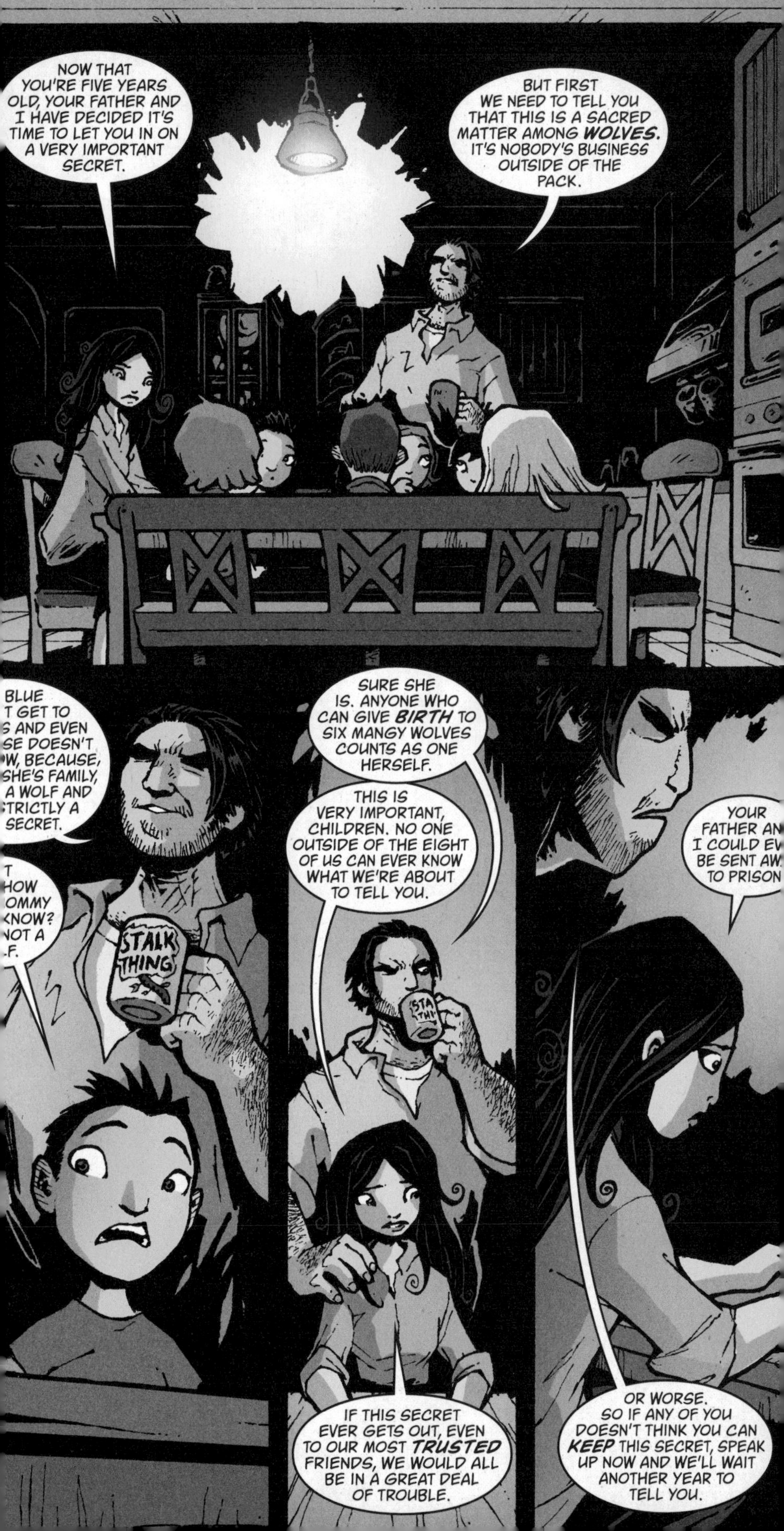
NOW THAT YOU'RE FIVE YEARS OLD, YOUR FATHER AND I HAVE DECIDED IT'S TIME TO LET YOU IN ON A VERY IMPORTANT SECRET.
BUT FIRST WE NEED TO TELL YOU THAT THIS IS A SACRED MATTER AMONG **WOLVES.** IT'S NOBODY'S BUSINESS OUTSIDE OF THE PACK.
BLUE T GET TO S AND EVEN SE DOESN'T W, BECAUSE, SHE'S FAMILY, A WOLF AND STRICTLY A SECRET.
T HOW OMMY KNOW? NOT A .F.
STALK THING
SURE SHE IS. ANYONE WHO CAN GIVE **BIRTH** TO SIX MANGY WOLVES COUNTS AS ONE HERSELF.
THIS IS VERY IMPORTANT, CHILDREN. NO ONE OUTSIDE OF THE EIGHT OF US CAN EVER KNOW WHAT WE'RE ABOUT TO TELL YOU.
IF THIS SECRET EVER GETS OUT, EVEN TO OUR MOST **TRUSTED** FRIENDS, WE WOULD ALL BE IN A GREAT DEAL OF TROUBLE.
YOUR FATHER AN I COULD EV BE SENT AW TO PRISON
OR WORSE. SO IF ANY OF YOU DOESN'T THINK YOU CAN **KEEP** THIS SECRET, SPEAK UP NOW AND WE'LL WAIT ANOTHER YEAR TO TELL YOU.

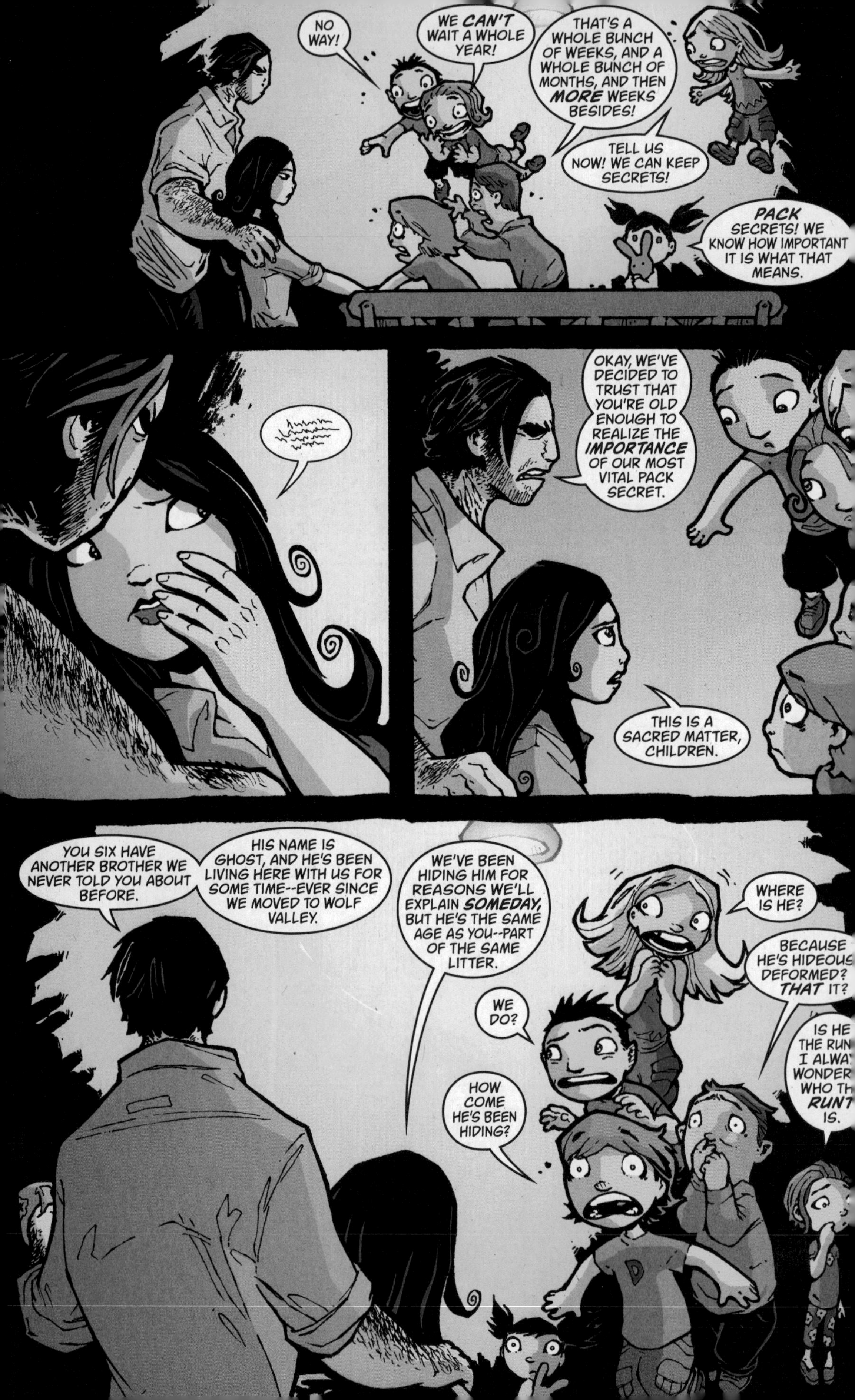
NO WAY!
WE CAN'T WAIT A WHOLE YEAR!
THAT'S A WHOLE BUNCH OF WEEKS, AND A WHOLE BUNCH OF MONTHS, AND THEN MORE WEEKS BESIDES!
TELL US NOW! WE CAN KEEP SECRETS!
PACK SECRETS! WE KNOW HOW IMPORTANT IT IS WHAT THAT MEANS.
OKAY, WE'VE DECIDED TO TRUST THAT YOU'RE OLD ENOUGH TO REALIZE THE IMPORTANCE OF OUR MOST VITAL PACK SECRET.
THIS IS A SACRED MATTER, CHILDREN.
YOU SIX HAVE ANOTHER BROTHER WE NEVER TOLD YOU ABOUT BEFORE.
HIS NAME IS GHOST, AND HE'S BEEN LIVING HERE WITH US FOR SOME TIME--EVER SINCE WE MOVED TO WOLF VALLEY.
WE'VE BEEN HIDING HIM FOR REASONS WE'LL EXPLAIN SOMEDAY, BUT HE'S THE SAME AGE AS YOU--PART OF THE SAME LITTER.
WHERE IS HE?
BECAUSE HE'S HIDEOUS DEFORMED? THAT IT?
WE DO?
HOW COME HE'S BEEN HIDING?

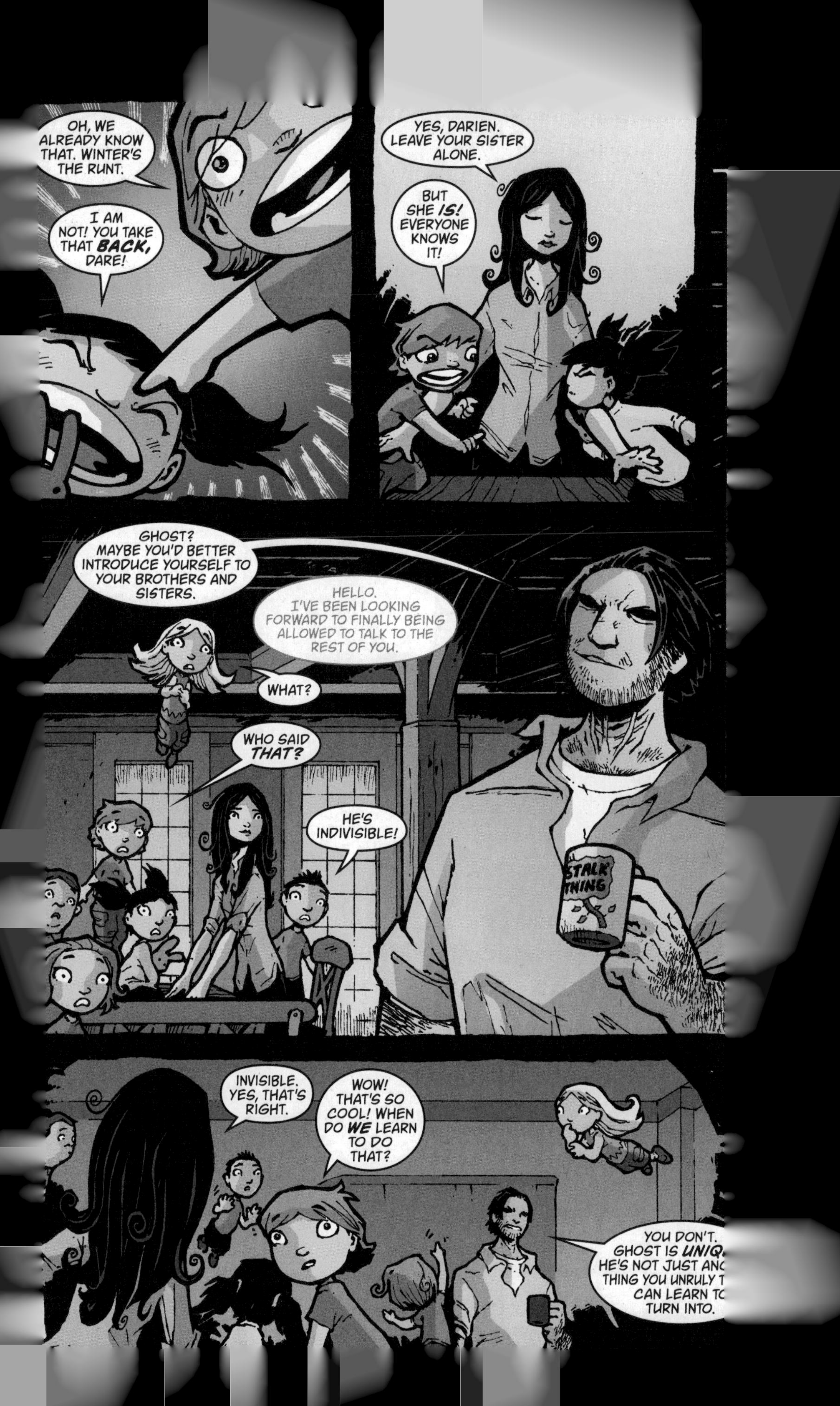

OH, WE ALREADY KNOW THAT. WINTER'S THE RUNT.
I AM NOT! YOU TAKE THAT BACK, DARE!
YES, DARIEN. LEAVE YOUR SISTER ALONE.
BUT SHE IS! EVERYONE KNOWS IT!
GHOST? MAYBE YOU'D BETTER INTRODUCE YOURSELF TO YOUR BROTHERS AND SISTERS.
HELLO. I'VE BEEN LOOKING FORWARD TO FINALLY BEING ALLOWED TO TALK TO THE REST OF YOU.
WHAT?
WHO SAID THAT?
HE'S INDIVISIBLE!
STALK THING
INVISIBLE. YES, THAT'S RIGHT.
WOW! THAT'S SO COOL! WHEN DO WE LEARN TO DO THAT?
YOU DON'T. GHOST IS UNIQ
HE'S NOT JUST ANO
THING YOU UNRULY T
CAN LEARN TO
TURN INTO.

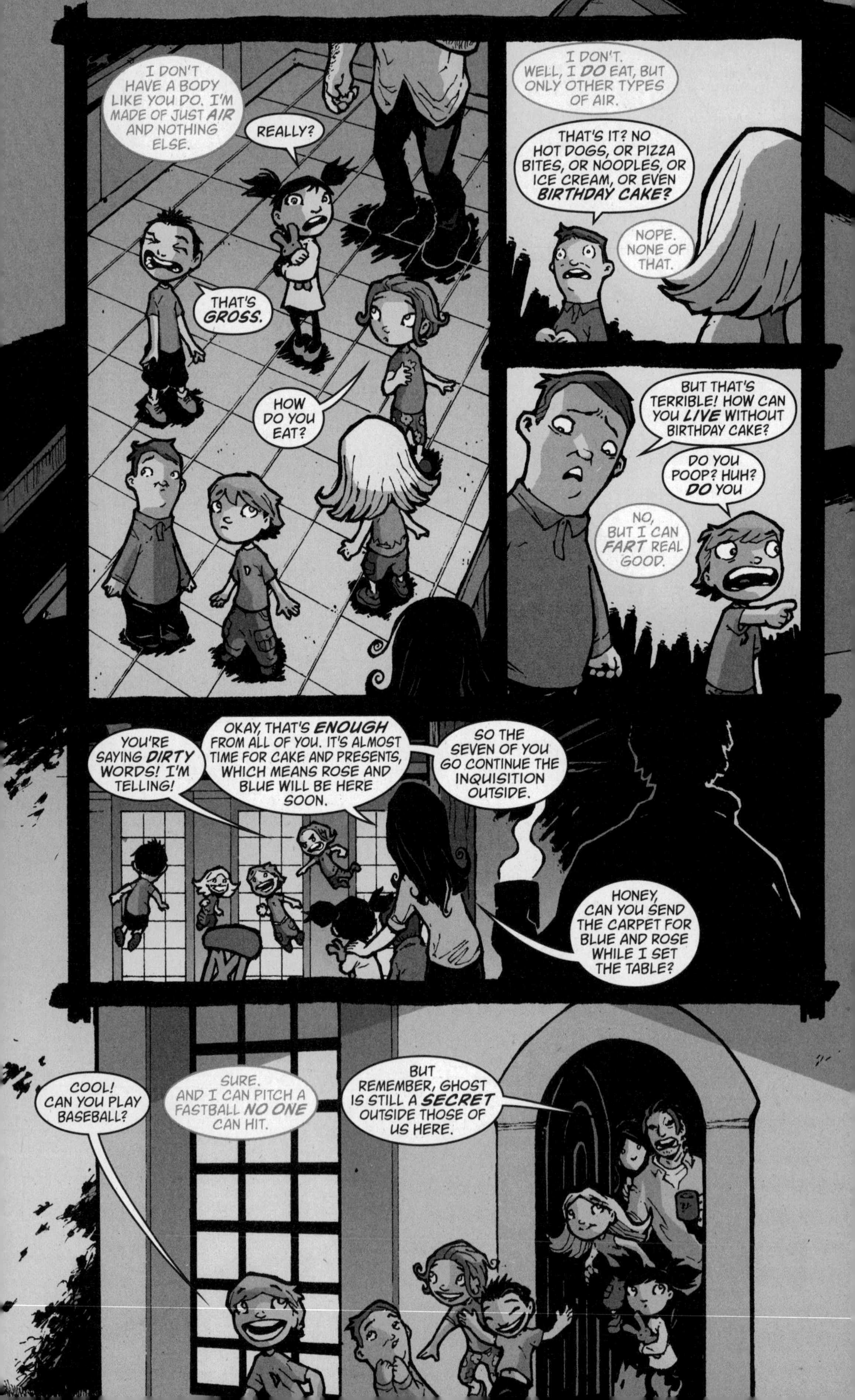

I DON'T HAVE A BODY LIKE YOU DO. I'M MADE OF JUST AIR AND NOTHING ELSE.
REALLY?
THAT'S GROSS.
HOW DO YOU EAT?
I DON'T. WELL, I DO EAT, BUT ONLY OTHER TYPES OF AIR.
THAT'S IT? NO HOT DOGS, OR PIZZA BITES, OR NOODLES, OR ICE CREAM, OR EVEN BIRTHDAY CAKE?
NOPE. NONE OF THAT.
BUT THAT'S TERRIBLE! HOW CAN YOU LIVE WITHOUT BIRTHDAY CAKE?
DO YOU POOP? HUH? DO YOU
NO, BUT I CAN FART REAL GOOD.
YOU'RE SAYING DIRTY WORDS! I'M TELLING!
OKAY, THAT'S ENOUGH FROM ALL OF YOU. IT'S ALMOST TIME FOR CAKE AND PRESENTS, WHICH MEANS ROSE AND BLUE WILL BE HERE SOON.
SO THE SEVEN OF YOU GO CONTINUE THE INQUISITION OUTSIDE.
HONEY, CAN YOU SEND THE CARPET FOR BLUE AND ROSE WHILE I SET THE TABLE?
COOL! CAN YOU PLAY BASEBALL?
SURE. AND I CAN PITCH A FASTBALL NO ONE CAN HIT.
BUT REMEMBER, GHOST IS STILL A SECRET OUTSIDE THOSE OF US HERE.

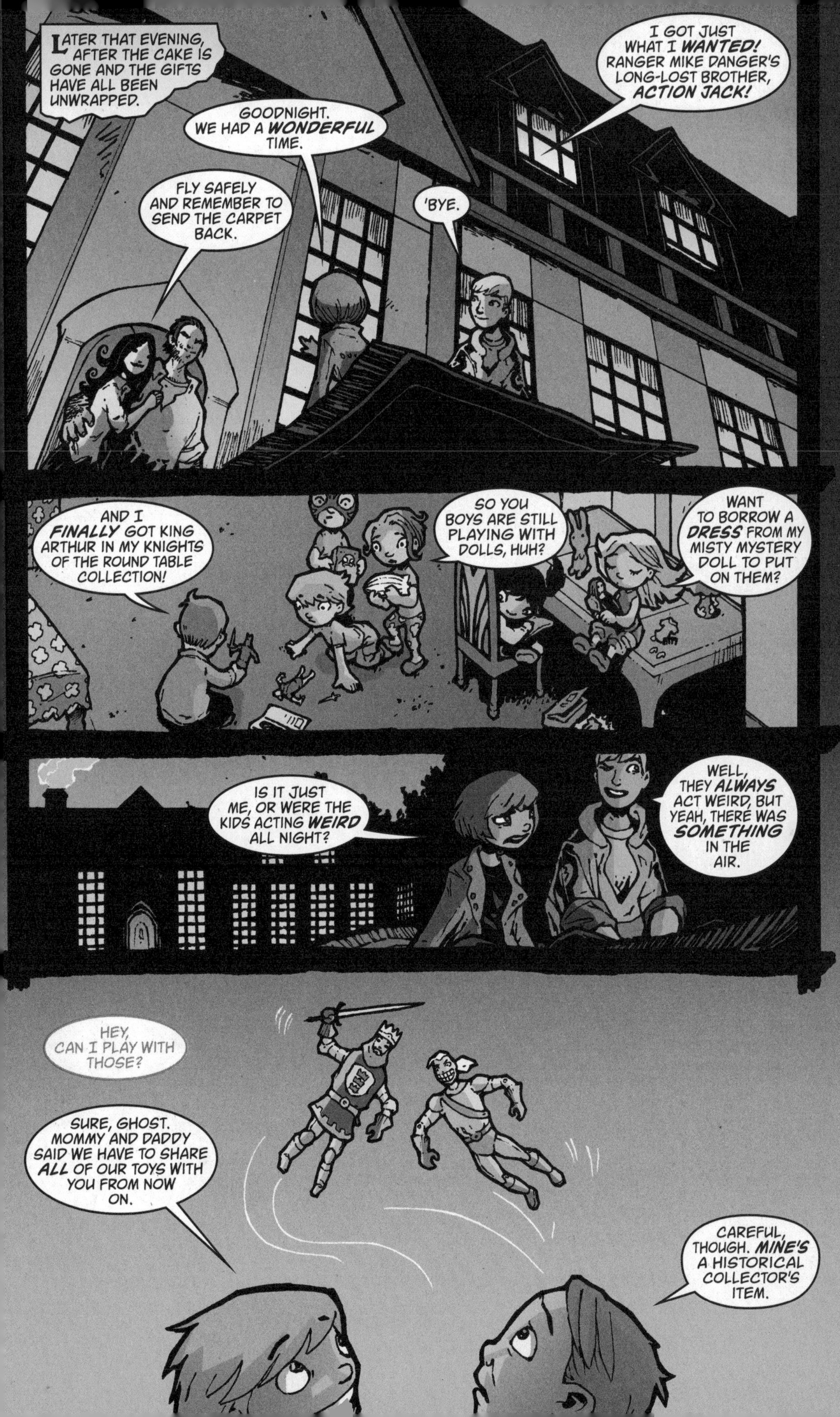
LATER THAT EVENING, AFTER THE CAKE IS GONE AND THE GIFTS HAVE ALL BEEN UNWRAPPED.
GOODNIGHT. WE HAD A WONDERFUL TIME.
FLY SAFELY AND REMEMBER TO SEND THE CARPET BACK.
'BYE.
I GOT JUST WHAT I WANTED! RANGER MIKE DANGER'S LONG-LOST BROTHER, ACTION JACK!
AND I FINALLY GOT KING ARTHUR IN MY KNIGHTS OF THE ROUND TABLE COLLECTION!
SO YOU BOYS ARE STILL PLAYING WITH DOLLS, HUH?
WANT TO BORROW A DRESS FROM MY MISTY MYSTERY DOLL TO PUT ON THEM?
IS IT JUST ME, OR WERE THE KIDS ACTING WEIRD ALL NIGHT?
WELL, THEY ALWAYS ACT WEIRD, BUT YEAH, THERE WAS SOMETHING IN THE AIR.
HEY, CAN I PLAY WITH THOSE?
SURE, GHOST. MOMMY AND DADDY SAID WE HAVE TO SHARE ALL OF OUR TOYS WITH YOU FROM NOW ON.
CAREFUL, THOUGH. MINE'S A HISTORICAL COLLECTOR'S ITEM.

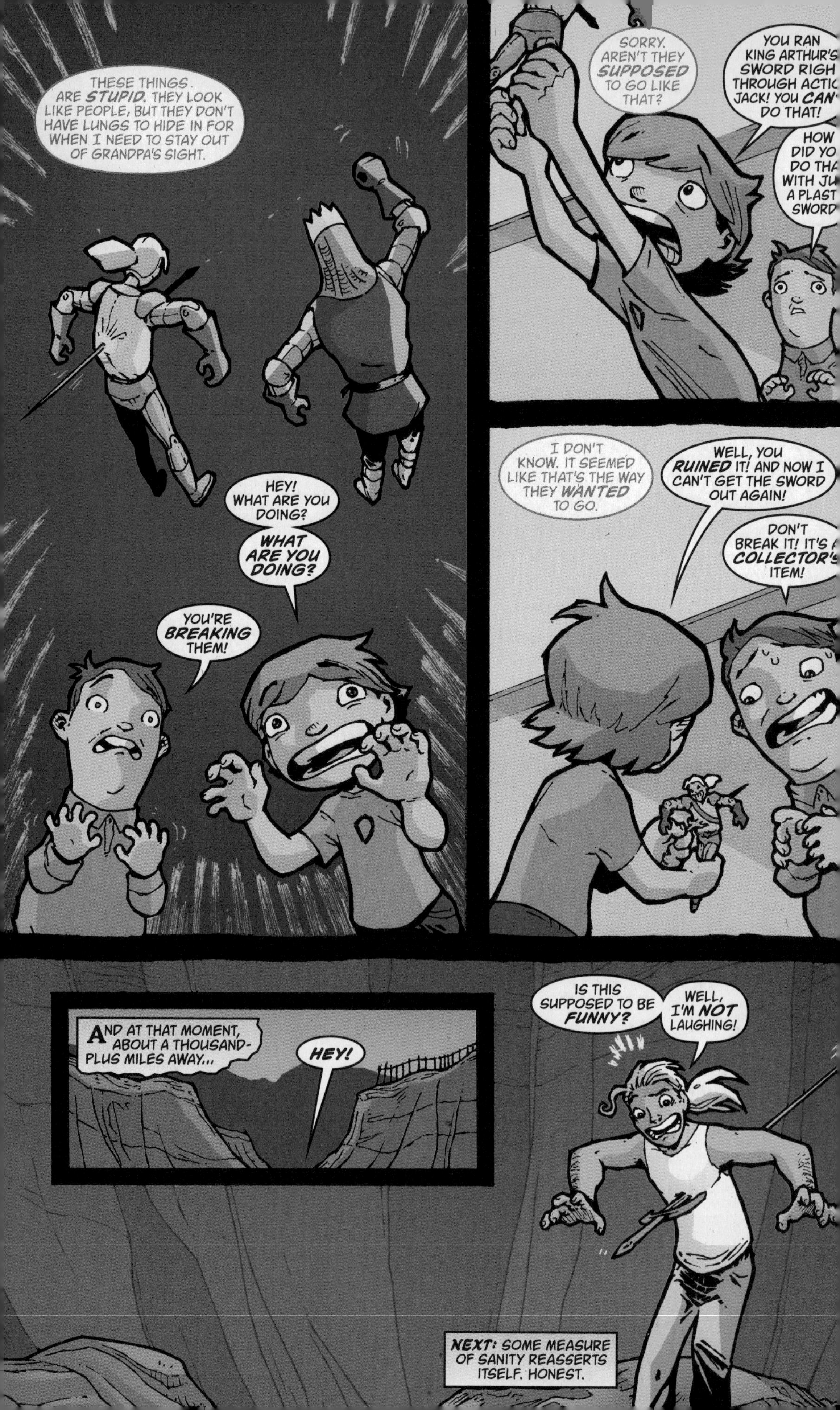

THESE THINGS. ARE STUPID. THEY LOOK LIKE PEOPLE, BUT THEY DON'T HAVE LUNGS TO HIDE IN FOR WHEN I NEED TO STAY OUT OF GRANDPA'S SIGHT.
HEY! WHAT ARE YOU DOING?
WHAT ARE YOU DOING?
YOU'RE BREAKING THEM!
SORRY. AREN'T THEY SUPPOSED TO GO LIKE THAT?
YOU RAN KING ARTHUR'S SWORD RIGH THROUGH ACTIC JACK! YOU CAN DO THAT!
HOW DID YO DO THA WITH JU A PLAST SWORD
I DON'T KNOW. IT SEEMED LIKE THAT'S THE WAY THEY WANTED TO GO.
WELL, YOU RUINED IT! AND NOW I CAN'T GET THE SWORD OUT AGAIN!
DON'T BREAK IT! IT'S A COLLECTOR'S ITEM!
AND AT THAT MOMENT, ABOUT A THOUSAND-PLUS MILES AWAY...
HEY!
IS THIS SUPPOSED TO BE FUNNY?
WELL, I'M NOT LAUGHING!
NEXT: SOME MEASURE OF SANITY REASSERTS ITSELF. HONEST.

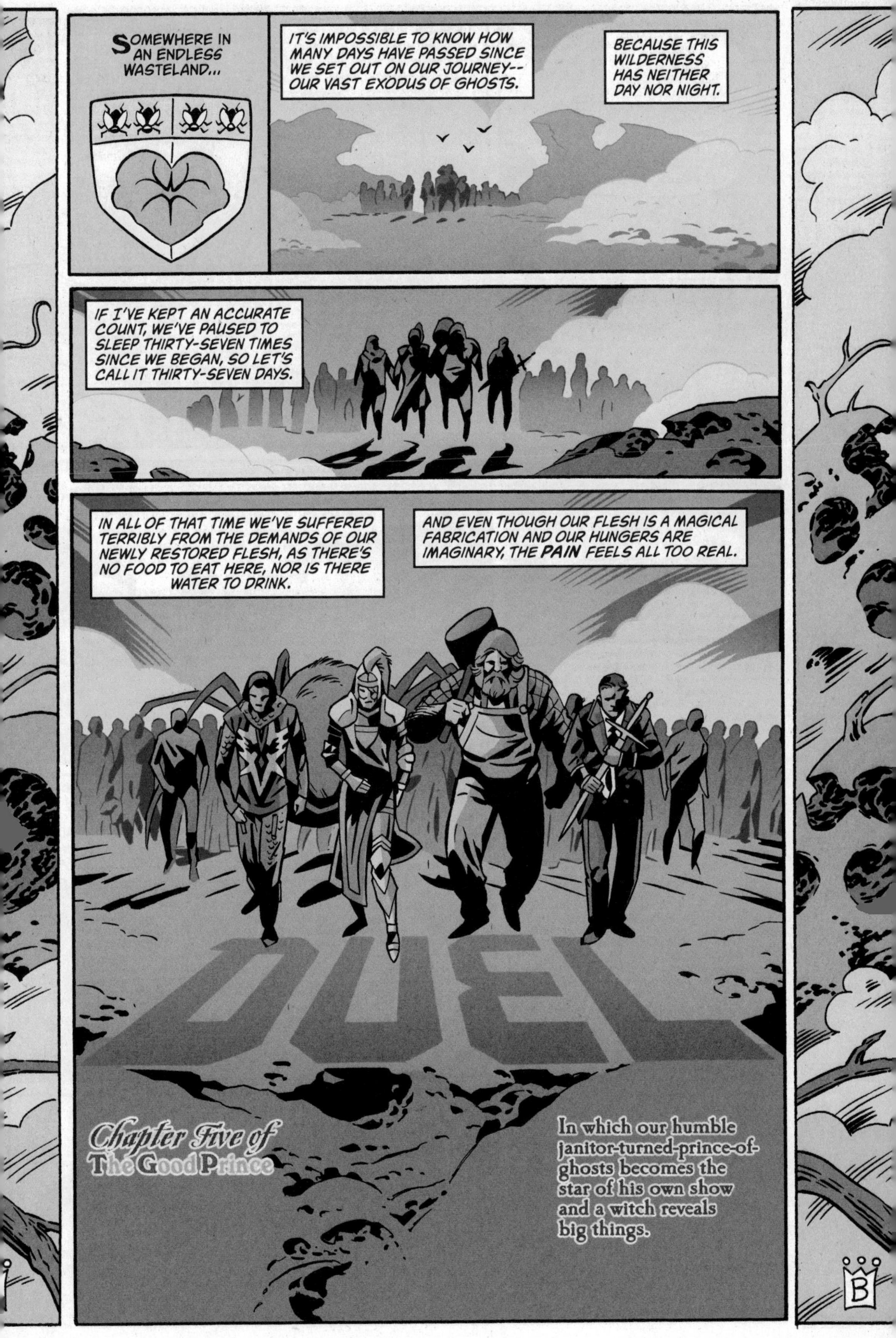
SOMEWHERE IN AN ENDLESS WASTELAND...
IT'S IMPOSSIBLE TO KNOW HOW MANY DAYS HAVE PASSED SINCE WE SET OUT ON OUR JOURNEY--OUR VAST EXODUS OF GHOSTS.
BECAUSE THIS WILDERNESS HAS NEITHER DAY NOR NIGHT.
IF I'VE KEPT AN ACCURATE COUNT, WE'VE PAUSED TO SLEEP THIRTY-SEVEN TIMES SINCE WE BEGAN, SO LET'S CALL IT THIRTY-SEVEN DAYS.
IN ALL OF THAT TIME WE'VE SUFFERED TERRIBLY FROM THE DEMANDS OF OUR NEWLY RESTORED FLESH, AS THERE'S NO FOOD TO EAT HERE, NOR IS THERE WATER TO DRINK.
AND EVEN THOUGH OUR FLESH IS A MAGICAL FABRICATION AND OUR HUNGERS ARE IMAGINARY, THE PAIN FEELS ALL TOO REAL.
DUEL
Chapter Five of The Good Prince
In which our humble janitor-turned-prince-of-ghosts becomes the star of his own show and a witch reveals big things.

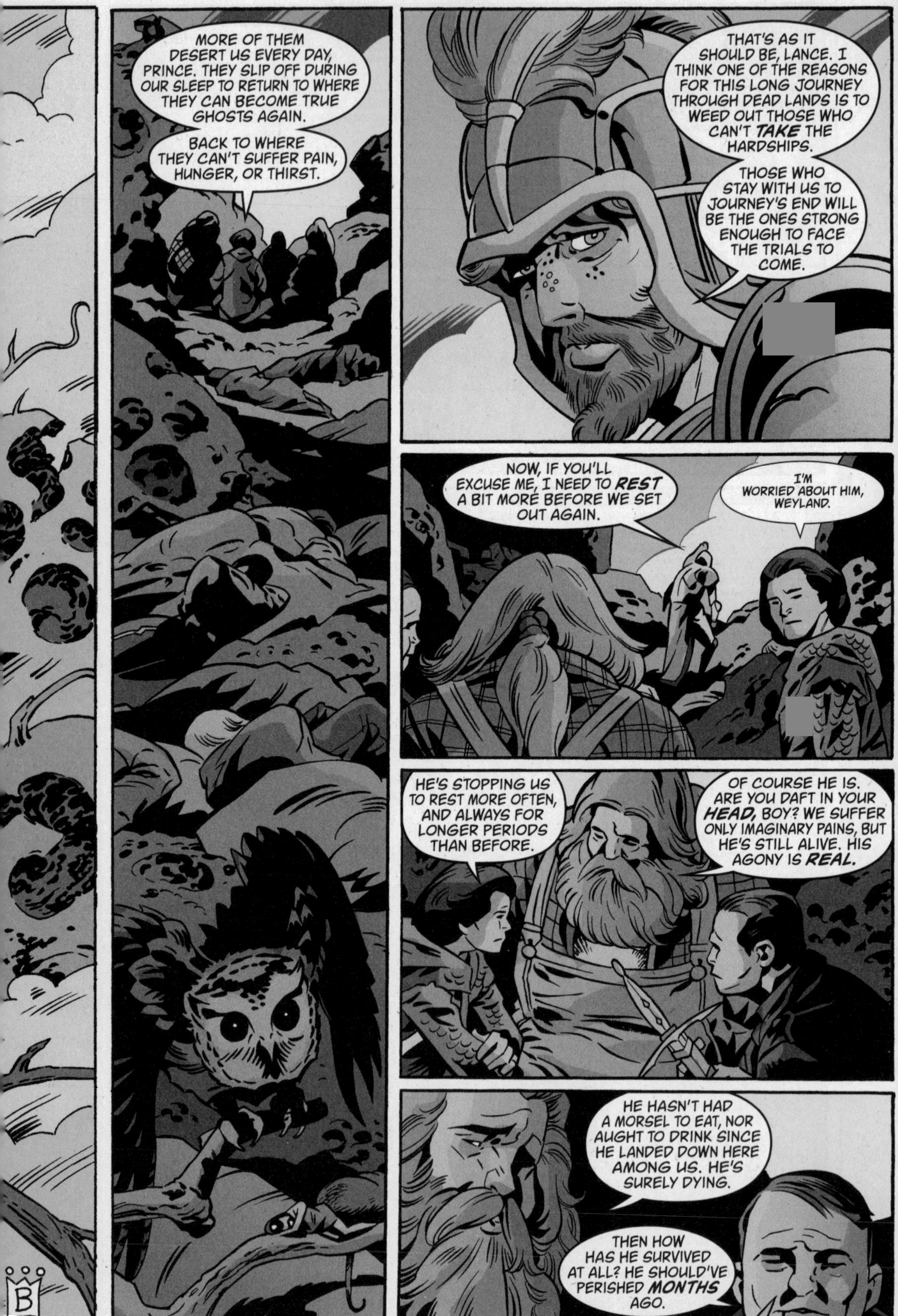
MORE OF THEM DESERT US EVERY DAY, PRINCE. THEY SLIP OFF DURING OUR SLEEP TO RETURN TO WHERE THEY CAN BECOME TRUE GHOSTS AGAIN.
BACK TO WHERE THEY CAN'T SUFFER PAIN, HUNGER, OR THIRST.
THAT'S AS IT SHOULD BE, LANCE. I THINK ONE OF THE REASONS FOR THIS LONG JOURNEY THROUGH DEAD LANDS IS TO WEED OUT THOSE WHO CAN'T TAKE THE HARDSHIPS.
THOSE WHO STAY WITH US TO JOURNEY'S END WILL BE THE ONES STRONG ENOUGH TO FACE THE TRIALS TO COME.
NOW, IF YOU'LL EXCUSE ME, I NEED TO REST A BIT MORE BEFORE WE SET OUT AGAIN.
I'M WORRIED ABOUT HIM, WEYLAND.
HE'S STOPPING US TO REST MORE OFTEN, AND ALWAYS FOR LONGER PERIODS THAN BEFORE.
OF COURSE HE IS. ARE YOU DAFT IN YOUR HEAD, BOY? WE SUFFER ONLY IMAGINARY PAINS, BUT HE'S STILL ALIVE. HIS AGONY IS REAL.
HE HASN'T HAD A MORSEL TO EAT, NOR AUGHT TO DRINK SINCE HE LANDED DOWN HERE AMONG US. HE'S SURELY DYING.
THEN HOW HAS HE SURVIVED AT ALL? HE SHOULD'VE PERISHED MONTHS AGO.

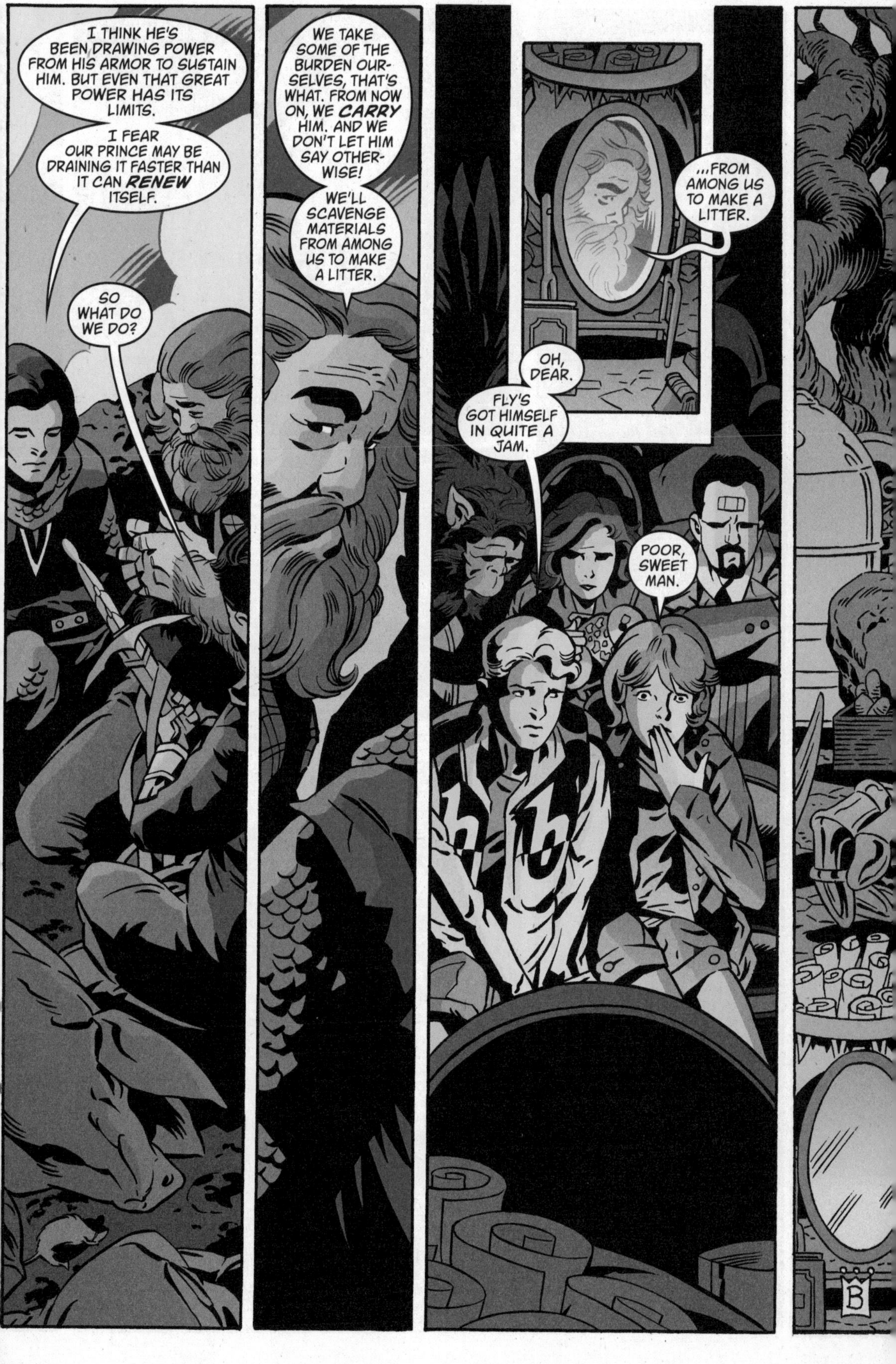
I THINK HE'S BEEN DRAWING POWER FROM HIS ARMOR TO SUSTAIN HIM. BUT EVEN THAT GREAT POWER HAS ITS LIMITS.
I FEAR OUR PRINCE MAY BE DRAINING IT FASTER THAN IT CAN *RENEW* ITSELF.
SO WHAT DO WE DO?
WE TAKE SOME OF THE BURDEN OURSELVES, THAT'S WHAT. FROM NOW ON, WE *CARRY* HIM. AND WE DON'T LET HIM SAY OTHERWISE!
WE'LL SCAVENGE MATERIALS FROM AMONG US TO MAKE A LITTER.
...FROM AMONG US TO MAKE A LITTER.
OH, DEAR.
FLY'S GOT HIMSELF IN QUITE A JAM.
POOR, SWEET MAN.

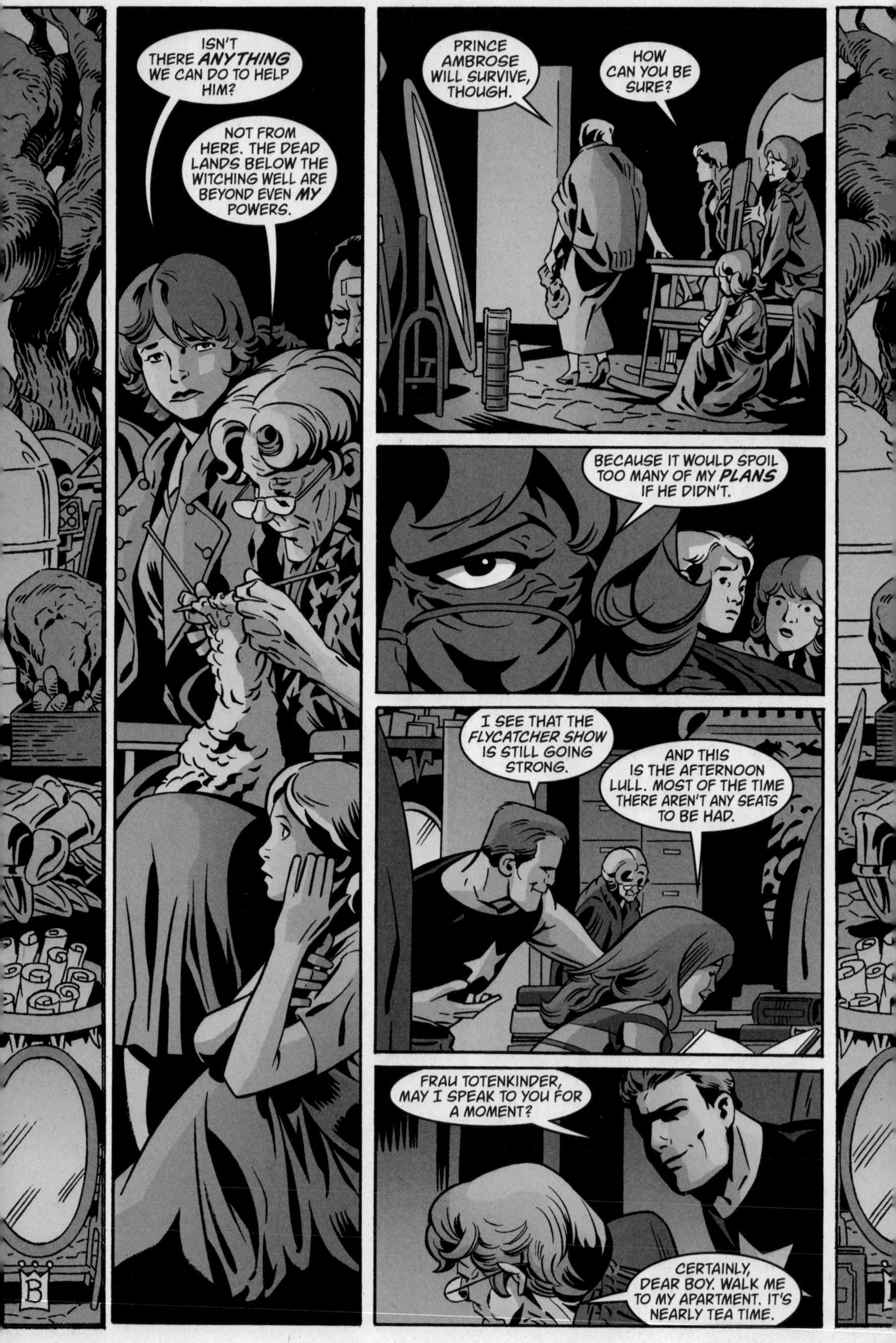
ISN'T THERE ANYTHING WE CAN DO TO HELP HIM?
NOT FROM HERE. THE DEAD LANDS BELOW THE WITCHING WELL ARE BEYOND EVEN MY POWERS.
PRINCE AMBROSE WILL SURVIVE, THOUGH.
HOW CAN YOU BE SURE?
BECAUSE IT WOULD SPOIL TOO MANY OF MY PLANS IF HE DIDN'T.
I SEE THAT THE FLYCATCHER SHOW IS STILL GOING STRONG.
AND THIS IS THE AFTERNOON LULL. MOST OF THE TIME THERE AREN'T ANY SEATS TO BE HAD.
FRAU TOTENKINDER, MAY I SPEAK TO YOU FOR A MOMENT?
CERTAINLY, DEAR BOY. WALK ME TO MY APARTMENT. IT'S NEARLY TEA TIME.

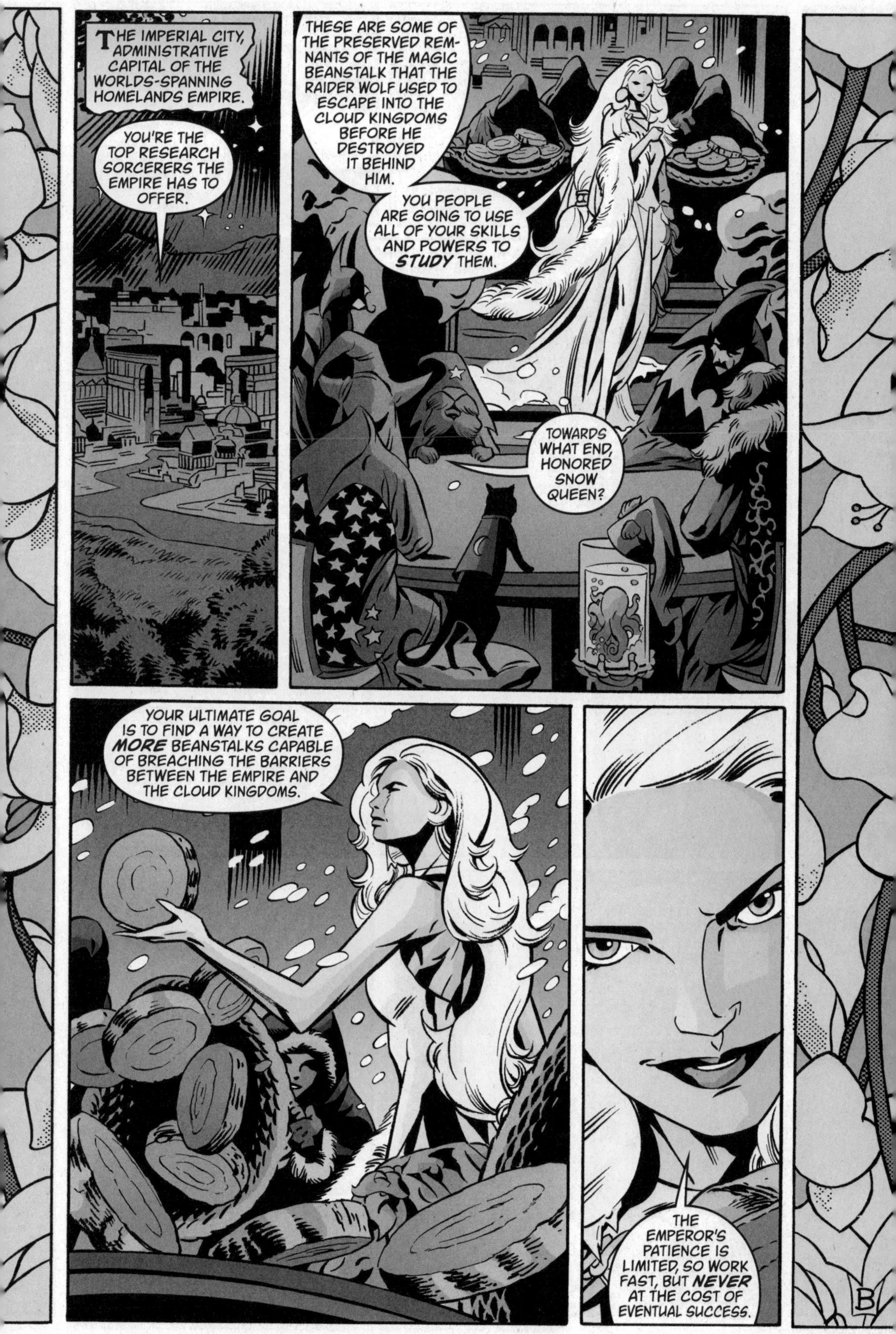
THE IMPERIAL CITY, ADMINISTRATIVE CAPITAL OF THE WORLDS-SPANNING HOMELANDS EMPIRE.
YOU'RE THE TOP RESEARCH SORCERERS THE EMPIRE HAS TO OFFER.
THESE ARE SOME OF THE PRESERVED REMNANTS OF THE MAGIC BEANSTALK THAT THE RAIDER WOLF USED TO ESCAPE INTO THE CLOUD KINGDOMS BEFORE HE DESTROYED IT BEHIND HIM.
YOU PEOPLE ARE GOING TO USE ALL OF YOUR SKILLS AND POWERS TO STUDY THEM.
TOWARDS WHAT END, HONORED SNOW QUEEN?
YOUR ULTIMATE GOAL IS TO FIND A WAY TO CREATE MORE BEANSTALKS CAPABLE OF BREACHING THE BARRIERS BETWEEN THE EMPIRE AND THE CLOUD KINGDOMS.
THE EMPEROR'S PATIENCE IS LIMITED, SO WORK FAST, BUT NEVER AT THE COST OF EVENTUAL SUCCESS.

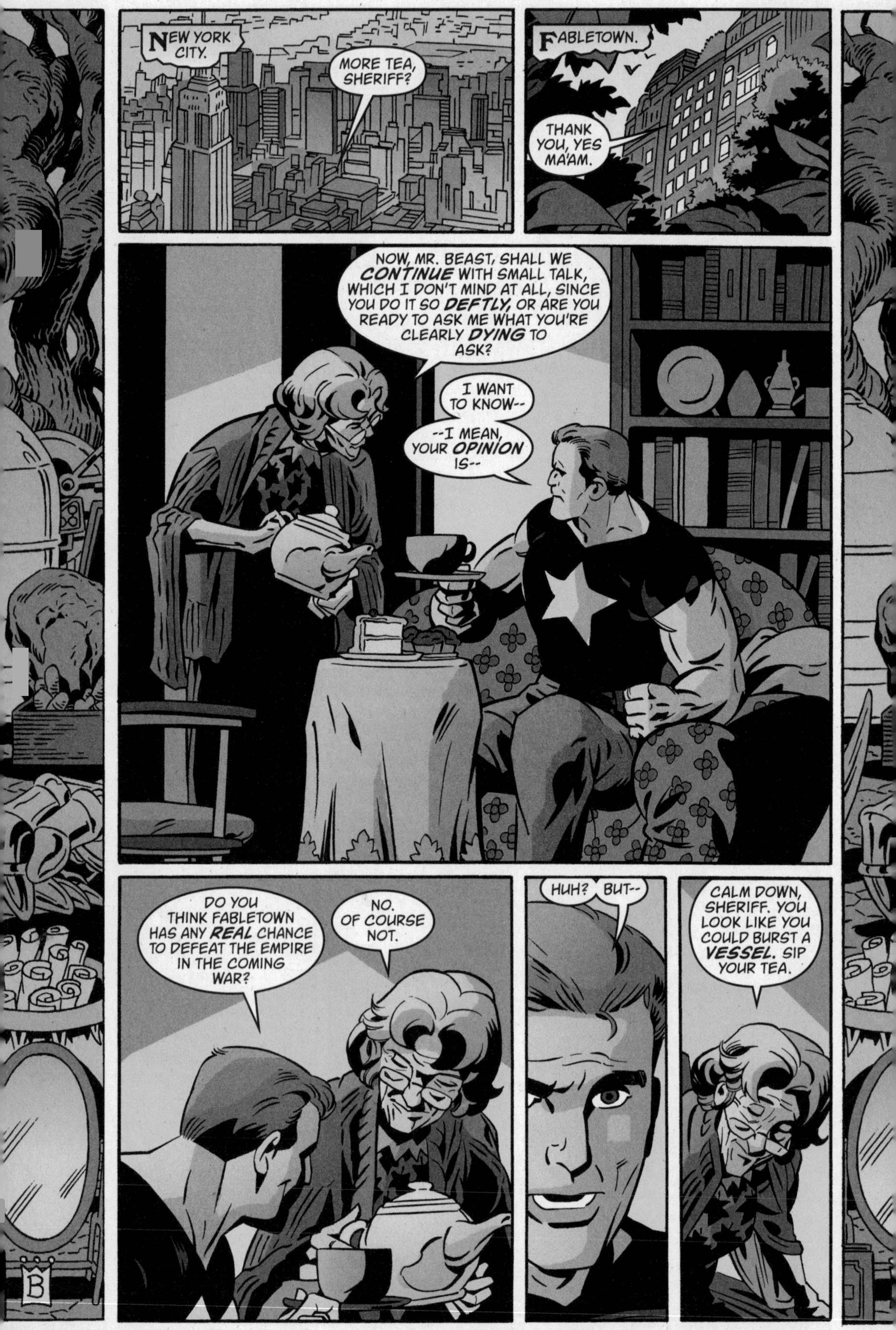
NEW YORK CITY.
MORE TEA, SHERIFF?
FABLETOWN.
THANK YOU, YES MA'AM.
NOW, MR. BEAST, SHALL WE CONTINUE WITH SMALL TALK, WHICH I DON'T MIND AT ALL, SINCE YOU DO IT SO DEFTLY, OR ARE YOU READY TO ASK ME WHAT YOU'RE CLEARLY DYING TO ASK?
I WANT TO KNOW--
--I MEAN, YOUR OPINION IS--
DO YOU THINK FABLETOWN HAS ANY REAL CHANCE TO DEFEAT THE EMPIRE IN THE COMING WAR?
NO. OF COURSE NOT.
HUH? BUT--
CALM DOWN, SHERIFF. YOU LOOK LIKE YOU COULD BURST A VESSEL. SIP YOUR TEA.

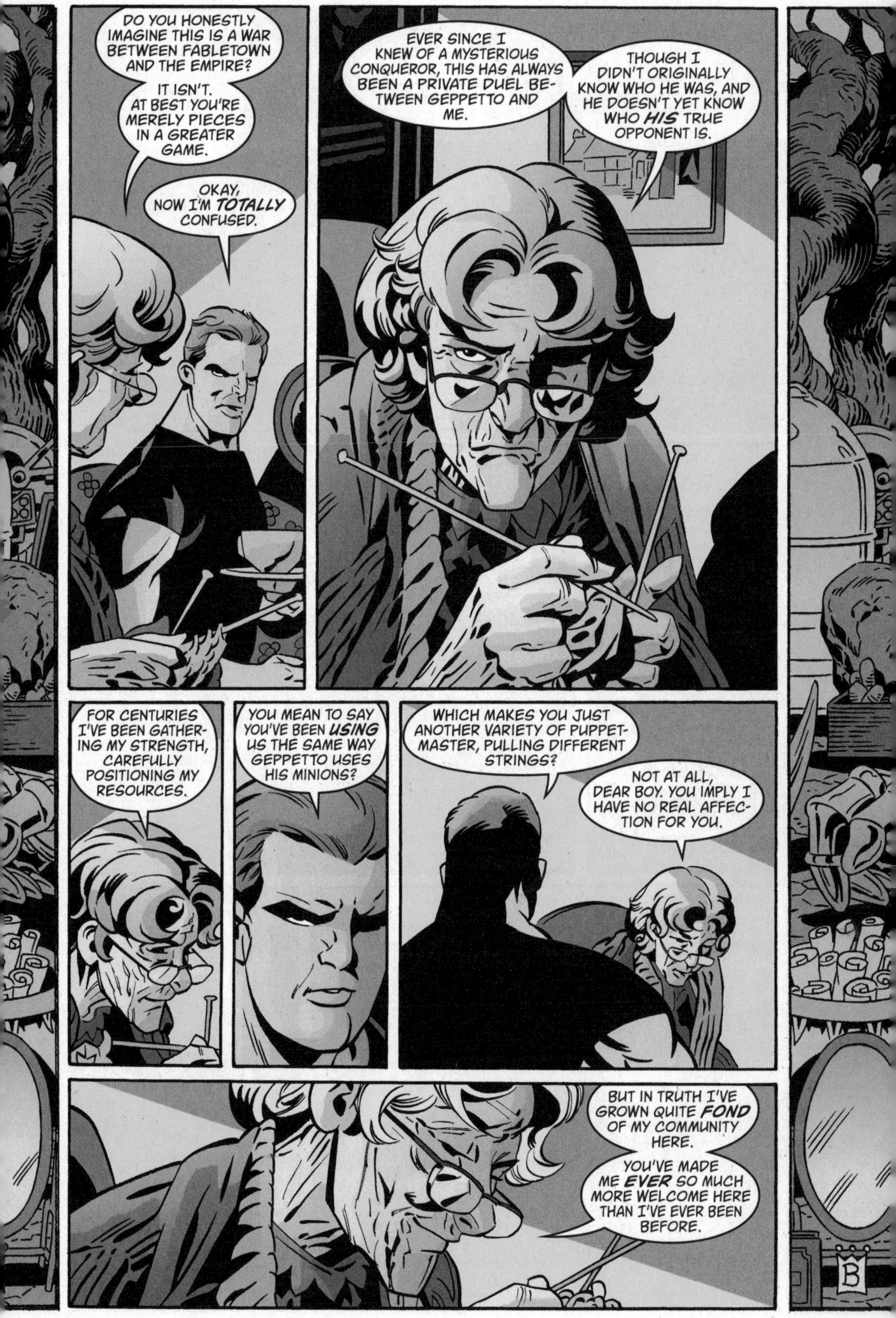

DO YOU HONESTLY IMAGINE THIS IS A WAR BETWEEN FABLETOWN AND THE EMPIRE?
IT ISN'T. AT BEST YOU'RE MERELY PIECES IN A GREATER GAME.
OKAY, NOW I'M TOTALLY CONFUSED.
EVER SINCE I KNEW OF A MYSTERIOUS CONQUEROR, THIS HAS ALWAYS BEEN A PRIVATE DUEL BETWEEN GEPPETTO AND ME.
THOUGH I DIDN'T ORIGINALLY KNOW WHO HE WAS, AND HE DOESN'T YET KNOW WHO HIS TRUE OPPONENT IS.
FOR CENTURIES I'VE BEEN GATHERING MY STRENGTH, CAREFULLY POSITIONING MY RESOURCES.
YOU MEAN TO SAY YOU'VE BEEN USING US THE SAME WAY GEPPETTO USES HIS MINIONS?
WHICH MAKES YOU JUST ANOTHER VARIETY OF PUPPET-MASTER, PULLING DIFFERENT STRINGS?
NOT AT ALL, DEAR BOY. YOU IMPLY I HAVE NO REAL AFFECTION FOR YOU.
BUT IN TRUTH I'VE GROWN QUITE FOND OF MY COMMUNITY HERE.
YOU'VE MADE ME EVER SO MUCH MORE WELCOME HERE THAN I'VE EVER BEEN BEFORE.

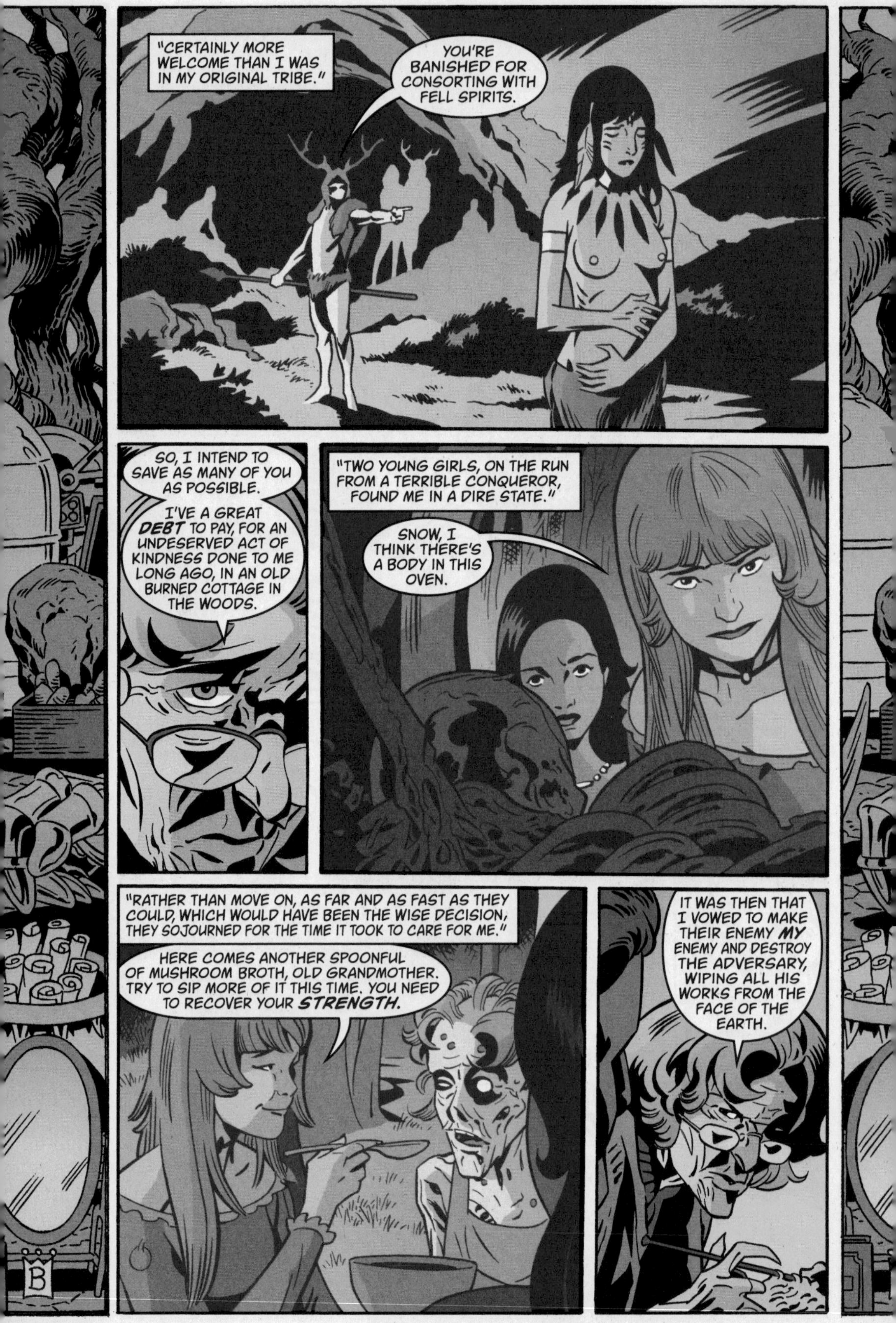
"CERTAINLY MORE WELCOME THAN I WAS IN MY ORIGINAL TRIBE."
YOU'RE BANISHED FOR CONSORTING WITH FELL SPIRITS.
SO, I INTEND TO SAVE AS MANY OF YOU AS POSSIBLE.
I'VE A GREAT DEBT TO PAY, FOR AN UNDESERVED ACT OF KINDNESS DONE TO ME LONG AGO, IN AN OLD BURNED COTTAGE IN THE WOODS.
"TWO YOUNG GIRLS, ON THE RUN FROM A TERRIBLE CONQUEROR, FOUND ME IN A DIRE STATE."
SNOW, I THINK THERE'S A BODY IN THIS OVEN.
"RATHER THAN MOVE ON, AS FAR AND AS FAST AS THEY COULD, WHICH WOULD HAVE BEEN THE WISE DECISION, THEY SOJOURNED FOR THE TIME IT TOOK TO CARE FOR ME."
HERE COMES ANOTHER SPOONFUL OF MUSHROOM BROTH, OLD GRANDMOTHER. TRY TO SIP MORE OF IT THIS TIME. YOU NEED TO RECOVER YOUR STRENGTH.
IT WAS THEN THAT I VOWED TO MAKE THEIR ENEMY MY ENEMY AND DESTROY THE ADVERSARY, WIPING ALL HIS WORKS FROM THE FACE OF THE EARTH.

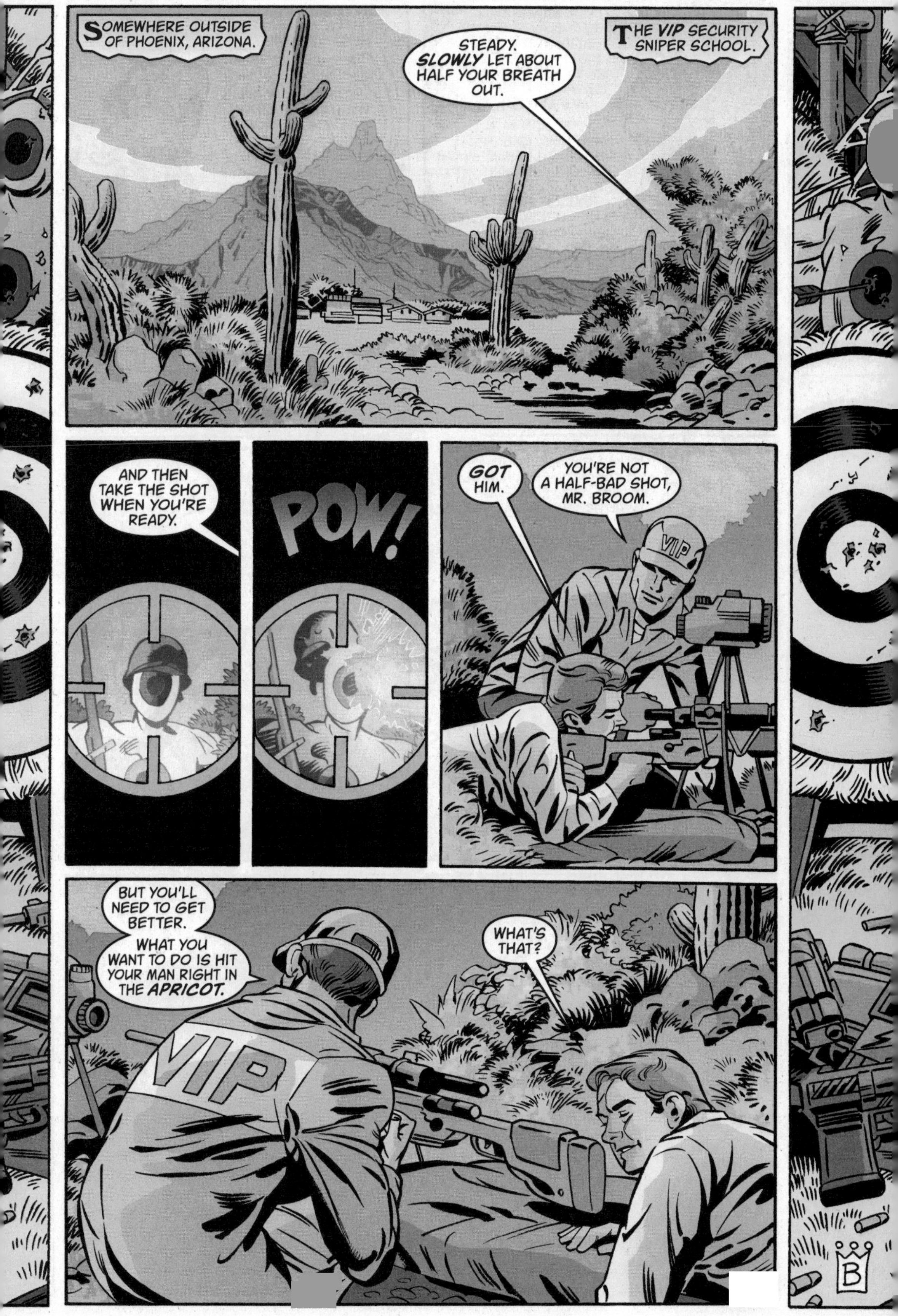
SOMEWHERE OUTSIDE OF PHOENIX, ARIZONA.
THE VIP SECURITY SNIPER SCHOOL.
STEADY. SLOWLY LET ABOUT HALF YOUR BREATH OUT.
AND THEN TAKE THE SHOT WHEN YOU'RE READY.
POW!
GOT HIM.
YOU'RE NOT A HALF-BAD SHOT, MR. BROOM.
BUT YOU'LL NEED TO GET BETTER.
WHAT YOU WANT TO DO IS HIT YOUR MAN RIGHT IN THE APRICOT.
WHAT'S THAT?
VIP

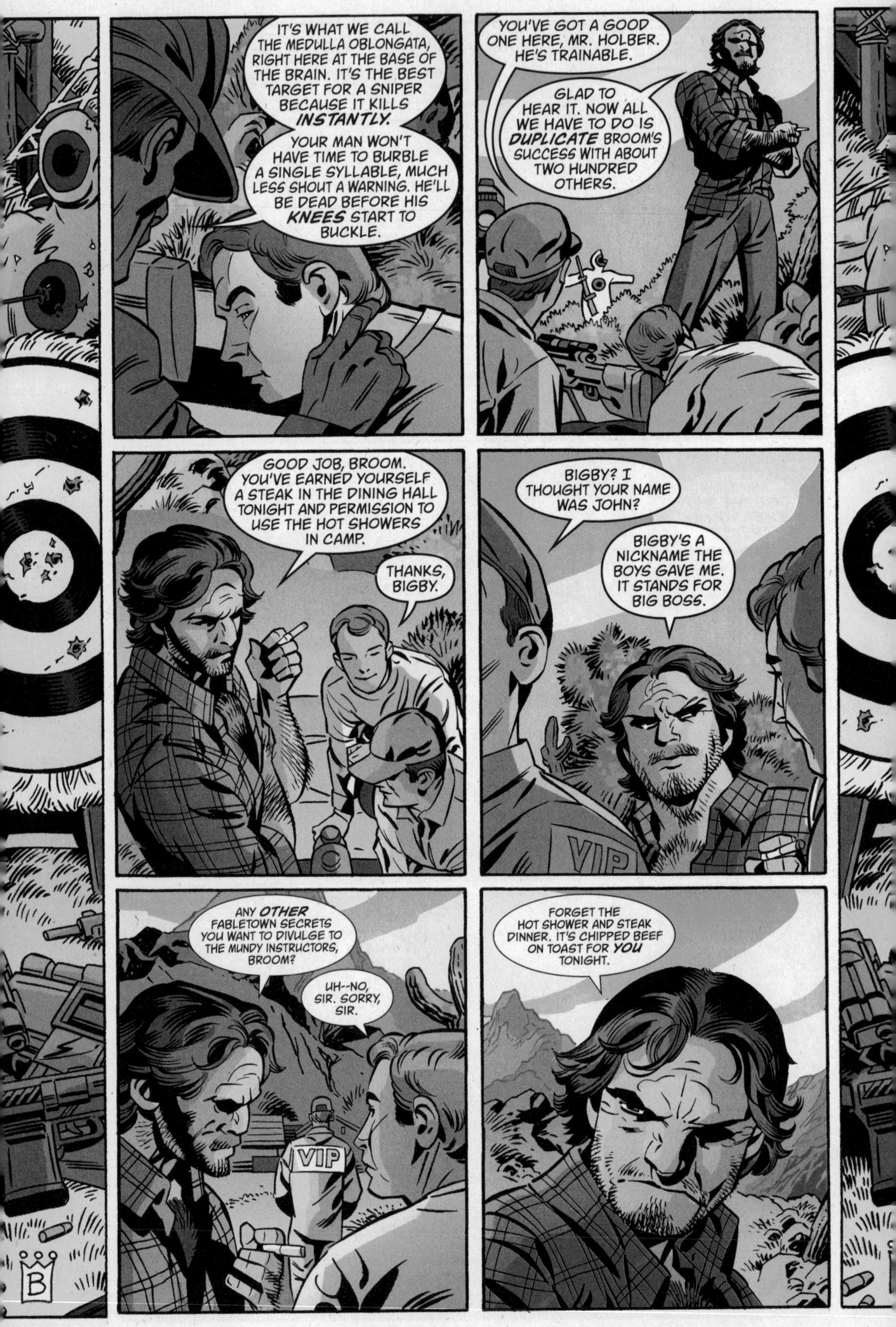
IT'S WHAT WE CALL THE MEDULLA OBLONGATA, RIGHT HERE AT THE BASE OF THE BRAIN. IT'S THE BEST TARGET FOR A SNIPER BECAUSE IT KILLS INSTANTLY.
YOUR MAN WON'T HAVE TIME TO BURBLE A SINGLE SYLLABLE, MUCH LESS SHOUT A WARNING. HE'LL BE DEAD BEFORE HIS KNEES START TO BUCKLE.
YOU'VE GOT A GOOD ONE HERE, MR. HOLBER. HE'S TRAINABLE.
GLAD TO HEAR IT. NOW ALL WE HAVE TO DO IS DUPLICATE BROOM'S SUCCESS WITH ABOUT TWO HUNDRED OTHERS.
GOOD JOB, BROOM. YOU'VE EARNED YOURSELF A STEAK IN THE DINING HALL TONIGHT AND PERMISSION TO USE THE HOT SHOWERS IN CAMP.
THANKS, BIGBY.
BIGBY? I THOUGHT YOUR NAME WAS JOHN?
BIGBY'S A NICKNAME THE BOYS GAVE ME. IT STANDS FOR BIG BOSS.
VIP
ANY OTHER FABLETOWN SECRETS YOU WANT TO DIVULGE TO THE MUNDY INSTRUCTORS, BROOM?
UH--NO, SIR. SORRY, SIR.
VIP
FORGET THE HOT SHOWER AND STEAK DINNER. IT'S CHIPPED BEEF ON TOAST FOR YOU TONIGHT.

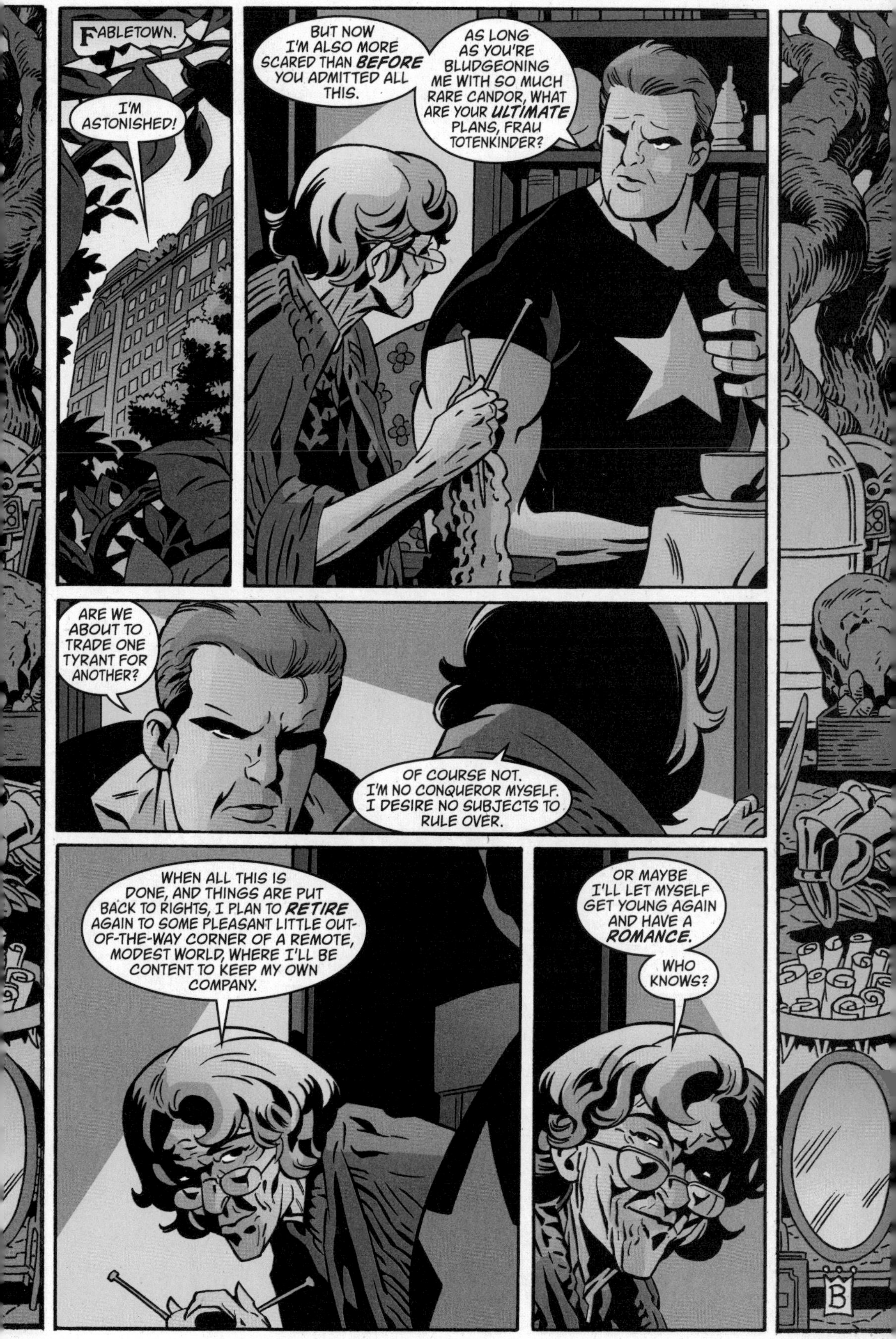
FABLETOWN.
I'M ASTONISHED!
BUT NOW I'M ALSO MORE SCARED THAN BEFORE YOU ADMITTED ALL THIS.
AS LONG AS YOU'RE BLUDGEONING ME WITH SO MUCH RARE CANDOR, WHAT ARE YOUR ULTIMATE PLANS, FRAU TOTENKINDER?
ARE WE ABOUT TO TRADE ONE TYRANT FOR ANOTHER?
OF COURSE NOT. I'M NO CONQUEROR MYSELF. I DESIRE NO SUBJECTS TO RULE OVER.
WHEN ALL THIS IS DONE, AND THINGS ARE PUT BACK TO RIGHTS, I PLAN TO RETIRE AGAIN TO SOME PLEASANT LITTLE OUT-OF-THE-WAY CORNER OF A REMOTE, MODEST WORLD, WHERE I'LL BE CONTENT TO KEEP MY OWN COMPANY.
OR MAYBE I'LL LET MYSELF GET YOUNG AGAIN AND HAVE A ROMANCE.
WHO KNOWS?

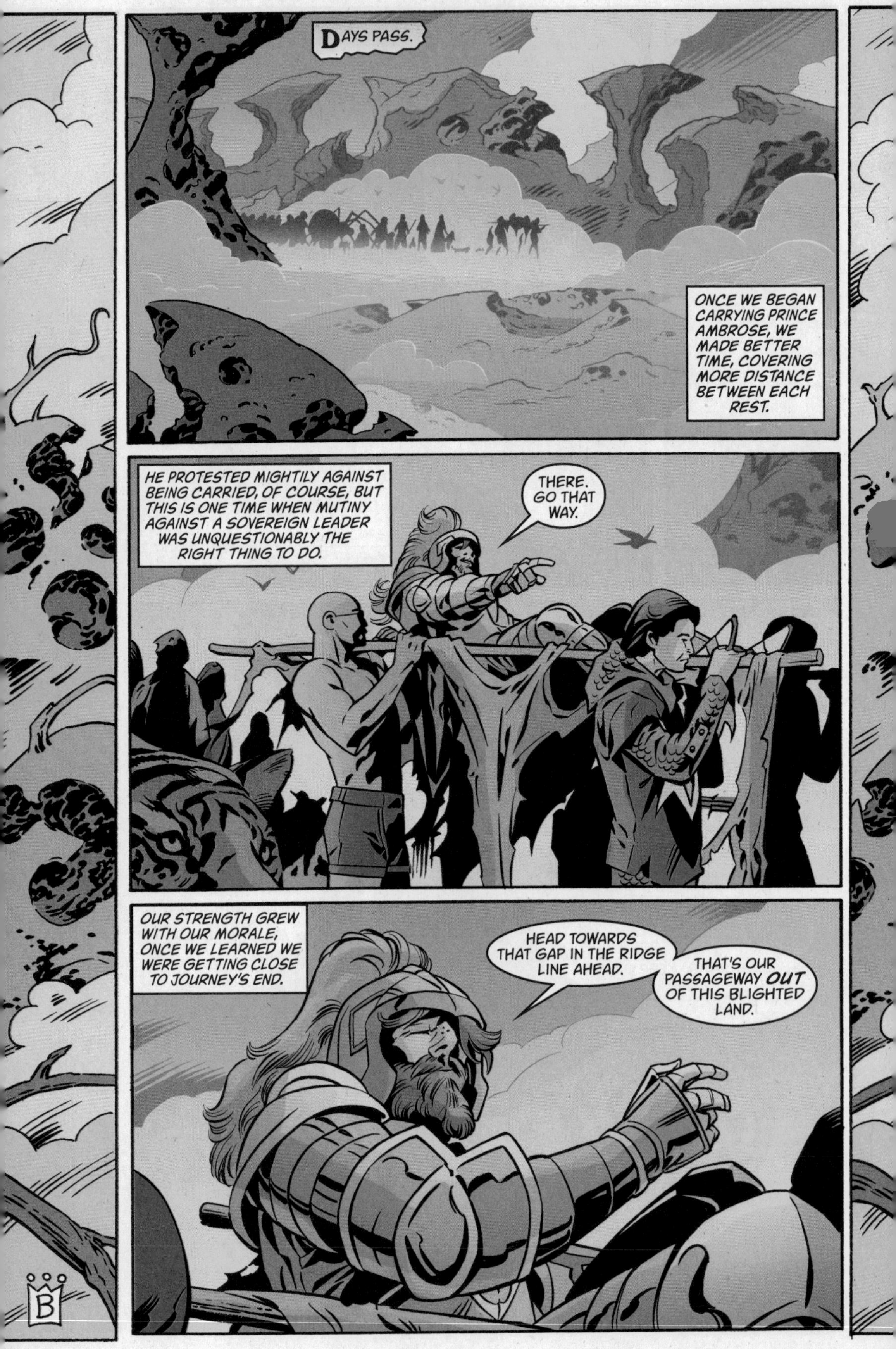
DAYS PASS.
ONCE WE BEGAN CARRYING PRINCE AMBROSE, WE MADE BETTER TIME, COVERING MORE DISTANCE BETWEEN EACH REST.
HE PROTESTED MIGHTILY AGAINST BEING CARRIED, OF COURSE, BUT THIS IS ONE TIME WHEN MUTINY AGAINST A SOVEREIGN LEADER WAS UNQUESTIONABLY THE RIGHT THING TO DO.
THERE. GO THAT WAY.
OUR STRENGTH GREW WITH OUR MORALE, ONCE WE LEARNED WE WERE GETTING CLOSE TO JOURNEY'S END.
HEAD TOWARDS THAT GAP IN THE RIDGE LINE AHEAD.
THAT'S OUR PASSAGEWAY OUT OF THIS BLIGHTED LAND.

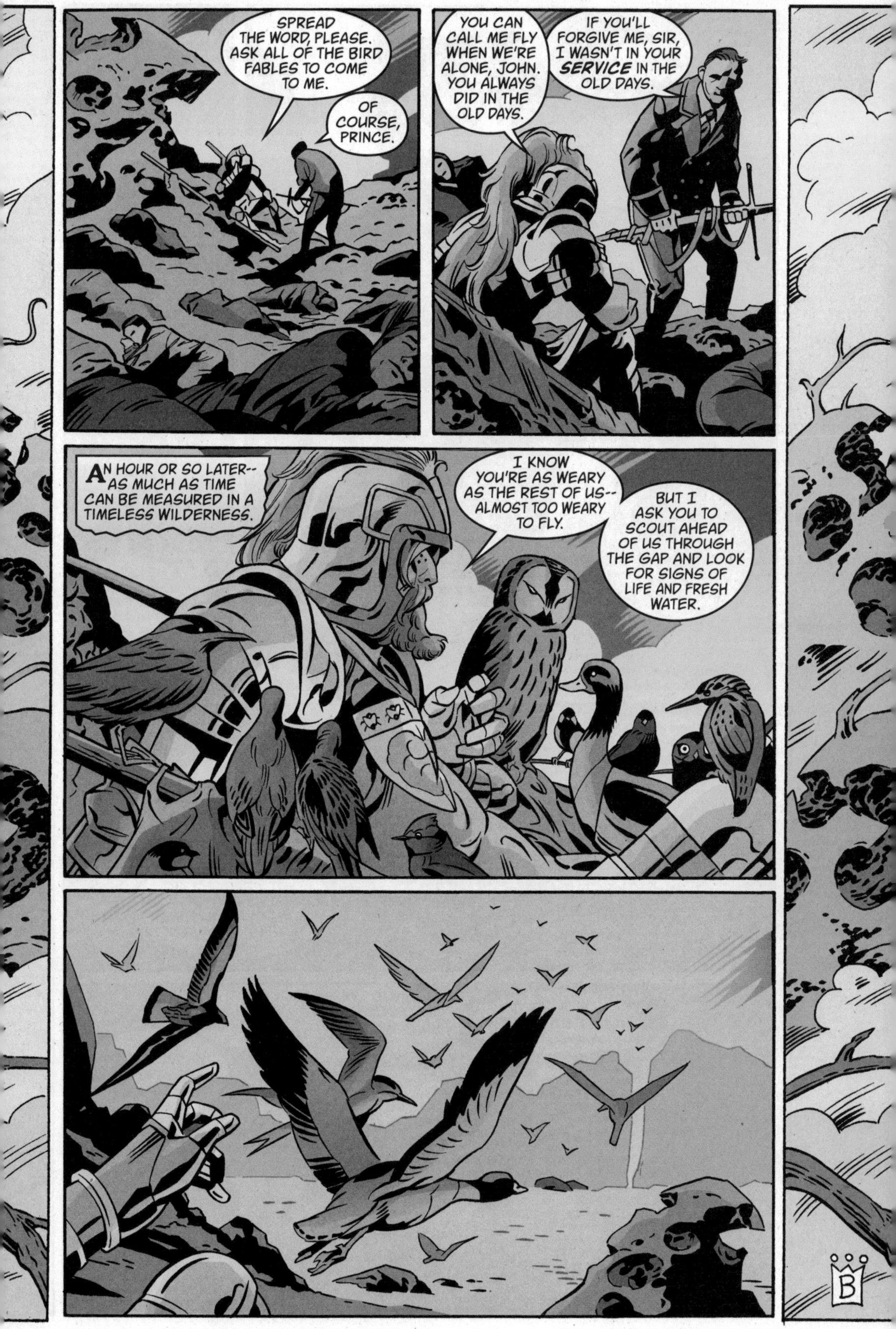
SPREAD THE WORD, PLEASE. ASK ALL OF THE BIRD FABLES TO COME TO ME.
OF COURSE, PRINCE.
YOU CAN CALL ME FLY WHEN WE'RE ALONE, JOHN. YOU ALWAYS DID IN THE OLD DAYS.
IF YOU'LL FORGIVE ME, SIR, I WASN'T IN YOUR SERVICE IN THE OLD DAYS.
AN HOUR OR SO LATER-- AS MUCH AS TIME CAN BE MEASURED IN A TIMELESS WILDERNESS.
I KNOW YOU'RE AS WEARY AS THE REST OF US-- ALMOST TOO WEARY TO FLY.
BUT I ASK YOU TO SCOUT AHEAD OF US THROUGH THE GAP AND LOOK FOR SIGNS OF LIFE AND FRESH WATER.

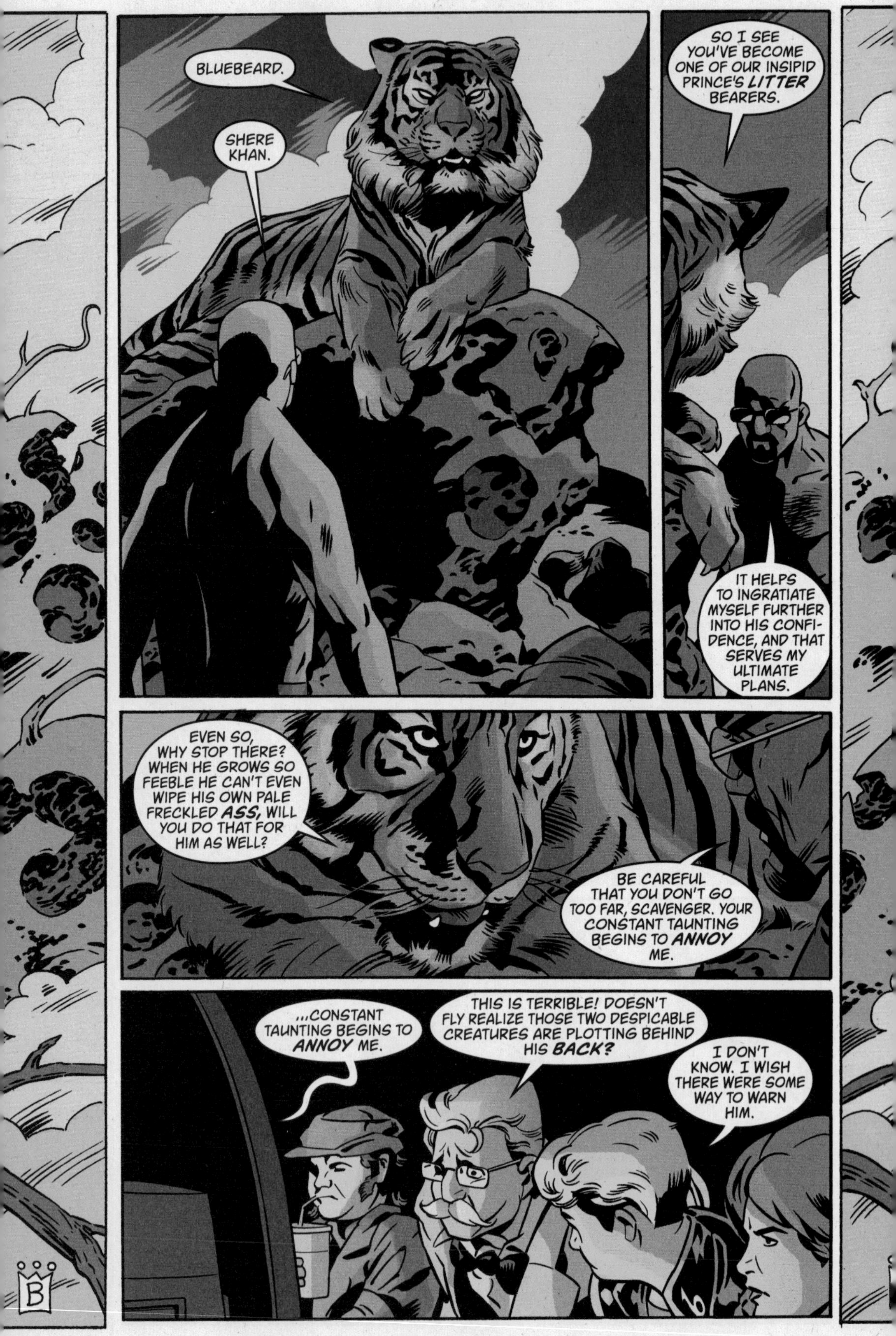

BLUEBEARD.
SHERE KHAN.
SO I SEE YOU'VE BECOME ONE OF OUR INSIPID PRINCE'S LITTER BEARERS.
IT HELPS TO INGRATIATE MYSELF FURTHER INTO HIS CONFI-DENCE, AND THAT SERVES MY ULTIMATE PLANS.
EVEN SO, WHY STOP THERE? WHEN HE GROWS SO FEEBLE HE CAN'T EVEN WIPE HIS OWN PALE FRECKLED ASS, WILL YOU DO THAT FOR HIM AS WELL?
BE CAREFUL THAT YOU DON'T GO TOO FAR, SCAVENGER. YOUR CONSTANT TAUNTING BEGINS TO ANNOY ME.
...CONSTANT TAUNTING BEGINS TO ANNOY ME.
THIS IS TERRIBLE! DOESN'T FLY REALIZE THOSE TWO DESPICABLE CREATURES ARE PLOTTING BEHIND HIS BACK?
I DON'T KNOW. I WISH THERE WERE SOME WAY TO WARN HIM.

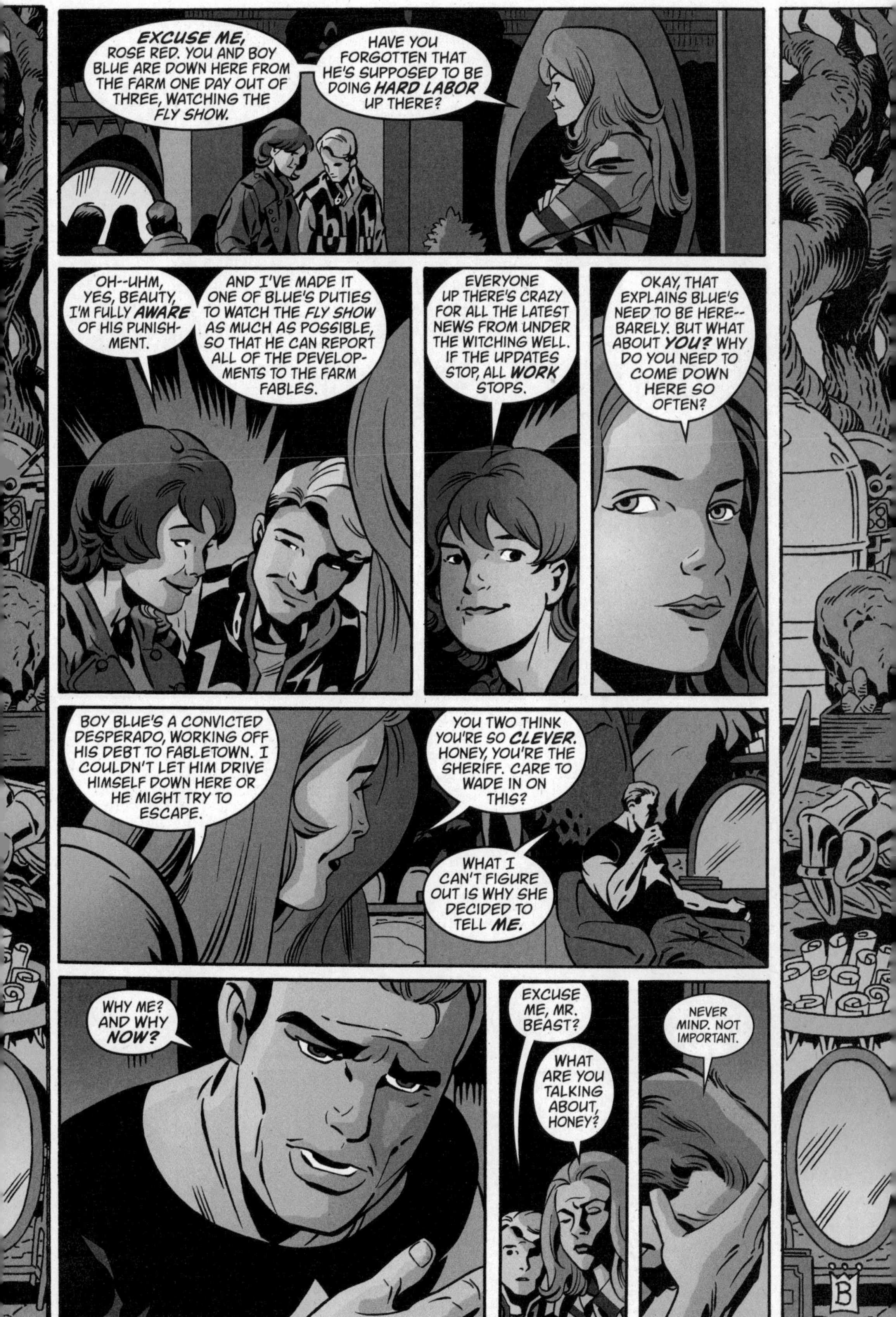
EXCUSE ME, ROSE RED. YOU AND BOY BLUE ARE DOWN HERE FROM THE FARM ONE DAY OUT OF THREE, WATCHING THE FLY SHOW.
HAVE YOU FORGOTTEN THAT HE'S SUPPOSED TO BE DOING HARD LABOR UP THERE?
OH--UHM, YES, BEAUTY, I'M FULLY AWARE OF HIS PUNISHMENT.
AND I'VE MADE IT ONE OF BLUE'S DUTIES TO WATCH THE FLY SHOW AS MUCH AS POSSIBLE, SO THAT HE CAN REPORT ALL OF THE DEVELOPMENTS TO THE FARM FABLES.
EVERYONE UP THERE'S CRAZY FOR ALL THE LATEST NEWS FROM UNDER THE WITCHING WELL. IF THE UPDATES STOP, ALL WORK STOPS.
OKAY, THAT EXPLAINS BLUE'S NEED TO BE HERE--BARELY. BUT WHAT ABOUT YOU? WHY DO YOU NEED TO COME DOWN HERE SO OFTEN?
BOY BLUE'S A CONVICTED DESPERADO, WORKING OFF HIS DEBT TO FABLETOWN. I COULDN'T LET HIM DRIVE HIMSELF DOWN HERE OR HE MIGHT TRY TO ESCAPE.
YOU TWO THINK YOU'RE SO CLEVER. HONEY, YOU'RE THE SHERIFF. CARE TO WADE IN ON THIS?
WHAT I CAN'T FIGURE OUT IS WHY SHE DECIDED TO TELL ME.
WHY ME? AND WHY NOW?
EXCUSE ME, MR. BEAST?
WHAT ARE YOU TALKING ABOUT, HONEY?
NEVER MIND. NOT IMPORTANT.

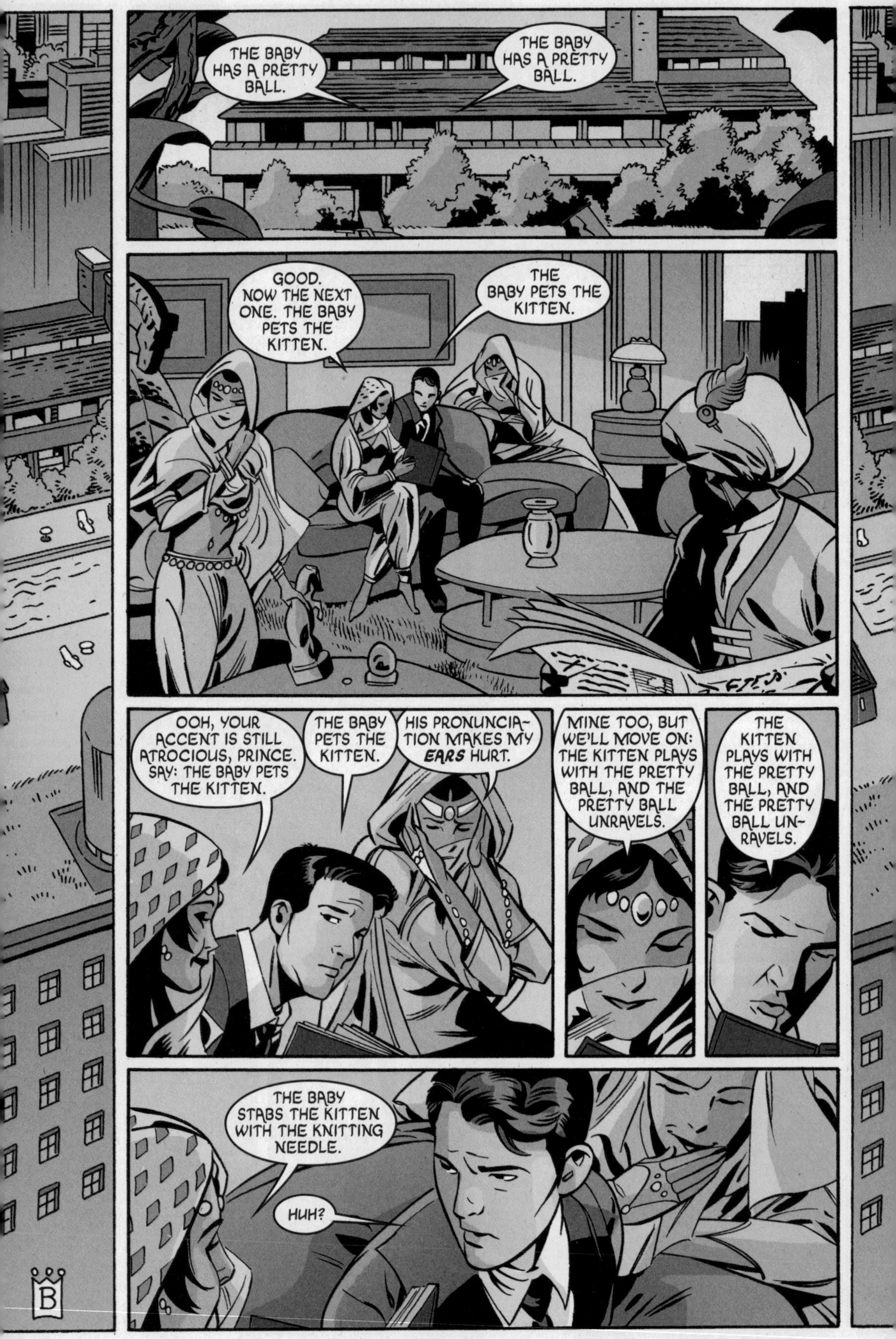
THE BABY HAS A PRETTY BALL.
THE BABY HAS A PRETTY BALL.
GOOD. NOW THE NEXT ONE. THE BABY PETS THE KITTEN.
THE BABY PETS THE KITTEN.
OOH, YOUR ACCENT IS STILL ATROCIOUS, PRINCE. SAY: THE BABY PETS THE KITTEN.
THE BABY PETS THE KITTEN.
HIS PRONUNCIA-TION MAKES MY EARS HURT.
MINE TOO, BUT WE'LL MOVE ON: THE KITTEN PLAYS WITH THE PRETTY BALL, AND THE PRETTY BALL UNRAVELS.
THE KITTEN PLAYS WITH THE PRETTY BALL, AND THE PRETTY BALL UN-RAVELS.
THE BABY STABS THE KITTEN WITH THE KNITTING NEEDLE.
HUH?

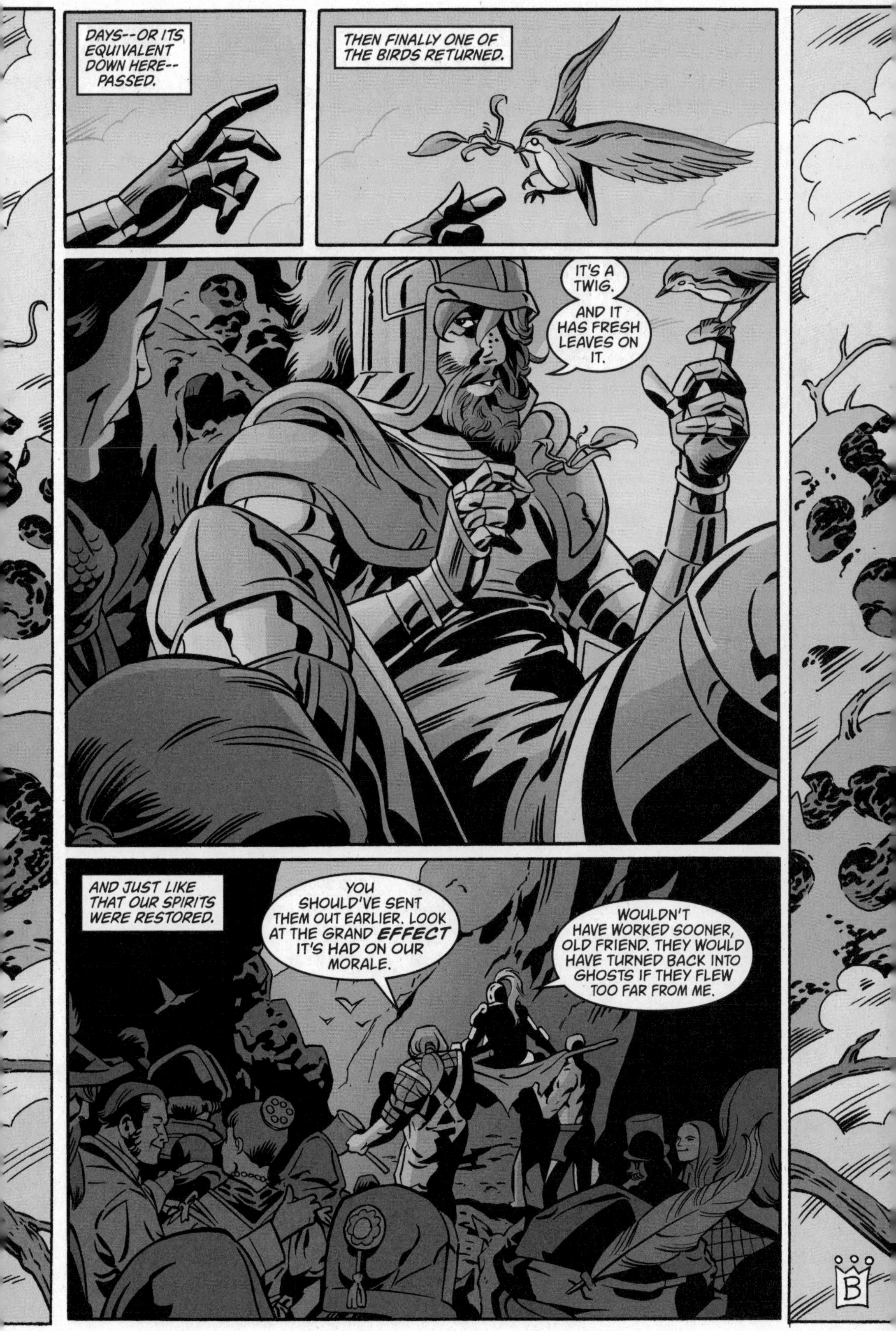
DAYS--OR ITS EQUIVALENT DOWN HERE--PASSED.
THEN FINALLY ONE OF THE BIRDS RETURNED.
IT'S A TWIG.
AND IT HAS FRESH LEAVES ON IT.
AND JUST LIKE THAT OUR SPIRITS WERE RESTORED.
YOU SHOULD'VE SENT THEM OUT EARLIER. LOOK AT THE GRAND EFFECT IT'S HAD ON OUR MORALE.
WOULDN'T HAVE WORKED SOONER, OLD FRIEND. THEY WOULD HAVE TURNED BACK INTO GHOSTS IF THEY FLEW TOO FAR FROM ME.

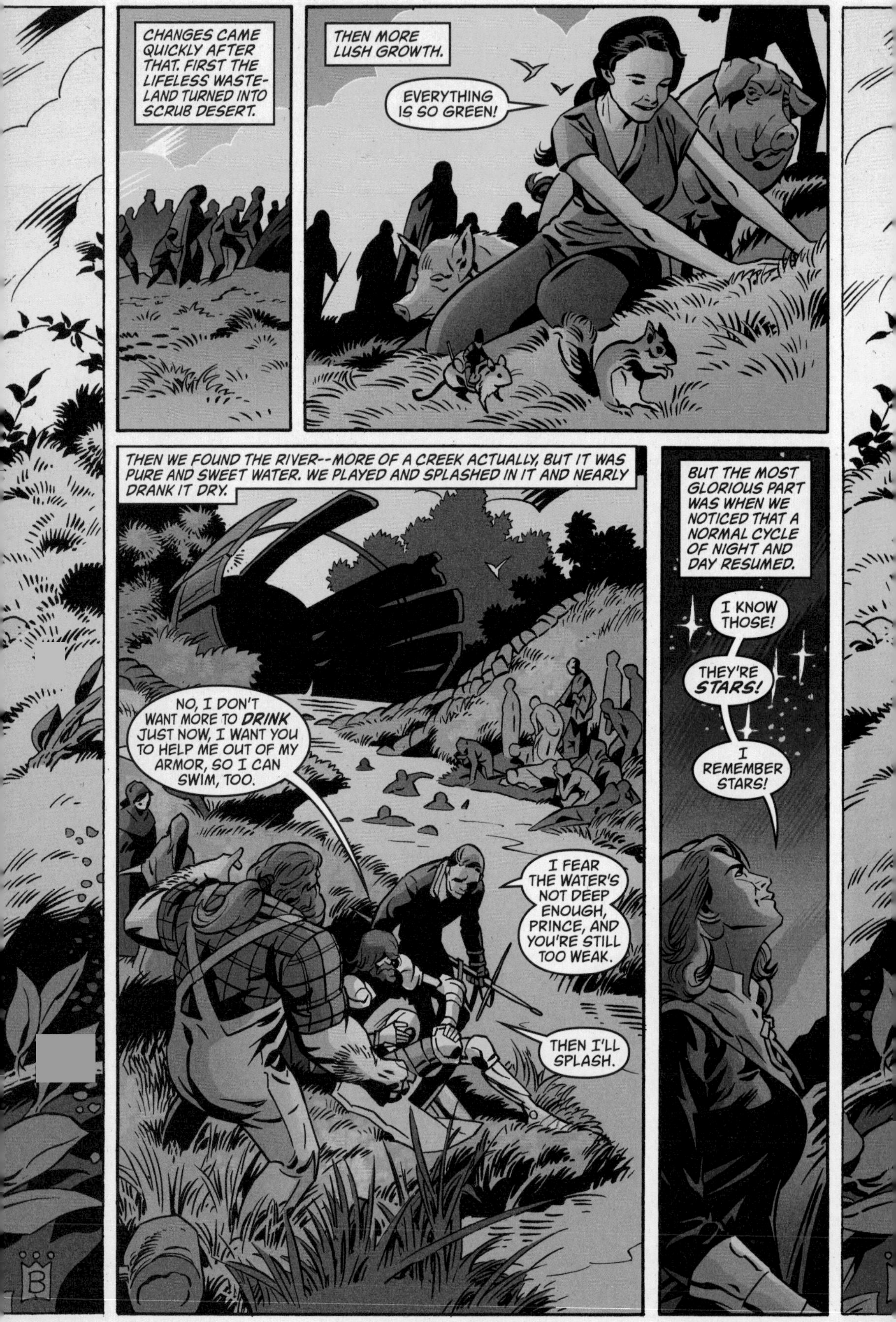

CHANGES CAME QUICKLY AFTER THAT. FIRST THE LIFELESS WASTE-LAND TURNED INTO SCRUB DESERT.
THEN MORE LUSH GROWTH.
EVERYTHING IS SO GREEN!
THEN WE FOUND THE RIVER--MORE OF A CREEK ACTUALLY, BUT IT WAS PURE AND SWEET WATER. WE PLAYED AND SPLASHED IN IT AND NEARLY DRANK IT DRY.
NO, I DON'T WANT MORE TO DRINK JUST NOW, I WANT YOU TO HELP ME OUT OF MY ARMOR, SO I CAN SWIM, TOO.
I FEAR THE WATER'S NOT DEEP ENOUGH, PRINCE, AND YOU'RE STILL TOO WEAK.
THEN I'LL SPLASH.
BUT THE MOST GLORIOUS PART WAS WHEN WE NOTICED THAT A NORMAL CYCLE OF NIGHT AND DAY RESUMED.
I KNOW THOSE!
THEY'RE STARS!
I REMEMBER STARS!

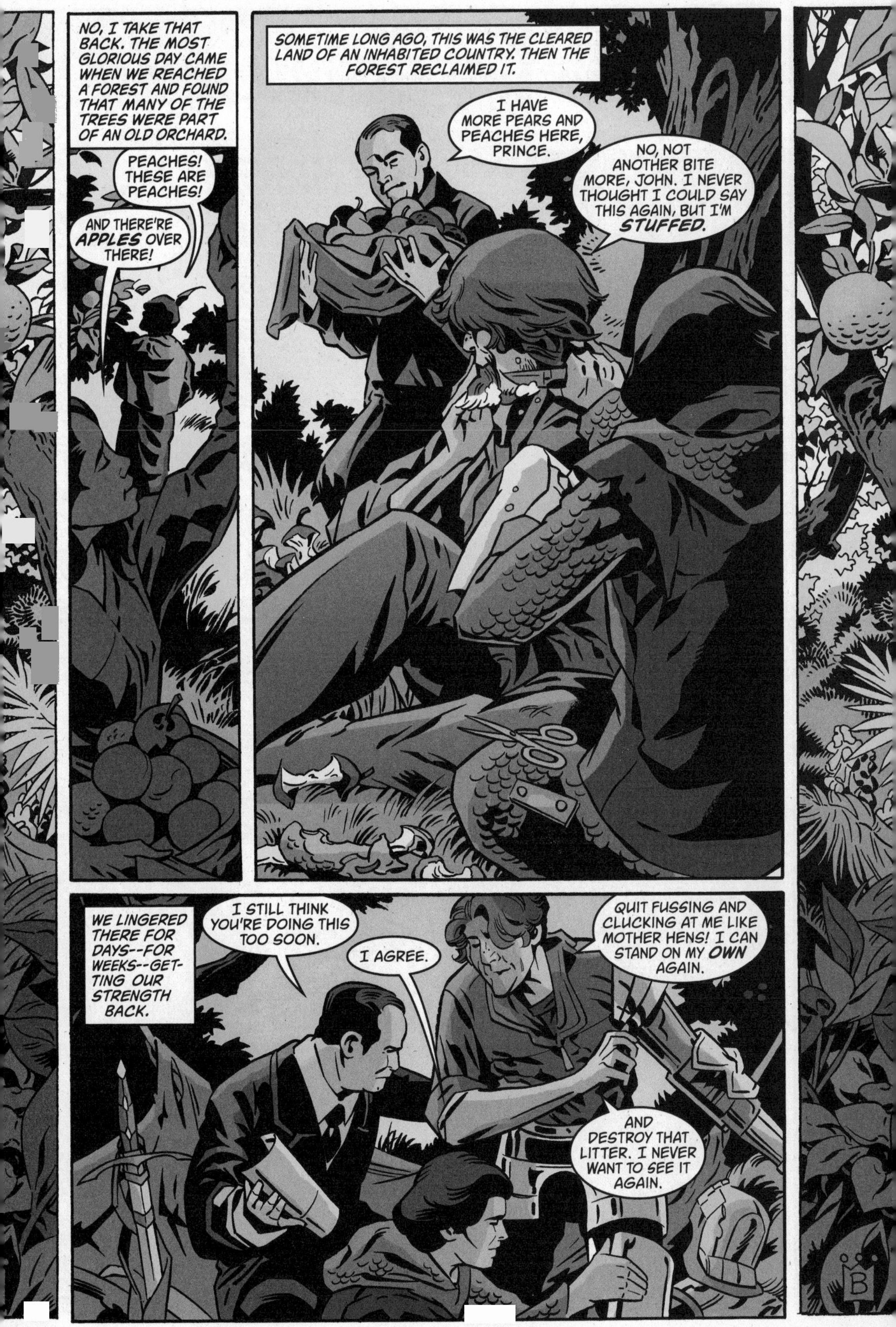

NO, I TAKE THAT BACK. THE MOST GLORIOUS DAY CAME WHEN WE REACHED A FOREST AND FOUND THAT MANY OF THE TREES WERE PART OF AN OLD ORCHARD.
PEACHES! THESE ARE PEACHES!
AND THERE'RE APPLES OVER THERE!
SOMETIME LONG AGO, THIS WAS THE CLEARED LAND OF AN INHABITED COUNTRY. THEN THE FOREST RECLAIMED IT.
I HAVE MORE PEARS AND PEACHES HERE, PRINCE.
NO, NOT ANOTHER BITE MORE, JOHN. I NEVER THOUGHT I COULD SAY THIS AGAIN, BUT I'M STUFFED.
WE LINGERED THERE FOR DAYS--FOR WEEKS--GETTING OUR STRENGTH BACK.
I STILL THINK YOU'RE DOING THIS TOO SOON.
I AGREE.
QUIT FUSSING AND CLUCKING AT ME LIKE MOTHER HENS! I CAN STAND ON MY OWN AGAIN.
AND DESTROY THAT LITTER. I NEVER WANT TO SEE IT AGAIN.

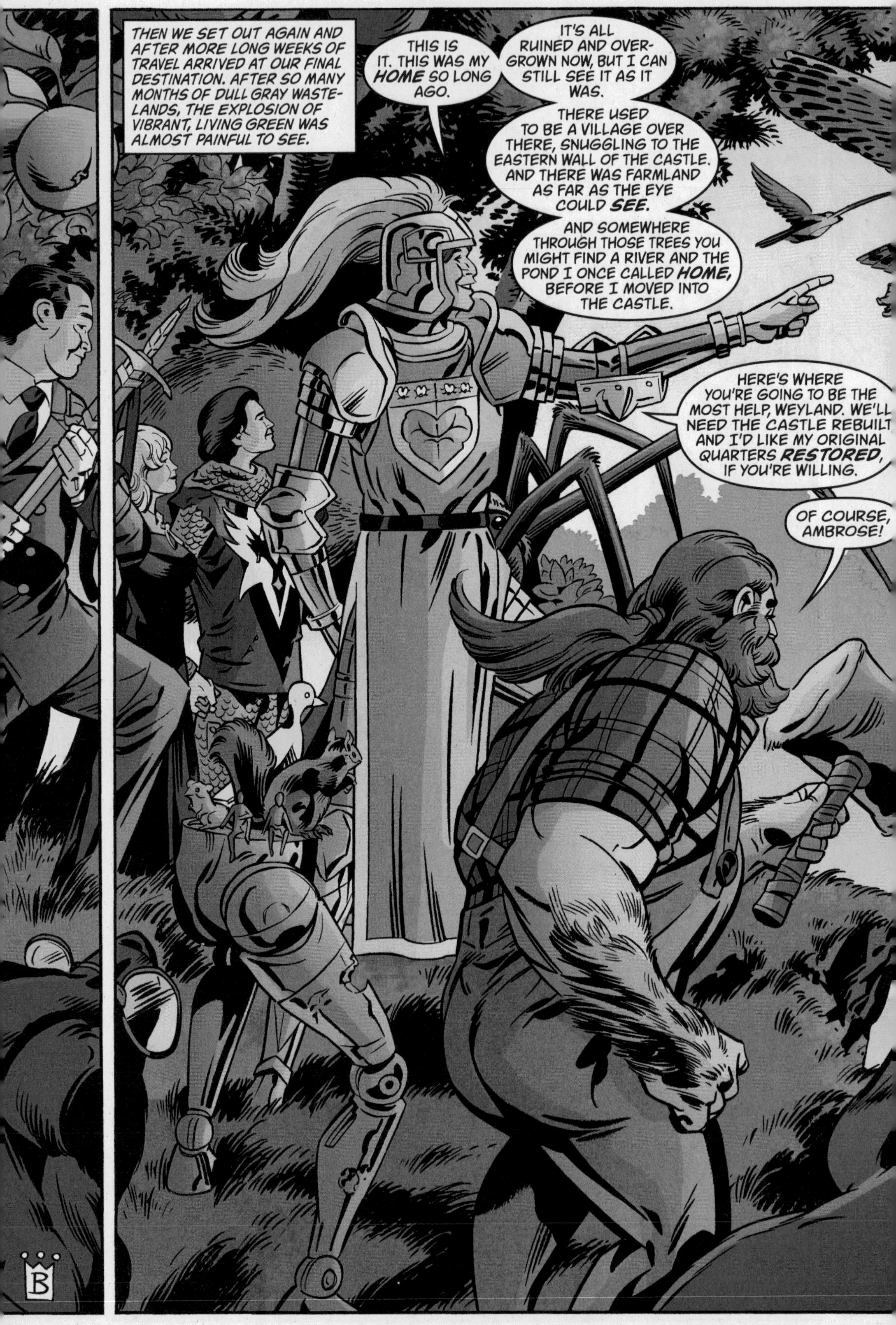
THEN WE SET OUT AGAIN AND AFTER MORE LONG WEEKS OF TRAVEL ARRIVED AT OUR FINAL DESTINATION. AFTER SO MANY MONTHS OF DULL GRAY WASTELANDS, THE EXPLOSION OF VIBRANT, LIVING GREEN WAS ALMOST PAINFUL TO SEE.
THIS IS IT. THIS WAS MY **HOME** SO LONG AGO.
IT'S ALL RUINED AND OVERGROWN NOW, BUT I CAN STILL SEE IT AS IT WAS.
THERE USED TO BE A VILLAGE OVER THERE, SNUGGLING TO THE EASTERN WALL OF THE CASTLE. AND THERE WAS FARMLAND AS FAR AS THE EYE COULD **SEE.**
AND SOMEWHERE THROUGH THOSE TREES YOU MIGHT FIND A RIVER AND THE POND I ONCE CALLED **HOME,** BEFORE I MOVED INTO THE CASTLE.
HERE'S WHERE YOU'RE GOING TO BE THE MOST HELP, WEYLAND. WE'LL NEED THE CASTLE REBUILT AND I'D LIKE MY ORIGINAL QUARTERS **RESTORED,** IF YOU'RE WILLING.
OF COURSE, AMBROSE!

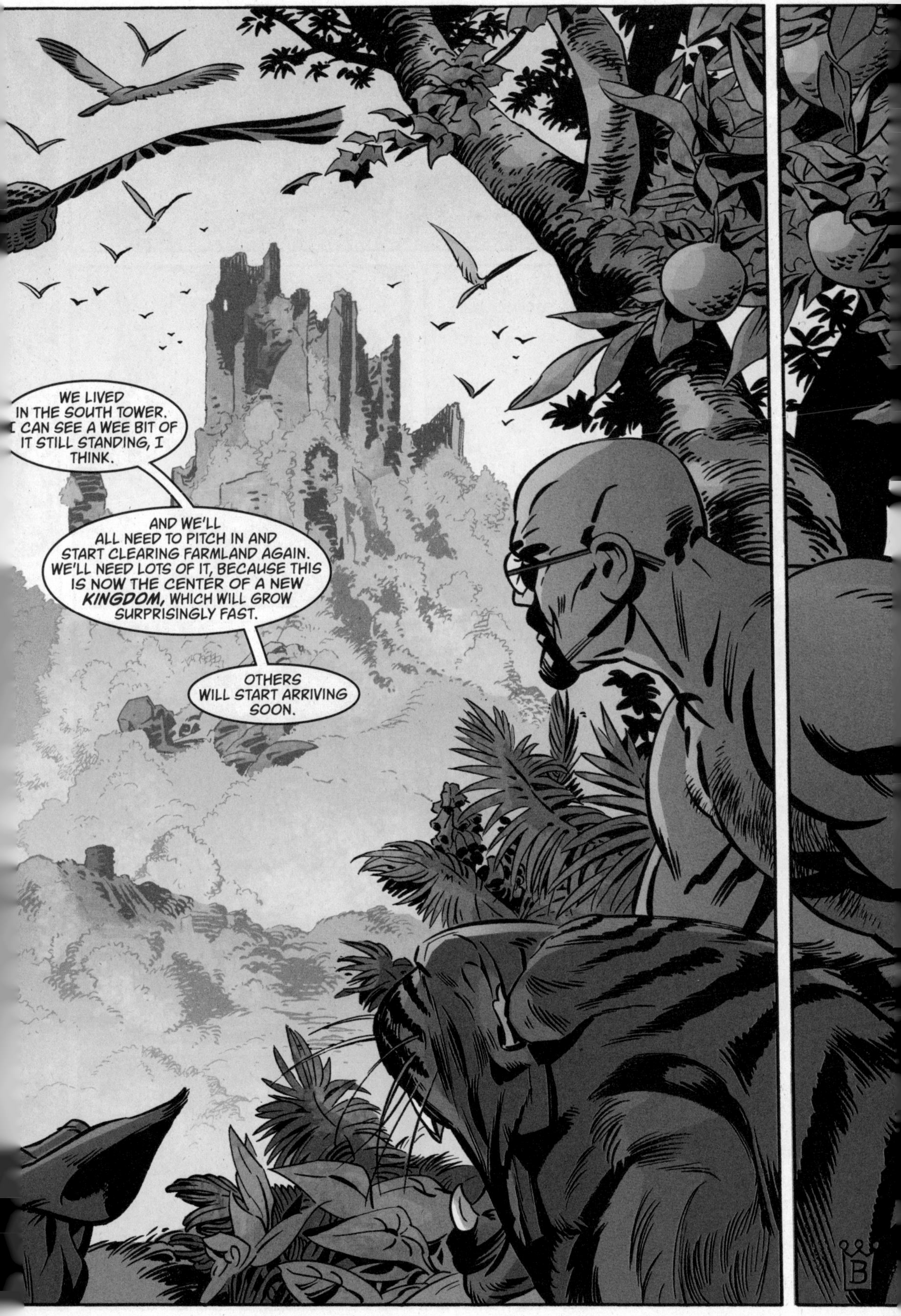
WE LIVED IN THE SOUTH TOWER. I CAN SEE A WEE BIT OF IT STILL STANDING, I THINK.
AND WE'LL ALL NEED TO PITCH IN AND START CLEARING FARMLAND AGAIN. WE'LL NEED LOTS OF IT, BECAUSE THIS IS NOW THE CENTER OF A NEW ***KINGDOM,*** WHICH WILL GROW SURPRISINGLY FAST.
OTHERS WILL START ARRIVING SOON.

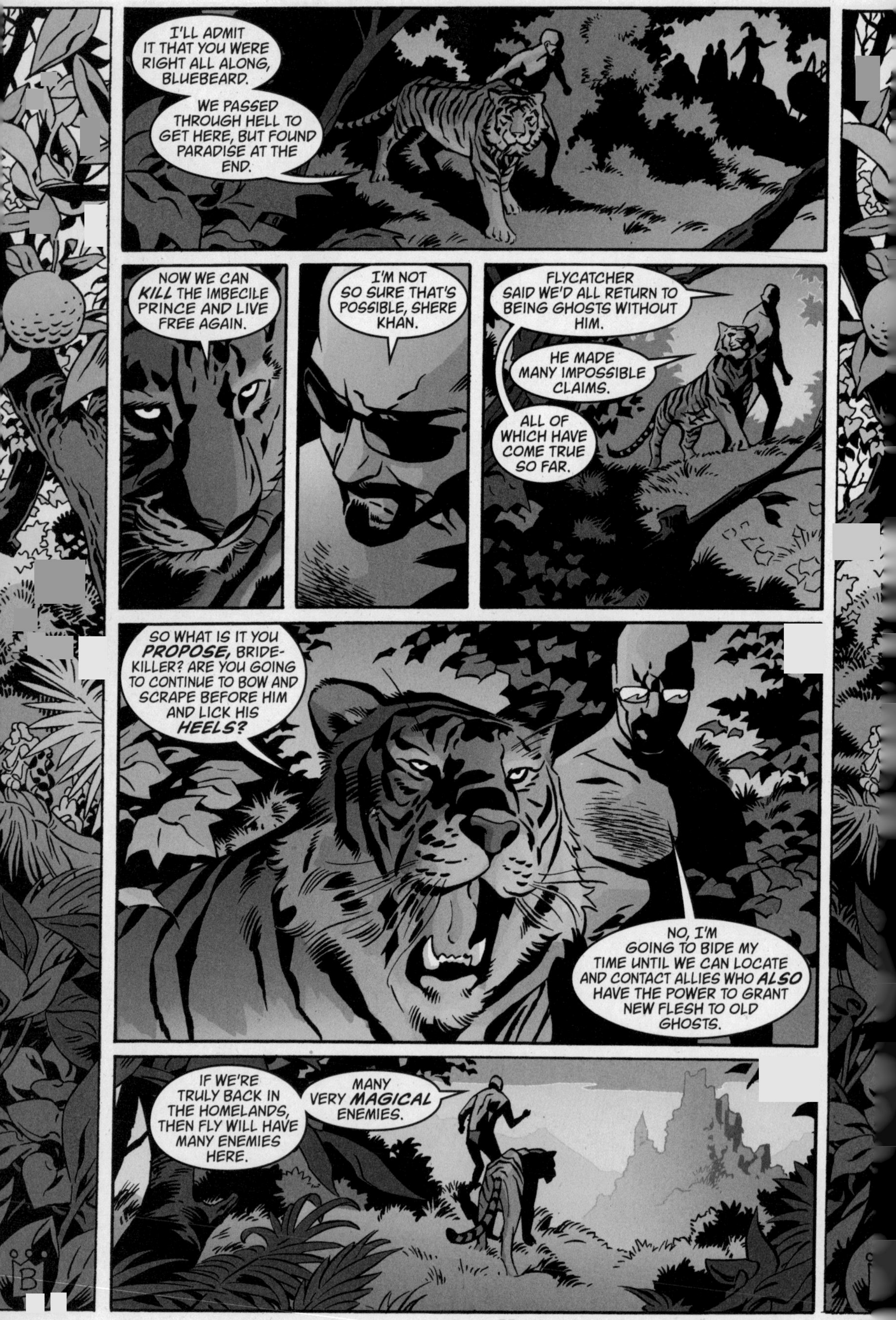
I'LL ADMIT IT THAT YOU WERE RIGHT ALL ALONG, BLUEBEARD.
WE PASSED THROUGH HELL TO GET HERE, BUT FOUND PARADISE AT THE END.
NOW WE CAN KILL THE IMBECILE PRINCE AND LIVE FREE AGAIN.
I'M NOT SO SURE THAT'S POSSIBLE, SHERE KHAN.
FLYCATCHER SAID WE'D ALL RETURN TO BEING GHOSTS WITHOUT HIM.
HE MADE MANY IMPOSSIBLE CLAIMS.
ALL OF WHICH HAVE COME TRUE SO FAR.
SO WHAT IS IT YOU PROPOSE, BRIDE-KILLER? ARE YOU GOING TO CONTINUE TO BOW AND SCRAPE BEFORE HIM AND LICK HIS HEELS?
NO, I'M GOING TO BIDE MY TIME UNTIL WE CAN LOCATE AND CONTACT ALLIES WHO ALSO HAVE THE POWER TO GRANT NEW FLESH TO OLD GHOSTS.
IF WE'RE TRULY BACK IN THE HOMELANDS, THEN FLY WILL HAVE MANY ENEMIES HERE.
MANY VERY MAGICAL ENEMIES.

NEXT: **How to really anger an empire.**

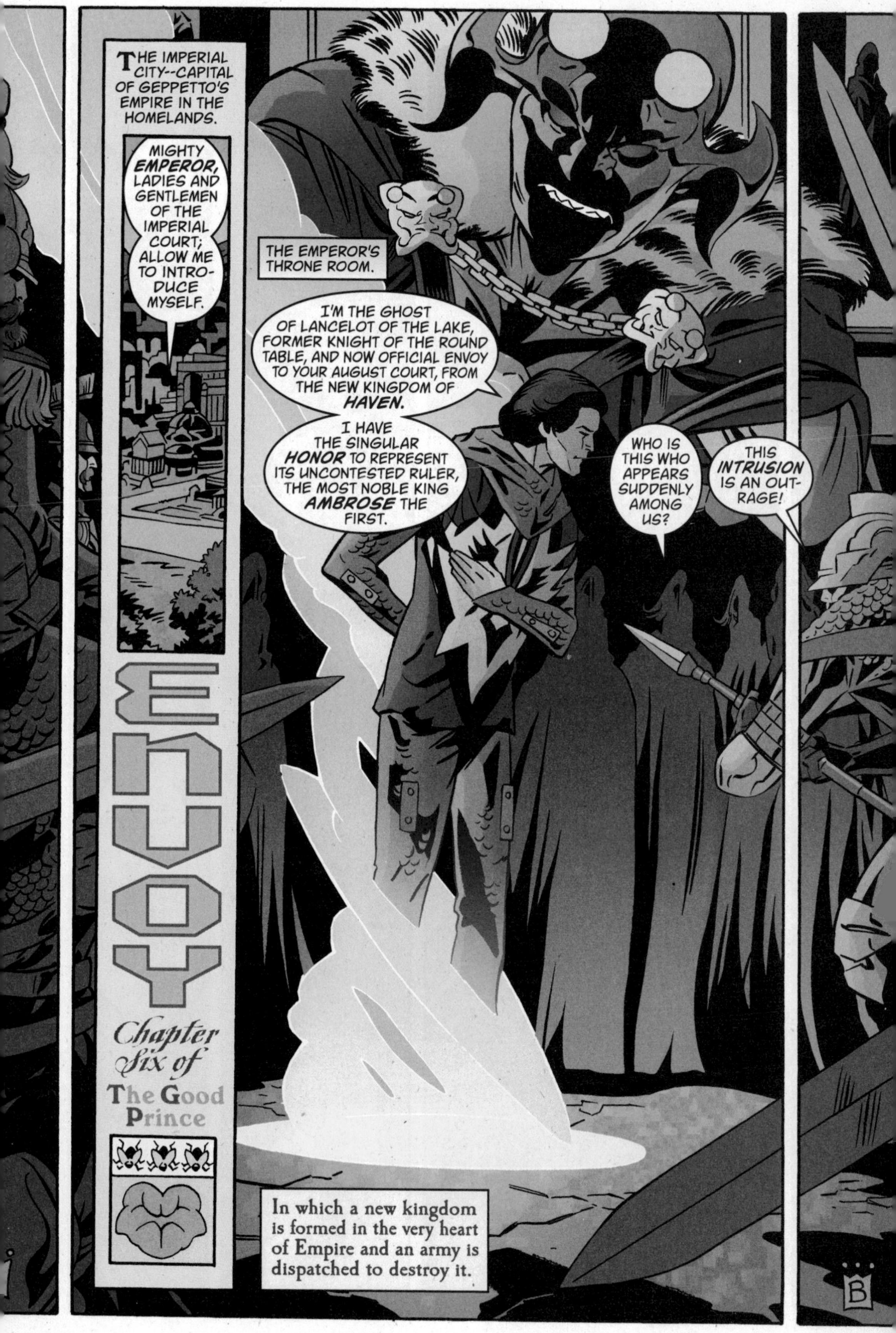

THE IMPERIAL CITY--CAPITAL OF GEPPETTO'S EMPIRE IN THE HOMELANDS.
MIGHTY EMPEROR, LADIES AND GENTLEMEN OF THE IMPERIAL COURT; ALLOW ME TO INTRO-DUCE MYSELF.
THE EMPEROR'S THRONE ROOM.
I'M THE GHOST OF LANCELOT OF THE LAKE, FORMER KNIGHT OF THE ROUND TABLE, AND NOW OFFICIAL ENVOY TO YOUR AUGUST COURT, FROM THE NEW KINGDOM OF HAVEN.
I HAVE THE SINGULAR HONOR TO REPRESENT ITS UNCONTESTED RULER, THE MOST NOBLE KING AMBROSE THE FIRST.
WHO IS THIS WHO APPEARS SUDDENLY AMONG US?
THIS INTRUSION IS AN OUT-RAGE!
ENVOY
Chapter Six of The Good Prince
In which a new kingdom is formed in the very heart of Empire and an army is dispatched to destroy it.

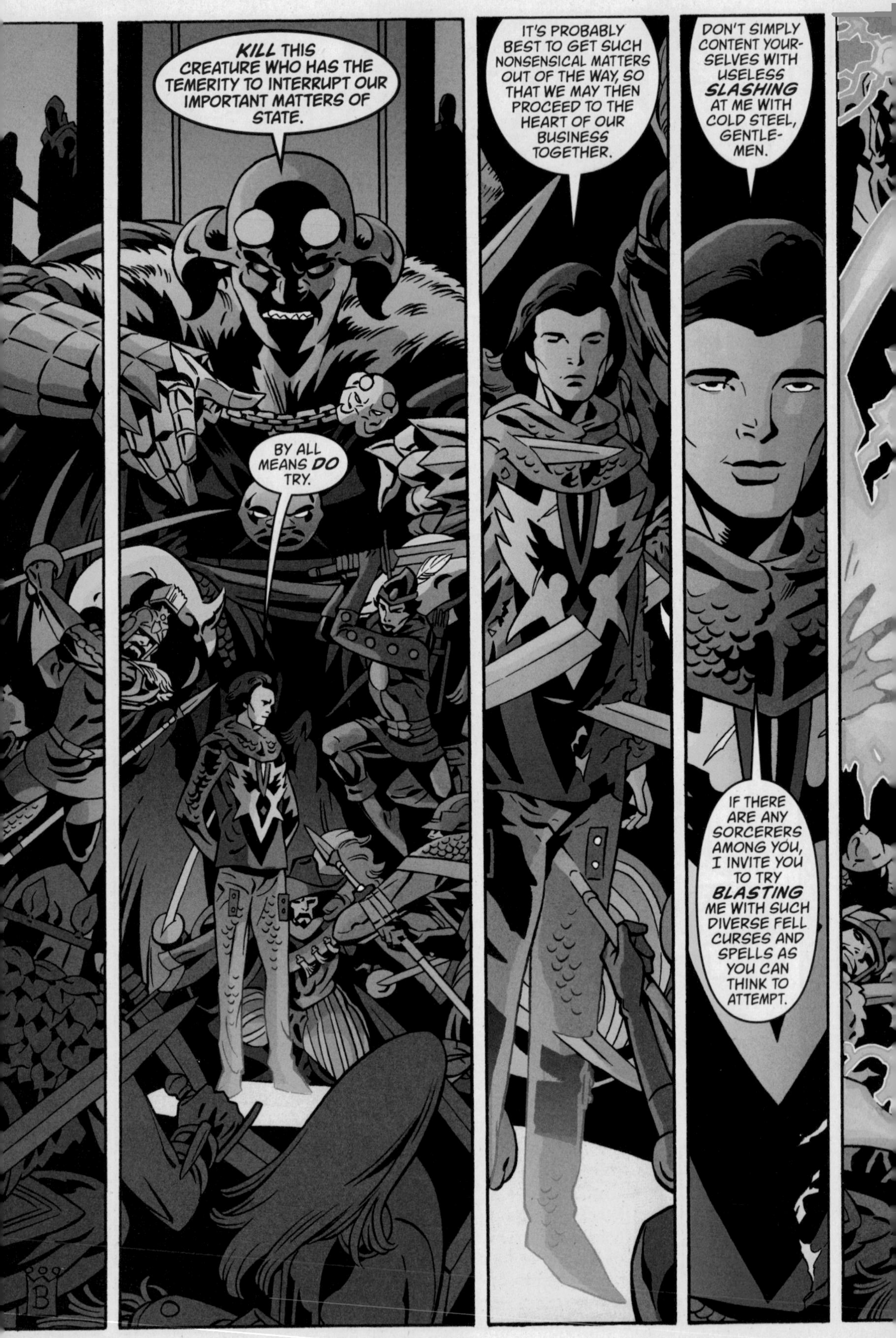
KILL THIS CREATURE WHO HAS THE TEMERITY TO INTERRUPT OUR IMPORTANT MATTERS OF STATE.
BY ALL MEANS DO TRY.
IT'S PROBABLY BEST TO GET SUCH NONSENSICAL MATTERS OUT OF THE WAY, SO THAT WE MAY THEN PROCEED TO THE HEART OF OUR BUSINESS TOGETHER.
DON'T SIMPLY CONTENT YOURSELVES WITH USELESS SLASHING AT ME WITH COLD STEEL, GENTLEMEN.
IF THERE ARE ANY SORCERERS AMONG YOU, I INVITE YOU TO TRY BLASTING ME WITH SUCH DIVERSE FELL CURSES AND SPELLS AS YOU CAN THINK TO ATTEMPT.

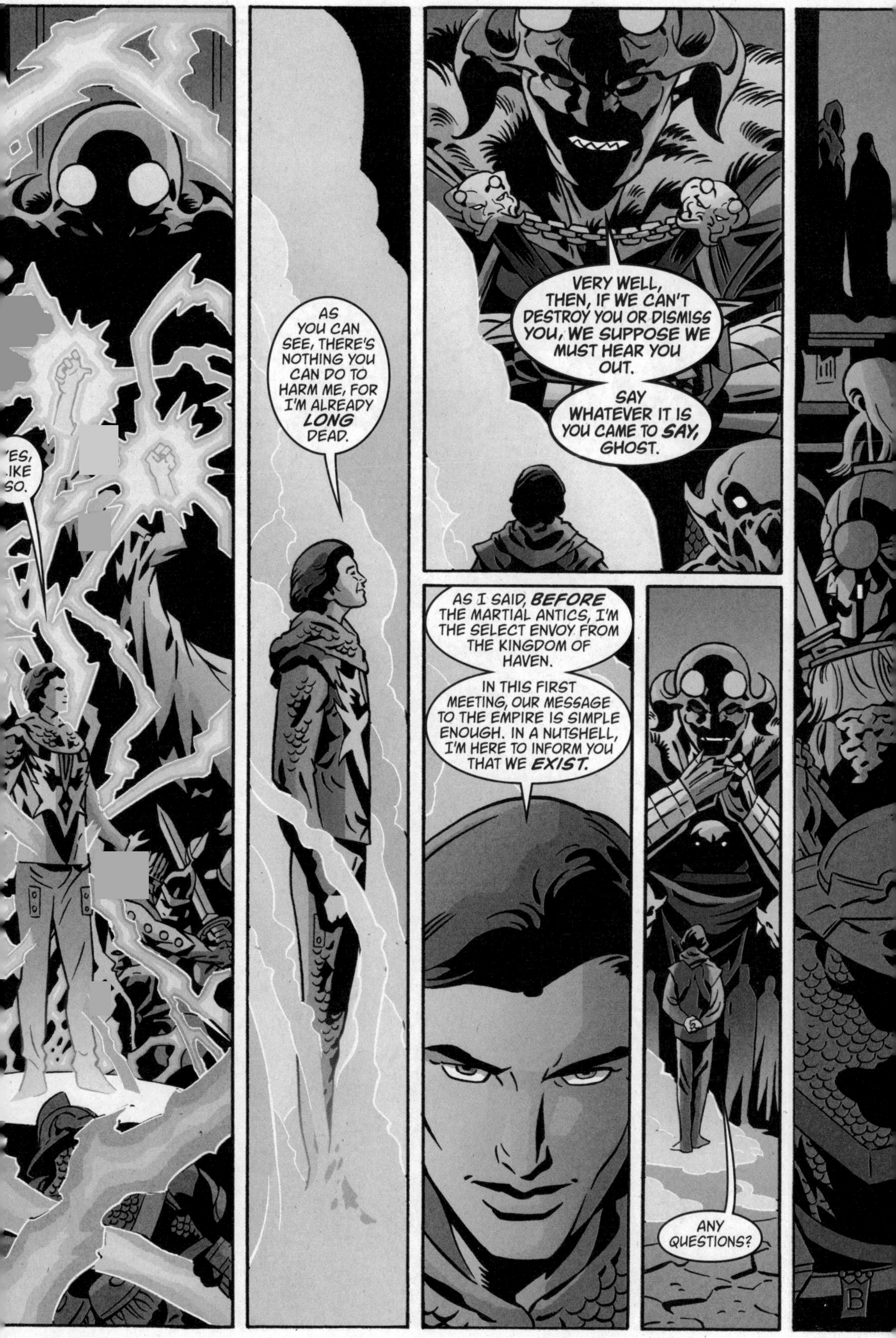

YES, LIKE SO.
AS YOU CAN SEE, THERE'S NOTHING YOU CAN DO TO HARM ME, FOR I'M ALREADY LONG DEAD.
VERY WELL, THEN, IF WE CAN'T DESTROY YOU OR DISMISS YOU, WE SUPPOSE WE MUST HEAR YOU OUT.
SAY WHATEVER IT IS YOU CAME TO SAY, GHOST.
AS I SAID, BEFORE THE MARTIAL ANTICS, I'M THE SELECT ENVOY FROM THE KINGDOM OF HAVEN.
IN THIS FIRST MEETING, OUR MESSAGE TO THE EMPIRE IS SIMPLE ENOUGH. IN A NUTSHELL, I'M HERE TO INFORM YOU THAT WE EXIST.
ANY QUESTIONS?

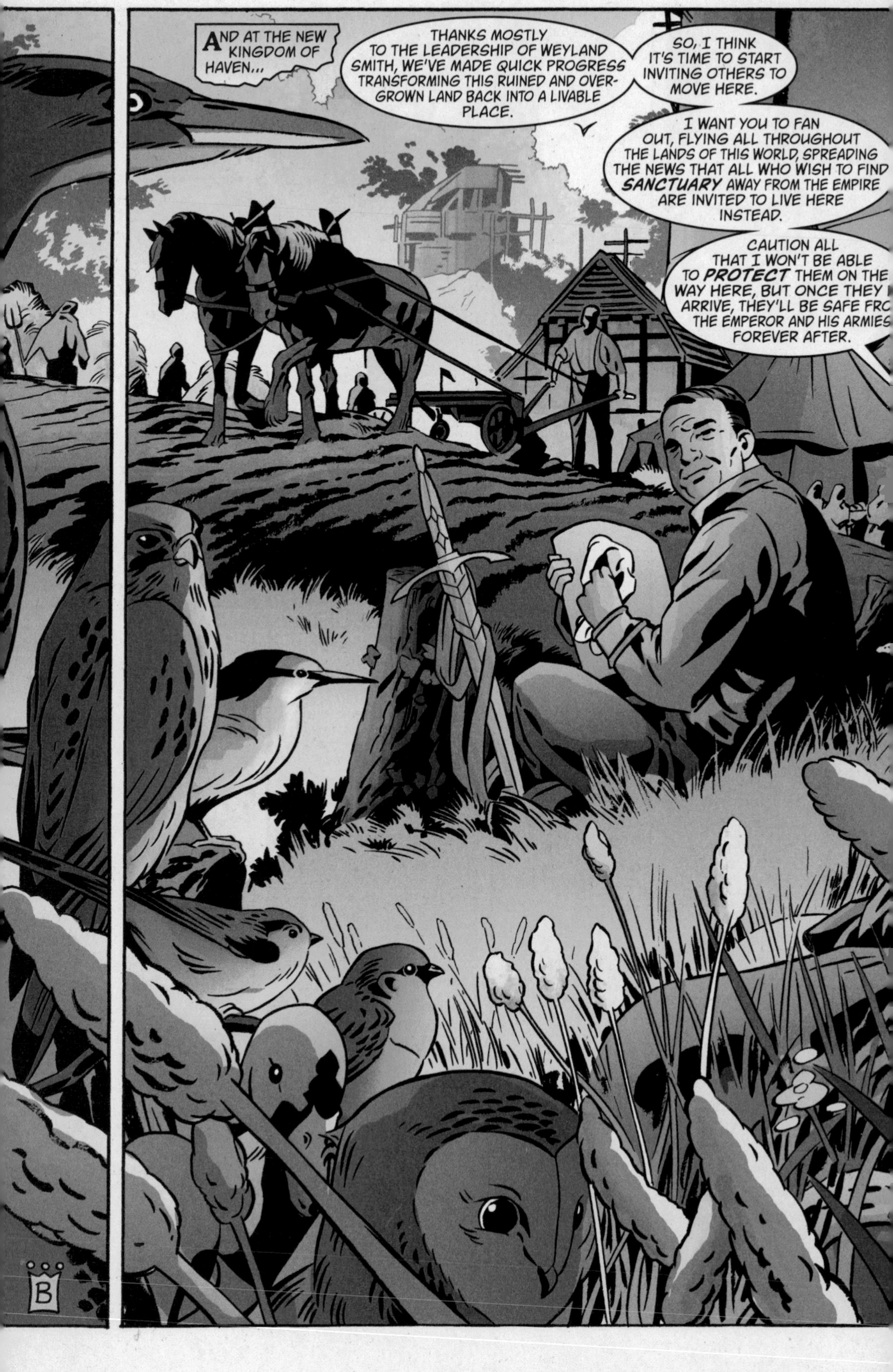

AND AT THE NEW KINGDOM OF HAVEN...
THANKS MOSTLY TO THE LEADERSHIP OF WEYLAND SMITH, WE'VE MADE QUICK PROGRESS TRANSFORMING THIS RUINED AND OVER-GROWN LAND BACK INTO A LIVABLE PLACE.
SO, I THINK IT'S TIME TO START INVITING OTHERS TO MOVE HERE.
I WANT YOU TO FAN OUT, FLYING ALL THROUGHOUT THE LANDS OF THIS WORLD, SPREADING THE NEWS THAT ALL WHO WISH TO FIND SANCTUARY AWAY FROM THE EMPIRE ARE INVITED TO LIVE HERE INSTEAD.
CAUTION ALL THAT I WON'T BE ABLE TO PROTECT THEM ON THE WAY HERE, BUT ONCE THEY ARRIVE, THEY'LL BE SAFE FRO THE EMPEROR AND HIS ARMIES FOREVER AFTER.

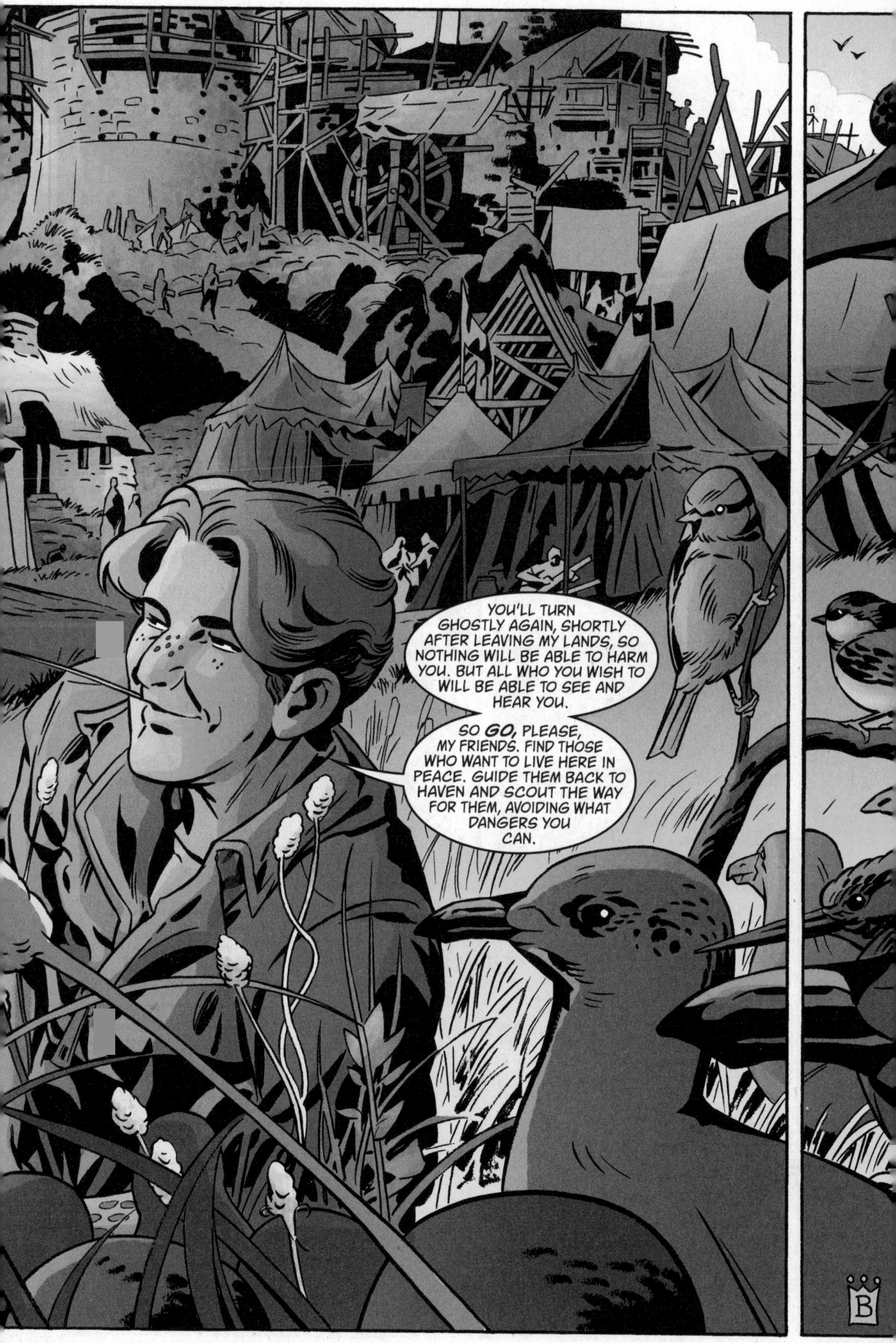
YOU'LL TURN GHOSTLY AGAIN, SHORTLY AFTER LEAVING MY LANDS, SO NOTHING WILL BE ABLE TO HARM YOU. BUT ALL WHO YOU WISH TO WILL BE ABLE TO SEE AND HEAR YOU.
SO *GO,* PLEASE, MY FRIENDS. FIND THOSE WHO WANT TO LIVE HERE IN PEACE. GUIDE THEM BACK TO HAVEN AND SCOUT THE WAY FOR THEM, AVOIDING WHAT DANGERS YOU CAN.

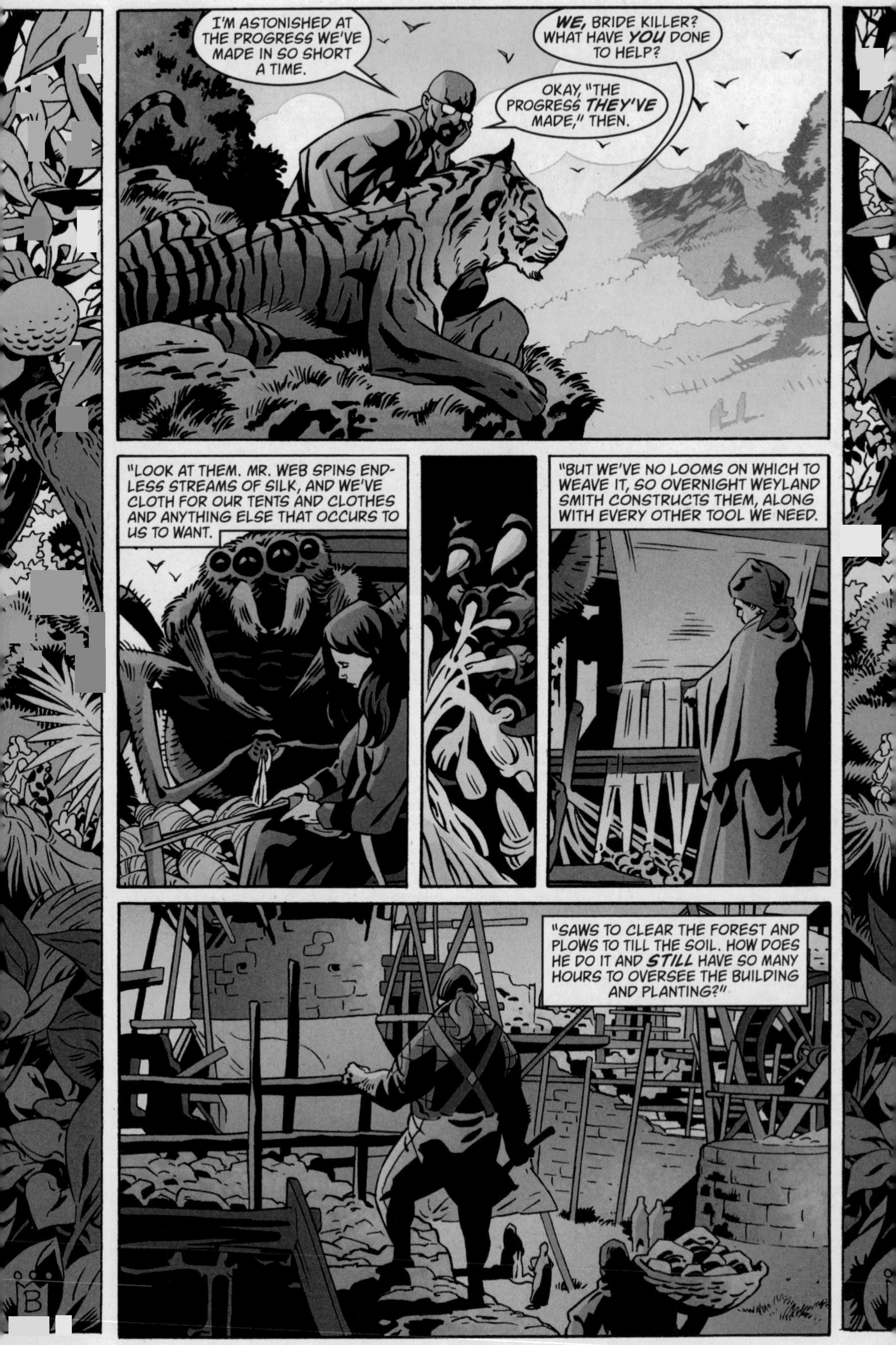
I'M ASTONISHED AT THE PROGRESS WE'VE MADE IN SO SHORT A TIME.
WE, BRIDE KILLER? WHAT HAVE YOU DONE TO HELP?
OKAY, "THE PROGRESS THEY'VE MADE," THEN.
"LOOK AT THEM. MR. WEB SPINS ENDLESS STREAMS OF SILK, AND WE'VE CLOTH FOR OUR TENTS AND CLOTHES AND ANYTHING ELSE THAT OCCURS TO US TO WANT.
"BUT WE'VE NO LOOMS ON WHICH TO WEAVE IT, SO OVERNIGHT WEYLAND SMITH CONSTRUCTS THEM, ALONG WITH EVERY OTHER TOOL WE NEED.
"SAWS TO CLEAR THE FOREST AND PLOWS TO TILL THE SOIL. HOW DOES HE DO IT AND STILL HAVE SO MANY HOURS TO OVERSEE THE BUILDING AND PLANTING?"

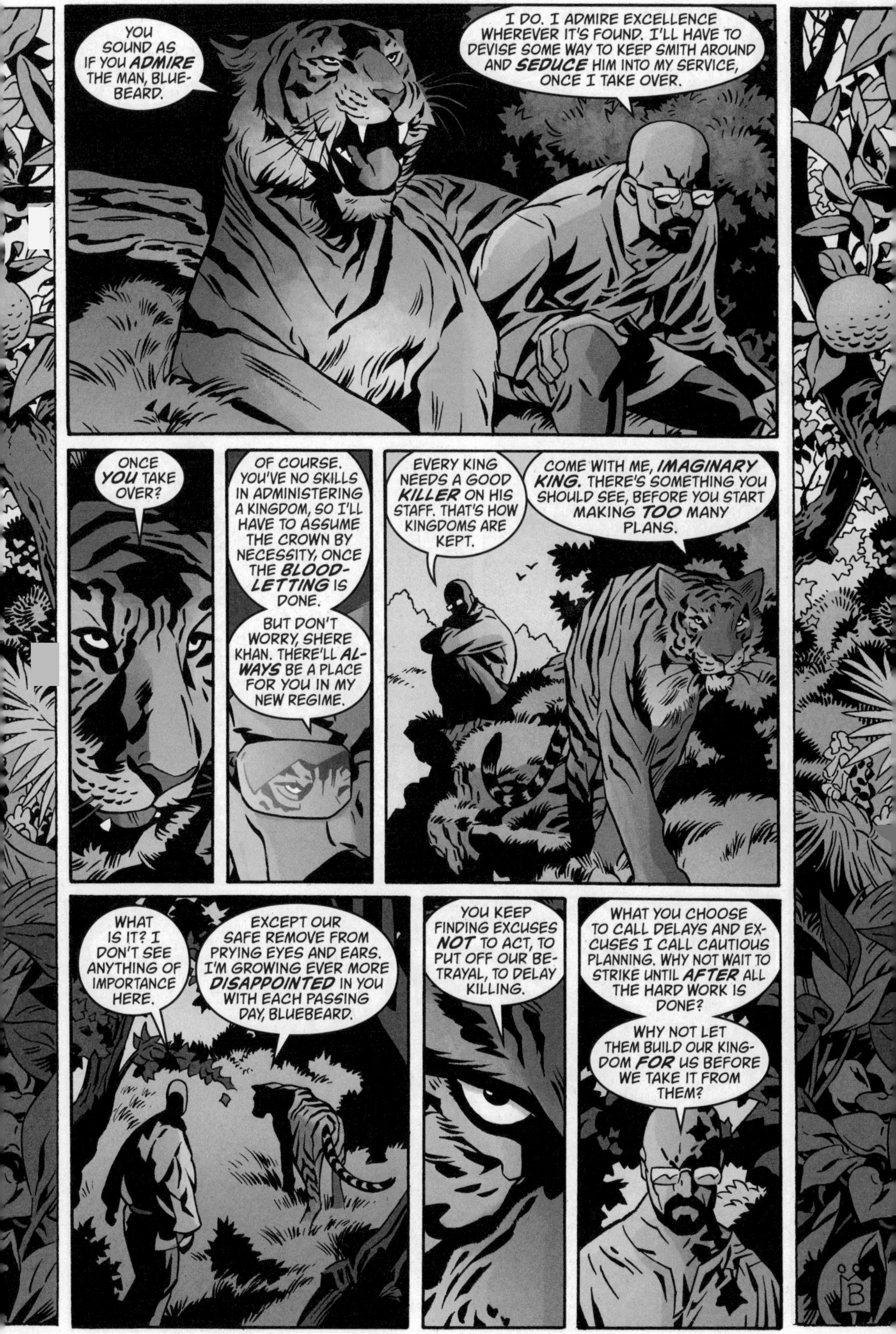
YOU SOUND AS IF YOU ADMIRE THE MAN, BLUE-BEARD.
I DO. I ADMIRE EXCELLENCE WHEREVER IT'S FOUND. I'LL HAVE TO DEVISE SOME WAY TO KEEP SMITH AROUND AND SEDUCE HIM INTO MY SERVICE, ONCE I TAKE OVER.
ONCE YOU TAKE OVER?
OF COURSE. YOU'VE NO SKILLS IN ADMINISTERING A KINGDOM, SO I'LL HAVE TO ASSUME THE CROWN BY NECESSITY, ONCE THE BLOOD-LETTING IS DONE.
BUT DON'T WORRY, SHERE KHAN. THERE'LL AL-WAYS BE A PLACE FOR YOU IN MY NEW REGIME.
EVERY KING NEEDS A GOOD KILLER ON HIS STAFF. THAT'S HOW KINGDOMS ARE KEPT.
COME WITH ME, IMAGINARY KING. THERE'S SOMETHING YOU SHOULD SEE, BEFORE YOU START MAKING TOO MANY PLANS.
WHAT IS IT? I DON'T SEE ANYTHING OF IMPORTANCE HERE.
EXCEPT OUR SAFE REMOVE FROM PRYING EYES AND EARS. I'M GROWING EVER MORE DISAPPOINTED IN YOU WITH EACH PASSING DAY, BLUEBEARD.
YOU KEEP FINDING EXCUSES NOT TO ACT, TO PUT OFF OUR BE-TRAYAL, TO DELAY KILLING.
WHAT YOU CHOOSE TO CALL DELAYS AND EX-CUSES I CALL CAUTIOUS PLANNING. WHY NOT WAIT TO STRIKE UNTIL AFTER ALL THE HARD WORK IS DONE?
WHY NOT LET THEM BUILD OUR KING-DOM FOR US BEFORE WE TAKE IT FROM THEM?

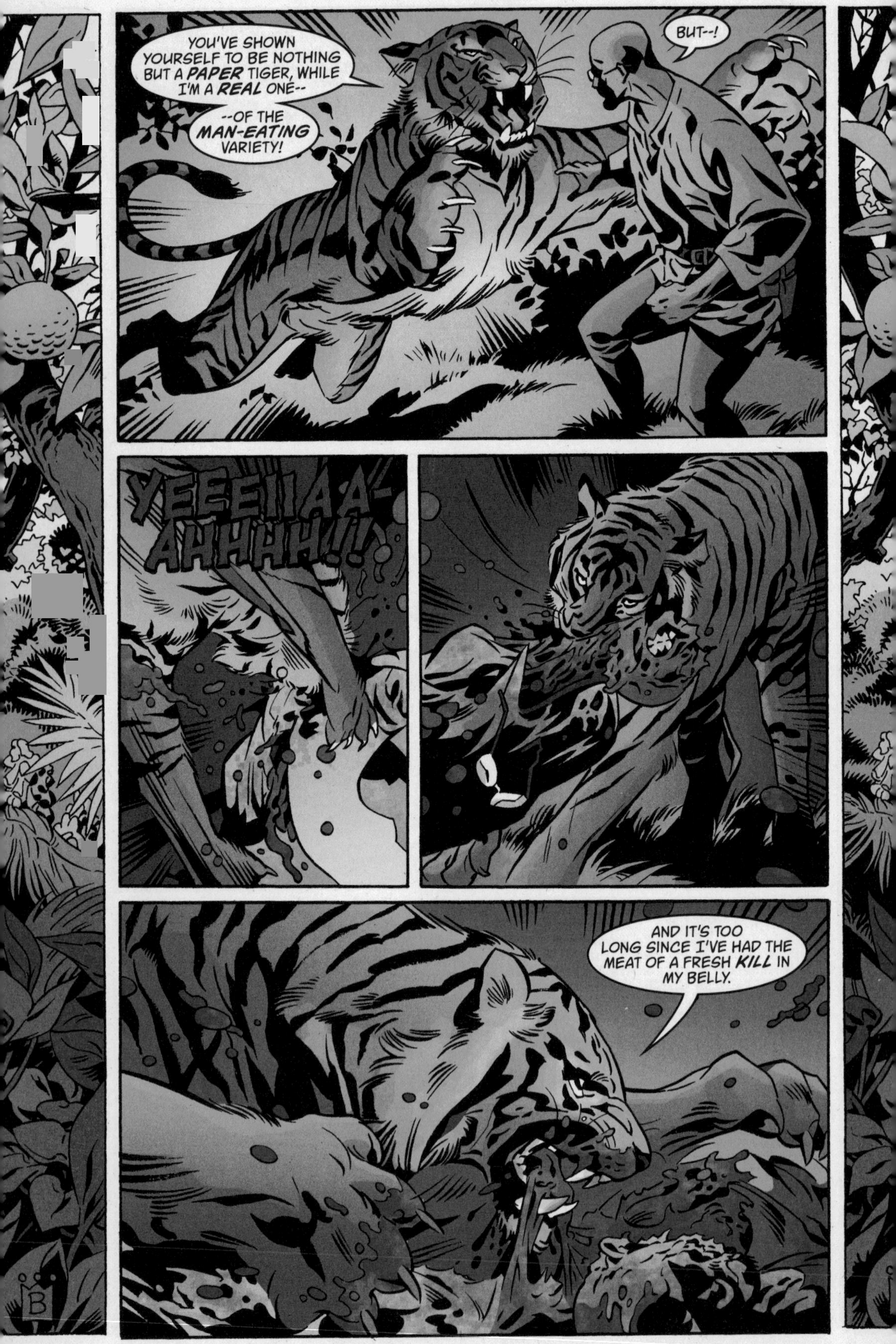
YOU'VE SHOWN YOURSELF TO BE NOTHING BUT A PAPER TIGER, WHILE I'M A REAL ONE--
BUT--!
--OF THE MAN-EATING VARIETY!
YEEEIIAA-AHHHH!!!
AND IT'S TOO LONG SINCE I'VE HAD THE MEAT OF A FRESH KILL IN MY BELLY.

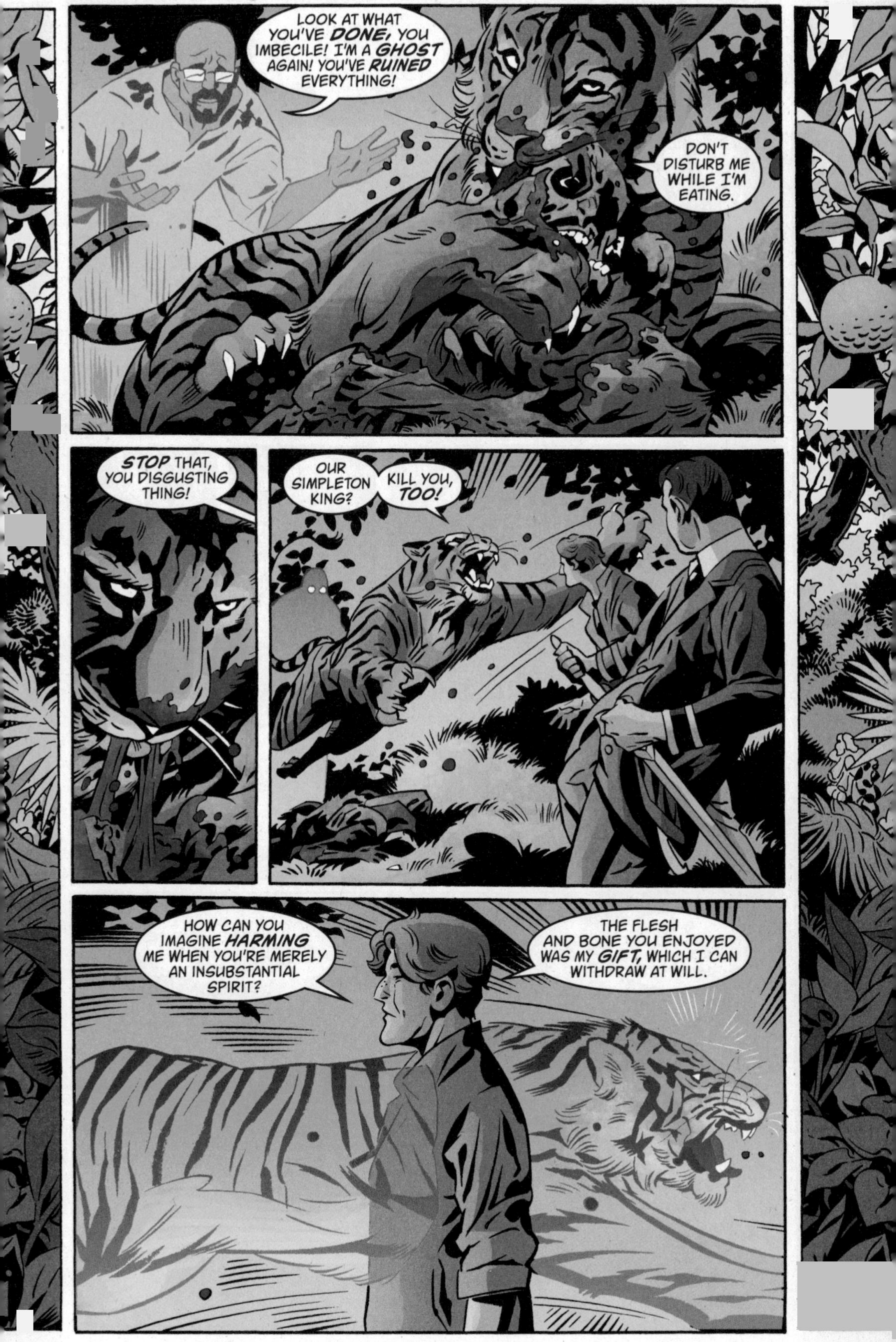
LOOK AT WHAT YOU'VE DONE, YOU IMBECILE! I'M A GHOST AGAIN! YOU'VE RUINED EVERYTHING!
DON'T DISTURB ME WHILE I'M EATING.
STOP THAT, YOU DISGUSTING THING!
OUR SIMPLETON KING?
KILL YOU, TOO!
HOW CAN YOU IMAGINE HARMING ME WHEN YOU'RE MERELY AN INSUBSTANTIAL SPIRIT?
THE FLESH AND BONE YOU ENJOYED WAS MY GIFT, WHICH I CAN WITHDRAW AT WILL.

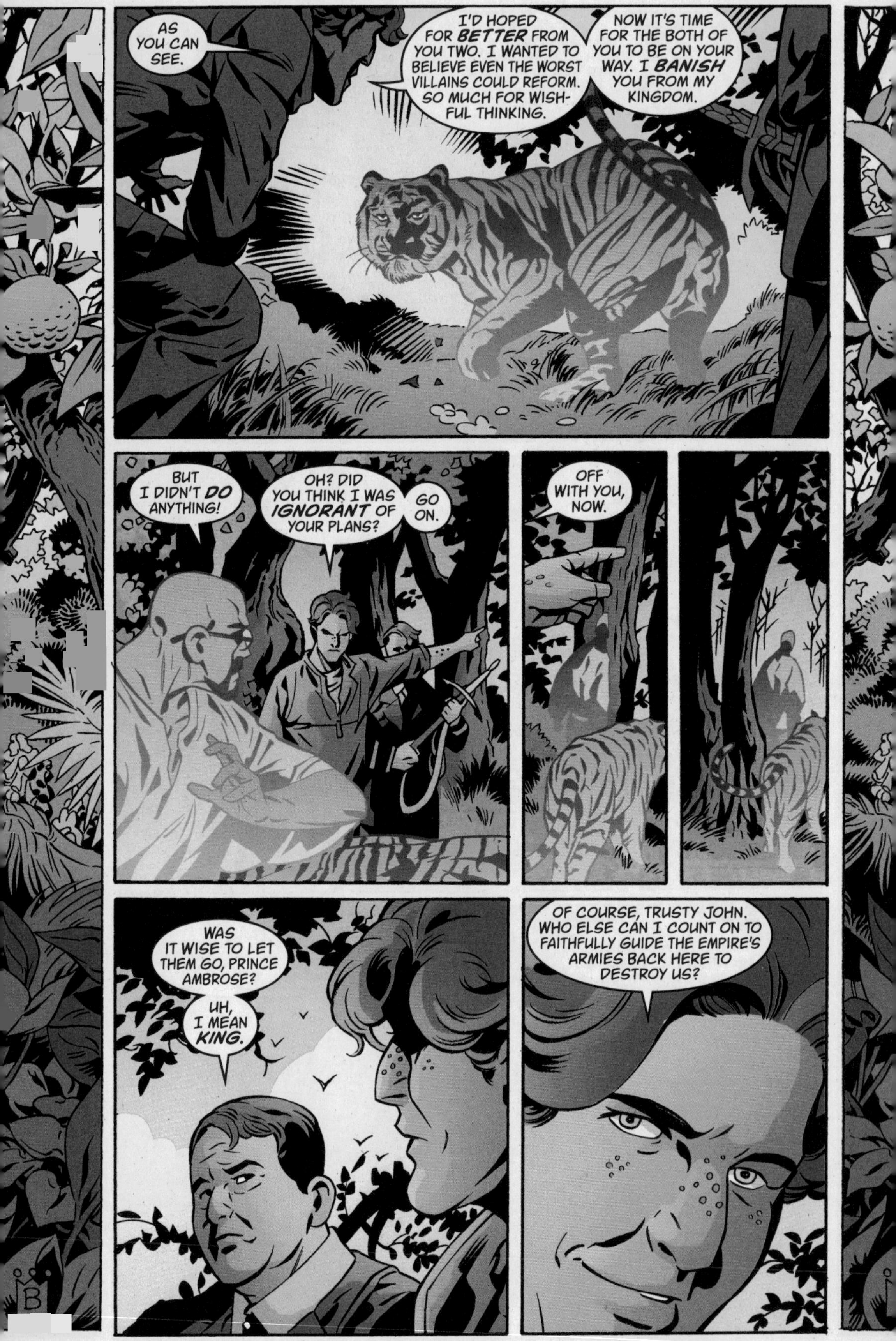
AS YOU CAN SEE.
I'D HOPED FOR BETTER FROM YOU TWO. I WANTED TO BELIEVE EVEN THE WORST VILLAINS COULD REFORM. SO MUCH FOR WISH-FUL THINKING.
NOW IT'S TIME FOR THE BOTH OF YOU TO BE ON YOUR WAY. I BANISH YOU FROM MY KINGDOM.
BUT I DIDN'T DO ANYTHING!
OH? DID YOU THINK I WAS IGNORANT OF YOUR PLANS?
GO ON.
OFF WITH YOU, NOW.
WAS IT WISE TO LET THEM GO, PRINCE AMBROSE?
UH, I MEAN KING.
OF COURSE, TRUSTY JOHN. WHO ELSE CAN I COUNT ON TO FAITHFULLY GUIDE THE EMPIRE'S ARMIES BACK HERE TO DESTROY US?

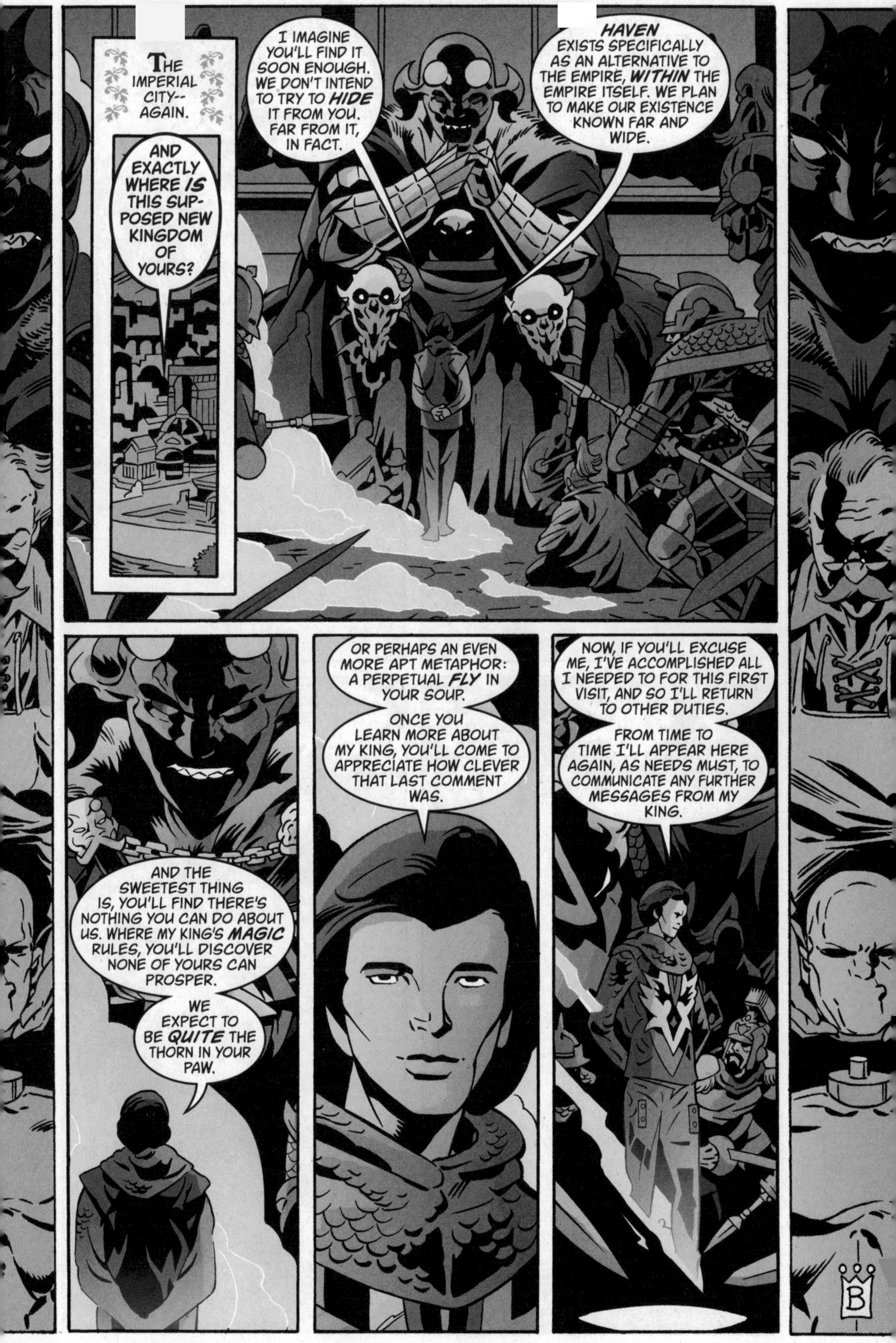
THE IMPERIAL CITY-- AGAIN.
AND EXACTLY WHERE *IS* THIS SUPPOSED NEW KINGDOM OF YOURS?
I IMAGINE YOU'LL FIND IT SOON ENOUGH. WE DON'T INTEND TO TRY TO *HIDE* IT FROM YOU. FAR FROM IT, IN FACT.
HAVEN EXISTS SPECIFICALLY AS AN ALTERNATIVE TO THE EMPIRE, *WITHIN* THE EMPIRE ITSELF. WE PLAN TO MAKE OUR EXISTENCE KNOWN FAR AND WIDE.
AND THE SWEETEST THING IS, YOU'LL FIND THERE'S NOTHING YOU CAN DO ABOUT US. WHERE MY KING'S *MAGIC* RULES, YOU'LL DISCOVER NONE OF YOURS CAN PROSPER.
WE EXPECT TO BE *QUITE* THE THORN IN YOUR PAW.
OR PERHAPS AN EVEN MORE APT METAPHOR: A PERPETUAL *FLY* IN YOUR SOUP.
ONCE YOU LEARN MORE ABOUT MY KING, YOU'LL COME TO APPRECIATE HOW CLEVER THAT LAST COMMENT WAS.
NOW, IF YOU'LL EXCUSE ME, I'VE ACCOMPLISHED ALL I NEEDED TO FOR THIS FIRST VISIT, AND SO I'LL RETURN TO OTHER DUTIES.
FROM TIME TO TIME I'LL APPEAR HERE AGAIN, AS NEEDS MUST, TO COMMUNICATE ANY FURTHER MESSAGES FROM MY KING.

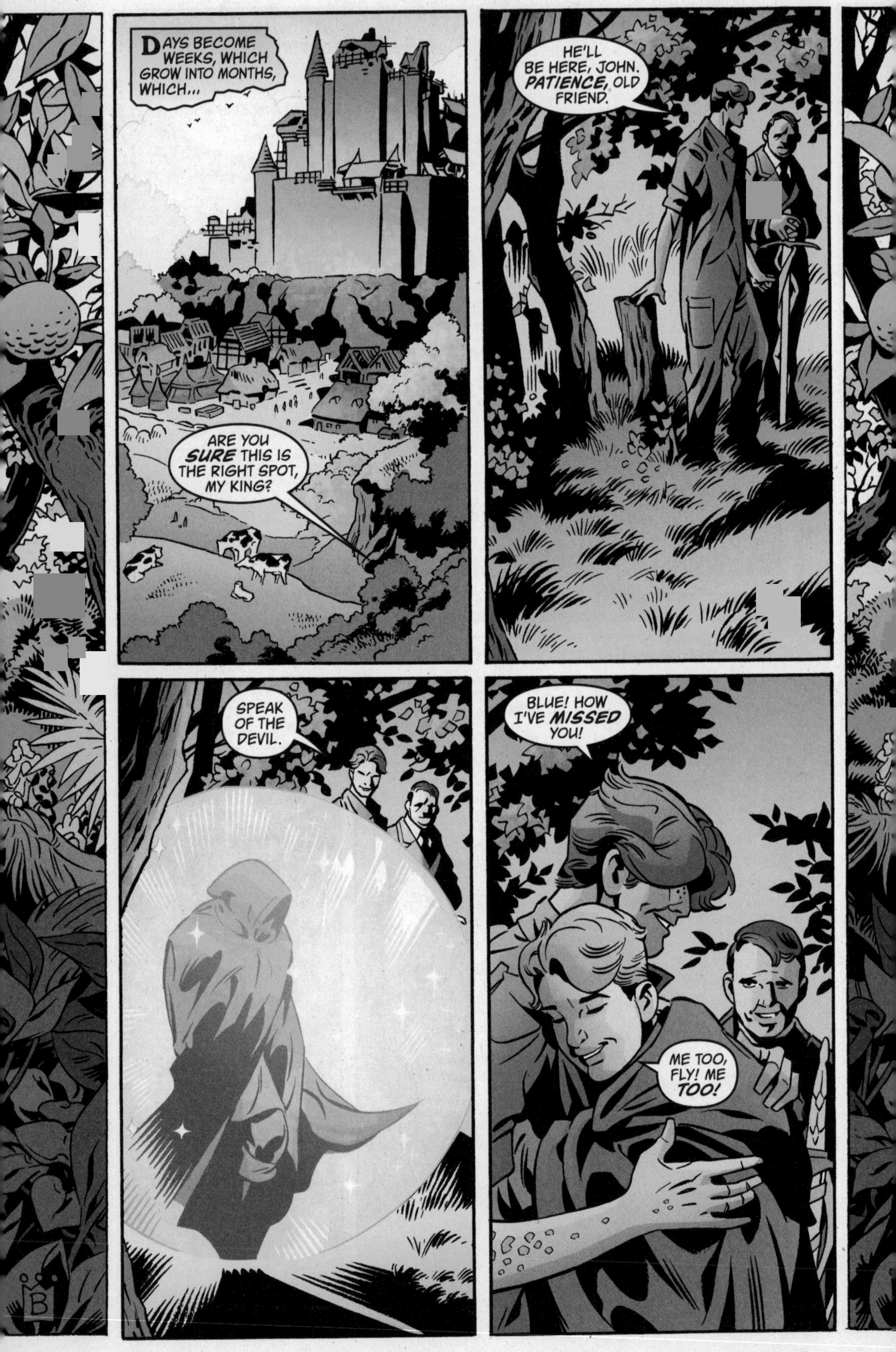
DAYS BECOME WEEKS, WHICH GROW INTO MONTHS, WHICH...
ARE YOU SURE THIS IS THE RIGHT SPOT, MY KING?
HE'LL BE HERE, JOHN. PATIENCE, OLD FRIEND.
SPEAK OF THE DEVIL.
BLUE! HOW I'VE MISSED YOU!
ME TOO, FLY! ME TOO!

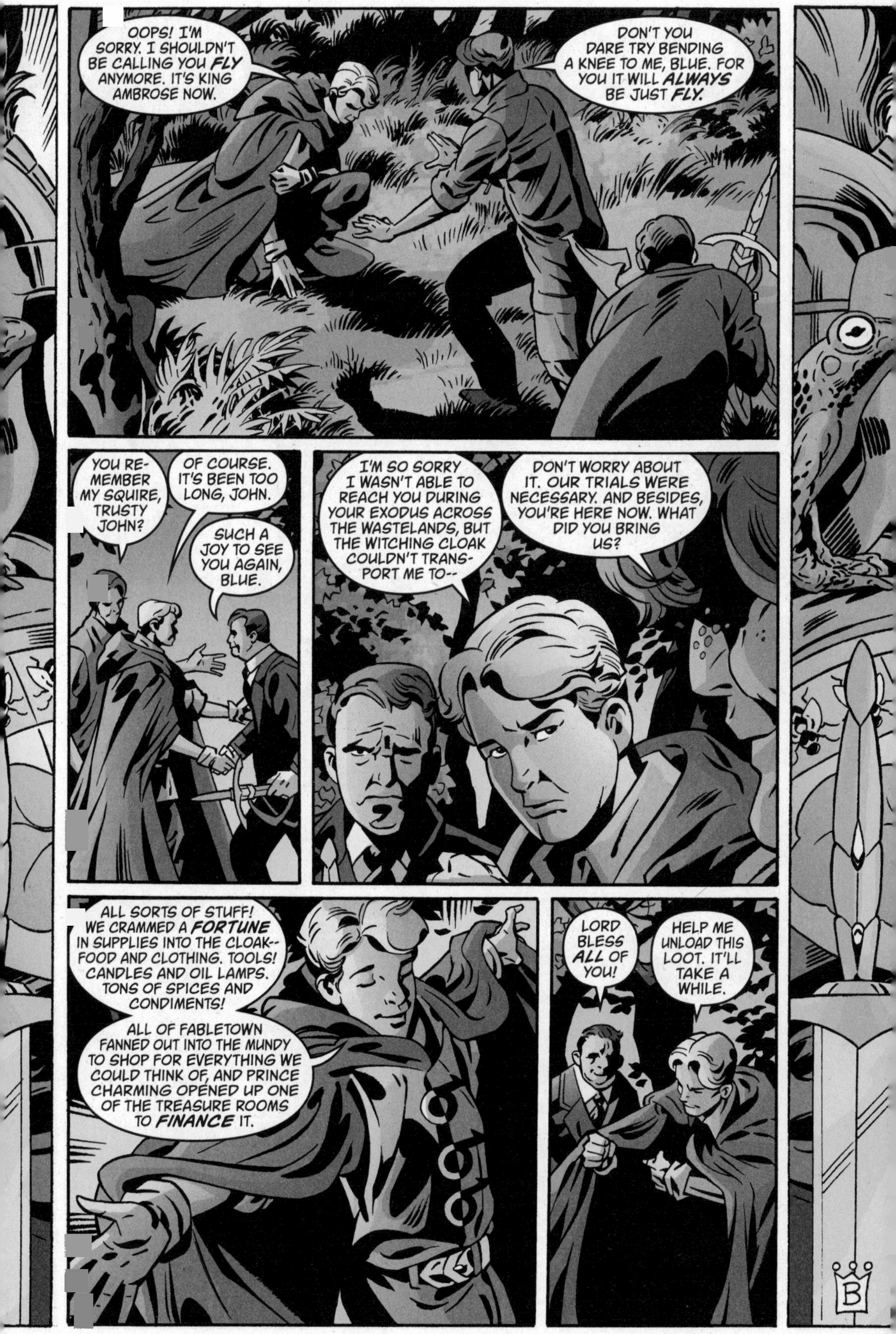
OOPS! I'M SORRY. I SHOULDN'T BE CALLING YOU FLY ANYMORE. IT'S KING AMBROSE NOW.
DON'T YOU DARE TRY BENDING A KNEE TO ME, BLUE. FOR YOU IT WILL ALWAYS BE JUST FLY.
YOU REMEMBER MY SQUIRE, TRUSTY JOHN?
OF COURSE. IT'S BEEN TOO LONG, JOHN.
SUCH A JOY TO SEE YOU AGAIN, BLUE.
I'M SO SORRY I WASN'T ABLE TO REACH YOU DURING YOUR EXODUS ACROSS THE WASTELANDS, BUT THE WITCHING CLOAK COULDN'T TRANSPORT ME TO--
DON'T WORRY ABOUT IT. OUR TRIALS WERE NECESSARY. AND BESIDES, YOU'RE HERE NOW. WHAT DID YOU BRING US?
ALL SORTS OF STUFF! WE CRAMMED A FORTUNE IN SUPPLIES INTO THE CLOAK-- FOOD AND CLOTHING. TOOLS! CANDLES AND OIL LAMPS. TONS OF SPICES AND CONDIMENTS!
ALL OF FABLETOWN FANNED OUT INTO THE MUNDY TO SHOP FOR EVERYTHING WE COULD THINK OF, AND PRINCE CHARMING OPENED UP ONE OF THE TREASURE ROOMS TO FINANCE IT.
LORD BLESS ALL OF YOU!
HELP ME UNLOAD THIS LOOT. IT'LL TAKE A WHILE.

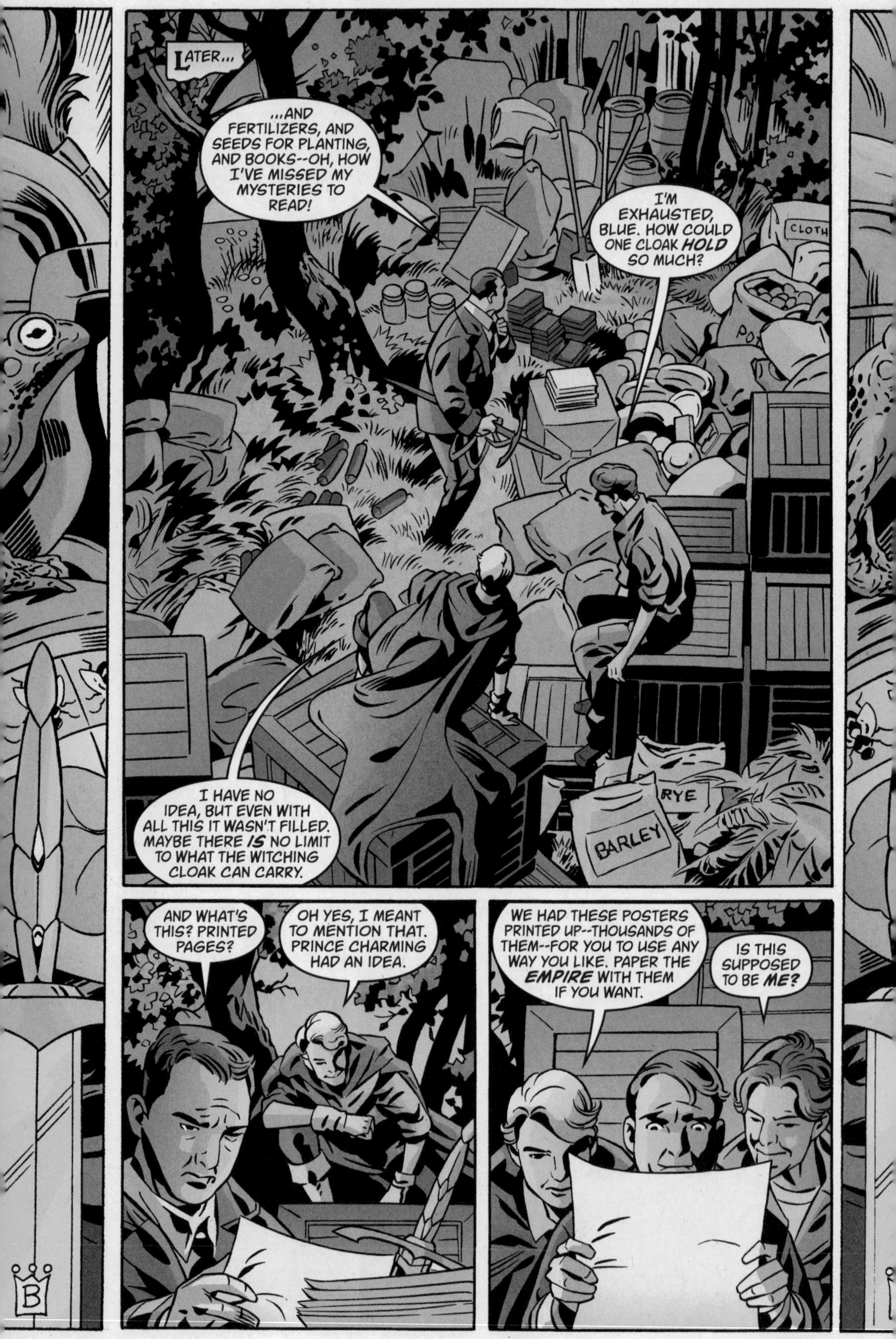
LATER...
...AND FERTILIZERS, AND SEEDS FOR PLANTING, AND BOOKS--OH, HOW I'VE MISSED MY MYSTERIES TO READ!
I'M EXHAUSTED, BLUE. HOW COULD ONE CLOAK HOLD SO MUCH?
CLOTH
I HAVE NO IDEA, BUT EVEN WITH ALL THIS IT WASN'T FILLED. MAYBE THERE IS NO LIMIT TO WHAT THE WITCHING CLOAK CAN CARRY.
RYE
BARLEY
AND WHAT'S THIS? PRINTED PAGES?
OH YES, I MEANT TO MENTION THAT. PRINCE CHARMING HAD AN IDEA.
WE HAD THESE POSTERS PRINTED UP--THOUSANDS OF THEM--FOR YOU TO USE ANY WAY YOU LIKE. PAPER THE EMPIRE WITH THEM IF YOU WANT.
IS THIS SUPPOSED TO BE ME?

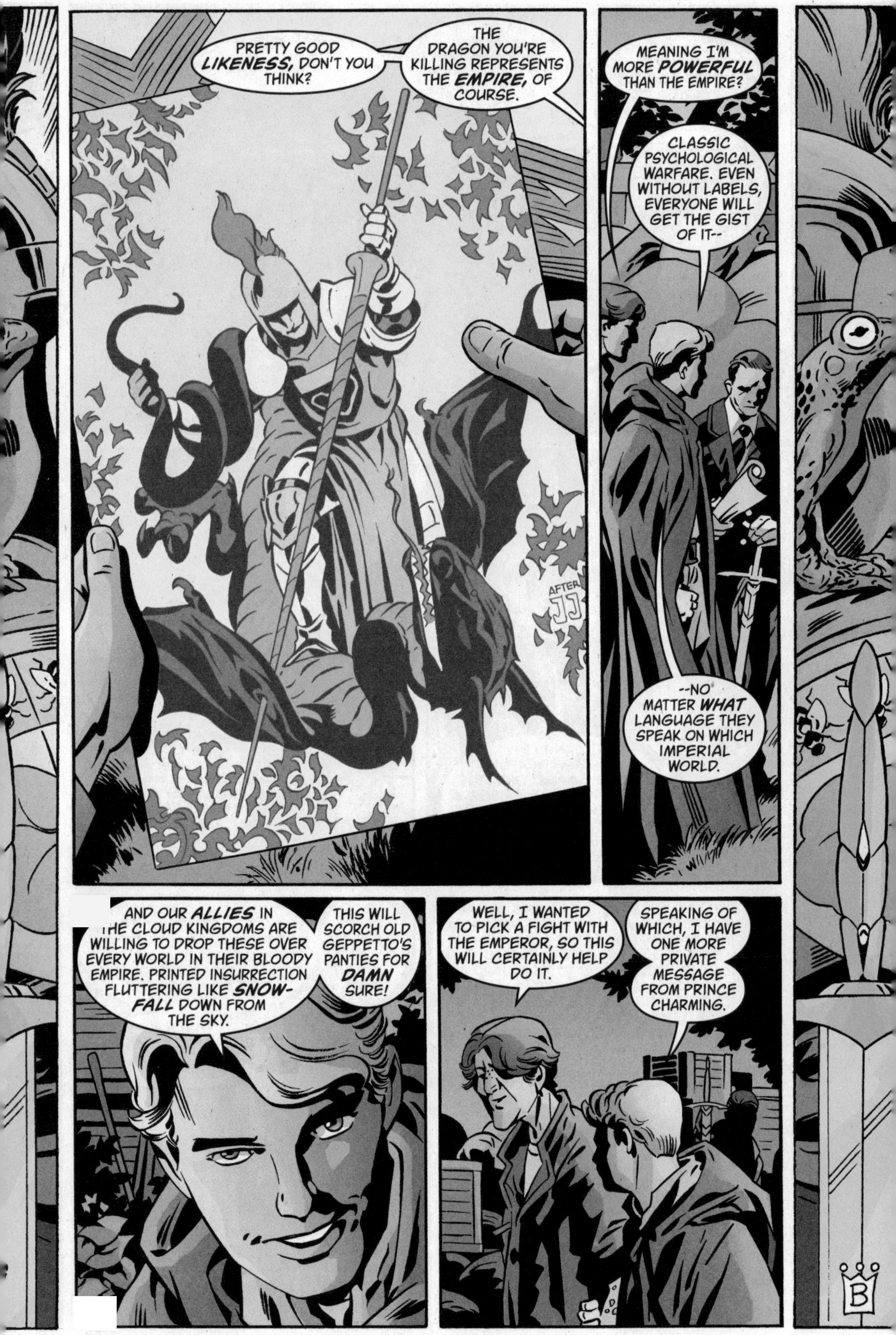
PRETTY GOOD LIKENESS, DON'T YOU THINK?
THE DRAGON YOU'RE KILLING REPRESENTS THE EMPIRE, OF COURSE.
AFTER JJ
MEANING I'M MORE POWERFUL THAN THE EMPIRE?
CLASSIC PSYCHOLOGICAL WARFARE. EVEN WITHOUT LABELS, EVERYONE WILL GET THE GIST OF IT--
--NO MATTER WHAT LANGUAGE THEY SPEAK ON WHICH IMPERIAL WORLD.
AND OUR ALLIES IN THE CLOUD KINGDOMS ARE WILLING TO DROP THESE OVER EVERY WORLD IN THEIR BLOODY EMPIRE. PRINTED INSURRECTION FLUTTERING LIKE SNOW-FALL DOWN FROM THE SKY.
THIS WILL SCORCH OLD GEPPETTO'S PANTIES FOR DAMN SURE!
WELL, I WANTED TO PICK A FIGHT WITH THE EMPEROR, SO THIS WILL CERTAINLY HELP DO IT.
SPEAKING OF WHICH, I HAVE ONE MORE PRIVATE MESSAGE FROM PRINCE CHARMING.

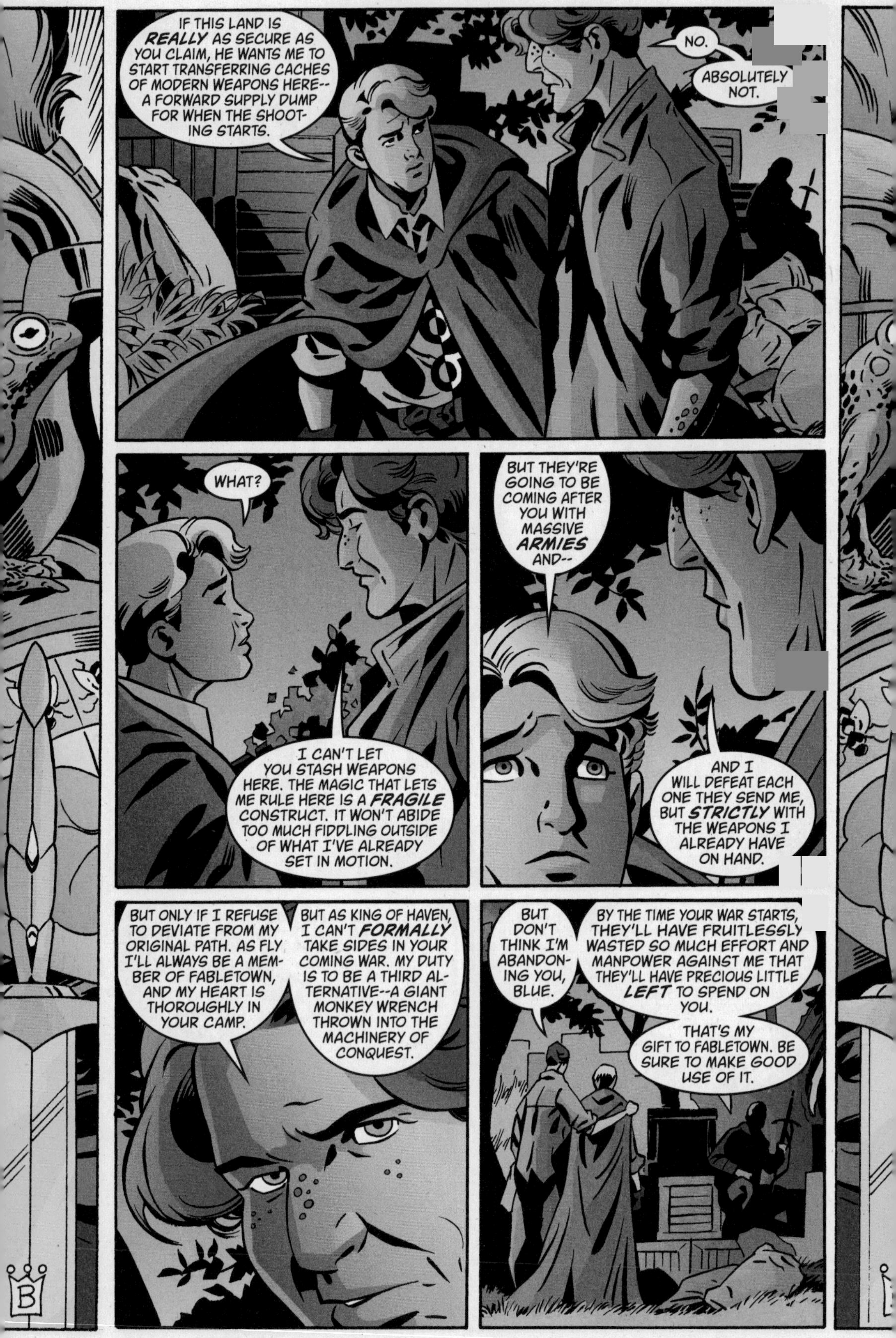
IF THIS LAND IS REALLY AS SECURE AS YOU CLAIM, HE WANTS ME TO START TRANSFERRING CACHES OF MODERN WEAPONS HERE--A FORWARD SUPPLY DUMP FOR WHEN THE SHOOTING STARTS.
NO.
ABSOLUTELY NOT.
WHAT?
I CAN'T LET YOU STASH WEAPONS HERE. THE MAGIC THAT LETS ME RULE HERE IS A FRAGILE CONSTRUCT. IT WON'T ABIDE TOO MUCH FIDDLING OUTSIDE OF WHAT I'VE ALREADY SET IN MOTION.
BUT THEY'RE GOING TO BE COMING AFTER YOU WITH MASSIVE ARMIES AND--
AND I WILL DEFEAT EACH ONE THEY SEND ME, BUT STRICTLY WITH THE WEAPONS I ALREADY HAVE ON HAND.
BUT ONLY IF I REFUSE TO DEVIATE FROM MY ORIGINAL PATH. AS FLY I'LL ALWAYS BE A MEMBER OF FABLETOWN, AND MY HEART IS THOROUGHLY IN YOUR CAMP.
BUT AS KING OF HAVEN, I CAN'T FORMALLY TAKE SIDES IN YOUR COMING WAR. MY DUTY IS TO BE A THIRD ALTERNATIVE--A GIANT MONKEY WRENCH THROWN INTO THE MACHINERY OF CONQUEST.
BUT DON'T THINK I'M ABANDONING YOU, BLUE.
BY THE TIME YOUR WAR STARTS, THEY'LL HAVE FRUITLESSLY WASTED SO MUCH EFFORT AND MANPOWER AGAINST ME THAT THEY'LL HAVE PRECIOUS LITTLE LEFT TO SPEND ON YOU.
THAT'S MY GIFT TO FABLETOWN. BE SURE TO MAKE GOOD USE OF IT.

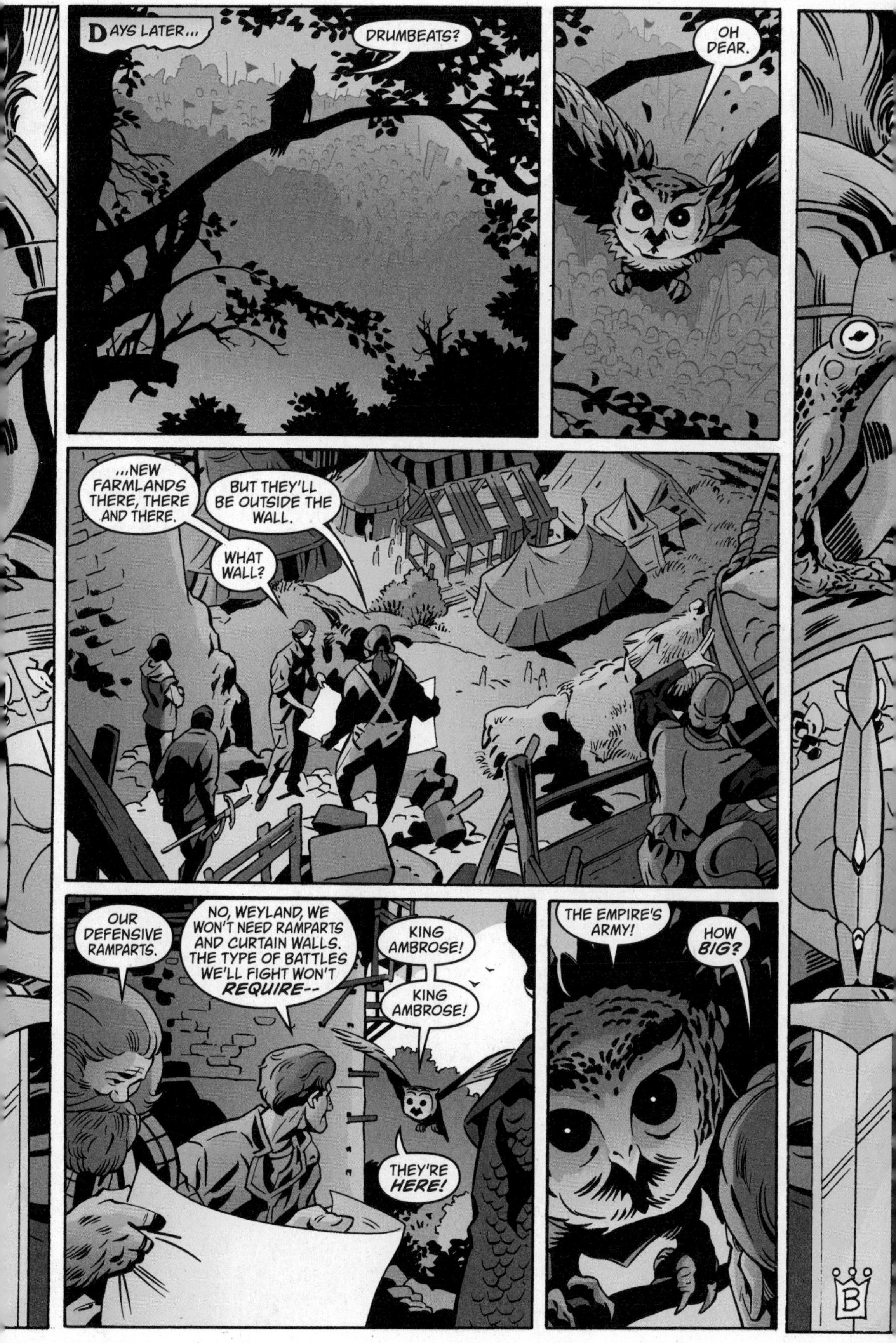
DAYS LATER...
DRUMBEATS?
OH DEAR.
...NEW FARMLANDS THERE, THERE AND THERE.
BUT THEY'LL BE OUTSIDE THE WALL.
WHAT WALL?
OUR DEFENSIVE RAMPARTS.
NO, WEYLAND, WE WON'T NEED RAMPARTS AND CURTAIN WALLS. THE TYPE OF BATTLES WE'LL FIGHT WON'T *REQUIRE--*
KING AMBROSE!
KING AMBROSE!
THEY'RE *HERE!*
THE EMPIRE'S ARMY!
HOW *BIG?*
B

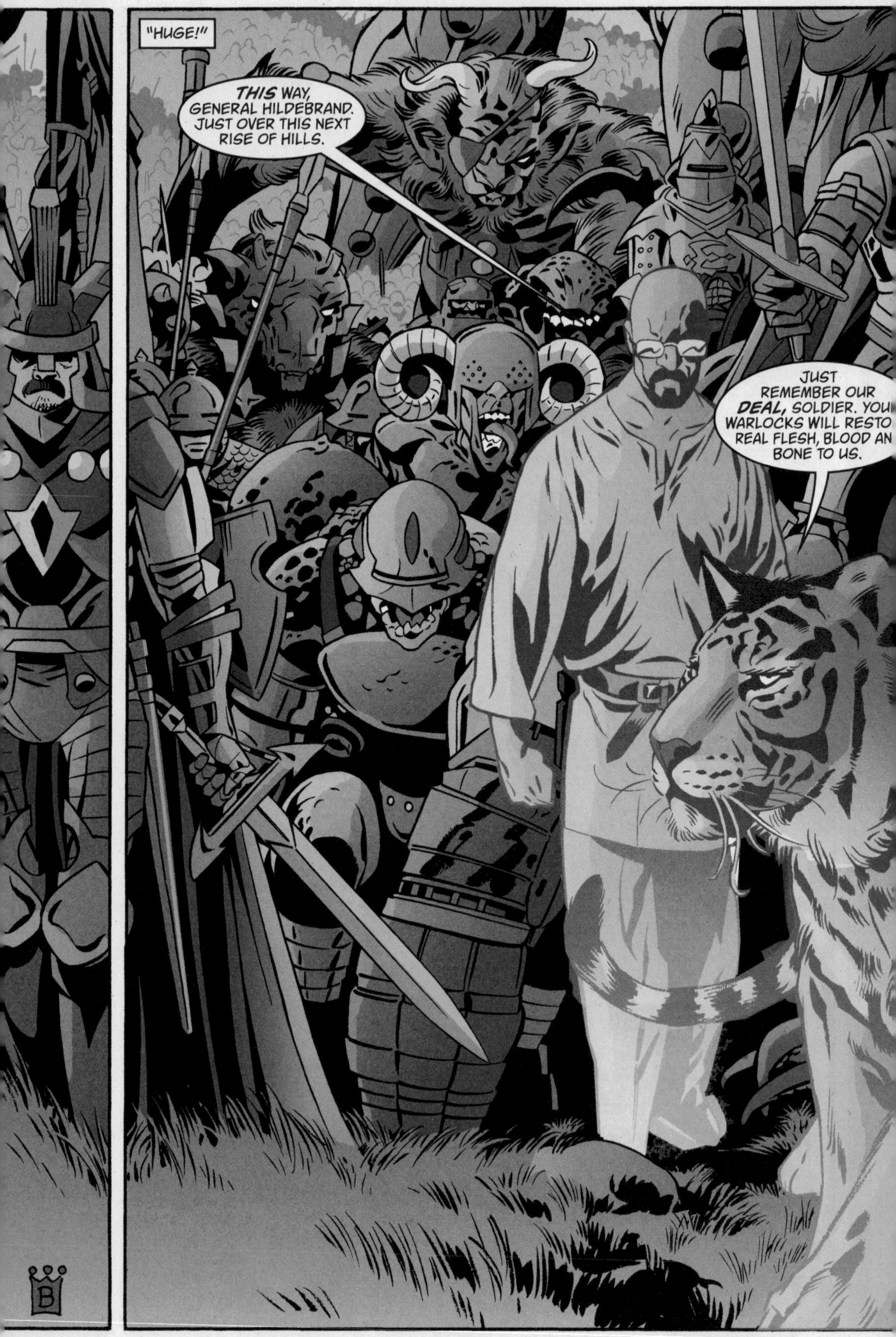
"HUGE!"
THIS WAY, GENERAL HILDEBRAND. JUST OVER THIS NEXT RISE OF HILLS.
JUST REMEMBER OUR DEAL, SOLDIER. YOU WARLOCKS WILL RESTO REAL FLESH, BLOOD AN BONE TO US.

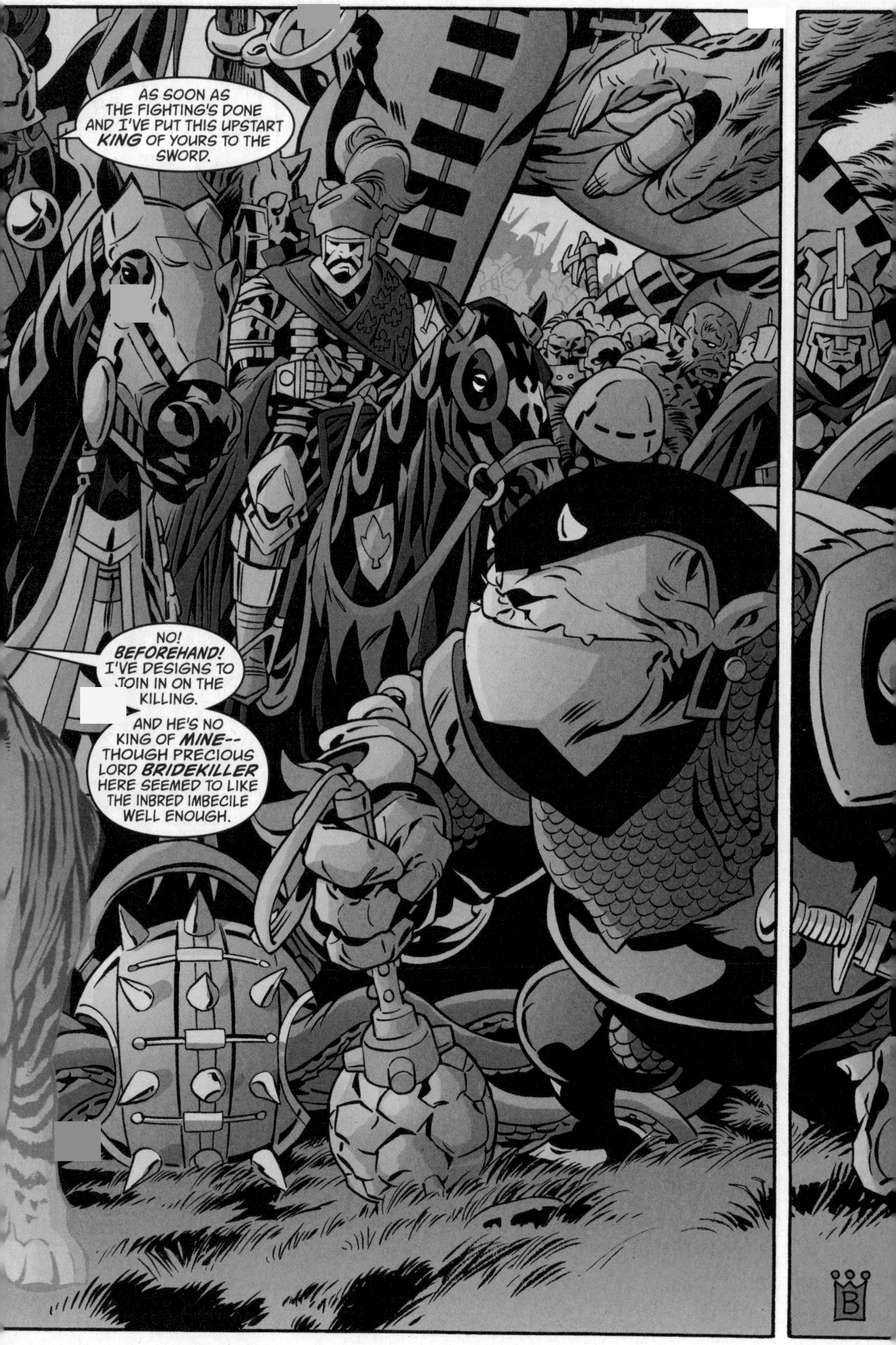
AS SOON AS THE FIGHTING'S DONE AND I'VE PUT THIS UPSTART KING OF YOURS TO THE SWORD.
NO! BEFOREHAND! I'VE DESIGNS TO JOIN IN ON THE KILLING.
AND HE'S NO KING OF MINE-- THOUGH PRECIOUS LORD BRIDEKILLER HERE SEEMED TO LIKE THE INBRED IMBECILE WELL ENOUGH.

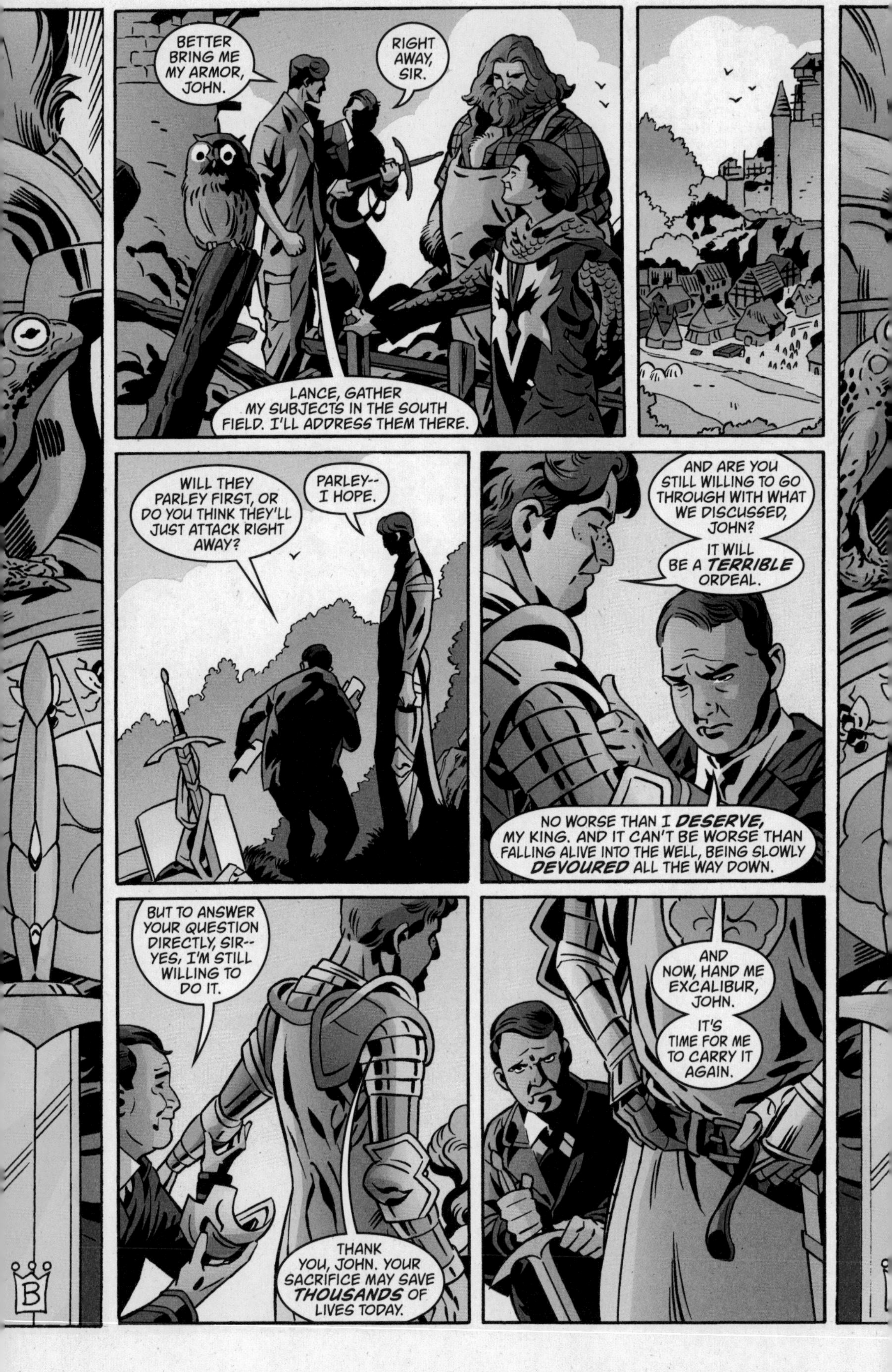
BETTER BRING ME MY ARMOR, JOHN.
RIGHT AWAY, SIR.
LANCE, GATHER MY SUBJECTS IN THE SOUTH FIELD. I'LL ADDRESS THEM THERE.
WILL THEY PARLEY FIRST, OR DO YOU THINK THEY'LL JUST ATTACK RIGHT AWAY?
PARLEY-- I HOPE.
AND ARE YOU STILL WILLING TO GO THROUGH WITH WHAT WE DISCUSSED, JOHN?
IT WILL BE A TERRIBLE ORDEAL.
NO WORSE THAN I DESERVE, MY KING. AND IT CAN'T BE WORSE THAN FALLING ALIVE INTO THE WELL, BEING SLOWLY DEVOURED ALL THE WAY DOWN.
BUT TO ANSWER YOUR QUESTION DIRECTLY, SIR-- YES, I'M STILL WILLING TO DO IT.
THANK YOU, JOHN. YOUR SACRIFICE MAY SAVE THOUSANDS OF LIVES TODAY.
AND NOW, HAND ME EXCALIBUR, JOHN.
IT'S TIME FOR ME TO CARRY IT AGAIN.

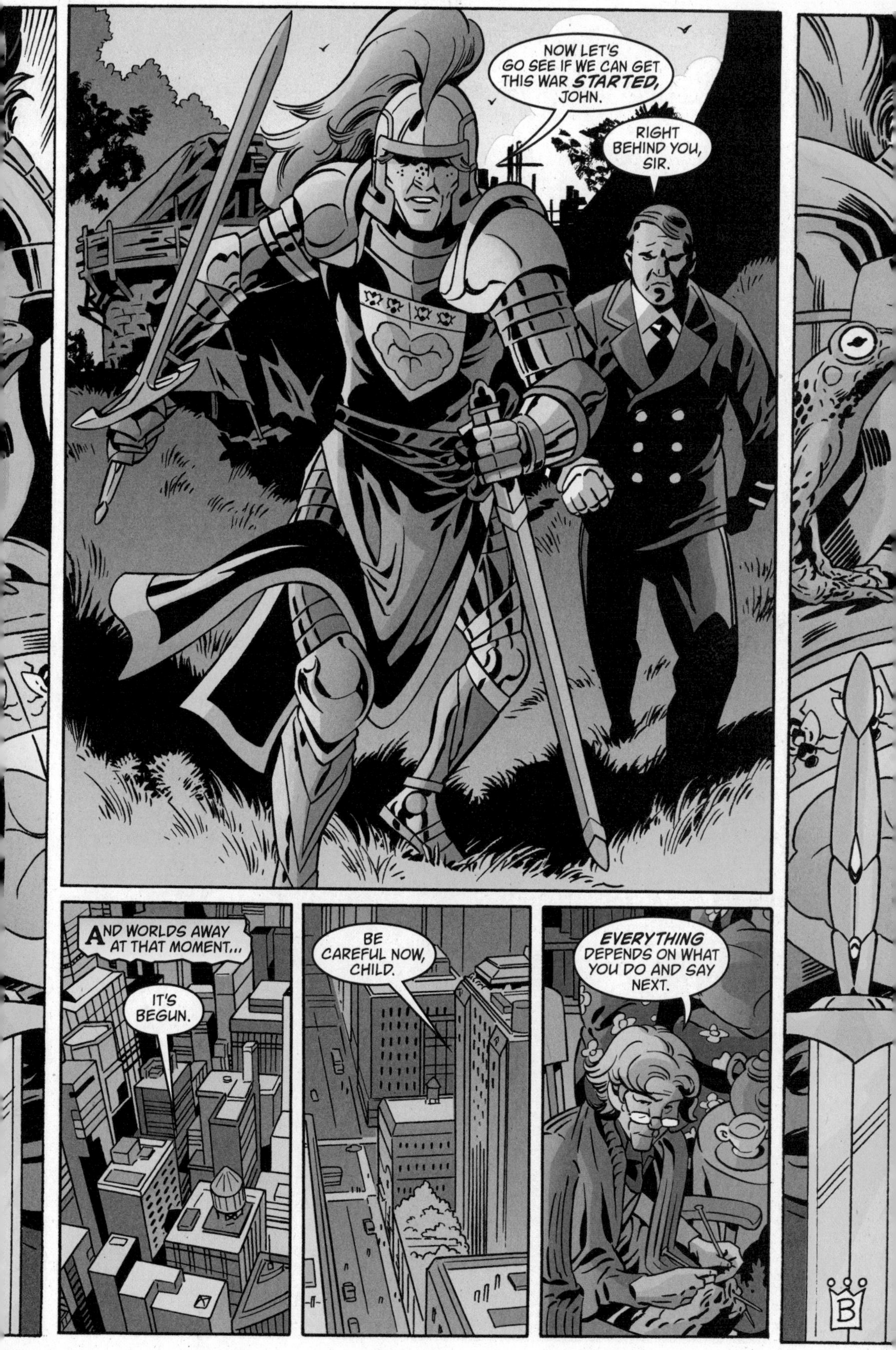
NOW LET'S GO SEE IF WE CAN GET THIS WAR STARTED, JOHN.
RIGHT BEHIND YOU, SIR.
AND WORLDS AWAY AT THAT MOMENT...
IT'S BEGUN.
BE CAREFUL NOW, CHILD.
EVERYTHING DEPENDS ON WHAT YOU DO AND SAY NEXT.

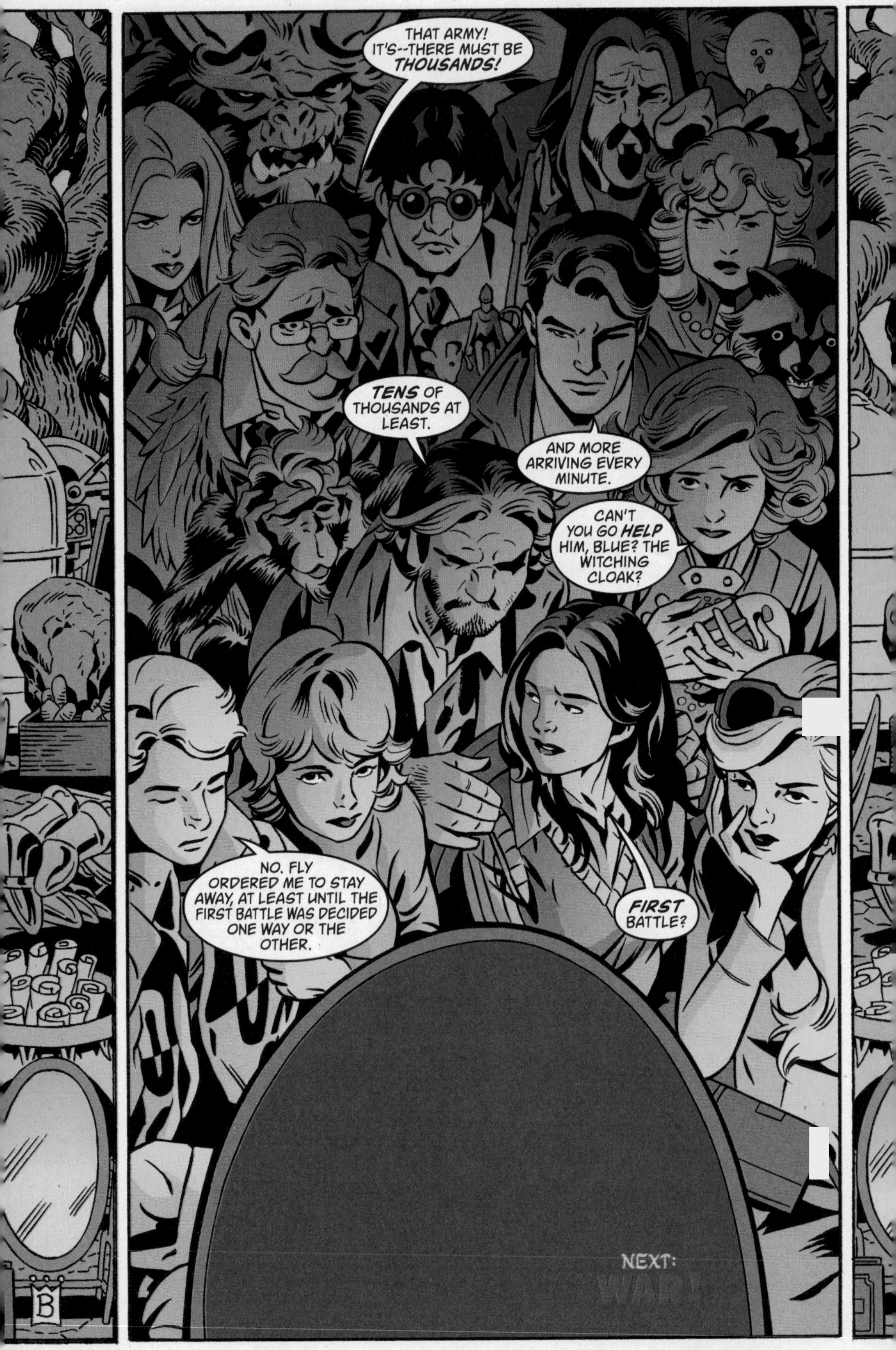
THAT ARMY! IT'S--THERE MUST BE THOUSANDS!
TENS OF THOUSANDS AT LEAST.
AND MORE ARRIVING EVERY MINUTE.
CAN'T YOU GO HELP HIM, BLUE? THE WITCHING CLOAK?
NO. FLY ORDERED ME TO STAY AWAY, AT LEAST UNTIL THE FIRST BATTLE WAS DECIDED ONE WAY OR THE OTHER.
FIRST BATTLE?
NEXT: WAR!

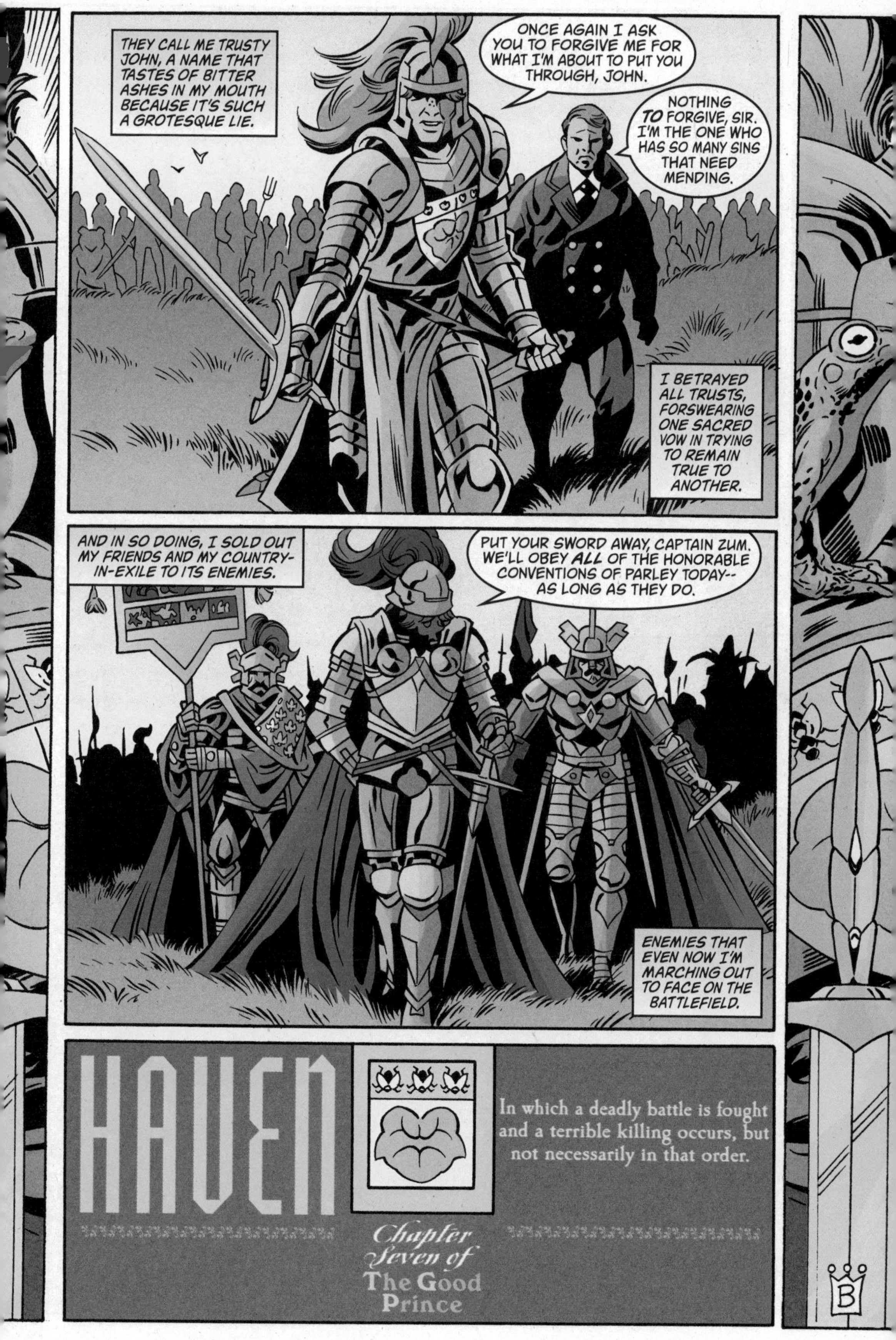
THEY CALL ME TRUSTY JOHN, A NAME THAT TASTES OF BITTER ASHES IN MY MOUTH BECAUSE IT'S SUCH A GROTESQUE LIE.
ONCE AGAIN I ASK YOU TO FORGIVE ME FOR WHAT I'M ABOUT TO PUT YOU THROUGH, JOHN.
NOTHING TO FORGIVE, SIR. I'M THE ONE WHO HAS SO MANY SINS THAT NEED MENDING.
I BETRAYED ALL TRUSTS, FORSWEARING ONE SACRED VOW IN TRYING TO REMAIN TRUE TO ANOTHER.
AND IN SO DOING, I SOLD OUT MY FRIENDS AND MY COUNTRY-IN-EXILE TO ITS ENEMIES.
PUT YOUR SWORD AWAY, CAPTAIN ZUM. WE'LL OBEY ALL OF THE HONORABLE CONVENTIONS OF PARLEY TODAY-- AS LONG AS THEY DO.
ENEMIES THAT EVEN NOW I'M MARCHING OUT TO FACE ON THE BATTLEFIELD.
HAVEN
In which a deadly battle is fought and a terrible killing occurs, but not necessarily in that order.
Chapter Seven of The Good Prince
B

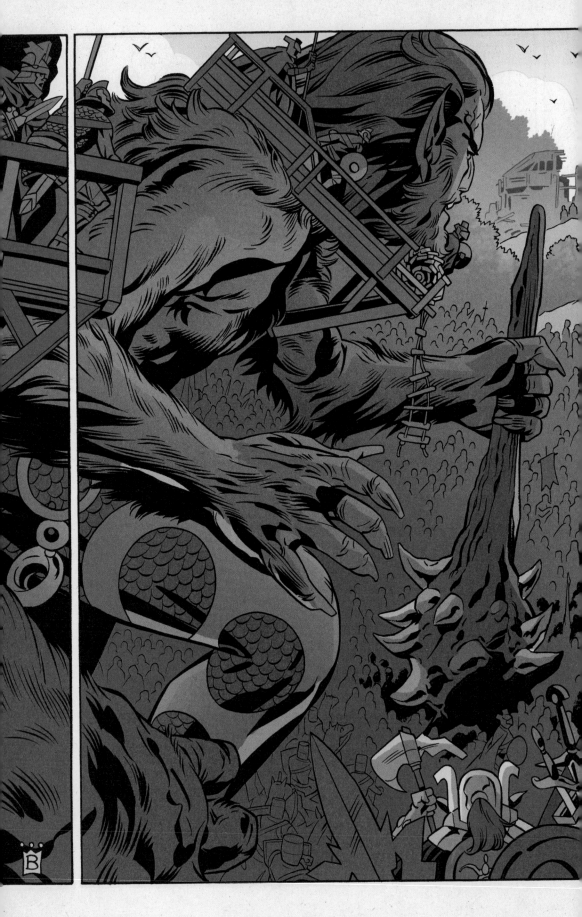

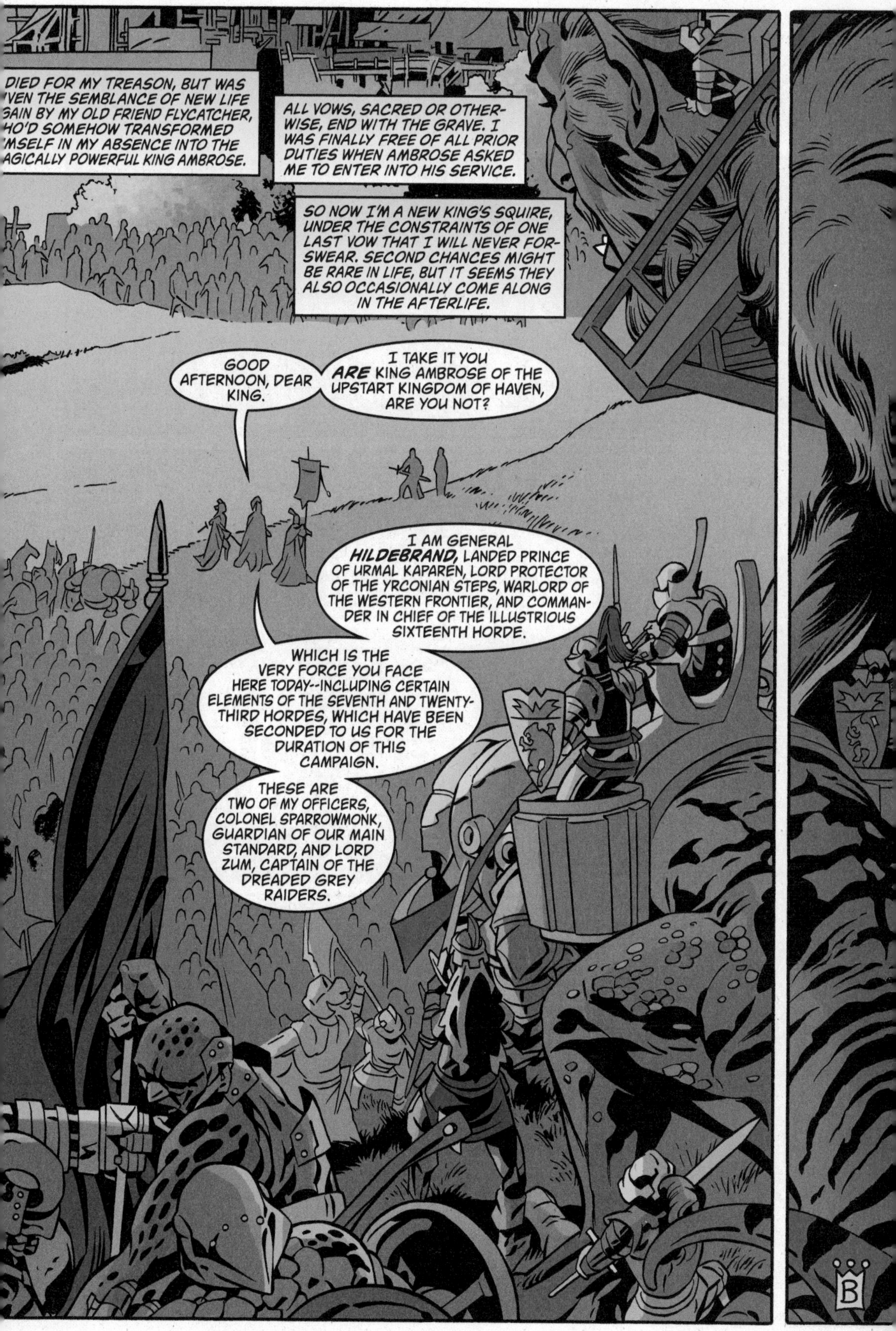
DIED FOR MY TREASON, BUT WAS 'VEN THE SEMBLANCE OF NEW LIFE GAIN BY MY OLD FRIEND FLYCATCHER, HO'D SOMEHOW TRANSFORMED 'MSELF IN MY ABSENCE INTO THE AGICALLY POWERFUL KING AMBROSE.
ALL VOWS, SACRED OR OTHER-WISE, END WITH THE GRAVE. I WAS FINALLY FREE OF ALL PRIOR DUTIES WHEN AMBROSE ASKED ME TO ENTER INTO HIS SERVICE.
SO NOW I'M A NEW KING'S SQUIRE, UNDER THE CONSTRAINTS OF ONE LAST VOW THAT I WILL NEVER FOR-SWEAR. SECOND CHANCES MIGHT BE RARE IN LIFE, BUT IT SEEMS THEY ALSO OCCASIONALLY COME ALONG IN THE AFTERLIFE.
GOOD AFTERNOON, DEAR KING.
I TAKE IT YOU ARE KING AMBROSE OF THE UPSTART KINGDOM OF HAVEN, ARE YOU NOT?
I AM GENERAL HILDEBRAND, LANDED PRINCE OF URMAL KAPAREN, LORD PROTECTOR OF THE YRCONIAN STEPS, WARLORD OF THE WESTERN FRONTIER, AND COMMAN-DER IN CHIEF OF THE ILLUSTRIOUS SIXTEENTH HORDE.
WHICH IS THE VERY FORCE YOU FACE HERE TODAY--INCLUDING CERTAIN ELEMENTS OF THE SEVENTH AND TWENTY-THIRD HORDES, WHICH HAVE BEEN SECONDED TO US FOR THE DURATION OF THIS CAMPAIGN.
THESE ARE TWO OF MY OFFICERS, COLONEL SPARROWMONK, GUARDIAN OF OUR MAIN STANDARD, AND LORD ZUM, CAPTAIN OF THE DREADED GREY RAIDERS.

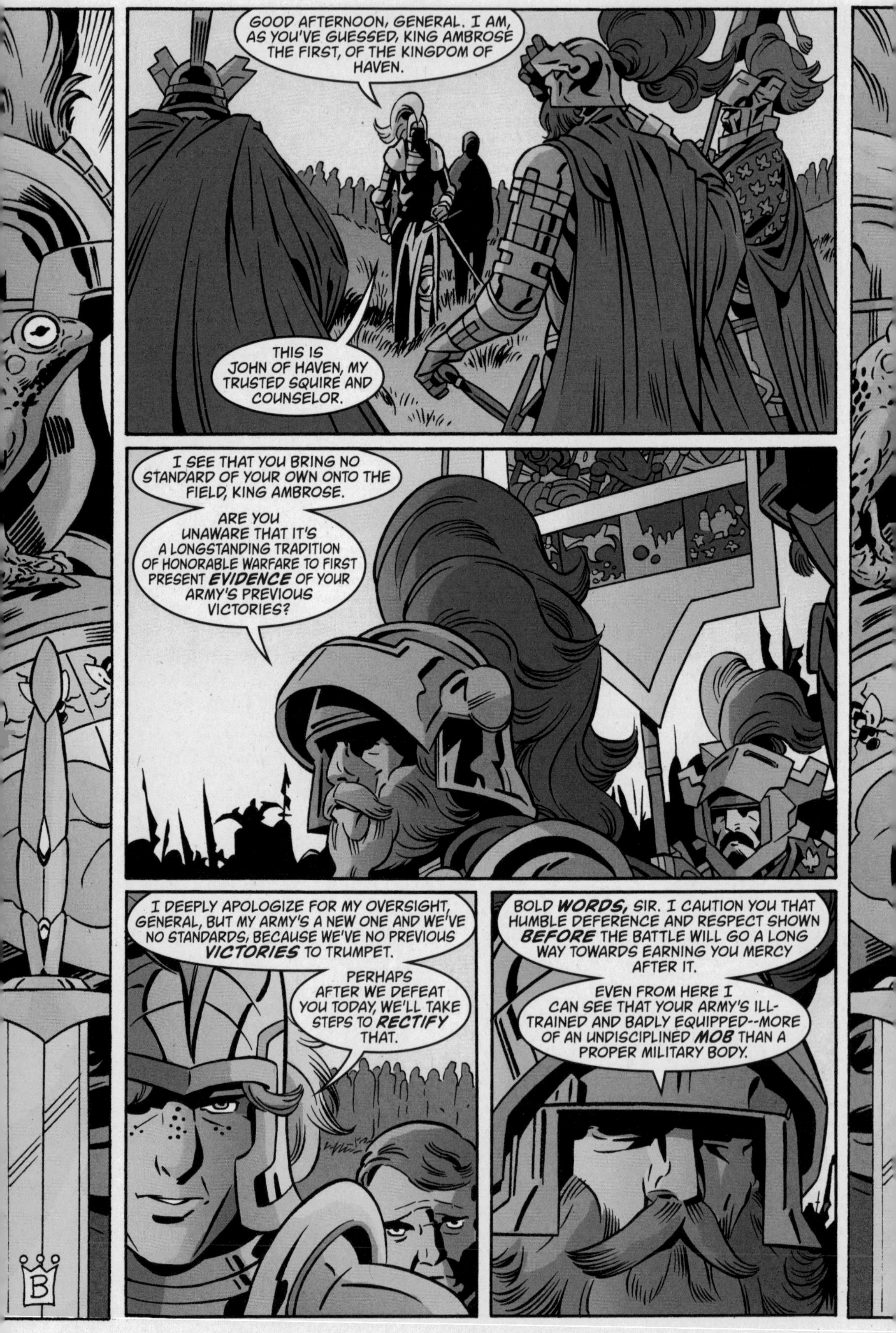
GOOD AFTERNOON, GENERAL. I AM, AS YOU'VE GUESSED, KING AMBROSE THE FIRST, OF THE KINGDOM OF HAVEN.
THIS IS JOHN OF HAVEN, MY TRUSTED SQUIRE AND COUNSELOR.
I SEE THAT YOU BRING NO STANDARD OF YOUR OWN ONTO THE FIELD, KING AMBROSE.
ARE YOU UNAWARE THAT IT'S A LONGSTANDING TRADITION OF HONORABLE WARFARE TO FIRST PRESENT EVIDENCE OF YOUR ARMY'S PREVIOUS VICTORIES?
I DEEPLY APOLOGIZE FOR MY OVERSIGHT, GENERAL, BUT MY ARMY'S A NEW ONE AND WE'VE NO STANDARDS, BECAUSE WE'VE NO PREVIOUS VICTORIES TO TRUMPET.
PERHAPS AFTER WE DEFEAT YOU TODAY, WE'LL TAKE STEPS TO RECTIFY THAT.
BOLD WORDS, SIR. I CAUTION YOU THAT HUMBLE DEFERENCE AND RESPECT SHOWN BEFORE THE BATTLE WILL GO A LONG WAY TOWARDS EARNING YOU MERCY AFTER IT.
EVEN FROM HERE I CAN SEE THAT YOUR ARMY'S ILL-TRAINED AND BADLY EQUIPPED--MORE OF AN UNDISCIPLINED MOB THAN A PROPER MILITARY BODY.

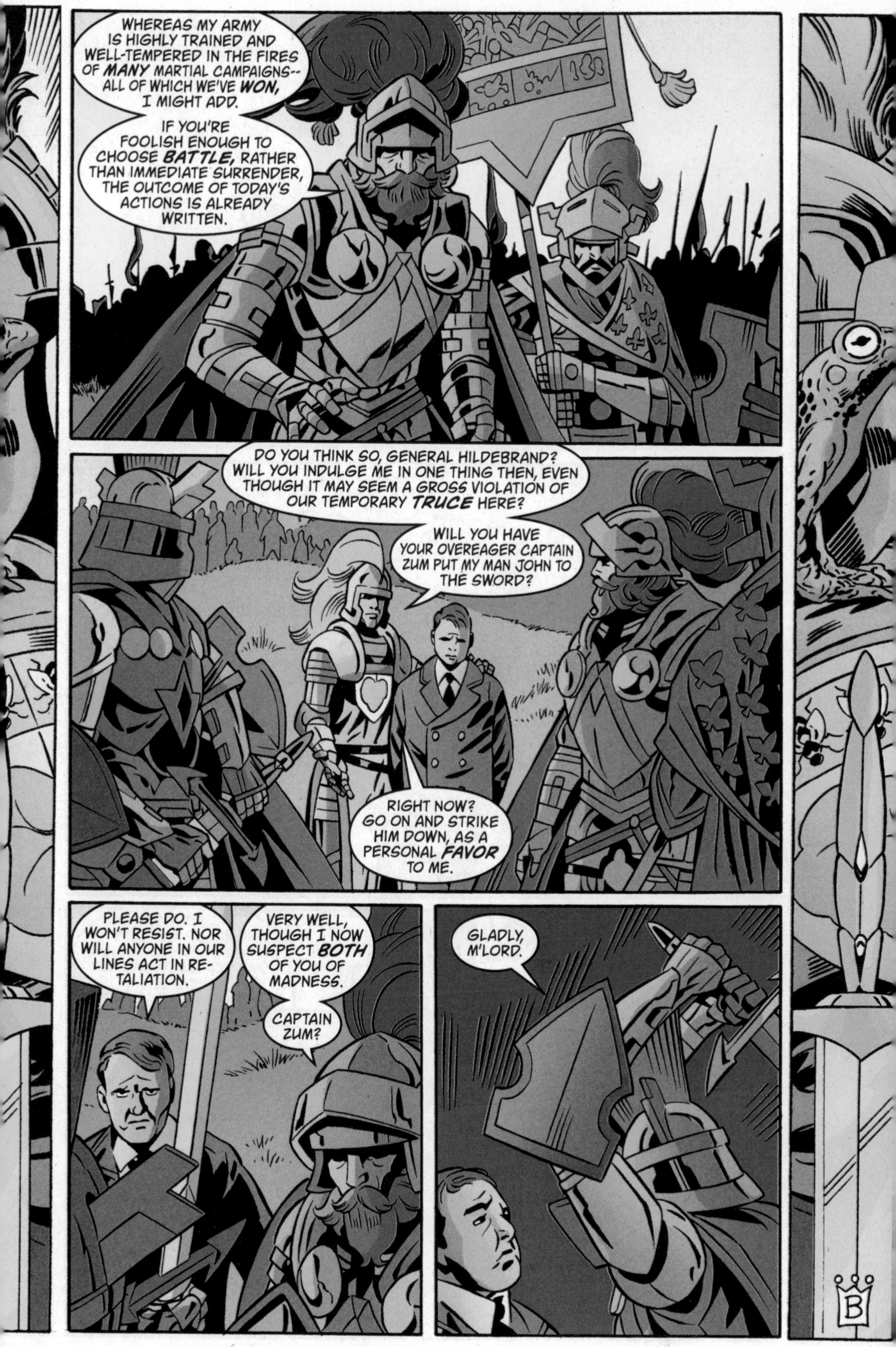
WHEREAS MY ARMY IS HIGHLY TRAINED AND WELL-TEMPERED IN THE FIRES OF MANY MARTIAL CAMPAIGNS-- ALL OF WHICH WE'VE WON, I MIGHT ADD.
IF YOU'RE FOOLISH ENOUGH TO CHOOSE BATTLE, RATHER THAN IMMEDIATE SURRENDER, THE OUTCOME OF TODAY'S ACTIONS IS ALREADY WRITTEN.
DO YOU THINK SO, GENERAL HILDEBRAND? WILL YOU INDULGE ME IN ONE THING THEN, EVEN THOUGH IT MAY SEEM A GROSS VIOLATION OF OUR TEMPORARY TRUCE HERE?
WILL YOU HAVE YOUR OVEREAGER CAPTAIN ZUM PUT MY MAN JOHN TO THE SWORD?
RIGHT NOW? GO ON AND STRIKE HIM DOWN, AS A PERSONAL FAVOR TO ME.
PLEASE DO. I WON'T RESIST. NOR WILL ANYONE IN OUR LINES ACT IN RE-TALIATION.
VERY WELL, THOUGH I NOW SUSPECT BOTH OF YOU OF MADNESS.
CAPTAIN ZUM?
GLADLY, M'LORD.

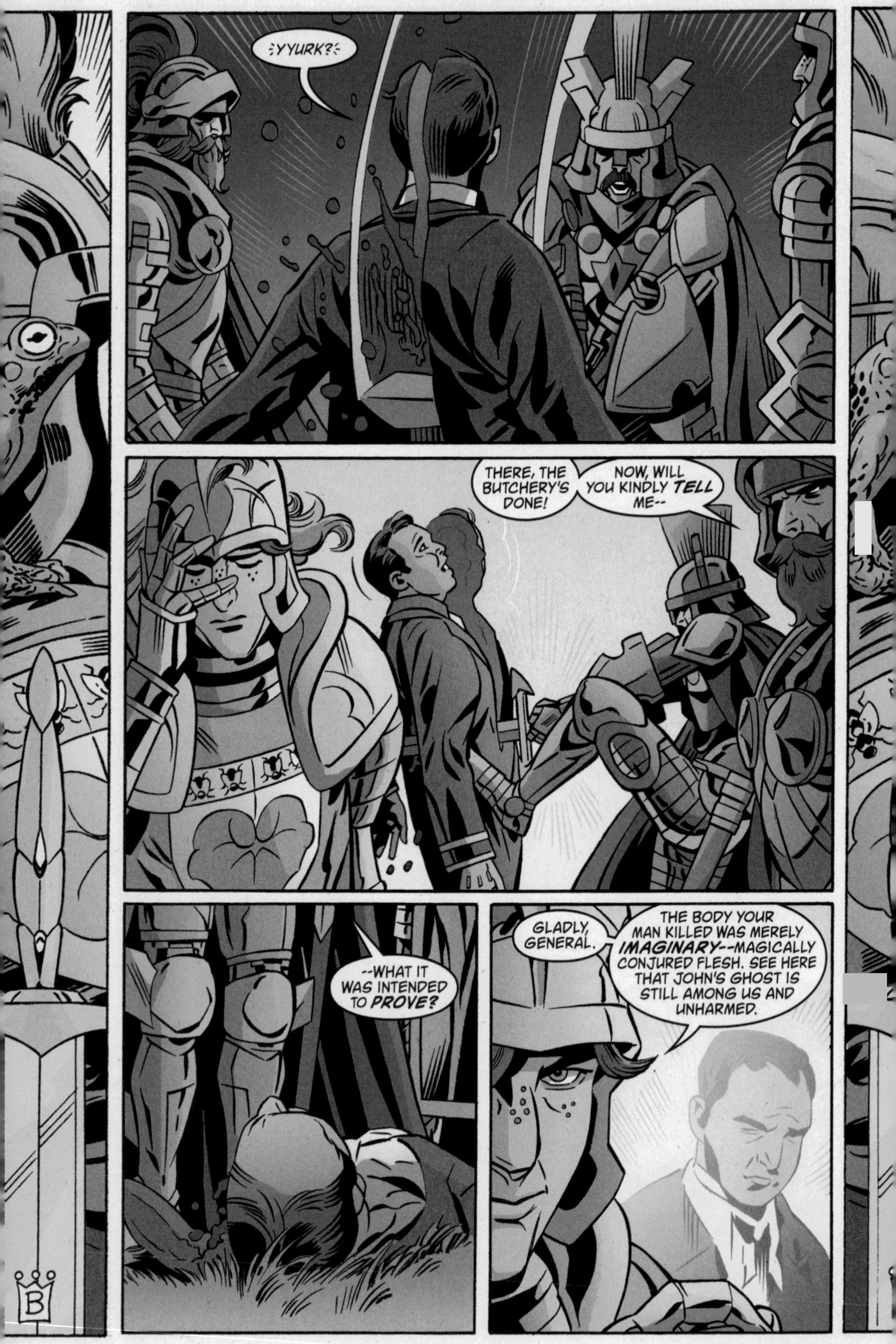
YYURK?
THERE, THE BUTCHERY'S DONE!
NOW, WILL YOU KINDLY TELL ME--
--WHAT IT WAS INTENDED TO PROVE?
GLADLY, GENERAL.
THE BODY YOUR MAN KILLED WAS MERELY IMAGINARY--MAGICALLY CONJURED FLESH. SEE HERE THAT JOHN'S GHOST IS STILL AMONG US AND UNHARMED.

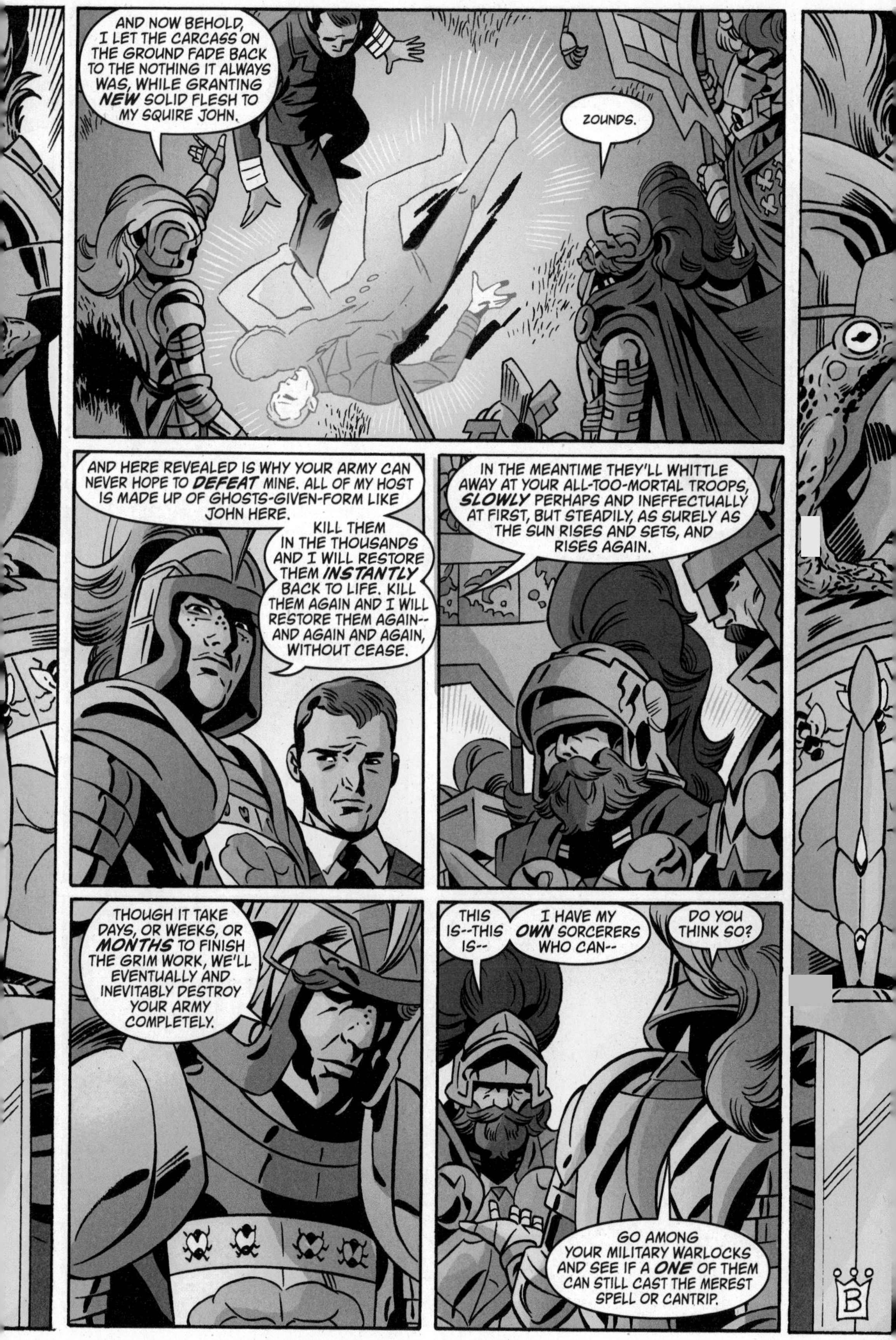
AND NOW BEHOLD, I LET THE CARCASS ON THE GROUND FADE BACK TO THE NOTHING IT ALWAYS WAS, WHILE GRANTING NEW SOLID FLESH TO MY SQUIRE JOHN.
ZOUNDS.
AND HERE REVEALED IS WHY YOUR ARMY CAN NEVER HOPE TO DEFEAT MINE. ALL OF MY HOST IS MADE UP OF GHOSTS-GIVEN-FORM LIKE JOHN HERE.
KILL THEM IN THE THOUSANDS AND I WILL RESTORE THEM INSTANTLY BACK TO LIFE. KILL THEM AGAIN AND I WILL RESTORE THEM AGAIN-- AND AGAIN AND AGAIN, WITHOUT CEASE.
IN THE MEANTIME THEY'LL WHITTLE AWAY AT YOUR ALL-TOO-MORTAL TROOPS, SLOWLY PERHAPS AND INEFFECTUALLY AT FIRST, BUT STEADILY, AS SURELY AS THE SUN RISES AND SETS, AND RISES AGAIN.
THOUGH IT TAKE DAYS, OR WEEKS, OR MONTHS TO FINISH THE GRIM WORK, WE'LL EVENTUALLY AND INEVITABLY DESTROY YOUR ARMY COMPLETELY.
THIS IS--THIS IS--
I HAVE MY OWN SORCERERS WHO CAN--
DO YOU THINK SO?
GO AMONG YOUR MILITARY WARLOCKS AND SEE IF A ONE OF THEM CAN STILL CAST THE MEREST SPELL OR CANTRIP.

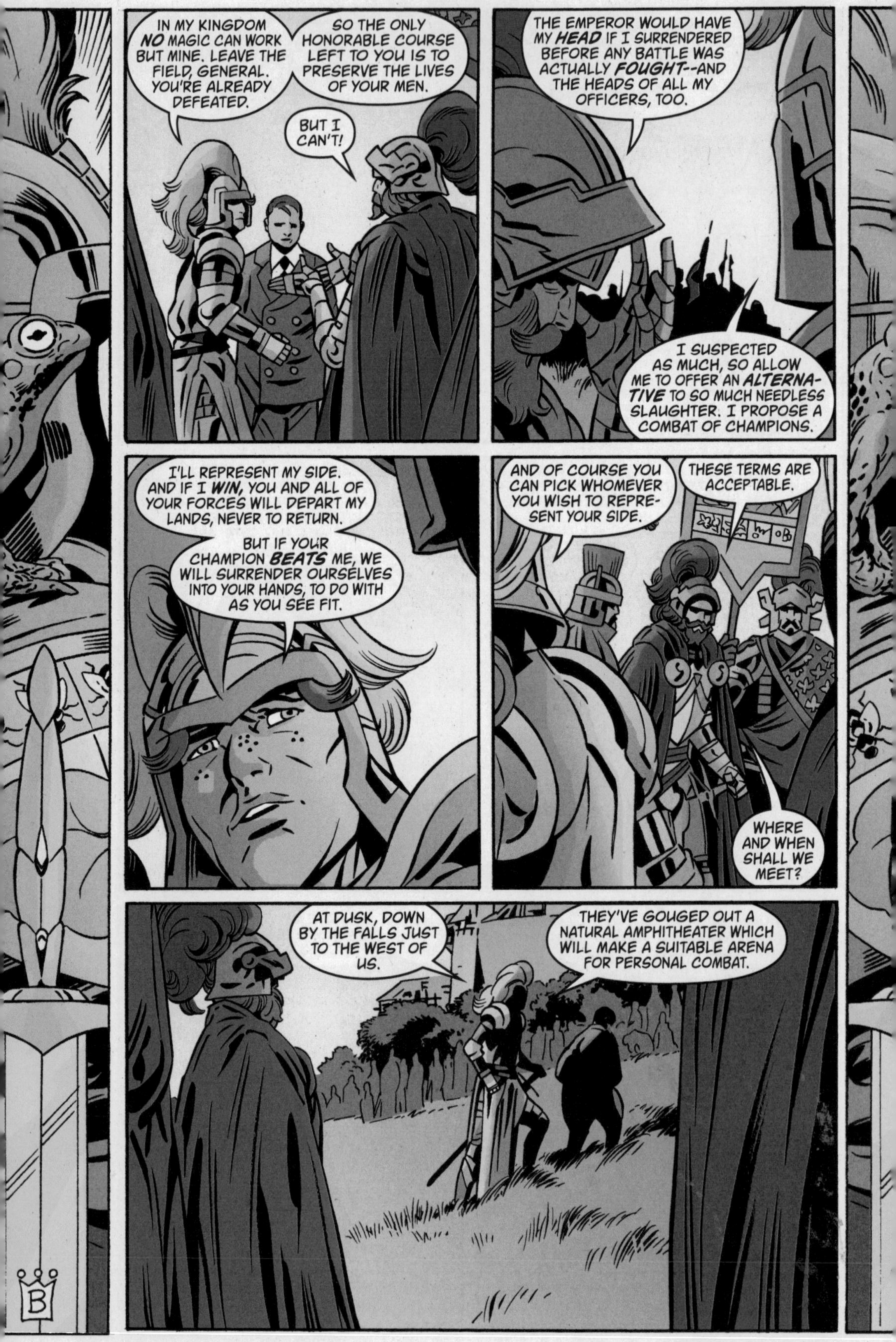
IN MY KINGDOM NO MAGIC CAN WORK BUT MINE. LEAVE THE FIELD, GENERAL. YOU'RE ALREADY DEFEATED.
SO THE ONLY HONORABLE COURSE LEFT TO YOU IS TO PRESERVE THE LIVES OF YOUR MEN.
BUT I CAN'T!
THE EMPEROR WOULD HAVE MY HEAD IF I SURRENDERED BEFORE ANY BATTLE WAS ACTUALLY FOUGHT--AND THE HEADS OF ALL MY OFFICERS, TOO.
I SUSPECTED AS MUCH, SO ALLOW ME TO OFFER AN ALTERNATIVE TO SO MUCH NEEDLESS SLAUGHTER. I PROPOSE A COMBAT OF CHAMPIONS.
I'LL REPRESENT MY SIDE. AND IF I WIN, YOU AND ALL OF YOUR FORCES WILL DEPART MY LANDS, NEVER TO RETURN.
BUT IF YOUR CHAMPION BEATS ME, WE WILL SURRENDER OURSELVES INTO YOUR HANDS, TO DO WITH AS YOU SEE FIT.
AND OF COURSE YOU CAN PICK WHOMEVER YOU WISH TO REPRESENT YOUR SIDE.
THESE TERMS ARE ACCEPTABLE.
WHERE AND WHEN SHALL WE MEET?
AT DUSK, DOWN BY THE FALLS JUST TO THE WEST OF US.
THEY'VE GOUGED OUT A NATURAL AMPHITHEATER WHICH WILL MAKE A SUITABLE ARENA FOR PERSONAL COMBAT.

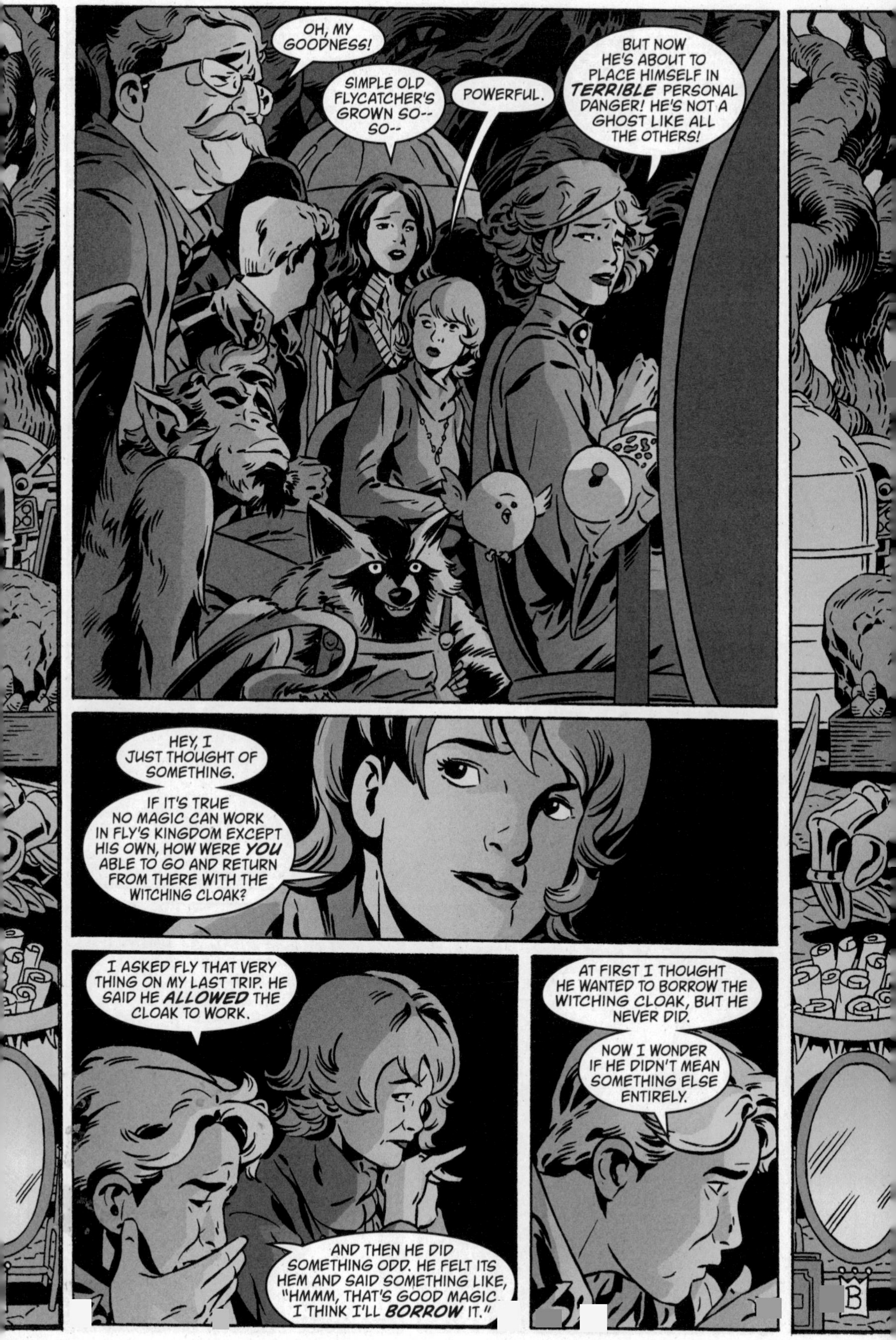
OH, MY GOODNESS!
SIMPLE OLD FLYCATCHER'S GROWN SO-- SO--
POWERFUL.
BUT NOW HE'S ABOUT TO PLACE HIMSELF IN TERRIBLE PERSONAL DANGER! HE'S NOT A GHOST LIKE ALL THE OTHERS!
HEY, I JUST THOUGHT OF SOMETHING.
IF IT'S TRUE NO MAGIC CAN WORK IN FLY'S KINGDOM EXCEPT HIS OWN, HOW WERE YOU ABLE TO GO AND RETURN FROM THERE WITH THE WITCHING CLOAK?
I ASKED FLY THAT VERY THING ON MY LAST TRIP. HE SAID HE ALLOWED THE CLOAK TO WORK.
AND THEN HE DID SOMETHING ODD. HE FELT ITS HEM AND SAID SOMETHING LIKE, "HMMM, THAT'S GOOD MAGIC. I THINK I'LL BORROW IT."
AT FIRST I THOUGHT HE WANTED TO BORROW THE WITCHING CLOAK, BUT HE NEVER DID.
NOW I WONDER IF HE DIDN'T MEAN SOMETHING ELSE ENTIRELY.

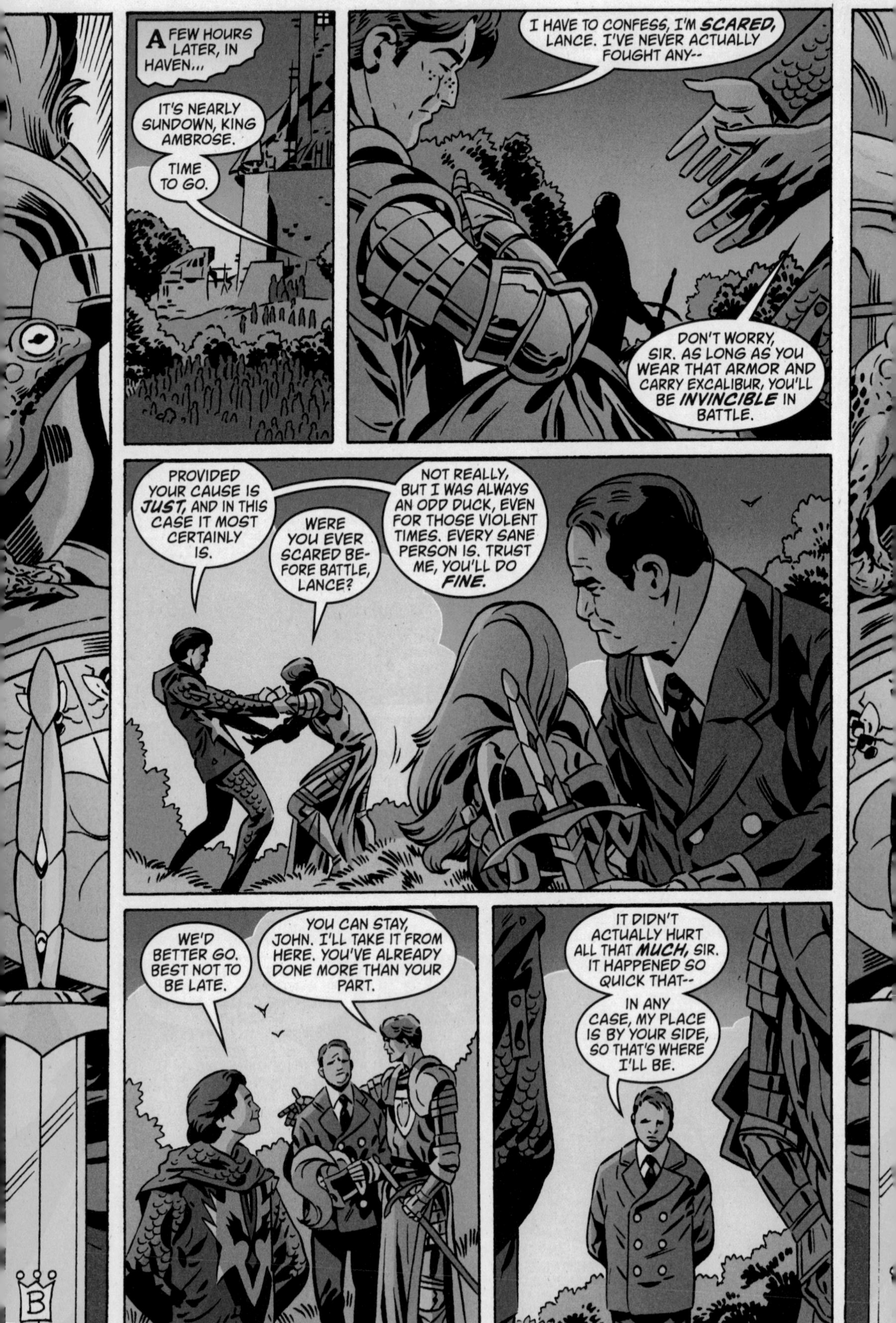

A FEW HOURS LATER, IN HAVEN...
IT'S NEARLY SUNDOWN, KING AMBROSE.
TIME TO GO.
I HAVE TO CONFESS, I'M SCARED, LANCE. I'VE NEVER ACTUALLY FOUGHT ANY--
DON'T WORRY, SIR. AS LONG AS YOU WEAR THAT ARMOR AND CARRY EXCALIBUR, YOU'LL BE INVINCIBLE IN BATTLE.
PROVIDED YOUR CAUSE IS JUST, AND IN THIS CASE IT MOST CERTAINLY IS.
WERE YOU EVER SCARED BEFORE BATTLE, LANCE?
NOT REALLY, BUT I WAS ALWAYS AN ODD DUCK, EVEN FOR THOSE VIOLENT TIMES. EVERY SANE PERSON IS. TRUST ME, YOU'LL DO FINE.
WE'D BETTER GO. BEST NOT TO BE LATE.
YOU CAN STAY, JOHN. I'LL TAKE IT FROM HERE. YOU'VE ALREADY DONE MORE THAN YOUR PART.
IT DIDN'T ACTUALLY HURT ALL THAT MUCH, SIR. IT HAPPENED SO QUICK THAT--
IN ANY CASE, MY PLACE IS BY YOUR SIDE, SO THAT'S WHERE I'LL BE.

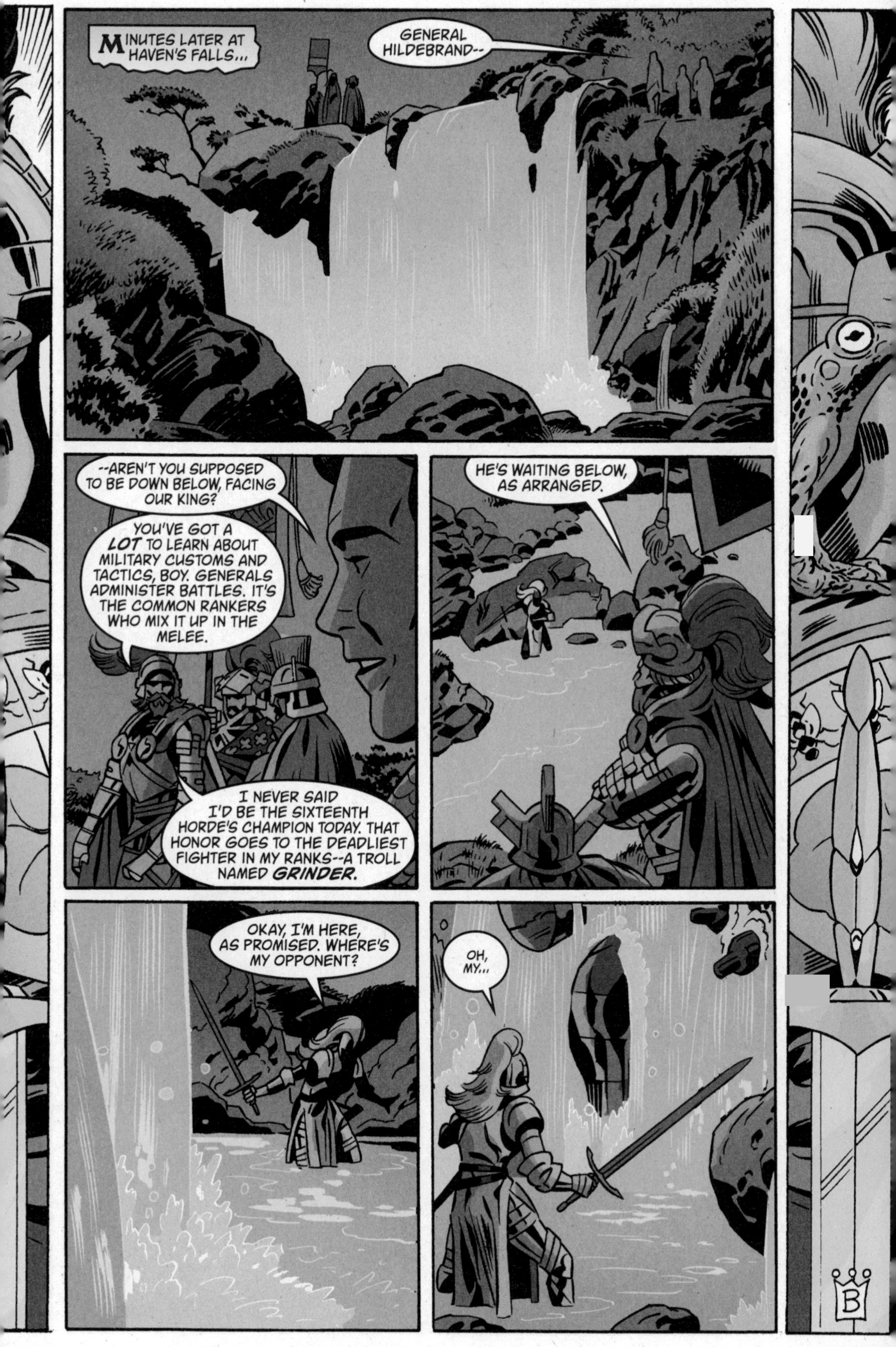
MINUTES LATER AT HAVEN'S FALLS...
GENERAL HILDEBRAND--
--AREN'T YOU SUPPOSED TO BE DOWN BELOW, FACING OUR KING?
YOU'VE GOT A LOT TO LEARN ABOUT MILITARY CUSTOMS AND TACTICS, BOY. GENERALS ADMINISTER BATTLES. IT'S THE COMMON RANKERS WHO MIX IT UP IN THE MELEE.
I NEVER SAID I'D BE THE SIXTEENTH HORDE'S CHAMPION TODAY. THAT HONOR GOES TO THE DEADLIEST FIGHTER IN MY RANKS--A TROLL NAMED GRINDER.
HE'S WAITING BELOW, AS ARRANGED.
OKAY, I'M HERE, AS PROMISED. WHERE'S MY OPPONENT?
OH, MY...

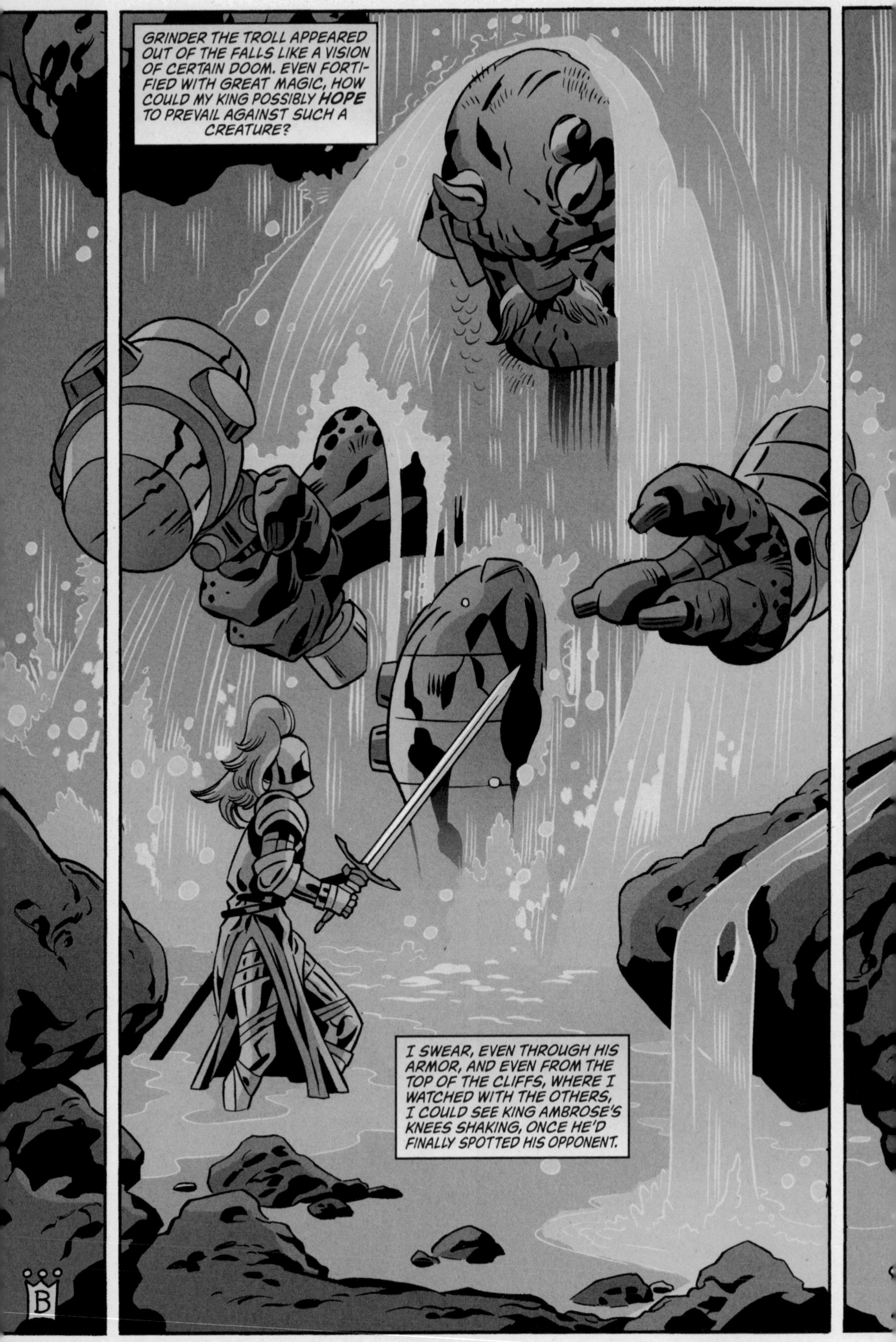
GRINDER THE TROLL APPEARED OUT OF THE FALLS LIKE A VISION OF CERTAIN DOOM. EVEN FORTIFIED WITH GREAT MAGIC, HOW COULD MY KING POSSIBLY HOPE TO PREVAIL AGAINST SUCH A CREATURE?
I SWEAR, EVEN THROUGH HIS ARMOR, AND EVEN FROM THE TOP OF THE CLIFFS, WHERE I WATCHED WITH THE OTHERS, I COULD SEE KING AMBROSE'S KNEES SHAKING, ONCE HE'D FINALLY SPOTTED HIS OPPONENT.

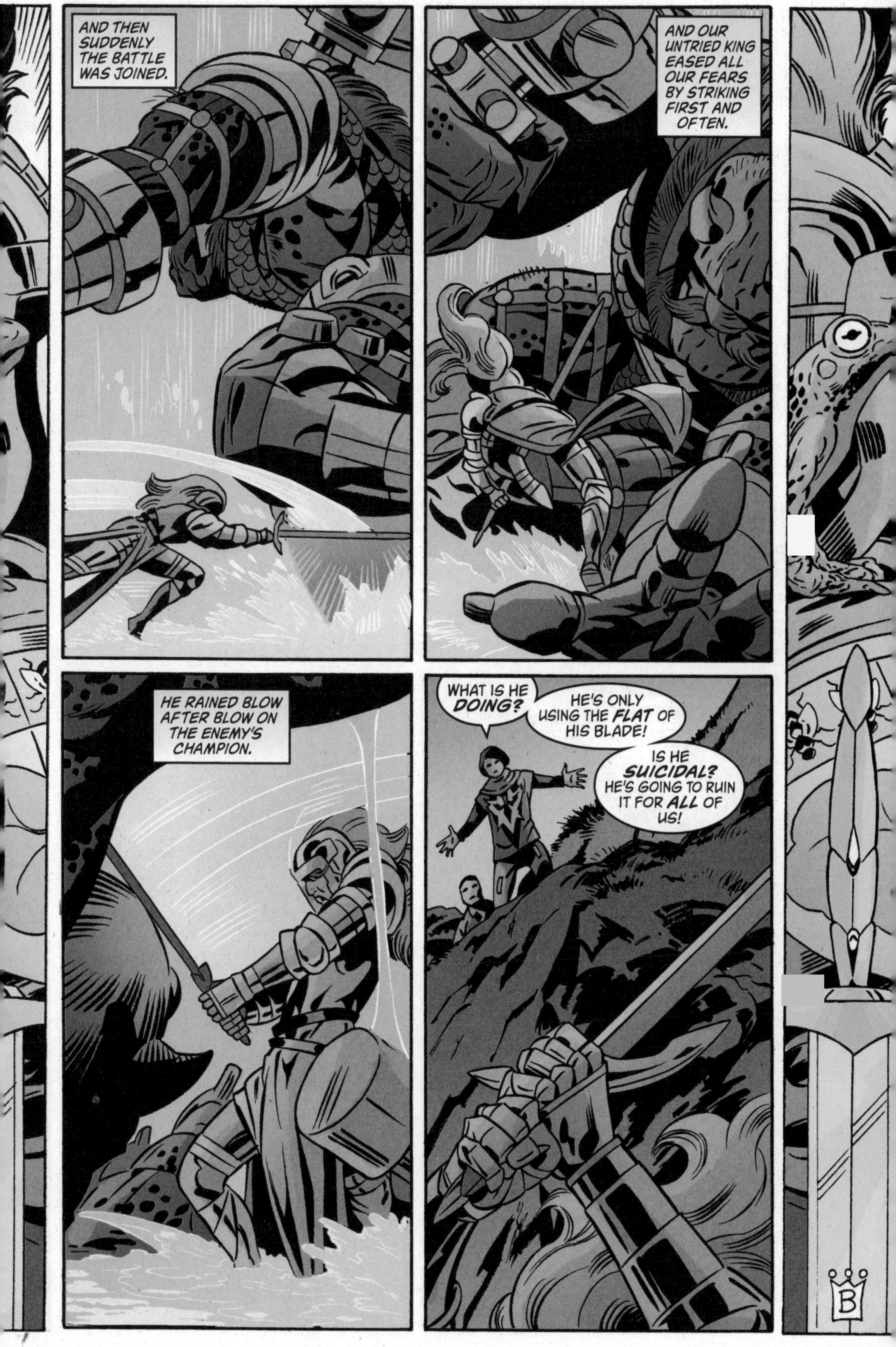
AND THEN SUDDENLY THE BATTLE WAS JOINED.
AND OUR UNTRIED KING EASED ALL OUR FEARS BY STRIKING FIRST AND OFTEN.
HE RAINED BLOW AFTER BLOW ON THE ENEMY'S CHAMPION.
WHAT IS HE DOING?
HE'S ONLY USING THE FLAT OF HIS BLADE!
IS HE SUICIDAL? HE'S GOING TO RUIN IT FOR ALL OF US!

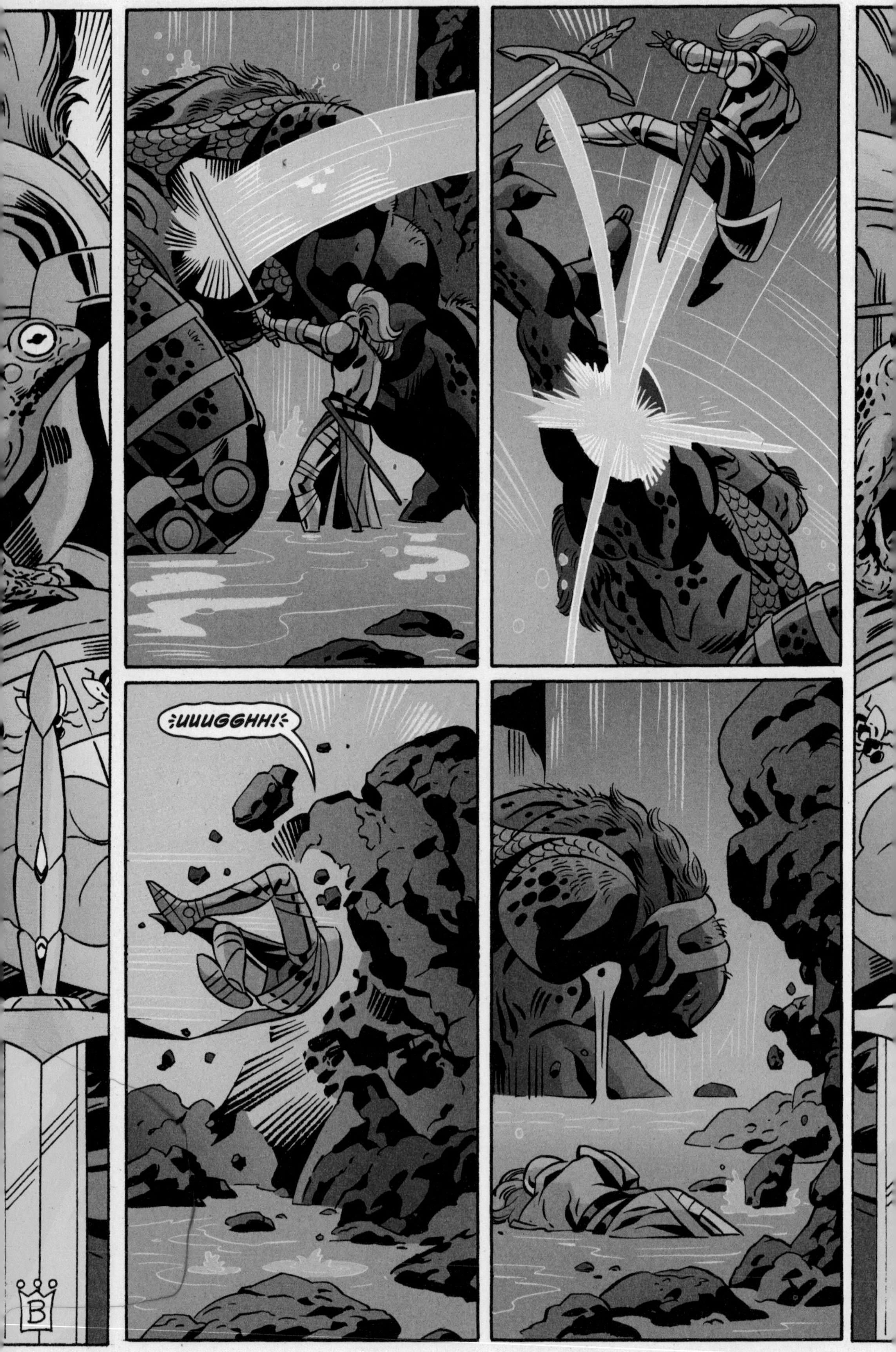
UUUGGHH!

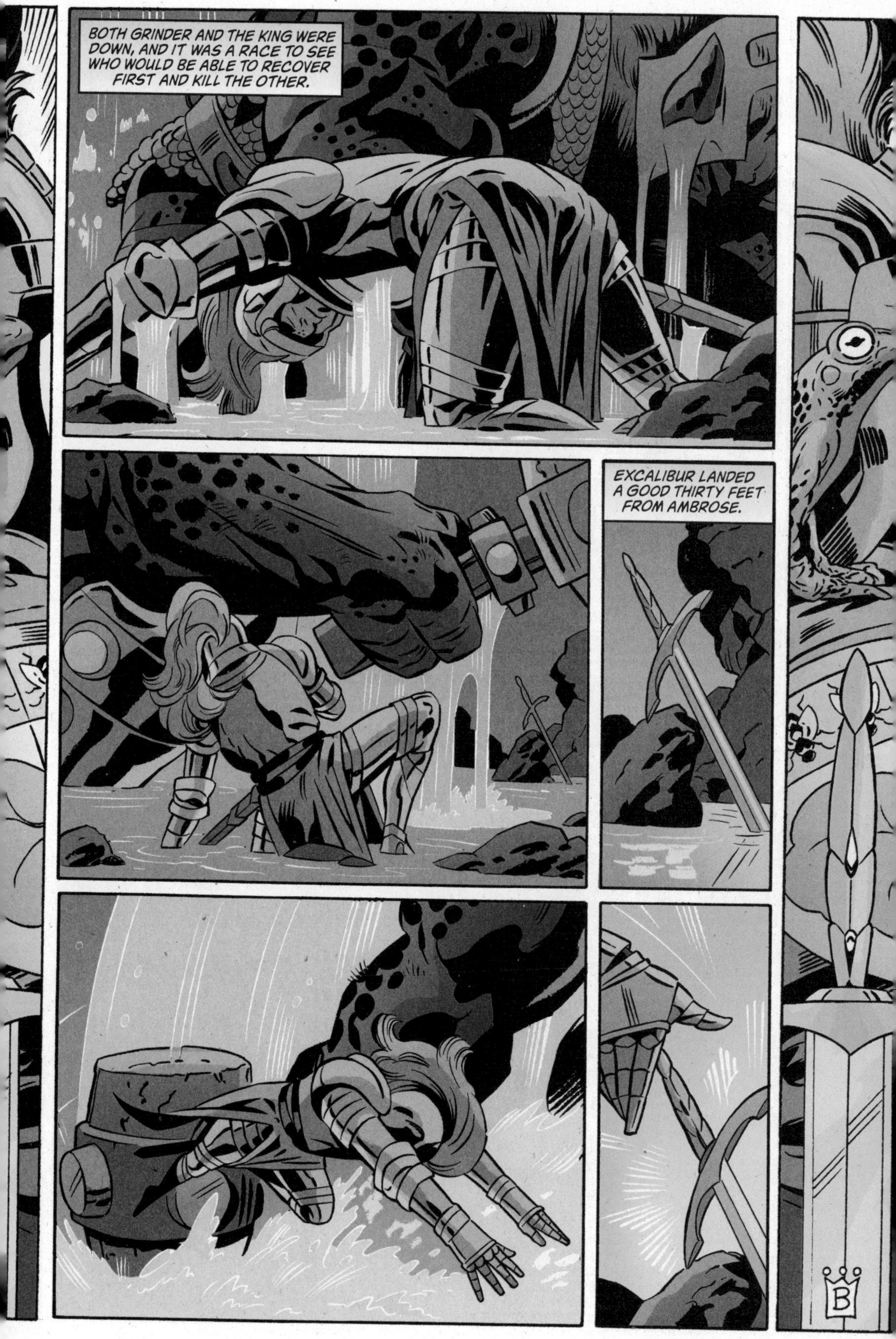
BOTH GRINDER AND THE KING WERE DOWN, AND IT WAS A RACE TO SEE WHO WOULD BE ABLE TO RECOVER FIRST AND KILL THE OTHER.
EXCALIBUR LANDED A GOOD THIRTY FEET FROM AMBROSE.

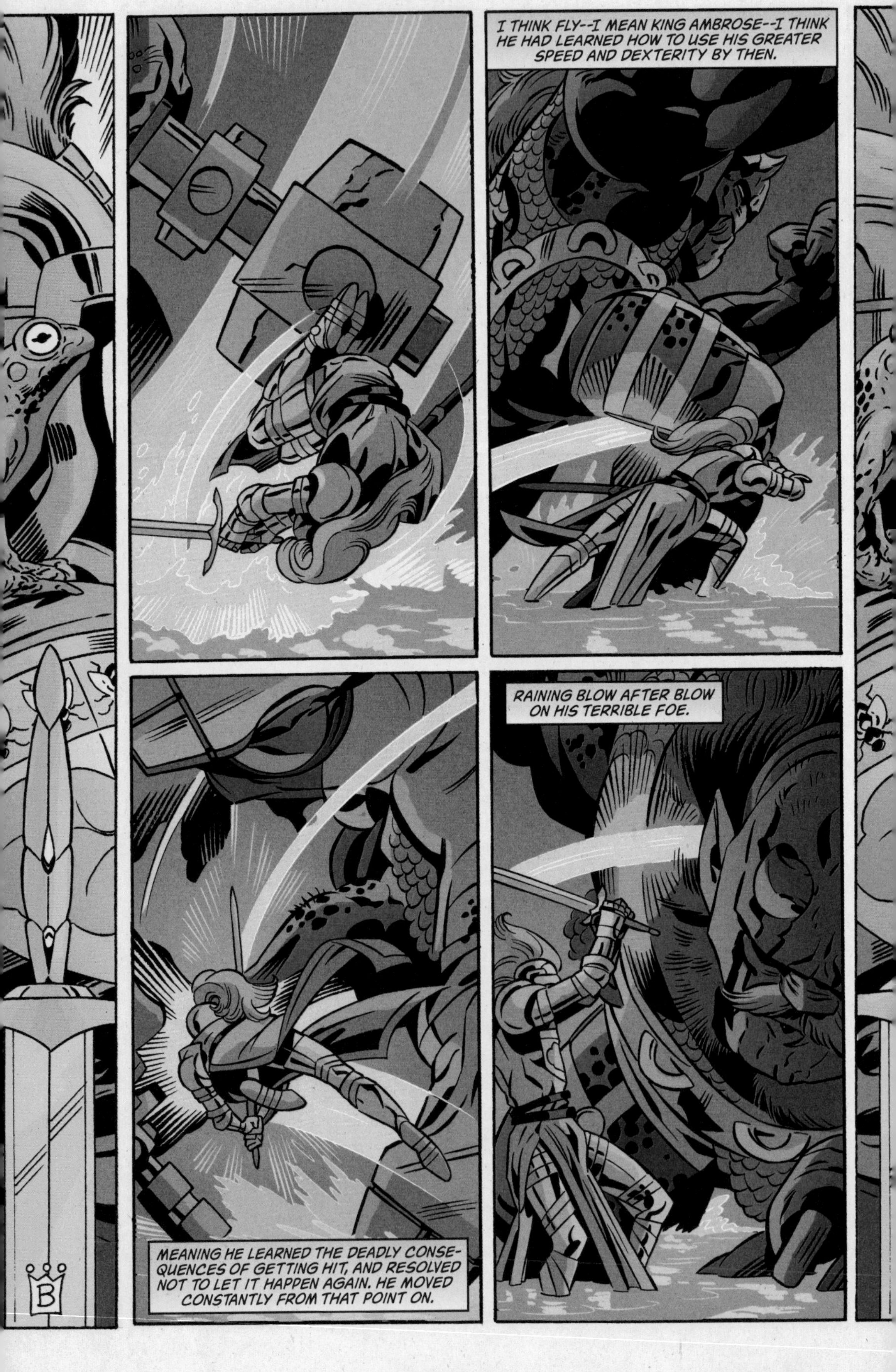

I THINK FLY--I MEAN KING AMBROSE--I THINK HE HAD LEARNED HOW TO USE HIS GREATER SPEED AND DEXTERITY BY THEN.
MEANING HE LEARNED THE DEADLY CONSE-QUENCES OF GETTING HIT, AND RESOLVED NOT TO LET IT HAPPEN AGAIN. HE MOVED CONSTANTLY FROM THAT POINT ON.
RAINING BLOW AFTER BLOW ON HIS TERRIBLE FOE.
B

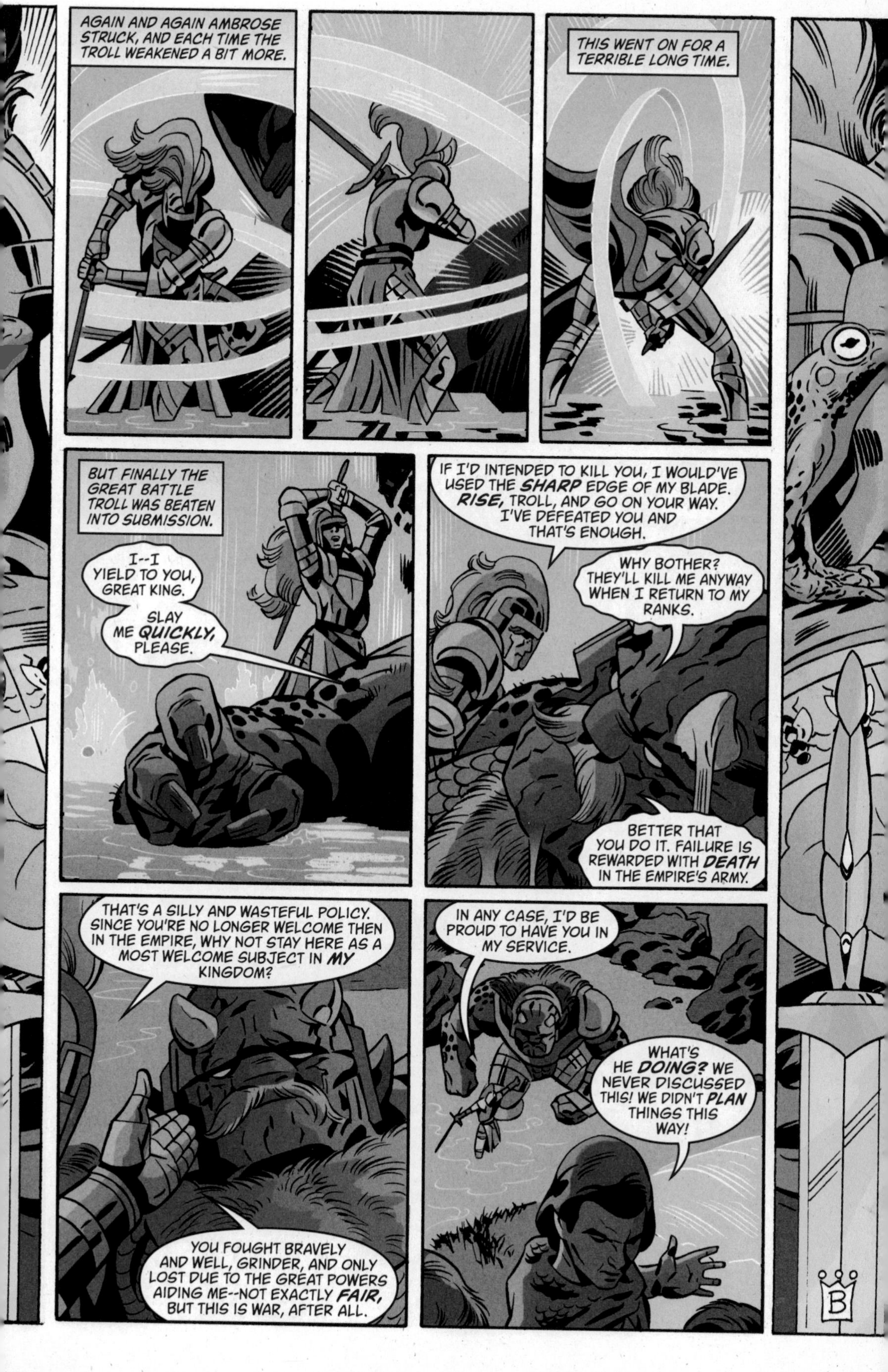
AGAIN AND AGAIN AMBROSE STRUCK, AND EACH TIME THE TROLL WEAKENED A BIT MORE.
THIS WENT ON FOR A TERRIBLE LONG TIME.
BUT FINALLY THE GREAT BATTLE TROLL WAS BEATEN INTO SUBMISSION.
I--I YIELD TO YOU, GREAT KING.
SLAY ME QUICKLY, PLEASE.
IF I'D INTENDED TO KILL YOU, I WOULD'VE USED THE SHARP EDGE OF MY BLADE. RISE, TROLL, AND GO ON YOUR WAY. I'VE DEFEATED YOU AND THAT'S ENOUGH.
WHY BOTHER? THEY'LL KILL ME ANYWAY WHEN I RETURN TO MY RANKS.
BETTER THAT YOU DO IT. FAILURE IS REWARDED WITH DEATH IN THE EMPIRE'S ARMY.
THAT'S A SILLY AND WASTEFUL POLICY. SINCE YOU'RE NO LONGER WELCOME THEN IN THE EMPIRE, WHY NOT STAY HERE AS A MOST WELCOME SUBJECT IN MY KINGDOM?
YOU FOUGHT BRAVELY AND WELL, GRINDER, AND ONLY LOST DUE TO THE GREAT POWERS AIDING ME--NOT EXACTLY FAIR, BUT THIS IS WAR, AFTER ALL.
IN ANY CASE, I'D BE PROUD TO HAVE YOU IN MY SERVICE.
WHAT'S HE DOING? WE NEVER DISCUSSED THIS! WE DIDN'T PLAN THINGS THIS WAY!
B

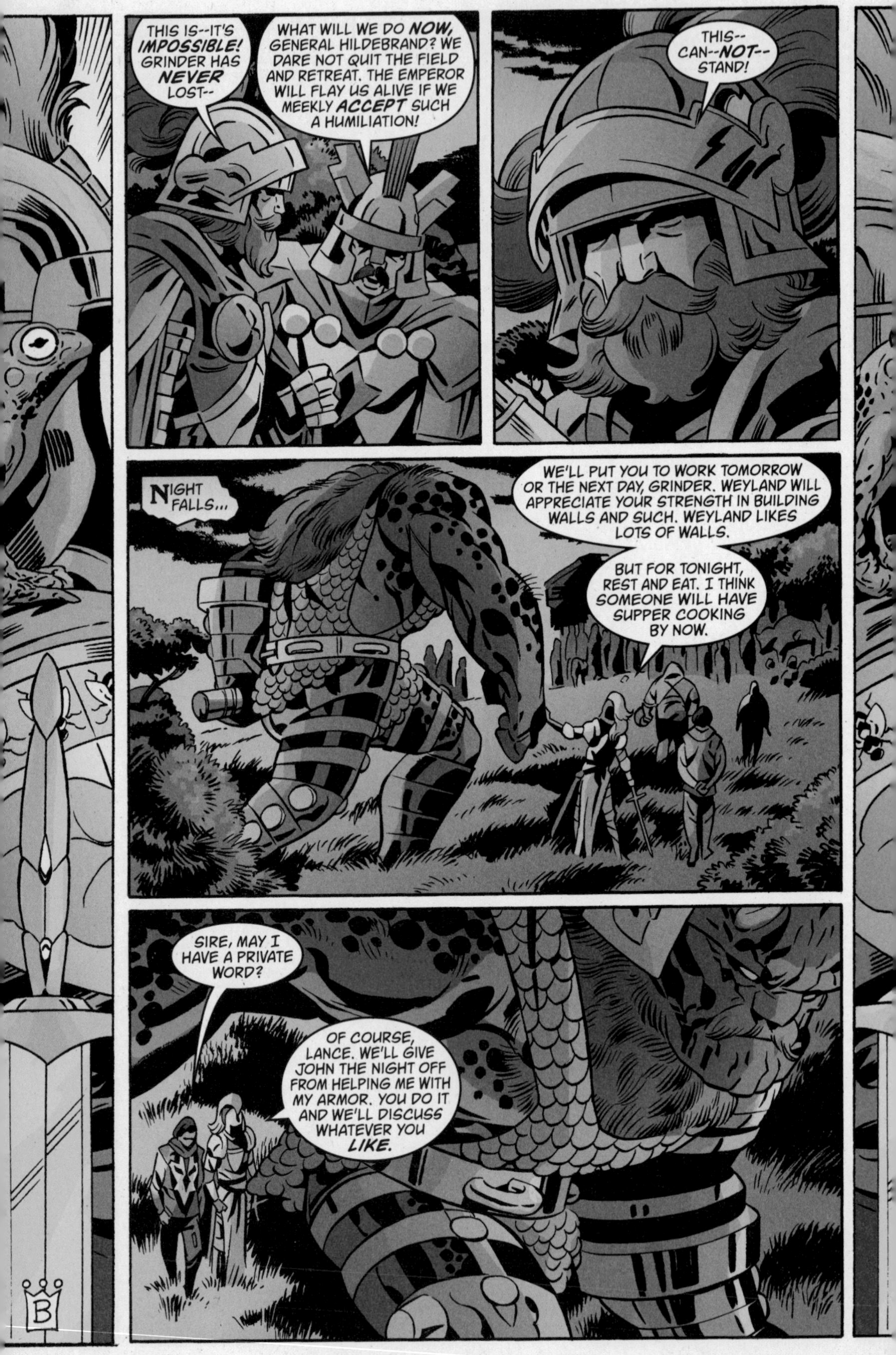
THIS IS--IT'S IMPOSSIBLE! GRINDER HAS NEVER LOST--
WHAT WILL WE DO NOW, GENERAL HILDEBRAND? WE DARE NOT QUIT THE FIELD AND RETREAT. THE EMPEROR WILL FLAY US ALIVE IF WE MEEKLY ACCEPT SUCH A HUMILIATION!
THIS-- CAN--NOT-- STAND!
NIGHT FALLS...
WE'LL PUT YOU TO WORK TOMORROW OR THE NEXT DAY, GRINDER. WEYLAND WILL APPRECIATE YOUR STRENGTH IN BUILDING WALLS AND SUCH. WEYLAND LIKES LOTS OF WALLS.
BUT FOR TONIGHT, REST AND EAT. I THINK SOMEONE WILL HAVE SUPPER COOKING BY NOW.
SIRE, MAY I HAVE A PRIVATE WORD?
OF COURSE, LANCE. WE'LL GIVE JOHN THE NIGHT OFF FROM HELPING ME WITH MY ARMOR. YOU DO IT AND WE'LL DISCUSS WHATEVER YOU LIKE.

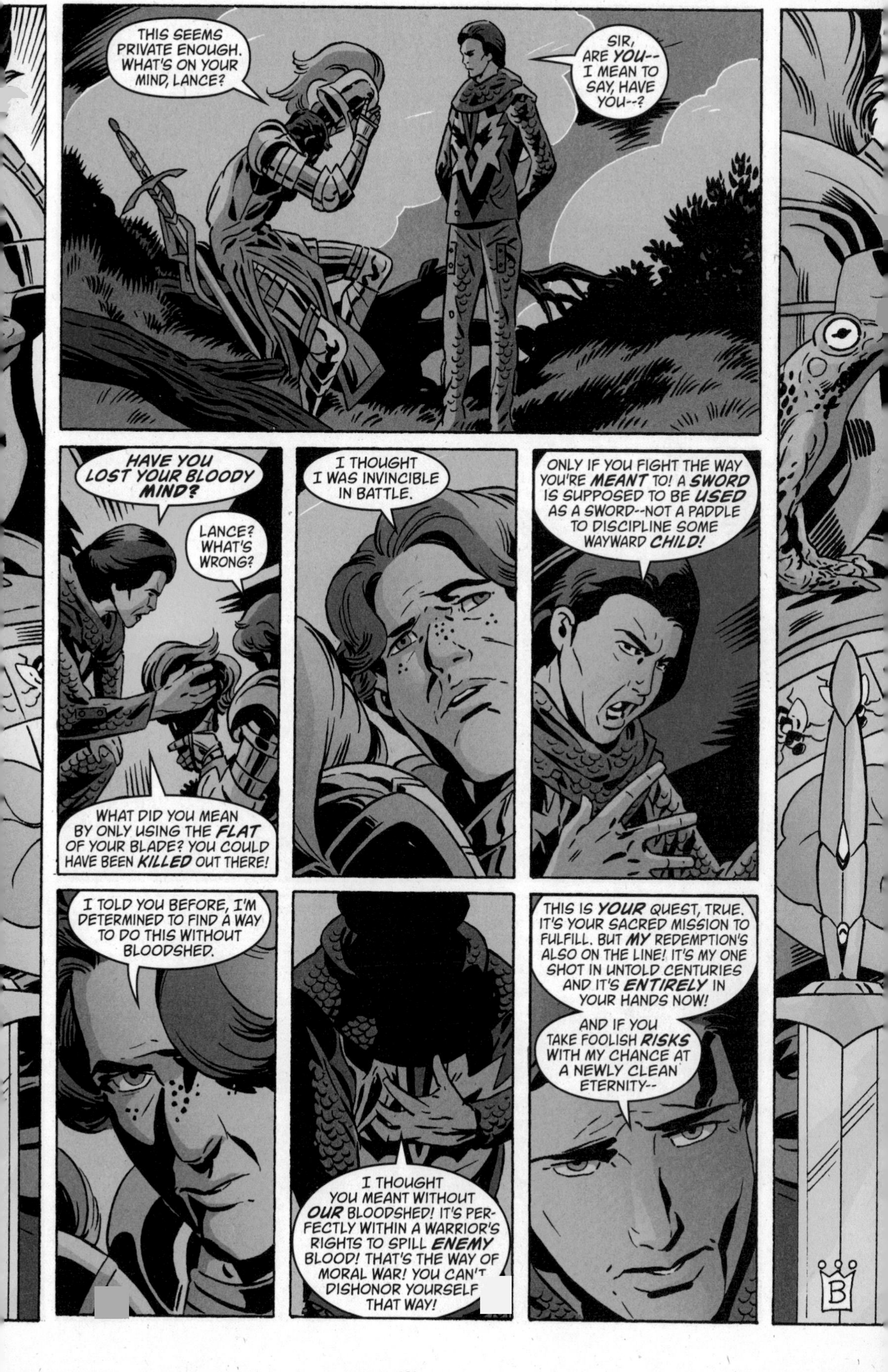
THIS SEEMS PRIVATE ENOUGH. WHAT'S ON YOUR MIND, LANCE?
SIR, ARE YOU-- I MEAN TO SAY, HAVE YOU--?
HAVE YOU LOST YOUR BLOODY MIND?
LANCE? WHAT'S WRONG?
WHAT DID YOU MEAN BY ONLY USING THE FLAT OF YOUR BLADE? YOU COULD HAVE BEEN KILLED OUT THERE!
I THOUGHT I WAS INVINCIBLE IN BATTLE.
ONLY IF YOU FIGHT THE WAY YOU'RE MEANT TO! A SWORD IS SUPPOSED TO BE USED AS A SWORD--NOT A PADDLE TO DISCIPLINE SOME WAYWARD CHILD!
I TOLD YOU BEFORE, I'M DETERMINED TO FIND A WAY TO DO THIS WITHOUT BLOODSHED.
I THOUGHT YOU MEANT WITHOUT OUR BLOODSHED! IT'S PERFECTLY WITHIN A WARRIOR'S RIGHTS TO SPILL ENEMY BLOOD! THAT'S THE WAY OF MORAL WAR! YOU CAN'T DISHONOR YOURSELF THAT WAY!
THIS IS YOUR QUEST, TRUE. IT'S YOUR SACRED MISSION TO FULFILL. BUT MY REDEMPTION'S ALSO ON THE LINE! IT'S MY ONE SHOT IN UNTOLD CENTURIES AND IT'S ENTIRELY IN YOUR HANDS NOW!
AND IF YOU TAKE FOOLISH RISKS WITH MY CHANCE AT A NEWLY CLEAN ETERNITY--

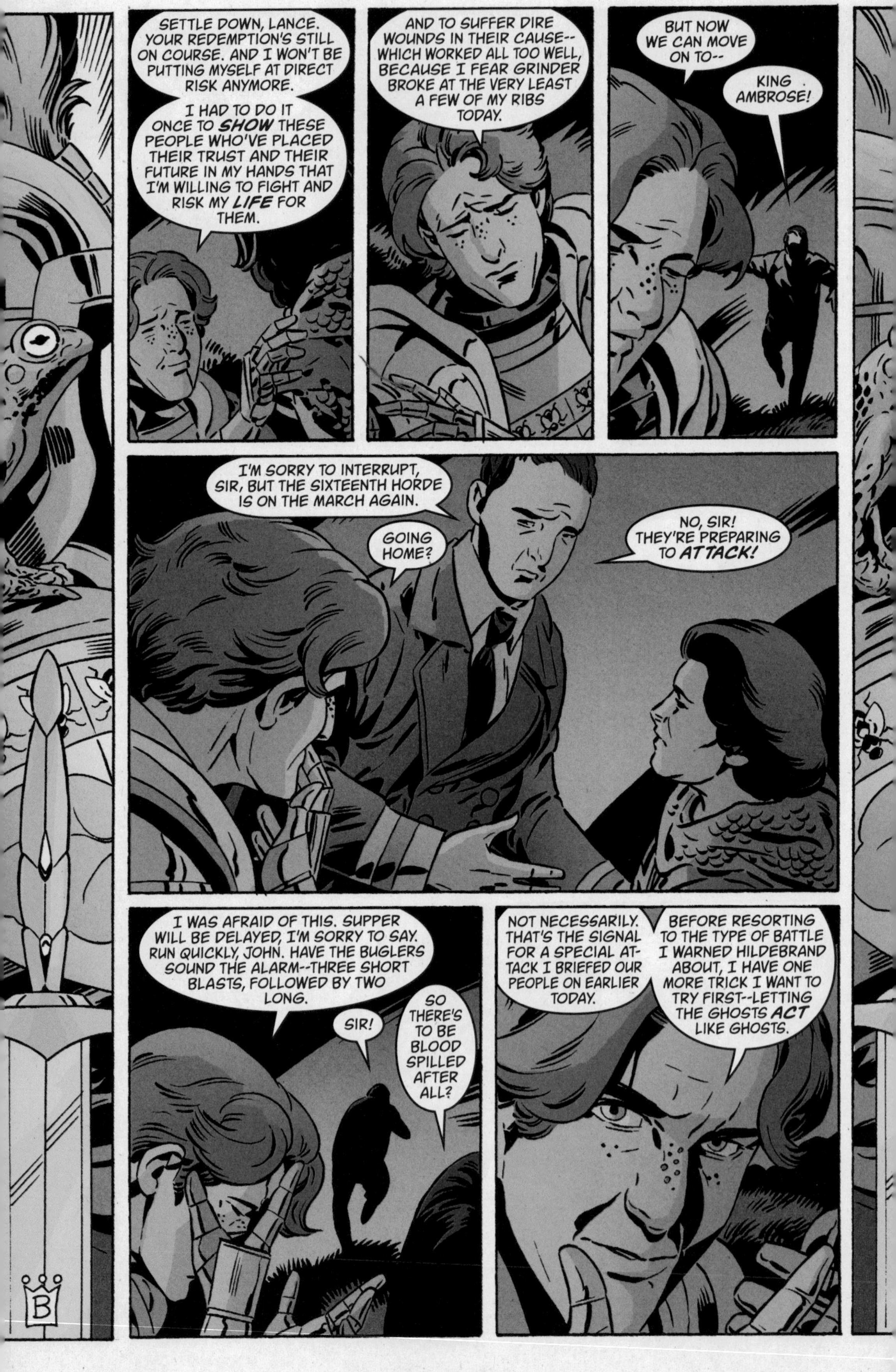
SETTLE DOWN, LANCE. YOUR REDEMPTION'S STILL ON COURSE. AND I WON'T BE PUTTING MYSELF AT DIRECT RISK ANYMORE.
I HAD TO DO IT ONCE TO SHOW THESE PEOPLE WHO'VE PLACED THEIR TRUST AND THEIR FUTURE IN MY HANDS THAT I'M WILLING TO FIGHT AND RISK MY LIFE FOR THEM.
AND TO SUFFER DIRE WOUNDS IN THEIR CAUSE--WHICH WORKED ALL TOO WELL, BECAUSE I FEAR GRINDER BROKE AT THE VERY LEAST A FEW OF MY RIBS TODAY.
BUT NOW WE CAN MOVE ON TO--
KING AMBROSE!
I'M SORRY TO INTERRUPT, SIR, BUT THE SIXTEENTH HORDE IS ON THE MARCH AGAIN.
GOING HOME?
NO, SIR! THEY'RE PREPARING TO ATTACK!
I WAS AFRAID OF THIS. SUPPER WILL BE DELAYED, I'M SORRY TO SAY. RUN QUICKLY, JOHN. HAVE THE BUGLERS SOUND THE ALARM--THREE SHORT BLASTS, FOLLOWED BY TWO LONG.
SIR!
SO THERE'S TO BE BLOOD SPILLED AFTER ALL?
NOT NECESSARILY. THAT'S THE SIGNAL FOR A SPECIAL AT-TACK I BRIEFED OUR PEOPLE ON EARLIER TODAY.
BEFORE RESORTING TO THE TYPE OF BATTLE I WARNED HILDEBRAND ABOUT, I HAVE ONE MORE TRICK I WANT TO TRY FIRST--LETTING THE GHOSTS ACT LIKE GHOSTS.
B

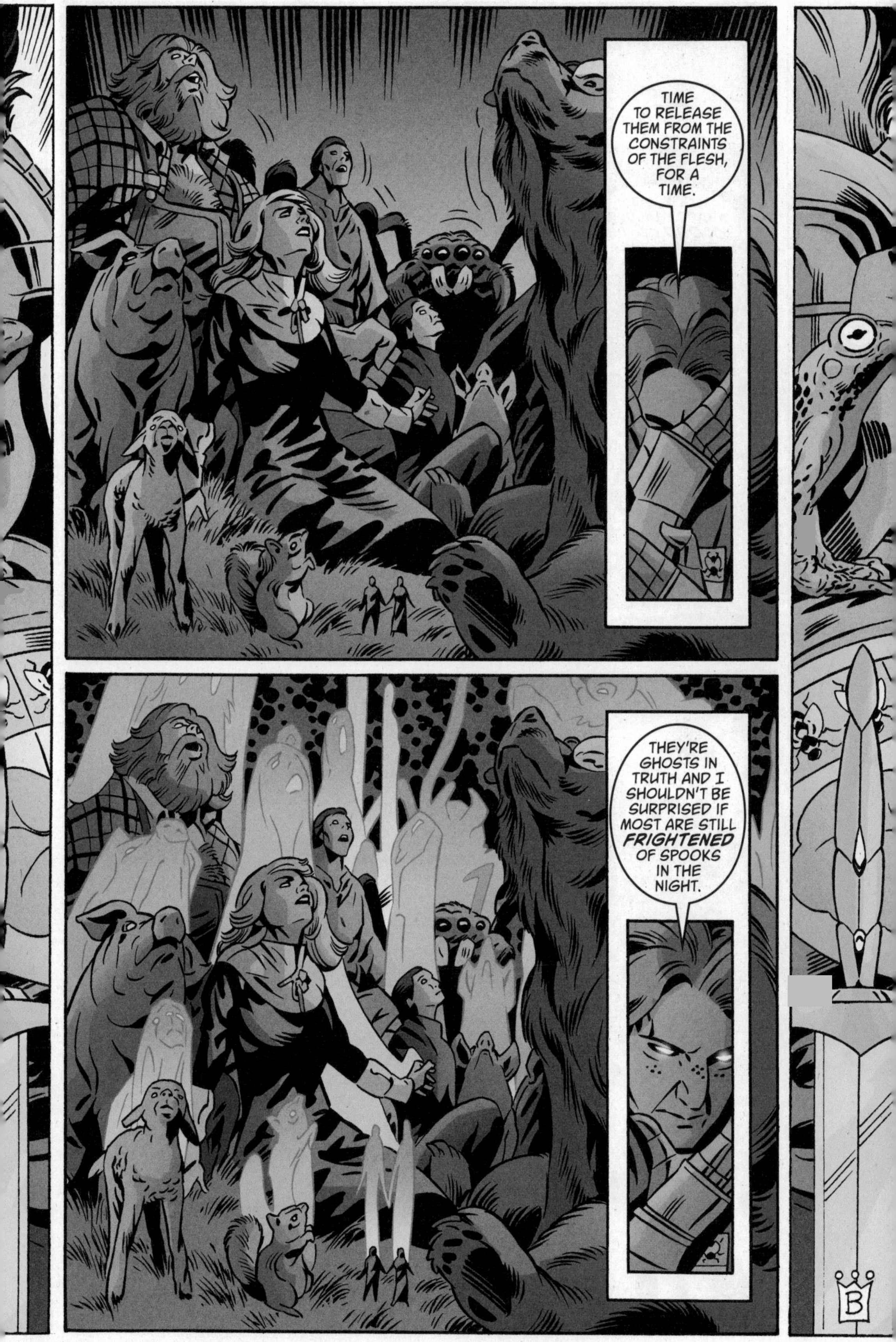
TIME TO RELEASE THEM FROM THE CONSTRAINTS OF THE FLESH, FOR A TIME.
THEY'RE GHOSTS IN TRUTH AND I SHOULDN'T BE SURPRISED IF MOST ARE STILL **FRIGHTENED** OF SPOOKS IN THE NIGHT.

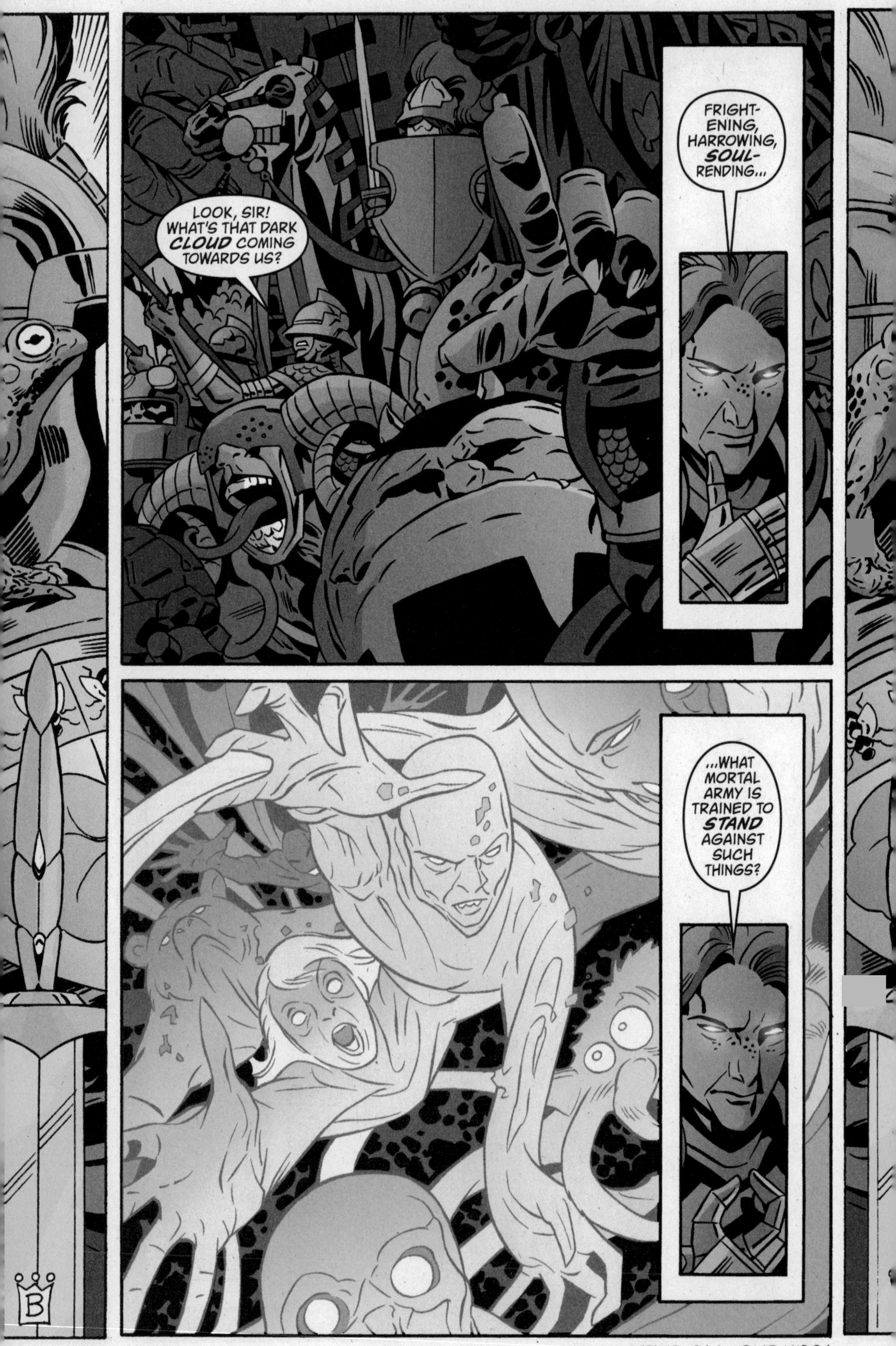
FRIGHT-ENING, HARROWING, SOUL-RENDING...
LOOK, SIR! WHAT'S THAT DARK CLOUD COMING TOWARDS US?
...WHAT MORTAL ARMY IS TRAINED TO STAND AGAINST SUCH THINGS?
NEXT: ALL-OUT WAR!

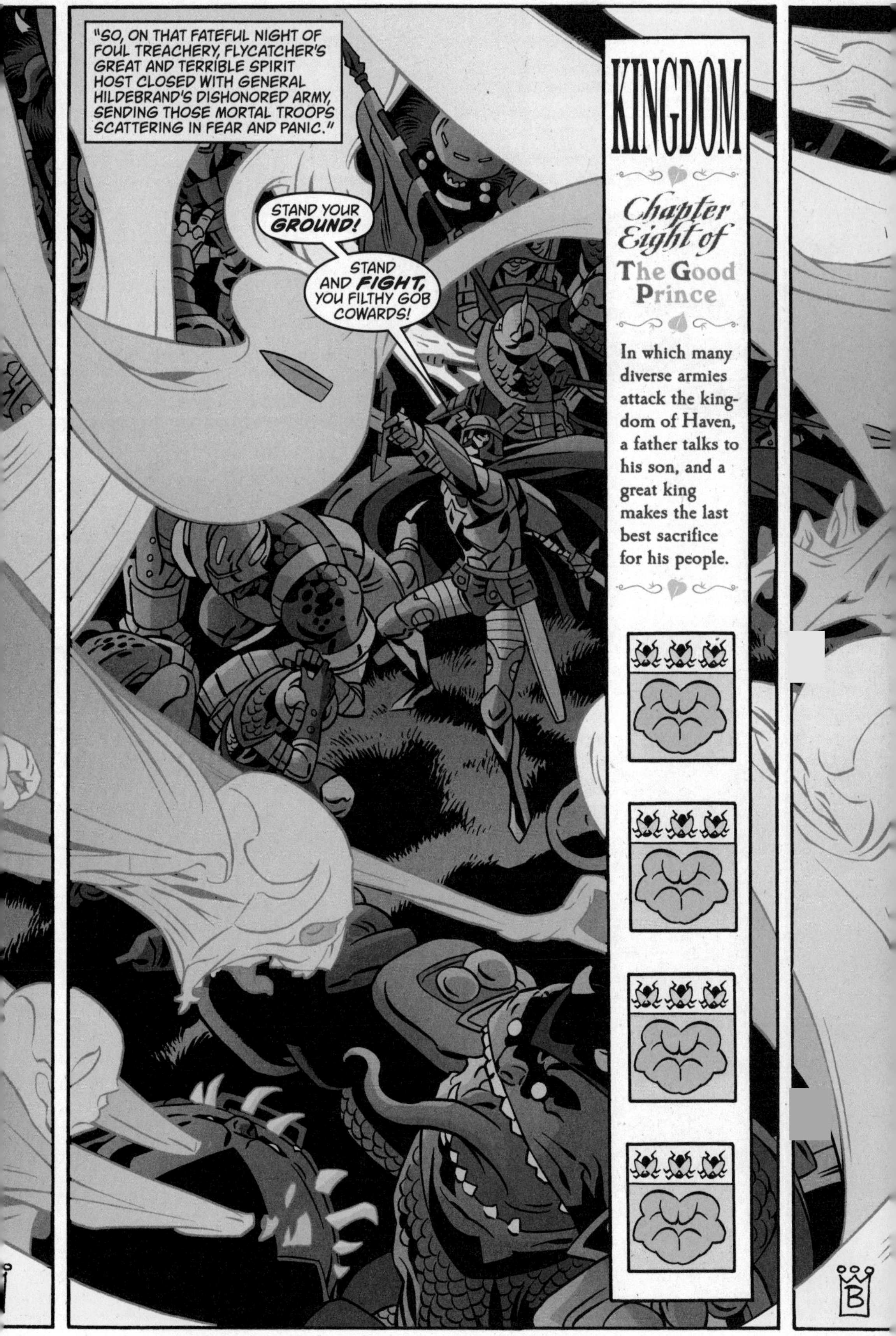
"SO, ON THAT FATEFUL NIGHT OF FOUL TREACHERY, FLYCATCHER'S GREAT AND TERRIBLE SPIRIT HOST CLOSED WITH GENERAL HILDEBRAND'S DISHONORED ARMY, SENDING THOSE MORTAL TROOPS SCATTERING IN FEAR AND PANIC."
STAND YOUR GROUND!
STAND AND FIGHT, YOU FILTHY GOB COWARDS!
KINGDOM
Chapter Eight of The Good Prince
In which many diverse armies attack the kingdom of Haven, a father talks to his son, and a great king makes the last best sacrifice for his people.

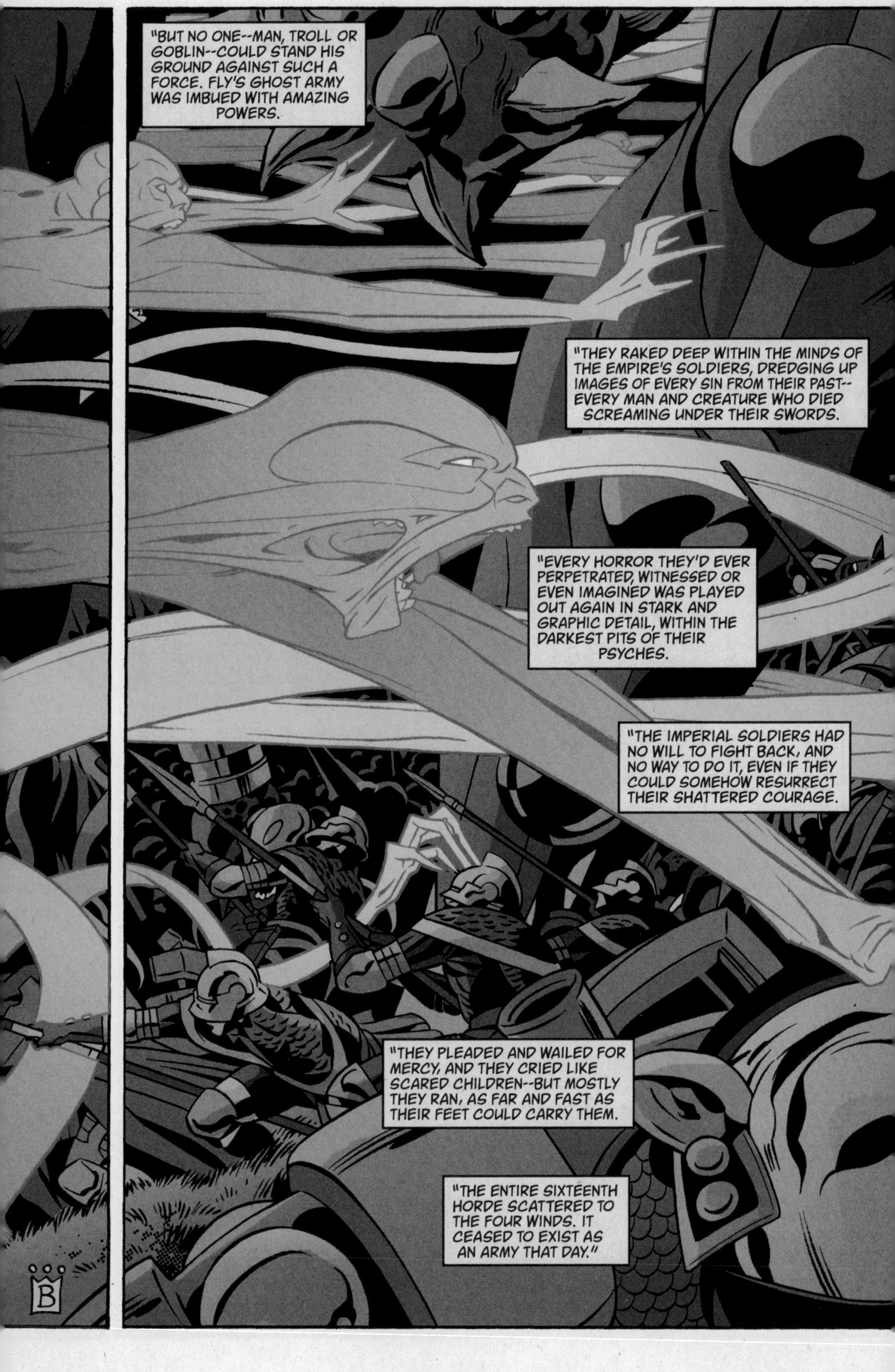
"BUT NO ONE--MAN, TROLL OR GOBLIN--COULD STAND HIS GROUND AGAINST SUCH A FORCE. FLY'S GHOST ARMY WAS IMBUED WITH AMAZING POWERS.
"THEY RAKED DEEP WITHIN THE MINDS OF THE EMPIRE'S SOLDIERS, DREDGING UP IMAGES OF EVERY SIN FROM THEIR PAST--EVERY MAN AND CREATURE WHO DIED SCREAMING UNDER THEIR SWORDS.
"EVERY HORROR THEY'D EVER PERPETRATED, WITNESSED OR EVEN IMAGINED WAS PLAYED OUT AGAIN IN STARK AND GRAPHIC DETAIL, WITHIN THE DARKEST PITS OF THEIR PSYCHES.
"THE IMPERIAL SOLDIERS HAD NO WILL TO FIGHT BACK, AND NO WAY TO DO IT, EVEN IF THEY COULD SOMEHOW RESURRECT THEIR SHATTERED COURAGE.
"THEY PLEADED AND WAILED FOR MERCY, AND THEY CRIED LIKE SCARED CHILDREN--BUT MOSTLY THEY RAN, AS FAR AND FAST AS THEIR FEET COULD CARRY THEM.
"THE ENTIRE SIXTEENTH HORDE SCATTERED TO THE FOUR WINDS. IT CEASED TO EXIST AS AN ARMY THAT DAY."
B

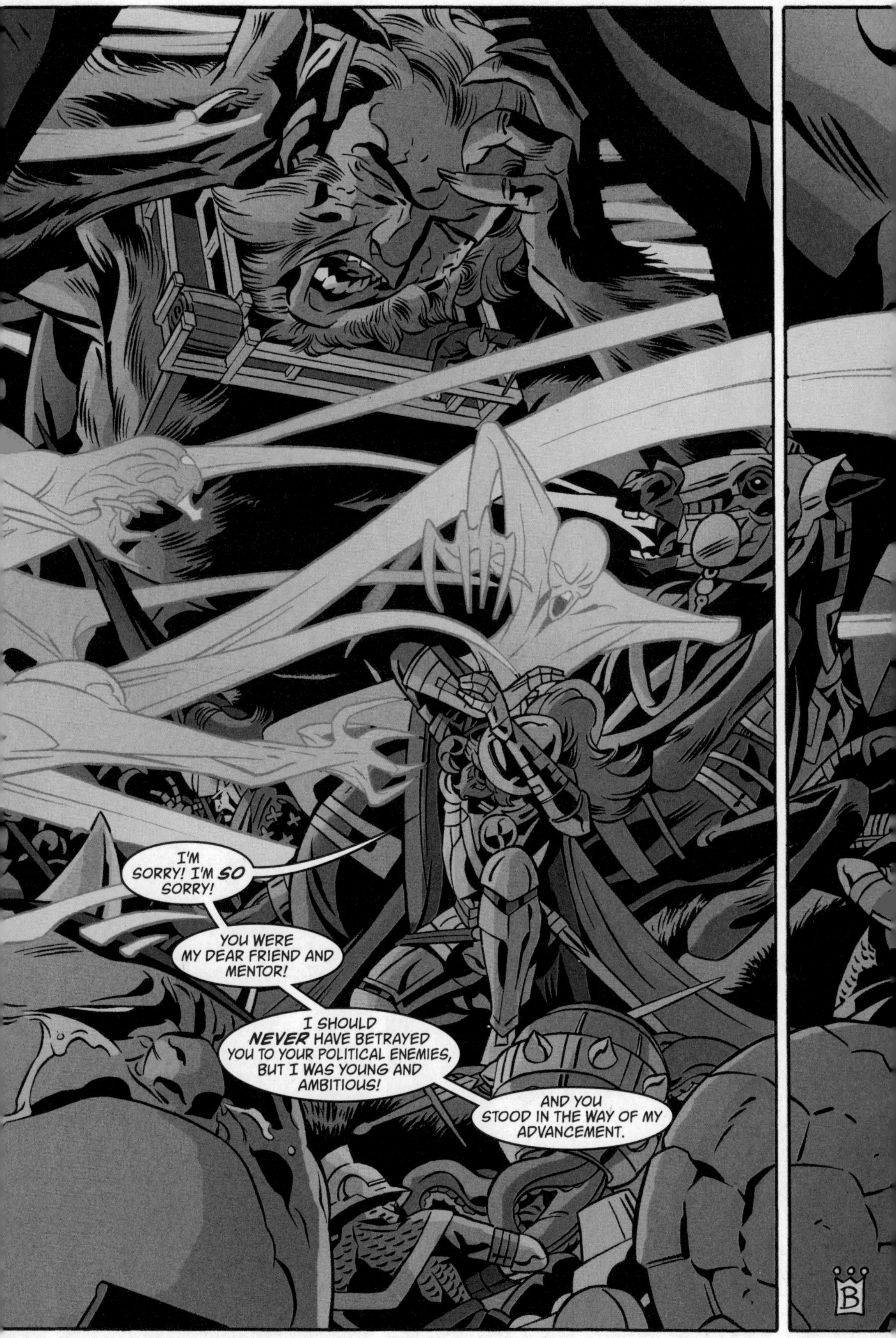
I'M SORRY! I'M SO SORRY!
YOU WERE MY DEAR FRIEND AND MENTOR!
I SHOULD NEVER HAVE BETRAYED YOU TO YOUR POLITICAL ENEMIES, BUT I WAS YOUNG AND AMBITIOUS!
AND YOU STOOD IN THE WAY OF MY ADVANCEMENT.

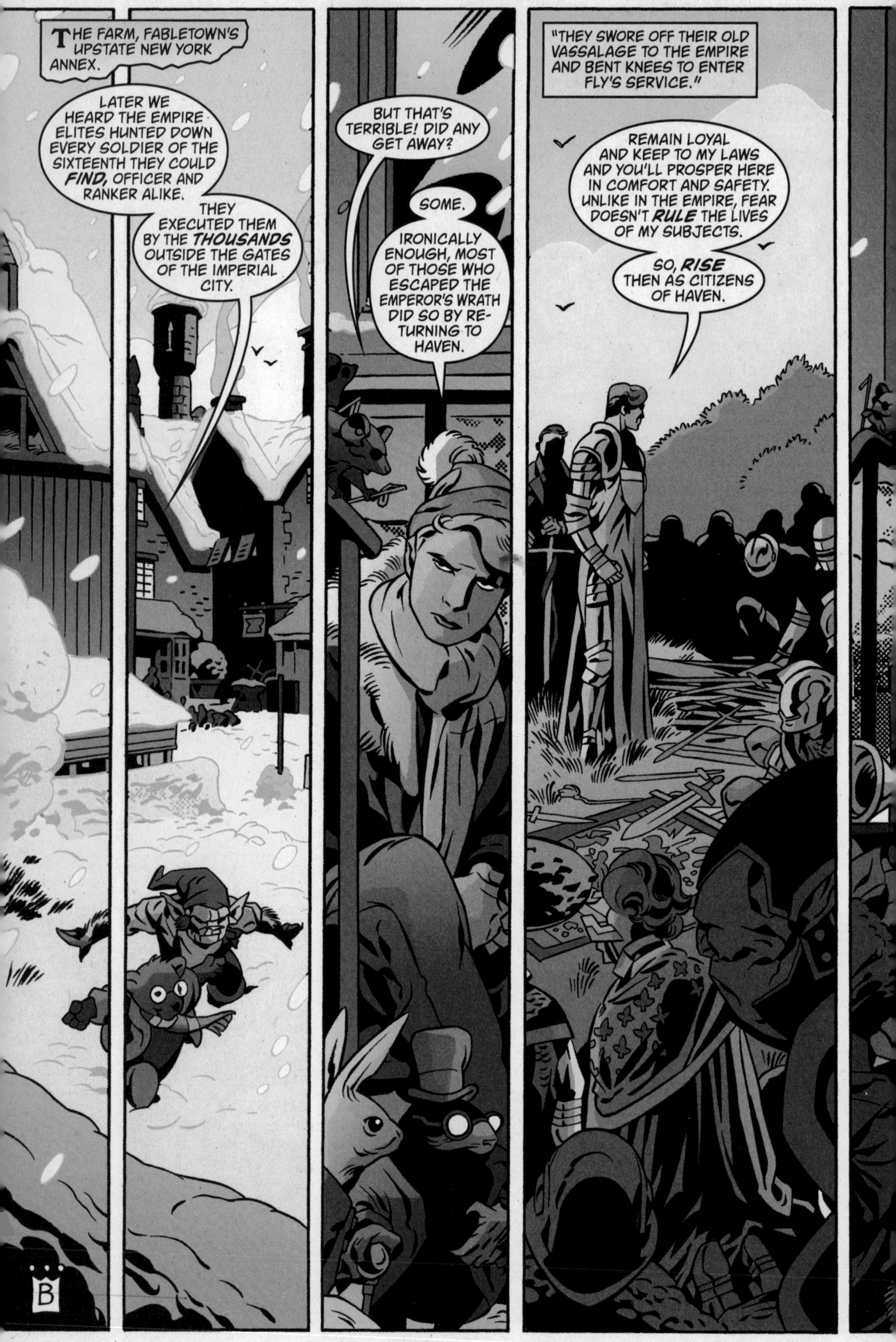
THE FARM, FABLETOWN'S UPSTATE NEW YORK ANNEX.
LATER WE HEARD THE EMPIRE ELITES HUNTED DOWN EVERY SOLDIER OF THE SIXTEENTH THEY COULD FIND, OFFICER AND RANKER ALIKE.
THEY EXECUTED THEM BY THE THOUSANDS OUTSIDE THE GATES OF THE IMPERIAL CITY.
BUT THAT'S TERRIBLE! DID ANY GET AWAY?
SOME.
IRONICALLY ENOUGH, MOST OF THOSE WHO ESCAPED THE EMPEROR'S WRATH DID SO BY RE-TURNING TO HAVEN.
"THEY SWORE OFF THEIR OLD VASSALAGE TO THE EMPIRE AND BENT KNEES TO ENTER FLY'S SERVICE."
REMAIN LOYAL AND KEEP TO MY LAWS AND YOU'LL PROSPER HERE IN COMFORT AND SAFETY. UNLIKE IN THE EMPIRE, FEAR DOESN'T RULE THE LIVES OF MY SUBJECTS.
SO, RISE THEN AS CITIZENS OF HAVEN.

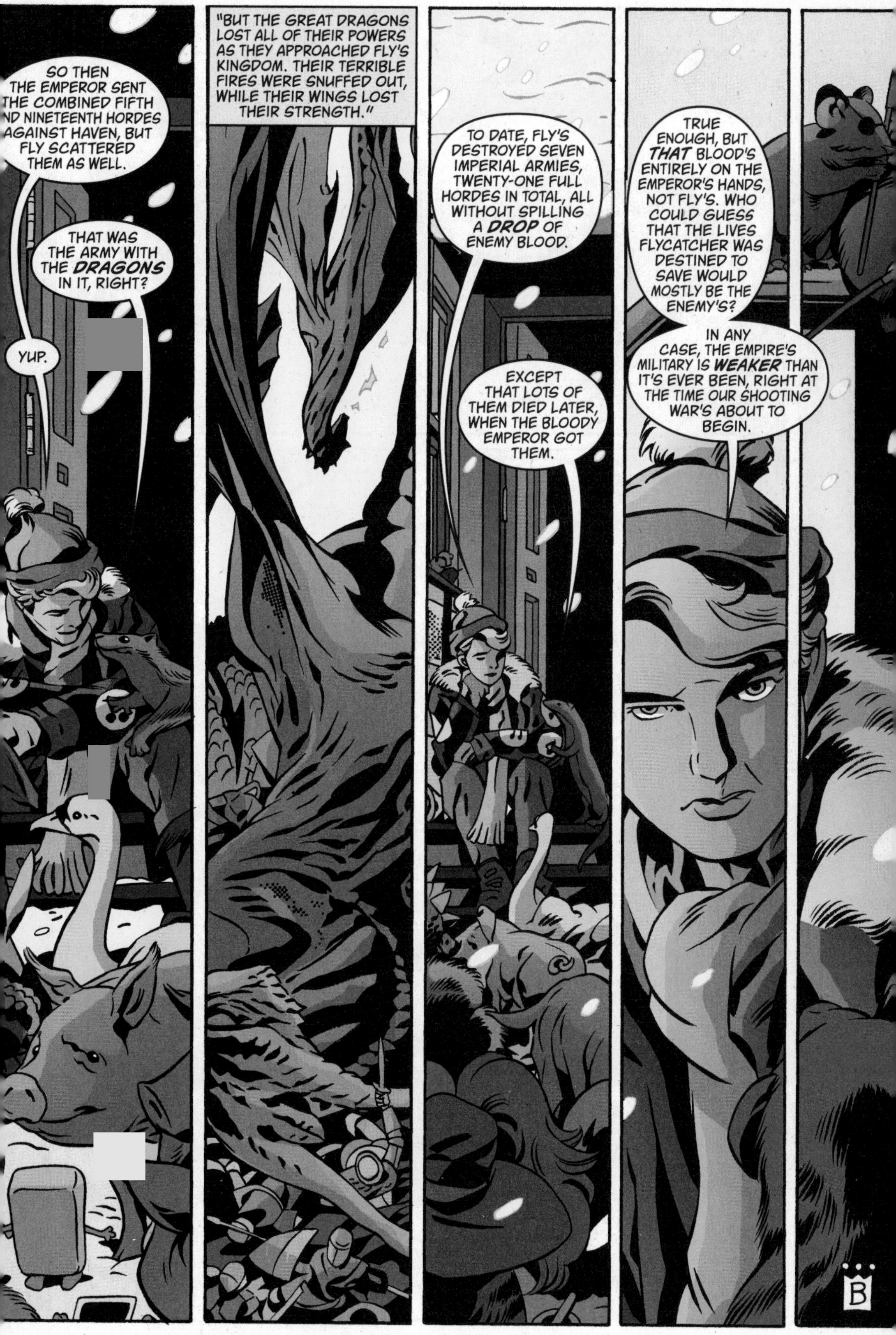
SO THEN THE EMPEROR SENT THE COMBINED FIFTH AND NINETEENTH HORDES AGAINST HAVEN, BUT FLY SCATTERED THEM AS WELL.
THAT WAS THE ARMY WITH THE DRAGONS IN IT, RIGHT?
YUP.
"BUT THE GREAT DRAGONS LOST ALL OF THEIR POWERS AS THEY APPROACHED FLY'S KINGDOM. THEIR TERRIBLE FIRES WERE SNUFFED OUT, WHILE THEIR WINGS LOST THEIR STRENGTH."
TO DATE, FLY'S DESTROYED SEVEN IMPERIAL ARMIES, TWENTY-ONE FULL HORDES IN TOTAL, ALL WITHOUT SPILLING A DROP OF ENEMY BLOOD.
EXCEPT THAT LOTS OF THEM DIED LATER, WHEN THE BLOODY EMPEROR GOT THEM.
TRUE ENOUGH, BUT THAT BLOOD'S ENTIRELY ON THE EMPEROR'S HANDS, NOT FLY'S. WHO COULD GUESS THAT THE LIVES FLYCATCHER WAS DESTINED TO SAVE WOULD MOSTLY BE THE ENEMY'S?
IN ANY CASE, THE EMPIRE'S MILITARY IS WEAKER THAN IT'S EVER BEEN, RIGHT AT THE TIME OUR SHOOTING WAR'S ABOUT TO BEGIN.

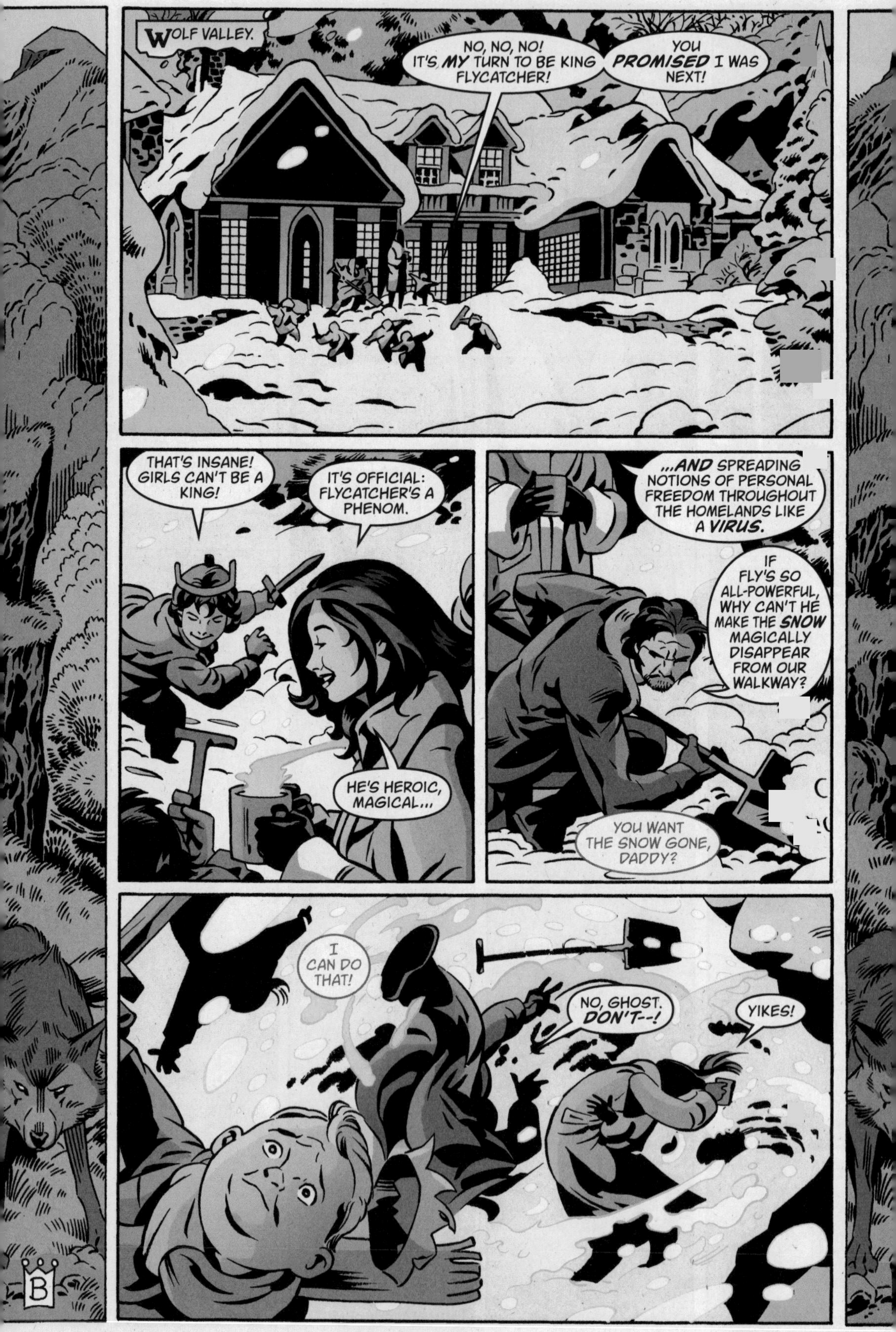
WOLF VALLEY.
NO, NO, NO! IT'S MY TURN TO BE KING FLYCATCHER!
YOU PROMISED I WAS NEXT!
THAT'S INSANE! GIRLS CAN'T BE A KING!
IT'S OFFICIAL: FLYCATCHER'S A PHENOM.
HE'S HEROIC, MAGICAL...
...AND SPREADING NOTIONS OF PERSONAL FREEDOM THROUGHOUT THE HOMELANDS LIKE A VIRUS.
IF FLY'S SO ALL-POWERFUL, WHY CAN'T HE MAKE THE SNOW MAGICALLY DISAPPEAR FROM OUR WALKWAY?
YOU WANT THE SNOW GONE, DADDY?
I CAN DO THAT!
NO, GHOST. DON'T--!
YIKES!

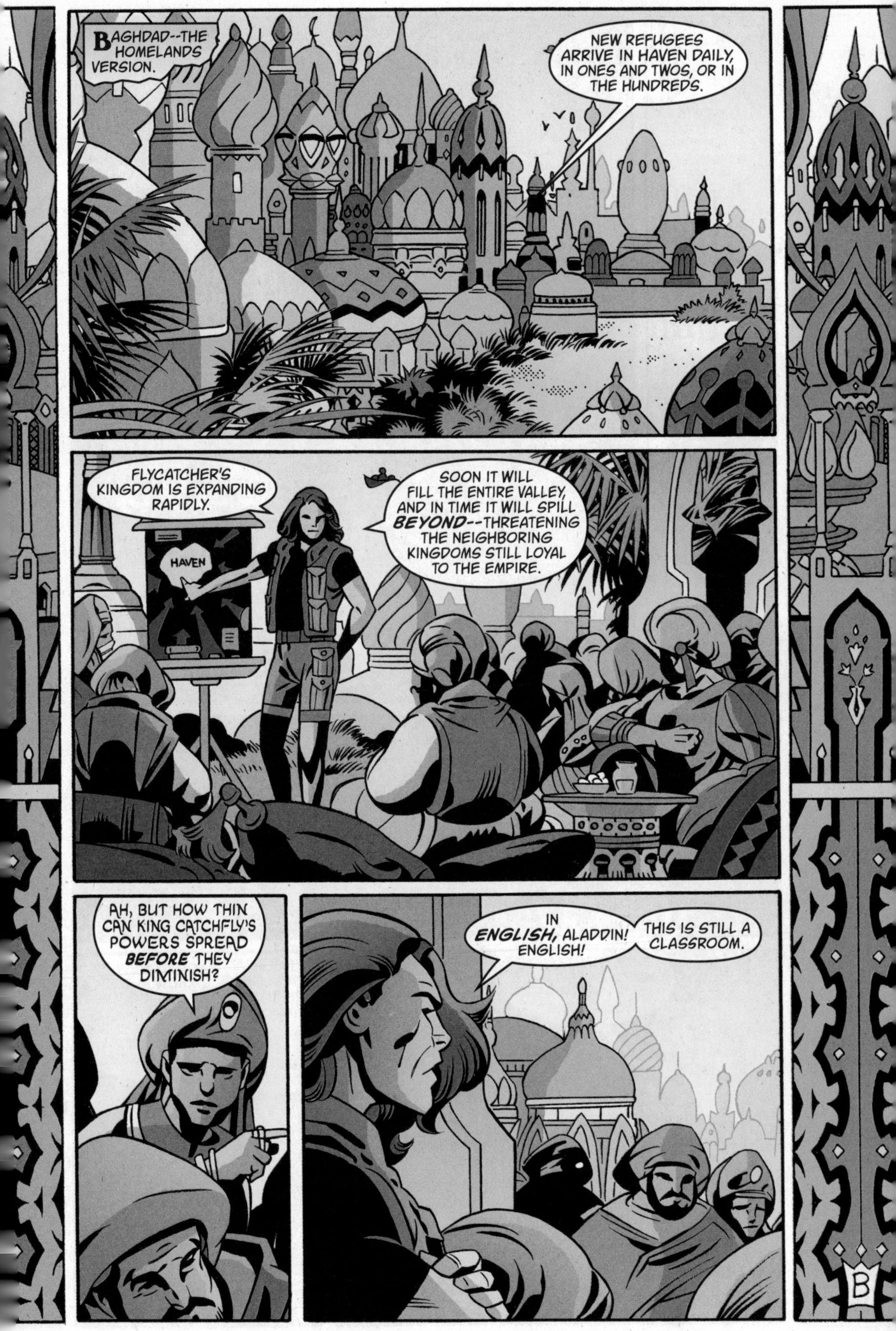
BAGHDAD--THE HOMELANDS VERSION.
NEW REFUGEES ARRIVE IN HAVEN DAILY, IN ONES AND TWOS, OR IN THE HUNDREDS.
FLYCATCHER'S KINGDOM IS EXPANDING RAPIDLY.
SOON IT WILL FILL THE ENTIRE VALLEY, AND IN TIME IT WILL SPILL BEYOND--THREATENING THE NEIGHBORING KINGDOMS STILL LOYAL TO THE EMPIRE.
HAVEN
AH, BUT HOW THIN CAN KING CATCHFLY'S POWERS SPREAD BEFORE THEY DIMINISH?
IN ENGLISH, ALADDIN! ENGLISH!
THIS IS STILL A CLASSROOM.

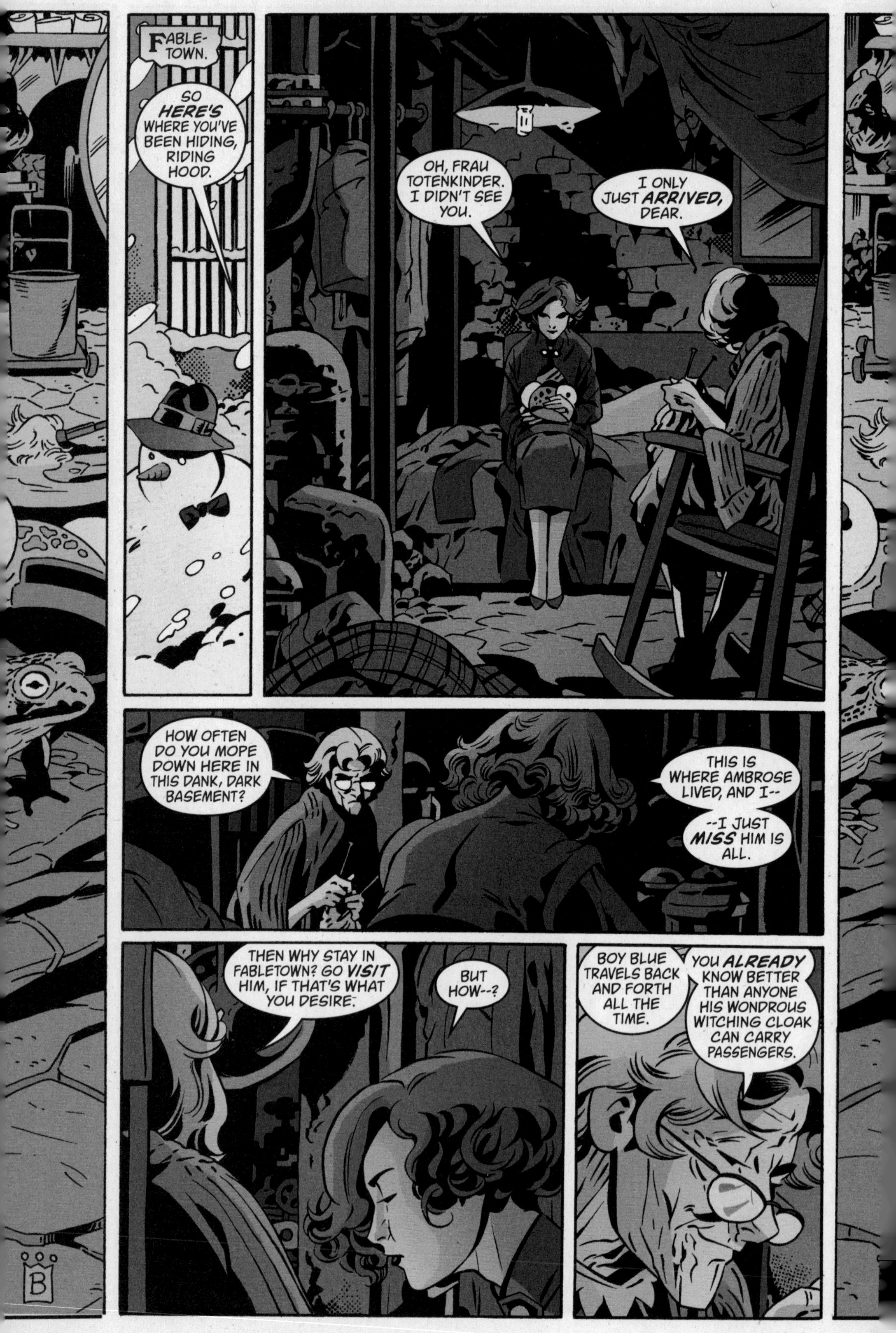
FABLE-TOWN.
SO HERE'S WHERE YOU'VE BEEN HIDING, RIDING HOOD.
OH, FRAU TOTENKINDER. I DIDN'T SEE YOU.
I ONLY JUST ARRIVED, DEAR.
HOW OFTEN DO YOU MOPE DOWN HERE IN THIS DANK, DARK BASEMENT?
THIS IS WHERE AMBROSE LIVED, AND I--
--I JUST MISS HIM IS ALL.
THEN WHY STAY IN FABLETOWN? GO VISIT HIM, IF THAT'S WHAT YOU DESIRE.
BUT HOW--?
BOY BLUE TRAVELS BACK AND FORTH ALL THE TIME.
YOU ALREADY KNOW BETTER THAN ANYONE HIS WONDROUS WITCHING CLOAK CAN CARRY PASSENGERS.

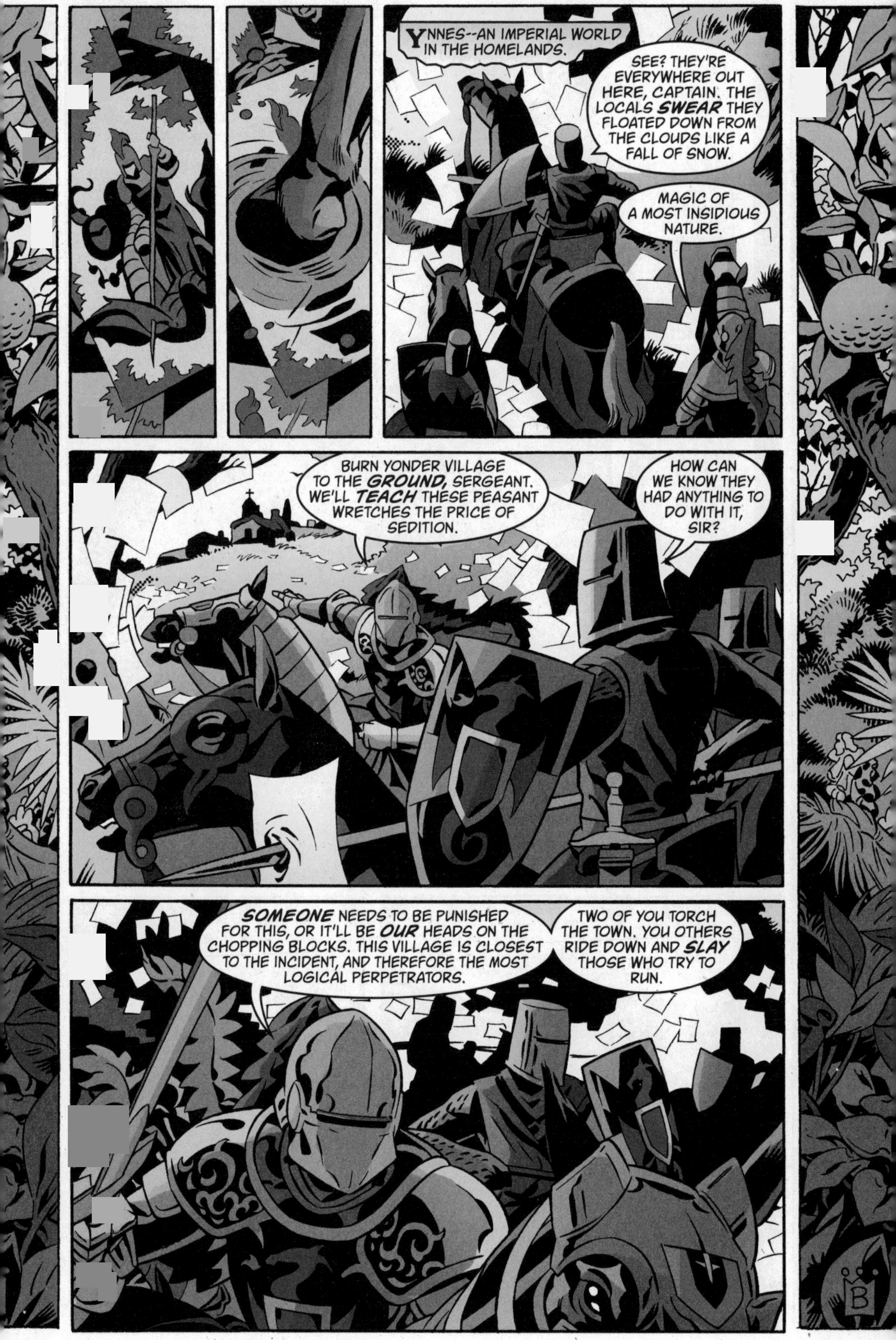
YNNES--AN IMPERIAL WORLD IN THE HOMELANDS.
SEE? THEY'RE EVERYWHERE OUT HERE, CAPTAIN. THE LOCALS SWEAR THEY FLOATED DOWN FROM THE CLOUDS LIKE A FALL OF SNOW.
MAGIC OF A MOST INSIDIOUS NATURE.
BURN YONDER VILLAGE TO THE GROUND, SERGEANT. WE'LL TEACH THESE PEASANT WRETCHES THE PRICE OF SEDITION.
HOW CAN WE KNOW THEY HAD ANYTHING TO DO WITH IT, SIR?
SOMEONE NEEDS TO BE PUNISHED FOR THIS, OR IT'LL BE OUR HEADS ON THE CHOPPING BLOCKS. THIS VILLAGE IS CLOSEST TO THE INCIDENT, AND THEREFORE THE MOST LOGICAL PERPETRATORS.
TWO OF YOU TORCH THE TOWN. YOU OTHERS RIDE DOWN AND SLAY THOSE WHO TRY TO RUN.

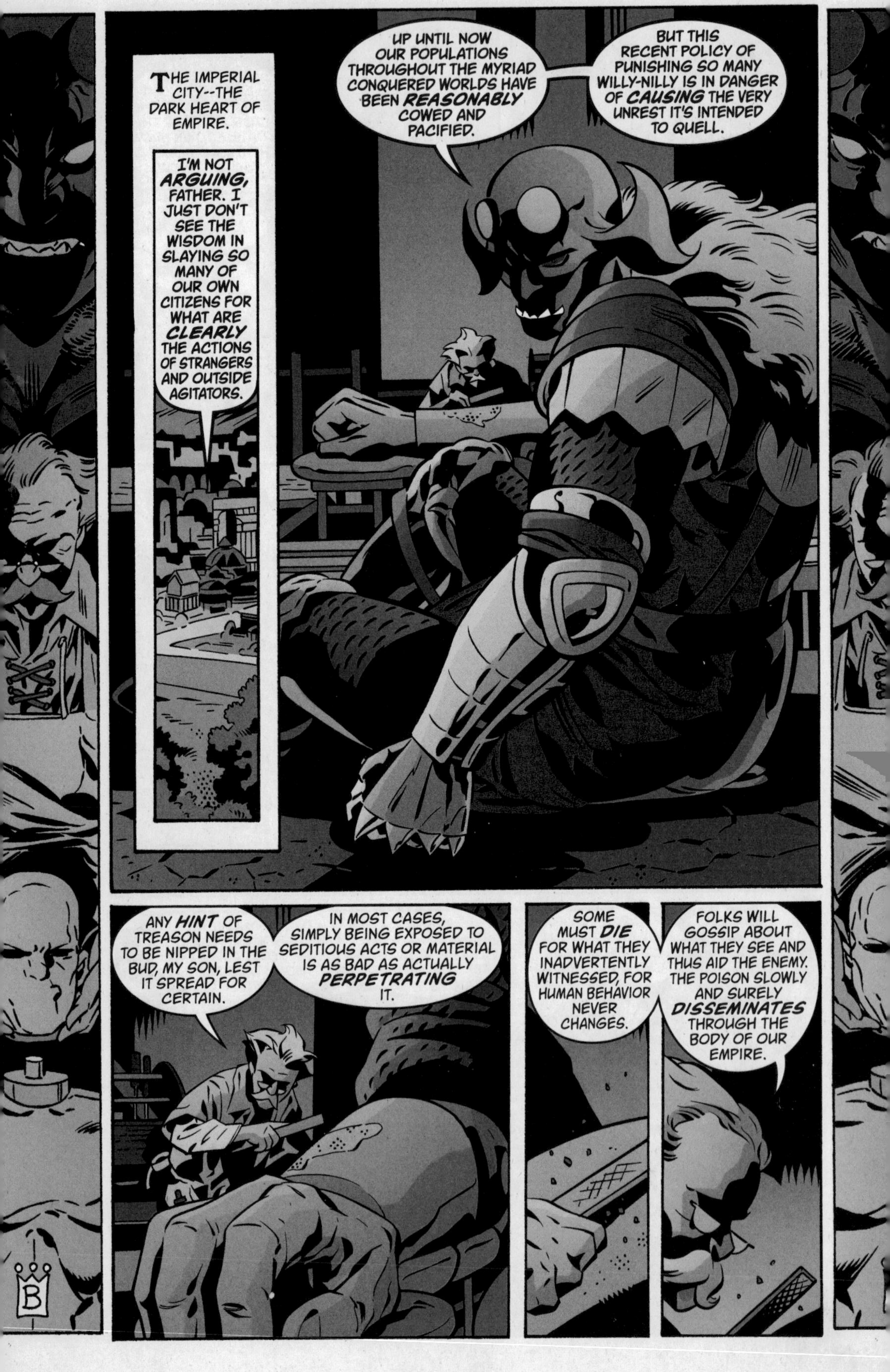
THE IMPERIAL CITY--THE DARK HEART OF EMPIRE.
I'M NOT ARGUING, FATHER. I JUST DON'T SEE THE WISDOM IN SLAYING SO MANY OF OUR OWN CITIZENS FOR WHAT ARE CLEARLY THE ACTIONS OF STRANGERS AND OUTSIDE AGITATORS.
UP UNTIL NOW OUR POPULATIONS THROUGHOUT THE MYRIAD CONQUERED WORLDS HAVE BEEN REASONABLY COWED AND PACIFIED.
BUT THIS RECENT POLICY OF PUNISHING SO MANY WILLY-NILLY IS IN DANGER OF CAUSING THE VERY UNREST IT'S INTENDED TO QUELL.
ANY HINT OF TREASON NEEDS TO BE NIPPED IN THE BUD, MY SON, LEST IT SPREAD FOR CERTAIN.
IN MOST CASES, SIMPLY BEING EXPOSED TO SEDITIOUS ACTS OR MATERIAL IS AS BAD AS ACTUALLY PERPETRATING IT.
SOME MUST DIE FOR WHAT THEY INADVERTENTLY WITNESSED, FOR HUMAN BEHAVIOR NEVER CHANGES.
FOLKS WILL GOSSIP ABOUT WHAT THEY SEE AND THUS AID THE ENEMY. THE POISON SLOWLY AND SURELY DISSEMINATES THROUGH THE BODY OF OUR EMPIRE.
B

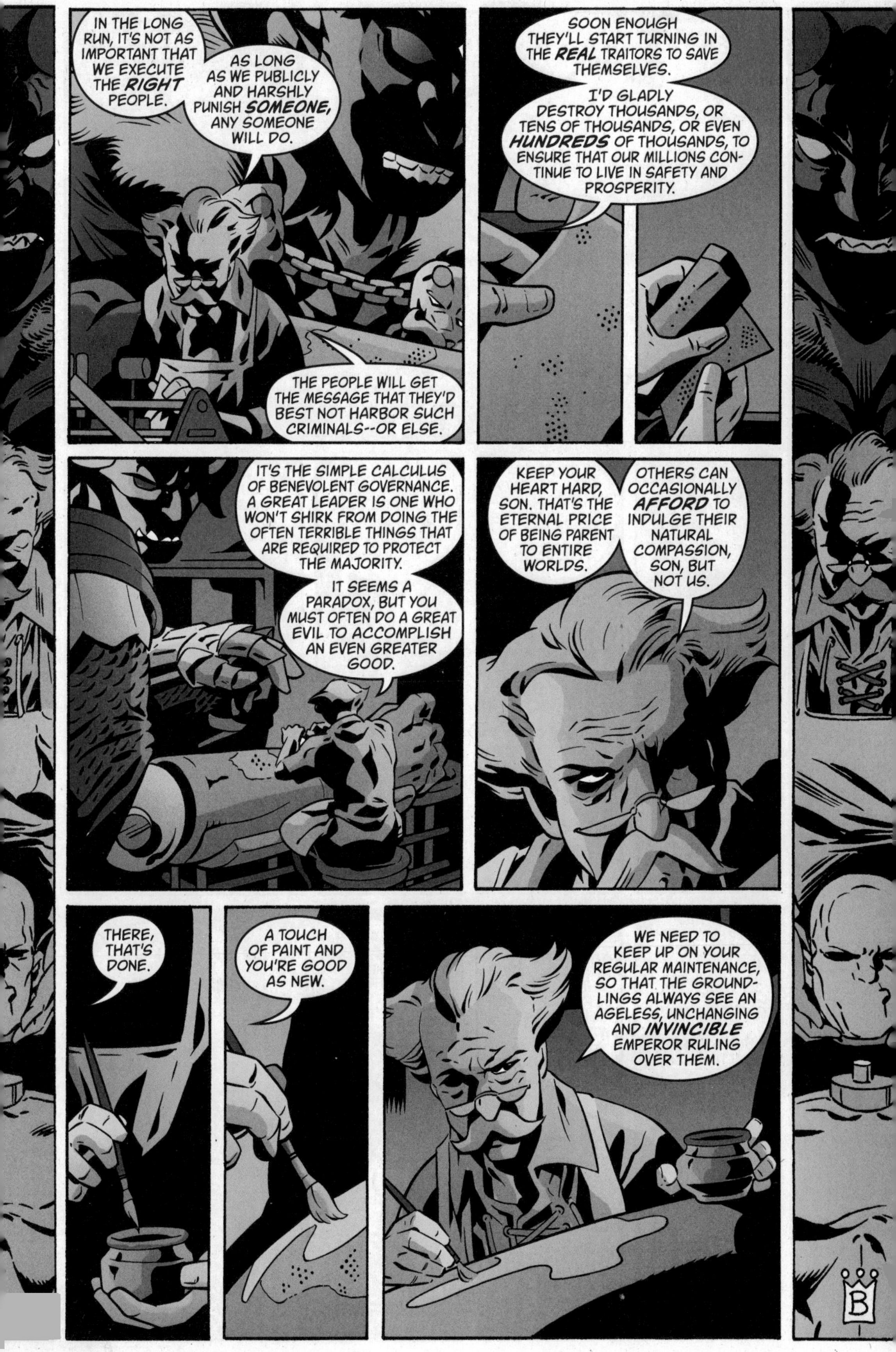
IN THE LONG RUN, IT'S NOT AS IMPORTANT THAT WE EXECUTE THE RIGHT PEOPLE.
AS LONG AS WE PUBLICLY AND HARSHLY PUNISH SOMEONE, ANY SOMEONE WILL DO.
THE PEOPLE WILL GET THE MESSAGE THAT THEY'D BEST NOT HARBOR SUCH CRIMINALS--OR ELSE.
SOON ENOUGH THEY'LL START TURNING IN THE REAL TRAITORS TO SAVE THEMSELVES.
I'D GLADLY DESTROY THOUSANDS, OR TENS OF THOUSANDS, OR EVEN HUNDREDS OF THOUSANDS, TO ENSURE THAT OUR MILLIONS CONTINUE TO LIVE IN SAFETY AND PROSPERITY.
IT'S THE SIMPLE CALCULUS OF BENEVOLENT GOVERNANCE. A GREAT LEADER IS ONE WHO WON'T SHIRK FROM DOING THE OFTEN TERRIBLE THINGS THAT ARE REQUIRED TO PROTECT THE MAJORITY.
IT SEEMS A PARADOX, BUT YOU MUST OFTEN DO A GREAT EVIL TO ACCOMPLISH AN EVEN GREATER GOOD.
KEEP YOUR HEART HARD, SON. THAT'S THE ETERNAL PRICE OF BEING PARENT TO ENTIRE WORLDS.
OTHERS CAN OCCASIONALLY AFFORD TO INDULGE THEIR NATURAL COMPASSION, SON, BUT NOT US.
THERE, THAT'S DONE.
A TOUCH OF PAINT AND YOU'RE GOOD AS NEW.
WE NEED TO KEEP UP ON YOUR REGULAR MAINTENANCE, SO THAT THE GROUNDLINGS ALWAYS SEE AN AGELESS, UNCHANGING AND INVINCIBLE EMPEROR RULING OVER THEM.

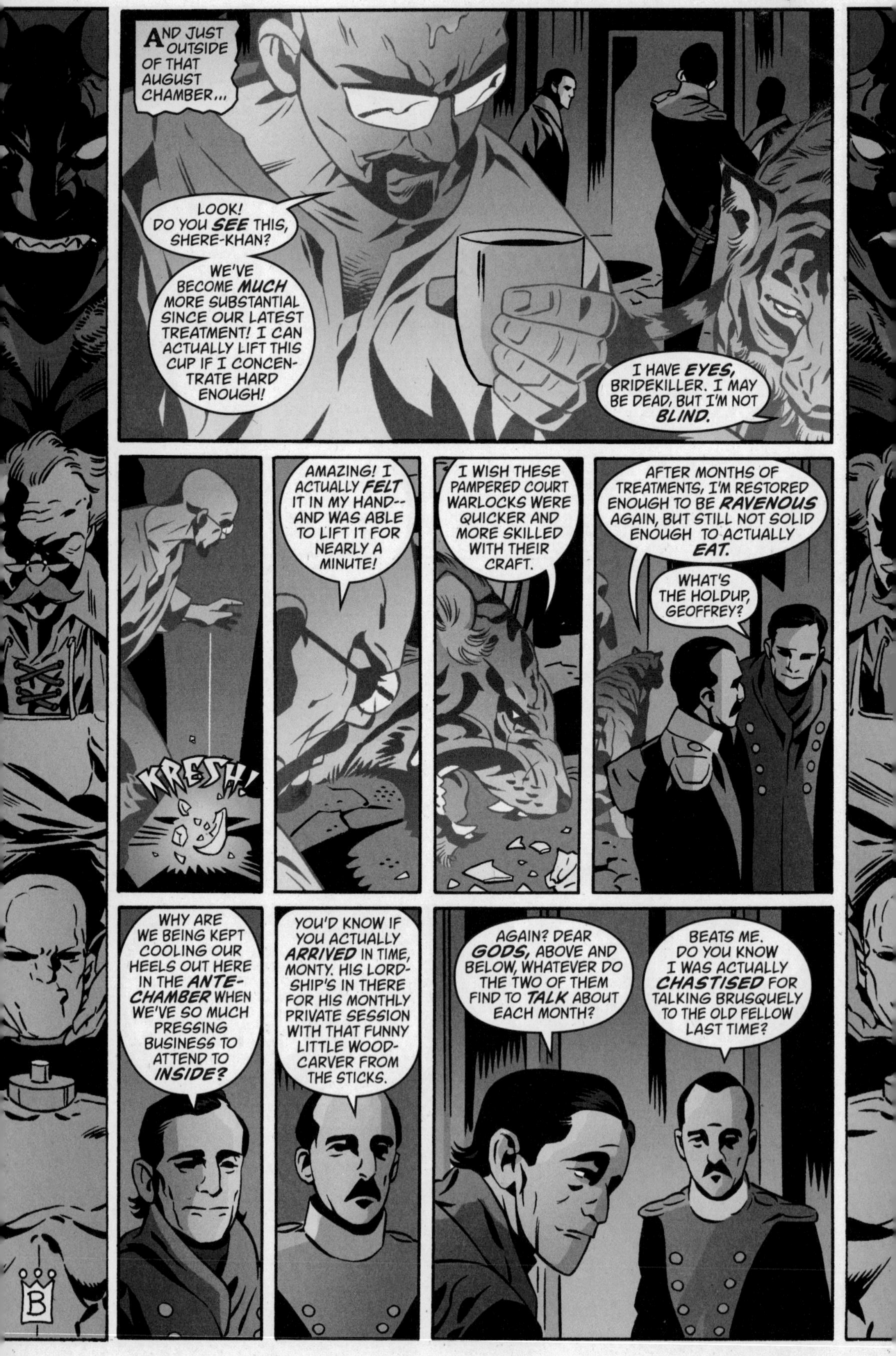
AND JUST OUTSIDE OF THAT AUGUST CHAMBER...
LOOK! DO YOU SEE THIS, SHERE-KHAN?
WE'VE BECOME MUCH MORE SUBSTANTIAL SINCE OUR LATEST TREATMENT! I CAN ACTUALLY LIFT THIS CUP IF I CONCENTRATE HARD ENOUGH!
I HAVE EYES, BRIDEKILLER. I MAY BE DEAD, BUT I'M NOT BLIND.
KRESH!
AMAZING! I ACTUALLY FELT IT IN MY HAND--AND WAS ABLE TO LIFT IT FOR NEARLY A MINUTE!
I WISH THESE PAMPERED COURT WARLOCKS WERE QUICKER AND MORE SKILLED WITH THEIR CRAFT.
AFTER MONTHS OF TREATMENTS, I'M RESTORED ENOUGH TO BE RAVENOUS AGAIN, BUT STILL NOT SOLID ENOUGH TO ACTUALLY EAT.
WHAT'S THE HOLDUP, GEOFFREY?
WHY ARE WE BEING KEPT COOLING OUR HEELS OUT HERE IN THE ANTE-CHAMBER WHEN WE'VE SO MUCH PRESSING BUSINESS TO ATTEND TO INSIDE?
YOU'D KNOW IF YOU ACTUALLY ARRIVED IN TIME, MONTY. HIS LORDSHIP'S IN THERE FOR HIS MONTHLY PRIVATE SESSION WITH THAT FUNNY LITTLE WOOD-CARVER FROM THE STICKS.
AGAIN? DEAR GODS, ABOVE AND BELOW, WHATEVER DO THE TWO OF THEM FIND TO TALK ABOUT EACH MONTH?
BEATS ME. DO YOU KNOW I WAS ACTUALLY CHASTISED FOR TALKING BRUSQUELY TO THE OLD FELLOW LAST TIME?
B

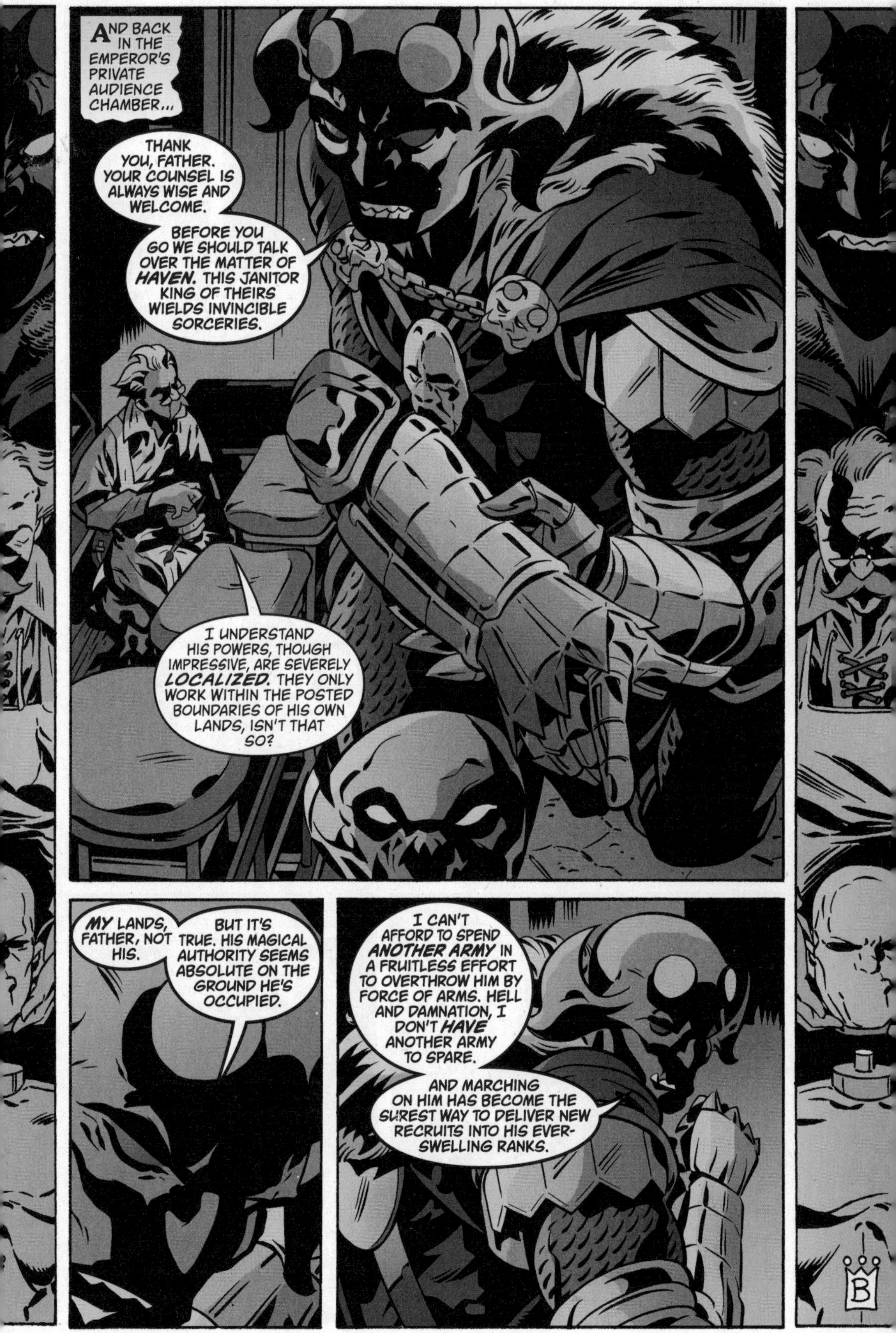
AND BACK IN THE EMPEROR'S PRIVATE AUDIENCE CHAMBER...
THANK YOU, FATHER. YOUR COUNSEL IS ALWAYS WISE AND WELCOME.
BEFORE YOU GO WE SHOULD TALK OVER THE MATTER OF HAVEN. THIS JANITOR KING OF THEIRS WIELDS INVINCIBLE SORCERIES.
I UNDERSTAND HIS POWERS, THOUGH IMPRESSIVE, ARE SEVERELY LOCALIZED. THEY ONLY WORK WITHIN THE POSTED BOUNDARIES OF HIS OWN LANDS, ISN'T THAT SO?
MY LANDS, FATHER, NOT HIS.
BUT IT'S TRUE. HIS MAGICAL AUTHORITY SEEMS ABSOLUTE ON THE GROUND HE'S OCCUPIED.
I CAN'T AFFORD TO SPEND ANOTHER ARMY IN A FRUITLESS EFFORT TO OVERTHROW HIM BY FORCE OF ARMS. HELL AND DAMNATION, I DON'T HAVE ANOTHER ARMY TO SPARE.
AND MARCHING ON HIM HAS BECOME THE SUREST WAY TO DELIVER NEW RECRUITS INTO HIS EVER-SWELLING RANKS.

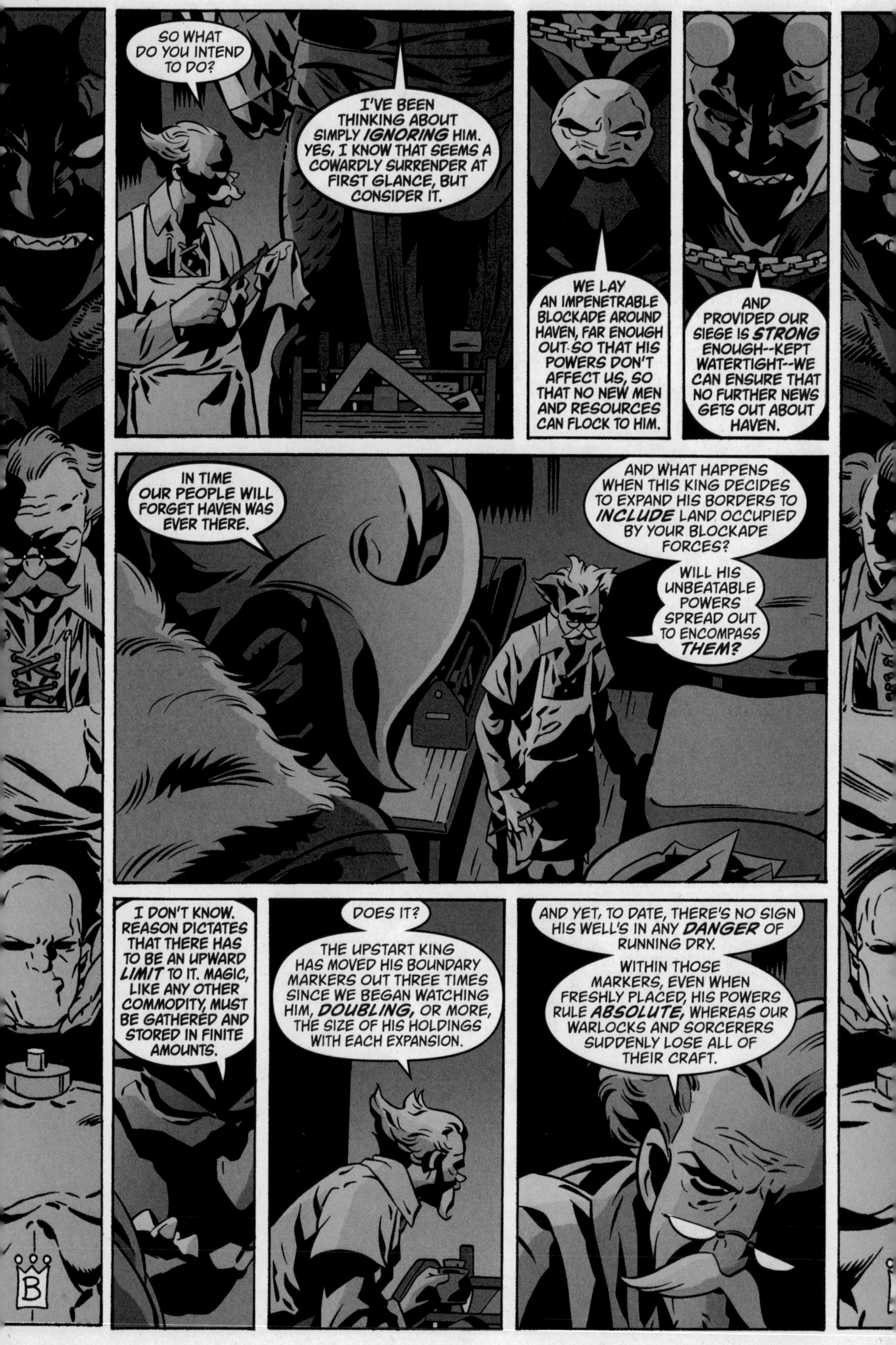
SO WHAT DO YOU INTEND TO DO?
I'VE BEEN THINKING ABOUT SIMPLY IGNORING HIM. YES, I KNOW THAT SEEMS A COWARDLY SURRENDER AT FIRST GLANCE, BUT CONSIDER IT.
WE LAY AN IMPENETRABLE BLOCKADE AROUND HAVEN, FAR ENOUGH OUT SO THAT HIS POWERS DON'T AFFECT US, SO THAT NO NEW MEN AND RESOURCES CAN FLOCK TO HIM.
AND PROVIDED OUR SIEGE IS STRONG ENOUGH--KEPT WATERTIGHT--WE CAN ENSURE THAT NO FURTHER NEWS GETS OUT ABOUT HAVEN.
IN TIME OUR PEOPLE WILL FORGET HAVEN WAS EVER THERE.
AND WHAT HAPPENS WHEN THIS KING DECIDES TO EXPAND HIS BORDERS TO INCLUDE LAND OCCUPIED BY YOUR BLOCKADE FORCES?
WILL HIS UNBEATABLE POWERS SPREAD OUT TO ENCOMPASS THEM?
I DON'T KNOW. REASON DICTATES THAT THERE HAS TO BE AN UPWARD LIMIT TO IT. MAGIC, LIKE ANY OTHER COMMODITY, MUST BE GATHERED AND STORED IN FINITE AMOUNTS.
DOES IT?
THE UPSTART KING HAS MOVED HIS BOUNDARY MARKERS OUT THREE TIMES SINCE WE BEGAN WATCHING HIM, DOUBLING, OR MORE, THE SIZE OF HIS HOLDINGS WITH EACH EXPANSION.
AND YET, TO DATE, THERE'S NO SIGN HIS WELL'S IN ANY DANGER OF RUNNING DRY.
WITHIN THOSE MARKERS, EVEN WHEN FRESHLY PLACED, HIS POWERS RULE ABSOLUTE, WHEREAS OUR WARLOCKS AND SORCERERS SUDDENLY LOSE ALL OF THEIR CRAFT.
B

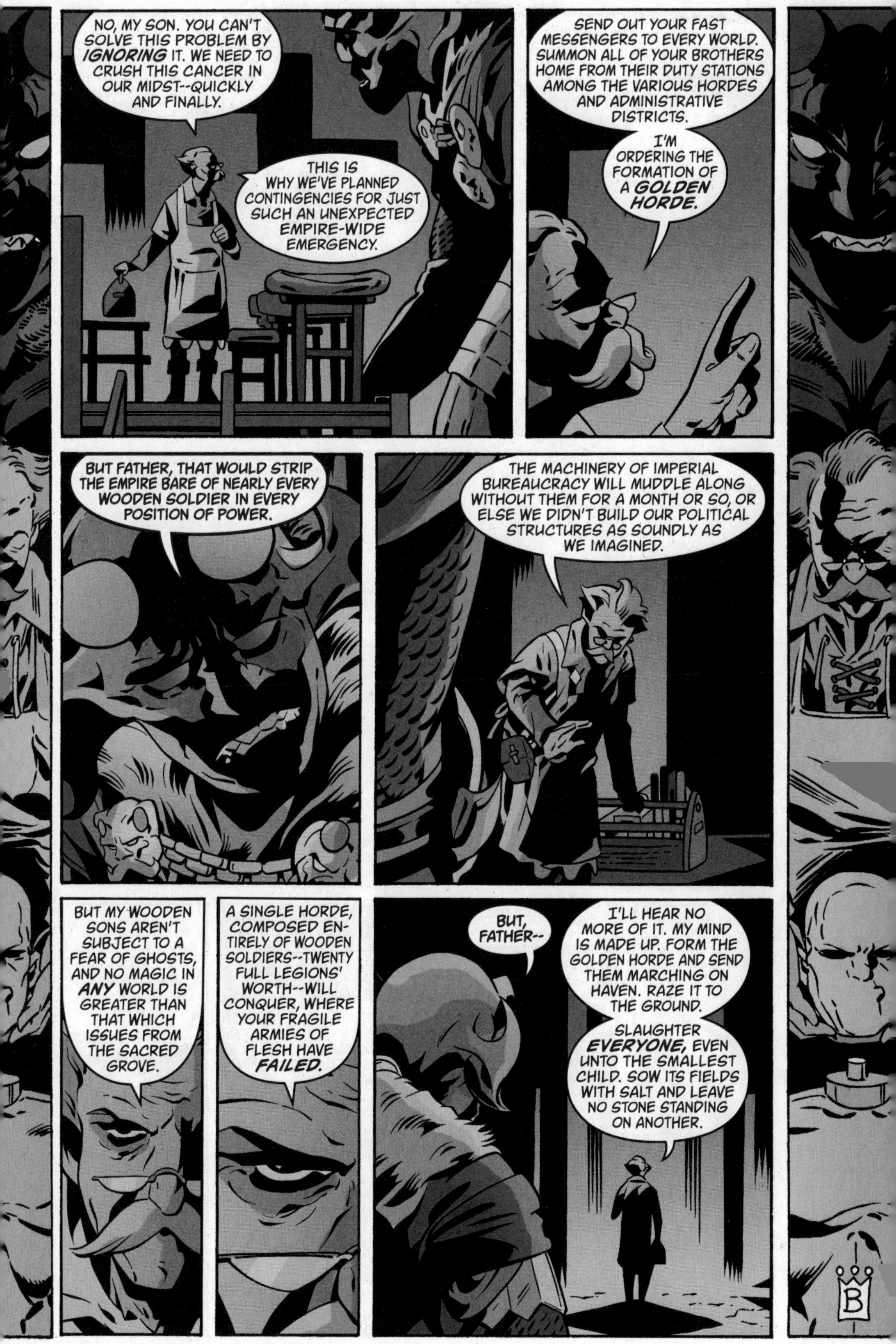
NO, MY SON. YOU CAN'T SOLVE THIS PROBLEM BY *IGNORING* IT. WE NEED TO CRUSH THIS CANCER IN OUR MIDST--QUICKLY AND FINALLY.
THIS IS WHY WE'VE PLANNED CONTINGENCIES FOR JUST SUCH AN UNEXPECTED EMPIRE-WIDE EMERGENCY.
SEND OUT YOUR FAST MESSENGERS TO EVERY WORLD. SUMMON ALL OF YOUR BROTHERS HOME FROM THEIR DUTY STATIONS AMONG THE VARIOUS HORDES AND ADMINISTRATIVE DISTRICTS.
I'M ORDERING THE FORMATION OF A *GOLDEN HORDE.*
BUT FATHER, THAT WOULD STRIP THE EMPIRE BARE OF NEARLY EVERY WOODEN SOLDIER IN EVERY POSITION OF POWER.
THE MACHINERY OF IMPERIAL BUREAUCRACY WILL MUDDLE ALONG WITHOUT THEM FOR A MONTH OR SO, OR ELSE WE DIDN'T BUILD OUR POLITICAL STRUCTURES AS SOUNDLY AS WE IMAGINED.
BUT MY WOODEN SONS AREN'T SUBJECT TO A FEAR OF GHOSTS, AND NO MAGIC IN *ANY* WORLD IS GREATER THAN THAT WHICH ISSUES FROM THE SACRED GROVE.
A SINGLE HORDE, COMPOSED ENTIRELY OF WOODEN SOLDIERS--TWENTY FULL LEGIONS' WORTH--WILL CONQUER, WHERE YOUR FRAGILE ARMIES OF FLESH HAVE *FAILED.*
BUT, FATHER--
I'LL HEAR NO MORE OF IT. MY MIND IS MADE UP. FORM THE GOLDEN HORDE AND SEND THEM MARCHING ON HAVEN. RAZE IT TO THE GROUND.
SLAUGHTER *EVERYONE,* EVEN UNTO THE SMALLEST CHILD. SOW ITS FIELDS WITH SALT AND LEAVE NO STONE STANDING ON ANOTHER.

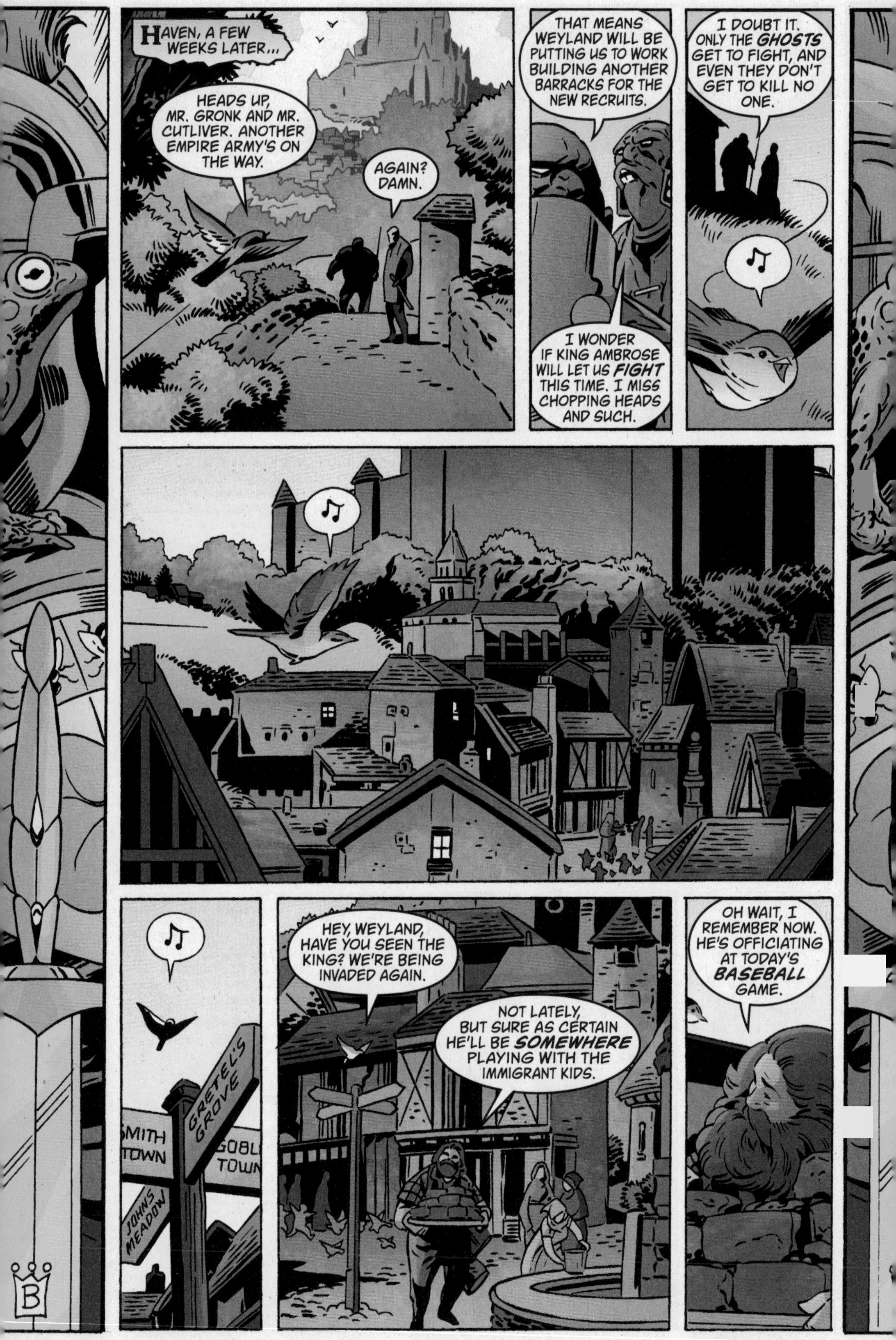
HAVEN, A FEW WEEKS LATER...
HEADS UP, MR. GRONK AND MR. CUTLIVER. ANOTHER EMPIRE ARMY'S ON THE WAY.
AGAIN? DAMN.
THAT MEANS WEYLAND WILL BE PUTTING US TO WORK BUILDING ANOTHER BARRACKS FOR THE NEW RECRUITS.
I WONDER IF KING AMBROSE WILL LET US FIGHT THIS TIME. I MISS CHOPPING HEADS AND SUCH.
I DOUBT IT. ONLY THE GHOSTS GET TO FIGHT, AND EVEN THEY DON'T GET TO KILL NO ONE.
♫
♫
♫
SMITH TOWN
GRETEL'S GROVE
GOBL TOWN
JOHNS MEADOW
HEY, WEYLAND, HAVE YOU SEEN THE KING? WE'RE BEING INVADED AGAIN.
NOT LATELY, BUT SURE AS CERTAIN HE'LL BE SOMEWHERE PLAYING WITH THE IMMIGRANT KIDS.
OH WAIT, I REMEMBER NOW. HE'S OFFICIATING AT TODAY'S BASEBALL GAME.

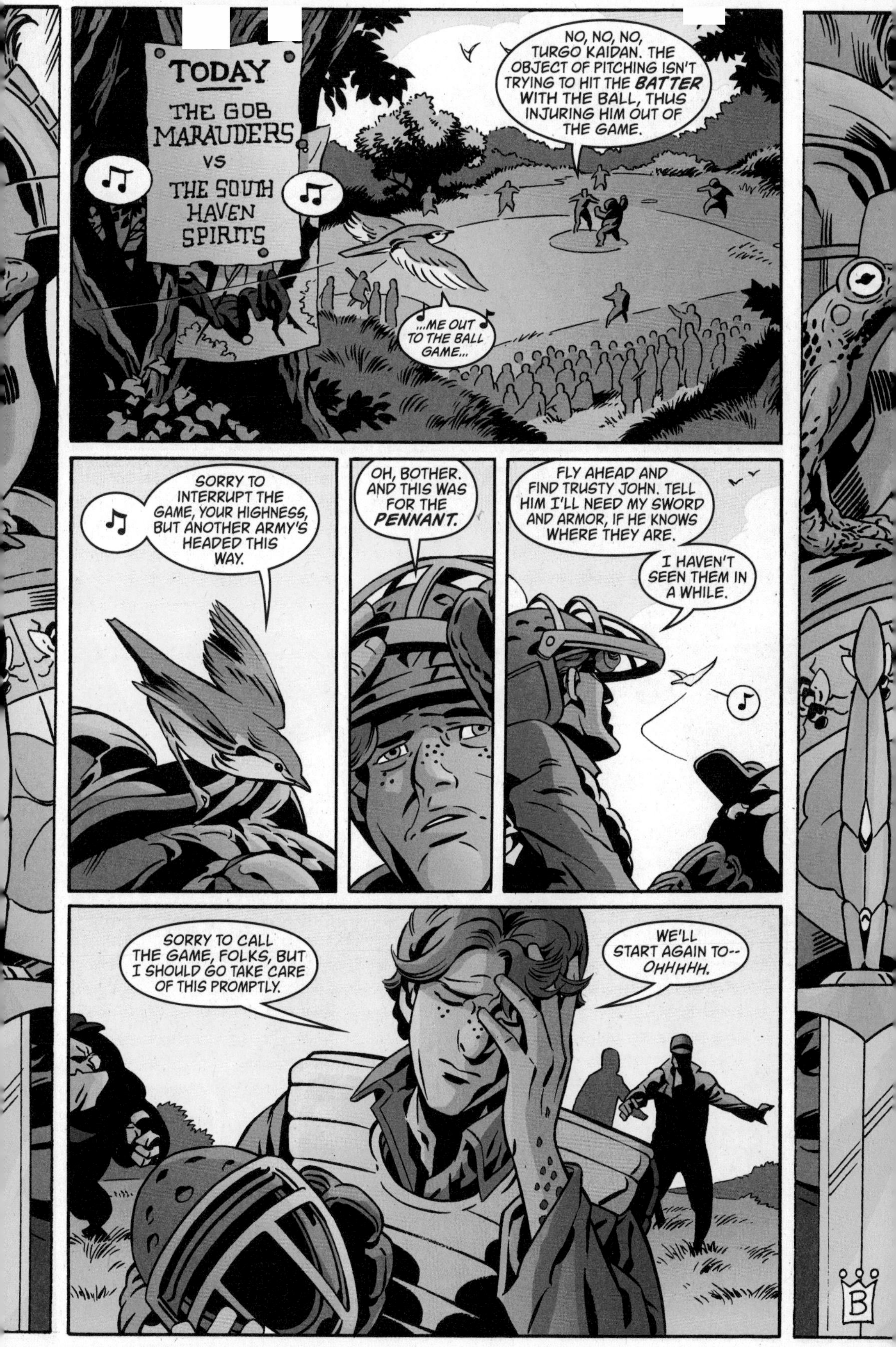
TODAY
THE GOB MARAUDERS VS THE SOUTH HAVEN SPIRITS
NO, NO, NO, TURGO KAIDAN. THE OBJECT OF PITCHING ISN'T TRYING TO HIT THE BATTER WITH THE BALL, THUS INJURING HIM OUT OF THE GAME.
...ME OUT TO THE BALL GAME...
SORRY TO INTERRUPT THE GAME, YOUR HIGHNESS, BUT ANOTHER ARMY'S HEADED THIS WAY.
OH, BOTHER. AND THIS WAS FOR THE PENNANT.
FLY AHEAD AND FIND TRUSTY JOHN. TELL HIM I'LL NEED MY SWORD AND ARMOR, IF HE KNOWS WHERE THEY ARE.
I HAVEN'T SEEN THEM IN A WHILE.
SORRY TO CALL THE GAME, FOLKS, BUT I SHOULD GO TAKE CARE OF THIS PROMPTLY.
WE'LL START AGAIN TO-- OHHHHH.

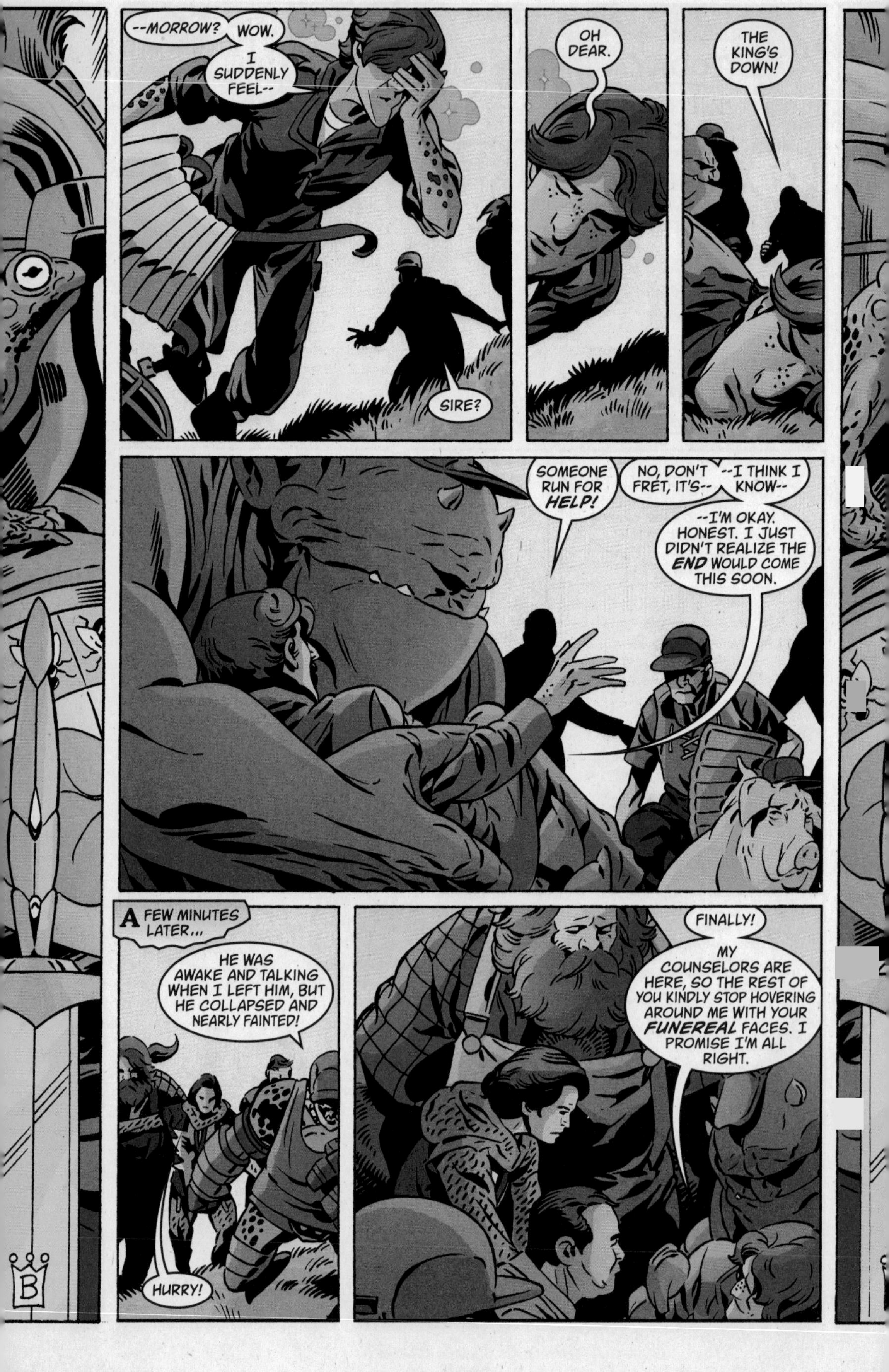
--MORROW?
WOW. I SUDDENLY FEEL--
SIRE?
OH DEAR.
THE KING'S DOWN!
SOMEONE RUN FOR HELP!
NO, DON'T FRET, IT'S--
--I THINK I KNOW--
--I'M OKAY. HONEST. I JUST DIDN'T REALIZE THE END WOULD COME THIS SOON.
A FEW MINUTES LATER...
HE WAS AWAKE AND TALKING WHEN I LEFT HIM, BUT HE COLLAPSED AND NEARLY FAINTED!
HURRY!
FINALLY!
MY COUNSELORS ARE HERE, SO THE REST OF YOU KINDLY STOP HOVERING AROUND ME WITH YOUR FUNEREAL FACES. I PROMISE I'M ALL RIGHT.

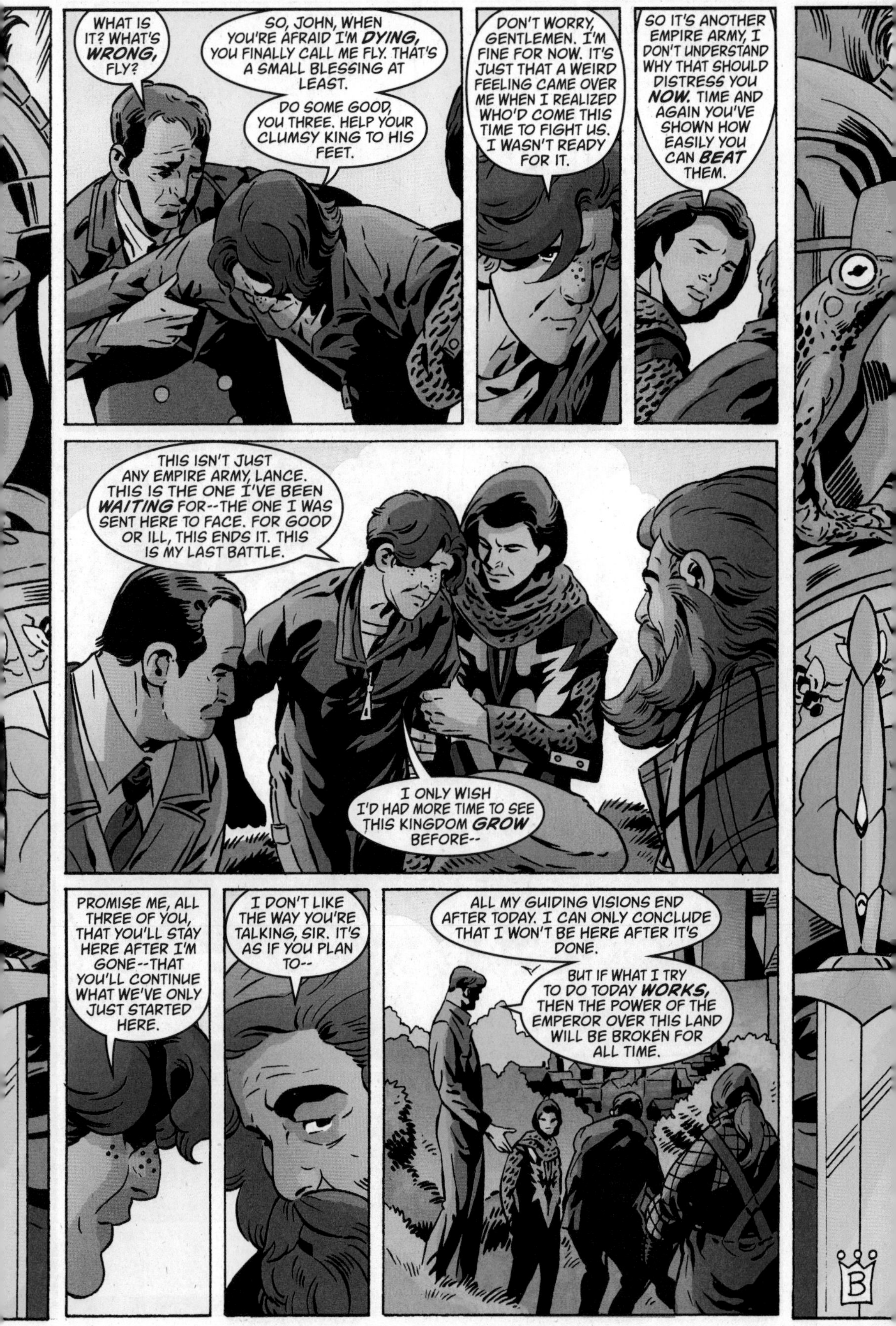
WHAT IS IT? WHAT'S WRONG, FLY?
SO, JOHN, WHEN YOU'RE AFRAID I'M DYING, YOU FINALLY CALL ME FLY. THAT'S A SMALL BLESSING AT LEAST.
DO SOME GOOD, YOU THREE. HELP YOUR CLUMSY KING TO HIS FEET.
DON'T WORRY, GENTLEMEN. I'M FINE FOR NOW. IT'S JUST THAT A WEIRD FEELING CAME OVER ME WHEN I REALIZED WHO'D COME THIS TIME TO FIGHT US. I WASN'T READY FOR IT.
SO IT'S ANOTHER EMPIRE ARMY, I DON'T UNDERSTAND WHY THAT SHOULD DISTRESS YOU NOW. TIME AND AGAIN YOU'VE SHOWN HOW EASILY YOU CAN BEAT THEM.
THIS ISN'T JUST ANY EMPIRE ARMY, LANCE. THIS IS THE ONE I'VE BEEN WAITING FOR--THE ONE I WAS SENT HERE TO FACE. FOR GOOD OR ILL, THIS ENDS IT. THIS IS MY LAST BATTLE.
I ONLY WISH I'D HAD MORE TIME TO SEE THIS KINGDOM GROW BEFORE--
PROMISE ME, ALL THREE OF YOU, THAT YOU'LL STAY HERE AFTER I'M GONE--THAT YOU'LL CONTINUE WHAT WE'VE ONLY JUST STARTED HERE.
I DON'T LIKE THE WAY YOU'RE TALKING, SIR. IT'S AS IF YOU PLAN TO--
ALL MY GUIDING VISIONS END AFTER TODAY. I CAN ONLY CONCLUDE THAT I WON'T BE HERE AFTER IT'S DONE.
BUT IF WHAT I TRY TO DO TODAY WORKS, THEN THE POWER OF THE EMPEROR OVER THIS LAND WILL BE BROKEN FOR ALL TIME.
B

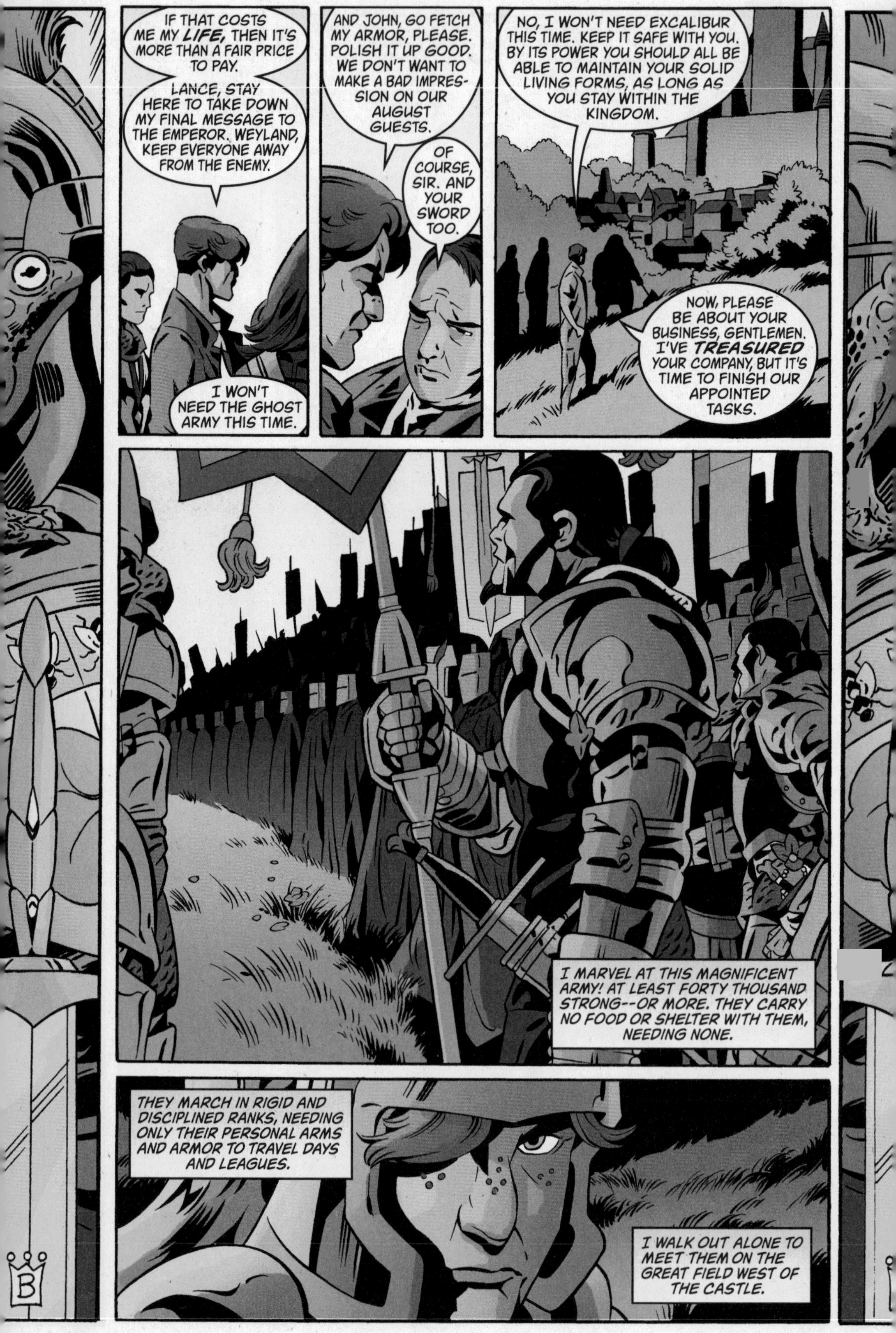

IF THAT COSTS ME MY *LIFE,* THEN IT'S MORE THAN A FAIR PRICE TO PAY.
LANCE, STAY HERE TO TAKE DOWN MY FINAL MESSAGE TO THE EMPEROR. WEYLAND, KEEP EVERYONE AWAY FROM THE ENEMY.
I WON'T NEED THE GHOST ARMY THIS TIME.
AND JOHN, GO FETCH MY ARMOR, PLEASE. POLISH IT UP GOOD. WE DON'T WANT TO MAKE A BAD IMPRESSION ON OUR AUGUST GUESTS.
OF COURSE, SIR. AND YOUR SWORD TOO.
NO, I WON'T NEED EXCALIBUR THIS TIME. KEEP IT SAFE WITH YOU. BY ITS POWER YOU SHOULD ALL BE ABLE TO MAINTAIN YOUR SOLID LIVING FORMS, AS LONG AS YOU STAY WITHIN THE KINGDOM.
NOW, PLEASE BE ABOUT YOUR BUSINESS, GENTLEMEN. I'VE *TREASURED* YOUR COMPANY, BUT IT'S TIME TO FINISH OUR APPOINTED TASKS.
I MARVEL AT THIS MAGNIFICENT ARMY! AT LEAST FORTY THOUSAND STRONG--OR MORE. THEY CARRY NO FOOD OR SHELTER WITH THEM, NEEDING NONE.
THEY MARCH IN RIGID AND DISCIPLINED RANKS, NEEDING ONLY THEIR PERSONAL ARMS AND ARMOR TO TRAVEL DAYS AND LEAGUES.
I WALK OUT ALONE TO MEET THEM ON THE GREAT FIELD WEST OF THE CASTLE.

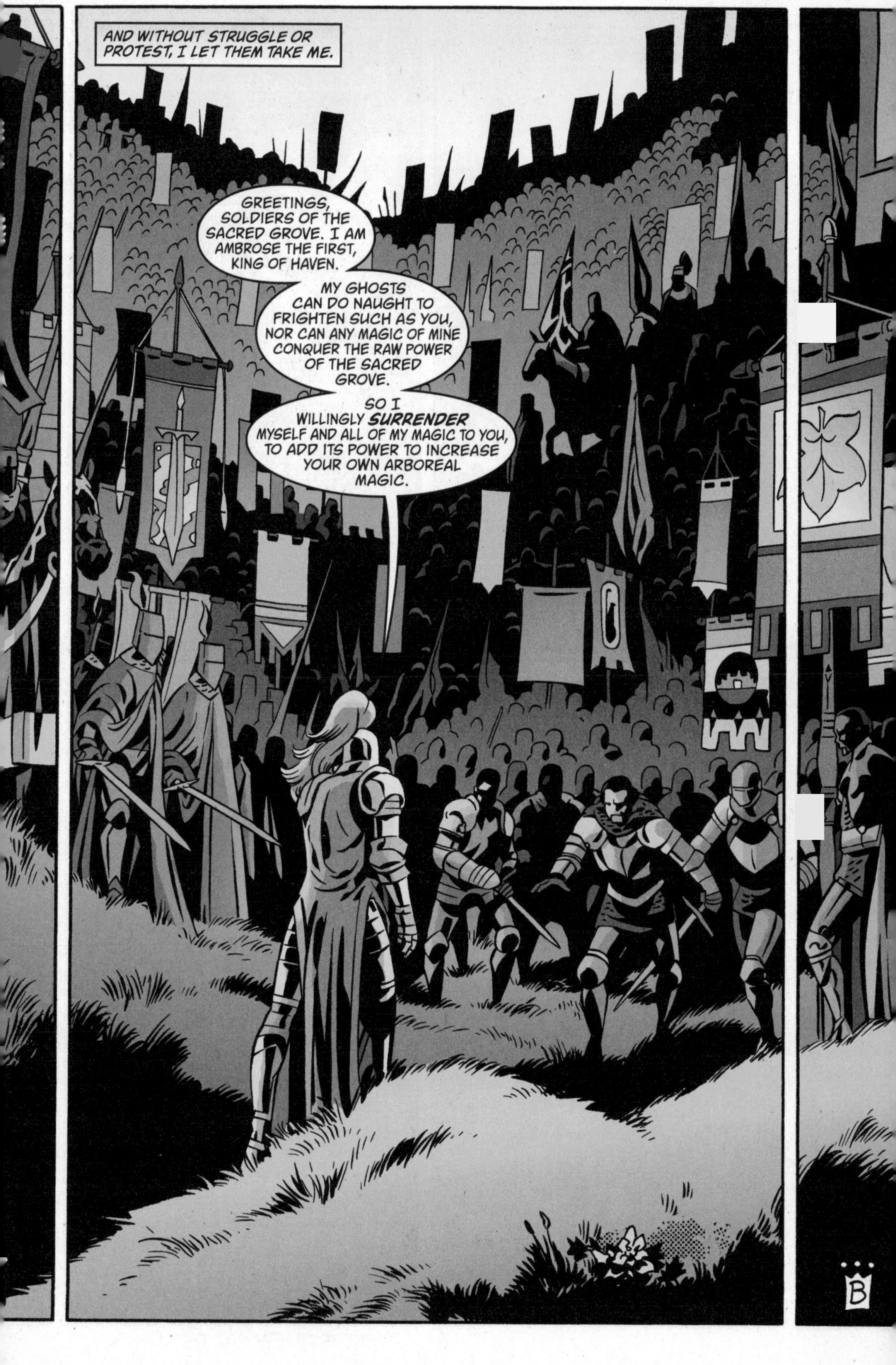

AND WITHOUT STRUGGLE OR PROTEST, I LET THEM TAKE ME.
GREETINGS, SOLDIERS OF THE SACRED GROVE. I AM AMBROSE THE FIRST, KING OF HAVEN.
MY GHOSTS CAN DO NAUGHT TO FRIGHTEN SUCH AS YOU, NOR CAN ANY MAGIC OF MINE CONQUER THE RAW POWER OF THE SACRED GROVE.
SO I WILLINGLY ***SURRENDER*** MYSELF AND ALL OF MY MAGIC TO YOU, TO ADD ITS POWER TO INCREASE YOUR OWN ARBOREAL MAGIC.

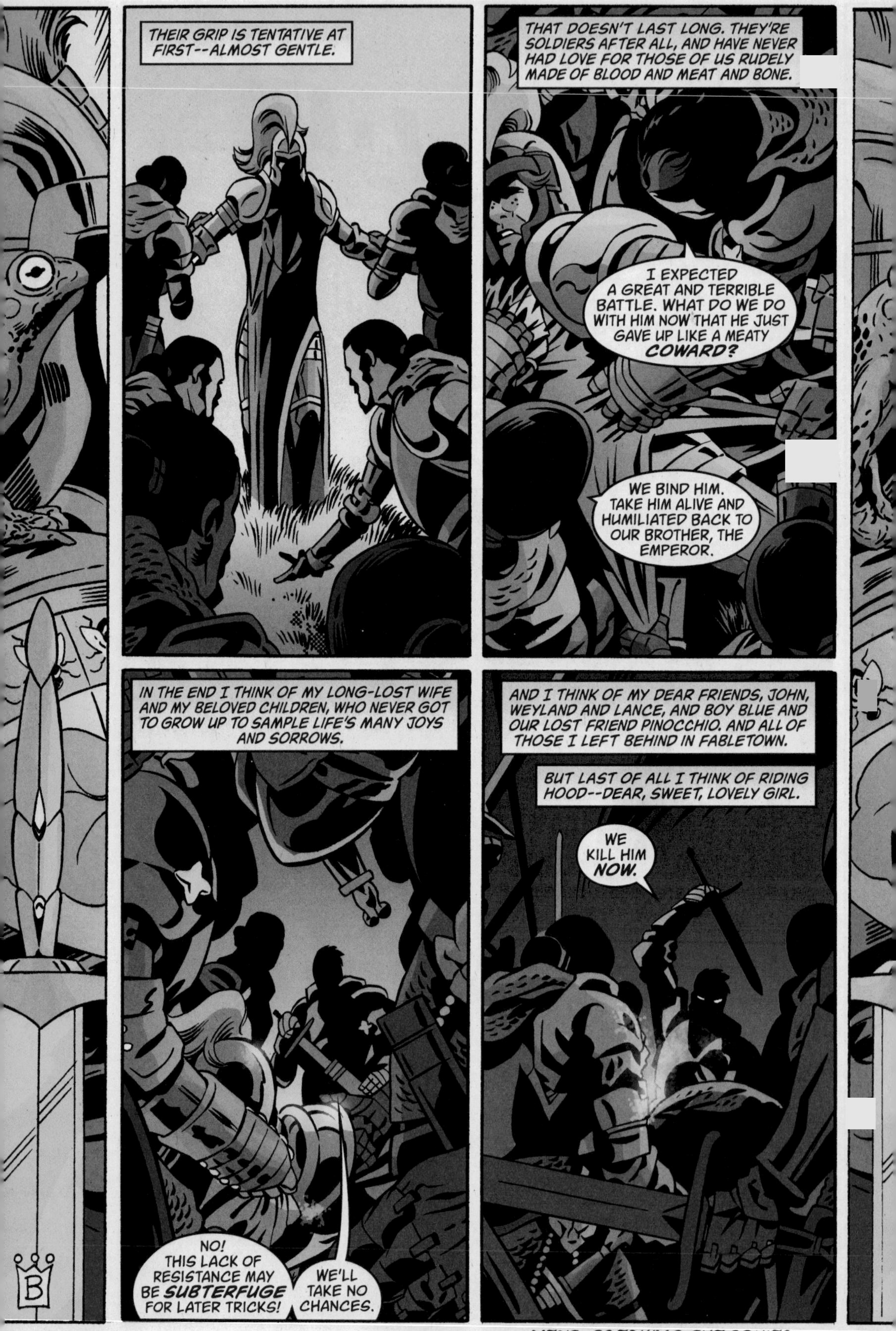
THEIR GRIP IS TENTATIVE AT FIRST--ALMOST GENTLE.
THAT DOESN'T LAST LONG. THEY'RE SOLDIERS AFTER ALL, AND HAVE NEVER HAD LOVE FOR THOSE OF US RUDELY MADE OF BLOOD AND MEAT AND BONE.
I EXPECTED A GREAT AND TERRIBLE BATTLE. WHAT DO WE DO WITH HIM NOW THAT HE JUST GAVE UP LIKE A MEATY COWARD?
WE BIND HIM. TAKE HIM ALIVE AND HUMILIATED BACK TO OUR BROTHER, THE EMPEROR.
IN THE END I THINK OF MY LONG-LOST WIFE AND MY BELOVED CHILDREN, WHO NEVER GOT TO GROW UP TO SAMPLE LIFE'S MANY JOYS AND SORROWS.
NO! THIS LACK OF RESISTANCE MAY BE SUBTERFUGE FOR LATER TRICKS!
WE'LL TAKE NO CHANCES.
AND I THINK OF MY DEAR FRIENDS, JOHN, WEYLAND AND LANCE, AND BOY BLUE AND OUR LOST FRIEND PINOCCHIO. AND ALL OF THOSE I LEFT BEHIND IN FABLETOWN.
BUT LAST OF ALL I THINK OF RIDING HOOD--DEAR, SWEET, LOVELY GIRL.
WE KILL HIM NOW.

NEXT: *BREAKING THE POWER*

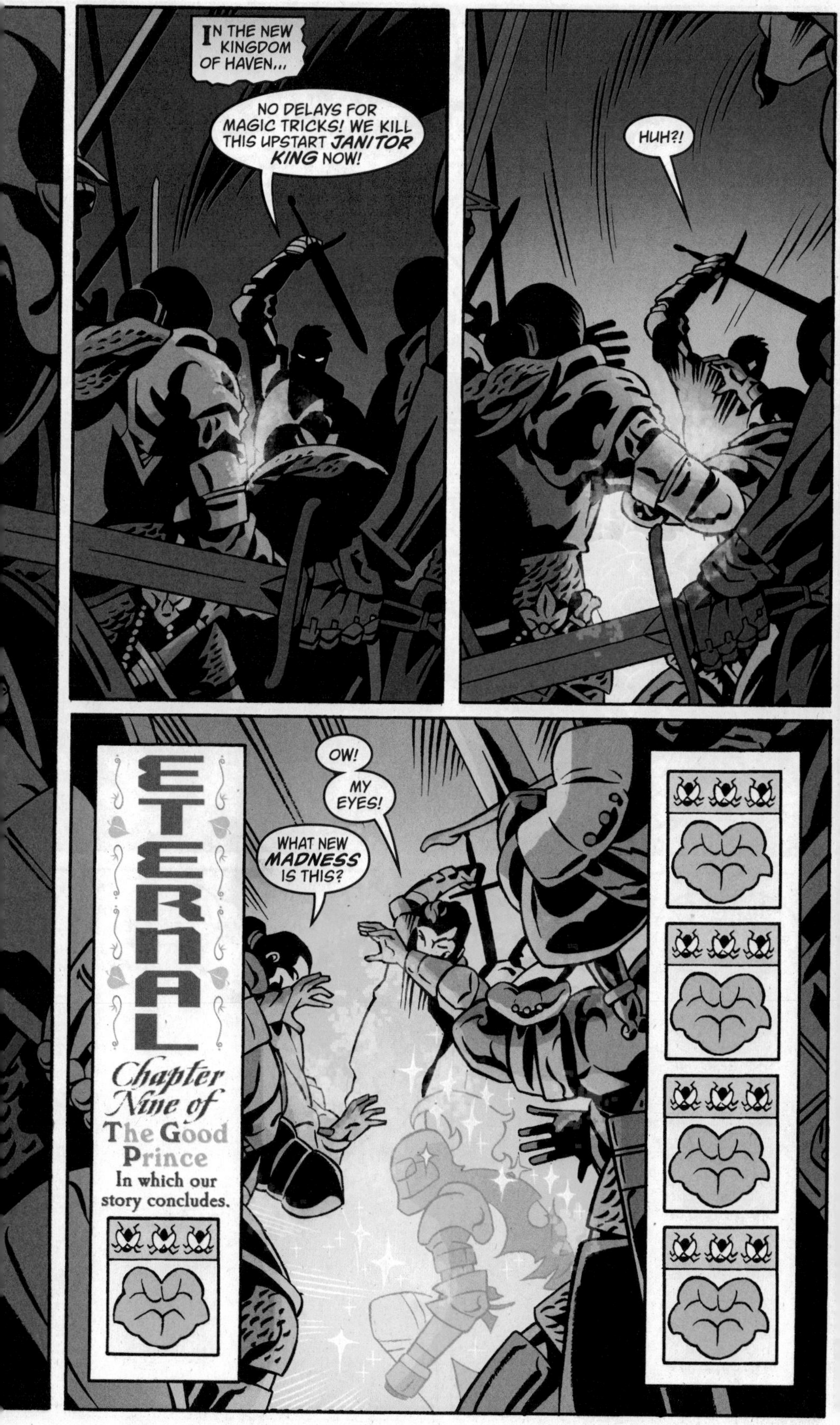

IN THE NEW KINGDOM OF HAVEN...
NO DELAYS FOR MAGIC TRICKS! WE KILL THIS UPSTART JANITOR KING NOW!
HUH?!
OW! MY EYES!
WHAT NEW MADNESS IS THIS?
ETERNAL
Chapter Nine of The Good Prince
In which our story concludes.

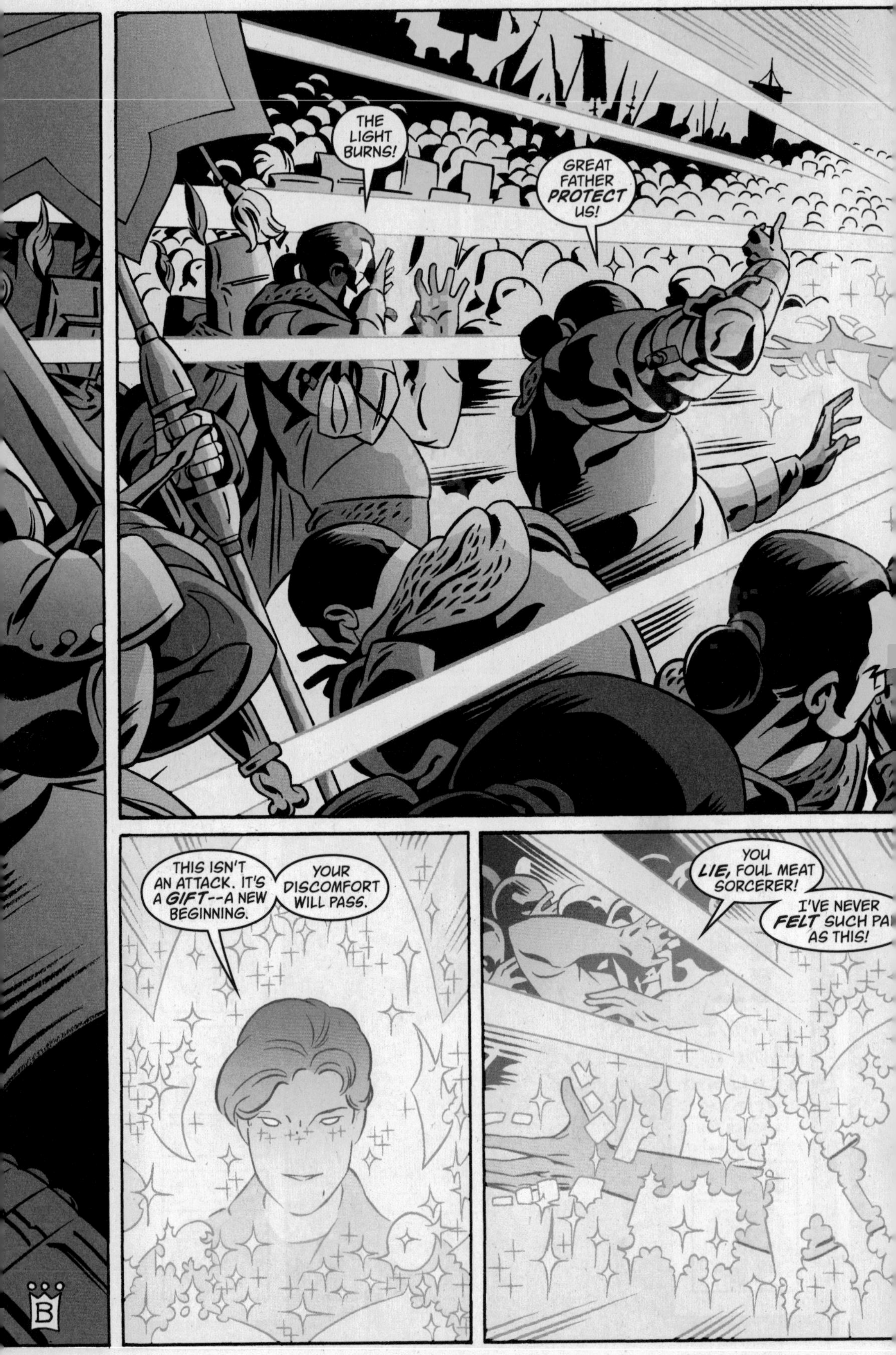
THE LIGHT BURNS!
GREAT FATHER PROTECT US!
THIS ISN'T AN ATTACK. IT'S A GIFT--A NEW BEGINNING.
YOUR DISCOMFORT WILL PASS.
YOU LIE, FOUL MEAT SORCERER!
I'VE NEVER FELT SUCH PA AS THIS!

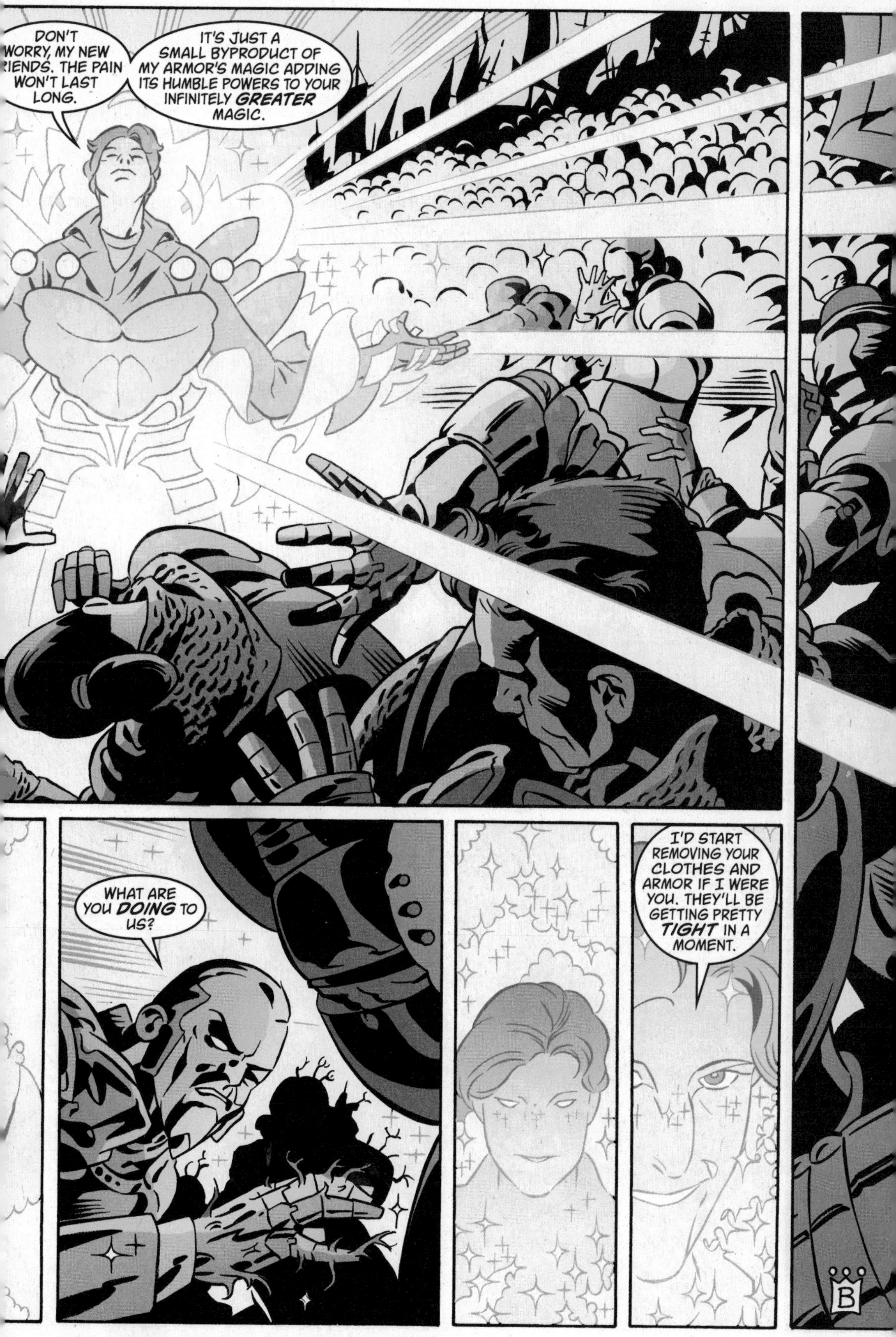
DON'T WORRY, MY NEW FRIENDS. THE PAIN WON'T LAST LONG.
IT'S JUST A SMALL BYPRODUCT OF MY ARMOR'S MAGIC ADDING ITS HUMBLE POWERS TO YOUR INFINITELY GREATER MAGIC.
WHAT ARE YOU DOING TO US?
I'D START REMOVING YOUR CLOTHES AND ARMOR IF I WERE YOU. THEY'LL BE GETTING PRETTY TIGHT IN A MOMENT.

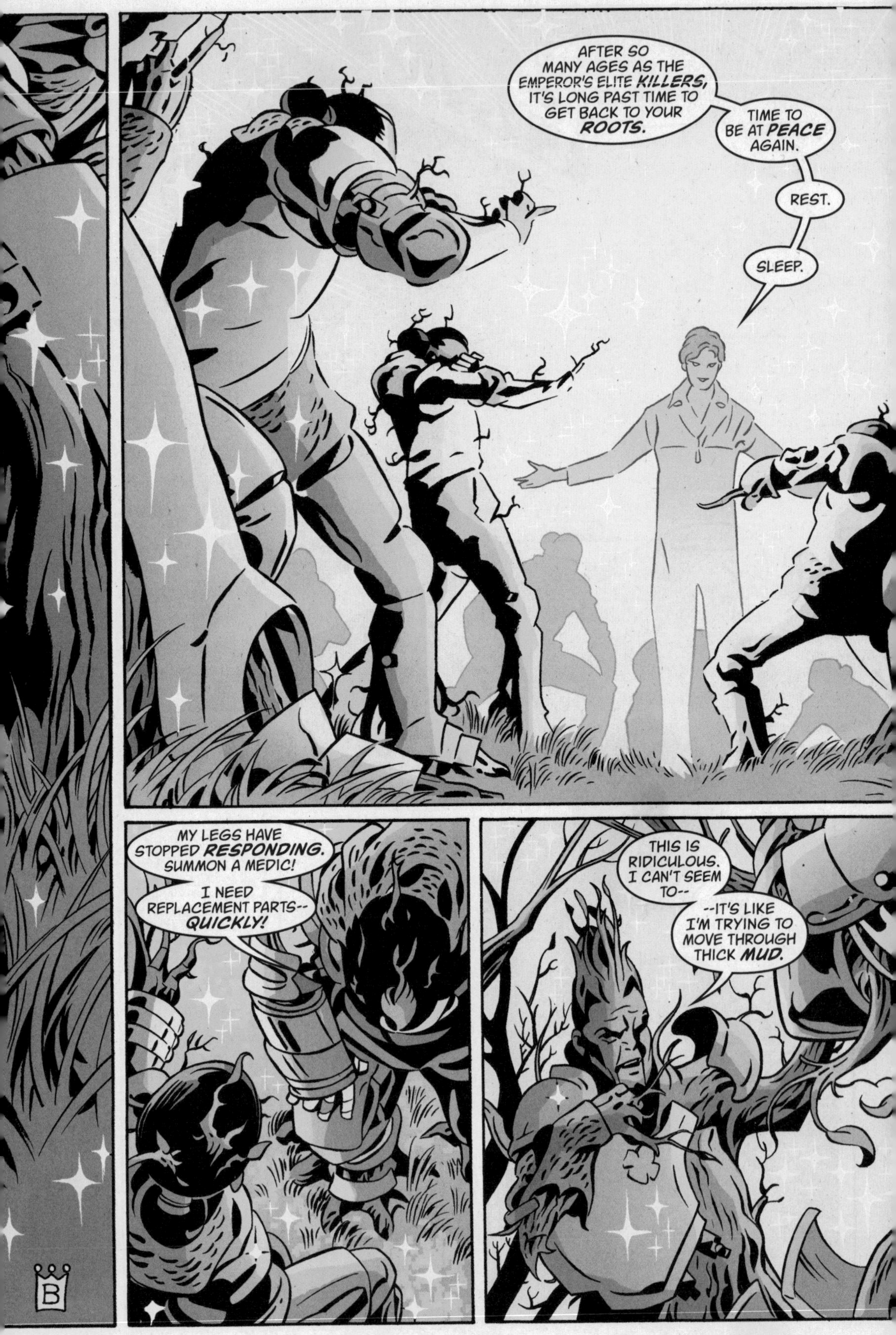
AFTER SO MANY AGES AS THE EMPEROR'S ELITE KILLERS, IT'S LONG PAST TIME TO GET BACK TO YOUR ROOTS.
TIME TO BE AT PEACE AGAIN.
REST.
SLEEP.
MY LEGS HAVE STOPPED RESPONDING. SUMMON A MEDIC!
I NEED REPLACEMENT PARTS-- QUICKLY!
THIS IS RIDICULOUS. I CAN'T SEEM TO--
--IT'S LIKE I'M TRYING TO MOVE THROUGH THICK MUD.

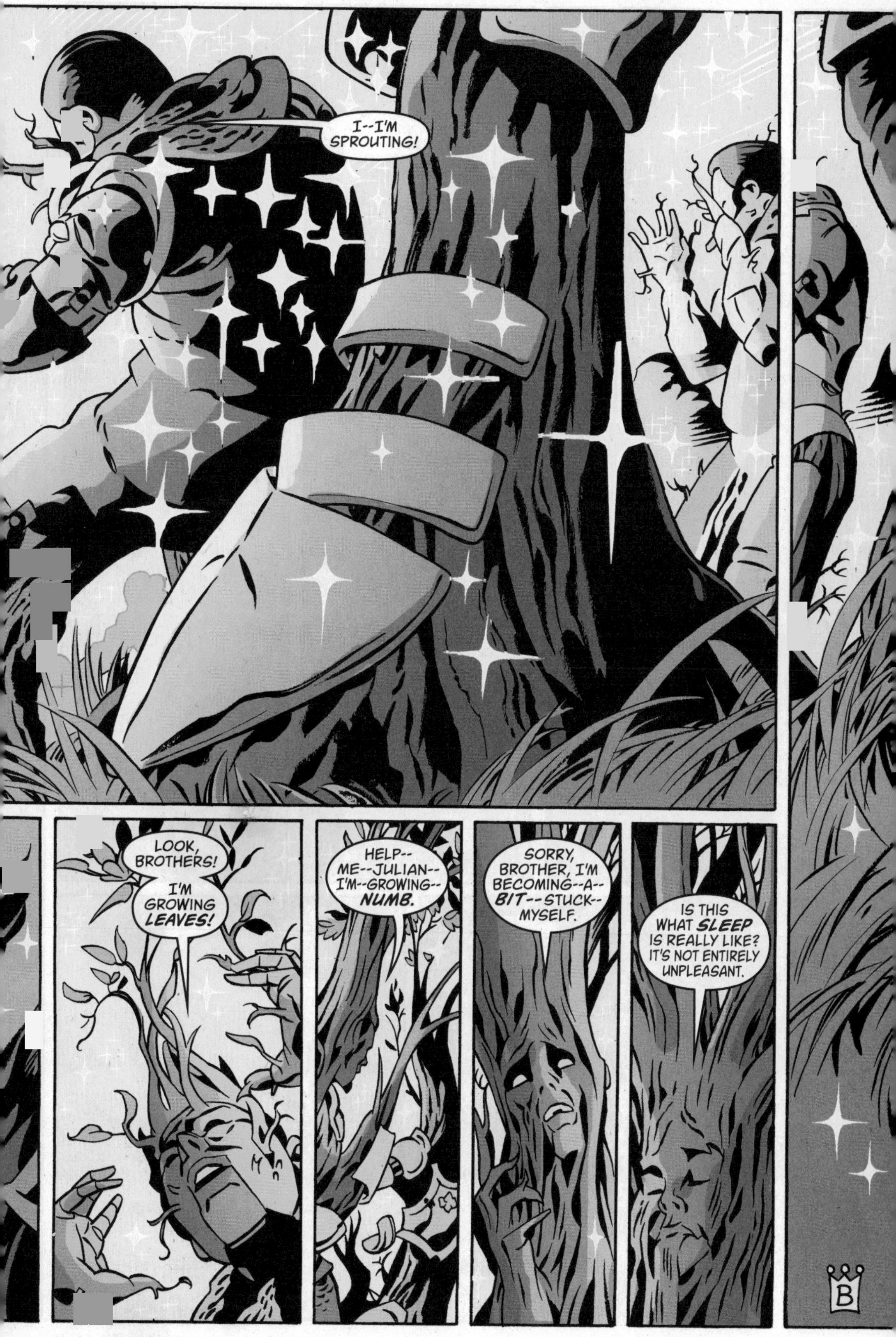
I--I'M SPROUTING!
LOOK, BROTHERS!
I'M GROWING LEAVES!
HELP-- ME--JULIAN-- I'M--GROWING-- NUMB.
SORRY, BROTHER, I'M BECOMING--A-- BIT--STUCK-- MYSELF.
IS THIS WHAT SLEEP IS REALLY LIKE? IT'S NOT ENTIRELY UNPLEASANT.

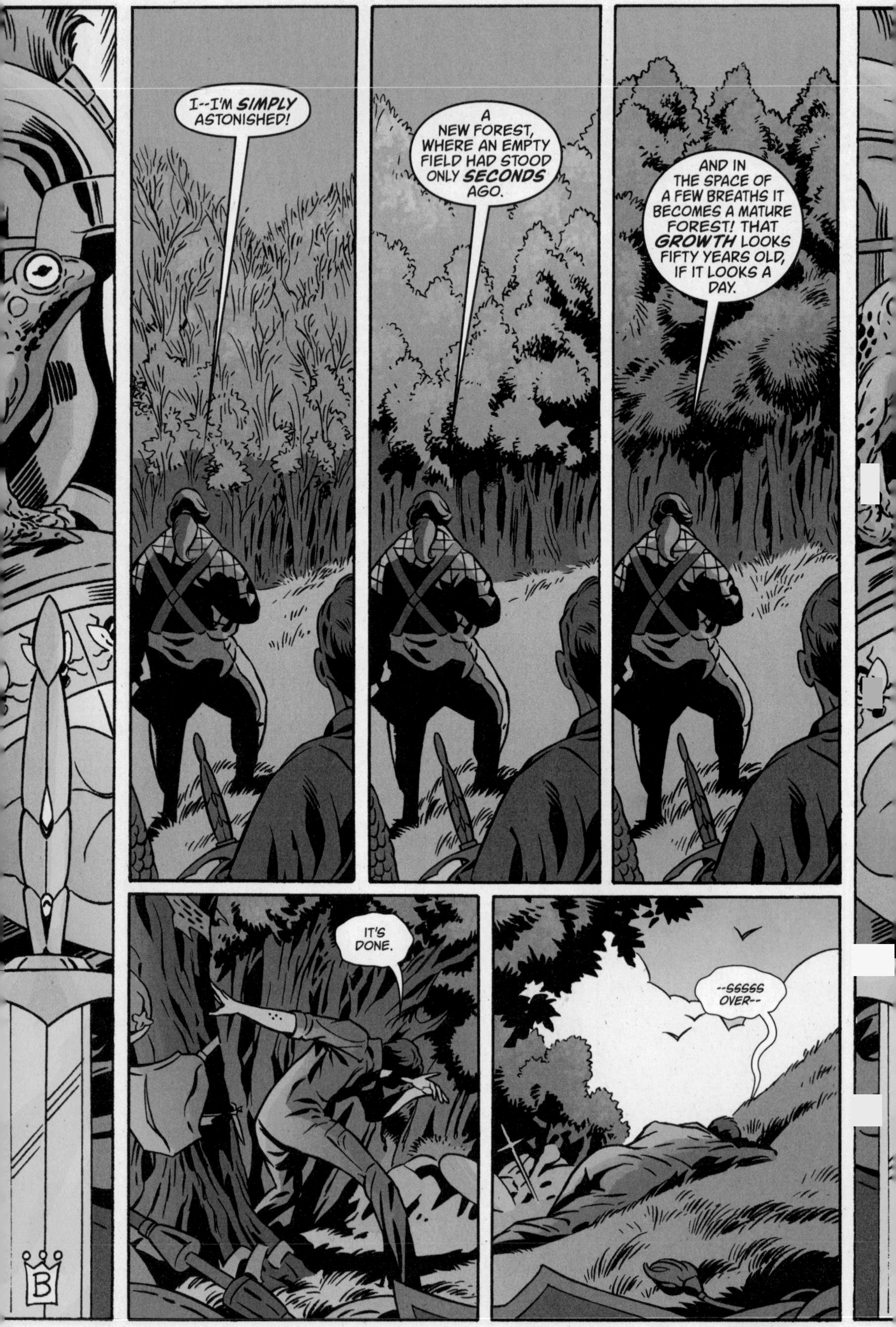
I--I'M *SIMPLY* ASTONISHED!
A NEW FOREST, WHERE AN EMPTY FIELD HAD STOOD ONLY *SECONDS* AGO.
AND IN THE SPACE OF A FEW BREATHS IT BECOMES A MATURE FOREST! THAT *GROWTH* LOOKS FIFTY YEARS OLD, IF IT LOOKS A DAY.
IT'S DONE.
--SSSSS OVER--

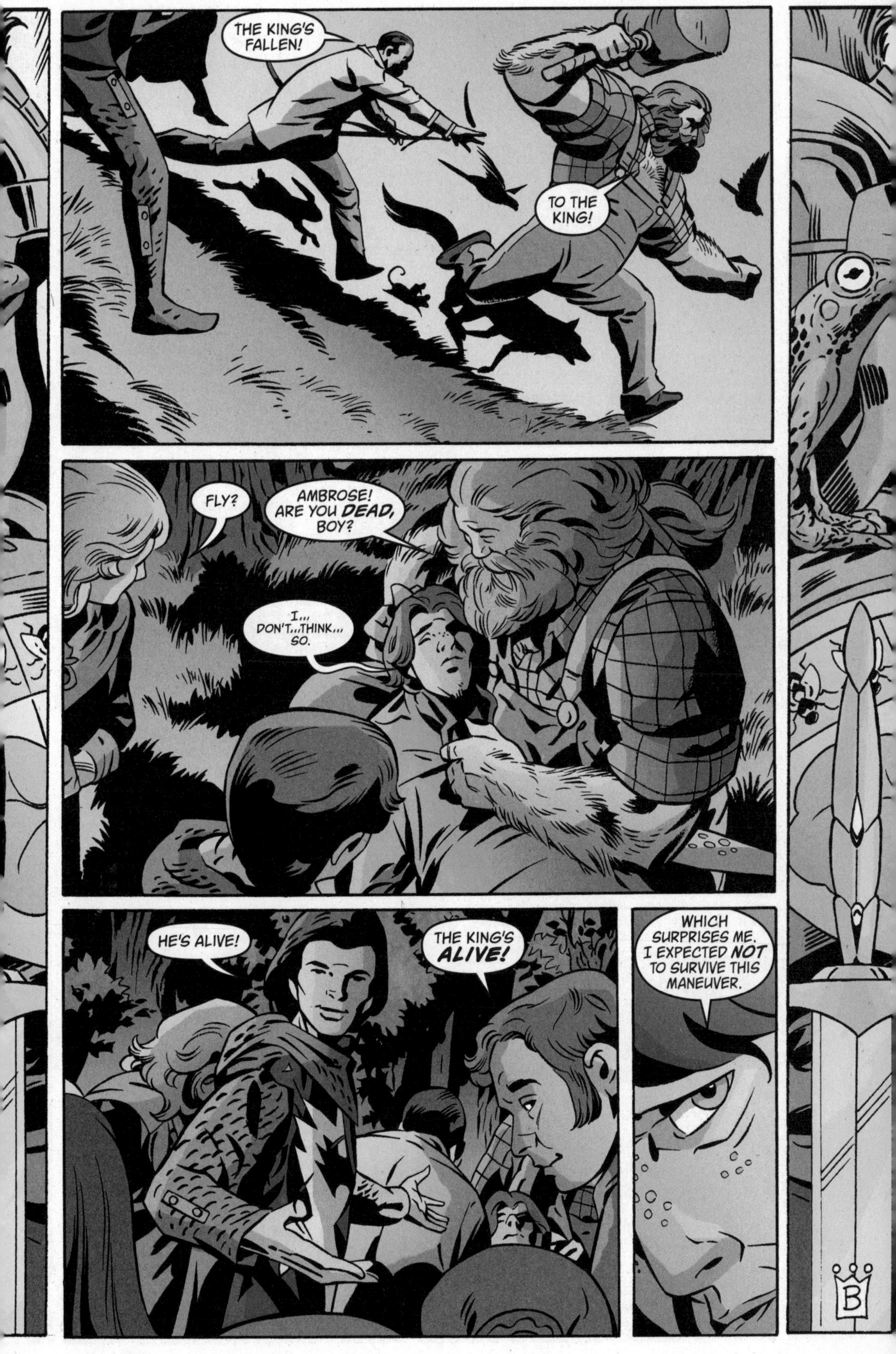
THE KING'S FALLEN!
TO THE KING!
FLY?
AMBROSE! ARE YOU DEAD, BOY?
I... DON'T...THINK... SO.
HE'S ALIVE!
THE KING'S ALIVE!
WHICH SURPRISES ME. I EXPECTED NOT TO SURVIVE THIS MANEUVER.

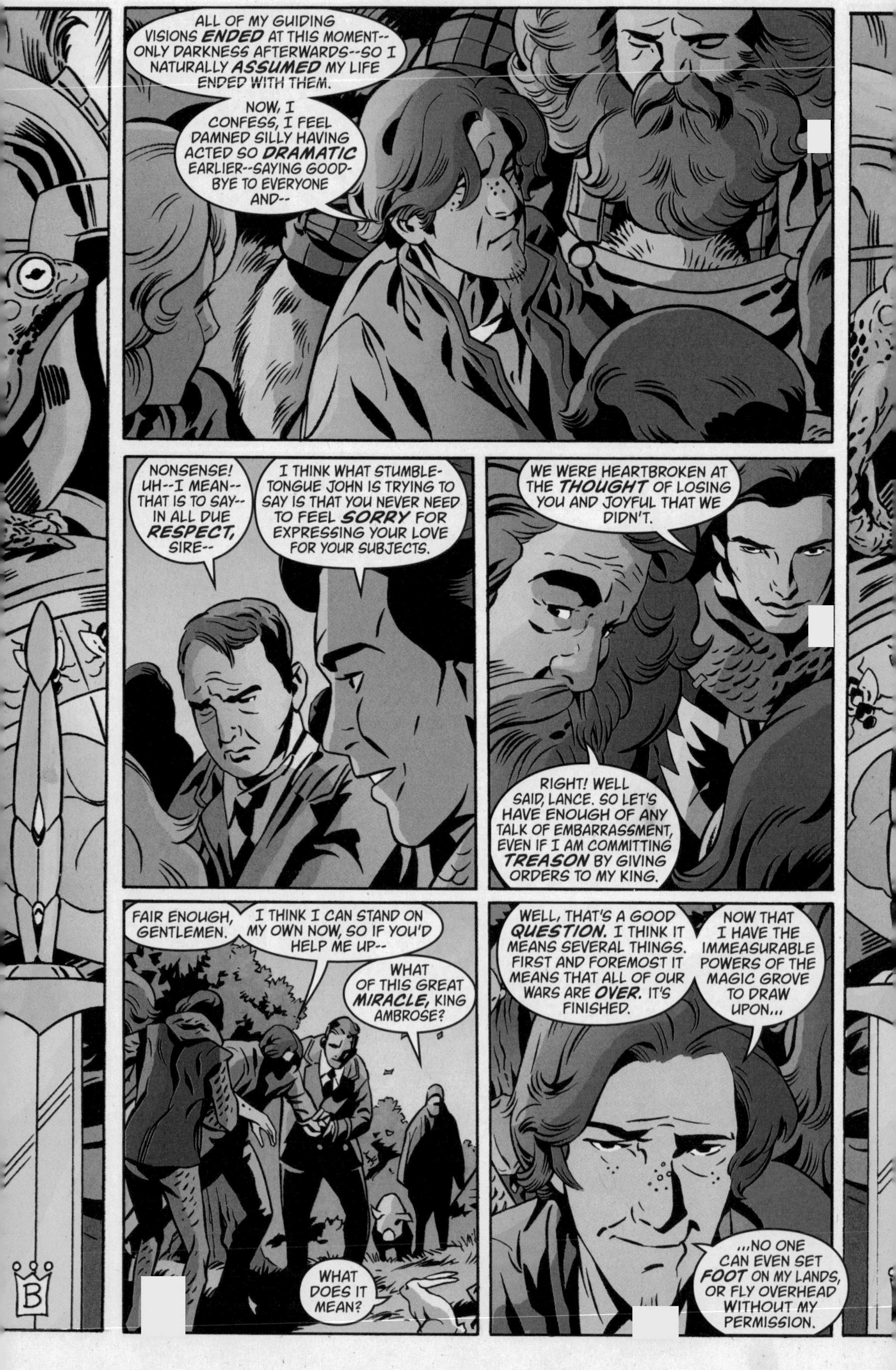

ALL OF MY GUIDING VISIONS ENDED AT THIS MOMENT--ONLY DARKNESS AFTERWARDS--SO I NATURALLY ASSUMED MY LIFE ENDED WITH THEM.
NOW, I CONFESS, I FEEL DAMNED SILLY HAVING ACTED SO DRAMATIC EARLIER--SAYING GOOD-BYE TO EVERYONE AND--
NONSENSE! UH--I MEAN--THAT IS TO SAY--IN ALL DUE RESPECT, SIRE--
I THINK WHAT STUMBLE-TONGUE JOHN IS TRYING TO SAY IS THAT YOU NEVER NEED TO FEEL SORRY FOR EXPRESSING YOUR LOVE FOR YOUR SUBJECTS.
WE WERE HEARTBROKEN AT THE THOUGHT OF LOSING YOU AND JOYFUL THAT WE DIDN'T.
RIGHT! WELL SAID, LANCE. SO LET'S HAVE ENOUGH OF ANY TALK OF EMBARRASSMENT, EVEN IF I AM COMMITTING TREASON BY GIVING ORDERS TO MY KING.
FAIR ENOUGH, GENTLEMEN.
I THINK I CAN STAND ON MY OWN NOW, SO IF YOU'D HELP ME UP--
WHAT OF THIS GREAT MIRACLE, KING AMBROSE?
WHAT DOES IT MEAN?
WELL, THAT'S A GOOD QUESTION. I THINK IT MEANS SEVERAL THINGS. FIRST AND FOREMOST IT MEANS THAT ALL OF OUR WARS ARE OVER. IT'S FINISHED.
NOW THAT I HAVE THE IMMEASURABLE POWERS OF THE MAGIC GROVE TO DRAW UPON...
...NO ONE CAN EVEN SET FOOT ON MY LANDS, OR FLY OVERHEAD WITHOUT MY PERMISSION.

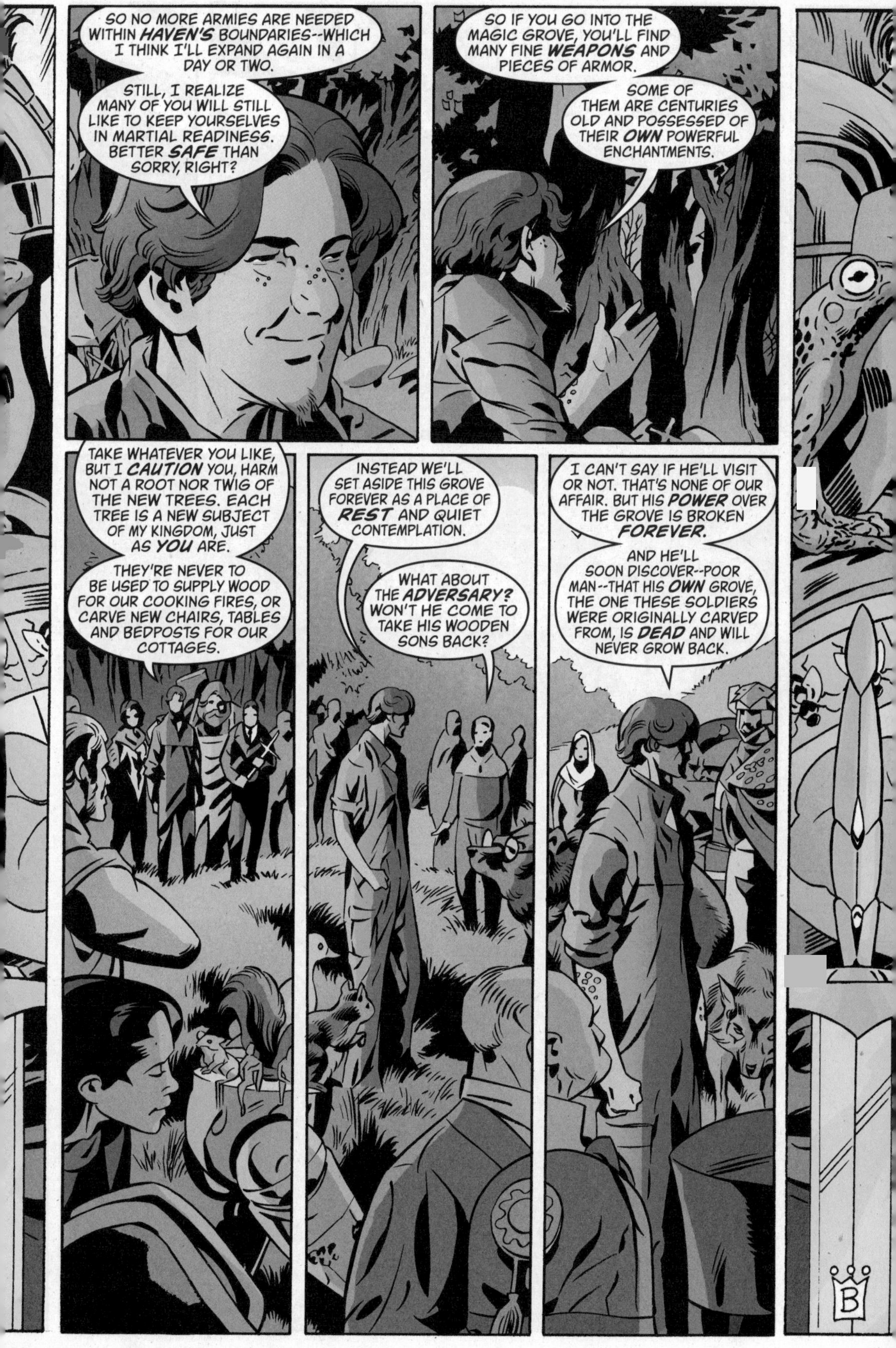
SO NO MORE ARMIES ARE NEEDED WITHIN HAVEN'S BOUNDARIES--WHICH I THINK I'LL EXPAND AGAIN IN A DAY OR TWO.
STILL, I REALIZE MANY OF YOU WILL STILL LIKE TO KEEP YOURSELVES IN MARTIAL READINESS. BETTER SAFE THAN SORRY, RIGHT?
SO IF YOU GO INTO THE MAGIC GROVE, YOU'LL FIND MANY FINE WEAPONS AND PIECES OF ARMOR.
SOME OF THEM ARE CENTURIES OLD AND POSSESSED OF THEIR OWN POWERFUL ENCHANTMENTS.
TAKE WHATEVER YOU LIKE, BUT I CAUTION YOU, HARM NOT A ROOT NOR TWIG OF THE NEW TREES. EACH TREE IS A NEW SUBJECT OF MY KINGDOM, JUST AS YOU ARE.
THEY'RE NEVER TO BE USED TO SUPPLY WOOD FOR OUR COOKING FIRES, OR CARVE NEW CHAIRS, TABLES AND BEDPOSTS FOR OUR COTTAGES.
INSTEAD WE'LL SET ASIDE THIS GROVE FOREVER AS A PLACE OF REST AND QUIET CONTEMPLATION.
WHAT ABOUT THE ADVERSARY? WON'T HE COME TO TAKE HIS WOODEN SONS BACK?
I CAN'T SAY IF HE'LL VISIT OR NOT. THAT'S NONE OF OUR AFFAIR. BUT HIS POWER OVER THE GROVE IS BROKEN FOREVER.
AND HE'LL SOON DISCOVER--POOR MAN--THAT HIS OWN GROVE, THE ONE THESE SOLDIERS WERE ORIGINALLY CARVED FROM, IS DEAD AND WILL NEVER GROW BACK.
B

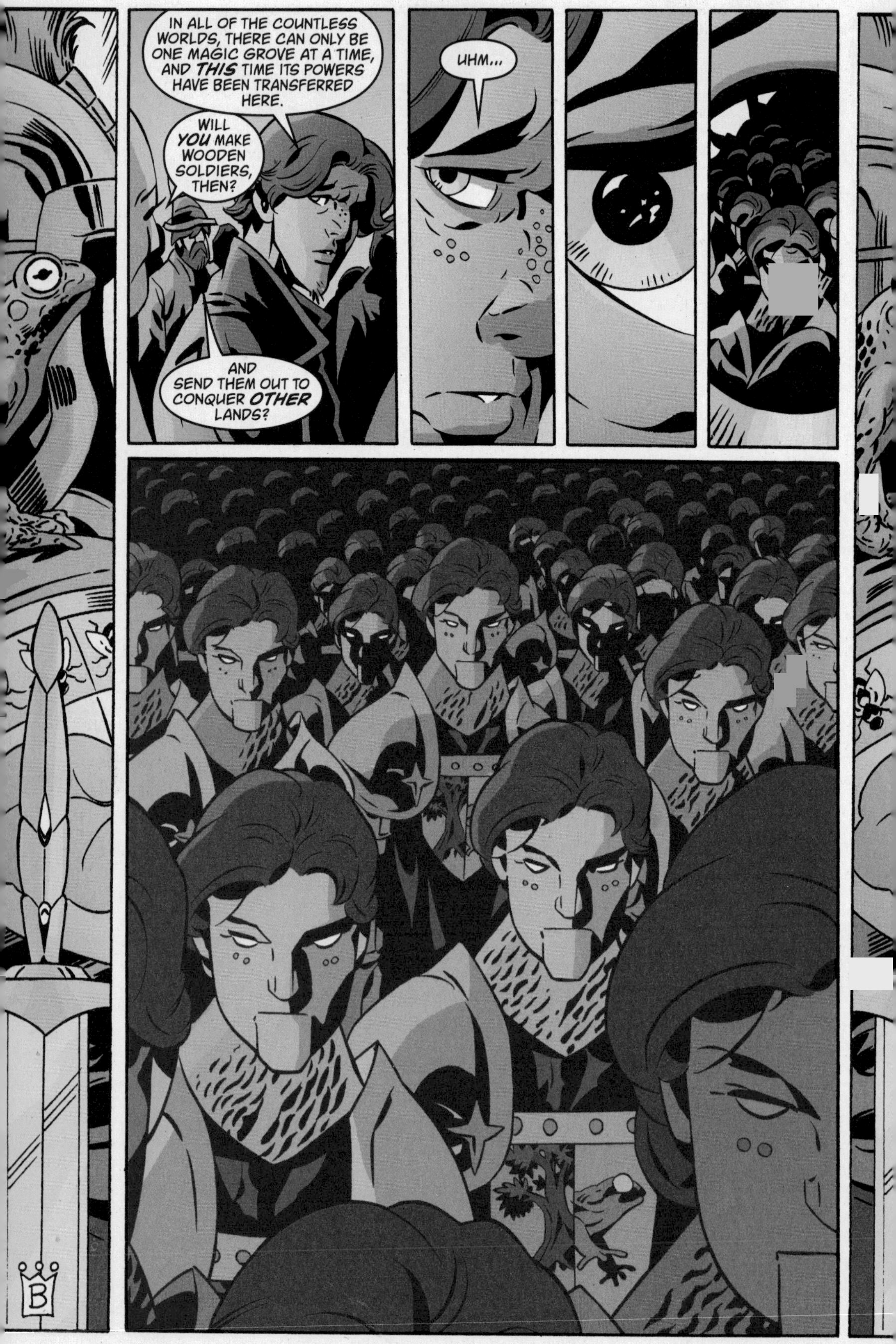
IN ALL OF THE COUNTLESS WORLDS, THERE CAN ONLY BE ONE MAGIC GROVE AT A TIME, AND THIS TIME ITS POWERS HAVE BEEN TRANSFERRED HERE.
WILL YOU MAKE WOODEN SOLDIERS, THEN?
AND SEND THEM OUT TO CONQUER OTHER LANDS?
UHM...

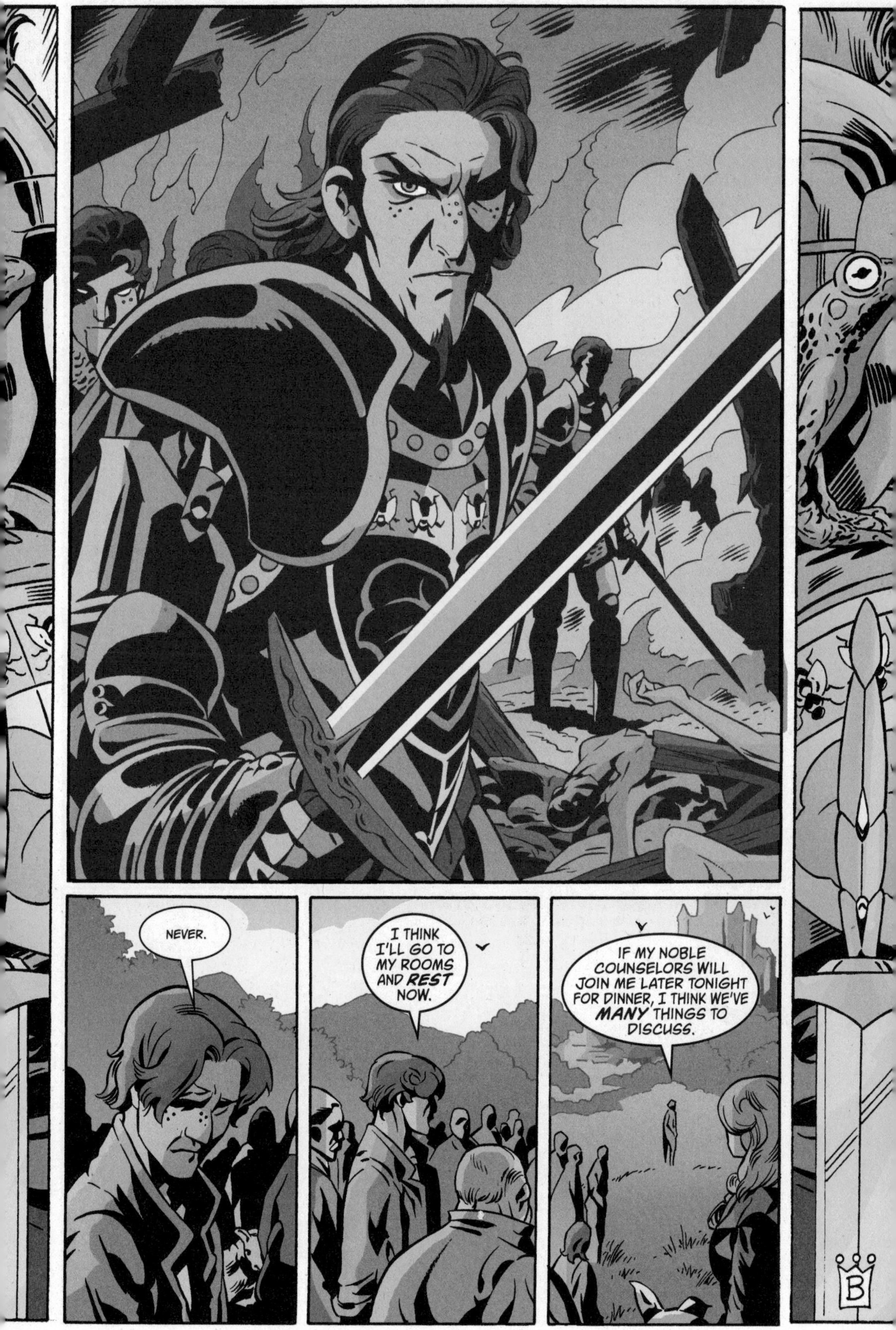
NEVER.
I THINK I'LL GO TO MY ROOMS AND REST NOW.
IF MY NOBLE COUNSELORS WILL JOIN ME LATER TONIGHT FOR DINNER, I THINK WE'VE MANY THINGS TO DISCUSS.

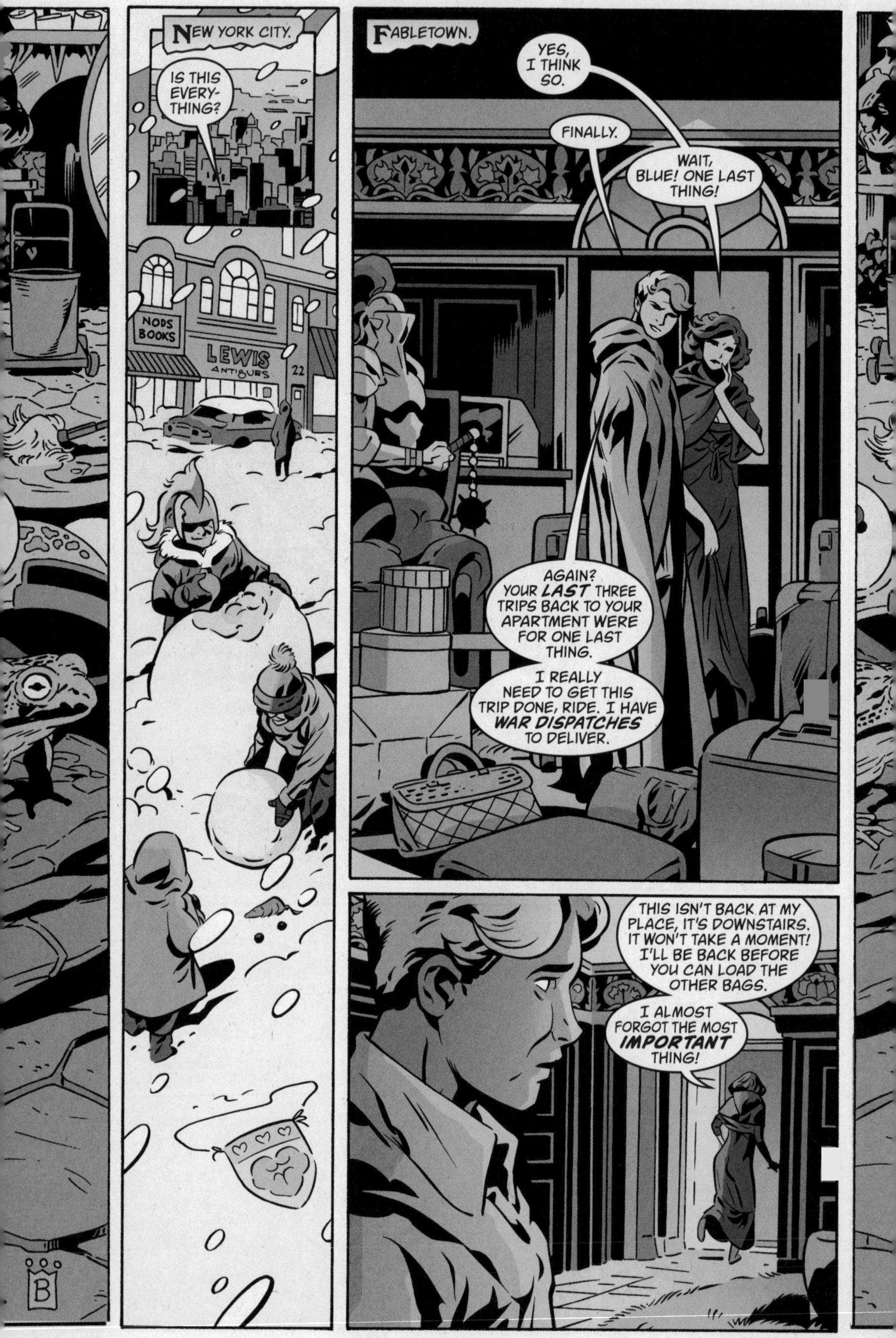
NEW YORK CITY.
IS THIS EVERY-THING?
NODS BOOKS
LEWIS ANTIQUES
22
FABLETOWN.
YES, I THINK SO.
FINALLY.
WAIT, BLUE! ONE LAST THING!
AGAIN? YOUR LAST THREE TRIPS BACK TO YOUR APARTMENT WERE FOR ONE LAST THING.
I REALLY NEED TO GET THIS TRIP DONE, RIDE. I HAVE WAR DISPATCHES TO DELIVER.
THIS ISN'T BACK AT MY PLACE, IT'S DOWNSTAIRS. IT WON'T TAKE A MOMENT! I'LL BE BACK BEFORE YOU CAN LOAD THE OTHER BAGS.
I ALMOST FORGOT THE MOST IMPORTANT THING!

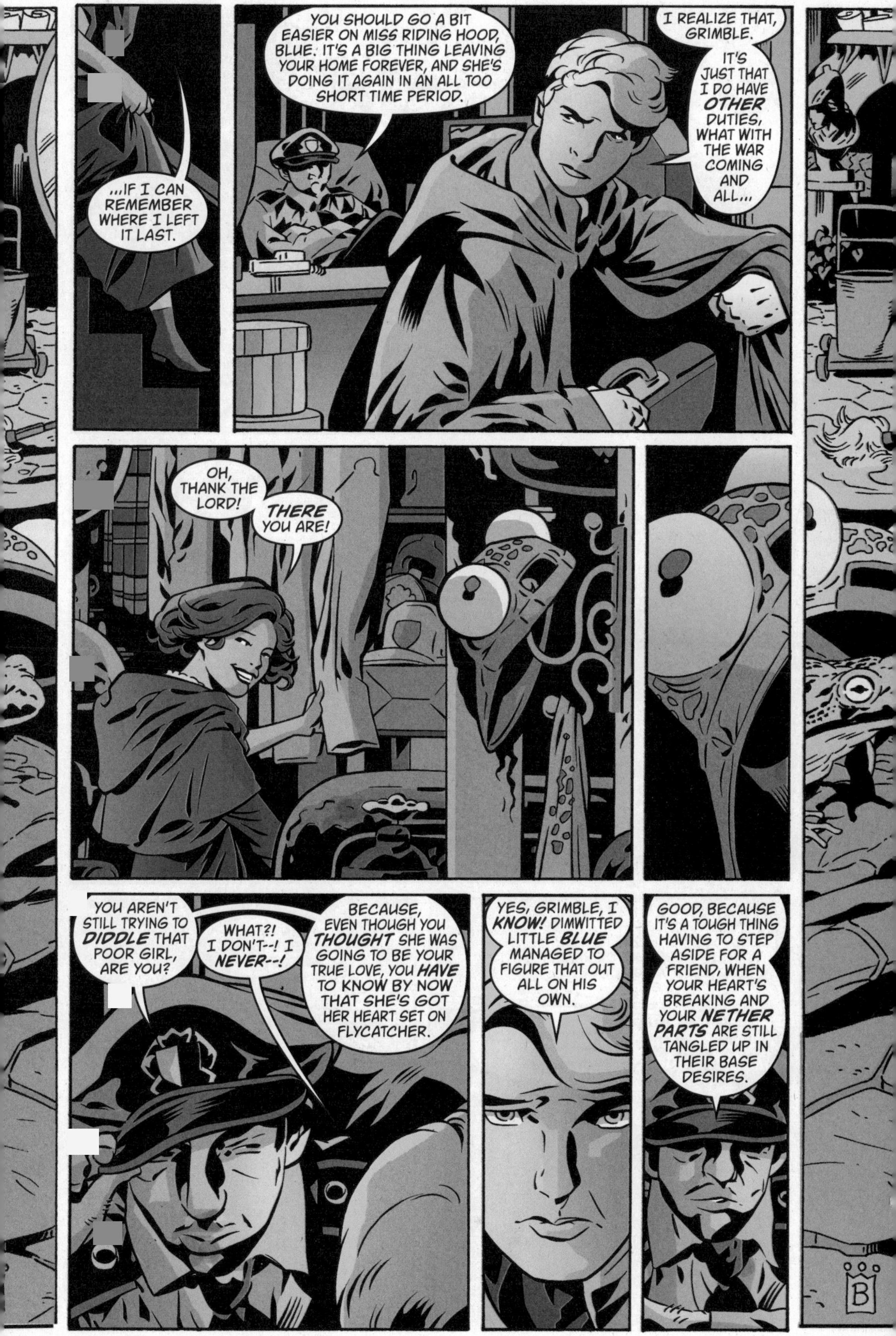
...IF I CAN REMEMBER WHERE I LEFT IT LAST.
YOU SHOULD GO A BIT EASIER ON MISS RIDING HOOD, BLUE. IT'S A BIG THING LEAVING YOUR HOME FOREVER, AND SHE'S DOING IT AGAIN IN AN ALL TOO SHORT TIME PERIOD.
I REALIZE THAT, GRIMBLE.
IT'S JUST THAT I DO HAVE OTHER DUTIES, WHAT WITH THE WAR COMING AND ALL...
OH, THANK THE LORD!
THERE YOU ARE!
YOU AREN'T STILL TRYING TO DIDDLE THAT POOR GIRL, ARE YOU?
WHAT?! I DON'T--! I NEVER--!
BECAUSE, EVEN THOUGH YOU THOUGHT SHE WAS GOING TO BE YOUR TRUE LOVE, YOU HAVE TO KNOW BY NOW THAT SHE'S GOT HER HEART SET ON FLYCATCHER.
YES, GRIMBLE, I KNOW! DIMWITTED LITTLE BLUE MANAGED TO FIGURE THAT OUT ALL ON HIS OWN.
GOOD, BECAUSE IT'S A TOUGH THING HAVING TO STEP ASIDE FOR A FRIEND, WHEN YOUR HEART'S BREAKING AND YOUR NETHER PARTS ARE STILL TANGLED UP IN THEIR BASE DESIRES.

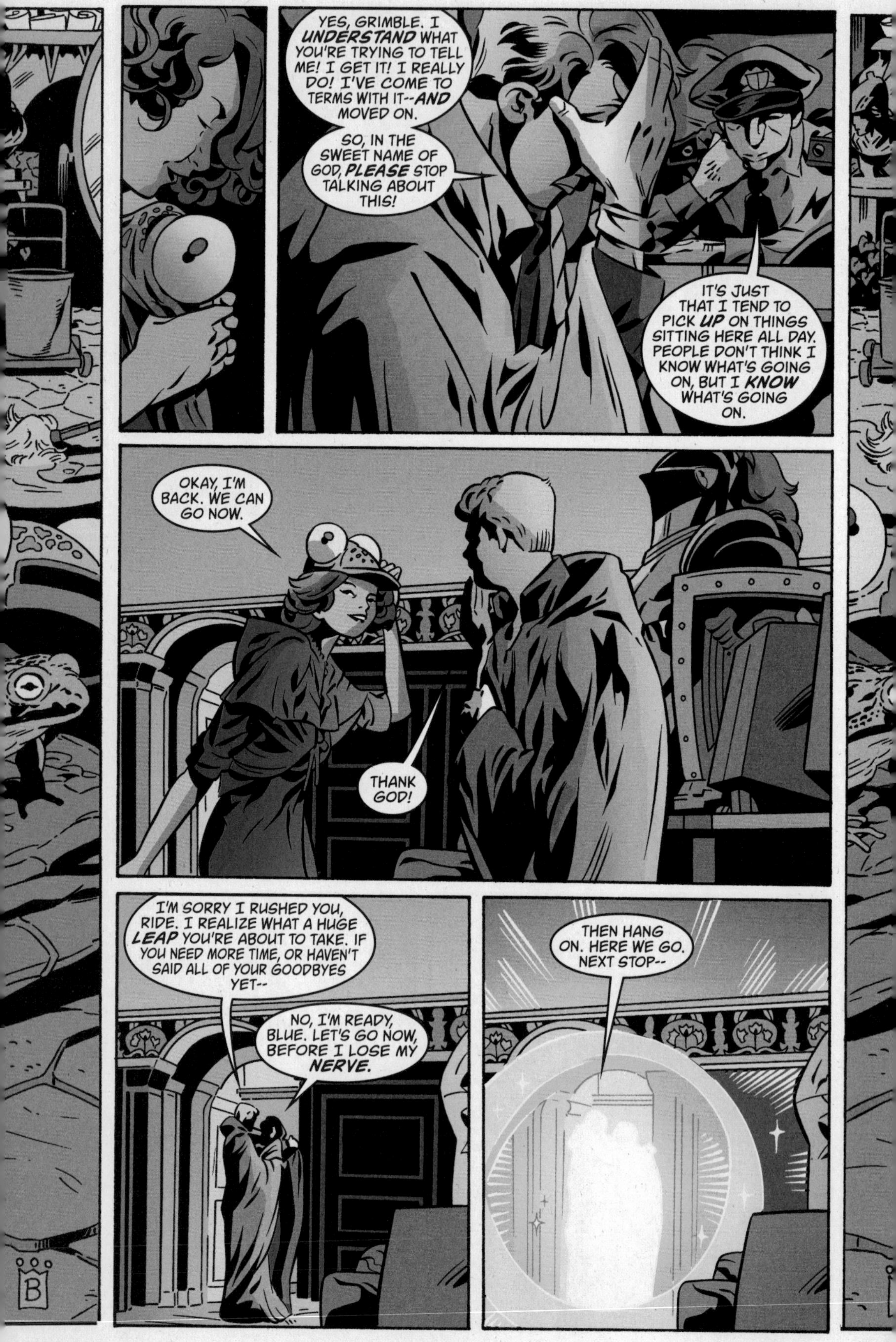
YES, GRIMBLE. I UNDERSTAND WHAT YOU'RE TRYING TO TELL ME! I GET IT! I REALLY DO! I'VE COME TO TERMS WITH IT--AND MOVED ON.
SO, IN THE SWEET NAME OF GOD, PLEASE STOP TALKING ABOUT THIS!
IT'S JUST THAT I TEND TO PICK UP ON THINGS SITTING HERE ALL DAY. PEOPLE DON'T THINK I KNOW WHAT'S GOING ON, BUT I KNOW WHAT'S GOING ON.
OKAY, I'M BACK. WE CAN GO NOW.
THANK GOD!
I'M SORRY I RUSHED YOU, RIDE. I REALIZE WHAT A HUGE LEAP YOU'RE ABOUT TO TAKE. IF YOU NEED MORE TIME, OR HAVEN'T SAID ALL OF YOUR GOODBYES YET--
NO, I'M READY, BLUE. LET'S GO NOW, BEFORE I LOSE MY NERVE.
THEN HANG ON. HERE WE GO. NEXT STOP--

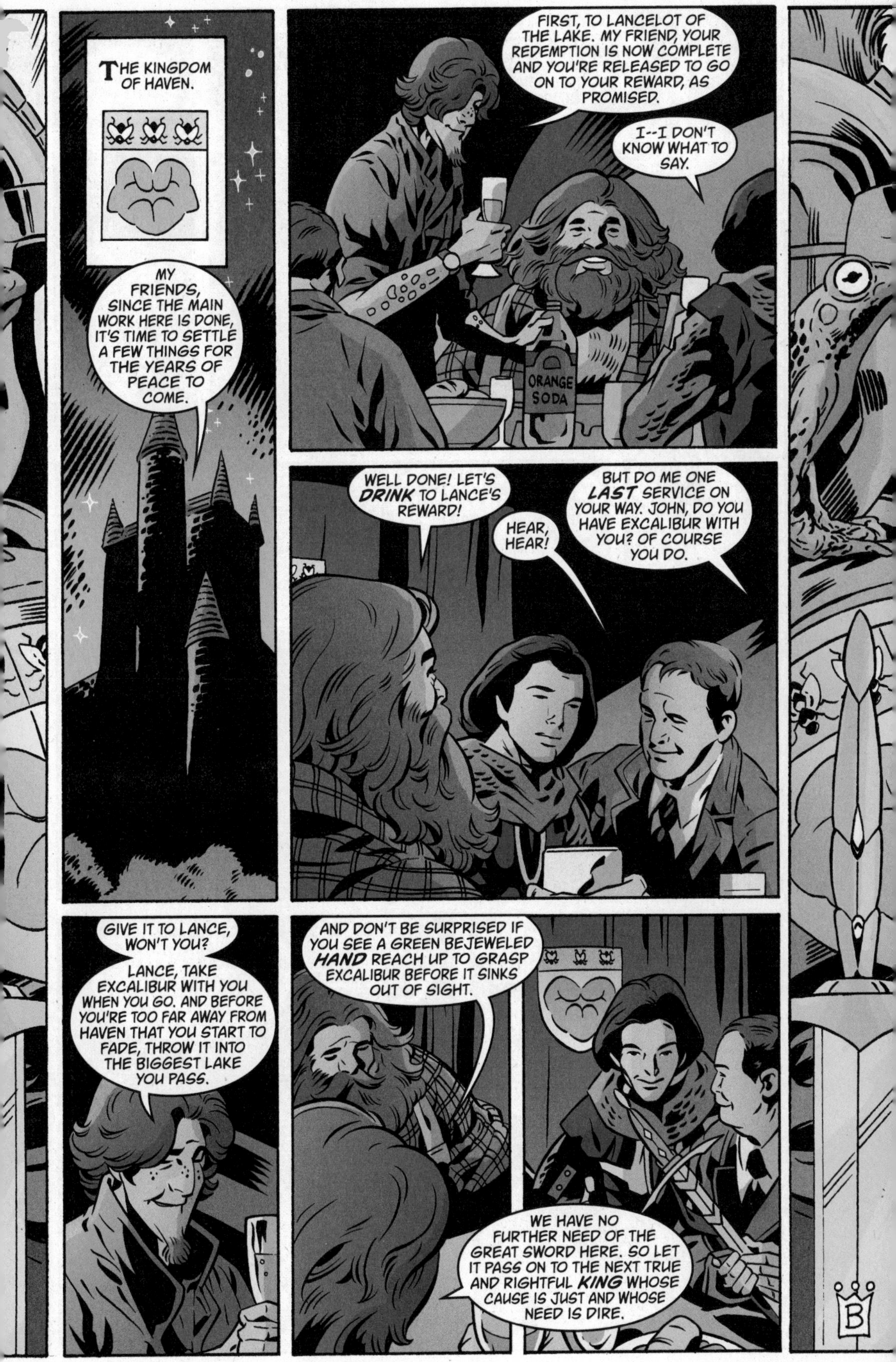
THE KINGDOM OF HAVEN.
MY FRIENDS, SINCE THE MAIN WORK HERE IS DONE, IT'S TIME TO SETTLE A FEW THINGS FOR THE YEARS OF PEACE TO COME.
FIRST, TO LANCELOT OF THE LAKE. MY FRIEND, YOUR REDEMPTION IS NOW COMPLETE AND YOU'RE RELEASED TO GO ON TO YOUR REWARD, AS PROMISED.
I--I DON'T KNOW WHAT TO SAY.
ORANGE SODA
WELL DONE! LET'S DRINK TO LANCE'S REWARD!
HEAR, HEAR!
BUT DO ME ONE LAST SERVICE ON YOUR WAY. JOHN, DO YOU HAVE EXCALIBUR WITH YOU? OF COURSE YOU DO.
GIVE IT TO LANCE, WON'T YOU?
LANCE, TAKE EXCALIBUR WITH YOU WHEN YOU GO. AND BEFORE YOU'RE TOO FAR AWAY FROM HAVEN THAT YOU START TO FADE, THROW IT INTO THE BIGGEST LAKE YOU PASS.
AND DON'T BE SURPRISED IF YOU SEE A GREEN BEJEWELED HAND REACH UP TO GRASP EXCALIBUR BEFORE IT SINKS OUT OF SIGHT.
WE HAVE NO FURTHER NEED OF THE GREAT SWORD HERE. SO LET IT PASS ON TO THE NEXT TRUE AND RIGHTFUL KING WHOSE CAUSE IS JUST AND WHOSE NEED IS DIRE.

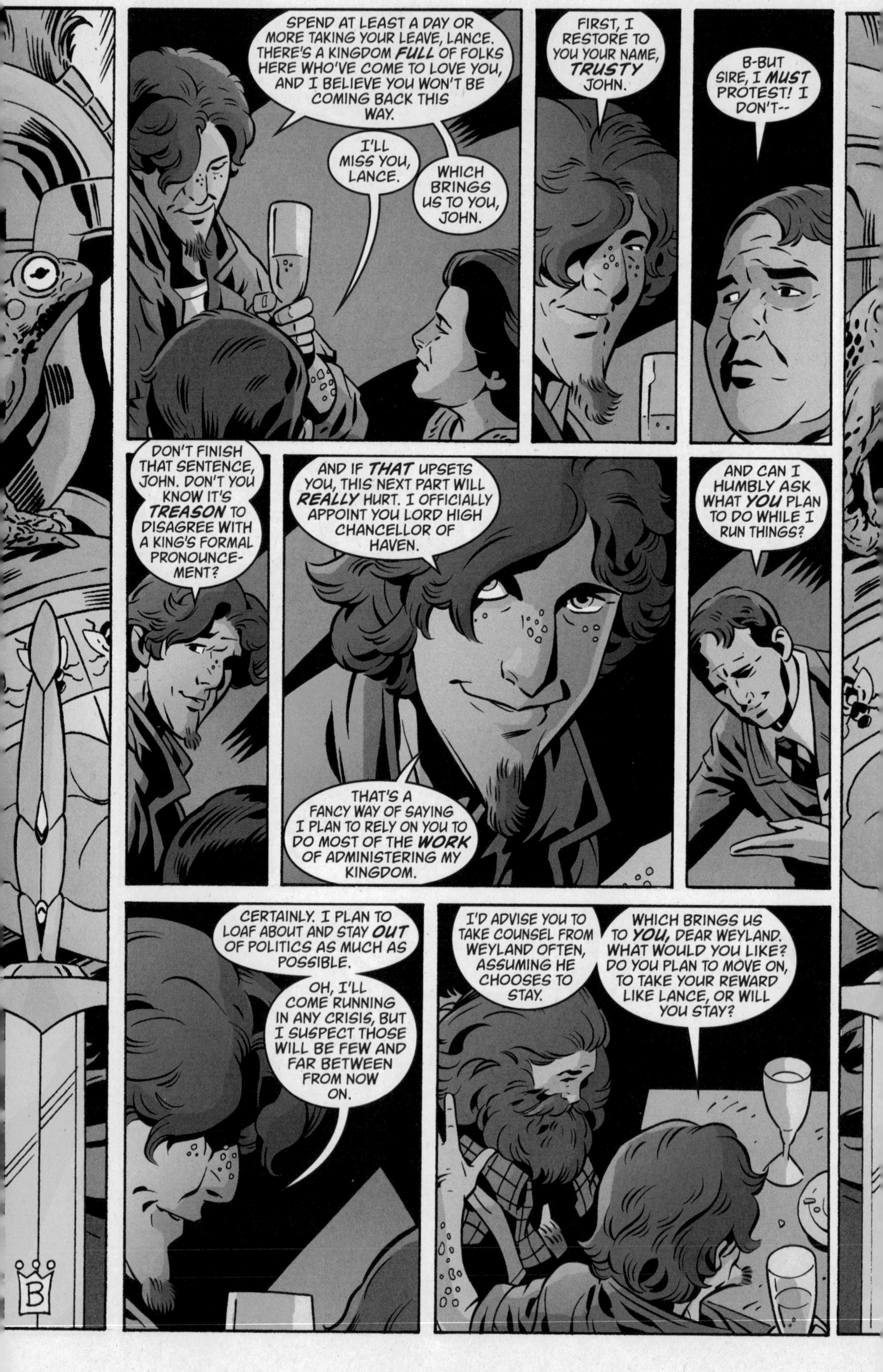
SPEND AT LEAST A DAY OR MORE TAKING YOUR LEAVE, LANCE. THERE'S A KINGDOM FULL OF FOLKS HERE WHO'VE COME TO LOVE YOU, AND I BELIEVE YOU WON'T BE COMING BACK THIS WAY.
I'LL MISS YOU, LANCE.
WHICH BRINGS US TO YOU, JOHN.
FIRST, I RESTORE TO YOU YOUR NAME, TRUSTY JOHN.
B-BUT SIRE, I MUST PROTEST! I DON'T--
DON'T FINISH THAT SENTENCE, JOHN. DON'T YOU KNOW IT'S TREASON TO DISAGREE WITH A KING'S FORMAL PRONOUNCEMENT?
AND IF THAT UPSETS YOU, THIS NEXT PART WILL REALLY HURT. I OFFICIALLY APPOINT YOU LORD HIGH CHANCELLOR OF HAVEN.
THAT'S A FANCY WAY OF SAYING I PLAN TO RELY ON YOU TO DO MOST OF THE WORK OF ADMINISTERING MY KINGDOM.
AND CAN I HUMBLY ASK WHAT YOU PLAN TO DO WHILE I RUN THINGS?
CERTAINLY. I PLAN TO LOAF ABOUT AND STAY OUT OF POLITICS AS MUCH AS POSSIBLE.
OH, I'LL COME RUNNING IN ANY CRISIS, BUT I SUSPECT THOSE WILL BE FEW AND FAR BETWEEN FROM NOW ON.
I'D ADVISE YOU TO TAKE COUNSEL FROM WEYLAND OFTEN, ASSUMING HE CHOOSES TO STAY.
WHICH BRINGS US TO YOU, DEAR WEYLAND. WHAT WOULD YOU LIKE? DO YOU PLAN TO MOVE ON, TO TAKE YOUR REWARD LIKE LANCE, OR WILL YOU STAY?
B

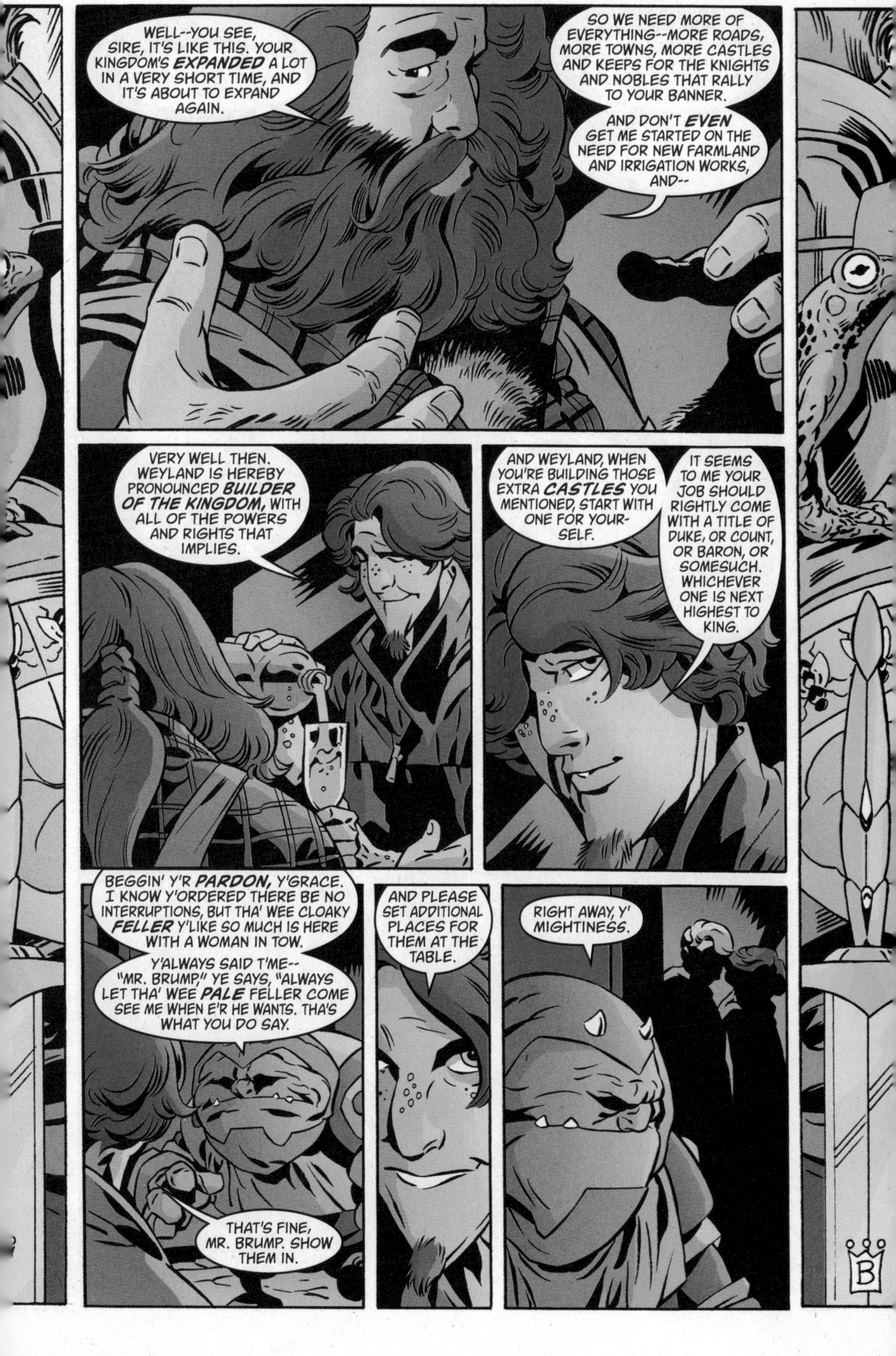
WELL--YOU SEE, SIRE, IT'S LIKE THIS. YOUR KINGDOM'S EXPANDED A LOT IN A VERY SHORT TIME, AND IT'S ABOUT TO EXPAND AGAIN.
SO WE NEED MORE OF EVERYTHING--MORE ROADS, MORE TOWNS, MORE CASTLES AND KEEPS FOR THE KNIGHTS AND NOBLES THAT RALLY TO YOUR BANNER.
AND DON'T EVEN GET ME STARTED ON THE NEED FOR NEW FARMLAND AND IRRIGATION WORKS, AND--
VERY WELL THEN. WEYLAND IS HEREBY PRONOUNCED BUILDER OF THE KINGDOM, WITH ALL OF THE POWERS AND RIGHTS THAT IMPLIES.
AND WEYLAND, WHEN YOU'RE BUILDING THOSE EXTRA CASTLES YOU MENTIONED, START WITH ONE FOR YOURSELF.
IT SEEMS TO ME YOUR JOB SHOULD RIGHTLY COME WITH A TITLE OF DUKE, OR COUNT, OR BARON, OR SOMESUCH. WHICHEVER ONE IS NEXT HIGHEST TO KING.
BEGGIN' Y'R PARDON, Y'GRACE. I KNOW Y'ORDERED THERE BE NO INTERRUPTIONS, BUT THA' WEE CLOAKY FELLER Y'LIKE SO MUCH IS HERE WITH A WOMAN IN TOW.
Y'ALWAYS SAID T'ME-- "MR. BRUMP," YE SAYS, "ALWAYS LET THA' WEE PALE FELLER COME SEE ME WHEN E'R HE WANTS. THA'S WHAT YOU DO SAY.
THAT'S FINE, MR. BRUMP. SHOW THEM IN.
AND PLEASE SET ADDITIONAL PLACES FOR THEM AT THE TABLE.
RIGHT AWAY, Y' MIGHTINESS.

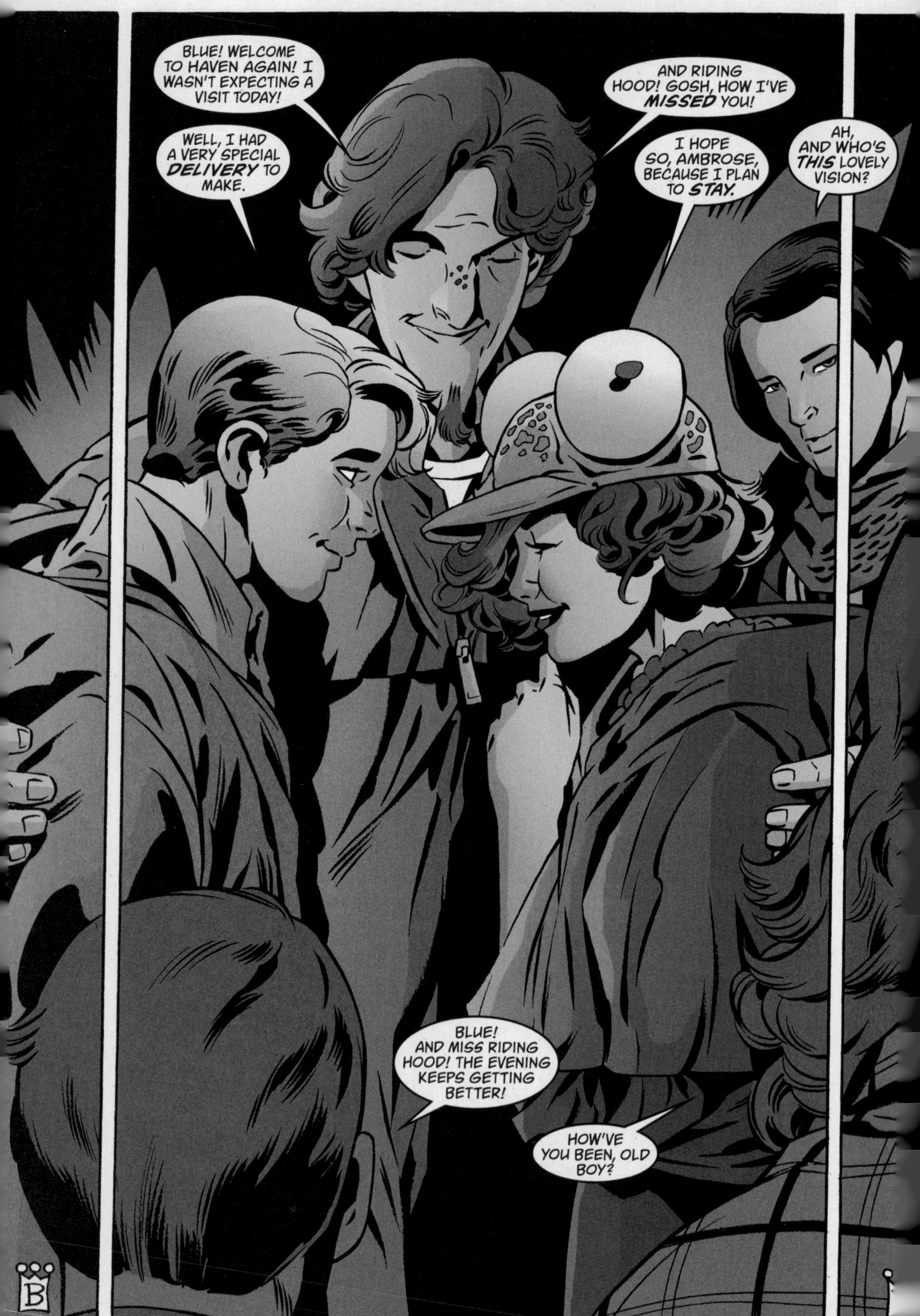
BLUE! WELCOME TO HAVEN AGAIN! I WASN'T EXPECTING A VISIT TODAY!
WELL, I HAD A VERY SPECIAL DELIVERY TO MAKE.
AND RIDING HOOD! GOSH, HOW I'VE MISSED YOU!
I HOPE SO, AMBROSE, BECAUSE I PLAN TO STAY.
AH, AND WHO'S THIS LOVELY VISION?
BLUE! AND MISS RIDING HOOD! THE EVENING KEEPS GETTING BETTER!
HOW'VE YOU BEEN, OLD BOY?

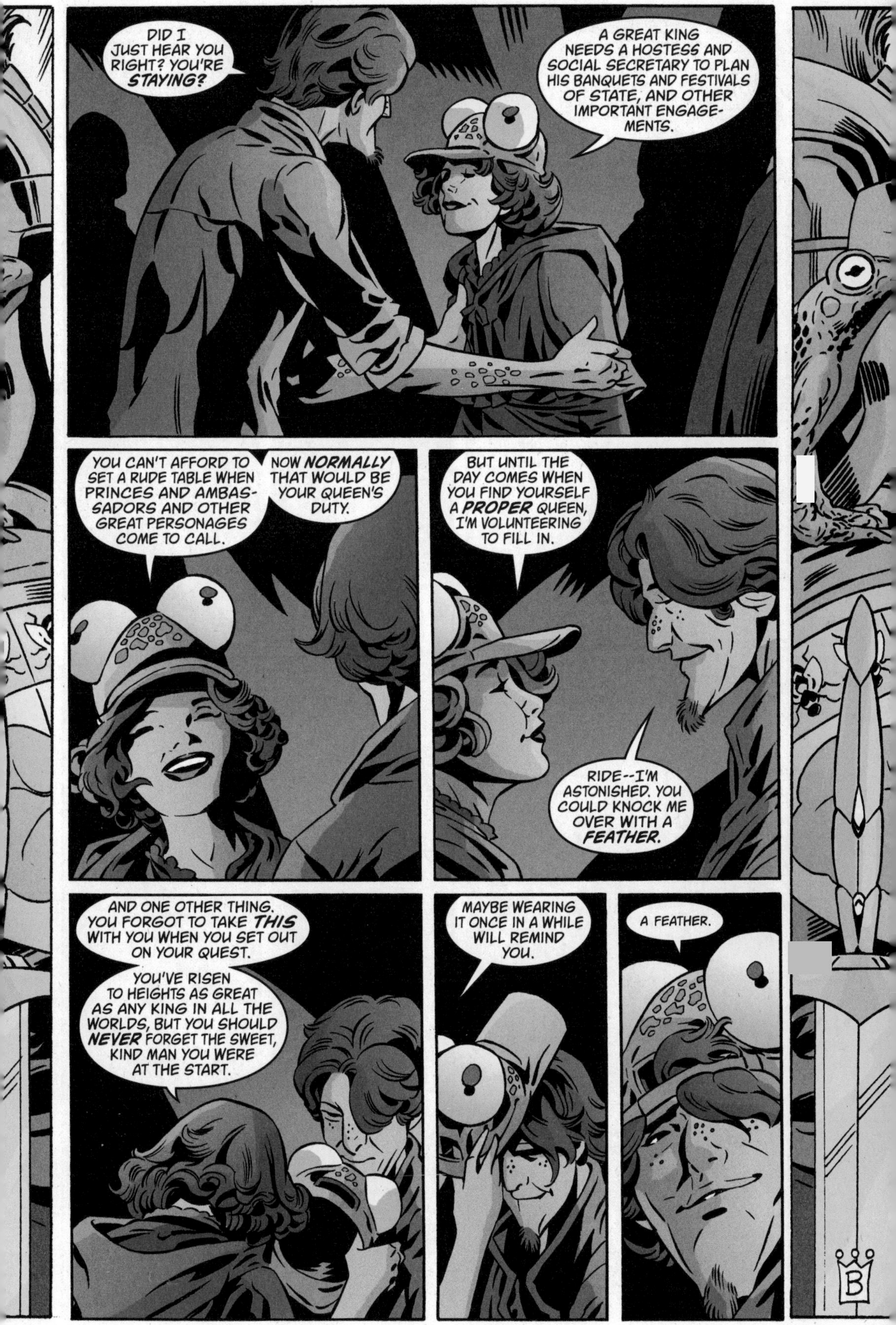
DID I JUST HEAR YOU RIGHT? YOU'RE STAYING?
A GREAT KING NEEDS A HOSTESS AND SOCIAL SECRETARY TO PLAN HIS BANQUETS AND FESTIVALS OF STATE, AND OTHER IMPORTANT ENGAGE-MENTS.
YOU CAN'T AFFORD TO SET A RUDE TABLE WHEN PRINCES AND AMBAS-SADORS AND OTHER GREAT PERSONAGES COME TO CALL.
NOW NORMALLY THAT WOULD BE YOUR QUEEN'S DUTY.
BUT UNTIL THE DAY COMES WHEN YOU FIND YOURSELF A PROPER QUEEN, I'M VOLUNTEERING TO FILL IN.
RIDE--I'M ASTONISHED. YOU COULD KNOCK ME OVER WITH A FEATHER.
AND ONE OTHER THING. YOU FORGOT TO TAKE THIS WITH YOU WHEN YOU SET OUT ON YOUR QUEST.
YOU'VE RISEN TO HEIGHTS AS GREAT AS ANY KING IN ALL THE WORLDS, BUT YOU SHOULD NEVER FORGET THE SWEET, KIND MAN YOU WERE AT THE START.
MAYBE WEARING IT ONCE IN A WHILE WILL REMIND YOU.
A FEATHER.
B

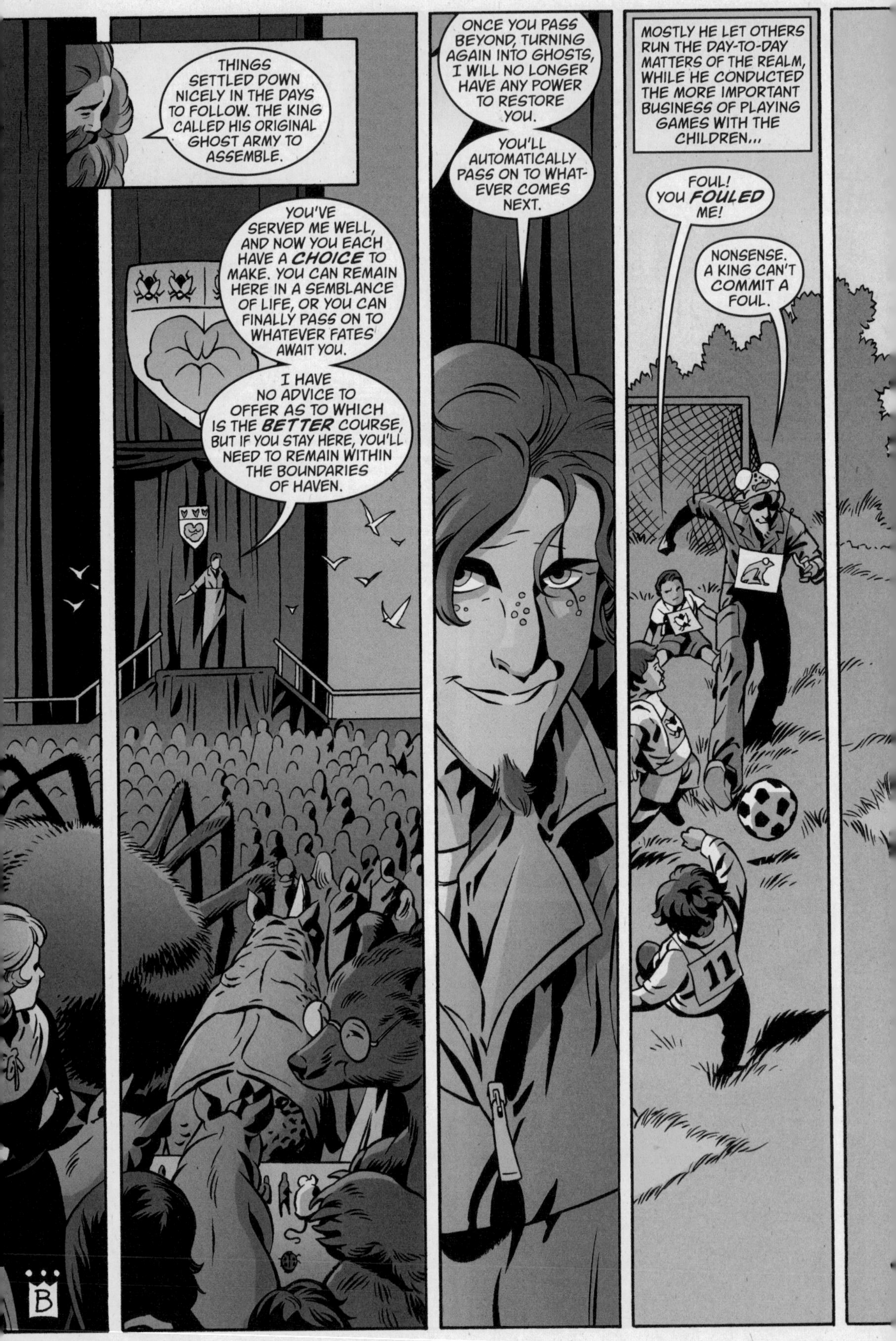
THINGS SETTLED DOWN NICELY IN THE DAYS TO FOLLOW. THE KING CALLED HIS ORIGINAL GHOST ARMY TO ASSEMBLE.
YOU'VE SERVED ME WELL, AND NOW YOU EACH HAVE A *CHOICE* TO MAKE. YOU CAN REMAIN HERE IN A SEMBLANCE OF LIFE, OR YOU CAN FINALLY PASS ON TO WHATEVER FATES AWAIT YOU.
I HAVE NO ADVICE TO OFFER AS TO WHICH IS THE *BETTER* COURSE, BUT IF YOU STAY HERE, YOU'LL NEED TO REMAIN WITHIN THE BOUNDARIES OF HAVEN.
ONCE YOU PASS BEYOND, TURNING AGAIN INTO GHOSTS, I WILL NO LONGER HAVE ANY POWER TO RESTORE YOU.
YOU'LL AUTOMATICALLY PASS ON TO WHATEVER COMES NEXT.
MOSTLY HE LET OTHERS RUN THE DAY-TO-DAY MATTERS OF THE REALM, WHILE HE CONDUCTED THE MORE IMPORTANT BUSINESS OF PLAYING GAMES WITH THE CHILDREN...
FOUL! YOU *FOULED* ME!
NONSENSE. A KING CAN'T COMMIT A FOUL.
11

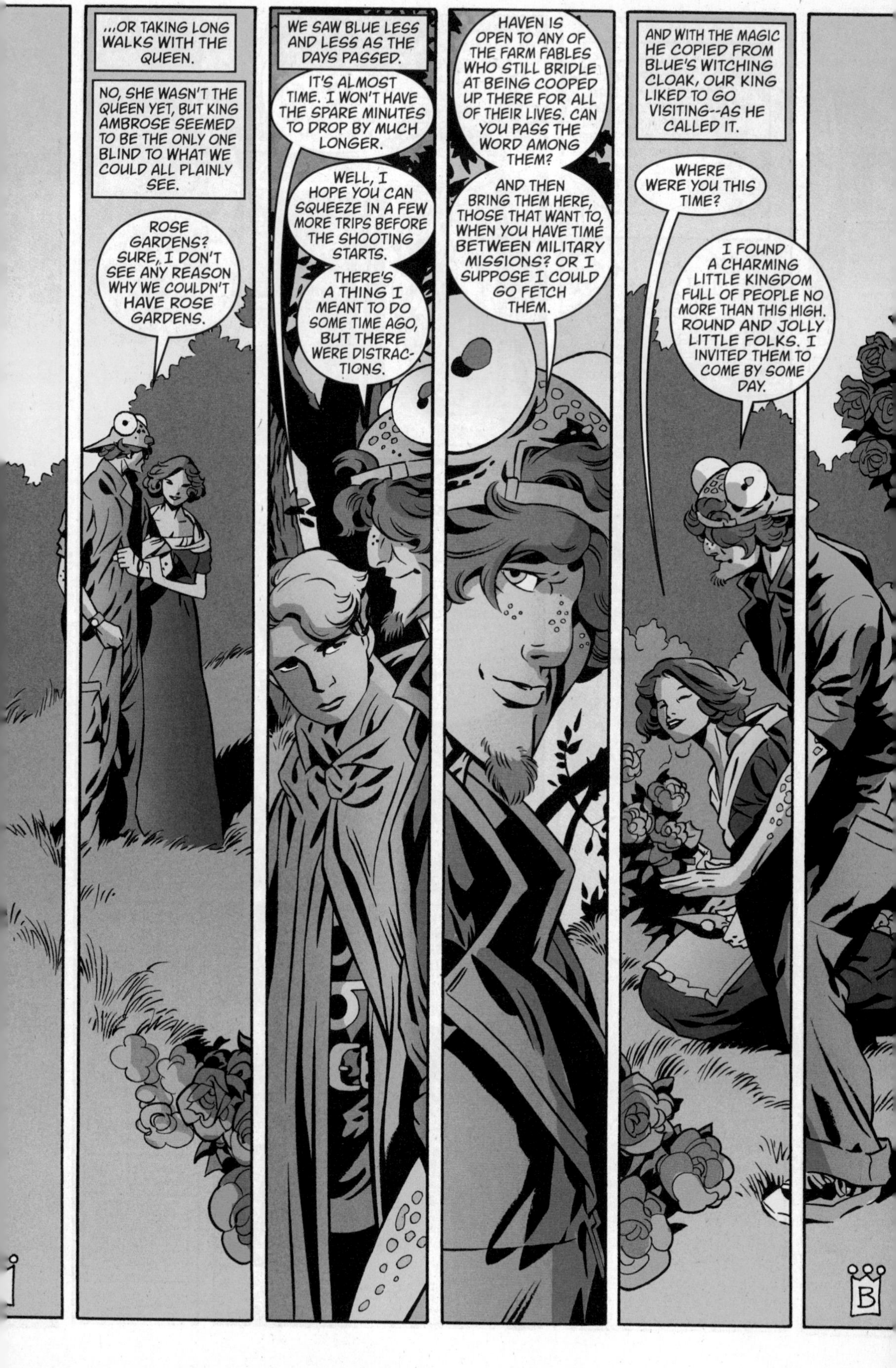
...OR TAKING LONG WALKS WITH THE QUEEN.
NO, SHE WASN'T THE QUEEN YET, BUT KING AMBROSE SEEMED TO BE THE ONLY ONE BLIND TO WHAT WE COULD ALL PLAINLY SEE.
ROSE GARDENS? SURE, I DON'T SEE ANY REASON WHY WE COULDN'T HAVE ROSE GARDENS.
WE SAW BLUE LESS AND LESS AS THE DAYS PASSED.
IT'S ALMOST TIME. I WON'T HAVE THE SPARE MINUTES TO DROP BY MUCH LONGER.
WELL, I HOPE YOU CAN SQUEEZE IN A FEW MORE TRIPS BEFORE THE SHOOTING STARTS.
THERE'S A THING I MEANT TO DO SOME TIME AGO, BUT THERE WERE DISTRACTIONS.
HAVEN IS OPEN TO ANY OF THE FARM FABLES WHO STILL BRIDLE AT BEING COOPED UP THERE FOR ALL OF THEIR LIVES. CAN YOU PASS THE WORD AMONG THEM?
AND THEN BRING THEM HERE, THOSE THAT WANT TO, WHEN YOU HAVE TIME BETWEEN MILITARY MISSIONS? OR I SUPPOSE I COULD GO FETCH THEM.
AND WITH THE MAGIC HE COPIED FROM BLUE'S WITCHING CLOAK, OUR KING LIKED TO GO VISITING--AS HE CALLED IT.
WHERE WERE YOU THIS TIME?
I FOUND A CHARMING LITTLE KINGDOM FULL OF PEOPLE NO MORE THAN THIS HIGH. ROUND AND JOLLY LITTLE FOLKS. I INVITED THEM TO COME BY SOME DAY.

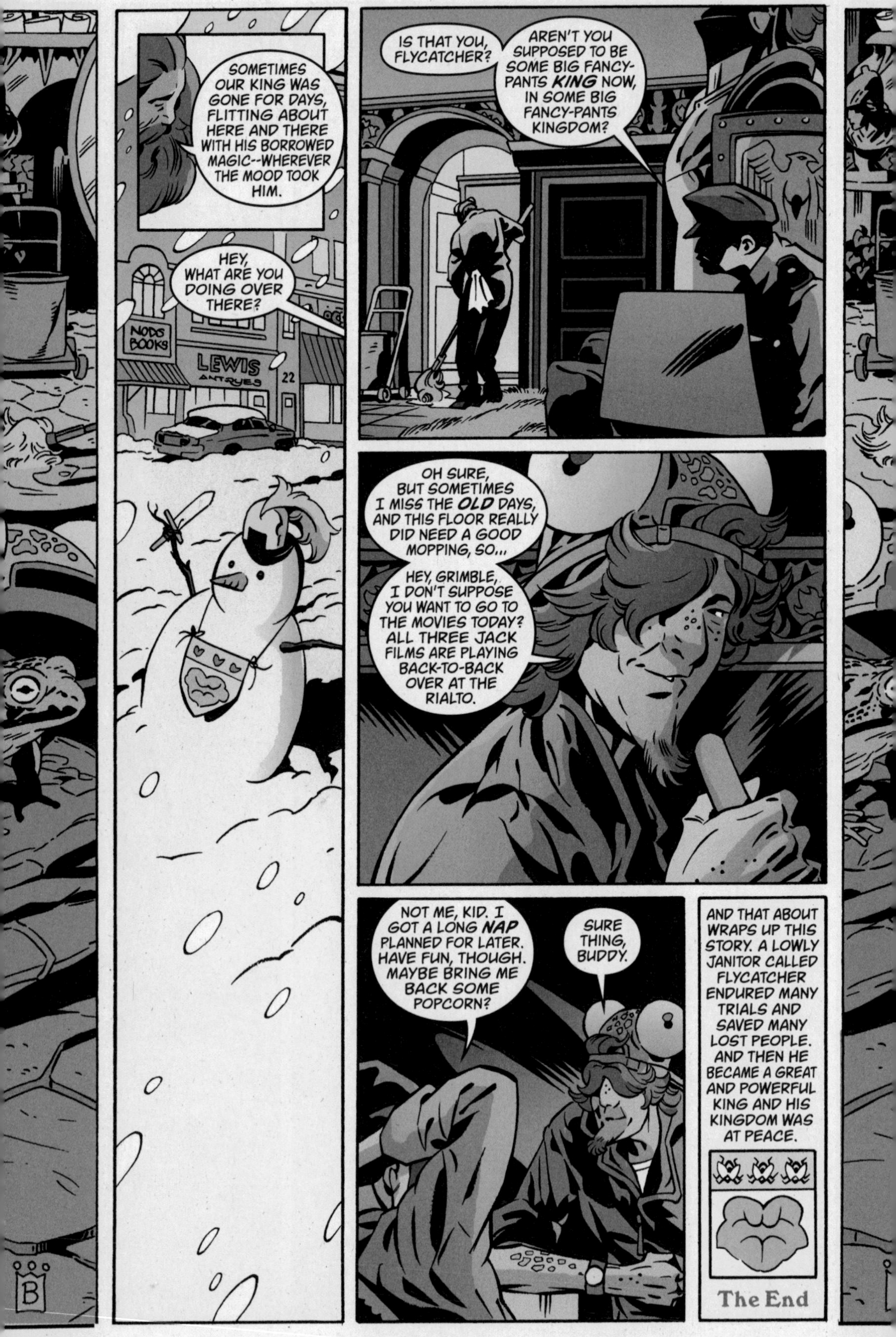
SOMETIMES OUR KING WAS GONE FOR DAYS, FLITTING ABOUT HERE AND THERE WITH HIS BORROWED MAGIC--WHEREVER THE MOOD TOOK HIM.
HEY, WHAT ARE YOU DOING OVER THERE?
NODS BOOKS
LEWIS ANTIQUES
22
IS THAT YOU, FLYCATCHER?
AREN'T YOU SUPPOSED TO BE SOME BIG FANCY-PANTS KING NOW, IN SOME BIG FANCY-PANTS KINGDOM?
OH SURE, BUT SOMETIMES I MISS THE OLD DAYS, AND THIS FLOOR REALLY DID NEED A GOOD MOPPING, SO...
HEY, GRIMBLE, I DON'T SUPPOSE YOU WANT TO GO TO THE MOVIES TODAY? ALL THREE JACK FILMS ARE PLAYING BACK-TO-BACK OVER AT THE RIALTO.
NOT ME, KID. I GOT A LONG NAP PLANNED FOR LATER. HAVE FUN, THOUGH. MAYBE BRING ME BACK SOME POPCORN?
SURE THING, BUDDY.
AND THAT ABOUT WRAPS UP THIS STORY. A LOWLY JANITOR CALLED FLYCATCHER ENDURED MANY TRIALS AND SAVED MANY LOST PEOPLE. AND THEN HE BECAME A GREAT AND POWERFUL KING AND HIS KINGDOM WAS AT PEACE.
The End

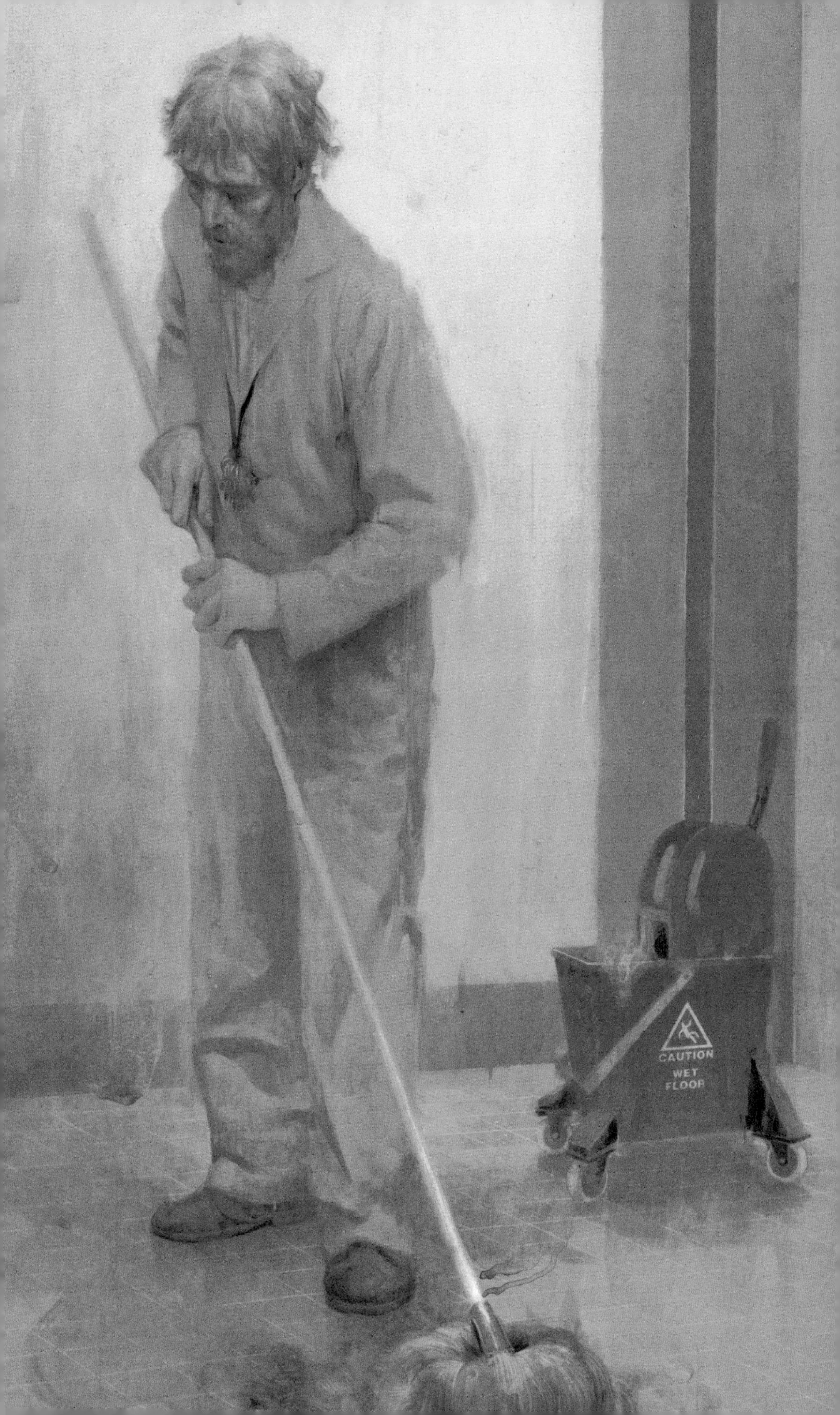
CAUTION
WET
FLOOR

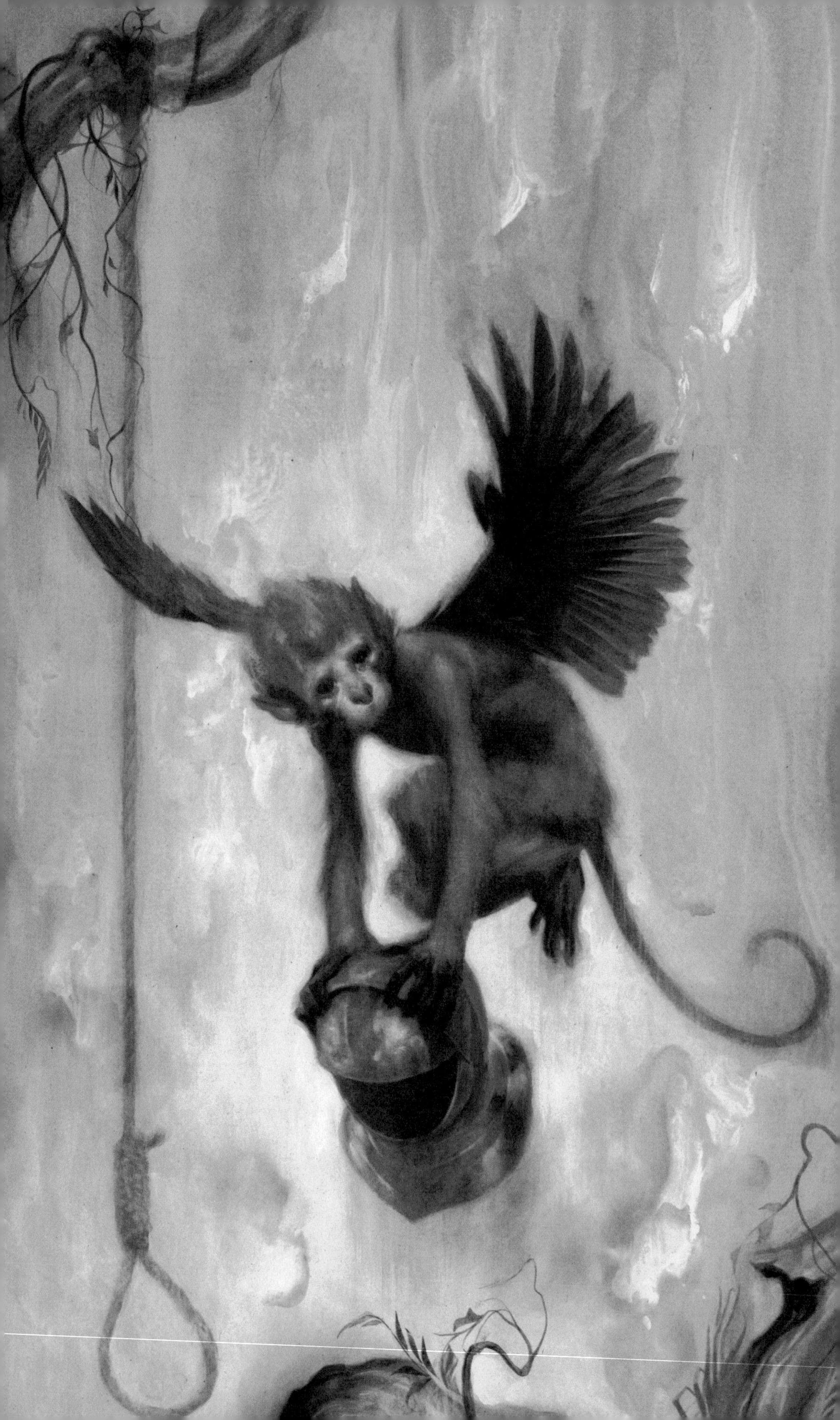

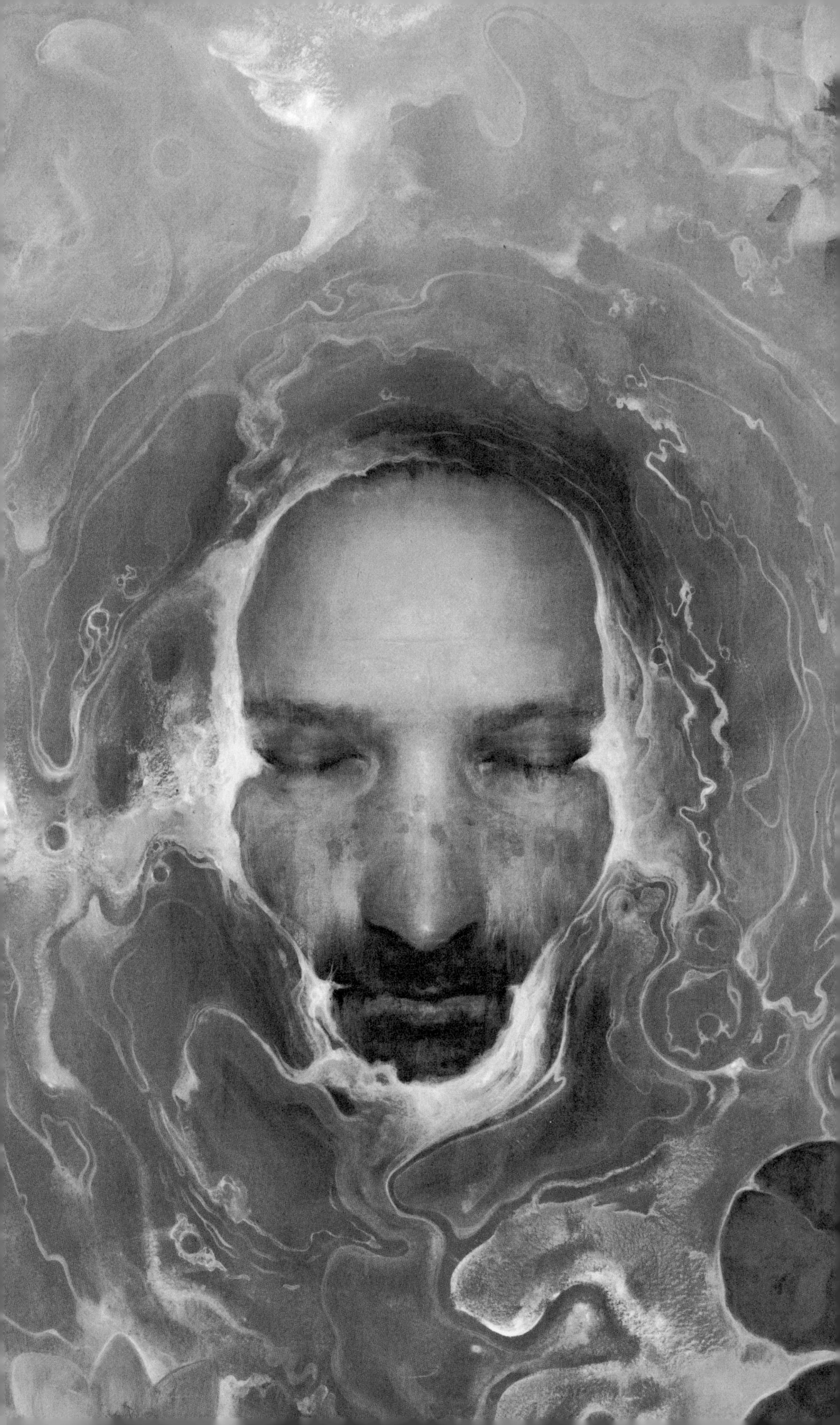

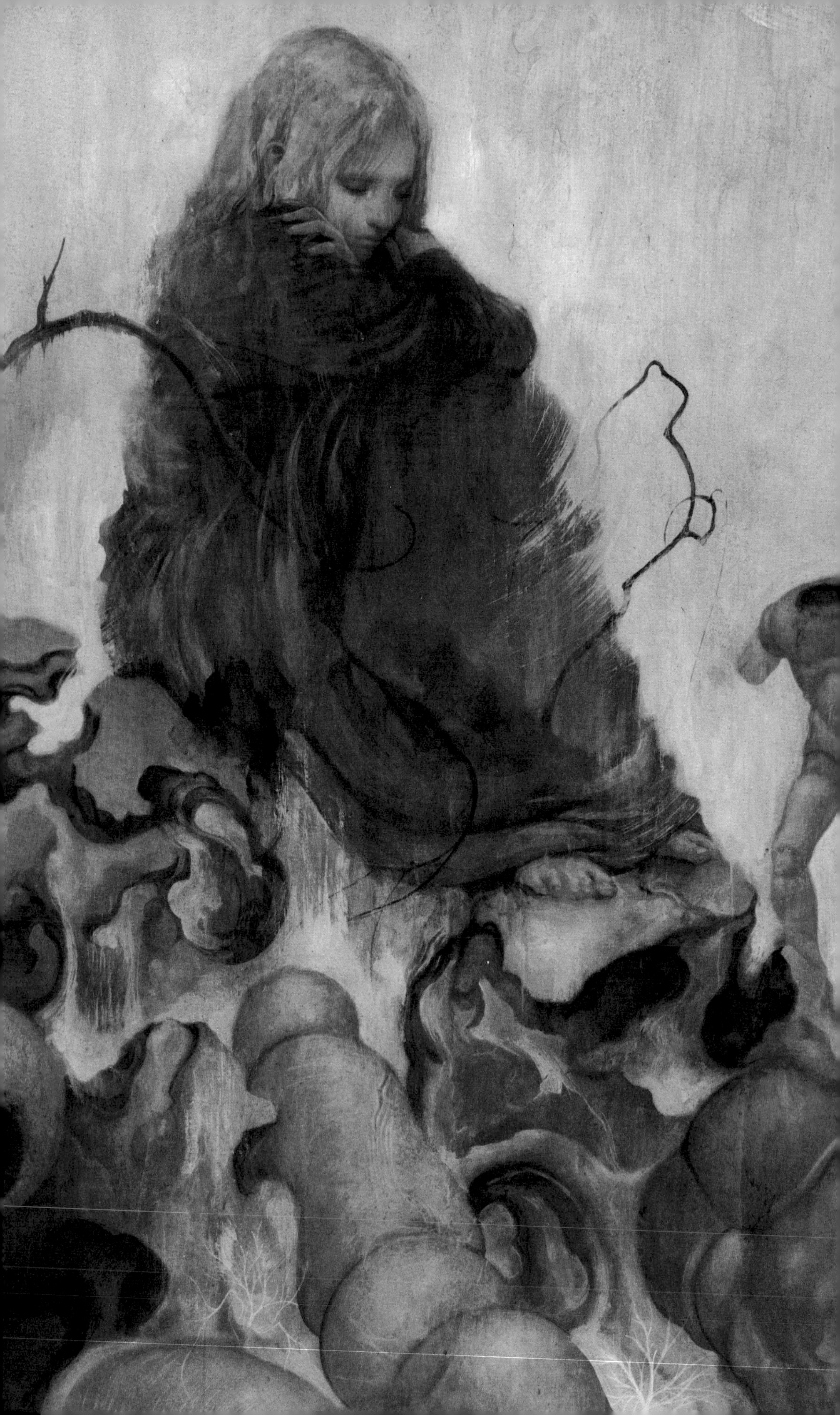

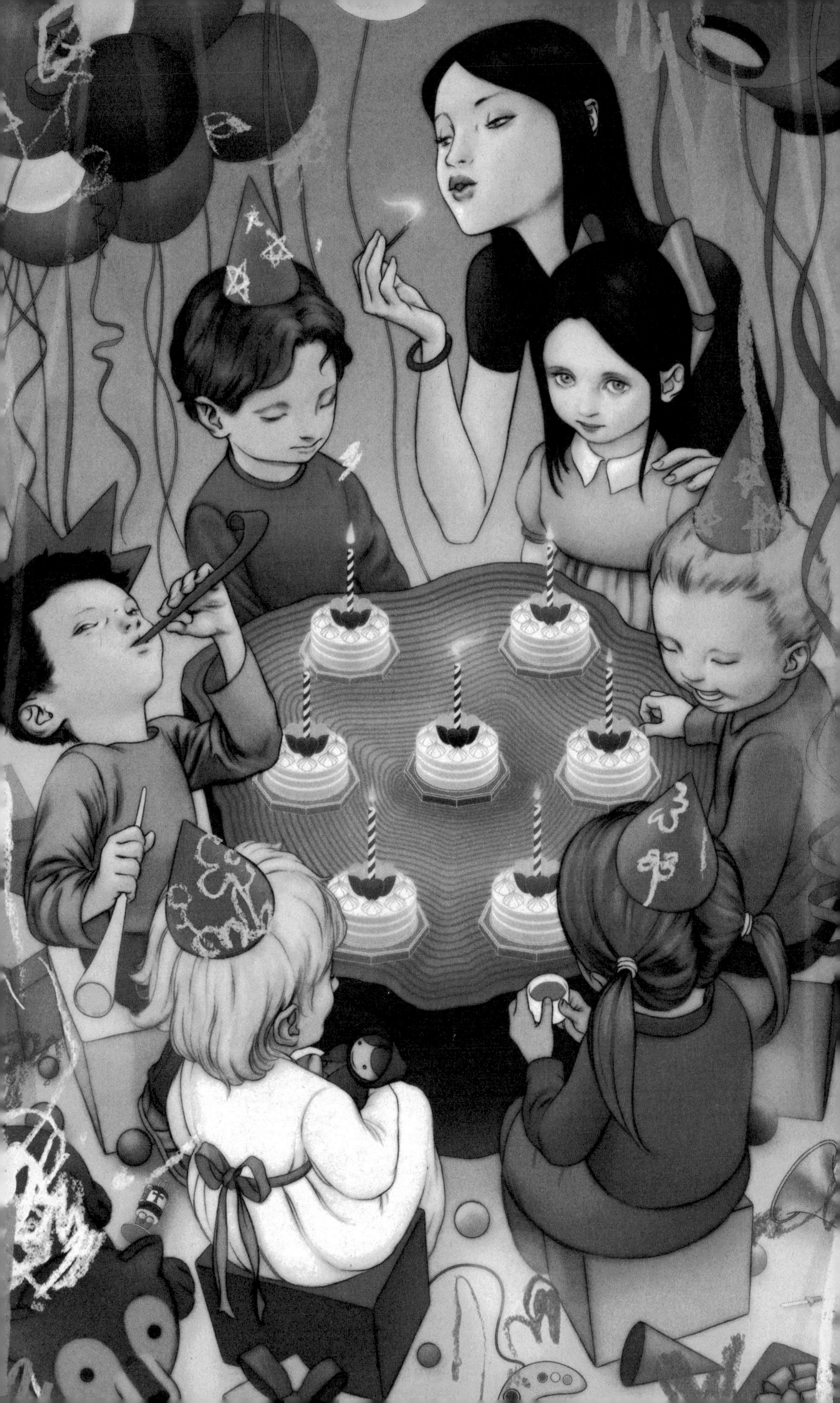

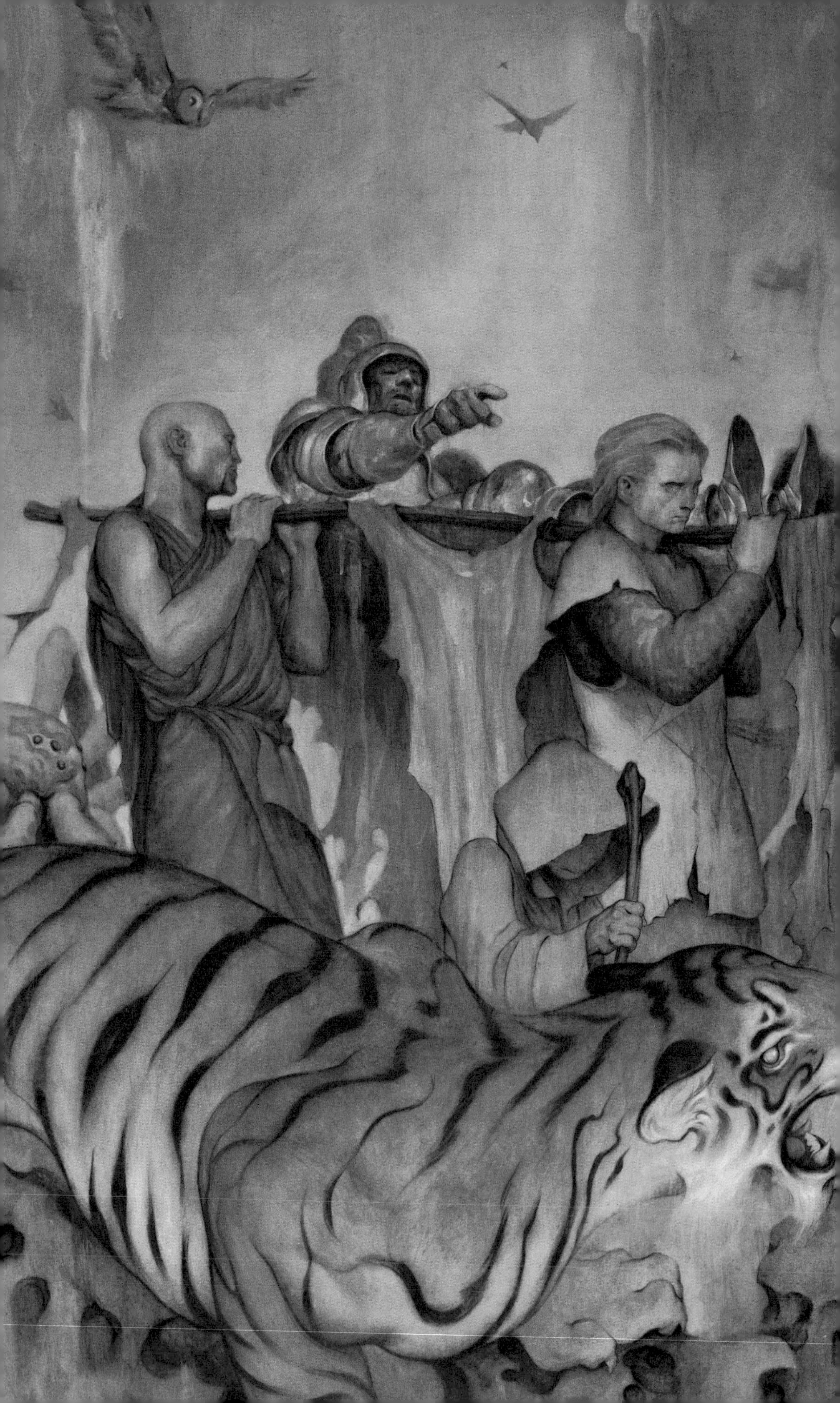

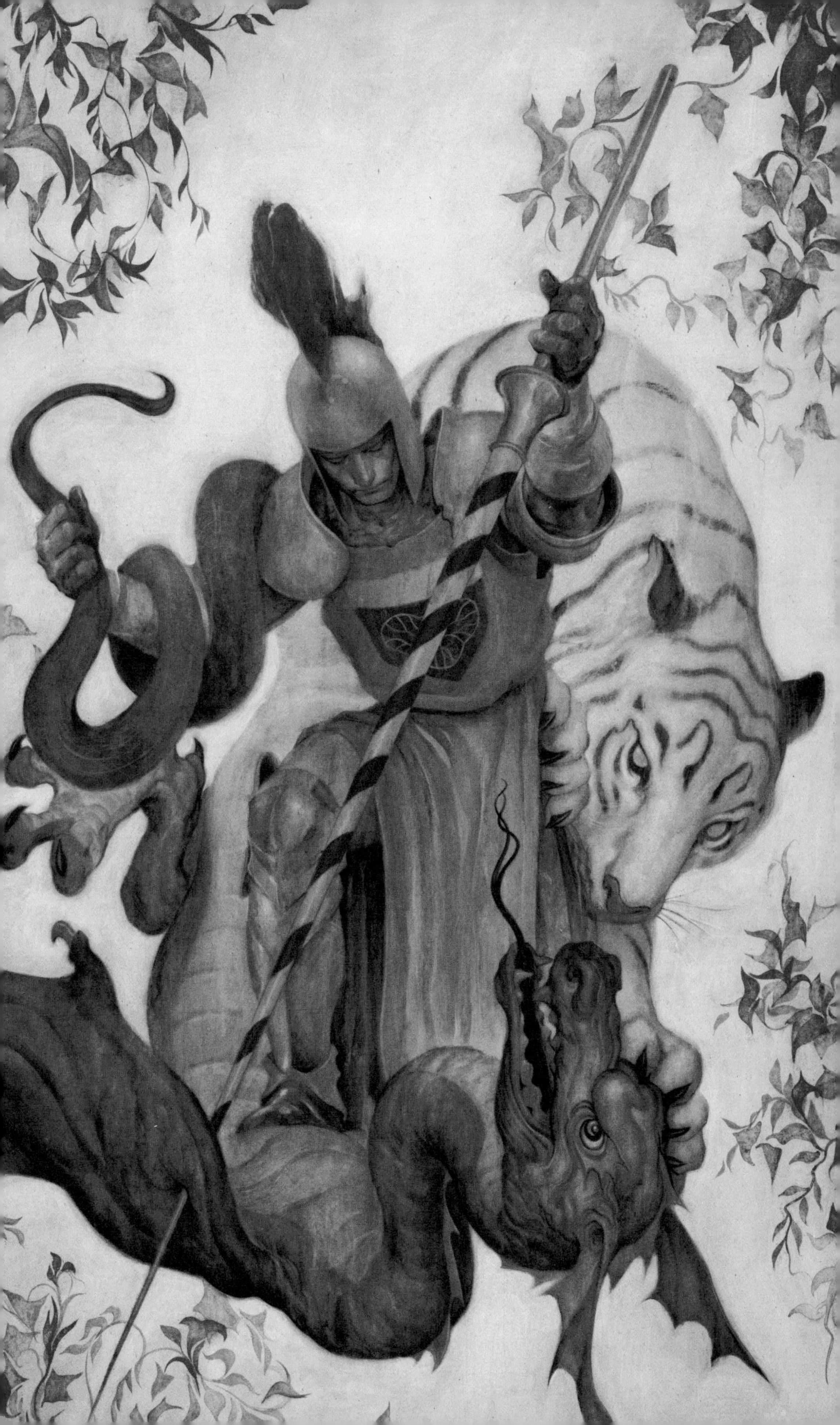

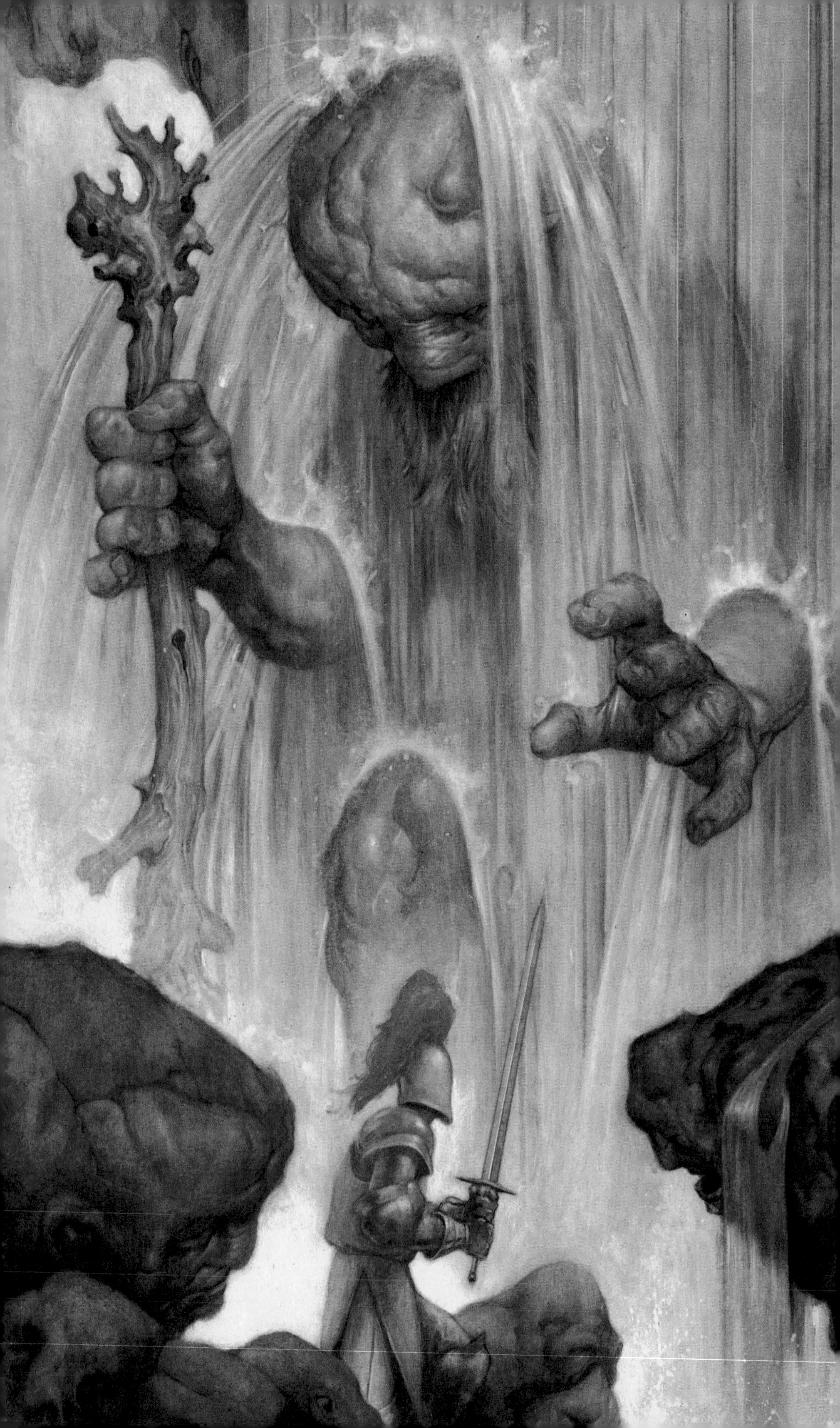

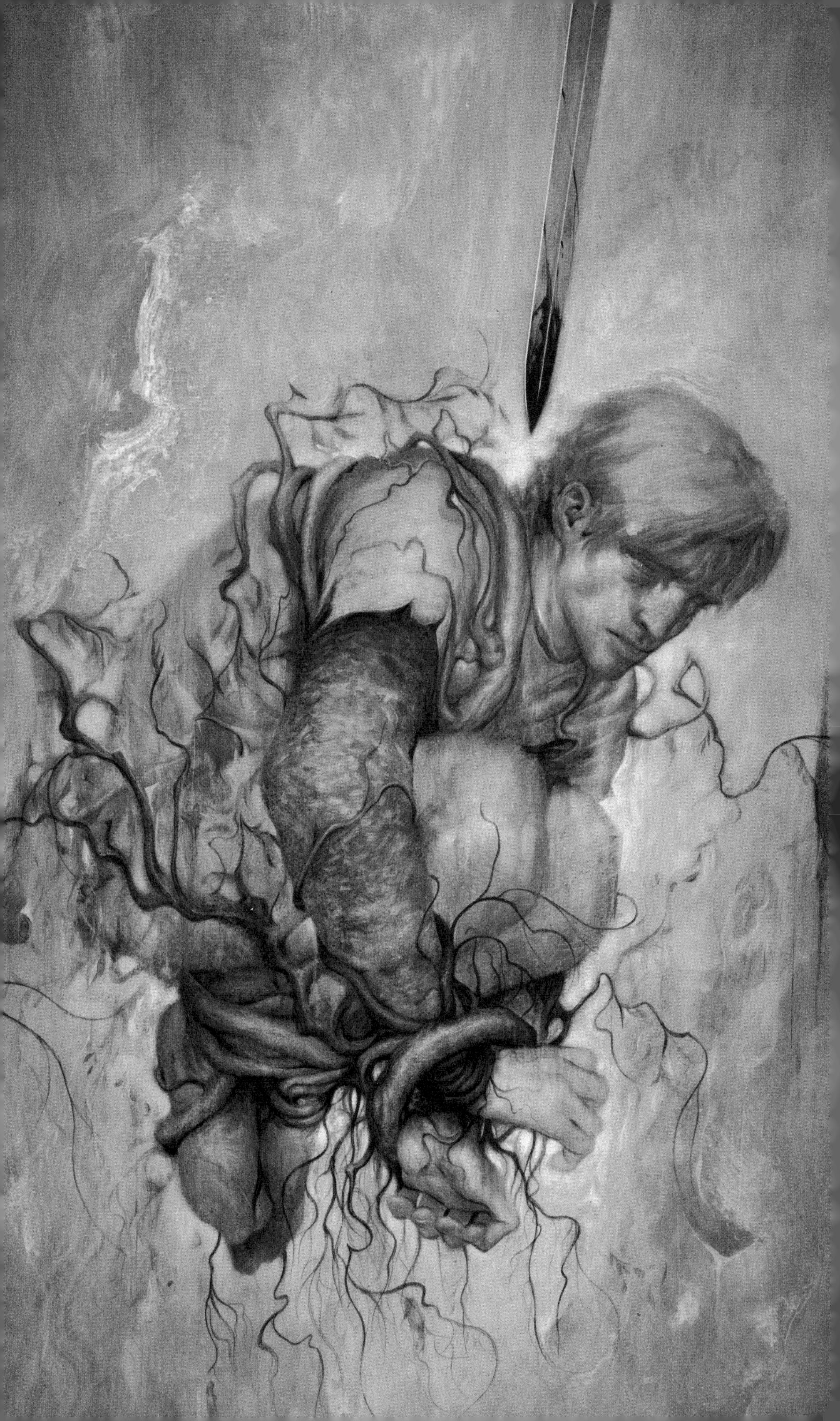

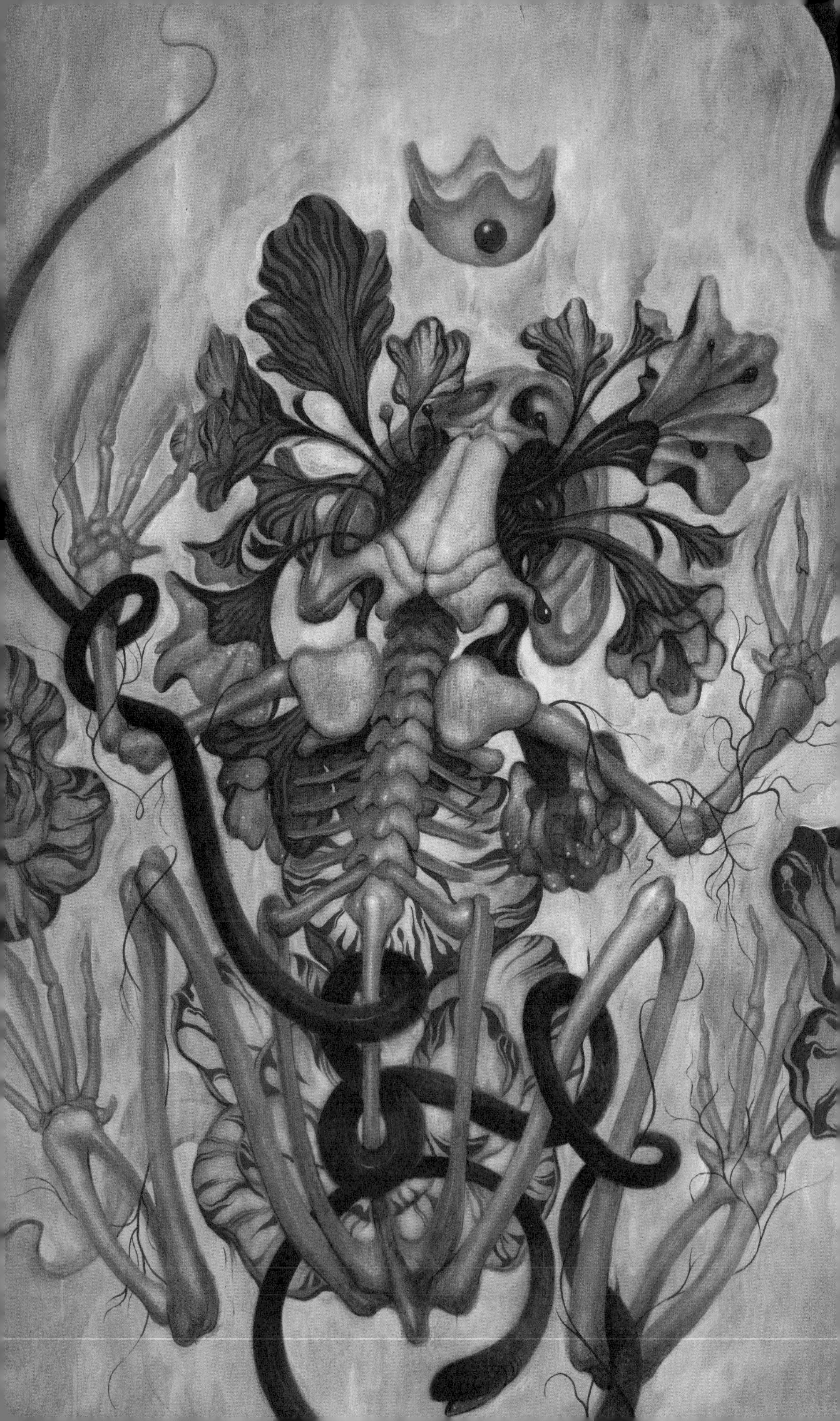